# AutoCAD 2004 VBA:
# A Programmer's Reference

JOE SUTPHIN

**Apress**™

AutoCAD 2004 VBA: A Programmer's Reference
Copyright © 2004 by Joe Sutphin

ISBN (pbk): 1-59059-272-7

Printed and bound in the United States of America 12345678910

Technical Reviewer: David Stein

Editorial Board: Dan Appleman, Craig Berry, Gary Cornell, Tony Davis, Steven Rycroft, Julian Skinner, Martin Streicher, Jim Sumser, Karen Watterson, Gavin Wray, John Zukowski

Assistant Publisher: Grace Wong

Project Manager: Sofia Marchant

Copy Editors: Nicole LeClerc, Jim Grey, Ami Knox

Production Manager: Kari Brooks

Production Editor: Kelly Winquist

Proofreader: Lori Bring

Compositor: Molly Sharp

Indexer: Valerie Hanes Perry

Artist: April Milne

Cover Designer: Kurt Krames

Manufacturing Manager: Tom Debolski

Distributed to the book trade in the United States by Springer-Verlag New York, Inc., 175 Fifth Avenue, New York, NY, 10010 and outside the United States by Springer-Verlag GmbH & Co. KG, Tiergartenstr. 17, 69112 Heidelberg, Germany.

In the United States: phone 1-800-SPRINGER, email orders@springer-ny.com, or visit http://www.springer-ny.com. Outside the United States: fax +49 6221 345229, email orders@springer.de, or visit http://www.springer.de.

For information on translations, please contact Apress directly at 2560 Ninth Street, Suite 219, Berkeley, CA 94710. Phone 510-549-5930, fax 510-549-5939, email info@apress.com, or visit http://www.apress.com.

The source code for this book is available to readers at http://www.apress.com in the Downloads section. You will need to answer questions pertaining to this book in order to successfully download the code.

*This book is dedicated to my wife, Grace. Without her,*
*I would not be able to accomplish the task of writing a book.*

# Contents at a Glance

# Contents

# Appendix B AutoCAD Constants Reference ............... 763

# About the Author

**Joe Sutphin**'s background includes more than 25 years in the machinery manufacturing industry. He has more than 18 years of CAD experience with 12+ years of AutoCAD-specific experience. Joe is an Autodesk Registered Developer, and his work has appeared in the pages of *CADENCE* and *CADALYST* magazines. He has been programming for over 15 years, with the last 10 years being Visual Basic–specific experience. In 1998 he collaborated with Microsoft on a Visual Basic application case study. He is the author of the best-selling book titled *AutoCAD 2000 VBA Programmer's Reference*.

# Acknowledgments

There are many, many people to thank on this project. Please forgive me if I miss mentioning your name or misspell it. First, the people at Apress. Without them I would not have had the opportunity to create this work. Thanks to Gary Cornell and Dan Appleman for their initial acceptance and input, Beth Christmas for coordinating things, and Karen Watterson for continuing to give me opportunities for achievement.

A great big thank you to the editorial and production staff: Grace Wong, Sofia Marchant, Nicole LeClerc, Jim Grey, Ami Knox, and Kelly Winquist. Thanks to Doris Wong for putting up with my demands for the web site content, and thanks to Jessica Dolcourt for coordinating the book cover. I enjoyed working with each of you.

A special thanks to my technical reviewer, David Stein.

A special thank you to my children, Stephen, Clair, David, and Emily, for understanding when daddy had to work.

A special thank you to Rod Ellis for helping me with the picture for this book.

Lastly, thanks to those who helped and whose names I forgot to include here. To everyone in the AutoCAD community with whom I've had the pleasure of crossing paths, from the bottom of my heart, thanks!

# Introduction

THIS BOOK PROVIDES A CONCISE GUIDE for programmers to the kind of customization you can achieve with AutoCAD 2004. It demonstrates the use of AutoCAD through short code examples written in Visual Basic for Applications (VBA). It also includes a full reference section for quick reference on all the events, methods, and properties are available with AutoCAD.

## What Is AutoCAD?

So, what is AutoCAD? First released in 1982 under the name MicroCAD, AutoCAD has become a powerful tool for drafting and design purposes. AutoCAD 2004 incorporates many new features to enhance flexibility and drawing control. To reflect this extra functionality, many new ActiveX objects, properties, methods, and events have been included for improved programmability.

## What Is This Book About?

This book is about AutoCAD 2004 and how to use AutoCAD VBA in your applications to handle all your drawing tasks more efficiently. It shows you how to programmatically control the creation and editing of individual drawing objects, manipulate linetypes and layers, control text and dimension styles, and much more. As you encounter each of these topics, you'll cover all the associated objects including their properties, methods, and events.

By interfacing into AutoCAD, you can exploit all of AutoCAD's functionality that would have taken you a long time to write yourself. This book will first help you learn how to make use of this functionality. Then it will become a handy reference for later when you have a question that you just can't remember the answer to.

This book offers you, the reader, an easy-to-follow tutorial and reference to AutoCAD 2004, by splitting the whole topic into neat and intuitive segments. This also makes it easier to find specific information later when you need it (i.e., when you're coding real-world applications). To aid you in finding this information as quickly as possible, a comprehensive quick reference section is included. The reference section lists all of the properties, methods, and events of each of the AutoCAD 2004 objects.

This book is divided into three main parts:

- The first part (Chapters 1 through 3) provides a rapid introduction to AutoCAD, its object model, and VBA, and it explains the notation and commands particular to AutoCAD VBA projects.

- The middle part (Chapters 4 through 19) supplies a detailed breakdown of most of the object model, covering common tasks complete with many and varied code examples demonstrating the use of the relevant objects' methods and properties.

- Finally, there's a quick reference section (Appendixes A through D), which gives you a description of all the members of all AutoCAD objects at a glance.

## Who Is This Book For?

The book is a reference guide for AutoCAD programmers, and it's primarily designed to explain and demonstrate the features of AutoCAD 2004. As such, this isn't a beginner's guide, though if you've programmed in any language that can interface with other COM objects, you should be able to easily understand and use this book.

In particular, the book is aimed at programmers who use AutoCAD for daily tasks and can see the benefits of customizing and automating these tasks. Programming techniques needed to create and modify AutoCAD drawings, customize preferences, query and set system variables, and so on using the built-in VBA are presented.

AutoCAD may be customized to virtually any degree of sophistication. If you can think it up, then I bet you can use AutoCAD VBA to help you achieve your goal.

## Tell Us What You Think

We've worked hard on this book to make it enjoyable and useful. Our best reward would be to hear from you that you liked it and that it was worth the money you paid for it. We've done our best to try to understand and match your expectations.

Please let us know what you think about it. Tell us what you liked best and what we could have done better. If you think this is just a marketing gimmick, then test us out—drop us a line! We'll answer, and we'll take whatever you say under consideration for future editions. The easiest way to do so is to send e-mail to feedback@apress.com.

You can also find more details about Apress on our web site. There you'll find the code from our latest books, sneak previews of forthcoming titles, and information about the authors and the editors. You can order Apress titles or find out where your nearest local bookstore with Apress titles is located. The address of our site is http://www.apress.com.

## Customer Support

If you find a mistake in the book, your first port of call should be the errata page for this book on our web site. You can see any errata already posted there or submit your own.

If you can't find an answer there, send an e-mail to support@apress.com telling us about the problem. We'll do everything we can to answer promptly. Please remember to let us know the book your query relates to and, if possible, the page number as well. This will help us to reply to you quickly.

CHAPTER 1

# The VBA Integrated Development Environment (VBAIDE)

**WITHIN AUTOCAD,** you develop VBA programs in the Visual Basic for Applications (VBA) Integrated Development Environment (IDE). Like the Visual LISP IDE, Autodesk provides the VBAIDE as an integral part of many of its products, including AutoCAD. Unlike the Visual LISP IDE, however, Microsoft licenses the VBAIDE to Autodesk for inclusion in their products. As such, its features are from Microsoft, not Autodesk.

This chapter explores this environment's facets and shows you how to take advantage of its tools. It covers these topics:

- Visual Basic concepts

- Starting the editor

- Exploring the user interface

- Managing projects

- Using the text editor

- The Object Browser

## Visual Basic Concepts

Since VBA is a Microsoft Windows development environment, you'll find developing in VBA easiest if you have some knowledge of Windows. If you are new to Windows, you'll find fundamental differences between programming in Windows and programming in other environments, such as Visual LISP. The next sections outline concepts of Windows programming that may be new to you.

## Windows, Events, and Messages

Explaining the inner workings of Windows requires much more space than is available in this book. But you don't need an extensive knowledge of Windows' workings to create useful applications. The Windows operating system can be simplified to 3 basic concepts: windows, events, and messages.

A window is a rectangular region on the screen that has its own border. The AutoCAD drawing window, Notepad, a Word document, and the place where you compose an e-mail are all windows.

Windows can have hierarchy. A dialog form, which is a window within a distinct application, contains relevant ActiveX components and code. A drawing window is the parent of a dialog form window, and AutoCAD is the parent of the drawing windows within it. The operating system is the parent "window" of all applications running in it, including AutoCAD.

Each window recognizes and controls the programs that execute inside them or their subordinate windows. To manage windows, Windows assigns a unique ID known as a *handle*, or *hWnd* in programming jargon, to each window. Windows uses *events* to constantly monitor each window for signs of activity. Events change the application environment or *system state*. They occur when a user acts, such as by clicking the mouse or pressing a key; programmatically; or by another window through system processes.

Each time an event is triggered, Windows sends a message to the hosting application. Windows processes the message and broadcasts it to the windows. Then, based on its own instructions, each window can take appropriate action such as repainting itself when uncovered by another window. In the case of VBA in AutoCAD, the VBA workspace intercepts event messages. VBA programs can then respond directly or pass the event up to AutoCAD or to Windows if necessary. VBA provides a controlling environment within AutoCAD in which to execute and respond to events, either directly or by allowing AutoCAD or Windows to respond.

Although this seems like a lot of work, VBA hides most of the low-level details from you and exposes event procedures, which are routines that execute when a particular event occurs, for your convenience. You can quickly create very powerful applications without being concerned with low-level details.

## Event-Driven vs. Procedural Programming

When a traditional procedural application runs, it follows a predetermined path that controls the portions and sequence of code executed. It starts with the first line of code and progresses from the top down, calling each procedure when needed, until reaching the end of the code. This predetermined path is the major difference between procedural and event-driven applications.

Event-driven applications do not have a predetermined destiny. Different sections of code are executed based upon the events triggered in whatever order they occur. Depending on what events occur when the application runs, some sections of code may not get executed at all.

You can't predict the sequence of events, so you must make assumptions about the application's "state" at any moment. This seems like it would be difficult, but it's really not. Typically, you have a set of possibilities to work with, such as the Click, DblClick, KeyPress, and LostFocus events. For example, you might require the user to type a value in a TextBox before enabling a CommandButton that allows further processing. The TextBox control's Change event would contain code that enables the CommandButton control, as shown in this sample code:

```
Private Sub TextBox1_Change()
  If Len(TextBox1.Text) > 0 Then
    CommandButton1.Enabled = True

    Else
      CommandButton1.Enabled = False
  End If
End Sub
```

Each time you add or delete text from the TextBox control, the program executes this event procedure. The code checks the length of the text and if it is greater than zero, meaning there is something in the TextBox, then it enables the CommandButton. Otherwise, it disables the CommandButton.

Programmatically changing the text in the TextBox triggers the Change event. If you allow for this occurrence, you might get unexpected results. Using events is very powerful, but you must know what each event might trigger elsewhere in your application.

## *Interactively Developing Your Applications*

In more traditional development environments, most developers follow a distinct 3-step process: writing, compiling, and testing. However, uses a more interactive approach to development that makes it easier for both beginning and experienced developers.

Languages such as C++ require you to write all the code then compile it. During the compile, you may uncover numerous errors from simple typing errors to more complex syntax errors. The Visual Basic programming environment, on the other hand, interprets your code every line of the way alerting you to potential problems now instead of during a lengthy compile cycle.

Because Visual Basic is partially compiling your code as you type it, it takes very little time to finish compiling the code and execute your application. Unlike other languages, you will find that you are constantly writing, executing, and refining your application. In addition, the Visual Basic environment employs a graphical environment. You most often work in the graphical interface first and on the code second. This lets you spend more time creating and less time compiling and recompiling.

## Starting the Editor

One of the first questions that you will face is "How do I enter source code (structured commands) or develop a user interface (forms or dialog boxes)?" The answer is the IDE, a graphical user interface you use to develop applications. It is similar to development environments provided in other applications such as Microsoft Access and Microsoft Excel.

To display the VBAIDE, choose Tools ➤ Macro ➤ Visual Basic Editor or press Alt+F11. Alternatively, you can start the editor by typing **VBAIDE** at the AutoCAD command prompt, as shown in Figure 1-1.

*Figure 1-1. The AutoCAD command prompt*

## Exploring the User Interface

The editor is composed of several different windows. The first time you open it, it looks like Figure 1-2. Use the View menu to control which windows are visible. To get context-sensitive help on any window, click in it and press F1.

The rest of this section discusses the most frequently used windows.

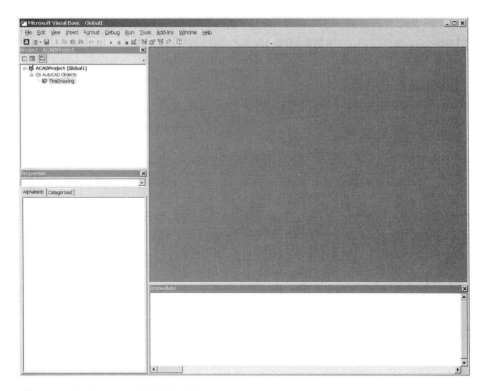

*Figure 1-2. The AutoCAD VBAIDE*

## The Project Explorer

The Project Explorer window displays a hierarchical view called a *treeview* of your project's components that are loaded in the IDE. The view lists all of the UserForms, code, and class modules associated with each project. Use this window to keep track of and move components between projects. Figure 1-3 shows what a typical Project Explorer window looks like.

*Figure 1-3. Project Properties*

As you add, create, and remove files, the Project Explorer reflects those changes. You can save each project with a .dvb extension or you can embed it directly into a drawing file. You can't delete the required ThisDrawing object, which represents the active drawing, but nothing requires you to place code in this module.

You can close the Project Explorer window to gain more space in the IDE. To reopen it, choose View ➤ Project Explorer or press Ctrl+R.

## The Code Window

The Code window is where you'll do most of your development work to manipulate AutoCAD. You can have a window open for each module in the project, as shown in Figure 1-4.

*Figure 1-4. Cascaded VBAIDE windows*

Alternatively, you can see one window at a time by clicking the window's Maximize button, shown in Figure 1-5, which is in its upper-right corner.

*Figure 1-5. Maximize window example*

Later, this chapter discusses features such as Auto List Members and Auto Quick Info that make writing code easier and less prone to common typing errors.

## The Properties Window

Properties control an object's behavior. You can query or control properties of AutoCAD entities, such as the color or linetype of a `Line` object, using the `Color` or `Linetype` properties.

The Properties window displays an object's design-time properties. You can change design-time properties while you develop your application. Changing properties during development has no effect on what you do in the IDE. However, any of these property changes could affect how well (and sometimes whether) your application will run. Figure 1-6 shows the properties of a typical `UserForm` object.

*Figure 1-6. Properties dialog box*

**NOTE**  *Design time is when you develop your application in the IDE, writing code and adding forms and controls.*

If you need to set a particular property once, set it at design time in the Properties window, But you will sometimes need to set a property's value at run time. Additionally, some properties are read-only and some are available only at run time. Each situation requires that you set the property value programmatically (using code).

You can close the Properties window to gain more space in the IDE. To reopen the Properties window, choose View ➤ Properties Window or press F4.

## The Object and Procedure Boxes

The Object box (on the left, see Figure 1-7) lists all the objects and controls in your project. The Procedure box (on the right) lists all the procedures and events implemented in your application.

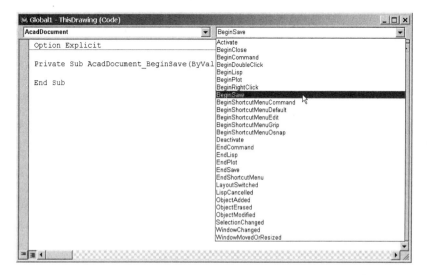

*Figure 1-7. Object and procedure boxes*

When you select an object from the Object box, the procedures associated with that object appear in the Procedure box. Figure 1-8 shows that after you choose a procedure, the IDE adds its basic framework to your code window, where you write your source code.

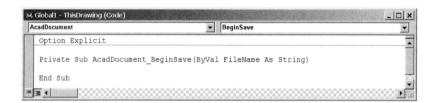

*Figure 1-8. VBAIDE procedure example*

When a procedure or event does not appear in **bold** type in the Procedure box, then it contains no code. Incidentally, when you choose an object, the IDE adds its default event procedure to the Code window. You may or may not choose to use the default procedure.

## The Immediate Window

The Immediate window serves as a convenient place to send output from a running application during development. Alternatively, you can use it to set variables when you run an application, or to check a variable's value, such as the path to the AutoCAD executable file as shown in Figure 1-9.

*Figure 1-9. Executing in the Immediate window*

In this example, use a question mark (?) to ask the VBAIDE to tell you a variable's value. To set a variable's value in the Immediate window, type the statement just as you would in the Code window. Figure 1-10 shows how it's done.

*Figure 1-10. Setting a variable in Immediate window*

 **NOTE** *You can't declare variables in the Immediate window. Also, a variable's scope and valid VBA commands in the Immediate window are equally important. Chapter 2 covers variable scope.*

## The Options dialog box

The Options dialog box, shown in Figure 1-11, lets you customize the IDE's look and feel, including syntax color scheme, source code font, and tab spacing. To open the Options dialog box, choose Tools ➤ Options. This section covers the most commonly used options.

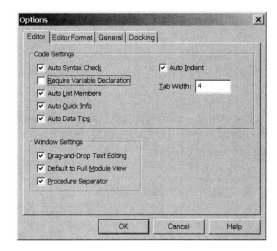

*Figure 1-11. Options dialog box*

For most developers, the default settings are fine. However, you should consider changing two settings on the Editor tab: Auto Syntax Check and Require Variable Declaration.

When the Auto Syntax Check option is checked, syntax errors in your code generate an error message similar to Figure 1-12.

*Figure 1-12. Error message dialog box*

As you begin to develop more complex applications and reuse lines of code from other places in your application, these error messages will become a nuisance. Anytime you move the cursor off the offending line of code, you get one of these error messages. But if you uncheck Auto Syntax Check, the VBAIDE notifies you of errors by changing the color of the offending line of code to red.

The Require Variable Declaration option is unchecked by default, meaning that the VBAIDE does not require that you properly declare your variables before you use them. This isn't much of a concern when you write a simple macro, but when you start developing larger and more complex applications you'll find this option indispensable. Checking this option forces you to think about each variable and its data type. When you check this option, the VBAIDE adds a line of code to the start of each module as shown in Figure 1-13.

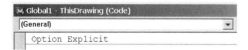

*Figure 1-13. Option Explicit example*

After you check this option, exit and restart AutoCAD to make it take effect.

By declaring variables to be a specific data type, you save memory resources. Undeclared variables are, by default, assigned the variant data type. This data type uses the most memory and could lead to memory resource problems when users run your application. As a rule of thumb, always declare each variable you use in your application, and choose data type that uses the least possible memory. Chapter 2 discusses data types and memory in more detail.

## Managing Projects

Managing your code components is critical to successfully developing applications. This section discusses adding components to your project, saving your project, and loading and executing an application.

## *Project Structure*

A VBA project contains several different types of files, including:

- UserForm module

- Standard module

- Class module

- Reference .dvb file

### UserForm Module

UserForm modules (files with an `.frm` extension) contain a text description of your form, controls placement, and property settings. They also include `UserForm`-level declarations of constants, variables, and procedures; and event procedures.

### Standard Module

Standard modules (files with a `.bas` extension) contain module-level declarations of programmer-defined data types, constants, variables, and public procedures. A standard module typically contains those routines that don't fit nicely into a class definition.

### Class Module

Use class modules (files with a `.cls` extension) to create your own objects, including methods, properties, and events. Class modules are similar to UserForm modules except that they have a visible user interface. Class modules are very versatile and vital to VBA and AutoCAD. As you progress through this book, you'll see that classes and objects are everywhere.

### Reference .dvb File

You can reference the code of another `.dvb` file in your current project. This feature lets you easily reuse code among several projects. You can't create a circular reference, which is a reference to one project and a reference in that project to the current project. If you accidentally create a circular reference, AutoCAD tells you of the error. You have to undo the reference before you can continue.

## Creating, Opening, and Saving Projects

To extract, embed, create, save, load, and unload VBA projects, open the VBA Manager dialog box, shown in Figure 1-14. To open it, either type **VBAMAN** at the AutoCAD command prompt or choose Tools ➤ Macros ➤ VBA Manager.

You must explicitly load all `.dvb` projects. AutoCAD loads embedded projects automatically when the drawing containing them is opened, depending upon how you configure AutoCAD's security options. Clicking New creates a new project in the VBAIDE that you can access by clicking the Visual Basic Editor button. To load an existing project, click the Load button. The Open VBA Project dialog box in Figure 1-15 appears, letting you choose the project to load.

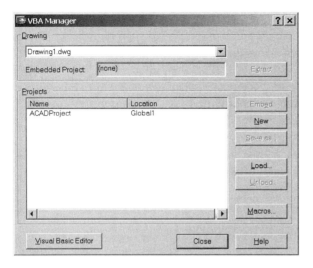

*Figure 1-14. VBA Manager dialog box*

**TIP**   *Embedding VBA macros within drawings is fine for drawings that remain within your organization. Avoid embedding macros when you'll deliver the drawings to outside users or customers as it imposes a security risk on their part to trust your macros in their environment.*

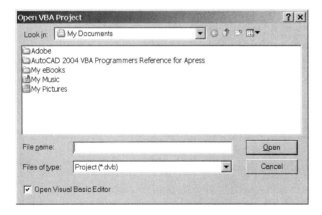

*Figure 1-15. Open VBA Project dialog box*

This dialog box is similar to the standard File Open dialog box in Windows. Similar to creating a new project, when you choose the .dvb project you want, click the Visual Basic Editor button to start working on your project.

There are two other ways to create and load DVB project files:

- Type **VBAIDE** at the AutoCAD command prompt or press Alt+F11 to open or create a DVB project file.

- Type **VBALOAD** at the AutoCAD command prompt to open the Open VBA Project dialog box so you can choose a project to load.

To save your project, choose File ➤ Save or press Ctrl+S. If you have not previously saved your project, the standard Save As dialog box appears, as shown in Figure 1-16.

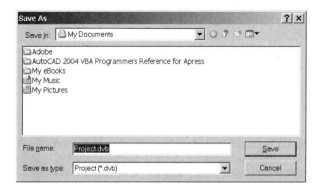

*Figure 1-16. Save As dialog box*

Unlike in Visual Basic, you don't need to save each project module separately. AutoCAD saves them all in a `.dvb` file. However, as the next section illustrates, you can export each module to a separate file.

**TIP** *Avoid saving your custom program files under the AutoCAD installation folder tree. Instead, create a separate folder tree for them. This prevents AutoCAD installations and updates from affecting your program files.*

## Adding, Removing, and Saving Files

You will sometimes want to add to your VBA project a file such as a common UserForm module or a collection of routines in a standard module. To do this, choose File ➤ Insert File or press Ctrl+M. The Import File dialog box appears, as shown in Figure 1-17.

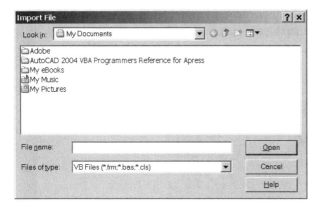

*Figure 1-17. Import File dialog box*

To remove a file from your project, highlight the module name in the Project
Explorer window. Then choose File ➤ Remove. You can also highlight the mod-
ule name, right-click to invoke the popup menu in Figure 1-18, and then choose
Remove.

*Figure 1-18. Remove module popup menu*

Notice that this menu includes an Export File option. Use this option to
export a module to a separate file. Highlight the module name in the Project
Explorer window, and then either choose File ➤ Export File or press Ctrl+E.
A Save As dialog box appears for the type of file to export. Alternatively, you can
highlight the module name in the Project Explorer window, right click to invoke
the popup menu, and choose Export File.

## Adding ActiveX Controls and Code Components

When you start a project and add a UserForm module, a common toolbox
appears. It contains a standard collection of ActiveX controls called *intrinsic*

*controls.* Chapter 3 covers intrinsic controls in more detail. If you want to insert an ActiveX control that is not in the toolbox, choose Tools ➤ Additional Controls or right-click in the Toolbox window and choose Additional Controls. The Additional Controls dialog box shown in Figure 1-19 appears.

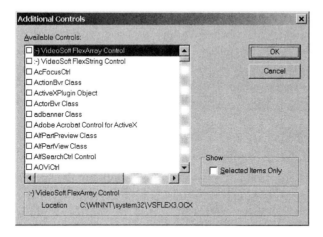

*Figure 1-19. Additional Controls dialog box*

This dialog box lists all the ActiveX controls that are properly registered on your machine. However, if you want to use a particular ActiveX control, check its End User License Agreement (EULA) to determine whether you have a license to use it in a VBA host application. Many ActiveX controls installed with Microsoft Visual Basic, including TreeView, ListView, File, Directory, and Drive, are not licensed for use in a VBA host application. However, Chapter 19 explains some easy ways you can use the Windows application programming interface (API) to get around this dilemma.

You can add more than ActiveX controls—code components are perhaps even more common. This is the means by which your application can gain access to other ActiveX automation applications such as Microsoft Excel, Access, and Word. ActiveX automation is your key to building powerful applications that take advantage of objects exposed by other applications.

To use the objects, methods, properties, and events that other applications expose, first add a reference to that application. Choose Tools ➤ References to open the References dialog box, shown in Figure 1-20.

Check the reference you want to add. The dialog box lists alphabetically the references your application doesn't use. Later, when you write your own objects using class modules, this is where you'll add them to your project.

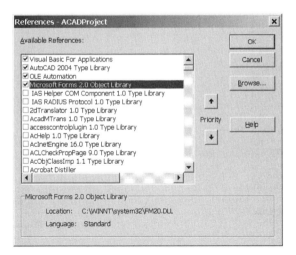

*Figure 1-20. References dialog box*

To improve performance, deselect any references your application doesn't use. Each reference must be resolved before your project loads. Depending on your project's size, this could greatly decrease how long your user waits for the application to load and run.

**NOTE**   *If your application uses an object of another application, you can't remove the reference to it without first removing the object.*

## The Object Browser

When you set a reference to an application's object library, the Object Browser lists all the objects, methods, properties, constants, and events that application exposes. To open the Object Browser, choose View ➤ Object Browser or press F2. By default, the Object Browser lists all libraries your project currently references. To view just the AutoCAD library, for example, click AutoCAD in the drop-down list in the Object Browser, as shown in Figure 1-21. The Object Browser gives you a perspective of the objects an application exposes and the methods, properties, events, and constants those objects expose for your application to manipulate.

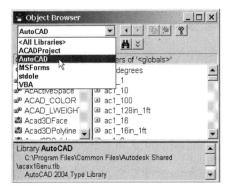

*Figure 1-21. Object Browser dialog box*

## Loading and Running Applications

You can load and subsequently execute your VBA applications in many different ways. This section explains the most common ways.

### Acad.dvb

AutoCAD searches the support file search path for the file acad.dvb. If AutoCAD finds this file, it loads it into the current session. The following example illustrates how to implement this feature.

```
Public Sub Start()
    Application.ActiveDocument.SetVariable "OSMODE", 35
End Sub
```

Place this code in the ThisDrawing module and save the file as acad.dvb. Save this file in any subdirectory specified in the support file search path. Now each time that you start an AutoCAD session, AutoCAD loads this file. Also, if you include a routine called AcadStartup, AutoCAD executes it when it loads acad.dvb.

The example in Figure 1-22 shows how to use the macros that you have stored in the acad.dvb file.

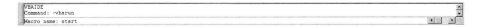

*Figure 1-22. AutoCAD command prompt*

Type -vbarun then the name of the macro to run (Start in this instance). In this example, the value of the system variable OSMODE is set to 35. This is a convenient way to store macros that will invoke AutoCAD with a particular setup.

## Acaddoc.lsp

AutoCAD automatically searches the default search path (a combination of the support/file path list, the current working folder, and the shortcut's startup folder) for a file named acaddoc.lsp. If AutoCAD finds this file, it loads it into the current drawing. Unlike acad.dvb, which loads only when you start a new AutoCAD session, AutoCAD loads acaddoc.lsp each time you open or create a drawing.

**TIP**   *To verify the actual search path list, go to the command prompt, type **–insert**, enter a meaningless string of characters such as **sdfsdfsdf** (keep it less than 31 characters, though), and press Enter. AutoCAD displays a list of folders in which it tried to find your file when it fails.*

AutoCAD provides a special programmer-defined function called S::STARTUP that, if included in acaddoc.lsp or any default startup LISP file, is automatically executed when you open or create a drawing. You can define S::STARTUP in acaddoc.lsp to perform setup operations for each drawing.

You can define an S::STARTUP function in several different places, including acad.lsp, acaddoc.lsp, an .mnl file, or any AutoLISP file loaded from any of these files. You can overwrite a previously defined S::STARTUP function—which means that another definition can overwrite your S::STARTUP routine.

**NOTE**   *Never modify or replace the files acad2000doc.lsp, acad2004.lsp, or acad2004doc.lsp as they may be overwritten by a service pack installation without warning. It is also a good idea to append the S::STARTUP function instead of defining it, as many third party products rely upon S::STARTUP to initialize their environments. If you define a new S::STARTUP, you could disable some or all of another loaded product in the process.*

The following example shows how to ensure that your startup function works with other functions.

```
(defun-q Startup ()
  (command "-vbarun" "Start")
)
(setq S::STARTUP (append S::STARTUP Startup))
```

This code appends your startup function to any existing S::STARTUP function, and then redefines the S::STARTUP function to include your startup code. This works regardless of any other existence of an S::STARTUP function.

---

**NOTE** *In AutoLISP, you must use* defun-q *as opposed to* defun *for this example to work properly. Visual LISP constructs functions differently from AutoLISP between* defun *and* defun-q.

---

## Embedded Projects

AutoCAD lets you embed a VBA project into a drawing. Each time the drawing is loaded, AutoCAD also loads the VBA project embedded in the drawing. Of all the options to load VBA projects automatically, this is the worst one. It stores the VBA project with the drawing, making your drawing file that much bigger. If you copy the drawing file to create a new drawing, you also copy its VBA project. If you want to change the VBA project, you need to change each VBA project in every drawing file that you created from the original. In addition, delivering drawings with embedded macros to customers imposes a serious potential security risk on their part. Well, you get the picture of why this is the worst option to choose.

## VBARUN and the Macros Dialog Box

The dialog-box version of the VBARUN command features several options that extend how you create and execute a VBA macro.

You can execute a VBA macro at the AutoCAD command prompt. To execute a macro from the AutoCAD command prompt, type **–VBARUN**, press Enter, and type the macro name, similar to the example in Figure 1-23.

*Figure 1-23. AutoCAD Command prompt*

In this example, AutoCAD would execute the Start macro.

If the macro you wish to execute is unique among all the VBA projects loaded, then just specify the macro name after the –VBARUN command. However, if you have multiple macros loaded with the same name, specify the macro to execute using either of these syntaxes:

```
ProjectName.ModuleName.MacroName    or    ModuleName.MacroName
```

How far down inside your project and modules your macro is placed, and whether you have multiple projects loaded, determine which syntax is appropriate.

You can also execute a macro through the Macros dialog box, shown in Figure 1-24. To open this dialog box, type **VBARUN** at the AutoCAD command prompt. You can also choose Tools ➤ Macro ➤ Macros or press Alt+F8. For the beginner or end user, this is an excellent way to execute macros.

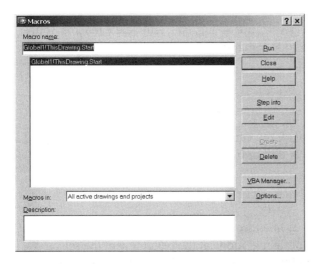

*Figure 1-24. Macros dialog box*

### Macros

Tasks that occur frequently or are of a complex nature are ideal candidates for a macro. Using a macro gives you a more consistent and convenient way to accomplish these tasks. Macros let you create this process once and then reuse it multiple times.

You can create macros in one of two places, either the ThisDrawing module or in a standard module. In either case, always declare them as Public subprocedures and not functions that return a value and can't receive arguments. Despite these limitations, macros are a powerful tool for increasing AutoCAD end-user productivity.

An example of where you might want to use a macro is in initializing user preferences whenever a drawing is created or opened, as in the following code:

```
Public Sub Setup()
  Application.Preferences.OpenSave.AutoSaveInterval = 15
End Sub
```

In this example, AutoCAD will save the user's work every 15 minutes. You might consider using a macro similar to this to set various system variables for each drawing that you work on or perhaps for when each AutoCAD session begins. The previous section explained how to make VBA routines execute automatically for the start of either an AutoCAD session or a drawing.

## The Macros Dialog Box

Use the Macros dialog box to create, run, debug, edit, and delete macros. You can also control how a macro runs using several options. This section explains each button in this dialog box.

### Run

This button executes your macro. You can also execute your macro from within the VBAIDE by choosing Run ➤ Run or by pressing F5.

### Step Into

This button lets you step line by line through the code of the macro you select. It enters the VBAIDE in step (or debug) mode at the beginning of the selected macro. You can also start Step Into from within the VBAIDE by choosing Debug ➤ Step Into or by pressing F8.

### Edit

This button lets you edit your macro's code. It opens the VBAIDE in edit mode at the beginning of the selected macro. This is identical to typing **VBAIDE** at the AutoCAD command prompt and navigating to the appropriate project, module, and macro.

### Create

To create a macro, enter a name in the Macros dialog box and press the Create button. This opens a dialog box that lets you choose where you want to create your macro. You can also specify the project in which to create the macro. If you do not specify a project name, the Select Project dialog box, shown in Figure 1-25, appears. Choose from the list of loaded projects.

*Figure 1-25. Select Project dialog box*

### Delete

To delete a macro from the project file, select the Delete button... If you accidentally delete a macro, retrieve it by *immediately* switching to the VBA editor, bring the module that contained your source code into focus, and either choose Edit ➤ Undo or press Ctrl+Z.

 **CAUTION**   *This command deletes the source code associated with the macro. Be careful!*

### VBA Manager

This button opens the VBA Manager dialog box, which lets you create, edit, load, unload, close, embed, and extract your VBA projects.

 **NOTE**   *For more about this dialog box, see "Creating, Opening, and Saving Projects," earlier in this chapter.*

### *Options*

AutoCAD VBA provides three options for controlling how AutoCAD handles VBA projects by default. Table 1-1 explains these options.

*Table 1-1. VBA options in AutoCAD*

| OPTION | MEANING | DEFAULT VALUE |
| --- | --- | --- |
| Enable Auto Embedding | Determines whether a VBA project will be embedded in the current drawing. | `False` or unchecked. |
| Allow Break on Errors | Determines whether VBA is instructed to enter Break mode when an error occurs in your application. | `True` or checked. |
| Enable Macro Virus Protection | Determines whether macro virus protection is enabled. | `True` or checked. |

## Using the Text Editor

Fortunately, the VBA text editor is not just a plain old text editor. It has some pretty nice features that make your application development efforts more efficient. This section tells you how to take advantage of their usefulness.

## Auto List Members

When you type a valid object name in your code and then type a period (.), VBA drops down a list of properties and methods available for that object, as shown in Figure 1-26. Typing the first few letters of the property or method name moves you to that selection in the list. Pressing the Tab key completes the typing for you. You can also press the Complete Word button on the Edit toolbar. This option is also helpful when you aren't sure which properties are available for an object.

Visual Basic 6 and VB.NET programmers know this feature by its other name: IntelliSense.

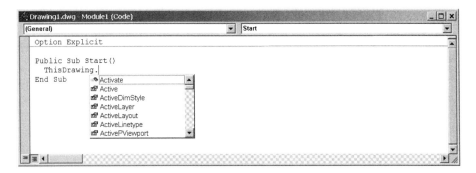

*Figure 1-26. Auto List Members example*

 **TIP** *If you disable this feature, you can still access it by pressing CTRL+J.*

## Auto Quick Info

Auto Quick Info displays the syntax of statements, procedures, and functions that are early bound (there is a reference set to the object library you're using). This feature is not available for late bound objects (no reference set to the object library). When you type the name of a valid Visual Basic statement, procedure, or function, the IDE shows the syntax immediately below the current line, with the first argument in **boldface**, as shown in Figure 1-27. After entering the first argument value, the second argument appears in **boldface**, and so on.

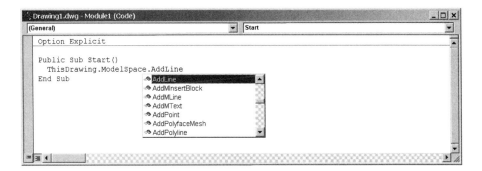

*Figure 1-27. Auto Quick Info example*

**TIP** *If you disable this feature, you can still access it by pressing CTRL+I.*

You may have noticed that this feature also provides you with a function's return value, which can be very helpful when you use an unfamiliar function for the first time.

## Summary of AutoCAD VBA Commands

AutoCAD provides a number of commands to access the VBA editor and execute VBA code. The following table, Table 1-2, summarizes these commands that you can enter at the AutoCAD command prompt.

*Table 1-2. VBA editor commands*

| COMMAND | DESCRIPTION |
| --- | --- |
| VBALOAD | Loads a VBA (.dvb) project file into AutoCAD memory. If you are going to edit your project, you may want to click the Visual Basic Editor option. This puts you inside the VBA editor for immediate editing. |
| VBAIDE | Opens the VBAIDE. If you have loaded a project, this opens the VBA editor so you can begin editing. |
| VBAUNLOAD | Unloads the current project. If you made changes without saving them, AutoCAD asks you to save your VBA project first. |
| VBARUN | Opens a dialog box from which you can choose a VBA macro to run. This option has a number of features you may choose. |
| -VBARUN | Runs a VBA macro from the AutoCAD command prompt. If you have macros with the same name in more than one module file, then you must use the *<modulename.macroname>* syntax. |
| VBAMAN | Invokes the VBA Manager dialog box, which lets you view, create, load, close, embed, and extract projects. |
| VBASTMT | Executes a VBA expression from the AutoCAD command prompt |

## Summary

This chapter covered a tremendous amount of information about the Visual Basic for Applications Integrated Development Environment, or VBAIDE. While this is sufficient for most of your AutoCAD VBA development needs, you can get more help from the AutoCAD help files.

The next chapter introduces you to the Visual Basic programming language and its variables, constants, control structures, and more. It also introduces you to the basics of object-oriented programming.

# CHAPTER 2

# Introduction to Visual Basic Programming

**A VISUAL BASIC APPLICATION CONTAINS** several components:

- UserForm modules, which contain an application's visual interface, including ActiveX controls and the form's Visual Basic code

- Standard (.bas) and Class (.cls) modules, which contain customized routines and classes

- Intrinsic and custom ActiveX controls (.ocx) and code components in ActiveX DLLs (.dll)

By default, an AutoCAD VBA project contains a single module called ThisDrawing. You can then add UserForms, standard and class modules, and ActiveX controls as needed. Chapter 3 describes how to add these elements to an application. If you are an experienced VBA developer in AutoCAD 2000 or 2002, read the documentation in AutoCAD 2004 for new, changed, and removed features for ActiveX, VBA, system variables, and drawing data classes. Each new release brings considerable changes that often affect program development in good and bad ways.

## Variables

Variables let you retain values for use *locally* in a procedure or *globally* in your entire application. For example, you might retrieve user input for drawing a LINE entity, saving the coordinates the user selected. You might also ask the user to select a color for an entity using a drop-down combo box or a list box.

Visual Basic refers to variables by name, such as InsertionPoint or LayerName. It's best to avoid using variable names that coincide with predefined property or event names. Variables are known by their *data type*; that is, the kind of data that they can store. The data type determines the amount of memory required to store the variable's value.

## Declaring Variables

Use the `Dim` statement in a procedure to declare a variable. Here's the syntax:

```
Dim <VariableName> [As DataType]
```

Variable names must

- Begin with a letter

- Not contain a period (.)

- Be no longer than 255 characters

- Be unique in the same scope

Declare the variable's data type in the optional `As` *DataType* clause in the `Dim` statement. A variable's data type determines the kind of information a variable holds, such as *String*, *Integer*, or *Object*. See the "Data Types" section later in this chapter for more information.

### Implicit Declaration

You don't have to declare variables as a specific data type before you use them. If you use a variable without explicitly declaring it, Visual Basic creates a variable with that name and assigns it the `Variant` data type. This is the largest data type available in terms of memory usage and could lead to memory resource problems. When you use an undeclared variable, accidentally misspelling the variable name creates another undeclared variable. These kinds of errors can lead to poor performance and a lot of wasted time debugging your code.

### Explicit Declaration

To avoid the hazards mentioned above, force Visual Basic to require that you declare all variables before you use them. To do so, place the following line at the top of your code module:

```
Option Explicit
```

Alternatively, you can turn on explicit data type checking by choosing Tools ➤ Options and checking the Require Variable Declaration box, as shown in Figure 2-1.

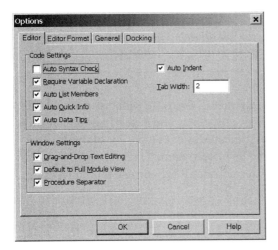

*Figure 2-1. The Options dialog box*

## Variable Names

You can name variables almost any way you want, but there are some restrictions. Follow these rules in variable names:

- You must use a letter as the first character.

- You can't use a space; a period (.); an exclamation mark (!); or the characters @, &, $, or # in the name.

- The name can't be longer than 255 characters.

- Generally, don't use names that are the same as Visual Basic's functions, statements, and methods. To use an intrinsic language function, statement, or method that conflicts with an assigned name, explicitly identify it. Precede the intrinsic function, statement, or method name with the name of the associated type library. For example, if you have a variable called Left, you can only invoke the **Left** function using VBA.Left.

- You can't repeat names in the same scope. For example, you can't declare two variables named age in the same procedure. However, you can declare a private variable named age and a procedure-level variable named age in the same module.

**NOTE** *Visual Basic isn't case-sensitive, but preserves a variable's capitalization in the statement where you declare it.*

In addition to restrictions and requirements, there are widely accepted best practices for naming variables to ensure consistency and ease of reading. Begin each variable's name with a prefix that indicates its data type. For example, a String variable named FirstName should be instead named strFirstName. Table 2-1 lists some commonly used prefixes. Not only does this book use this convention, but so does most sample code elsewhere.

*Table 2-1. Commonly Used Variable Prefixes*

| DATA TYPE | PREFIX | EXAMPLE |
| --- | --- | --- |
| String | str | strFirstName |
| Label | lbl | lblProperties |
| Double | dbl | dblXcoordinate |
| Integer | int | intFloorLevel |
| ListBox | lst | lstSystemNames |
| ComboBox | cbo | cboElecSystems |
| Button | btn | btnChoice |
| CheckBox | chk | chkSaveBackup |
| OptionButton | opt | optSaveFormat |
| Frame | frm | frmSaveOptions |

## Variable Scope and Lifetime

If you declare a variable in a procedure, only code in that procedure can access it. This is known as *local scope*. But sometimes you'll want procedures throughout a module or throughout the application to access one of your variables. Visual Basic lets you specify this broader scope when you declare your variables.

## Scoping Variables

All procedures, variables, constants, and so on have a scope, also called a lifetime. Where you declare them determines when and from where you can access them. You can declare variables as procedure (local) or module, as Table 2-2 explains.

*Table 2-2. Variable Scope*

| SCOPE | PRIVATE | PUBLIC |
|---|---|---|
| Procedure | The variable is accessible only in the procedure where you declared it. | You can't declare variables as Public in a procedure. |
| Module | The variable is accessible in the module where you declared it. | The variable is accessible by all procedures in the module |

### Procedure Variables

Procedure variables, also called local variables, are available only in the procedure in which you declare them. Declare them using either the `Dim` or `Static` keyword, as in this example:

```
Dim Line As AcadLine
```

or

```
Static Count As Integer
```

Variables that you declare in a procedure using the `Dim` keyword have scope only while you're inside that procedure. When you leave the procedure, the variable's value is gone. On the other hand, a variable declared in a procedure using the `Static` keyword lives as long as your application runs, much like a global variable but with local scope (that is, you can access it only when you are in that procedure).

Local variables are used for calculations pertinent to the procedure. Declare a local variable as `Static` only when you need to keep a running count, such as in a procedure, and don't want other procedures in the application to have access to the variable.

### *Module Variables*

By default, variables that you create in a UserForm, Standard or Class module are available only to procedures in that module. At the module level, the Private and Dim keywords are equal. However, it's better to use the Private keyword to make your code more understandable and easily distinguishable from variables declared using the Public keyword.

In the declarations section at the top of your module, declare Private module variables like this:

```
Private LayerOn As Boolean
```

### *Global Variables*

If you want to access module variables anywhere in your application, use the Public keyword as follows:

```
Public LayerOn As Boolean
```

When you do this, the variable is available to every module and procedure in your application. You can't declare Public variables in a procedure.

 **TIP**  *When you declare a variable, declare it as locally as possible. Then as you find that particular variable needs to be accessible more globally, move its declaration out one level at a time.*

## Constants

Constants are values that never change. If you will use a value frequently in your application and its value will never change, declare it as a constant. For example:

```
'declare any constants used throughout applications
Public Const SAVETIME = 15        'public constant for default automatic save time
```

The following scope rules apply to constants:

- If you want a constant to be accessible in a procedure, you must declare it in that procedure.

- To make a constant accessible only in a module in the module's declaration section. Be sure to declare the constant as `Private`.

- You can declare constants as `Private` or `Public`, but they are most often `Public`.

- To make constants accessible to any module or procedure in your application, declare them in the module's declaration section using the `Public` keyword.

---

**TIP** *Typically, constant names are all capitals to distinguish them from variables.*

---

## Data Types

If you don't specify a variable's data type using the `As` keyword, as the following example shows, Visual Basic makes it a `Variant` data type.

```
Dim Variable
```

Although you can create variables this way, you should instead assign a data type to every variable you create. This makes your code more readable and removes ambiguity about what your intentions are in your application.

```
Dim InsertionPoint As Variant
Dim Counter As Integer
```

VBA provides a number of different data types. Each data type has a specific purpose that you should consider when you choose which one to use. Table 2-3 explains VBA's data types.

---

**NOTE** *Data type properties have been modified in Visual Basic.NET and Visual Studio for Applications. If you plan to work in a mixed environment where your VBA programs may interface with .NET programs, be sure to research the differences carefully!*

---

Table 2-3. *Visual Basic Data Types*

| DATA TYPE | RANGE OF VALUES | PURPOSE |
|-----------|-----------------|---------|
| Integer | -32768 to +32767 | Relatively small positive and negative whole numbers |
| Long | -2,147,483,648 to +2,147,483,647 | Relatively large positive and negative whole numbers |
| Single | Approximately 1.4E-45 to 3.4E+48 | Single-precision floating-point numbers that use 4 bytes of data |
| Double | Approximately 4.94E-324 to 1.8E+308 | Double precision floating point numbers that use 8 bytes of data |
| Currency | -922,337,203,685,477.5808 to +922,337,203,685,477.5807 | Money calculations where accuracy is important, giving 15 digits to the left of the decimal and 4 digits to the right of the decimal |
| String | Approximately 0 to 2 billion characters | Text characters |
| Boolean | 1 or 0 | True/False, Yes/No, On/Off values |
| Byte | 0 to 255 | A finite group of positive integers, usually used for character or color code values. |
| Date | 1/1/100 to 12/31/9999 and 0:00:00 to 23:59:59 | General date and time |
| Variant | Anything | The default data type if you don't specify one |

### *Exchanging Numbers and Strings*

You can assign string values that represent a numeric value to a numeric variable. You can also assign a numeric value to a string variable. The following code illustrates this:

```
Public Sub MyMacro()
Dim Count As Integer
Dim NumericString As String

  Count = 100
  NumericString = "555"
```

```
  MsgBox "Integer: " & Count & vbCrLf & _
          "String: " & NumericString

  Count = NumericString

  MsgBox "Integer: " & Count
End Sub
```

Place this code in a standard module file and run it from the AutoCAD command prompt. Caution should be the rule when using this strategy. Assigning a string data type that does not represent a valid number to a numeric variable causes a run-time error. This next section outlines the Visual Basic functions that check the values being converted and give you feedback about their validity.

### Converting Data Types

To help you convert one data type to another, Visual Basic provides the conversion functions shown in Table 2-4.

*Table 2-4. Data Type Conversion Functions*

| FUNCTION NAME | CONVERTS TO |
| --- | --- |
| CBool | Boolean |
| CByte | Byte |
| CCur | Currency |
| CDate | Date |
| CDbl | Double |
| CInt | Integer |
| CLng | Long |
| CSng | Single |
| CStr | String |
| CVar | Variant |
| CVErr | Error |

Using these conversion functions insures that you assign appropriate values to the different variables. The value that you convert must fit in the target data type's value range. If you try to convert to a smaller data type, you may encounter errors or your program may behave strangely.

## Introduction to Arrays

An array is a variable that can hold multiple values of the same data type, each value placed into a separate compartment. In contrast, a normal variable can hold only one value.

---

 **TIP**  *If you need to store an array of different kinds of values, create an array of* Variants.

---

You can work with arrays as a whole or by using an index value to access each element. AutoCAD uses arrays for 3-D WCS coordinates. Arrays are nothing more than a collection of values treated as a single unit, analogous to a List in Visual LISP.

### *Fixed-Length Arrays*

If you know how many elements your array will contain, then declare it with that many elements. The following example, typical of an AutoCAD VBA application, creates a three-element array:

```
Dim StartPoint(0 to 2) As Double
```

This example populates each element of the array with a value:

```
StartPoint(0) = 0
StartPoint(1) = 0
StartPoint(2) = 0
```

### *Detecting an Array's Bounds*

When you use an array to control a looping operation, you need to know the array's lower and upper bounds, or *dimension*. Going beyond an array's lower and upper bounds generates a run-time error. Visual Basic provides two functions, LBound and UBound, that tell you these two values. The following example uses an array of unknown size to control a For ... Next loop.

```
Dim Index As Integer

For Index = LBound(GivenArray) To UBound(GivenArray)
    .
```

·
·

```
Next Index
```

### *Dynamic Arrays*

Sometimes you either don't know how elements will be needed, and sometimes you just don't want to create more elements than you need. Visual Basic lets you create an array whose size you can change as your application runs. To do so, declare your array variable without specifying its dimensions in the parentheses, as in this example:

```
Dim Index() As Integer
```

When you define the array in your source code, use the ReDim statement:

```
ReDim Index(10)
```

ReDim can appear only in a procedure because it executes an action at run time, unlike the Dim and Static statements.

Whenever you redimension an array, the array's contents are erased. You can keep this from happening by using the Preserve keyword, as follows:

```
ReDim Preserve Index(UBound(Index) + 1)
```

This example uses UBound to find the current array's size and then adds one more element to it. Using ReDim imposes some performance issues (such as speed) because it copies the array in the background. Each time you change the array's dimensions, Visual Basic makes a new array, copies the contents into it, and then replaces the original array with the new array. The performance issues become evident when manipulating large arrays that contain large elements.

## Modules

VBA applications may consist of any number of UserForms and standard and/or class modules. This section briefly explains each component you can use in a project.

## UserForm

Although not contained in separate files as in a standalone Visual Basic application, the UserForm module is an integral part of your project. The UserForm module contains the procedures you write to react to the UserForm's events and the controls you place on your UserForm. The UserForm module contains UserForm-level procedures, variables, and constants specific to the project. Also, if you were to export the UserForm module to a file and look at it with a text editor, you would see descriptions of the UserForm and all the controls and their property settings.

To import a UserForm module file (.frm), choose File ➤ Import File or press Ctrl+M. The UserForm module file must have been created by AutoCAD or a similar VBA-enabled application, such as Microsoft Word. If you create the form module file in Visual Basic using the Microsoft Forms 2.0 form add-in, you can import them too. You can't, however, import a .frm file created by Visual Basic.

---

 **NOTE**  *UserForms in earlier versions of VBA are modal, meaning that you can't click away from them to other applications that might be running. To let the user access the AutoCAD window, you must first hide your application window. In AutoCAD 2004 with VBA 6.3, set the form window's ShowModal property at design time to make UserForms modal (True) or modeless (False).*

---

## Standard

The standard module file (.bas) generally contains procedures and declarations that other modules in your application can access. The standard module can contain global (available to the entire application) or module-level declarations of procedures, variables, constants, and programmer-defined data types. Your application does not have to use the code that you write in a standard module. The standard module gives you a place to put code that may be used frequently and that you would like to have handy when the need arises. Code modules may also include subroutines or functions that you will use frequently throughout your programs.

# Class

The foundation of object-oriented programming in Visual Basic is the *Class* module. You can create new objects by writing code in class modules that implement their own properties, methods, and events. They support the same features as the UserForm module, but allow a new level of functionality such as creating ActiveX controls, ActiveX documents, and so on. AutoCAD VBA can create only code components. To create components such as ActiveX controls and ActiveX documents, you need Visual Basic.

Class modules hold the key to creating new objects. These objects may contain their own properties and methods and may be instantiated more than once. Class modules let you combine functionality into a single source. Tasks such as API function calls and common database activities are prime candidates for Class modules.

## Procedures

Procedures are blocks of code that have a specific purpose. You will use three different kinds of procedures in most of your applications: Sub, Function, and Event. Each of these has a specific purpose.

## Sub

Sub procedures are blocks of code that another procedure in your application explicitly calls. They may contain parameters when called, but do not return a value.

The syntax of a Sub procedure is

```
[Private|Public|Static] Sub ProcedureName([argumentlist])
     <... block of statements ...>
End Sub
```

The statements between Sub and End Sub are executed each time the Sub procedure is called. By default, Sub procedures are Public, and therefore may be called from a UserForm, Class, or Standard module unless specified otherwise using the Private keyword.

The *argument list* is similar to the variables declared in a Sub procedure. These are variables that the calling procedure passes to the Sub procedure when it is executed. For more details on passing arguments to procedures, see "Passing Arguments To Procedures," later in this chapter.

The following example illustrates a typical Sub procedure. In this example, the Layers collection displays the name of each layer in the currently active document.

```
Public Sub IterateLayers()
Dim Layer As AcadLayer
   For Each Layer In ThisDrawing.Layers
      Debug.Print Layer.Name
   Next Layer
End Sub
```

## Function

Function procedures are similar to Sub procedures, except that they can return a value to the calling procedure.

The syntax of a Function procedure is

```
[Private|Public|Static] Function ProcedureName([argumentlist]) [As VariableType]
      <... block of statements ...>
End Function
```

This example illustrates calling a Function procedure and assigning the return value to a variable of the appropriate type.

```
ReturnValue = FunctionName([argumentlist])
```

The Function procedure's return value has a data type. If the data type is not specified, it is Variant by default.

FunctionName is used to return the Function procedure's value. The value becomes part of the function expression that called the Function procedure:

```
Public FunctionName(arguments) As DataType

      <... statements ...>

      FunctionName = ReturnValue
End Function
```

## Event

Event procedures are executed when events occur in an object. You can declare Event procedures in a class module or, more typically, as part of a UserForm module either attached to the UserForm itself or on ActiveX controls placed on the UserForm.

Event procedures use a unique naming convention that distinguishes them from other procedures:

```
ObjectVariable_EventName
```

This example shows the default event procedure for a typical UserForm:

```
Private Sub UserForm_Click()

End Sub
```

VBA passes arguments to some events when they occur, such as

```
Private Sub AcadDocument_BeginSave(ByVal FileName As String)

End Sub
```

This event is called just prior to AutoCAD saving the current drawing. VBA passes the current drawing's name as a string to the Event procedure. This may be useful if you have several drawings open and want to save only a particular drawing by checking the FileName parameter for that name.

Use Event procedures only when you must since they impose performance overhead by executing every time the event occurs. Overusing them can bring AutoCAD to a crawl or even crash it entirely.

## Calling Procedures

You can't call a Sub procedure in a Visual Basic expression, which means that you can't use one in an If ... Then statement in an assignment, or in a comparative statement. You call a Sub procedure as a standalone statement, similar to the following:

```
CreateLayer Name
```

However, a Function procedure is typically part of an expression as in the following:

```
If CheckForLayer("Layer1") Then
```

A Sub or Function procedure can modify the values of the arguments passed.

## Passing Arguments to Procedures

There are two methods of passing arguments to procedures: by value and by reference.

**By value.** When you pass arguments by value (ByVal), only a copy of the variable is passed to the procedure. If the procedure modifies the variable's value, only the copy is changed. The original variable still contains its original value. Calling a procedure using the ByVal keyword lets you pass a value to the procedure as follows

```
Public Sub ProcedureName(ByVal Variable)
.
.
.
End Sub
```

**By reference.** Passing arguments by reference (ByRef) is the Visual Basic default. Variables passed by reference let you change the original variable's value. Since ByRef is the default, you don't need to explicitly declare it as such when you call procedures.

---

 **NOTE** *Newer programming languages, such as VB .NET, C#, and VSA, have made* ByVal *the default.*

---

## Control Structures

Control structures control your application's flow and execution. Without control structures, your application would run from top to bottom. This may be suitable for the most simple applications, but the power of Visual Basic lets you control the flow and execution and effectively change its order.

## Decision Structures

Decision structures let you test the condition, value, or *state* of a variable and perform operations based on the test's result.

### If ... Then

Use an If ... Then statement to conditionally execute one or more other statements. The If ... Then statement is used in one of the following methods

```
If <condition> Then <statement>
```

or

```
If <condition> Then
    <statements>
End If
```

The <condition> can be an expression that evaluates to a numeric value. Visual Basic interprets the numeric value as either True (nonzero) or False (zero).

When the <condition> evaluates to True, then Visual Basic executes the <statement(s)> following the Then keyword, as in the following single-line If ... Then statement

```
If Count < 20 Then Count = Count + 1
```

To execute more than one statement after the conditional test, write it like this:

```
If Count < 20 Then
  Count = Count + 1
  Application.Visible = False
End If
```

The multiple-line version of the If ... Then statement requires that you end the statement with the End If keywords.

## *If ... Then ... Else*

To test several conditions, define several blocks of statements where a statement is executed only when its condition is met. For example:

```
If <condition1> Then
  <statement block 1>

  Else If
    <statement block 2>

  Else
    <statement block 3>
End If
```

If `<condition1>` returns `True`, Visual Basic executes the statements following the `Then` keyword. Visual Basic ignores the statements in `<statement block 2>` and `<statement block 3>`, continuing execution with the statements following the `End If` keywords.

If `<condition1>` returns `False`, Visual Basic executes the statements following the `Else If` keywords, if supplied. Visual Basic ignores the statements in `<statement block 1>` and `<statement block 3>`, continuing execution with the statements following the `End If` keywords.

You may use any number of `Else If` statements, but only one `Else` statement, in an `If ... Then ... Else` statement.

## *Select Case*

When you evaluate more than two conditions, it often makes more sense to use the `Select Case` control structure.

When you want to selectively execute a block of statements from a choice of many, use the `Select Case` structure, as in this example:

```
Select Case <TestExpression>
  Case <ExpressionList>
    <statements>
  .
  .
  .

  Case Else
    <statements>
End Select
```

The Select Case structure begins with a single test expression. Visual Basic evaluates it once and compares it with each Case statement in the structure. When Visual Basic finds a match, it executes the associated block of statements.

The <ExpressionList> may contain one or more values separated by commas. The statement may contain zero or more statements. Visual Basic executes only <statements> associated with the first match to the <TestExpression>. After those <statements> are completed, execution continues with any statements following the End Select keywords.

You can include an optional Case Else statement that Visual Basic executes if it finds no Case matches.

This example shows how the Select Case structure works:

```
Select Case UCase(ColorName)
  Case "RED"
    Layer.Color = acRed

  Case "YELLOW"
    Layer.Color = acYellow

  Case "GREEN"
    Layer.Color = acGreen

  Case "CYAN"
    Layer.Color = acCyan

  Case "BLUE"
    Layer.Color = acBlue

  Case "MAGENTA"
    Layer.Color = acMagenta

  Case "WHITE"
    Layer.Color = acWhite

  Case Else
    If CInt(ColorName) > 0 And CInt(ColorName) < 256 Then
      Layer.Color = CInt(ColorName)

    Else
      MsgBox UCase(ColorName) & " is an invalid color name", _
             vbCritical, "Invalid Color Selected"
    End If
End Select
```

Another way to format `Select Case` is to put the return statements on the same line as the Case statements. This keeps the code format simpler when you have a small set of cases. Type a colon (:) after the `Case` statement to separate it from the return statement code:

```
Select Case Ucase(ColorName)
    Case RED: Layer.Color = acRed
    Case BLUE: Layer.Color = acBlue
End Select
```

While the `Select Case` evaluates a single test expression at the top of the structure, the `If ... Then ... Else` structure evaluates a different expression for each `Else ... If` statement. Therefore, you replace an `If ... Then ... Else` structure with a `Select Case` statement if each `Else If` statement evaluates the same expression but looks for different values.

## Loop Structures

Use loop structures to execute a series of statements repeatedly. Loops execute based on conditions. Depending on their structure, they can stop executing at their beginning or end.

## *Do While ... Loop*

You can use a `Do While ... Loop` to execute a block of statements an infinite number of times. This loop first evaluates a numeric value. If it's `True` (nonzero), Visual Basic executes each statement in the loop. At the end of the loop, Visual Basic then reevaluates the condition and keeps executing the loop's statements until the condition is `False` (zero). When the condition is `False`, the loop skips over all its statements. Visual Basic executes the statements after the `Loop` keyword. Here's a `Do While ... Loop`'s syntax:

```
Do While <condition>
    <statements>
Loop
```

The following example first tests the `Index` value against a string's `Length`, then executes each statement and increments the `Index` variable at the end of the loop. Execution continues until it evaluates the entire string or detects an illegal value.

```
Do While Index - 1 < Length
  Character = Asc(Mid(Name, Index, 1))
  Select Case Character
    Case 36, 45, 48 To 57, 65 To 90, 95
      IsOK = True
    Case Else
      IsOK = False
      Exit Sub
  End Select
  Index = Index + 1
Loop
```

In the Do While ... Loop, evaluation takes place at the top of the loop. If the condition is False (zero), then Visual Basic executes none of the loop's statements.

## Do ... Loop While

Use the Do ... Loop While to execute the loop's statements at least one time before evaluating the condition. If the condition evaluates to True (nonzero), execution continues at the top of the loop. Otherwise, the condition is False (zero), and the loop stops. This loop has the following syntax:

```
Do
  <statements>
Loop While <condition>
```

## Do Until ... Loop and Do Loop ... Until

There are two other loop structures: Do Until ... Loop and Do Loop ... Until. These loops run while the condition is False (zero) rather than True (nonzero). These loops have the following syntax:

```
Do Until <condition>
  <statements>
Loop
```

and

```
Do
  <statements>
Loop Until <condition>
```

This example compares the Do While ... Loop to Do Until ... Loop, iterating an ADO database recordset collection until they reach the recordset's end of file (EOF) marker:

```
Do While Not Recordset.EOF
    Debug.Print Recordset.Fields("layername").Value
Recordset.MoveNext
Loop
```

and

```
Do Until Recordset.EOF
    Debug.Print Recordset.Fields("layername").Value
    Recordset.MoveNext
Loop
```

## *For ... Next*

Use a For ... Next loop when you know how many times you want to execute a block of statements. It uses a counter variable that you can either increase or decrease to control the number of cycles or times Visual Basic executes the loop. The For ... Next loop has this syntax:

```
For <counter> = <StartingValue> To <EndingValue> [Step <increment>]
  <statements>
Next [<counter>]
```

> **NOTE** *The optional* <increment> *value can be positive or negative. If it's positive, then* <StartingValue> *must be less than or equal to* <EndingValue>. *Otherwise, the statements in the loop never execute. If it's negative, then* <StartingValue> *must be greater than or equal to* <EndingValue>. *If you don't set a step, it defaults to 1.*

When a For ... Next loop executes, the following sequence of events occurs:

1. The <counter> variable is set to <StartingValue>.

2. If <counter> is greater than <EndingValue>, Visual Basic exits the loop. If the <increment> variable is negative, Visual Basic tests whether <counter> is less than <EndingValue>.

3. Visual Basic executes each statement in the loop.

4. Visual Basic increments or decrements the <counter> variable by 1 or by the [Step <increment>] value, if you specified one.

5. Visual Basic repeats steps 2 through 4 until the <condition> in step 2 is met, when it exits the loop.

The following example illustrates using the For ... Next loop:

```
Dim Point(0 To 2) As Double
Dim Index As Integer

  For Index = 0 To 2
    Point(Index) = 0
  Next Index
```

## For ... Each ... Next

Use a For ... Each ... Next structure to iterate through an object collection's elements or through an array, executing a block of statements for each element. This structure iterates through each element of the collection or array regardless of how many elements the collection or array contains. For ... Each ... Next has this syntax:

```
For Each <element> In <collection>
  <statements>
Next <element>
```

The following restrictions apply when using For ... Each ... Next:

- For collection objects, the element data type can be Variant, generic (late bound object), or a specific (early bound) object type.

- Arrays must contain only Variant data types.

- You can't use For ... Each ... Next with an array of programmer-defined data types. This is because the Variant data type can't contain user-defined data types.

The following example illustrates using this structure:

```
Public Sub DisplayLayers()
Dim Layer As AcadLayer

  For Each Layer In ThisDrawing.Layers
    Debug.Print Layer.Name
  Next Layer
End Sub
```

## Nested Control Structures

Placing one control structure in another is called *nesting*. You can nest control structures to any level you want, but indent each level for readability. The following example demonstrates nesting control structures:

```
Public Sub WhatColor()
Dim Layer As AcadLayer
Dim Answer As String

  For Each Layer In ThisDrawing.Layers
    Answer = InputBox("Enter color name: ")

    'user pressed cancel
    If Answer = "" Then Exit Sub

    Select Case UCase(ColorName)
      Case "RED"
        Layer.Color = acRed

      Case "YELLOW"
        Layer.Color = acYellow

      Case "GREEN"
        Layer.Color = acGreen

      Case "CYAN"
        Layer.Color = acCyan
```

```
      Case "BLUE"
         Layer.Color = acBlue

      Case "MAGENTA"
         Layer.Color = acMagenta

      Case "WHITE"
         Layer.Color = acWhite

      Case Else
         If CInt(ColorName) > 0 And CInt(ColorName) < 256 Then
            Layer.Color = CInt(ColorName)

         Else
            MsgBox UCase(ColorName) & " is an invalid color name", _
                  vbCritical, "Invalid Color Selected"
         End If
    End Select
  Next Layer
End Sub
```

# Exiting a Control Structure

Using the Exit statement immediately exits a For or Do loop. The syntax to exit a loop is as follows:

```
Do While <condition>
  <statements>

  Exit Do
Loop
```

**or**

```
For Count = 0 To 5
  <statements>

  Exit For
Next Count
```

## Exiting a Sub or Function Procedure

Using the Exit statement immediately exits a Sub or Function procedure. The syntax is simple:

```
Public Sub SubName()
.
  Exit Sub
.
End Sub
```

or

```
Public Function FunctionName() As Object
.
  Exit Function
.
End Function
```

It is useful to exit a Sub or Function procedure when a condition has been met and you don't want to execute any remaining code. This provides a means of exiting the procedure as soon as the condition is met.

## *With ... End With*

The With ... End With statement lets you shorten your coding work by telling the compiler to repeatedly use an implicit reference to a named object without having to restate the object each time you use it. Use this feature anywhere in a procedure that you repeatedly refer to an object. Consider the following example:

```
Dim mylayer As AcadLayer
mylayer = ThisDrawing.ActiveLayer
mylayer.Color = acBlue
mylayer.Linetype = "continuous"
mylayer.Lineweight = acLnWtByLwDefault
mylayer.Freeze = False
mylayer.LayerOn = True
mylayer.Lock = False
```

Using the With ... End With statement, you do less typing:

```
Dim mylayer As AcadLayer
mylayer = ThisDrawing.ActiveLayer
With mylayer
.Color = acBlue
.Linetype = "continuous"
.Lineweight = acLnWtByLwDefault
.Freeze = False
.LayerOn = True
.Lock = False
End With
```

# Application Writing Techniques

This section presents techniques for writing readable code. Failing to implement any of these techniques has no affect on your code's execution.

## *Writing Statements on Multiple Lines*

To write a long statement on more than one line, use the *line continuation character,* which is a space followed by an underscore ( _). Writing your code this way makes it more readable both in print and on the screen. This example shows the line continuation character in action:

```
'create the solid
Set AcadSolid = ThisDrawing.ModelSpace.AddExtrudedSolidAlongPath _
                (AcadRegion(0), AcadSpline)
'concatenate a long string value
Mypath = Application.Path & ?\My Custom Folders\VBA Programs? & _
                ?\Program 1\DVB Files?
```

 **NOTE** *Don't place comments after the line continuation character on the same line of code. There are also some restrictions as to where you can place a line continuation character, such as in the middle of an object or procedure name.*

Using this feature lets you format your code for easier reading. However, do not overuse this feature as too much of it can make your code unreadable.

## Combining Statements on a Single Line

Typically, you place only one statement on a line of source code. But sometimes combining more than one statement on a single line can make your code more readable, especially in AutoCAD. Consider these six lines of code:

```
StartPoint(0) = 0
StartPoint(1) = 0
StartPoint(2) = 0
EndPoint(0) = 1
EndPoint(1) = 1
EndPoint(2) = 0
```

You can make them more readable by placing similar statements on the same line:

```
StartPoint(0) = 0: StartPoint(1) = 0: StartPoint(2) = 0
EndPoint(0) = 1: EndPoint(1) = 1: EndPoint(2) = 0
```

Each statement is separated by a colon (:). The colon appears only between statements and not at the end of the line.

## Adding Comments to your Code

Making notes about how your code sections function is more a necessity than an option. Comments explain the purpose of the code not only to you, but to other developers. When you return to a section of code months later, if you have properly commented it, you won't have to guess or waste time trying to determine what is being executed.

Just as important as commenting functions and code blocks, always provide a comment for files themselves, usually at the top. This comment block explains what the file is for, who wrote it, and when it was written. You can also include notes about related files and dependent and specific requirements for using the program. The following example is just one way you could comment your program files:

```
?**********************************************************
? Filename: myProgramFile.dvb
? Author:   Joe Sutphin
? Date:     September 12, 2003
? Purpose:  This program inspires awe in my customers!
?**********************************************************
```

All comments begin with an apostrophe ('), called the *comment character*. Visual Basic ignores all text you type after the comment character to the end of the line.

The following example shows how you can use comments to document your program statements:

```
'define the Start and End point
StartPoint(0) = 0: StartPoint(1) = 0: StartPoint(2) = 0
EndPoint(0) = 1: EndPoint(1) = 1: EndPoint(2) = 0
```

## Overview of Object-Oriented Programming

When you create an application in VBA, you use objects whether you realize it or not. Both AutoCAD and VBA are objects. This section examines the fundamentals of object-oriented programming.

### Objects and Classes

An *object* is the creation or *instantiation* of a *class*. A class is a template or *definition* of a potential object. This template is used to create as many objects as needed based on a single class definition. Each object is an *instance* of the class. The action of creating a new object instance is referred to as *instantiation*.

The word class refers to classifying objects. For example, the entity objects Line and Circle are instances of the AcadLine and AcadCircle classes, respectively.

Visual Basic and VBA use class modules to define classes. An object, which is an instance of the class, is created based on the class module definition. Class modules consist of a declaration section followed by a series of Sub, Function, and Property subroutines similar to the UserForm and Standard modules. Variables and code in the class module can only be used by creating an object, which is an instance of the class.

### Object Data

An object contains data about itself. For example, an AcadLine object contains data about its starting and ending points, color, and thickness. The object also knows its linetype and the layer it sits on. These values are *properties* of the object. There may be many AcadLine objects, each having its own set of similar property values but each created from the same AcadLine class.

*Instance variables* store data values for each object instance. Each object instance contains its own set of variables, which were created from the same class. This is possible because each instance of the class, although created from the same class, must have a unique name. The Name property accesses each object and its properties. Each instance of a particular class has a unique name identifier.

Variables used in a class module are declared at the module level, as the following pseudocode shows:

```
Private StartPoint(0 To 2) As Double
Private EndPoint(0 To 2) As Double
```

You can declare variables in a class module as either Private or Public similar to UserForm and Standard modules.

## Private Variables

You can access variables you declare as Private only in the module in which you declare them. Their main use in the class module is to manage code specific to the object. Client programs can access class code only through the class interface. This adds a layer of security around your objects so that external applications can't circumvent the rules, haphazardly changing values without using the interface that you provide for accessing your object.

## Public Variables

You can access variables you declare as Public from within your class module and from a client application. It's generally bad practice to use Public variables in class modules. When you declare a variable as Public, you grant unrestricted access to it, trusting that the client application will not change them inappropriately or provide incorrect data. Using Public variables also means that there is no code to force control over how the client application manipulates the object.

One primary reason for using object-oriented programming techniques is that they hide or *encapsulate* the class's inner workings, exposing a client-application interface only for changing your objects.

Variables declared as Private force the client application to use the object's code to change the object's data, letting you change how the code is implemented with little or no change on the client application's part. Variables declared as

Public directly break the concept of encapsulation, providing a client with direct and uncontrolled access to the objects data.

## An Object's Behavior

The concept behind objects is to let applications interact with them. If the object's data is encapsulated in the object, then you must provide a means for a client application to access the object's data.

---

 **NOTE** *Autodesk makes a clear distinction between an entity and an object in terms of an entity being a graphic instance. For example, a Line object is the database representation of the Line entity, which is the selectable item in the drawing editor window. In general, Autodesk calls a graphic an entity and calls the entity's programmatic aspects an object.*

---

An object provides an interface that allows client applications to access its data. *Methods, properties,* and *events* provide a client application this access to the object.

The object's interface contains Property, Sub and Function routines and any events implemented in the object. Declaring any of these as Public makes them part of the object's interface. An object can contain multiple interfaces, just as in the real world, letting the client application access the object's data.

### Properties

Properties generally describe an object's characteristics such as height, width, length, and color, or the object's state such as On/Off or Thaw/Freeze. An object typically contains many properties that provide the client application with access to most, if not all, of its characteristics.

### Methods

Methods are Sub procedures or *functions* that act on the object, such as rotating, offsetting, or moving it. Most AutoCAD objects contain a small number of methods. Also, many of the methods are the same for similar objects, such as all the graphic objects or all the non-graphic objects.

## *Events*

Events are actions that the end user can perform while the application runs, including clicking the mouse button or pressing a key. No preset actions happen—you must provide the code to perform whatever tasks you want when an event occurs. This is perhaps the trickiest part of programming—several events can occur rapidly, and it is challenging to decide which event to supply code to respond to the event.

## *Debugging Basics*

This section discusses the basics of debugging your application. Debugging is more an art form then a science, and as such you'll need to decide what works best for you. These techniques give you a good understanding of the available tools and how to use them.

### *The Immediate Window*

Use the Immediate window to display the results of statements in your code. Sometimes referred to as the Debug window, its main purpose is to display debugging information. To open the Immediate window, choose View ➤ Immediate Window or press Ctrl+G.

To execute code in the Immediate window, type the statement into it and press the Enter key, as shown in Figure 2-2. To see the statement's return value, precede the statement with a question mark (?).

*Figure 2-2. Application.Path statement return value*

You typically use the Immediate window for these tasks:

- Testing new code

- Querying and/or changing a variable's value while your application is running

- Querying and/or changing a property value while your application is running

- Calling procedures similarly to calling them in code

- Viewing your program's debugging information while it runs

To can get help on syntax for functions, statements, properties, or methods in the Immediate window, select the keyword, property name, or method name and press F1.

### Adding a Watch

Adding a *watch* lets you watch the value of any valid Visual Basic expression. To create a watch, choose Debug ➤ Add Watch. The dialog box in Figure 2-3 appears.

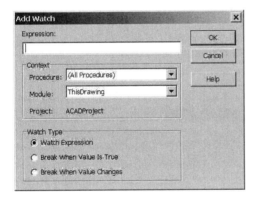

*Figure 2-3. The Add Watch dialog box*

If you have watches already defined in your code, the Watches window appears when the program's execution hits that watch. If a watch expression is out of scope, the Watches window contains no value. To display the Watches window, choose View ➤ Watch Window.

### The Call Stack

The Call Stack window, shown in Figure 2-4, lists started procedures that have not completed. This feature is available only in break mode, which is when program execution pauses. When the current procedure's code is executed, VBA adds the procedure to a list of active procedures. VBA also adds each `Sub`, `Function`, or `Property` procedure the procedure calls. As execution returns to the calling procedure, each procedure is removed from the list. The Immediate window procedures you execute are added to the Call Stack as well. To open the Call Stack window, when in break mode, click View ➤ Call Stack or press Ctrl+L.

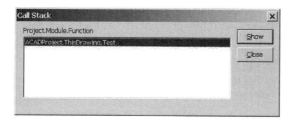

*Figure 2-4. The Call Stack dialog box*

### The Locals Window

The Locals window, shown in Figure 2-5, is similar to the Watches window, except that it displays *local* values—that is, variables declared in the current procedure. To open the Locals window, choose View ➤ Locals Window.

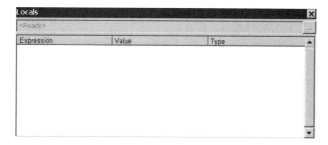

*Figure 2-5. The Locals window*

### Breakpoints

You use breakpoints to stop program execution at a statement in a procedure where you think a problem may exist. Breakpoints are cleared when they are no longer needed.

To set a breakpoint, follow these steps:

1. Place the insertion point somewhere on the line of code where you want to stop execution.

2. Choose Debug ➤ Toggle Breakpoint, press F9, or click next to the statement in the margin indicator bar if it's visible.

VBA adds the breakpoint and highlights the line using the breakpoint color defined on the Editor tab in the VBAIDE's Options dialog box.

**NOTE**   *Setting a breakpoint on a line that contains several statements separated by colons (:) breaks at the first statement on the line.*

To clear a breakpoint, follow these steps:

1. Place the insertion point somewhere on the line of code containing the breakpoint.

2. Choose Debug ➤ Toggle Breakpoint, press F9, or click next to the statement in the margin indicator bar if it's visible.

VBA clears the breakpoint and removes the highlighting.

To clear all the breakpoints in your application, choose Debug ➤ Clear All Breakpoints or press Ctrl+Shift+F9.

**NOTE**   *Breakpoints are not saved when you save your code.*

### Stepping Through Your Code

You can *step through* your code, which executes it one line at a time. Using this feature lets you monitor the effects of code on system and application variables. VBA gives you four different methods to step through your code; Step Into, Step Over, Step Out, and Run to Cursor, as shown in Table 2-5.

*Table 2-5. Methods for Stepping Through Code*

| METHOD | FUNCTION |
| --- | --- |
| Step Into | Executes your code one statement at a time. To use this method, choose Debug ➤ Step Into or press F8. |
| Step Over | Executes a procedure as a whole unit, then returns and steps to the next statement in the current procedure. To use this method, choose Debug ➤ Step Over or press Shift+F8. |
| Step Out | Executes the remaining code of a Sub or Function, then displays the statement following the procedure call. This feature is available in break mode only. To use this method, choose Debug ➤ Step Out or press Ctrl+Shift+F8. |
| Run to Cursor | Executes from the current statement in design mode to where you place the cursor. To use this method, click Debug ➤ Run to Cursor or press Ctrl+F8. |

## The On Error Statements

If you don't use an On Error statement, any run-time error is fatal—that is, an error message appears and execution stops.

> **NOTE** *An error-handling routine is a section of code marked by a line label such as* HandleError: *or a line number.*

On Error initiates *error handling*, which lets the application decide whether an error is fatal. It provides a structured means of controlling how execution will continue for non-fatal errors, and stops execution for fatal errors.

Error-handling routines typically rely on the value in the Err object's Number property. The error-handling routine should test or save relevant property values in the Err object before any other error can occur or before the program calls a procedure that might cause an error. The Err object's property values reflect only the most recent error. Err.Description contains the error message associated with Err.Number.

**NOTE** *VBA, VBScript, Visual Basic and Visual Basic.NET differ significantly between each other in terms of error handling features and capabilities.*

### On Error Resume Next

The On Error Resume Next statement allows execution to continue despite a run-time error. Execution can continue either with the statement right after the statement that caused the run-time error, or with the statement right after the most recent call out of the procedure that contains the On Error Resume Next statement. You can place the error-handling routine inline with where the error would occur, rather than transferring control to another location in the procedure:

```
Dim oLayer As AcadLayer
  On Error Resume Next
  Set oLayer = Application.ActiveDocument.Layers.Add(Name)
  If Err = 0 Then
    Set CreateLayer = oLayer
  End If
```

The On Error Resume Next statement becomes inactive when another procedure is called, so use an On Error Resume Next statement in each called routine if you want inline error handling in that routine.

**NOTE** *The* On Error Resume Next *structure may be preferable to* On Error GoTo *when handling errors generated during access to other objects. Checking* Err *after each interaction with an object removes ambiguity about which object the code accessed, which object placed the error code in* Err.Number, *and which object originally generated the error (specified in* Err.Source).

### On Error GoTo 0

On Error GoTo 0 disables the current procedure's error handling. It doesn't specify line 0 as the start of the error-handling code, even if the procedure contains a line numbered 0. Without an On Error GoTo 0 statement, Visual Basic disables error handling when it exits the procedure.

### *Exit Sub, Exit Function, and Exit Property*

To prevent error-handling code from running when no error has occurred, place an Exit Sub, Exit Function, or Exit Property statement immediately before the error-handling routine, as in this example:

```
Public Function ConnectToAutoCAD(WindowState As AcWindowState) As AcadApplication
    On Error GoTo HandleError
    . . .
    Exit Function

ExitHere:
    Exit Function

HandleError:
    . . .
    Resume ExitHere
End Function
```

In this example, the error-handling code follows the Exit Function statement and precedes the End Function statement to separate it from the procedure flow. You can place error-handling code anywhere in a procedure, but you typically place it at the end for easy maintenance.

## The Err Object

The Err object contains information about run-time errors. You will use the Err object quite a bit to keep your applications from crashing on the end user at run time. Typically, you'll most frequently use the Err object's Description and Number properties, and its Clear method.

### *The Description Property*

The Description property is a string describing the error. Users will appreciate you displaying this property in a MsgBox control instead of crashing the program.

### *The Number Property*

The Number property is the error's number. Some errors give you only a number to work with. All of this book's the examples list both the Description and Number properties.

To use the Err object, include the following statement in your procedure, which executes if an error should occur:

```
On Error GoTo HandleError
```

If an error occurs, execution goes directly to the error handler, as shown in this example:

```
ExitHere:
  Exit Sub

HandleError:
  MsgBox Error:  & Err.Description &  ( & Err.Number & )
  Resume ExitHere
```

If an error should happen, this example successfully traps the error and lets your application exit gracefully. Include this construct where the user is likely to make an error. The Resume statement tells Visual Basic where to continue execution after handling the error.

**NOTE** *For a more detailed list of* Number *property values and their meanings, search for "trappable errors" in AutoCAD VBA's online help. Most OLE objects return errors whose numbers are in a unique range; you usually have to convert them to get their descriptions.*

### *The Clear Property*

The Clear property clears any error's Err object. The most common use of this property is when VB programmers try to connect or start an instance of AutoCAD, as in this example:

```
Dim Application As AcadApplication

On Error Resume Next

Set Application = GetObject(Class:="AutoCAD.Application")

If Err Then
  Err.Clear

  Set Application = CreateObject(Class:="AutoCAD.Application")

  If Err Then
    MsgBox "Error connecting to AutoCAD", vbCritical, "AutoCAD Fatal Error"
    Exit Sub
  End If
End If
```

In this example, the `On Error Resume Next` statement tells Visual Basic to keep executing code should an error occur. This lets you gracefully handle the error. This example first tries to connect to an already running instance of AutoCAD. If that attempt fails, then the `Err` object holds the error code. The `Err` object's `Clear` method then clears the error. It then tries to start AutoCAD. If that attempt fails, then the application can't continue.

## Summary

This chapter presented the essence of the Visual Basic programming language. It also discussed common techniques for debugging your applications. The next chapter covers your application's user interface, including graphic elements such as using ActiveX controls and designing and handling your application's visual aspects.

# CHAPTER 3

# Application Elements

**AUTOCAD VBA PROVIDES SUPPORT** for creating complete applications, including dialog box interfaces. This chapter examines how to create and manipulate these dialog boxes and how to place and manipulate ActiveX control components such as text boxes and list boxes.

## Designing a UserForm

The UserForm object is the canvas upon which you visually design your application, and it provides the windows your users interact with when they run the application. UserForms have their own properties, methods, and events you can use to control their appearance and behavior.

The first step in designing a UserForm is to set its properties, such as width and height. You may set a UserForm's properties at design time or at run time using code.

### Adding a UserForm to Your Application

If your application requires a user interface or dialog with the user, then you need to add a UserForm. A *UserForm,* or *dialog box,* is a window in which several bits of information can be gathered or displayed at once. A login dialog box is a simple example of a form, whereas the AutoCAD Select File dialog box in Figure 3-1 represents a more complex application example.

To add a UserForm to your project, select Insert ➤ UserForm. Alternatively, you can use a drop-down toolbar button, shown in Figure 3-2, that enables you to add these four basic components: UserForm, Module, Class Module, and Procedure.

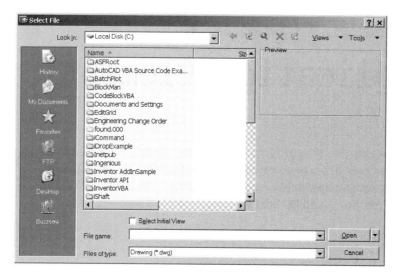

Figure 3-1. The Select File dialog box

Figure 3-2. The drop-down toolbar button showing various modules

Once you've chosen to add a UserForm to your project, your project should look something like Figure 3-3.

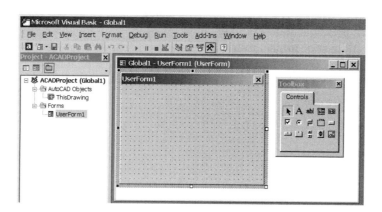

Figure 3-3. The AutoCAD VBAIDE

## Setting UserForm Properties

UserForm properties control a form's physical appearance. The UserForm.Caption property defines the text that appears on the left-hand side of the UserForm title bar, as shown in Figure 3-4.

Caption ⟶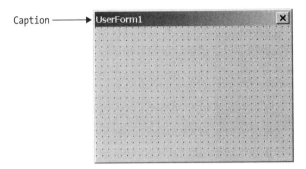

*Figure 3-4. The Caption property of UserForm*

UserForms in AutoCAD 2000 VBA are modal and therefore don't contain a minimize or maximize button on the right side of the UserForm title bar. UserForms in AutoCAD 2002 and 2004 VBA (VBA 6.3), however, can be either modal or modeless.

The UserForm.Height and UserForm.Width properties control the initial UserForm height and width, respectively, as shown in Figure 3-5.

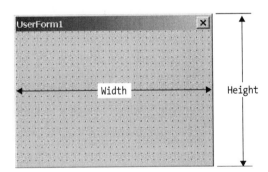

*Figure 3-5. The Width and Height properties of UserForm*

However, you may change these properties at run time as demonstrated in the following example:

```
Private Sub UserForm_Activate()
    UserForm1.Width = 200
    UserForm1.Height = 150
End Sub
```

In this example, the UserForm's Width and Height properties are changed when the UserForm is activated through the Activate method.

As you can see in Figure 3-6, the UserForm.Left and UserForm.Top properties control the initial UserForm position relative to the upper-left corner of the screen.

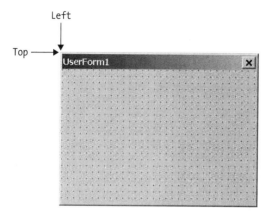

*Figure 3-6. The Top and Left properties of UserForm*

## Adding a Control to a Form

When you add a UserForm to your project, another window immediately appears. This window, called the *Toolbox,* is where you'll find the *intrinsic,* or default, ActiveX controls that are available for you to design your user interface (see Figure 3-7).

*Figure 3-7. The ActiveX Toolbox*

Placing an ActiveX control on a form is simply a matter of clicking the control in the Toolbox and then clicking the area of the UserForm where you want to place the control. Each time you drop a new control onto a form, VBA automatically provides a default name and index number for the control. For example, the first TextBox control will be named TextBox1 by default. You can rename controls by modifying their Name property.

When you click the ActiveX control you want, the cursor becomes a plus (+) sign, with the icon of the control appearing to the lower right of the plus sign, when the cursor is moved over the UserForm. The middle of this plus sign signifies the upper-left corner (the Left and Top properties) of the control. By default, the control will snap to the closest grid point displayed on your UserForm.

For example, pick the TextBox control, as shown in Figure 3-8.

*Figure 3-8. Toolbox with IntelliSense displayed*

Place the control in the upper-left corner of the UserForm similar to what you see in Figure 3-9.

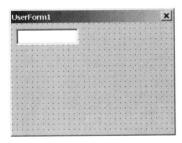

*Figure 3-9. UserForm with a TextBox control*

Now, create a dialog box interface that looks something like the example depicted in Figure 3-10. (Don't worry about making it look exactly like the illustration; you just need to have the same controls on a form for this example.) Table 3-1 lists the controls and their respective property settings.

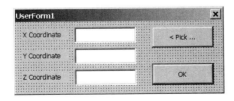

*Figure 3-10. Completed UserForm*

*Table 3-1. Class Controls and Their Property Settings*

| CONTROL CLASS | NAME | CAPTION |
|---|---|---|
| Label | Label1 | X Coordinate |
| Label | Label2 | Y Coordinate |
| Label | Label3 | Z Coordinate |
| CommandButton | cmdPick | < Pick … |
| CommandButton | cmdOK | OK |
| TextBox | txtX | |
| TextBox | txtY | |
| TextBox | txtZ | |

Next, you'll enter some code and see how to make this dialog box interface work. First, you need to open the UserForm code module by selecting View ➤ Code or pressing F7. Or you may start by double-clicking the < Pick … command button and entering the code listed here:

```
Private Sub cmdPick_Click()
Dim Point As Variant
   On Error Resume Next
   'hide the UserForm
   UserForm1.Hide
   'ask user to select a point
   Point = ThisDrawing.Utility.GetPoint(, "Select a point")
   If Err Then Exit Sub
   'assign values to appropriate textbox
   txtX = Point(0): txtY = Point(1): txtZ = Point(2)
   'redisplay the UserForm
   UserForm1.Show
End Sub
```

This is all the code you need to make this example work. Execute this example by selecting Run ➤ Run Sub/UserForm or by pressing F5. Alternatively, you can run the example by clicking the Run toolbar button as shown in Figure 3-11.

*Figure 3-11. The VBAIDE Run, Pause, and Stop icons*

This final bit of code allows you to exit your application gracefully:

```
Private Sub cmdOK_Click()
  Unload Me
End Sub
```

## Visual Basic ActiveX Controls

In this section, you'll be presented with each of the ActiveX controls that are available for use by default. You'll take a look at code examples demonstrating how you might use each of these controls within your own application.

The AutoCAD VBA environment provides you with 14 ActiveX controls. In this section I briefly explain what the most commonly used ActiveX controls do and how you may use them. Each of the controls appears in the Toolbox, shown in Figure 3-12, that is displayed whenever you have a UserForm active.

*Figure 3-12. The Toolbox window*

You can close the Toolbox window if needed. To redisplay the Toolbox window, select View ➤ Toolbox.

### *Label*

Used to convey information back to the user, the Label control looks similar to what you see in Figure 3-13 when you place it on a UserForm.

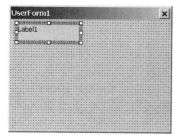

*Figure 3-13. A UserForm with a Label control*

Typically, you use this type of control to display error messages, entity counts, etc. Labels prove most useful when you control them at run time by changing the Caption property, as in the following snippet:

```
Private Sub UserForm_Activate()
  Label1.Caption = "# of Blocks = " & ThisDrawing.Blocks.Count
End Sub
```

Executing this bit of code produces the dialog box output shown in Figure 3-14.

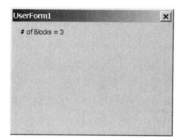

*Figure 3-14. A UserForm at run time with a Label control*

When you use a Label control, you may need to adjust the Label1.Width and/or Label1.Height properties to compensate for the amount of text to be displayed.

## TextBox

You use TextBox controls for data entry by the user (see Figure 3-15). Usually these controls enable the user to enter a single line of text, but you can change them to allow multiline text entry.

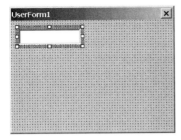

*Figure 3-15. A UserForm with a TextBox control*

Typically, you'll trap the KeyDown, KeyUp, and KeyPress events for a TextBox control. The KeyDown and KeyUp events occur in sequence when any key is pressed.

A KeyPress event may occur when any of the following keys or key combinations are pressed:

- Any printable keyboard character

- Ctrl combined with a character from the standard alphabet

- Ctrl combined with any special character

- Backspace

- Esc

A KeyPress event won't occur under any of the following situations:

- Pressing the Tab key

- Pressing the Enter key

- Pressing an arrow key

- When a keystroke causes the focus to move from one control to another

**NOTE**   *Backspace is part of the ANSI character set, but Delete isn't. Deleting a character in a control using Backspace causes a* KeyPress *event; deleting a character using Delete doesn't trigger a* KeyPress *event.*

The following example waits until the user presses the Enter key, and then prints the text entered in a standard Visual Basic MsgBox dialog box:

```
Private Sub TextBox1_KeyUp(ByVal KeyCode As MSForms.ReturnInteger, _
                         ByVal Shift As Integer)
  If KeyCode = 13 Then
    MsgBox "You entered: " & TextBox1.Text
  End If
End Sub
```

## ComboBox

Use the ComboBox control, an example of which appears in Figure 3-16, allows a selection from a standard group of possible responses presented in a drop-down list. The *DropDown List* style is very useful in controlling what the user enters. This style of ComboBox doesn't allow the user to enter any response; the user may only pick from the list. This means you don't need to check for invalid values in your code. Conversely, the *DropDown Combo* style allows users to enter a value if what they want isn't in the list. As the programmer, you'll have to decide which style to use.

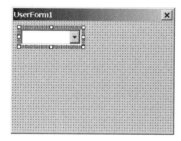

*Figure 3-16. A UserForm with a ComboBox control*

Here's an example of populating a drop-down list with values and then responding to the user's choice by displaying what was picked in a standard Visual Basic MsgBox dialog box:

```
Private Sub UserForm_Activate()
  With ComboBox1
    .AddItem "Item 1"
    .AddItem "Item 2"
```

```
      .AddItem "Item 3"
   End With
End Sub

Private Sub ComboBox1_Click()
   MsgBox "You choose: " & ComboBox1.List(ComboBox1.ListIndex)
End Sub
```

## ListBox

The ListBox control, shown in Figure 3-17, allows a selection from a standard group of possible responses. The difference between the ListBox control and the ComboBox control is the ListBox control displays more than a single choice at a time in a list format. Also, you can't type values into a ListBox control.

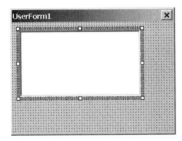

*Figure 3-17. A UserForm with a ListBox control*

The following example illustrates how to populate a ListBox control and then respond to the Click event:

```
Private Sub UserForm_Activate()
   With ListBox1
      .AddItem "Item 1"
      .AddItem "Item 2"
      .AddItem "Item 3"
   End With
End Sub

Private Sub ListBox1_Click()
   MsgBox "You clicked on: " & ListBox1.List(ListBox1.ListIndex)
End Sub
```

## CheckBox

Use the CheckBox control to determine if an item is selected (see Figure 3-18). If the box is unchecked, then the item isn't selected. If the box is checked, then the user has selected that item. You may have any number of CheckBox controls on a UserForm; each CheckBox control's checked state is independent of any other CheckBox control.

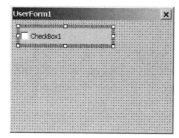

*Figure 3-18. A UserForm with a CheckBox control*

The following example uses the Click event of the CheckBox control to determine the current state of the control:

```
Private Sub CheckBox1_Click()
   If CheckBox1.Value Then
     MsgBox "Checked"

     Else
        MsgBox "Unchecked"
   End If
End Sub
```

## OptionButton

The OptionButton control is ideal for situations in which you want your user to choose just one item. Most AutoCAD users know these as *radio buttons*. The OptionButton control is usually placed inside a Frame control for grouping, as Figure 3-19 demonstrates. On a UserForm or within a Frame control, only one OptionButton may be selected at a time.

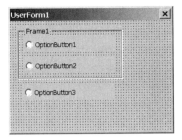

*Figure 3-19. A UserForm with OptionButtons*

In the following example, the `Click` event of each of the `OptionButton` controls contains code that is executed depending on which `OptionButton` is clicked:

```
Private Sub OptionButton1_Click()
  MsgBox "OptionButton1"
End Sub

Private Sub OptionButton2_Click()
  MsgBox "OptionButton2"
End Sub
```

## ToggleButton

Use a `ToggleButton` control to enable an option and leave it that way until the user depresses the button again (see Figure 3-20). This control presents an on/off switch whose appearance changes depending on whether or not it the user has depressed it. The `ToggleButton` control has a `Picture` property you could change depending on the state of the button.

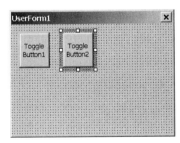

*Figure 3-20. A UserForm with ToggleButtons*

In the following example, the condition of the ToggleButton control is tested using a Select … Case statement and an appropriate message is displayed:

```
Private Sub ToggleButton1_Click()
  Select Case ToggleButton1.Value
    Case False
       MsgBox "ToggleButton1 is Off"
    Case True
       MsgBox "ToggleButton1 is On"
  End Select
End Sub
```

## *Frame*

The Frame control, shown in Figure 3-21, is a container for other controls, similar to the UserForm. Controls placed within a Frame control will move when you move the Frame control. Also, if you set the Frame control's Enabled property to False, then all the controls within the Frame control are disabled. Coordinate placement within the Frame is based on the Frame and not the UserForm. The Frame control provides a means of grouping related controls together for easier user selection.

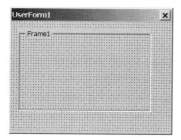

*Figure 3-21. A UserForm with a Frame control*

## *CommandButton*

Use CommandButton controls, shown in Figure 3-22, to allow users to signify that they have made all the selections and text entries they want to make and either want to continue on with the application or want to cancel the operation. The most common use of this control is for OK and Cancel button operations.

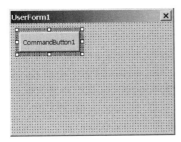

*Figure 3-22. A UserForm with a CommandButton*

The following is the most common method of ending a running application:

```
Private Sub cmdOK_Click()
   Unload Me
End Sub
```

## Additional ActiveX Controls

This section briefly explains the remaining five ActiveX controls available by default. Because these controls aren't commonly used, I don't cover them in as much detail as the previous controls. You can get further details about each of these ActiveX controls by placing one on a UserForm, highlighting it, and pressing F1.

### TabStrip

Use TabStrip controls when the data format between each tab is the same, but each tab represents a different entity (see Figure 3-23). A good analogy would be a custom control. All TextBox controls have the same property definitions (the data that appears on every tab selection). However, each instance of the control must have a different name (the tab name). Controls added to a TabStrip are actually added to the UserForm. When you move the TabStrip, the other controls do *not* move with it.

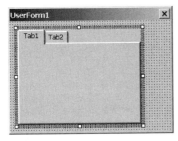

*Figure 3-23. A UserForm with a TabStrip control*

## MultiPage

The MultiPage control, shown in Figure 3-24, is similar to a UserForm. Each tab or page is separate from the others. For example, if you add a control to Page1, the same control doesn't appear on any other page. Nor is it a part of the UserForm. The MultiPage control is similar to a Frame control in that when you move the MultiPage control, all the controls contained within it move as well.

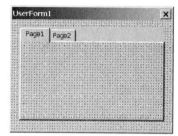

*Figure 3-24. A UserForm with a MultiPage control*

## ScrollBar

Use ScrollBar controls to allow the user to easily change values based on clicking the up and down arrows of the control (see Figure 3-25). Typically a ScrollBar increases or decreases counting values within a TextBox control. This control contains a slider bar indicating its relative position to the minimum and maximum values. The slider also allows the user to make very large changes quickly to the value.

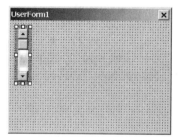

*Figure 3-25. A UserForm with a ScrollBar control*

## SpinButton

A SpinButton control allows the user to change values easily based on clicking the up and down arrows of the control (see Figure 3-26). Typically, you use this control to increase or decrease counting values with a TextBox control. Values may only be changed by clicking the up and down arrows. Unlike ScrollBar controls, SpinButton controls have no slider bar.

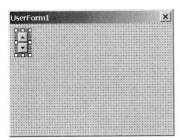

*Figure 3-26. A UserForm with a SpinButton control*

## Image

The Image control, shown in Figure 3-27, enables you to display pictures on your UserForm. The following types of images are supported: *.bmp, *.cur, *.gif, *.ico, *.jpg, and *.wmf. With the Image control's default event being Click, you could also use it as a fancy CommandButton control with a picture. In addition to specifying the picture to be displayed, you can define the Image control's display properties such as clip, stretch, and zoom, as well as apply 3-D border effects on the control itself, such as Flat, Raised, and Sunken.

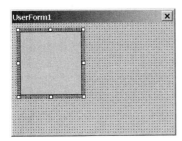

*Figure 3-27. A UserForm with an Image control*

## Summary

This chapter presented the essence of the visual portion of your application. The combinations of the different ActiveX controls provided by AutoCAD VBA are practically endless, and the right combination for you will depend on the needs of your application. You're somewhat forced to find your own way when creating your user interface. In this chapter I discussed UserForms, how to add controls to a UserForm, and the various ActiveX controls available to you. One thought you may want to keep in mind when designing your user interface is to keep it simple.

# CHAPTER 4

# AutoCAD Events

EVENTS OCCUR AS A RESULT OF actions happening while your program is running, such as opening or saving a drawing. They allow you to write source code that will execute whenever that event occurs. Messages such as "Would you like to save changes?" are the common results of a user action that has triggered an event.

AutoCAD 2004 supports three levels of events: application, document, and object. These event levels correspond to the three major areas of AutoCAD. Event handlers are Sub procedures that are executed automatically every time their associated event occurs. Some AutoCAD events allow information to be passed to the event handlers through parameters.

## Application-Level Events

Changes to the AutoCAD application environment results in application-level events. These include the opening and saving of drawings, running of AutoCAD commands, changes to system variables, and changes to the AutoCAD application window.

Application-level events aren't enabled when you load a VBA project. The following example illustrates the steps you need to take to enable application-level events.

First, insert a new class module by selecting Insert ➤ Class Module, and name the new class module appropriately, for example clsApplicationEvents. Then declare an object of type AcadApplication using the WithEvents keyword.

```
Public WithEvents objApp As AcadApplication
```

You should now see the new object objApp appears in the Object list box of the class module and all its event procedures are available in the Procedure list box, as shown in Figure 4-1.

You can then go ahead and write the code within these procedures that you want to be executed each time the events occur. However, these event handlers won't be triggered unless you've set the reference to correspond to the Application object.

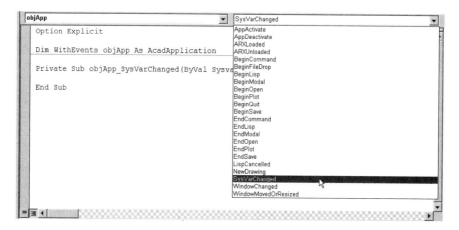

*Figure 4-1. The Object and Procedure boxes*

You can do this as follows. In the ThisDrawing or any code module declare a variable to be a new instance of the class module that you just created, and in a subroutine set this variable to hold a reference to the Application object.

```
Option Explicit
Public objApp As New clsApplicationEvents

Public Sub InitializeEvents()
  Set objApp.objApp = ThisDrawing.Application
End Sub
```

As soon as the InitializeEvents subroutine is called, in this case by running the App_StartMacro macro shown next, the application-level events are enabled.

```
Public Sub App_StartMacro()
  InitializeEvents
End Sub
```

The following examples illustrate writing code within the event procedures of the class module to execute when those events occur. The first informs the user when a system variable changes, and the second ensures that the AutoSave interval for a new drawing is always set to 30 minutes.

```
Private Sub objApp_SysVarChanged(ByVal SysvarName As String, _
                                 ByVal newVal As Variant)
  MsgBox "The System Variable: " & SysvarName & " has changed to " & newVal
End Sub
```

```
Private Sub objApp_NewDrawing()
    ThisDrawing.SetVariable "SAVETIME", 30
    MsgBox "The autosave interval is currently set to 30 mins"
End Sub
```

The following list summarizes the events available at the application level:

AppActivate

AppDeactivate

ARXLoaded

ARXUnloaded

BeginCommand

BeginFileDrop

BeginLisp

BeginModal

BeginOpen

BeginPlot

BeginQuit

BeginSave

EndCommand

EndLisp

EndModal

EndOpen

EndPlot

EndSave

LispCancelled

NewDrawing

SysVarChanged

WindowChanged

WindowMovedOrResized

**NOTE** *Unlike Visual LISP, VBA provides no "CommandCancelled" or "CancelledCommand" event to respond to. When a user presses the Esc key in most cases, it won't fire the* EndCommand *event.*

## Document-Level Events

Changes to a document or its contents result in document-level events. Adding or editing objects and regeneration of the drawing are just some examples of document-level events. Unlike application-level events, document-level events are available by default in the ThisDrawing module of an AutoCAD project. If you choose the AcadDocument object in the Object list box of the ThisDrawing module, the document-level events are listed in the Procedure list box, as shown in Figure 4-2.

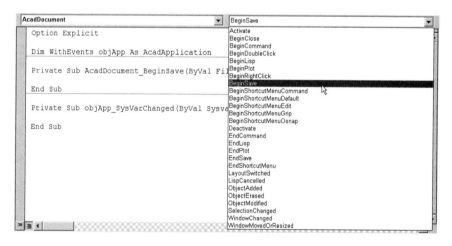

*Figure 4-2. The Procedure box showing document-level events*

The following is a summary of events available at the document level:

Activate

BeginClose

BeginCommand

```
BeginDoubleClick

BeginLisp

BeginPlot

BeginRightClick

BeginSave

BeginShortcutMenuCommand

BeginShortcutMenuDefault

BeginShortcutMenuEdit

BeginShortcutMenuGrip

BeginShortcutMenuOsnap

Deactivate

EndCommand

EndLisp

EndPlot

EndSave

EndShortcutMenu

LayoutSwitched

LispCancelled

ObjectAdded

ObjectErased

ObjectModified

SelectionChanged

WindowChanged

WindowMovedOrResized
```

Next you'll look at some of the document events and why you might want to add code to execute when they occur.

## The BeginCommand and EndCommand Events

When you issue an AutoCAD command such as LINE or DIM, the BeginCommand event is triggered. Any code that you've written inside the BeginCommand event procedure is then executed. Once the code associated with the BeginCommand event has finished executing and after the command itself has finished, the EndCommand event is triggered. Now, any code that you've written inside the EndCommand event procedure executes. You may have code associated with either, both, or neither event. If a command is canceled prior to completion, such as when a user presses the Esc key, it doesn't fire the EndCommand event.

The following BeginCommand event procedure illustrates creating a layer called Objects (if it doesn't exist) and making the layer active based on the user starting the LINE command:

```
Option Explicit
Public objCurrentLayer As AcadLayer
Public objPreviousLayer As AcadLayer

Private Sub AcadDocument_BeginCommand(ByVal CommandName As String)
   Set objPreviousLayer = ThisDrawing.ActiveLayer
   Select Case CommandName
     Case "LINE"
       If Not ThisDrawing.ActiveLayer.Name = "OBJECTS" Then
         Set objCurrentLayer = ThisDrawing.Layers.Add("OBJECTS")
         ThisDrawing.ActiveLayer = objCurrentLayer
       End If
   End Select
End Sub
```

The corresponding EndCommand event procedure puts the user back to the layer he or she was on if you had to change it in order to draw a line:

```
Private Sub AcadDocument_EndCommand(ByVal CommandName As String)
   Select Case CommandName
     Case "LINE"
         ThisDrawing.ActiveLayer = objPreviousLayer
     End Select
   Set objCurrentLayer = Nothing
   Set objPreviousLayer = Nothing
End Sub
```

The reason for using such code is that it brings continuity to your drawings. For example, all lines will be on the Objects layer, and by adding further code all text could be added automatically to a Text layer.

## The BeginOpen and EndOpen Events

When AutoCAD receives a request to open an existing drawing file, the `BeginOpen` event is triggered. Once AutoCAD has finished loading the drawing file and it's visible, an `EndOpen` event occurs. One possible use of this event procedure would be to store all the current system variables before you open a drawing. Then once the drawing is opened, you restore the system variables back to their previous values.

When AutoCAD receives a request to create a new drawing file, a slightly different sequence of events occurs. The `BeginOpen` event occurs as before, and then the `BeginSave` event occurs (see the section "The BeginSave and EndSave Events" for details). This is followed by an `EndSave` event and finally an `EndOpen` event.

## The BeginClose Event

The `BeginClose` event is triggered upon the closing of a drawing session within AutoCAD. Be careful when you use this event! If you attempt to perform a lengthy task, it can frustrate users due to slowness, or it could even result in serious problems with AutoCAD, causing it to become unstable, lock up, or crash entirely.

## The Activate and Deactivate Events

The `Activate` event is triggered when a drawing window gains focus. When only one drawing is currently opened in AutoCAD, it will always have focus. When multiple drawings are opened, this event is triggered when switching between drawing windows. The drawing window that loses focus triggers the `Deactivate` event as a result. Normally, the `Deactivate` event is triggered just before the `Activate` event as drawing window focus is switched.

Keep in mind that the `Deactivate` event indicates the drawing has lost focus. Firing off a procedure as a result of this event might not be a good idea, as it may not complete its task until the drawing regains focus (indicated by another `Activate` event). You can develop programs to work with what is called a *zero document state,* meaning there are no drawings opened. Consult the Autodesk developer guide for more information on this topic.

## The BeginSave and EndSave Events

Immediately before AutoCAD begins to save the current drawing, the `BeginSave` event is triggered. Once AutoCAD has completed saving the drawing file, the

EndSave event occurs. You might use the BeginSave event to query whether or not the user wants to purge his or her drawing before saving it. You could use the EndSave event to reinitialize standard layers, linetypes, and text styles that may have been purged because they weren't currently being used.

As you can see, AutoCAD has provided some very useful events that greatly enhance its controllability.

## Object-Level Events

Object-level events occur when changes are made to a specific entity that you've declared as having events. Modified is the only object-level event and, as you would expect, it occurs when the specified object is modified.

To use object-level events, you must first create a new class module and declare a variable to hold a reference to the object whose Modified event you want to code. You might call the new class module something like clsObjectEvent. The new class module contains the declaration of the object using the VBA keyword WithEvents, for example:

```
Public WithEvents objLine As AcadLine
```

The new object then appears in the Object list box of the class module and the event procedure for the new object may now be written within the class module in the same way as for other subroutines. For your event procedures to be triggered, you must associate the declared object in the class module with the object of interest. For this Line object example, you could do this by placing the following code in the ThisDrawing module or any code module:

```
Dim objLine As New clsObjectEvent
Public Sub InitializeEvent()
Dim dblStart(2) As Double
Dim dblEnd(2) As Double
    dblEnd(0) = 1: dblEnd(1) = 1: dblEnd(2) = 0
    Set objLine.objLine = ThisDrawing.ModelSpace.AddLine(dblStart, dblEnd)
End Sub
```

You first declare your object to be a new instance of the class clsObjectEvent, and in the initial event procedure set the objLine variable to hold a reference to a newly created Line object. Now, as soon as this procedure is called, a new Line object is created that responds to any changes made to the line in question by executing the code in the Modified event procedure.

So if you put the following code in the `clsObjectEvent` class module, the new coordinates of the `Line` object will be displayed to the user, whenever the line is moved, rotated, scaled, etc.:

```
Private Sub objLine_Modified(ByVal pObject As AutoCAD.IAcadObject)
Dim varStartPoint As Variant
Dim varEndPoint As Variant

    varStartPoint = pObject.StartPoint
    varEndPoint = pObject.EndPoint
    MsgBox "New line runs from (" & varStartPoint(0) & ", " & _
        varStartPoint(1) & ", " & varStartPoint(2) & " ) to (" & _
        varEndPoint(0) & ", " & varEndPoint(1) & ", " & varEndPoint(2) & ")."

End Sub
```

## Summary

In this chapter you've seen how AutoCAD events can greatly increase program-ming flexibility. The steps involved in initializing events may seem a little complex to those first encountering events, but hopefully this won't deter you from taking full advantage of the power and flexibility they provide.

# CHAPTER 5

# User Preferences

THERE ARE ACTUALLY TWO "Preferences" objects within AutoCAD: AcadPreferences and DatabasePreferences. The AcadPreferences object is stored by AutoCAD and applies to all drawing sessions. The DatabasePreferences object (also called the "Document Preferences") is stored with each drawing file and only applies to the drawing in which it was saved.

This chapter covers a few aspects of the AcadPreferences object. A quick way to discern the differences between the AcadPreferences and DatabasePreferences objects is to look through the Options dialog box tabs and note the features with a drawing icon beside them. These indicate Document Preferences. All others are AcadPreferences features.

Users can set many different properties that affect the way they work with AutoCAD. For example, users can set the paths that are searched to find support files and programs, the properties affecting performance, and how the display is presented. You can view and set these properties through the Options dialog box, which you can access through the Tools ➤ Options menu, as shown in Figure 5-1, or by typing **OPTIONS** at the command prompt.

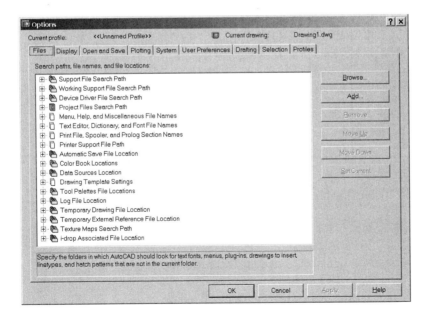

*Figure 5-1. The Options dialog box*

The `Preferences` collection object contains nine objects representing the nine tabs on the Options dialog box. These tabs roughly correspond to the objects contained within the `AcadPreferences` collection object. From left to right, they relate to the following `AcadPreferences` objects:

`PreferencesFiles`

`PreferencesDisplay`

`PreferencesOpenSave`

`PreferencesOutput`

`PreferencesSystem`

`PreferencesUser`

`PreferencesDrafting`

`PreferencesSelection`

`PreferencesProfiles`

AutoCAD 2000 and 2002 users will see a few new additions in AutoCAD 2004, such as color book locations, tool palette file settings, i-drop settings, hover grip colors, security options, right-click options, hidden line options, and more. Accessing these objects may seem a bit odd, as they're called "PreferencesFiles," but you request them from the `Preferences` object using their short name, such as "Files."

For example, the following code returns the `PreferencesProfiles` object used to save a custom profile file for later use with each session:

```
Dim PrefProfiles As AcadPreferencesProfiles

Set PrefProfiles = ThisDrawing.Application.Preferences.Profiles
```

In this chapter, I cover the following aspects of the `Preferences` object:

- Getting and setting the support path(s)

- Controlling the cursor size

- Getting and setting the `AutoSaveInterval` property

- Getting and setting the drawing template file path

- Getting and setting printer support path settings

- Getting and setting the file SaveAs type

- Enabling and disabling the Startup dialog box

- Saving and retrieving your personal preferences


# Getting and Setting Support Path(s)

Controlling support paths can be important if you're using custom applications during your AutoCAD session. Generally speaking, the default paths set by AutoCAD are probably not adequate because they don't include any paths for customs applications, for example. AutoCAD's saving grace is that you *can* change the default paths to accommodate your program needs. If you need to know the current path for your support files, you can read the SupportPath property of the PreferencesFiles object:

```
strSetPaths = ThisDrawing.Application.Preferences.Files.SupportPath
```

You can also append the SupportPath property as follows:

```
Dim strNewPath As String, strSetPath As String
strNewPath = ;c:\cadfiles\apress\dvb
strSetPath = ThisDrawing.Application.Preferences.Files.SupportPath
If Len(strSetPath & strNewPath) < 256 Then
   strNewPath = strSetPath & strNewPath
   ThisDrawing.Application.Preferences.Files.SupportPath = strNewPath
End If
```

Note that there is a 255-character limit on the cumulative length of the support path collection. This includes the semicolon delimiter used to store the value internally (it's actually stored as a single string and only shown as a list through the Options dialog form). If you exceed the limit, AutoCAD will truncate the paths, which may yield odd or unpredictable results.

In AutoCAD 2004, the support path list has changed, as well as other default path behaviors. This is due to Microsoft Windows XP logo certification requirements that Autodesk sought for its latest product releases. For example, you'll see two new default path entries under support paths that refer to the user profile path, as shown in Figure 5-2.

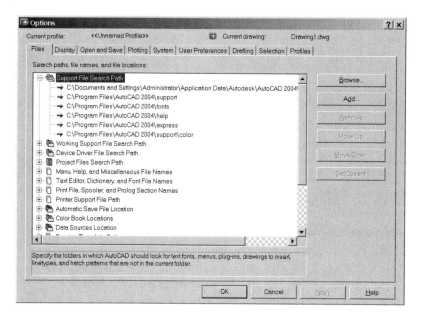

*Figure 5-2. Support File Search Path entries in the Options dialog box*

## Controlling Cursor Size

You may want to change the default cursor size to your particular preference. You can achieve this by using the `CursorSize` property of the `PreferencesDisplay` object:

```
intCursorSize = ThisDrawing.Application.Preferences.Display.CursorSize
```

The value of the `CursorSize` property is a positive integer that represents the percentage of the cursor size to the screen size. The default value is 5, the minimum is 1, and the maximum is 100. All other values will generate an error.

The following example prompts the user to enter a value for the cursor size, and if the returned value lies between 1 and 100, the size is changed. Otherwise, the user is informed that he or she has entered an invalid value.

```
Dim intCursorSize As Integer

intCursorSize = ThisDrawing.Utility.GetInteger(vbCrLf & _
    "Enter number for  size of cursor proportional to screen size" & vbCrLf)

If intCursorSize < 1 Or intCursorSize > 100 Then
    MsgBox "Cursor Size value must be between 1 and 100"
```

```
Else
    ThisDrawing.Application.Preferences.Display.CursorSize = intCursorSize
End If
```

## Getting and Setting the AutoSaveInterval Property

The AutoSaveInterval property is a positive integer value representing the number of whole minutes between automatic saves. The timer for automatic saves starts as soon as you make a change to the current drawing. Setting the AutoSaveInterval property to 0 (zero) means that you'll never get an automatic save operation. The maximum value allowed for the AutoSaveInterval property is 600 minutes.

The default value that AutoCAD uses for the time between automatic saves is 120 minutes. You can do a lot of work in 2 hours, all of which could potentially be lost if you don't initiate a save operation. Most users, then, will want to set the AutoSaveInterval property to a much shorter interval.

The following example retrieves the current setting, and if the autosave interval isn't set to 15 minutes, it's altered and the user is informed of the change:

```
If ThisDrawing.Application.Preferences.OpenSave.AutoSaveInterval <> 15 Then
    ThisDrawing.Application.Preferences.OpenSave.AutoSaveInterval = 15
    MsgBox "The autosave interval has been changed to 15 minutes."
End If
```

**TIP** *Autodesk recommends setting* IncrementalSavePercent *to 0 if you experience problems saving files across a network connection. This forces a full save at every automatic save, which may require a few more milliseconds but ensures a complete disk-write at every save. This can also help you avoid the dreaded automatic save backup files when you lose your sessions prematurely.*

## Getting and Setting the Drawing Template File Path

The TemplateDWGPath property is a string value specifying the path of template files used by the start-up wizards. The following example illustrates how to retrieve the current template files path:

```
strTemplatePath = ThisDrawing.Application.Preferences.Files.TemplateDwgPath
```

Setting the path to your specific value requires a fully qualified path, as shown here:

```
ThisDrawing.Application.Preferences.Files.TemplateDwgPath = _
"C:\Program " & _ "Files\AutoCAD 2004\Templates"
```

Manipulating the path settings can be helpful if you need to use various sets of templates from different customers or vendors, or if your internal departments must use different standards such as the metric system and English system of measurement or the ANSI and ISO industry standards.

## Getting and Setting Plotter Configuration Path Settings

One of the most common uses of the Preferences object is dealing with printer or plotter configuration aspects, as shown in Figure 5-3. Among these are the plot configuration support paths. These are displayed one way in the Options dialog form and somewhat differently in the AcadPreferences.Files object.

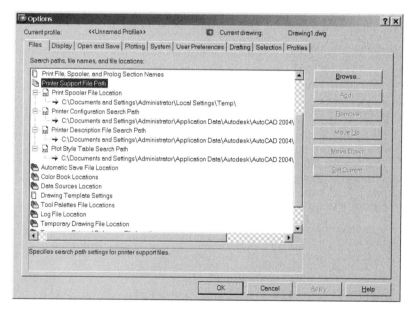

*Figure 5-3. Printer Support File Path options in the Options dialog box*

"Printer Configuration Search Path" is where the PC3 configuration files are stored and accessed from. This is linked to the PrinterConfigPath property. This is normally the "Plotters" folder in AutoCAD 2000 and 2002, but it has been moved in AutoCAD 2004.

"Printer Description File Search Path" is where the PMP paper size and plotter calibration files are stored. This is normally the "Drv" folder in AutoCAD 2000 and 2002; however, it has been moved in AutoCAD 2004. It's linked to the PrinterDescPath property.

"Plot Style Table Search Path" is where the CTB and STB plot style files are stored and accessed from. This is normally the "Plot Styles" folder in AutoCAD 2000 and 2002, but it has also been moved in AutoCAD 2004. This is linked to the PrinterStyleSheetPath property.

The following example shows how to modify the "Printer Configuration Search Path" using VBA and the AcadPreferences.File object:

```
Dim strPC3Path As String
strPC3Path = c:\cadfiles\plotconfigs
ThisDrawing.Application.Preferences.Files.PrinterConfigPath = strPC3Path
```

# Getting and Setting the File SaveAs Type

The SaveAsType property controls the format used when AutoCAD saves the current drawing. Table 5-1 shows the applicable values available for different formats supported by AutoCAD 2004 by using the acSaveAs enumeration. You can always explicitly override this setting either from the SAVEAS command or programmatically from the SaveAs method of the Document object in VBA.

*Table 5-1. acSaveAs Enumerations*

| NAME | VALUE | DESCRIPTION |
|---|---|---|
| acR12_dxf | 1 | AutoCAD Release12/LT2 DXF (*.dxf) |
| ac2000_dwg | 12 | AutoCAD 2000 DWG (*.dwg) |
| ac2000_dxf | 13 | AutoCAD 2000 DXF (*.dxf) |
| ac2000_Template | 14 | AutoCAD 2000 Drawing Template File (*.dwt) |
| ac2004_dwg | 24 | AutoCAD 2004 DWG (*.dwg) |
| ac2004_dxf | 25 | AutoCAD 2004 DXF (*.dxf) |
| ac2004_Template | 26 | AutoCAD 2004 Drawing Template File (*.dwt) |
| acNative | 24 | A synonym for the current drawing release format. If you want your application to save the drawing in the format of whatever version of AutoCAD the application is running on, then use the acNative format. |

> **NOTE** *The values shown in Table 5-1 are the only valid values that you can use. Valid values from earlier versions of AutoCAD not shown in the table. Other invalid values will generate an error.*

The following example determines the current file format that drawings will be saved as:

```
Public Sub SaveAsType()
Dim iSaveAsType As Integer
   iSaveAsType = ThisDrawing.Application.Preferences.OpenSave.SaveAsType
   Select Case iSaveAsType
      Case acR12_dxf
         MsgBox "Current save as format is R12_DXF", vbInformation
      Case ac2000_dwg
         MsgBox "Current save as format is 2000_DWG", vbInformation
      Case ac2000_dxf
         MsgBox "Current save as format is 2000_DXF", vbInformation
      Case ac2000_Template
         MsgBox "Current save as format is 2000_Template", vbInformation
      Case ac2004_dwg, acNative
         MsgBox "Current save as format is 2004_DWG", vbInformation
      Case ac2004_dxf
         MsgBox "Current save as format is 2004_DXF", vbInformation
      Case ac2004_Template
         MsgBox "Current save as format is 2004_Template", vbInformation
      Case acUnknown
         MsgBox "Current save as format is Unknown or Read-Only", vbInformation
   End Select
End Sub
```

You set the SaveAsType property by using the same enumerated types as shown in the following example:

```
ThisDrawing.Application.Preferences.OpenSave.SaveAsType = ac2000_dwg
```

The default value for the SaveAsType property for AutoCAD 2004 is ac2004_dwg.

**TIP** *In general, it's best (and safest) to leave the default SaveAsType setting as the current version and only convert drawing files at the end of the design phase, when you're preparing to deliver them to whomever requires the prior format. This eliminates the constant conversion process AutoCAD must do each time you open a drawing and save it. The repetitive conversion processes can impact performance and increase the risk of drawing database corruption. You can also batch-convert drawings using the Migration Assistance Batch Drawing Converter to save time at the end of a major project.*

## Enabling or Disabling the Startup Dialog Box

Some users may or may not want the Startup dialog box as shown in Figure 5-4 when they open an existing drawing or start a new drawing. This isn't an issue with most AutoCAD 2004 users because the Startup dialog box is disabled by default. Also, there is no more Today feature in AutoCAD 2004.

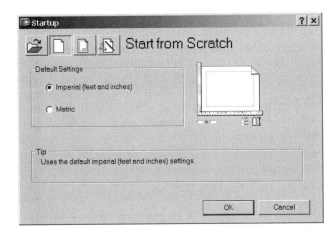

*Figure 5-4. The Startup dialog box*

You can control whether this dialog box is displayed using the EnableStartupDialog property of the PreferencesSystem object, as in the following example:

```
ThisDrawing.Application.Preferences.System.EnableStartupDialog = False
```

The initial value of the EnableStartupDialog property is True for versions up to AutoCAD 2002 only. It is False for AutoCAD 2004 products.

An AutoCAD 2004 quirk is that although the commands lines setting has been removed from the Display tab of the Options dialog box, the corresponding property is still exposed under the Display object (DockedVisibleLines). However, modifying its value has no effect whatsoever due to the command prompt being converted to a tool palette object.

## Saving and Retrieving Personal Preferences

Profiles are named environment configurations that allow you to load and change your entire desktop and support configurations at will. For example, you may create one for each project you work on, you may create one for each user on a shared workstation, or you may create one for each add-on application you use in AutoCAD.

Profiles are saved and recalled from the Windows Registry. You can save them and export them to .arg files, but they are actually Registry export files, having the same internal content and structure as a Windows .reg file. In fact, you can rename them as .reg files and double-click them to import them directly into the registry. AutoCAD, however, provides API access into the Profiles object to allow you to manage profiles from within AutoCAD.

Once you've settled on a standard for your preferences, you may want to save these settings in a file that you can later import for your current session. You should make all necessary changes to the preferences and then use the following code to export them to a file:

```
Dim strActiveProfile as String

strActiveProfile = ThisDrawing.Application.Preferences.Profiles.ActiveProfile
ThisDrawing.Application.Preferences.Profiles.ExportProfile _
    strActiveProfile, "C:\MYPROFILE.ARG"
```

Now that you've exported your preferences to a file, the following code will allow you to import these preferences into each of your AutoCAD sessions:

```
Dim strMyProfile As String

'name of profile
strMyProfile = "My Personal Profile"

ThisDrawing.Application.Preferences.Profiles.ImportProfile _
    strMyProfile, "C:\MYPROFILE.ARG", True
ThisDrawing.Application.Preferences.Profiles.ActiveProfile = strMyProfile
```

The True argument at the end of the ImportProfile method tells AutoCAD to preserve the path information from the .arg file and save this information into the Windows Registry. Also, notice that at the end of the preceding code I set the newly imported profile to be active. You must make your personal profile active for your settings to take effect.

If you attempt to import a profile from an .arg file, AutoCAD will always check to see if the profile name already exists within AutoCAD. If it exists, AutoCAD ignores the .arg file entirely. To force an import to take effect, you must either delete or rename the existing profile prior to importing. You can't delete the active profile, so it's usually easiest to rename it, import the new one, set it active, and delete the renamed profile, as shown in the following code:

```
Dim strActiveProfile As String
Dim strMyProfile As String
strMyProfile = "My Personal Profile"
strActiveProfile = ThisDrawing.Application.Preferences.Profiles.ActiveProfile
With ThisDrawing.Application.Preferences.Profiles
.RenameProfile strActiveProfile " MyBackupProfile"
.ImportProfile strMyProfile, "C:\MYPROFILE.ARG ",True
.ActiveProfile = strMyProfile
.DeleteProfile "MyBackupProfile"
End With
```

Obviously, the preceding example doesn't verify whether the active profile is the one you want to replace, so that's something else you should check if you use this method. It's interesting to note that whereas the Profiles object contains a logical collection of profiles, there is no Item or Count property. The ActiveProfile property returns a string name, not an object. The methods also are string based, not object based. This means that you can't access and manipulate profiles as objects. However, you can copy, delete, rename, import, export, and reset them.

## User Preferences Changes in AutoCAD 2004

AutoCAD 2004 adds, removes, and modifies quite a few Options dialog box features as well as many AcadPreferences objects. Be sure to read the online development documentation for changes in AutoCAD 2004. There are some interesting things to note, in addition to my comment earlier about the command prompt window. For example, although AutoCAD 2004 adds the new "hover grip" feature to the Options dialog box, the three color options are not represented cohesively under the hood. Figure 5-5 shows the Selection tab.

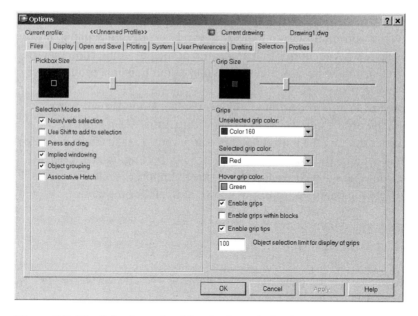

*Figure 5-5. The Selection tab of the Options dialog box*

The AcadPreferences.Selection object contains only GripColorSelected and GripColorUnselected. The GRIPHOVER system variable is the only means to access and modify the hover grip color. Another curious issue is that of tool palettes, which are new to AutoCAD 2004. These aren't exposed through the ActiveX model anywhere; they're actually stored as XML documents under the ToolPalettesPath property of the File object. There currently is no means to configure their display properties from VBA without invoking XML services.

## Summary

There's no way to cover every possible combination of preferences a typical user may use. Appendix A covers exact names and syntax of preferences. Please look there for more details on preferences.

# CHAPTER 6

# Controlling Layers and Linetypes

EFFECTIVE USE OF LAYERS AND LINETYPES is the key to creating structured drawings and manipulating AutoCAD in an efficient manner. In this chapter, you'll see how to access the Layers and Linetypes collections and their respective Layer and Linetype objects, and learn about their methods and properties. The code samples throughout this chapter demonstrate how to control these objects through VBA.

## Layers

A *layer* is a property of every AutoCAD drawing object. By using multiple layers, you may organize drawing data into logical categories. For example, when you design an office layout, you could use one layer to display the walls and other fixed structural objects, and you could use other layers to show the potential furniture or electrical arrangements. Alternatively, you could use a layer to hold dimensions (measurement annotations) or hidden lines. A Layer object represents one of these logical groupings.

Manipulating the state of layers makes it easier to manage complex drawings. For example, by making a layer visible or hidden, the user can choose to work with specific entity categories without being overwhelmed by all the other drawing entities.

Creating layers and controlling their state is the subject of the first part of this chapter. Later I discuss how to control linetypes.

The following list outlines the various actions that I cover with regard to layers:

- Accessing the Layers collection and Layer objects

- Checking for the existence of a specific layer

- Creating a new layer and making it the active layer

- Setting or returning the On/Off, Thawed/Frozen, Locked/Unlocked properties

- Renaming and deleting a layer

- Setting or returning a layer's Color and Linetype properties

## *Accessing Layers*

AutoCAD has a Layers collection that contains all the Layer objects in the drawing. You can create as many layers as you want by adding new Layer objects to the Layers collection.

You access the Layers collection via a Document object. In the following code, ThisDrawing is used as the active document:

```
Dim objLayers As AcadLayers
Set objLayers = ThisDrawing.Layers
```

To set a reference to an existing Layer object, use the Item method of the Layers collection as follows:

```
Dim objLayer As AcadLayer

Set objLayer = objLayers.Item(2)
Set objLayer = objLayers.Item("My Layer")
```

The parameter of this method is either an integer representing the position of the desired Layer object within the Layers collection or a string representing the name of the desired Layer object. If you use an index number, it must be between 0 and the value of the Layers.Count property minus 1.

Like other AutoCAD collections, Item is the default method for Layers. This means that the method name may be omitted, and the parameter passed straight to the Layers reference. This is often preferred, as it's simpler to type and read. The following code does the same thing as the prior example using the default method to specify the Layer object:

```
Dim objLayer As AcadLayer

Set objLayer = objLayers(2)
Set objLayer = objLayers("My Layer")
```

If you're just now learning Visual Basic or you've only been programming with it for a short while, it's recommended that you avoid using default methods and instead strive to use explicit properties and methods. Microsoft is making a strong commitment to explicit coding in all of its current and future programming technologies such as .NET. In fact, .NET doesn't support default methods or implicit data types by default.

## Iterating Layers

In some situations you'll want your program to step through each item in a collection—perhaps to check or alter some property of every element. This is termed *iteration*. Like all collections in VBA, Layers has built-in support for iteration using a For ... Each loop. The following example iterates the Layers collection, printing each Layer name to the Immediate or Debug window:

```
Public Sub ListLayers()
    Dim objLayer As AcadLayer

    For Each objLayer In ThisDrawing.Layers
        Debug.Print objLayer.Name
    Next
End Sub
```

You may also iterate the collection manually using the Count property in conjunction with the Item method. The Count property contains the total number of elements in the collection.

Remember, when you access a collection element using a number, the index must be between 0 and the value of the Layers.Count property minus 1. This is because all collections are by default zero-based. The following example prints each Layer name to the Debug window as before, but this time iterates the collection manually:

```
Public Sub ListLayersManually()
    Dim objLayers As AcadLayers
    Dim objLayer As AcadLayer
    Dim intI As Integer

    Set objLayers = ThisDrawing.Layers

    For intI = 0 To objLayers.Count - 1
        Set objLayer = objLayers(intI)
        Debug.Print objLayer.name
    Next
End Sub
```

You can see that the manual version is a bit more complex, with several variables involved. For most purposes, the For ... Each version is preferred, but because the manual version gives you full control over the iteration, it may be needed in some situations. For example, the following sample prints the Layer names to the Debug window by iterating the collection in *reverse* order:

```
Public Sub ListLayersBackwards()
    Dim objLayers As AcadLayers
    Dim objLayer As AcadLayer
    Dim intI As Integer

    Set objLayers = ThisDrawing.Layers

    For intI = objLayers.Count - 1 To 0 Step -1
        Set objLayer = objLayers(intI)
        Debug.Print objLayer.name
    Next
End Sub
```

## Checking for Existing Layers

At times your program may need to determine if an element is present in the collection. One way to do this is to search for the element while iterating the collection as described previously. The following example gets a layer name from the user and then checks for its existence by iterating the Layers collection:

```
Public Sub CheckForLayerByIteration()
    Dim objLayer As AcadLayer
    Dim strLayerName As String

    strLayername = InputBox("Enter a Layer name to search for: ")
    If "" = strLayername Then Exit Sub     ' exit if no name entered

    For Each objLayer In ThisDrawing.Layers     ' iterate layers
        If 0 = StrComp(objLayer.name, strLayername, vbTextCompare) Then
            MsgBox "Layer '" & strLayername & "' exists"
            Exit Sub                             ' exit after finding layer
        End If
    Next objLayer
    MsgBox "Layer '" & strLayername & "' does not exist"
End Sub
```

Unlike prior releases in which layer names were converted to uppercase, AutoCAD 2000 and higher allows the names to be mixed case. However, you can't have two layers with the same name but with a different combination of upper- and lowercase letters. For example, AutoCAD will treat "Objects" and "objects" as the same layer. This sample uses a case-insensitive string comparison of strLayerName and each Layer name to allow for capitalization differences.

A second technique is to let AutoCAD perform the search for you. This is quite a bit more efficient because AutoCAD can internally determine if the element is present, and it eliminates sending unneeded elements to your program. AutoCAD will also handle the case-insensitive name comparison for you. To use this technique you must employ the VBA error handler.

Like many AutoCAD VBA objects, the Layers collection uses run-time errors to signal unexpected conditions. These run-time errors, also called *exceptions*, must be handled by the calling program. If the exception isn't handled, the calling program halts and displays an error message to the user. In this case, Layers will raise an exception if you attempt to access an unknown Layer name. By detecting this exception, or more correctly the lack of the exception, your program is notified of the existence of the Layer. The following example gets a layer name from the user and uses AutoCAD to check for its existence:

```
Public Sub CheckForLayerByException()
    Dim strLayerName As String
    Dim objLayer As AcadLayer

    strLayerName = InputBox("Enter a Layer name to search for: ")
    If "" = strLayerName Then Exit Sub        ' exit if no name entered

    On Error Resume Next                ' handle exceptions inline
    Set objLayer = ThisDrawing.Layers(strLayerName)

    If objLayer Is Nothing Then            ' check if obj has been set
        MsgBox "Layer '" & strLayerName & "' does not exist"
    Else
        MsgBox "Layer '" & objLayer.Name & "' exists"
    End If
End Sub
```

## Creating a New Layer

You can create as many layers as needed using the criteria illustrated in Table 6-1. The Add method is used to create a Layer object and to add it to the Layers collection.

```
Set LayerObject = LayerCollection.Add(LayerName)
```

*Table 6-1. Layer Name Property*

| NAME | DATA TYPE | DESCRIPTION |
|------|-----------|-------------|
| LayerName | String | The name for the new layer. If the parameter isn't a valid layer name, an exception will be raised. If you attempt to add a new layer with the same name as an existing layer, a reference to the existing Layer is returned. |

The following example retrieves a layer name from the user and attempts to add it to the Layers collection:

```
Public Sub AddLayer()
    Dim strLayerName As String
    Dim objLayer As AcadLayer

    strLayerName = InputBox("Name of Layer to add: ")
    If "" = strLayerName Then Exit Sub       ' exit if no name entered

    On Error Resume Next                 ' handle exceptions inline
    'check to see if layer already exists
    Set objLayer = ThisDrawing.Layers(strLayerName)

    If objLayer Is Nothing Then
        Set objLayer = ThisDrawing.Layers.Add(strLayerName)
        If objLayer Is Nothing Then ' check if obj has been set
            MsgBox "Unable to Add '" & strLayerName & "'"
        Else
            MsgBox "Added Layer '" & objLayer.Name & "'"
        End If
    Else
        MsgBox "Layer already existed"
    End If
End Sub
```

In normal programming situations, it's usually best to define entity or object creation routines as functions rather than subroutines. This way, you can return the object to other functions or subroutines, making it possible to further manipulate the new object outside the function that creates it.

When a layer is first created, its properties are set to certain default values. Figure 6-1 shows what you would see in the Layer Properties Manager dialog box when a new layer called "Room Shell" is added with the preceding code.

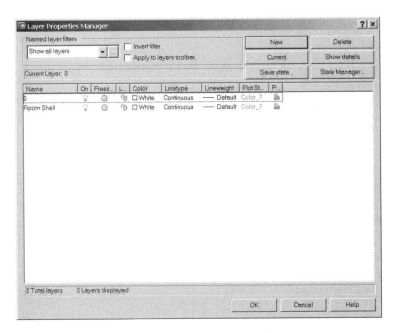

*Figure 6-1. The Layer Properties Manager dialog box*

Here you can see two layers. The first, layer "0," is created automatically by AutoCAD and may not be deleted or renamed. The second is the layer that was just created through code. The default attribute settings are shown.

We next examine how to change and retrieve the settings for some of these attributes and how to rename and delete a Layer object.

## Making a Layer Active

When you create new entities in AutoCAD, they're placed on the current or active layer. Therefore, to draw entities on a specific layer, you must first make that layer active.

> **NOTE** *You can't make a layer active if it's frozen. However, you can check for this condition before you attempt to make a layer active. For more details, see the section "Setting a Layer to Be Frozen/Thawed."*

The ActiveLayer property is a member of the Document object. To make a specific layer active, assign the Layer object to the ActiveLayer.

```
DocumentObject.ActiveLayer = LayerObject
```

The following code makes the layer named "Walls" the active layer for the current Document:

```
ThisDrawing.ActiveLayer = ThisDrawing.Layers("Walls")
```

New entities will now be placed on the "Walls" layer until another layer is made active. You can change the layer of existing entities by altering the Layer property of that particular entity. The Layer property is a string that corresponds to the name of a Layer object. The following example lets the user pick a drawing entity and specify a new layer name for that entity:

```
Public Sub ChangeEntityLayer()
    On Error Resume Next                 ' handle exceptions inline
    Dim objEntity As AcadEntity
    Dim varPick As Variant
    Dim strLayerName As String
    Dim objLayer As AcadLayer

    ThisDrawing.Utility.GetEntity objEntity, varPick, "Select an entity"
    If objEntity Is Nothing Then
        MsgBox "No entity was selected"
        Exit Sub  ' exit if no entity picked
    End If

    strLayerName = InputBox("Enter a new Layer name: ")
    If "" = strLayerName Then Exit Sub          ' exit if no name entered

    Set objLayer = ThisDrawing.Layers(strLayerName)
    If objLayer Is Nothing Then
        MsgBox "Layer was not recognized"
        Exit Sub    ' exit if layer not found
```

```
        End If
        objEntity.Layer = strLayerName              ' else change entity layer
End Sub
```

You can determine if a specific layer is active by comparing the string to the `ActiveLayer.Name` property:

```
If ThisDrawing.ActiveLayer.Name = "Walls" Then ...
```

This is a pretty common operation, so make it a function. You'll also want to allow for various combinations of upper- and lowercase letters, as AutoCAD does:

```
Public Function IsLayerActive(strLayerName As String) As Boolean
    IsLayerActive = False            'assume failure
    If 0 = StrComp(ThisDrawing.ActiveLayer.Name, strLayerName, _
                    vbTextCompare) Then
        IsLayerActive = True
    End If
End Function
```

This `IsLayerActive` function checks whether a particular string corresponds to the active layer name. `True` will be returned if the layer is active, otherwise `False` will be returned. The following gets a layer name from the user and employs the new function to see if it's active:

```
Public Sub LayerActive()
    Dim strLayerName As String
    strLayerName = InputBox("Name of the Layer to check: ")

    If IsLayerActive(strLayerName) Then
        MsgBox "'" & strLayerName & "' is active"
    Else
        MsgBox "'" & strLayerName & "' is not active"
    End If
End Sub
```

## Turning a Layer On/Off

Turning a layer on or off allows you to control its visibility on the screen. This feature affects only the layer being turned on/off and not the entire drawing. This can be useful if you want to work on some aspect of a complex drawing. By making certain layers invisible, you can ensure that the drawing entities on these layers don't obscure your current work.

You can also hide a layer by freezing it. This is more suitable if you want to hide a layer for a considerable length of time and is discussed later in this chapter in the section "Setting a Layer to Be Frozen/Thawed." Turning a layer on/off is more suited to situations in which the visibility will be changed frequently.

Layers that are turned off are regenerated with the rest of the drawing but won't be displayed or plotted. When a layer that's currently off is turned back on, the entities on the layer are redrawn but don't require regeneration of the entire drawing. Setting the LayerOn property will turn a layer on or off.

```
LayerObject.LayerOn = blnLayerOn
```

A value of True for this property will turn the layer on. Conversely, a value of False will turn the layer off.

The following code turns off every layer except the one specified by the user:

```
Public Sub ShowOnlyLayer()
    On Error Resume Next                    ' handle exceptions inline
    Dim strLayerName As String
    Dim objLayer As AcadLayer

    strLayerName = InputBox("Enter a Layer name to show: ")
    If "" = strLayerName Then Exit Sub         ' exit if no name entered

    For Each objLayer In ThisDrawing.Layers
        objLayer.LayerOn = False            ' turn off all the layers
    Next objLayer

    Set objLayer = ThisDrawing.Layers(strLayerName)
    If objLayer Is Nothing Then
        MsgBox "Layer does not exist"
        Exit Sub    ' exit if layer not found
    End If

    objLayer.LayerOn = True                 ' turn on the desired layer
End Sub
```

You may sometimes want to execute a particular chunk of code depending on the value of the LayerOn property, for example:

```
If objLayer.LayerOn Then ... 'executes if layer is On
```

## Setting a Layer to Be Frozen/Thawed

Freezing a layer makes the entities on that layer invisible. This improves the speed of display and reduces the amount of time needed to regenerate a drawing, because entities on frozen layers aren't regenerated with the rest of the drawing. Entities on frozen layers aren't considered when AutoCAD calculates the drawing extents either. When a frozen layer is thawed, AutoCAD forces a regeneration of the entire drawing.

The amount of performance improvement depends on the number of entities on the frozen layers. Also, if your drawing is complex with a lot of detail on different layers, freezing a layer that isn't frequently used will make your drawing less cluttered and improve entity selection.

Setting the Freeze property to True will freeze a layer, whereas setting it to False will thaw the layer. For example, the following freezes a specific Layer object:

```
objLayer.Freeze = True
```

Check the value of the Freeze property to determine the current state of a Layer object:

```
If objLayer.Freeze Then ... 'executes if layer is Frozen
```

Because of the resulting drawing regeneration, frequently resetting the Freeze property can greatly decrease performance. Thus, you should use Freeze only if you intend to hide a layer for an extended period. If you need to change the visibility of a layer often, LayerOn, as described earlier, is a better alternative.

## Locking/Unlocking a Layer

You can't select or edit entities on locked layers. However, the objects are still visible as long as the layer is on and thawed, and you can still use them in object snap selection, acting as an aid to the creation and modification of entities on other layers. Although you can't edit or select entities on a locked layer, you may add new entities to it. This feature can be very useful when you create an "overlay" or for reference data. Locking a layer doesn't preclude you from altering its on/off, freeze/thaw, plot/noplot, color, linetype, or lineweight properties.

The Lock property holds a Boolean value, and setting it to True will lock a layer. A value of False will unlock the layer, for example:

```
objLayer.Lock = False
```

Check the value of the `Lock` property to determine the current state of a Layer object:

```
If objLayer.Lock Then ...    'executes if layer is locked
```

## Making Layers Plottable or Not

You can control the ability to plot layers by manipulating the `Plottable` property of the `Layer` object. Setting it to `True` enables it to be processed for plotting. Setting it to `False` treats it as though it has been frozen with respect to plot output.

```
objlayer.Plottable = False
```

Note that some layers cannot be forced to plot even if you set their `Plottable` property to `True`. Certain layers created by the ACIS or ShapeManager solid-modeling engine as well as the layer DEFPOINTS are not plottable.

## Renaming a Layer

To rename a layer, simply assign a new name to the `Layer.Name` property. Take care to address the possible exceptions that may be raised: invalid name, existing name, etc.

 **NOTE** *You can't rename the AutoCAD-defined layer "0."*

The following example renames a `Layer` object based on user input:

```
Public Sub RenameLayer()
    On Error Resume Next                        ' handle exceptions inline
    Dim strLayerName As String
    Dim objLayer As AcadLayer

    strLayerName = InputBox("Original Layer name: ")
    If "" = strLayerName Then Exit Sub          ' exit if no old name

    Set objLayer = ThisDrawing.Layers(strLayerName)
    If objLayer Is Nothing Then                 ' exit if not found
        MsgBox "Layer '" & strLayerName & "' not found"
```

```
        Exit Sub
    End If

    strLayerName = InputBox("New Layer name: ")
    If "" = strLayerName Then Exit Sub          ' exit if no new name

    objLayer.Name = strLayerName                ' try and change name
    If Err Then                                 ' check if it worked
        MsgBox "Unable to rename layer: " & vbCr & Err.Description
    Else
        MsgBox "Layer renamed to '" & strLayerName & "'"
    End If
End Sub
```

## Deleting a Layer

The Layer.Delete method removes a Layer object from the Layers collection. This method takes no parameters and has no return value:

```
LayerObject.Delete
```

Within certain restrictions appearing in the following list, it's possible to delete a layer whenever you choose. A layer may not be deleted if

- It is the active layer.

- It is layer "0" (zero).

- It contains entities.

- It an Xref-dependent layer.

If a layer contains entities in model space, any paper space layout, or any block definition, it can't be deleted. There's no definitive way to tell which entities are referenced by a specific layer short of doing an exhaustive search of each of these collections. If all entities are moved to another layer, you can then delete the layer.

Xref-dependent layers are created when an external reference file is attached and activated. Entities in the current drawing can't reside on Xref-dependent layers. Furthermore, these layers are simply duplications of the layers in the external drawing and aren't saved with the current drawing, so there's no need to delete them.

Remember, AutoCAD creates certain layers automatically for its own purposes. An example of this is the special DEFPOINTS layer, which is created during dimensioning. I discuss dimensions in Chapter 11.

The following example deletes a layer based on user input:

```
Public Sub DeleteLayer()
    On Error Resume Next                        ' handle exceptions inline
    Dim strLayerName As String
    Dim objLayer As AcadLayer

    strLayerName = InputBox("Layer name to delete: ")
    If "" = strLayerName Then Exit Sub          ' exit if no old name

    Set objLayer = ThisDrawing.Layers(strLayerName)
    If objLayer Is Nothing Then                 ' exit if not found
        MsgBox "Layer '" & strLayerName & "' not found"
        Exit Sub
    End If

    objLayer.Delete                             ' try to delete it
    If Err Then                                 ' check if it worked
        MsgBox "Unable to delete layer: " & vbCr & Err.Description
    Else
        MsgBox "Layer '" & strLayerName & "' deleted"
    End If
End Sub
```

**TIP**  *Whenever you delete a collection member such as a layer, line-type, dimstyle, or text-style object, you should consider executing a* Purge *method against the drawing object to clean up the database.*

## Getting a Layer's Handle

AutoCAD assigns every object a unique handle or ID that remains constant for as long as the object exists. You access object handles are using the Handle property. For example:

```
Dim objLayer As AcadLayer
Dim strLayerHandle As String

Set objLayer = ThisDrawing.Layers("0")
strLayerHandle = objLayer.Handle
```

Handles are used extensively when working with extended entity data. *Extended entity data,* or *Xdata,* is nongraphical information that can be attached to objects by application programs.

## Layer Colors

Each layer has a `Color` property that provides the color for all entities drawn on the layer whose `Color` property is set to `ByLayer`. Unless an entity is set to a specific color, it will take on the color of the layer where it is drawn. This is very efficient—changing the layer color automatically changes the color of all entities whose `Color` property is set to `ByLayer`.

By default, a new layer's color will be white or black depending upon the drawing background color and is represented by the number 7. You can change the layer color at any time, and likewise you can assign individual entities their own color at any time.

A layer may take any one of 257 different color values; 9 of these have associated AutoCAD VBA constants, which are listed Table 6-2. You set the `Color` property by specifying either the constant or the AutoCAD color index number, ranging between 0 and 256. The following statements are equivalent:

```
objLayer.Color = acRed
```

or

```
objLayer.Color = 1
```

*Table 6-2. AutoCAD-Defined Color Constants*

| CONSTANT | COLOR INDEX | COLOR |
| --- | --- | --- |
| acByBlock | 0 | ByBlock |
| acRed | 1 | Red |
| acYellow | 2 | Yellow |
| acGreen | 3 | Green |
| acCyan | 4 | Cyan |
| acBlue | 5 | Blue |
| acMagenta | 6 | Magenta |
| acWhite | 7 | White/Black (depending on the screen background color) |
| acByLayer | 256 | ByLayer |

**CAUTION** *You shouldn't set the* Color *property of a layer to* ByBlock *or* ByLayer. *The results are unpredictable, and furthermore it doesn't make sense to do so.*

When you retrieve the value of the Color property, it's returned as an integer:

```
intColor = objLayer.Color
```

Therefore, if the color were red, for example, the value of the variable intColor would be equal to 1.

AutoCAD 2004 introduces support for RGB-based true color properties as well as Pantone color palettes and color books. Layer objects therefore expose a TrueColor property, which employs a new enumeration class called AcadAcCmColor.

## *Layer Linetypes*

Much like the color, each layer has a Linetype property that provides the default linetype of all entities drawn on the layer whose Linetype property is set to ByLayer. Unless an entity is set to a specific linetype, it will take on the linetype of the layer where it is drawn. Again, this is very efficient—changing the layer linetype automatically changes all entities whose Linetype property is set to ByLayer.

By default, a new layer's linetype will be Continuous, which is a solid line. You can change the layer's linetype at any time, and in addition you can assign individual entities their own linetypes at any time. The Layer.Linetype property is a string that you can access as follows:

```
Public Sub Layer0Linetype()
Dim objLayer As AcadLayer
Dim strLayerLinetype As String

    Set objLayer = ThisDrawing.Layers("0")
    objLayer.Linetype = "Continuous"
    strLayerLinetype = objLayer.Linetype

End Sub
```

Linetypes are generally loaded from files containing linetype definitions, which is demonstrated later in the section "Loading a Linetype."

## Layer Lineweights

Lineweights control the visible and plottable widths of entities. You can apply them to individual objects, groups, block insertions, Xrefs, layers, and more. You can toggle their display on or off, and you can scale them to suit viewport scales in paper space.

Lineweights themselves are somewhat of a unique animal. They're a list of varying widths, from thinnest to thickest; however, they're actually constructed from a mapping of an index list to a corresponding collection of explicit metric (millimeter) values. The index values are enumerations with integer values beginning with acLnWt, but the index simply points to an explicit value, such as 0.04 millimeters. This works very well, unless the default values are edited. So although acLnWt040 by default refers to a 0.04 millimeter thickness, it can't be guaranteed to be so in all cases. Refer to Appendix B for more information on Lineweight values.

The initial value for this property is acLnWtByBlock.

Lineweight values consist of standard enumeration including BYLAYER (acLnWtByLayer), BYBLOCK (acLnWtByBLock), and DEFAULT (acLnWtByLwDefault). The DEFAULT value is set by the LWDEFAULT system variable and defaults to a value of 0.01 in. or 0.25 mm. All new objects and layers have a default setting of DEFAULT. The lineweight value of 0 plots at the thinnest lineweight available on the specified plotting device and is displayed at 1 pixel wide in model space.

```
Public Sub GetLwt()
    Dim objLayer As AcadLayer
    Dim lwtLweight As Integer
    Set objLayer = ThisDrawing.ActiveLayer
    lwtLweight = objLayer.Lineweight
    Debug.Print "Lineweight is " & lwtLweight
End Sub
```

## Linetypes

As you would expect, linetypes characterize the different appearances that a line within a drawing may adopt. Linetypes are arranged in alternate patterns of dashes, dots, etc. to represent something specific to the user, such as process pipelines or railroad tracks, as shown in Figure 6-2.

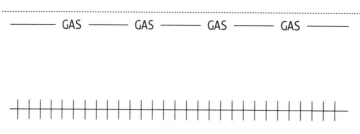

*Figure 6-2. Linetype examples*

You have a great deal of flexibility when it comes to linetypes—in fact, your imagination is virtually the limit.

Although it's possible to create new Linetype objects through VBA, *it isn't possible to control the line pattern directly through code.* However, VBA provides the Load method to load existing linetypes into your drawing. I discuss most of the methods and properties that AutoCAD provides for working with the Linetypes collection and Linetype objects.

You'll learn how to

- Access the Linetypes collection and Linetype objects.

- Check for the existence of a specific linetype.

- Load linetypes and make a specific linetype active.

- Rename and delete a linetype.

- Set or return a linetype's scale properties and description.

## *Accessing Linetypes*

Much like layers, AutoCAD has a Linetypes collection that contains all of the Linetype objects in the drawing. You can create as many Linetype objects as you want by adding to the Linetypes collection, but they'll be created with the default properties only.

The Linetypes collection is accessed via a Document object. In the following code, ThisDrawing is used as the active document:

```
Dim objLinetypes As AcadLineTypes
Set objLinetypes = ThisDrawing.Linetypes
```

To set a reference to an existing Linetype object, use the Item method of the Linetypes collection as follows:

```
Dim objLinetype As AcadLineType
Set objLinetype = objLinetypes.Item(2)
Set objLinetype = objLinetypes.Item("Dashed")
```

The parameter of this method is either an integer representing the position of the desired Linetype object within the Linetypes collection or a string representing the name of the desired Linetype object. If you use an index number, it must be between 0 and Linetypes.Count minus 1.

Like other AutoCAD collections, Item is the default method for Linetypes. This means that the method name may be omitted, and the parameter passed straight to the Linetypes reference. This is often preferred, as it's simpler to type and read. The following code does the same thing as the prior example using the default method to specify the Linetype object:

```
Dim objLinetype As AcadLinetype
Set objLinetype = objLinetypes(2)
Set objLinetype = objLinetypes("Dashed")
```

## Checking for Existing Linetypes

In some situations your program must determine if an element is present in the collection. One way to do this is to search for the element while iterating the collection, as described earlier in the chapter. The following example gets a linetype name from the user and then checks for its existence by iterating the Linetypes collection:

```
Public Sub CheckForLinetypeByIteration()
    Dim objLinetype As AcadLineType
    Dim strLinetypeName As String

    strLinetypeName = InputBox("Enter a Linetype name to search for: ")
    If "" = strLinetypeName Then Exit Sub          ' exit if no name entered

    For Each objLinetype In ThisDrawing.Linetypes
```

```
            If 0 = StrComp(objLinetype.Name, strLinetypeName, vbTextCompare) Then
                MsgBox "Linetype '" & strLinetypeName & "' exists"
                Exit Sub                        ' exit after finding linetype
            End If
        Next objLinetype

        MsgBox "Linetype '" & strLinetypeName & "' does not exist"
    End Sub
```

Unlike prior releases in which linetype names were converted to uppercase, AutoCAD 2000 and higher allow the names to be a mix of upper- and lowercase, although "Linetype1" and "LINETYPE1" will be treated as the same name. This sample uses a case-insensitive string comparison of strLinetypeName and each Linetype name to allow for capitalization differences.

A second technique is to let AutoCAD perform the search for you. This is quite a bit more efficient because AutoCAD can internally determine if the element is present, and it eliminates sending unneeded elements to your program. AutoCAD will also handle the case-insensitive name comparison for you. To use this technique you must employ the VBA error handler.

Like many AutoCAD ActiveX objects, the Linetypes collection uses run-time errors or exceptions to signal unexpected conditions. If an exception isn't handled, the calling program halts and displays an error message to the user. In this case, Linetypes will raise an exception if you attempt to access an unknown Linetype name. By detecting this exception, or more correctly the lack of the exception, your program is notified of the existence of the Linetype. The following example gets a linetype name from the user and uses AutoCAD to check for its existence:

```
Public Sub CheckForLinetypeByException()
    Dim strLinetypeName As String
    Dim objLinetype As AcadLineType

    strLinetypeName = InputBox("Enter a Linetype name to search for: ")
    If "" = strLinetypeName Then Exit Sub       ' exit if no name entered

    On Error Resume Next                ' handle exceptions inline
    Set objLinetype = ThisDrawing.Linetypes(strLinetypeName)

    If objLinetype Is Nothing Then      ' check if obj has been set
        MsgBox "Linetype '" & strLinetypeName & "' does not exist"
    Else
        MsgBox "Linetype '" & objLinetype.Name & "' exists"
    End If
End Sub
```

## Loading a Linetype

Linetype definitions are stored in linetype library files, which are external to drawing files and have the extension .lin. Linetypes are loaded by name from library files into similarly named Linetype objects in the drawing. Once loaded into a drawing, a Linetype object has no more connection to the library file. I don't cover the creation and definition of linetypes here, because no methods exist for customizing linetypes programmatically, but you can take a look at the AutoCAD Customization Guide in the online help files for details on creating custom linetypes. It's interesting to note that you can create custom linetypes by writing a linetype definition file programmatically and then loading it.

You can load a Linetype object into your drawing using the Load method shown in the following code and detailed in Table 6-3.

```
Set LinetypeObject = LinetypesCollection.Load(LinetypeName, _
                         LinetypeFilename)
```

*Table 6-3. Linetype Load Parameter Specifications*

| NAME | DATA TYPE | DESCRIPTION |
| --- | --- | --- |
| LineTypeName | String | The name of the linetype |
| LinetypeFilename | String | The path and file name of the linetype library file |

The AutoCAD default Linetype object definition file for standard linetypes is acad.lin. You can view the contents of this via the Linetype dialog box (click Format ➤ Linetype to bring it up) by clicking Load and browsing to the file (see Figure 6-3). You can also open a linetype definition file in any ASCII text editor such as Windows Notepad.

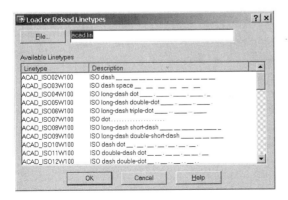

*Figure 6-3. The Linetype dialog box*

Once you determine the linetype library and the name of a specific linetype you'd like to load, you can use the following code to load it:

```
Public Sub LoadLinetype()
    Dim strLinetypeName As String
    Dim objLinetype As AcadLineType

    strLinetypeName = InputBox("Enter a Linetype name" & _
                        " to load from ACAD.LIN: ")
    If "" = strLinetypeName Then Exit Sub      ' exit if no name entered

    On Error Resume Next             ' handle exceptions inline
    ThisDrawing.Linetypes.Load strLinetypeName, "acad.lin"

    If Err Then                       ' check if err was thrown
        MsgBox "Error loading '" & strLinetypeName & "'" & vbCr & _
                Err.Description
    Else
        MsgBox "Loaded Linetype '" & strLinetypeName & "'"
    End If
End Sub
```

## Making a Linetype Active

The Linetype property for new entities is determined by the drawing linetype setting for the drawing. By default, this is set so that new entities are displayed using the linetype assigned to the layer that they're drawn on. By changing this setting, you may assign specific linetypes directly to entities rather than the layer setting, which normally takes precedence. You can change the linetype of an existing entity at any time by altering its Linetype property.

**NOTE**   *You can't make a linetype active if it's Xref dependent.*

You can use two special linetypes: ByLayer and ByBlock. The ByLayer option was described earlier in this chapter. This is the most commonly used method when creating drawing entities. If you use the ByBlock option, all new entities that you create will use the linetype associated with the block containing the entity. Block objects are considered in more detail in Chapter 13.

The `ActiveLinetype` property is a member of the `Document` object. To make a specific linetype active, assign the `Linetype` object to the `ActiveLinetype` property:

```
DocumentObject.ActiveLinetype = LinetypeObject
```

The following example makes the linetype named "TRACKS" the active linetype for the current `Document`:

```
ThisDrawing.ActiveLinetype = ThisDrawing.Linetypes("TRACKS")
```

Now, all the new entities will be created with this linetype until another linetype is activated. You can change the linetype of existing entities by altering the `Linetype` property of that particular entity. The `Linetype` property is a string that corresponds to the name of a `Linetype` object. The following example lets the user pick a drawing entity and specify a new linetype name for that entity:

```
Public Sub ChangeEntityLinetype()
    On Error Resume Next                    ' handle exceptions inline
    Dim objEntity As AcadEntity
    Dim varPick As Variant
    Dim strLinetypeName As String
    Dim objLinetype As AcadLineType

    ThisDrawing.Utility.GetEntity objEntity, varPick, "Select an entity"
    If objEntity Is Nothing Then Exit Sub      ' exit if no entity picked

    strLinetypeName = InputBox("Enter a new Linetype name: ")
    If "" = strLinetypeName Then Exit Sub      ' exit if no name entered

    Set objLinetype = ThisDrawing.Linetypes(strLinetypeName)
    If objLinetype Is Nothing Then
        MsgBox "Linetype is not loaded"
        Exit Sub    ' exit if linetype not found
    End If

    objEntity.Linetype = strLinetypeName         ' else change entity layer
End Sub
```

## Renaming a Linetype

To rename a linetype, simply assign a new name to the `Linetype.Name` property. Take care to address the possible exceptions that may be thrown up: invalid name, existing name, etc.

**NOTE** *You may not rename* ByLayer, ByBlock, Continuous, *and Xref-dependent linetypes.*

The following example renames a Linetype object based on user input:

```
Sub RenameLinetype()
    On Error Resume Next                    ' handle exceptions inline
    On Error Resume Next                    ' handle exceptions inline
    Dim strLinetypeName As String
    Dim objLinetype As AcadLineType

    strLinetypeName = InputBox("Original Linetype name: ")
    If "" = strLinetypeName Then Exit Sub          ' exit if no old name

    Set objLinetype = ThisDrawing.Linetypes(strLinetypeName)
    If objLinetype Is Nothing Then         ' exit if not found
        MsgBox "Linetype '" & strLinetypeName & "' not found"
        Exit Sub
    End If

    strLinetypeName = InputBox("New Linetype name: ")
    If "" = strLinetypeName Then Exit Sub          ' exit if no new name

    objLinetype.Name = strLinetypeName             ' try and change name
    If Err Then                            ' check if it worked
        MsgBox "Unable to rename Linetype: " & vbCr & Err.Description
    Else
        MsgBox "Linetype renamed to '" & strLinetypeName & "'"
    End If
End Sub
```

## Deleting a Linetype

The Linetype.Delete method removes a Linetype object from the Linetypes collection. This method takes no parameters and has no return value:

```
LinetypeObject.Delete
```

It's possible to delete a linetype practically whenever you choose; however, certain linetypes may not be deleted. A linetype may not be deleted if

- It is the active linetype.

- It is a ByLayer, ByBlock, or Continuous linetype.

- It is an Xref-dependent linetype.

Just as with layers, if a linetype is used by entities in model space, any paper space layout or any block definition, it can't be deleted. There's no definitive way to tell which entities are using a specific linetype short of doing an exhaustive search of each of these collections. If all entities using the linetype are assigned to another, you can then delete the linetype.

Xref-dependent linetypes are created when an external reference file is attached and activated. Entities in the current drawing can't use Xref-dependent linetypes. Furthermore, these linetypes are simply duplications of the linetypes in the external drawing and aren't saved with the current drawing, so you don't need to delete them.

The following example deletes a linetype based on user input:

```
Public Sub DeleteLinetype()
    On Error Resume Next                        ' handle exceptions inline
    Dim strLinetypeName As String
    Dim objLinetype As AcadLineType

    strLinetypeName = InputBox("Linetype name to delete: ")
    If "" = strLinetypeName Then Exit Sub        ' exit if no old name

    Set objLinetype = ThisDrawing.Linetypes(strLinetypeName)
    If objLinetype Is Nothing Then               ' exit if not found
        MsgBox "Linetype '" & strLinetypeName & "' not found"
        Exit Sub
    End If

    objLinetype.Delete                           ' try to delete it
    If Err Then                                  ' check if it worked
        MsgBox "Unable to delete linetype: " & vbCr & Err.Description
    Else
        MsgBox "Linetype '" & strLinetypeName & "' deleted"
    End If
End Sub
```

## Getting a Linetype's Handle

AutoCAD assigns to every object a unique handle or ID that remains constant for as long as the object exists. The handle of an object takes the form of a string and may be accessed via the read-only `Handle` property. For example:

```
Dim objLinetype As AcadLinetype
Dim strLinetypeHandle As String

Set objLinetype = ThisDrawing.Linetypes("Center")
strLinetypeHandle = objLinetype.Handle
```

You'll use handles extensively when working with extended entity data. *Extended entity data* is specific information that can be attached to an object or entity by an external application.

## Changing a Linetype's Description

AutoCAD allows you to read, add, or modify a linetype's description using the `Description` property of the `Linetype` object. This property is a string that typically describes the linetype, often with a simplified symbolized version of the actual linetype. The following code snippet shows the `Description` property being set and retrieved:

```
Dim objLineType As AcadLineType
Dim strLineTypeDescription As String

objLineType.Description = "Linetype Description: -.-.-."
strLineTypeDescription = objLineType.Description
```

The following example changes a `Linetype` description based on user input:

```
Public Sub DescribeLinetype()
    On Error Resume Next                        ' handle exceptions inline
    Dim strLinetypeName As String
    Dim strLinetypeDescription As String
    Dim objLinetype As AcadLineType

    strLinetypeName = InputBox("Enter the Linetype name: ")
    If "" = strLinetypeName Then Exit Sub           ' exit if no old name
```

```
Set objLinetype = ThisDrawing.Linetypes(strLinetypeName)
If objLinetype Is Nothing Then                  ' exit if not found
    MsgBox "Linetype '" & strLinetypeName & "' not found"
    Exit Sub
End If

strLinetypeDescription = InputBox("Enter the Linetype description: ")
If "" = strLinetypeDescription Then Exit Sub      ' exit if no new name

objLinetype.Description = strLinetypeDescription     ' try and change name
If Err Then                                    ' check if it worked
    MsgBox "Unable to alter Linetype: " & vbCr & Err.Description
Else
    MsgBox "Linetype '" & strLinetypeName & "' description changed"
End If
```

## Scaling Linetypes

The scale of a linetype determines how many times the pattern of a linetype is repeated over a given distance: the smaller the scale, the finer the pattern. You need to adjust the scale of linetypes to suitable values so that your drawings will display and plot sensibly.

Here I cover two types of scaling factors for linetypes: the global linetype scale or LTSCALE and the individual linetype scale or CELTSCALE. LTSCALE affects all objects within a drawing, and when it is changed, the lines of all existing objects are updated. CELTSCALE, on the other hand, affects only the objects that are created after it has been set. The scaling of a linetype depends on a combination of LTSCALE and CELTSCALE, as shown in Figure 6-4.

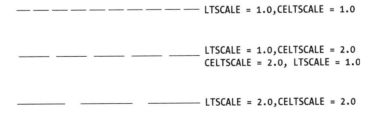

LTSCALE = 1.0,CELTSCALE = 1.0

LTSCALE = 1.0,CELTSCALE = 2.0
CELTSCALE = 2.0, LTSCALE = 1.0

LTSCALE = 2.0,CELTSCALE = 2.0

*Figure 6-4. An example of linetype scaling*

Because you're likely to assign the linetype scale a number such as 0.5 or 2.0, you might be tempted to use a single precision floating-point variable when reading the LTSCALE or CELTSCALE for a drawing. However, you might well find that the number returned isn't so simple and that you need more precision. Be proactive and use a double-precision variable type. Additionally, viewport scaling affects global and individual linetype scaling, as can plot-style configurations.

### Global Scale

The default for the global linetype LTSCALE system variable is 1.0, which means 1 linetype unit per drawing unit. A LTSCALE factor of 2.0 would mean 2 linetype units per drawing unit. Changing this value will change the linetype scale for all entities in the drawing. System variables are retrieved and set using the GetVariable and SetVariable methods of the Document object.

The following example demonstrates setting and reading the LTSCALE system variable, which holds a real number:

```
Dim dblNewLTScale As Double
ThisDrawing.SetVariable "LTSCALE", 2#
dblNewLTScale = ThisDrawing.GetVariable("LTSCALE")
```

### Individual Scale

The CELTSCALE system variable is set in a similar way to LTSCALE and also holds a real number.

```
Dim dblNewCELTScale As Double
ThisDrawing.SetVariable "CELTSCALE", 2#
dblNewCELTScale = ThisDrawing.GetVariable("CELTSCALE")
```

## Summary

In this chapter, I showed you the advantages of effective use of layers and linetypes. I discussed and gave code examples for many of the methods and properties of the Layers collection and Layer object and the Linetypes collection and Linetype object. For complete details of each of these AutoCAD objects, please refer to Appendix A.

CHAPTER 7

# User Interaction and the Utility Object

TO PROGRAM TRULY POWERFUL AutoCAD applications and macros, you need to
be able to interact with the user. The AutoCAD automation model provides
the Utility and SelectionSet objects to do just that. Chapter 12 discusses the
SelectionSet object. This chapter discusses the Utility object, which contains
a number of methods for obtaining user input via the AutoCAD command line
and graphics screen, such as picking points, entering distances and angles, and
picking a single entity.

In addition to these AutoCAD objects, you can, of course, interface with the
user through standard VBA functions and objects. The VBA InputBox and MsgBox
functions allow simple user input, while VBA UserForms and graphical controls
allow a level of sophistication limited only by your imagination.

This chapter covers:

- Controlling user keyword input

- Using GetXXX methods for all types of input

- Other interactive or interesting methods of the Utility object

## The Utility Object

The Utility object provides a number of useful methods for such things as
performing unit conversions, using the Internet from within AutoCAD, and
interacting with the user at the AutoCAD command line and graphics screen.
This section explains each method's syntax.

## Interface Methods

Interface methods present and retrieve information from the user. This section discusses the various methods made available through AutoCAD's Utility object.

### Input Methods and Dialogs

All of the AutoCAD input methods require that the user interact with the AutoCAD drawing or command window. To use these methods from a VBA UserForm, either hide the form before you call the input methods or set the UserForm to modeless operation. If you don't, an error will occur. This is because modal forms maintain the application focus while they're visible. As long as a modal VBA form is visible, there's no way for the user to get to the AutoCAD drawing or command window. UserForms can be modal or modeless only with AutoCAD 2002 and later versions.

The example below places the command button cmdGetReal on a UserForm, which is then hidden while the GetReal user input method executes:

```
Private Sub cmdGetReal_Click()
Dim dblInput As Double

    Me.Hide
    dblInput = ThisDrawing.Utility.GetReal("Enter a real value: ")
    Me.Show

End Sub
```

**NOTE** *Remember to* Show *the form after you hide it for user input, or your program will exit without completing any of the form's remaining code.*

The code in this chapter runs from the Macros dialog box. To work from a UserForm, you need to modify each sample. For example, change code from this:

```
Public Sub TestUserInput()
Dim strInput As String

    With ThisDrawing.Utility
        .InitializeUserInput 1, "Line Arc Circle laSt"
```

```
         strInput = .GetKeyword(vbCr & "Option [Line/Arc/Circle/laSt]: ")
         .Prompt "You selected '" & strInput & "'"
    End With
End Sub
```

to this:

```
Private Sub CommandButton1_Click()
Dim strInput As String

    Me.Hide
    With ThisDrawing.Utility
        .InitializeUserInput 1, "Line Arc Circle laSt"
        strInput = .GetKeyword(vbCr & "Option [Line/Arc/Circle/laSt]: ")
        MsgBox "You selected '" & strInput & "'"
    End With
    Me.Show

End Sub
```

Programs written using the full version of Visual Basic 6 or VBA 6.3 (AutoCAD 2002 and later) are not limited to modal dialog forms. But there still may be times where it makes sense to hide the form while interacting with the user at the AutoCAD command prompt. Try to think like your users when you design the interaction process and your forms' behavior.

## The Prompt Method

The Prompt method displays messages on the AutoCAD command line. It returns nothing.

```
UtilityObject.Prompt Message
```

The Message parameter is a string that contains the message to display at the command prompt.

**NOTE** *Remember to include carriage returns or linefeeds in the message string, or your message will just be appended to whatever text is on the command prompt.*

This example displays a simple message at the command prompt, as shown in Figure 7-1:

```
Public Sub TestPrompt()
    ThisDrawing.Utility.Prompt vbCrLf & "This is a simple message"
End Sub
```

*Figure 7-1. Command prompt output*

The remaining examples in this chapter make extensive use of the Prompt method to give the user feedback.

## The InitializeUserInput Method

The InitializeUserInput method establishes which keywords the program will accept during command line input. It also sets input criteria such as whether null values are allowed. It affects the very next call to an input function, after which the keywords and other input criteria are cleared.

The InitializeUserInput method has this syntax:

```
UtilityObject.InitializeUserInput OptionBits[, KeywordList]
```

Table 7-1 explains this method's parameters.

*Table 7-1. InitializeUserInput method parameters*

| NAME | TYPE | DESCRIPTION |
| --- | --- | --- |
| OptionBits | Long | Restricts what the user can input, as Table 7-2 explains |
| KeywordList | String | A list of the keywords delimited by spaces |

Table 7-2 explains valid OptionBits options.

*Table 7-2. Acceptable keyword list values*

| BIT VALUE | DESCRIPTION |
|---|---|
| 0 or not set | No control conditions are applied. |
| 1 | Prevents null input such as *Enter* or *Space*. |
| 2 | Prevents the user from entering a zero value. |
| 4 | Prevents the user from entering a negative value. |
| 8 | Lets the user enter a point outside the current drawing limits. AutoCAD won't check the drawing limits even if the LIMCHECK system variable is on. LIMCHECK controls whether entities may be created outside the drawing limits. |
| 16 | Not currently used. |
| 32 | For methods that allow input via the graphics screen, AutoCAD uses a dashed rather than solid line when it displays a rubber-band line or box. AutoCAD ignore this bit if the POPUPS system variable is set to zero. POPUPS indicates whether the currently configured display driver supports dialog boxes, the menu bar, and icon menus. |
| 64 | For the GetDistance method, ignores the Z-coordinate of 3-D points, thus returning a 2-D distance. |
| 128 | Accepts any user input. |

### Keywords

Command line keywords give the user various options. For instance, if you use AutoCAD Draw toolbar's rectangle command, you may either pick a point or use one of the five keywords to choose another command:

```
Specify first corner point or [Chamfer/Elevation/Fillet/Thickness/Width]:
```

The KeywordList parameter specifies a set of keywords available at the input prompt. It is a string that contains the keywords, each separated by a space. The capital letter in each keyword is the shortcut key the user can type.

It is common practice to give the user a list of valid keywords when prompting for input. You must supply this list in your input prompt, since AutoCAD does not indicate the active keywords in any other way. This example demonstrates these ideas by getting a keyword from the user and then printing it on the command line:

```
Public Sub TestUserInput()
Dim strInput As String

    With ThisDrawing.Utility
        .InitializeUserInput 1, "Line Arc Circle laSt"
        strInput = .GetKeyword(vbCr & "Option [Line/Arc/Circle/laSt]: ")
        .Prompt vbCr & "You selected '" & strInput & "'"
    End With
End Sub
```

In this example, you can type L for a line, A for an arc, C for a circle, or S for the last command. AutoCAD rejects any other single letter, whether in a keyword or otherwise. However, you can type a partial keyword, or even the entire keyword, if you wish. When you type partial keywords, you must supply enough of the keyword to uniquely distinguish it from all other keywords. The partial entry must also include at least up to the capital letter in the keyword. For example, AutoCAD rejects typing la, but typing **las** correctly returns laSt.

Regardless of how the user types a keyword, AutoCAD returns a string that exactly matches the capitalization used when you initialized the keyword. In the example above, typing S, LAS, Las, or any other variation returns laSt.

Keywords can be used in conjunction with these Utility input methods: GetKeyword, GetInteger, GetReal, GetDistance, GetAngle, GetOrientation, GetPoint, and GetCorner. Each of these methods can obtain keywords the InitialiseUserInput method set. See "The GetInput Method" later in this chapter to learn how to retrieve keywords from them.

## The GetXXX Methods

The GetXXX methods get specific types of data from the user. These methods make AutoCAD pause until the user supplies a value at the command prompt or picks a point in the drawing window. If the user supplies the wrong type of data, such as typing a string when a number is needed, AutoCAD displays a message at the command prompt that tells them to re-enter the data.

### The GetKeyword Method

The GetKeyword method gets a command line option from the user. You must call InitializeUserInput to establish the list of keywords before you use this method. It returns the keyword the user entered exactly as the keyword list specified it. If you want, you can include a prompt to display on the command line while the function waits for user input. This method has the following syntax:

```
strUserKeyWordInput = Object.GetKeyword([Prompt])
```

This method's Prompt parameter is a string that contains the prompt to display on the command line.

If the user tries to enter a string that's not in the keyword list, AutoCAD displays the error message Invalid option keyword in the command window. AutoCAD then tries to get valid user input by redisplaying the prompt if you specified one, or by displaying a blank command line if you didn't. If you allow null input, the user can press *Enter* to return an empty string.

This example asks the user for an option and then starts the specified command, using the SendCommand method outlined in Appendix A:

```
Sub TestGetKeyword()
Dim strInput As String

    With ThisDrawing.Utility
        .InitializeUserInput 0, "Line Arc Circle"
        strInput = .GetKeyword(vbCr & "Command [Line/Arc/Circle]: ")
    End With

    Select Case strInput

        Case "Line": ThisDrawing.SendCommand "_Line" & vbCr
        Case "Arc": ThisDrawing.SendCommand "_Arc" & vbCr
        Case "Circle": ThisDrawing.SendCommand "_Circle" & vbCr
        Case Else:  MsgBox "You pressed Enter."

    End Select

End Sub
```

### The GetString Method

The `GetString` method gets string values from the user. AutoCAD pauses until the user enters a value.

```
dblUserStringInput = UtilityObject.GetString(HasSpaces[ ,Prompt])
```

Table 7-3 lists this method's parameters.

*Table 7-3.* `GetString` *method parameters*

| NAME | TYPE | DESCRIPTION |
| --- | --- | --- |
| HasSpaces | Boolean | Specifies whether the user input may contain spaces. If set to True, spaces are valid and the user must press Enter to terminate the input. If set to False, spaces are not allowed and the user can terminate the input by typing either Enter or a space. |
| Prompt | String | An optional parameter used to display a prompt for input. |

This example gets a string from the user, including spaces, and then displays it:

```
Public Sub TestGetString()
Dim strInput As String

    With ThisDrawing.Utility
        strInput = .GetString(True, vbCr & "Enter a string: ")
        .Prompt vbCr & "You entered '" & strInput & "' "
    End With
End Sub
```

This method lets the user can enter up to 132 characters. Entering more than 132 characters generates the error `Method 'GetString' of object 'IAcadUtility' failed`, which is unfortunately the same description reported when a user issues a Cancel or Esc. If you need to distinguish between the overflow and the Cancel for this method, consider using the unique exception number instead of the description.

### The GetInteger Method

The GetInteger method gets an integer from the user. AutoCAD waits for the user to input an integer and returns the entered value. This method has the following syntax:

```
intUserIntegerInput = UtilityObject.GetInteger([Prompt])
```

This method has one parameter, Prompt, a string. Optionally use it to specify a prompt for input.

The user may enter either an integer in the range -32,768 to +32,767 or a keyword (see "The GetInput Method" later in the chapter for more information). If the user tries to enter any other value, AutoCAD returns the error message Requires an integer value or option keyword and asks the user enter another value. Here's an example of GetInteger:

```
Public Sub TestGetInteger()
Dim intInput As Integer

    With ThisDrawing.Utility
        intInput = .GetInteger(vbCr & "Enter an integer: ")
        .Prompt vbCr & "You entered " & intInput
    End With
End Sub
```

This method throws exceptions for null input, keyword entry, and canceled input.


### The GetReal Method

The GetReal method is similar to GetInteger but gets floating-point numbers. It returns a value of data type double.

```
dblUserRealInput = UtilityObject.GetReal([Prompt])
```

This method's Prompt parameter, a string, is optional. Use it to specify a prompt for input.

This method accepts any real (double-precision floating point) value or any previously set keyword. For more about these keywords, see "The GetInput Method," later in this chapter. If the user enters any other value, AutoCAD returns the error message `Requires numeric value` and asks the user to enter another value. This example retrieves and displays a real value from the user:

```
Public Sub TestGetReal()
Dim dblInput As Double

    With ThisDrawing.Utility
        dblInput = .GetReal(vbCrLf & "Enter an real: ")
        .Prompt vbCr & "You entered " & dblInput
    End With
End Sub
```

This method raises an exception for null input, keyword entry, and canceled input.

### The GetPoint Method

The `GetPoint` method gets a point from the user, either by typing coordinates at the command prompt or by picking points in the drawing area. The return value is a `Variant` and contains a three-element array of doubles holding the point's World Coordinate System (WCS) coordinates. This method has the following syntax:

```
varUserPointInput = UtilityObject.GetPoint([BasePoint] [,Prompt])
```

Table 7-4 explains this method's parameters.

*Table 7-4. GetPoint method parameters*

| NAME | TYPE | DESCRIPTION |
| --- | --- | --- |
| BasePoint | Variant | Optional. A three-element array of doubles that specifies the an angle vector's first point in WCS. |
| Prompt | String | Optional. A prompt for input. |

The optional `BasePoint` parameter sets a rubber-band line's start point. This line, which extends to the current crosshair position, can be a useful visual aid to the user during input.

This example gets a point from the user and displays its coordinate values:

```
Public Sub TestGetPoint()
Dim varPick As Variant
```

```
    With ThisDrawing.Utility
        varPick = .GetPoint(, vbCr & "Pick a point: ")
        .Prompt vbCr & varPick(0) & "," & varPick(1)
    End With
End Sub
```

This method raises exceptions for null input, keyword entry, and canceled input.

### The GetCorner Method

Given a base point in a rectangle, the GetCorner method gets the diagonally opposing corner point. It returns a Variant and contains a three-element array of doubles showing the corner point's WCS coordinates. This method has the following syntax:

```
varUserCornerInput = UtilityObject.GetCorner(BasePoint [,Prompt])
```

Table 7-5 explains this method's parameters.

*Table 7-5. GetCorner method parameters*

| NAME | TYPE | DESCRIPTION |
| --- | --- | --- |
| BasePoint | Variant | A three-element array of doubles specifying the rectangle's first corner in WCS. |
| Prompt | String | Optional. A prompt for input. |

If the user picks a point on the graphic screen, the GetCorner method ignores the point's Z-coordinate and sets it to the current elevation. This example gets a point and then a corner from the user and displays the rectangle's values:

```
Public Sub TestGetCorner()
Dim varBase As Variant
Dim varPick As Variant

    With ThisDrawing.Utility
        varBase = .GetPoint(, vbCr & "Pick the first corner: ")
        .Prompt vbCrLf & varBase(0) & "," & varBase(1)
        varPick = .GetCorner(varBase, vbLf & "Pick the second: ")
        .Prompt vbCr & varPick(0) & "," & varPick(1)
    End With
End Sub
```

This method throws exceptions for null input, keyword entry, and canceled input.

### The GetDistance Method

The `GetDistance` method gets a double from the user. It differs from `GetReal` in that the user can either type a distance in the current units format or pick the point(s) on the graphics screen. These two methods are otherwise similar, and most people prefer `GetDistance` because it's more flexible. This method has the following syntax:

```
dblUserDistanceInput = UtilityObject.GetDistance([BasePoint] [,Prompt])
```

Table 7-6 explains this method's parameters.

*Table 7-6. GetDistance method parameters*

| NAME | TYPE | DESCRIPTION |
| --- | --- | --- |
| BasePoint | Variant | Optional. A three-element array of doubles specifying a start point from which to begin measuring (in WCS). If you don't provide this parameter, the user must specify two points. |
| Prompt | String | Optional. A prompt for input. |

**NOTE**  *This method lets you enter a negative number at the command prompt and returns this negative number. But it calculates the absolute distance between points if you enter it on the graphics screen.*

If the user chooses to pick points from the screen, AutoCAD draws a rubber-band line as a visual aid from the base point, or first pick point, to the current crosshair position. By default, the points are three-dimensional. You may force AutoCAD to calculate a planar distance by first calling `InitializeUserInput` with bit code 16 in `OptionBits`. This makes AutoCAD ignore the Z-coordinates.

This example code sets the base point to the origin of WCS, prompts the user for input, and then displays the value:

```
Public Sub TestGetDistance()
Dim dblInput As Double
Dim dblBase(2) As Double

    dblBase(0) = 0:  dblBase(1) = 0:  dblBase(2) = 0

    With ThisDrawing.Utility
        dblInput = .GetDistance(dblBase, vbCr & "Enter a distance: ")
        .Prompt vbCr & "You entered " & dblInput
    End With
End Sub
```

This method raises an exception for null input, keyword entry, and canceled input.

### *The GetAngle Method*

Use the GetAngle to get an angle, in radians, from the user. The user may either type the angle at the command prompt or pick point(s) on the screen. VBA ignores the points' Z-coordinates. It measures the angle counterclockwise with respect to the ANGBASE system variable's current value. This method has the following syntax:

```
dblUserAngleInput = UtilityObject.GetAngle([BasePoint] [,Prompt])
```

Table 7-7 explains this method's parameters.

*Table 7-7.* GetAngle *method parameters*

| NAME | TYPE | DESCRIPTION |
| --- | --- | --- |
| BasePoint | Variant | Optional. A three-element array of doubles specifying an angle vector's first point in WCS. If not provided, the user must specify two points to specify the angle on the graphics screen. |
| Prompt | String | Optional. A prompt for input. |

This method returns the angle in radians regardless of the current setting of the DIMAUNIT angular units system variable or the angular unit type the user entered. In this way, it acts in a similar manner to the Utility object's AngleToReal conversion method.

This example sets the angular units to degrees, and then retrieves and displays an angle from the user:

```
Public Sub TestGetAngle()
Dim dblInput As Double

    ThisDrawing.SetVariable "DIMAUNIT", acDegrees

    With ThisDrawing.Utility
        dblInput = .GetAngle(, vbCr & "Enter an angle: ")
        .Prompt vbCr & "Angle in radians: " & dblInput
    End With
End Sub
```

This method throws exceptions for null input, keyword entry, and canceled input.

### The GetOrientation Method

The GetOrientation method is similar to GetAngle, except that the angle returned is always measured from the east, or three o'clock, regardless of the ANGBASE system variable setting. This method has the following syntax:

```
dblUserOrientationInput = UtilityObject.GetOrientation([BasePoint] [,Prompt])
```

Table 7-8 explains this method's parameters.

*Table 7-8. GetOrientation method parameters*

| NAME | TYPE | DESCRIPTION |
| --- | --- | --- |
| BasePoint | Variant | Optional. A three-element array of doubles specifying an angle vector's first point in WCS. If not provided, the user must specify two points if they wish to specify the angle on the graphics screen. |
| Prompt | String | Optional. A prompt for input. |

This method throws an exception for both null input or keyword entry if allowed and supplied.

### *The GetInput Method*

As was mentioned in the discussion of `GetKeyword`, you can use seven other input methods in conjunction with the keywords set using `InitializeUserInput`:

- `GetInteger`

- `GetReal`

- `GetDistance`

- `GetAngle`

- `GetOrientation`

- `GetPoint`

- `GetCorner`

When you set keywords for these methods, when they are executed the user can enter the data type requested or choose one of the available keywords. Because each of these input methods returns a specific data type, they can't also return the keyword string. Instead, the input methods use an exception with the description `User input is a keyword` to signal the presence of a keyword. Unless null input is disabled, VBA uses this same exception to indicate null input, such as when the user simply presses *Enter* at the input prompt.

Your code must handle the exception or the program will stop and display an error message. After detecting this exception, use `GetInput` to retrieve the keyword before calling any other `GetXXX` method. The `GetInput` method takes no parameters. It returns either a string containing the keyword in `InitializeUserInput` or an empty string in the case of null input.

```
StrUserKeywordInput = UtilityObject.GetInput()
```

As shown in the examples above, it is not necessary to call the `GetInput` method after the `GetXXX` methods when no keywords are offered to the user. If called independently, this method returns an empty string.

The following code retrieves either an integer or a keyword from the user. It uses GetInteger to demonstrate the GetInput method, but the technique is identical for each of the six other input methods:

```
Public Sub TestGetInput()
Dim intInput As Integer
Dim strInput As String

On Error Resume Next                    ' handle exceptions inline
    With ThisDrawing.Utility
        strInput = .GetInput()
        .InitializeUserInput 0, "Line Arc Circle"
        intInput = .GetInteger(vbCr & "Integer or [Line/Arc/Circle]: ")

        If Err.Description Like "*error*" Then
            .Prompt vbCr & "Input Cancelled"
        ElseIf Err.Description Like "*keyword*" Then
            strInput = .GetInput()
          Select Case strInput
                Case "Line": ThisDrawing.SendCommand "_Line" & vbCr
                Case "Arc": ThisDrawing.SendCommand "_Arc" & vbCr
                Case "Circle": ThisDrawing.SendCommand "_Circle" & vbCr
                Case Else: .Prompt vbCr & "Null Input entered"
            End Select
        Else
            .Prompt vbCr & "You entered " & intInput
        End If
    End With

End Sub
```

This example first sets the keywords using InitializeUserInput and then uses an input method to get the user's input. Because the code sets keywords, the input method either returns an integer or throws an exception when the user enters a keyword. If there was an exception and it contains the word "error," this code displays a cancel message. Otherwise, if the exception contains the word "keyword," the code uses GetInput to retrieve the keyword and takes an appropriate action based on the keyword. If no exception was thrown, this code uses the Integer value the GetInteger method returned.

There appears to be a bug that causes GetInput to return the keyword from earlier calls to InitializeUserInput when the user enters null input at a later input method that takes keywords. The following code demonstrates the problem. Choose any option at the first input prompt and then press Enter for the second input. In case the user enters a keyword, the second call to GetInput should return a null—but instead it returns the keyword you selected in the previous input.

```
Public Sub TestGetInputBug()

On Error Resume Next                    ' handle exceptions inline

    With ThisDrawing.Utility

        '' first keyword input
        .InitializeUserInput 1, "Alpha Beta Ship"
        .GetInteger vbCr & "Option [Alha/Beta/Ship]: "
        MsgBox "You entered: " & .GetInput()

        '' second keyword input - hit enter here
        .InitializeUserInput 0, "Bug May Slip"
        .GetInteger vbCr & "Hit enter [Bug/May/Slip]: "
        MsgBox "GetInput still returns: " & .GetInput()
    End With
End Sub
```

Because null and keyword input throw the same exceptions, GetInput's return value is the only way to determine which the user entered. But because of this odd persistence of the previous keyword entry, there is no sure way to determine whether the user entered a keyword or nothing at all.

The following code demonstrates a partial workaround for this problem. The technique is to grab the existing keyword from GetInput before calling InitializeUserInput for the second GetXXX method. If, after getting input from the user, the newly entered keyword matches the previous keyword, it's possible that the user entered a null.

```
Public Sub TestGetInputWorkaround()
Dim strBeforeKeyword As String
Dim strKeyword As String

On Error Resume Next                    ' handle exceptions inline
    With ThisDrawing.Utility
```

```
            '' first keyword input
            .InitializeUserInput 1, "This Bug Stuff"
            .GetInteger vbCrLf & "Option [This/Bug/Stuff]: "
            MsgBox "You entered: " & .GetInput()

            '' get lingering keyword
            strBeforeKeyword = .GetInput()

            '' second keyword input - press enter
            .InitializeUserInput 0, "Make Life Rough"
            .GetInteger vbCrLf & "Hit enter [Make/Life/Rough]: "
            strKeyword = .GetInput()

            '' if input = lingering it might be null input
            If strKeyword = strBeforeKeyword Then
                MsgBox "Looks like null input: " & strKeyword
            Else
                MsgBox "This time you entered: " & strKeyword
            End If
    End With

End Sub
```

### The GetEntity Method

Use the GetEntity method to select an AutoCAD object by letting the user pick an entity from the graphics screen.

**NOTE**   *Because the user may type L for the last entity in the draw-ing window, this method can return an invisible entity or an entity that's on a frozen layer.*

This method has the following syntax:

```
UtilityObject.GetEntity PickedEntity, PickedPoint[, Prompt]
```

Table 7-9 explains this method's parameters:

*Table 7-9. GetEntity method parameters*

| NAME | TYPE | DESCRIPTION |
|------|------|-------------|
| PickedEntity | AcadEntity object | Output. Returns a reference to the drawing object that the user picked. |
| PickPoint | Variant | Output. A three-element array of doubles that specifies the point by which the entity was picked in WCS. |
| Prompt | String | Optional. A prompt for input. |

This example gets an entity from the user and displays the point's object type and coordinates:

```
Public Sub TestGetEntity()
Dim objEnt As AcadEntity
Dim varPick As Variant

On Error Resume Next
    With ThisDrawing.Utility
        .GetEntity objEnt, varPick, vbCr & "Pick an entity: "
        If objEnt Is Nothing Then 'check if object was picked.
            .Prompt vbCrLf & "You did not pick as entity"
            Exit Sub
        End If
        .Prompt vbCr & "You picked a " & objEnt.ObjectName
        .Prompt vbCrLf & "At " & varPick(0) & "," & varPick(1)
    End With
End Sub
```

GetEntity raises an error if the input is null, such as when there is no entity at the picked point, or if the user presses *Enter* without selecting an entity. The example checks for this condition to avoid the error.

### The GetSubEntity Method

Use the GetSubEntity method in place of GetEntity when you need to obtain subentity information based on the user's selection. A subentities is an entity that another entity contains,, such as an entity in a block or a vertex entity contained in polylines. This method lets the user pick an entity or subentity from the graphics screen and returns details about that entity and any object(s) that contain it.

**NOTE**  *Like* GetEntity, *this method can return an entity even if it is not currently visible or is on a frozen layer because the user can type L to select the last entity in the drawing window.*

This method has the following syntax:

```
UtilityObject.GetSubEntity PickedEntity, PickPoint, Matrix, Context[, Prompt]
```

Table 7-10 explains this method's parameters:

*Table 7-10.* GetSubEntity *method parameters*

| NAME | TYPE | DESCRIPTION |
|------|------|-------------|
| PickedEntity | AcadEntity object | Output. Returns a reference to the drawing object that the user picked. |
| PickPoint | Variant | Output. A three-element array of doubles that specifies an angle vector's first point in WCS. |
| Matrix | Variant | Output. Returns a 4x4 element array of doubles that holds the selected entity's translation matrix. |
| Context | Variant | Output. Returns an array of long integers holding the ObjectIds for each parent block containing the selected entity, if the entity is in a block. |
| Prompt | String | Optional. A prompt for input. |

The Matrix output parameter is the selected entity's Model to World Transformation Matrix. It is a composite of all the transformations involved in the entity's visible representation. Imagine a line stored in a block, which is also stored in a block. The Matrix encapsulates each scale, rotation, and translation involved in the nested line's display. You can use it to translate points from the internal Model Coordinate System (MCS) to WCS.

The Context output parameter is an array of the ObjectIds for any objects that contain the selected entity. For our example line, this would be an array of two ObjectIds, one for each nesting level of the containing blocks. To get information about each containing entity, use the ObjectIdToObject method of the Document object to convert the ObjectId to an object reference.

This example uses the `Prompt` method to display information about the selected entity and any containing entities. Try it on a variety of entities, including those nested in blocks.

```
Public Sub TestGetSubEntity()
Dim objEnt As AcadEntity
Dim varPick As Variant
Dim varMatrix As Variant
Dim varParents As Variant
Dim intI As Integer
Dim intJ As Integer
Dim varID As Variant

    With ThisDrawing.Utility

        '' get the subentity from the user
        .GetSubEntity objEnt, varPick, varMatrix, varParents, _
            vbCr & "Pick an entity: "

        '' print some information about the entity
        .Prompt vbCr & "You picked a " & objEnt.ObjectName
        .Prompt vbCrLf & "At " & varPick(0) & "," & varPick(1)

        '' dump the varMatrix
        If Not IsEmpty(varMatrix) Then
            .Prompt vbLf & "MCS to WCS Translation varMatrix:"

            '' format varMatrix row
            For intI = 0 To 3
                .Prompt vbLf & "["

                '' format varMatrix column
                For intJ = 0 To 3
                    .Prompt "(" & varMatrix(intI, intJ) & ")"
                Next intJ

                .Prompt "]"
            Next intI
            .Prompt vbLf
        End If

        '' if it has a parent nest
        If Not IsEmpty(varParents) Then
```

*Chapter 7*

```
                        .Prompt vbLf & "Block nesting:"

                        '' depth counter
                        intI = -1

                        '' traverse most to least deep (reverse order)
                        For intJ = UBound(varParents) To LBound(varParents) Step -1

                            '' increment depth
                            intI = intI + 1

                            '' indent output
                            .Prompt vbLf & Space(intI * 2)

                            '' parent object id
                            varID = varParents(intJ)

                            '' parent entity
                            Set objEnt = ThisDrawing.ObjectIdToObject(varID)

                            '' print info about parent
                            .Prompt objEnt.ObjectName & " : " & objEnt.Name
                        Next intJ
                        .Prompt vbLf
                    End If
                    .Prompt vbCr
                End With
            End Sub
```

GetSubEntity throws an exception if the input is null, such as when there is no entity at the picked point or when the user presses *Enter* without selecting an entity.

Figure 7-2 shows the result of picking a line that forms part of a block reference named Window.

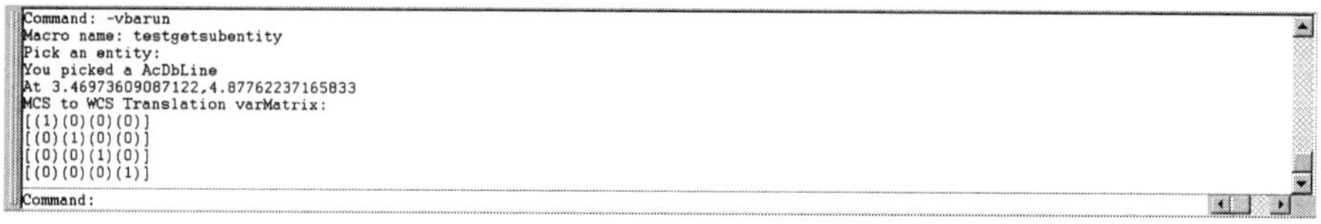

```
Command: -vbarun
Macro name: testgetsubentity
Pick an entity:
You picked a AcDbLine
At 3.46973609087122,4.87762237165833
MCS to WCS Translation varMatrix:
[(1)(0)(0)(0)]
[(0)(1)(0)(0)]
[(0)(0)(1)(0)]
[(0)(0)(0)(1)]
Command:
```

*Figure 7-2.* TestGetSubEntity *command line output*

## Handling Errors in User Input

Each AutoCAD command line user input method this chapter discusses uses run-time errors to signal input conditions such as null input, keyword input, or the user canceling the command-line input. Your code must handle these run-time errors, known as exceptions, or the program halts and displays an error message. VBA gives you two basic strategies for dealing with these exceptions.

On Error Goto. The first strategy is to use On Error Goto to jump to labeled sections of code called error handlers. This strategy has the advantage of keeping the main program logic very clean—all of the error handler code is separate from the program body. It has the disadvantage of becoming unwieldy as the program's size or complexity increases. As the complexity of errors increases, so too does the error handler's complexity. At a certain level of complexity, you reach a point of diminishing returns with labeled error handlers. They begin to take on a life of their own, with all their necessary conditions, loops, and jumps back and forth from the main program body.

On Error Resume Next. The second strategy is to use On Error Resume Next to handle the errors in the main program body. This is called inline error handling. It has the advantage of keeping the exception handling close to the method or function that generated the condition. This encourages, and in some ways forces, a more direct cause and effect framework for dealing with errors. Because inline error handling is woven into the main program execution, it has the disadvantage of clouding the pure algorithmic logic. Because of this interaction with the main program logic, it is also more difficult to retrofit existing code that lacks error handling with code that uses inline handling.

This chapter's examples in this chapter minimize error handling to focus all attention on the methods being described. However, because each input method generates exceptions for normal and expected conditions such as null input and keyword entry, be prepared to handle these errors in your program. See the sample code for the GetInput method for an example of handling these kinds of exceptions. You can apply this same framework to each input method.

## Conversion Methods

Several Utility methods do not involve direct user interaction, but are often used in conjunction with user input. These methods can be categorized as conversion methods. Use them to convert between common unit types or among AutoCAD's various coordinate systems.

## The AngleToReal Method

Use the AngleToReal method to convert a string that represents an angle into the equivalent radian value. This is useful, for example, for converting angles the user inputs as a string into a form compatible with most of AutoCAD's geometric methods. This method returns a double, giving the angle in radians.

```
dblAngle = UtilityObject.AngleToReal(Angle, Unit)
```

Table 7-11 explains this method's parameters.

*Table 7-11. AngleToReal method parameters*

| NAME | TYPE | DESCRIPTION |
|------|------|-------------|
| Angle | String | A string containing the angle to convert. |
| Unit | Long | The input angle's default unit format as one of AcAngleUnits' constants: acDegreeMinuteSeconds, acDegrees, acGrads, or acRadians. |

The Unit parameter specifies the conversion's default unit type. This default unit is assigned when the input specifies no units. For instance, the string 2.5 can be interpreted as degrees, grads, or radians. If the input contains an explicit unit type, AutoCAD uses it and ignores the Unit parameter. For instance, 2.5d, 2.5g, and 2.5r are each explicit, and AutoCAD reads them as degrees, grads, and radians respectively.

This example gets an angle from the user, converts it to a double using AngleToReal with a default of degrees, and then displays the results of the conversion to radians:

```
Public Sub TestAngleToReal()
Dim strInput As String
Dim dblAngle As Double

    With ThisDrawing.Utility
        strInput = .GetString(True, vbCr & "Enter an angle: ")
        dblAngle = .AngleToReal(strInput, acDegrees)
        .Prompt vbCr & "Radians: " & dblAngle
    End With
End Sub
```

An exception is thrown if AngleToReal is unable to convert the input string.

## The AngleToString Method

Use the AngleToString method to convert an angle in radians to a string representing the angle in angular units. This is useful for converting radian angles, used by most geometric properties and methods, into a form that the user can work with. This method returns a string that gives the angle in a specified unit type and precision. This method has the following syntax:

```
strAngle = UtilityObject.AngleToString(Angle, Unit, Precision)
```

Table 7-12 explains this method's parameters:

*Table 7-12. AngleToString method parameters*

| NAME | TYPE | DESCRIPTION |
|------|------|-------------|
| Angle | Double | The angle, in radians, to be converted. |
| Unit | Long | The angular unit for the output string as one of AcAngleUnits' constants: acDegreeMinuteSeconds, acDegrees, acGrads, or acRadians. |
| Precision | Long | Specifies the output's precision from 0 to 8 decimal places. |

This example gets an angle from the user, converts it to a double using AngleToReal with a default of degrees, and then converts and displays the results using AngleToString with a unit of degrees and a precision of 4 decimal places:

```
Public Sub TestAngleToString()
Dim strInput As String
Dim strOutput As String
Dim dblAngle As Double

    With ThisDrawing.Utility
        strInput = .GetString(True, vbCr & "Enter an angle: ")
        dblAngle = .AngleToReal(strInput, acDegrees)
        .Prompt vbCr & "Radians: " & dblAngle

        strOutput = .AngleToString(dblAngle, acDegrees, 4)
        .Prompt vbCrLf & "Degrees: " & strOutput
    End With
End Sub
Sub TestAngleToString()
```

## The DistanceToReal Method

Use the `DistanceToReal` method to convert a string that represents a linear distance into the equivalent double. This is useful, for example, for converting distances the user inputs as a string into their numeric equivalents. This method returns a double. It has the following syntax:

```
dblDistance = UtilityObject.DistanceToReal(Distance, Unit)
```

Table 7-13 explains this method's parameters.

*Table 7-13. `DistanceToReal` method parameters*

| NAME | TYPE | DESCRIPTION |
|------|------|-------------|
| Distance | String | A string that contains the angle to convert. |
| Unit | Long | The input's default unit format, as one of AcUnits' constants: acArchitectural, acDecimal, acDefaultUnits, acEngineering, acFractional, or acScientific. |

The `Unit` parameter specifies the conversion's default unit type. VBA assigns this default unit when the input specifies no units. If the input contains an explicit unit type, AutoCAD uses it and ignores the `Unit` parameter. For instance, `1'6-1/2"`, `1.54'`, `18 1/2`, and `0.185e+2` are each explicit and AutoCAD reads them as architectural, engineering, fractional, and scientific notation, respectively. The `acDefaultUnits` value uses whichever unit type the `LUNITS` system variable currently specifies.

This example gets a distance from the user, converts it using `DistanceToReal` with a default of architectural units, and then displays the results of the conversion to a double:

```
Public Sub TestDistanceToReal()
Dim strInput As String
Dim dblDist As Double

    With ThisDrawing.Utility
        strInput = .GetString(True, vbCr & "Enter a distance: ")
        dblDist = .DistanceToReal(strInput, acArchitectural)
        .Prompt vbCr & "Distance: " & dblDist
    End With
End Sub
```

An exception is thrown if `DistanceToReal` is unable to convert the input string.

## The RealToString Method

Use the `RealToString` method to convert a double to a string representing a distance in linear units. This is useful for converting the lengths, sizes, and locations that most AutoCAD geometric properties and methods use into a form that the user can work with. This method returns is a string containing the distance in a specified unit type and precision. It has the following syntax:

```
strDistance = UtilityObject.RealToString(Distance, Unit, Precision)
```

Table 7-14 explains this method's parameters.

*Table 7-14. RealToString method parameters*

| NAME | TYPE | DESCRIPTION |
| --- | --- | --- |
| Distance | Double | A double containing the distance. |
| Unit | Long | The linear unit format for the output string, as one of AcUnits' constants: acArchitectural, acDecimal, acDefaultUnits, acEngineering, acFractional, or acScientific |
| Precision | Long | The output's precision, from 0 to 8 decimal places. |

This example gets a distance from the user, converts it to a double using `DistanceToReal` with a default of architectural, and then converts and displays the results using `RealToString` with a unit of architectural and a precision of 4 decimal places:

```
Public Sub TestRealToString()
Dim strInput As String
Dim strOutput As String
Dim dblDist As Double

    With ThisDrawing.Utility
        strInput = .GetString(True, vbCr & "Enter a distance: ")
        dblDist = .DistanceToReal(strInput, acArchitectural)
        .Prompt vbCr & "Double: " & dblDist
```

```
            strOutput = .RealToString(dblDist, acArchitectural, 4)
            .Prompt vbCrLf & "Distance: " & strOutput
    End With
End Sub
```

## The AngleFromXAxis Method

Use the AngleFromXAxis method to measure the angle, in radians, between an imaginary line formed by two points and the WCS X-axis. This method returns a double. It has the following syntax:

```
dblAngle = UtilityObject.AngleFromXAxis(StartPoint, EndPoint)
```

Table 7-15 explains this method's parameters.

*Table 7-15. AngleFromXAxis method parameters*

| NAME | TYPE | DESCRIPTION |
| --- | --- | --- |
| StartPoint | Variant | A three-element array of doubles that specifies the first point of an imaginary line in WCS. |
| EndPoint | Variant | A three-element array of doubles that specifies the second point of an imaginary line in WCS. |

This example gets two points from the user, and then uses the AngleFromXAxis method to calculate the angle of a line formed by those points and the WCS X-axis:

```
Public Sub TestAngleFromXAxis()
Dim varStart As Variant
Dim varEnd As Variant
Dim dblAngle As Double

    With ThisDrawing.Utility
        varStart = .GetPoint(, vbCr & "Pick the start point: ")
        varEnd = .GetPoint(varStart, vbCr & "Pick the end point: ")
        dblAngle = .AngleFromXAxis(varStart, varEnd)
        .Prompt vbCr & "The angle from the X-axis is " _
            & .AngleToString(dblAngle, acDegrees, 2) & " degrees"
    End With
End Sub
```

## The PolarPoint Method

Use the `PolarPoint` method to get a new point that's a specified distance and angle from another point. This method returns a variant that holds a three-element array of doubles. It has the following syntax:

```
varPolarPoint = UtilityObject.PolarPoint(OriginalPoint, Angle, Distance)
```

Table 7-16 explains this method's parameters.

*Table 7-16. `PolarPoint` method parameters*

| NAME | TYPE | DESCRIPTION |
|------|------|-------------|
| OriginalPoint | Variant | A three-element array of doubles that specifies the point from which to begin the polar calculation. |
| Angle | Double | The angle in radians measured from WCS X-axis. |
| Distance | Double | The distance between the original and new point measured in current drawing units. |

In this example, the user specifies a start point and a rectangle's length, height, and angle. It uses the `PolarPoint` method and user input to calculate the rest of the points:

```
Public Sub TestPolarPoint()
Dim varpnt1 As Variant
Dim varpnt2 As Variant
Dim varpnt3 As Variant
Dim varpnt4 As Variant
Dim dblAngle As Double
Dim dblLength As Double
Dim dblHeight As Double
Dim dbl90Deg As Double

    '' get the point, length, height, and angle from user
    With ThisDrawing.Utility
```

```
'' get point, length, height, and angle from user
varpnt1 = .GetPoint(, vbCr & "Pick the start point: ")
dblLength = .GetDistance(varpnt1, vbCr & "Enter the length: ")
dblHeight = .GetDistance(varpnt1, vbCr & "Enter the height: ")
dblAngle = .GetAngle(varpnt1, vbCr & "Enter the angle: ")

'' calculate remaining rectangle points
dbl90Deg = .AngleToReal("90d", acDegrees)
varpnt2 = .PolarPoint(varpnt1, dblAngle, dblLength)
varpnt3 = .PolarPoint(varpnt2, dblAngle + dbl90Deg, dblHeight)
varpnt4 = .PolarPoint(varpnt3, dblAngle + (dbl90Deg * 2), dblLength)
End With

'' draw the rectangle
With ThisDrawing
    .ModelSpace.AddLine varpnt1, varpnt2
    .ModelSpace.AddLine varpnt2, varpnt3
    .ModelSpace.AddLine varpnt3, varpnt4
    .ModelSpace.AddLine varpnt4, varpnt1
End With

End Sub
```

Chapter 8 covers creating drawing objects.

## The TranslateCoordinates Method

Use the TranslateCoordinates method to translate a point from one coordinate system to another. This is often necessary when the user is working in a construction plane, for example. Most AutoCAD input and object-creation methods work exclusively in WCS, so you need to translate user input to correctly work in the construction plane.

This method returns an array of doubles. It has the following syntax:

```
dblAngle = UtilityObject.AngleFromXAxis(Point, From, To, Displacement [, Norm])
```

Table 7-17 explains this method's parameters:

*Table 7-17.* `TranslateCoordinates` *method parameters*

| NAME | TYPE | DESCRIPTION |
| --- | --- | --- |
| Point | Variant | A three-element array of doubles that specifies the point to translate. |
| From | Long | The source coordinate system. One of the AcCoordinateSystem constants: acDisplayDCS, acOCS, acPaperSpaceDCS, acUCS, or acWorld. |
| To | Long | The destination coordinate system. One of the AcCoordinateSystem constants: acDisplayDCS, acOCS, acPaperSpaceDCS, acUCS, or acWorld. |
| Displacement | Boolean | If True, the input is treated as a displacement vector. If False, the input is treated as a point. |
| Norm | Variant | Optional. A three-element array of doubles specifying the OCS normal. Use with an acOCS value in either the From or To parameters. |

The From and To parameters specify the point translation's source and desti-nation coordinate systems. For instance, to convert the Point from WCS to the current construction plane, set From to acWorld, and set To to acUCS. If either From or To is set to acOCS, you must pass the Norm to indicate the Object Coordinate System (OCS) normal vector.

NOTE   *Because you can pass only a single Normal into the method, points can't be translated from one OCS directly to another. Instead, translate the source OCS to an intermediate coordinate system, and then translate from the intermediate coordinate system to the desti-nation OCS.*

When the Displacement parameter is True, the Point parameter is treated like a displacement vector instead of like a point. Use this setting when you need to calculate offset values instead of a new point, such as when performing relative movement. For example, to move an entity by a specified amount, compose the X, Y, and Z displacements and pass them to TranslateCoordinates as a displace-ment vector.

The following example gets two points from the user and then uses the AngleFromXAxis method to calculate the angle of the line those points form and the WCS X-axis. It uses `TranslateCoordinates` to translate the first input point to User Coordinate System (UCS) for use in the basepoint of the second point acquisition:

```
Public Sub TestTranslateCoordinates()
Dim varpnt1 As Variant
Dim varpnt1Ucs As Variant
Dim varpnt2 As Variant

    '' get the point, length, height, and angle from user
    With ThisDrawing.Utility

        '' get start point
        varpnt1 = .GetPoint(, vbCr & "Pick the start point: ")

        '' convert to UCS for use in the basepoint rubberband line
        varpnt1Ucs = .TranslateCoordinates(varpnt1, acWorld, acUCS, False)

        '' get end point
        varpnt2 = .GetPoint(varpnt1Ucs, vbCr & "Pick the end point: ")
    End With

    '' draw the line
    With ThisDrawing
        .ModelSpace.AddLine varpnt1, varpnt2
    End With
End Sub
```

Try `TestTranslateCoordinates` from various coordinate systems and see that the rubber-band line in the second point input always starts in the correct position. Without the coordinate translation, the point is always expressed in WCS coordinates and appears incorrectly.

## Internet Methods

AutoCAD 2000 and higher has the ability to open and save drawing files from the Internet. The following methods let your program accept, return, or validate URLs. A Uniform Resource Locator (URL) is an Internet address that uniquely identifies remote files. The methods include a Web file browser, Internet file upload and downloading capabilities, and functions for validating URLs and determining if a file originated from the Internet.

## The IsURL Method

Use the IsURL method to determine if a string is a properly formed URL. It does not ensure that the URL is actually accessible, just that it is syntactically correct. It returns a Boolean. Its syntax is as follows:

```
blnStatus = UtilityObject.IsURL(InputURL)
```

This method has one parameter, InputURL, a string. Use it to specify the URL to check for validity.

This example gets a string from the user and then, using IsURL, displays whether it is a valid URL:

```
Public Sub TestIsURL()
Dim strInput As String

    With ThisDrawing.Utility
        strInput = .GetString(True, vbCr & "Enter a URL: ")
        If .IsURL(strInput) Then
            MsgBox "You entered a valid URL"
        Else
            MsgBox "That was not a URL"
        End If
    End With
End Sub
```

## The LaunchBrowserDialog Method

Use the LaunchBrowserDialog to perform an HTTP request, displaying a document using the default Web browser. It can't verify or validate URLs; it simply opens the browser and sends the request, exactly the way launching a Favorite works with Internet Explorer or a bookmark with Netscape. This method sets the OutputURL to the URL the user selects. It returns True if the Web browser successfully launched and the user selected a file, or False to indicate failure or that the user didn't select a file. This method has the following syntax:

```
blnStatus = UtilityObject.LaunchBrowserDialog(OutputURL, _
    Title, SelectCaption, StartingURL, PreferencesKey, SelectLinks)
```

Table 7-18 explains this method's parameters.

*Table 7-18.* `LaunchBrowserDialog` *method parameters*

| NAME | TYPE | DESCRIPTION |
|------|------|-------------|
| SelectedURL | String | Output. The URL of the remote file the user selected. |
| DialogTitle | String | A caption for the Web browser dialog. |
| OpenButtonCaption | String | A caption for the OK/Open button. |
| StartPageURL | String | The starting URL for the Web browser. |
| RegistryRootKey | String | The product root key for storing persistent Web browser dialog information. This key specifies where to store information about the size, position, and other preferences information of the dialog can be stored across sessions. Leave empty to disregard this functionality. |
| OpenButtonAlwaysEnabled | Boolean | (Input-Only) True: The Open button is enabled, allowing a file or link to be selected. False: The Open button is disabled and is only enabled when the user selects a file for download. |

The `RegistryRootKey` parameter stores the browser window's size and location in the Windows registry. This lets your application make the Web browser appear with the same size and location each time it is called. The information is stored in `HKEY_CURRENT_USER` and so is specific to each user. If you don't wish to use this capability, pass a null (empty) string in this parameter.

The `OpenButtonAlwaysEnabled` parameter enables URL link selection. If `True`, the Select button is enabled at all times and the browser can return any URL, whether it's an actual file or just a link. Use this if your program just needs to obtain a URL from the user, and doesn't need to actually open or work with the contents of a remote file.

This example uses `LaunchBrowserDialog` to get a URL from the user and displays the selection in a message box. Figure 7-3 illustrates this code in action.

```
Public Sub TestLaunchBrowserDialog()
Dim strStartUrl As String
Dim strInput As String
Dim blnStatus As Boolean

    strStartUrl = InputBox("Enter a URL", , "http://www.apress.com")
```

```
With ThisDrawing.Utility
    If .IsURL(strStartUrl) = False Then
        MsgBox "You did not enter a valid URL"
        Exit Sub
    End If

    blnStatus = .LaunchBrowserDialog(strInput, _
                                "Select a URL", _
                                "Select", _
                                strStartUrl, _
                                "ContractCADDgroup", _
                                True)
    If Not blnStatus Then
        MsgBox "You cancelled without selecting anything"
        Exit Sub
    End If

    If strStartUrl = strInput Then
        MsgBox "You selected the original URL"
    Else
        MsgBox "You selected: " & strInput
    End If
End With
```

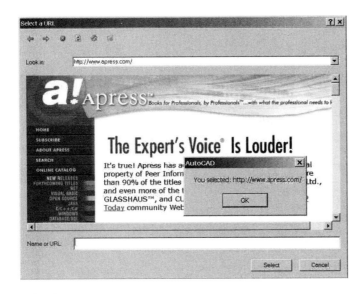

```
End Sub
```

*Figure 7-3.* TestLaunchBrowserDialog *output*

### The GetRemoteFile Method

Use the GetRemoteFile to retrieve a remote file given a URL. The file is downloaded to a temporary local file with the name being passed back in the LocalFile output parameter. This method returns nothing. It has the following syntax:

```
UtilityObject.GetRemoteFile InputURL, LocalFile, IgnoreCache
```

Table 7-19 explains this method's parameters.

*Table 7-19. GetRemoteFile method parameters*

| NAME | TYPE | DESCRIPTION |
| --- | --- | --- |
| InputURL | String | The URL from which to download the file. |
| LocalFile | String | Output. The temporary local copy's filename. |
| IgnoreCache | Boolean | Whether to use the browser's file cache to retrieve the file. |

If IgnoreCache is True, the file gets downloaded from the URL even if it is present in the local Browser file cache. Do this to ensure you have the most current copy of the file.

If InputURL is a secure URL, a dialog box asks the user for access information such as username and password.

This example gets a file from a user-specified URL and displays the temporary filename in a message box:

```
Public Sub TestGetRemoteFile()
Dim strUrl As String
Dim strLocalName As String
Dim blnStatus As Boolean

 strUrl = InputBox("Enter a URL of a drawing file")

    With ThisDrawing.Utility
        If .IsURL(strUrl) = False Then
            MsgBox "You did not enter a valid URL"
            Exit Sub
        End If
```

```
        .GetRemoteFile strUrl, strLocalName, True
        If Err Then
            MsgBox "Failed to download: " & strUrl & vbCr & Err.Description
        Else
            MsgBox "The file was downloaded to: " & strLocalName
        End If
    End With
End Sub
```

**NOTE**   *When you exit AutoCAD, the temporary file this method creates is deleted from your system.*

## The IsRemoteFile Method

Use the IsRemoteFile method to determine whether a local file was retrieved from a URL. The OutputURL parameter contains the file's original URL. This method returns True if the file was downloaded from a URL. This method has the following syntax:

```
blnStatus = UtilityObject.IsRemoteFile(LocalFile, OutputURL)
```

Table 7-20 explains this method's parameters:

*Table 7-20. IsRemoteFile method parameters*

| NAME | TYPE | DESCRIPTION |
|------|------|-------------|
| LocalFile | String | The filename of a local file to check. |
| OutputURL | String | Output. The original URL of the local file. |

This example gets a filename from the user, then displays a message telling whether the file was retrieved from a URL:

```
Public Sub TestIsRemoteFile()
Dim strOutputURL As String
Dim strLocalName As String

    strLocalName = InputBox("Enter the file and path name to check")
    If strLocalName = "" Then Exit Sub
    With ThisDrawing.Utility
        '' check if the local file is from a URL
        If .IsRemoteFile(strLocalName, strOutputURL) Then
            MsgBox "This file was downloaded from: " & strOutputURL
        Else
            MsgBox "This file was not downloaded from a URL"
        End If
    End With
End Sub
```

## The PutRemoteFile Method

Use the PutRemoteFile method to upload a local file to a URL. This method returns nothing. It has the following syntax:

```
UtilityObject.PutRemoteFile UploadURL, LocalFile
```

Table 7-21 explains this method's parameters:

*Table 7-21. PutRemoteFile method parameters*

| NAME | TYPE | DESCRIPTION |
| --- | --- | --- |
| UploadURL | String | The URL to upload the file to. |
| LocalFile | String | The filename to upload. |

If UploadURL is a secure URL, the method displays a dialog box to ask the user for their access information such as username and password.

For more extensive Web-enabled capabilities, look at Autodesk I-Drop technology and related API tools. I-Drop lets you publish content to Web sites and drag and drop selected items (and associated metadata) directly into drawings.

## Summary

While this chapter didn't cover every conceivable user interaction scenario, it did cover the most commonly used methods. The user interface is unique to each situation and as a programmer you have to decide how best to use AutoCAD VBA's methods and properties to create the ideal user interface.

# CHAPTER 8

# Drawing Objects

**AUTOCAD PROVIDES YOU WITH** a number of methods to create the drawing entities users normally access through the application window. Nearly every drawing entity that you can create and manipulate through the AutoCAD GUI has an equivalent object with associated properties and methods in the AutoCAD object model.

In this chapter I cover the majority of drawing entities that you can create as single AutoCAD objects, including the following:

- The `Arc`, `Circle`, and `Ellipse` objects

- Lines of finite and infinite length, such as the `Line`, `Ray`, and `Polyline` objects

- `Solid`, `Hatch`, and `Region` compound objects

The code samples in this chapter demonstrate how to create these objects through VBA. Realistically, though, before you create drawing entities you need to understand how to control the drawing space where you place and view these objects. You'll start, then, in the next section by examining how to toggle between the model space and paper space.

## Controlling the Drawing Space

AutoCAD segregates entities that users create into one of several collections. The two primary collections separate objects that make up the model geometry and objects used to describe the geometry for printing or plotting purposes. The model is stored in the `ModelSpace` collection, and the printing/plotting layout is stored in the `PaperSpace` collection.

*Model space* is the drawing area where users create the objects that they're designing or rendering. It typically contains everything that would exist in reality— each of the components in an assembly, or all of the physical elements of a building, for instance. Scaled views (or *viewports*) of specific areas of the model are then placed in *paper space*. Each of the views is dynamic, and changes to the model are automatically reflected in the paper space views.

Users will typically place items that describe the views of the model, such as dimensions, annotation, labels, and textual tables, into paper space. Title blocks and sheet borders are also placed here, and the complete page layout is formatted for output to a printer or plotter.

AutoCAD does nothing to enforce the division between the model space and the paper space—in fact, users may draw anything they want in either space. The spaces are simply provided to assist in the format and page layout for presentation and output purposes.

In AutoCAD 2000, users may create any number of paper space pages, which are called *layouts*. The layouts, each of which generally represents a single formatted page, are given unique names and are shown as a series of tabs at the bottom of each drawing window. AutoCAD automatically generates a model space layout named Model and a paper space layout named Layout1, but users may create as many as they'd like. Every layout except Model is a paper space layout, and the last of these accessed is always referred to by the PaperSpace property of the Document object.

---

 **NOTE**   *You can't rename or delete the* Model *layout. If you delete the last paper space layout, AutoCAD automatically creates a new* Layout1.

---

Internally, AutoCAD stores model space and each of the paper space layouts as special block definitions. Therefore, you may use all the operations noted in this chapter equally well with ModelSpace, PaperSpace, or Block objects with only occasional, minor differences.

## The ModelSpace and PaperSpace Collections

One of the first things you need to know to use the ModelSpace and PaperSpace collections is which space—model or paper—is currently active. This information is held in the ActiveSpace property of the Document object. This is an integer property, and it may hold one of the two values shown in Table 8-1, along with that value's associated AutoCAD constants.

*Table 8-1. ModelSpace and PaperSpace Constants*

| CONSTANT | VALUE |
|---|---|
| acModelSpace | 1 |
| acPaperSpace | 0 |

The following code snippet uses a message box to inform you of the active space for the current document:

```
If ThisDrawing.ActiveSpace = acModelSpace Then
    MsgBox "The active space is model space"
Else
    MsgBox "The active space is paper space"
End If
```

To change the active space, you need to set the value of the ActiveSpace property. The following code contains a macro you can use to toggle between the two spaces:

```
Public Sub ToggleSpace()
    With ThisDrawing
        If .ActiveSpace = acModelSpace Then
            .ActiveSpace = acPaperSpace
        Else
            .ActiveSpace = acModelSpace
        End If
    End With
End Sub
```

Alternatively, you can simply use the following line of code:

```
ThisDrawing.ActiveSpace = (ThisDrawing.ActiveSpace + 1) Mod 2
```

# Creating Objects

As mentioned previously, the Add*XXX* methods apply equally to the PaperSpace, ModelSpace, and Block objects. Therefore, when I present the syntax of each method in this section, the word Object denotes any one of these collections. For example:

```
Set CircleObject = Object.AddCircle(CenterPoint, Radius)
```

Each of the AddXXX methods returns an object reference to the newly created entity, so you must use the VBA Set operator if you want to assign this return to a variable.

When you create or modify an entity, the changes to the drawing don't display until the Update method of that object, the Update method of the Application object, or the Regen method of the Document object is called. In some cases, AutoCAD will update the display once your macro or program is complete; however, it's always safest to ensure the update takes place in your code. In the examples presented here, I use the Update method of the newly created entity to update the drawing display.

## Circular Objects

This section demonstrates how to create the various circular-shaped objects.

### The Arc Object

You create an Arc object by using the AddArc method. This method takes four arguments that determine the position and size of the arc:

```
Set ArcObject = Object.AddArc(CenterPoint, Radius, StartAngle, EndAngle)
```

Table 8-2 provides a brief description of each argument.

*Table 8-2. AddArc Method Parameters*

| NAME | DATA TYPE | DESCRIPTION |
| --- | --- | --- |
| CenterPoint | Variant | A three-element array of doubles specifying the center of the arc in the WCS |
| Radius | Double | The radius of the arc |
| StartAngle | Double | The start angle of the arc given in radians with respect to the X-axis of the WCS |
| EndAngle | Double | The end angle of the arc given in radians with respect to the X-axis of the WCS |

Arcs are drawn counterclockwise from the start angle to the end angle, as shown in Figure 8-1.

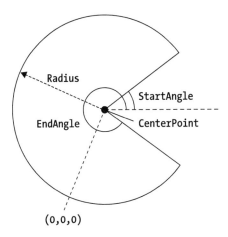

*Figure 8-1. The Arc object*

The following example creates an arc in the active drawing space (model or paper space) using user input:

```
Public Sub TestAddArc()
Dim varCenter As Variant
Dim dblRadius As Double
Dim dblStart As Double
Dim dblEnd As Double
Dim objEnt As AcadArc

    On Error Resume Next
    '' get input from user
    With ThisDrawing.Utility
        varCenter = .GetPoint(, vbCr & "Pick the center point: ")
        dblRadius = .GetDistance(varCenter, vbCr & "Enter the radius: ")
        dblStart = .GetAngle(varCenter, vbCr & "Enter the start angle: ")
        dblEnd = .GetAngle(varCenter, vbCr & "Enter the end angle: ")
    End With
```

```
'' draw the arc
If ThisDrawing.ActiveSpace = acModelSpace Then
    Set objEnt = ThisDrawing.ModelSpace.AddArc(varCenter, dblRadius, _
                                         dblStart, dblEnd)
Else
Set objEnt = ThisDrawing.PaperSpace.AddArc(varCenter, dblRadius, dblStart, dblEnd)
End If
    objEnt.Update
End Sub
```

## The Circle Object

You can create a Circle object by specifying the position of the center and the radius, and using the AddCircle method:

```
Set CircleObject = Object.AddCircle(CenterPoint, Radius)
```

Table 8-3 provides a brief description of each argument.

*Table 8-3. AddCircle Method Parameters*

| NAME | DATA TYPE | DESCRIPTION |
|------|-----------|-------------|
| CenterPoint | Variant | A three-element array of doubles specifying the center of the circle in the WCS |
| Radius | Double | The radius of the circle |

Figure 8-2 illustrates the Circle object.

The following example creates a circle based on user input:

```
Public Sub TestAddCircle()
Dim varCenter As Variant
Dim dblRadius As Double
Dim objEnt As AcadCircle

On Error Resume Next
    '' get input from user
```

```
    With ThisDrawing.Utility
        varCenter = .GetPoint(, vbCr & "Pick the centerpoint: ")
        dblRadius = .GetDistance(varCenter, vbCr & "Enter the radius: ")
    End With


    '' draw the entity
If ThisDrawing.ActiveSpace = acModelSpace Then
  Set objEnt = ThisDrawing.ModelSpace.AddCircle(varCenter, dblRadius)
Else
  Set objEnt = ThisDrawing.PaperSpace.AddCircle(varCenter, dblRadius)
End If
    objEnt.Update
End Sub
```

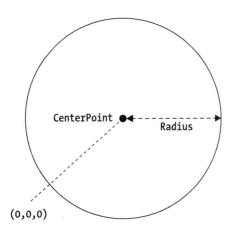

*Figure 8-2. The Circle object*

## The Ellipse Object

You use the AddEllipse method to create a fully closed Ellipse object. This method takes three parameters:

```
Set EllipseObject = Object.AddEllipse(CenterPoint, MajorAxis, RadiusRatio)
```

Table 8-4 describes the AddEllipse method's parameters.

*Table 8-4. AddEllipse Method Parameters*

| NAME | DATA TYPE | DESCRIPTION |
| --- | --- | --- |
| CenterPoint | Variant | A three-element array of doubles specifying the center of the ellipse in the WCS. |
| MajorAxis | Variant | A three-element array of doubles specifying the vector of the major axis of the ellipse from the CenterPoint. |
| RadiusRatio | Double | The ratio of the lengths of the minor to major axis vectors: 0 < RadiusRatio ≤ 1. A value of 1 generates a circle. |

If you want to create an elliptical arc, set the StartAngle and EndAngle properties after you create the full Ellipse object, as shown in Figure 8-3.

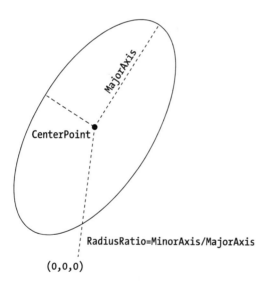

*Figure 8-3. The Ellipse object*

The following example creates a new `Ellipse` object by first setting the center axis, major axis, and radius ratio. It then gets a start and end angles from the user to convert the closed `Ellipse` into an elliptical arc.

```
Public Sub TestAddEllipse()
Dim dblCenter(0 To 2) As Double
Dim dblMajor(0 To 2) As Double
Dim dblRatio As Double
Dim dblStart As Double
Dim dblEnd As Double
Dim objEnt As AcadEllipse

On Error Resume Next

    '' setup the ellipse parameters
    dblCenter(0) = 0: dblCenter(1) = 0: dblCenter(2) = 0
    dblMajor(0) = 10: dblMajor(1) = 0: dblMajor(2) = 0
    dblRatio = 0.5

    '' draw the ellipse
If ThisDrawing.ActiveSpace = acModelSpace Then
  Set objEnt = ThisDrawing.ModelSpace.AddEllipse(dblCenter, dblMajor, dblRatio)
Else
  Set objEnt = ThisDrawing.PaperSpace.AddEllipse(dblCenter, dblMajor, dblRatio)
End If
    objEnt.Update

    '' get angular input from user
    With ThisDrawing.Utility
        dblStart = .GetAngle(dblCenter, vbCr & "Enter the start angle: ")
        dblEnd = .GetAngle(dblCenter, vbCr & "Enter the end angle: ")
    End With

    '' convert the ellipse into elliptical arc
With objEnt
    .StartAngle = dblStart
    .EndAngle = dblEnd
    .Update
End With
End Sub
```

## Line Objects

This section demonstrates how to create the various line-shaped objects.

### The Line Object

The AddLine method creates a Line object, which is a single, straight line running between two points:

```
Set LineObject = Object.AddLine(StartPoint, EndPoint)
```

Table 8-5 provides a brief description of each argument.

*Table 8-5. AddLine Method Parameters*

| NAME | DATA TYPE | DESCRIPTION |
| --- | --- | --- |
| StartPoint | Variant | A three-element array of doubles specifying the line's start in the WCS |
| EndPoint | Variant | A three-element array of doubles specifying the line's end in the WCS |

Figure 8-4 illustrates the Line object.

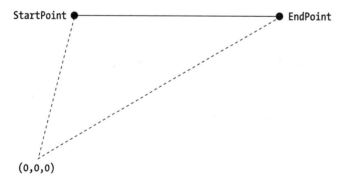

*Figure 8-4. The Line object*

This example gets a start and end point from the user and then creates a new line:

```
Public Sub TestAddLine()
Dim varStart As Variant
Dim varEnd As Variant
Dim objEnt As AcadLine

On Error Resume Next
    '' get input from user
    With ThisDrawing.Utility
        varStart = .GetPoint(, vbCr & "Pick the start point: ")
        varEnd = .GetPoint(varStart, vbCr & "Pick the end point: ")
    End With

    '' draw the entity
If ThisDrawing.ActiveSpace = acModelSpace Then
  Set objEnt = ThisDrawing.ModelSpace.AddLine(varStart, varEnd)
Else
  Set objEnt = ThisDrawing.PaperSpace.AddLine(varStart, varEnd)
End If
    objEnt.Update
End Sub
```

## The LWPolyline Object

A *lightweight polyline* is a 2-D line consisting of straight and arced segments. It's functionally similar to the legacy Polyline entity, but it's internally represented in a "flat" data structure as opposed to the tree-structured Polyline entity. This results in a more compact data size per entity and faster graphics regeneration, hence the "lightweight" name.

You create a new LWPolyline object using the AddLightWeightPolyline method, as follows:

```
Set LWPolylineObject = Object.AddLightWeightPolyline(Vertices)
```

Table 8-6 provides a brief description of each argument.

*Table 8-6. AddLightWeightPolyline Method Parameter*

| NAME | DATA TYPE | DESCRIPTION |
| --- | --- | --- |
| Vertices | Variant | An array of doubles specifying a list of 2-D vertex points in WCS coordinates. It's a simple array with a single dimension composed of alternating X and Y values (i.e., p1x, p1y, p2x, p2y, etc.). Because you must supply at least two points to create a polyline, this array must have a minimum of four elements. |

 **NOTE** *Lightweight polylines don't store Z-axis or elevation information with each vertex point. Instead, the* Polyline *object has an* Elevation *property that specifies the z elevation relative to the coordinate system for all vertices.*

Figure 8-5 illustrates the LightweightPolyline object.

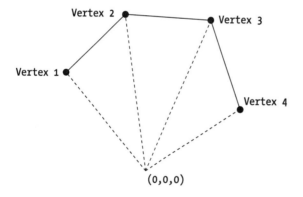

*Figure 8-5. The LightweightPolyline object*

When you create an LWPolyline object, it's open as shown in Figure 8-5. To close the polyline (i.e., to join the first vertex to the last), set its Closed property to True. All the segments are straight lines by default. See the section titled "Polyline Arc Segments" later in this chapter for details on how to optionally create arcs.

The following example creates a new lightweight polyline:

```
Public Sub TestAddLWPolyline()
Dim objEnt As AcadLWPolyline
Dim dblVertices() As Double

    '' setup initial points
    ReDim dblVertices(11)
    dblVertices(0) = 0#: dblVertices(1) = 0#
    dblVertices(2) = 10#: dblVertices(3) = 0#
    dblVertices(4) = 10#: dblVertices(5) = 10#
    dblVertices(6) = 5#: dblVertices(7) = 5#
    dblVertices(8) = 2#: dblVertices(9) = 2#
    dblVertices(10) = 0#: dblVertices(11) = 10#

    '' draw the entity
If ThisDrawing.ActiveSpace = acModelSpace Then
  Set objEnt = ThisDrawing.ModelSpace.AddLightWeightPolyline(dblVertices)
Else
  Set objEnt = ThisDrawing.PaperSpace.AddLightWeightPolyline(dblVertices)
End If
    objEnt.Closed = True
    objEnt.Update
End Sub
```

To add vertices to an LWPolyline object one at a time instead of all at once, use the AddVertex method. The following example uses this method in a loop, adding vertices to a selected polyline until the user is satisfied. Try using it on the polyline you created in the previous example:

```
Public Sub TestAddVertex()
    On Error Resume Next
    Dim objEnt As AcadLWPolyline
    Dim dblNew(0 To 1) As Double
    Dim lngLastVertex As Long
    Dim varPick As Variant
    Dim varWCS As Variant

    With ThisDrawing.Utility

        '' get entity from user
        .GetEntity objEnt, varPick, vbCr & "Pick a polyline <exit>: "
```

```
        '' exit if no pick
        If objEnt Is Nothing Then Exit Sub

        '' exit if not a lwpolyline
        If objEnt.ObjectName <> "AcDbPolyline" Then
            MsgBox "You did not pick a polyline"
            Exit Sub
        End If

        '' copy last vertex of pline into pickpoint to begin loop
        ReDim varPick(2)
        varPick(0) = objEnt.Coordinates(UBound(objEnt.Coordinates) - 1)
        varPick(1) = objEnt.Coordinates(UBound(objEnt.Coordinates))
        varPick(2) = 0

        '' append vertexes in a loop
        Do
            '' translate picked point to UCS for basepoint below
            varWCS = .TranslateCoordinates(varPick, acWorld, acUCS, True)

            '' get user point for new vertex, use last pick as basepoint
            varPick = .GetPoint(varWCS, vbCr & "Pick another point <exit>: ")

            '' exit loop if no point picked
            If Err Then Exit Do

            '' copy picked point X and Y into new 2d point
            dblNew(0) = varPick(0):  dblNew(1) = varPick(1)

            '' get last vertex offset.  it is one half the array size
            lngLastVertex = (UBound(objEnt.Coordinates) + 1) / 2

            '' add new vertex to pline at last offset
            objEnt.AddVertex lngLastVertex, dblNew
        Loop
    End With
    objEnt.Update
End Sub
```

## The MLine Object

The MLine object is a single graphic entity that consists of multiple parallel straight-line segments. The maximum number of parallel lines is 16. You use the AddMLine method to create a new MLine object:

```
Set MLineObject = Object.AddMLine(Vertices)
```

Table 8-7 provides a brief description of each argument.

*Table 8-7. AddMLine Method Parameter*

| NAME | DATA TYPE | DESCRIPTION |
| --- | --- | --- |
| Vertices | Variant | An array of doubles specifying a list of 3-D vertex points in WCS coordinates. It's a simple array with a single dimension composed of alternating X, Y, and Z values (i.e., p1x, p1y, p1z, p2x, p2y, p2z, etc.). Because you must supply at least two points to create an MLine, this array must have a minimum of six elements. |

Although an MLine object consists of multiple parallel lines, the AutoCAD Automation model doesn't expose those lines to VBA. Similarly, MLine styles aren't directly accessible from VBA. However, you have a limited amount of control when you use the CMLJUST, CMLSCALE, and CMLSTYLE system variables to control the justification, scale, and style of newly created MLines.

**NOTE** *You may create or load additional multiline styles using the* MLSTYLE *command.*

The following example illustrates the AddMLine method:

```
Public Sub TestAddMLine()
Dim objEnt As AcadMLine
Dim dblVertices(17) As Double
```

```
'' setup initial points
dblVertices(0) = 0: dblVertices(1) = 0: dblVertices(2) = 0
dblVertices(3) = 10: dblVertices(4) = 0: dblVertices(5) = 0
dblVertices(6) = 10: dblVertices(7) = 10: dblVertices(8) = 0
dblVertices(9) = 5: dblVertices(10) = 10: dblVertices(11) = 0
dblVertices(12) = 5: dblVertices(13) = 5: dblVertices(14) = 0
dblVertices(15) = 0: dblVertices(16) = 5: dblVertices(17) = 0

    '' draw the entity
If ThisDrawing.ActiveSpace = acModelSpace Then
   Set objEnt = ThisDrawing.ModelSpace.AddMLine(dblVertices)
Else
   Set objEnt = ThisDrawing.PaperSpace.AddMLine(dblVertices)
End If
    objEnt.Update
End Sub
```

## The Polyline Object

The Polyline object is similar in function to the LWPolyline object, but it's stored in an alternate format. It's a 2-D or 3-D line consisting of straight and arced segments, but the segments are stored as distinct entities. Each segment in an AcadPolyline object has a start point, an end point, and several other unique properties. This object is less efficient than the lightweight polyline object, in which segments are defined as a collection of vertex points.

Use the AddPolyline method to create a Polyline defined by a set of vertices, as follows:

```
Set PolylineObject = Object.AddPolyline(Vertices)
```

Table 8-8 provides a brief description of each argument.

*Table 8-8. AddPolyline Method Parameter*

| NAME | DATA TYPE | DESCRIPTION |
| --- | --- | --- |
| Vertices | Variant | An array of doubles specifying a list of 3-D vertex points in WCS coordinates. It's a simple array with a single dimension composed of alternating X, Y, and Z values (i.e., p1x, p1y, p1z, p2x, p2y, p2z, etc.). Because you must supply at least two points to create a polyline, this array must have a minimum of six elements. |

The following example illustrates the `AddPolyline` method and shows how to close the polyline and set its type:

```
Public Sub TestAddPolyline()
Dim objEnt As AcadPolyline
Dim dblVertices(17) As Double

    '' setup initial points
    dblVertices(0) = 0: dblVertices(1) = 0: dblVertices(2) = 0
    dblVertices(3) = 10: dblVertices(4) = 0: dblVertices(5) = 0
    dblVertices(6) = 7: dblVertices(7) = 10: dblVertices(8) = 0
    dblVertices(9) = 5: dblVertices(10) = 7: dblVertices(11) = 0
    dblVertices(12) = 6: dblVertices(13) = 2: dblVertices(14) = 0
    dblVertices(15) = 0: dblVertices(16) = 4: dblVertices(17) = 0

    '' draw the entity
If ThisDrawing.ActiveSpace = acModelSpace Then
  Set objEnt = ThisDrawing.ModelSpace.AddPolyline(dblVertices)
Else
  Set objEnt = ThisDrawing.PaperSpace.AddPolyline(dblVertices)
End If
    objEnt.Type = acFitCurvePoly
    objEnt.Closed = True
    objEnt.Update
End Sub
```

AutoCAD is set to draw lightweight polylines by default because of their efficiency; you may change this default setting using the `PLINETYPE` system variable. You can convert existing polylines from lightweight to heavy and vice versa by using the `Convertpoly` command.

Although it's less efficient for simple polyline representations, the `Polyline` object has features not present in the lightweight form, such as the capability to represent splines and other smoothly curved shapes. The following example allows the user to change a specified `Polyline` curve type from the command line. Try it on the polyline you created in the preceding example:

```
Public Sub TestPolylineType()
Dim objEnt As AcadPolyline
Dim varPick As Variant
Dim strType As String
Dim intType As Integer

On Error Resume Next
```

```
    With ThisDrawing.Utility
        .GetEntity objEnt, varPick, vbCr & "Pick a polyline: "
        If Err Then
            MsgBox "That is not a Polyline"
            Exit Sub
        End If

        .InitializeUserInput 1, "Simple Fit Quad Cubic"
        strType = .GetKeyword(vbCr & "Change type [Simple/Fit/Quad/Cubic]: ")

        Select Case strType
            Case "Simple": intType = acSimplePoly
            Case "Fit": intType = acFitCurvePoly
            Case "Quad": intType = acQuadSplinePoly
            Case "Cubic": intType = acCubicSplinePoly
        End Select
    End With

    objEnt.Type = intType
    objEnt.Closed = True
    objEnt.Update
End Sub
```

### *Polyline Arc Segments*

When you first create them, both the `LWPolyline` and `Polyline` objects consist of only straight-line segments. Each polyline segment has an arc *bulge factor* that determines the segment's arc radius. By default, all segments have a bulge factor of 0, which is a straight line. A positive bulge factor denotes a counterclockwise arc relative to the start and end points of the polyline segment, and a negative bulge factor denotes a clockwise arc.

You derive the bulge factor from the arc radius by calculating the tangent of one-fourth of the included angle between the polyline segment's start and end points, as shown in Figure 8-6.

Because AutoCAD is already storing the segment points, a bulge factor is a very efficient way to capture the arc radius. Further, because the bulge factor is calculated using the segment's start and end points, the resulting arc is automatically scaled as the distance between these points changes (e.g., when the user scales or grip-edits the polyline).

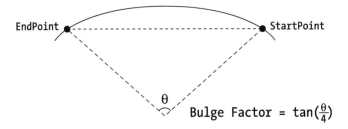

*Figure 8-6. Polyline segment*

To assign a bulge factor to the polyline segments, use the `SetBulge` method. The following example sets the bulge on a `Polyline` segment:

```
Public Sub TestAddBulge()
Dim objEnt As AcadPolyline
Dim dblVertices(17) As Double

    '' setup initial points
    dblVertices(0) = 0: dblVertices(1) = 0: dblVertices(2) = 0
    dblVertices(3) = 10: dblVertices(4) = 0: dblVertices(5) = 0
    dblVertices(6) = 7: dblVertices(7) = 10: dblVertices(8) = 0
    dblVertices(9) = 5: dblVertices(10) = 7: dblVertices(11) = 0
    dblVertices(12) = 6: dblVertices(13) = 2: dblVertices(14) = 0
    dblVertices(15) = 0: dblVertices(16) = 4: dblVertices(17) = 0

    '' draw the entity
If ThisDrawing.ActiveSpace = acModelSpace Then
  Set objEnt = ThisDrawing.ModelSpace.AddPolyline(dblVertices)
Else
  Set objEnt = ThisDrawing.PaperSpace.AddPolyline(dblVertices)
End If
    objEnt.Type = acSimplePoly
    'add bulge to the fourth segment
    objEnt.SetBulge 3, 0.5
    objEnt.Update
End Sub
```

## The Ray Object

The Ray object represents a line that extends to infinity in one direction from a specified start point. The AddRay method uses the following syntax to create a new ray:

```
Set RayObject = Object.AddRay(StartPoint, SecondPoint)
```

Table 8-9 provides a brief description of each argument.

*Table 8-9. AddRay Method Parameters*

| NAME | DATA TYPE | DESCRIPTION |
|------|-----------|-------------|
| StartPoint | Variant | A three-element array of doubles that specifies the ray's start with respect to the WCS. |
| SecondPoint | Variant | A three-element array of doubles that specifies a second point through which the ray passes. This point simply determines the ray's direction. |

Figure 8-7 illustrates the Ray object.

The following example uses the AddRay method with points obtained from the user:

```
Public Sub TestAddRay()
Dim varStart As Variant
Dim varEnd As Variant
Dim objEnt As AcadRay

On Error Resume Next
    '' get input from user
    With ThisDrawing.Utility
        varStart = .GetPoint(, vbCr & "Pick the start point: ")
        varEnd = .GetPoint(varStart, vbCr & "Indicate a direction: ")
    End With

    '' draw the entity
```

```
If ThisDrawing.ActiveSpace = acModelSpace Then
   Set objEnt = ThisDrawing.ModelSpace.AddRay(varStart, varEnd)
Else
   Set objEnt = ThisDrawing.PaperSpace.AddRay(varStart, varEnd)
End If
     objEnt.Update
End Sub
```

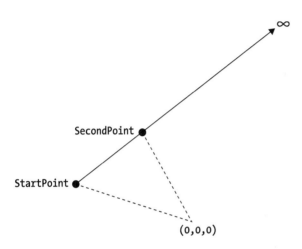

*Figure 8-7. The Ray object*

## The Spline Object

The Spline object represents a nonuniform rational B-spline (NURBS) quadratic or cubic curve. You use the AddSpline method to create a new Spline object:

```
Set SplineObject = Object.AddSpline(FitPoints, StartTangent, EndTangent)
```

Table 8-10 provides a brief description of each argument.

*Table 8-10. AddSpline Method Parameters*

| NAME | DATA TYPE | DESCRIPTION |
| --- | --- | --- |
| FitPoints | Variant | An array of doubles specifying a list of 3-D fit points in WCS coordinates. It's a simple array with a single dimension composed of alternating X, Y, and Z values (i.e., p1x, p1y, p1z, p2x, p2y, p2z, etc.). Because you must supply at least two points to create a spline, this array must have a minimum of six elements. |
| StartTangent | Variant | A three-element array of doubles that determines the tangent of the spline at its first fit point. |
| EndTangent | Variant | A three-element array of doubles that determines the tangent of the spline at its last fit point. |

Figure 8-8 illustrates the Spline object.

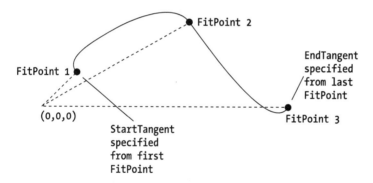

*Figure 8-8. The Spline object*

The following code sample demonstrates the AddSpline method:

```
Public Sub TestAddSpline()
Dim objEnt As AcadSpline
Dim dblBegin(0 To 2) As Double
Dim dblEnd(0 To 2) As Double
Dim dblPoints(14) As Double
```

```
    '' set tangencies
    dblBegin(0) = 1.5:    dblBegin(1) = 0#:    dblBegin(2) = 0
    dblEnd(0) = 1.5:   dblEnd(1) = 0#:   dblEnd(2) = 0

    '' set the fit dblPoints
    dblPoints(0) = 0: dblPoints(1) = 0: dblPoints(2) = 0
    dblPoints(3) = 3: dblPoints(4) = 5: dblPoints(5) = 0
    dblPoints(6) = 5: dblPoints(7) = 0: dblPoints(8) = 0
    dblPoints(9) = 7: dblPoints(10) = -5: dblPoints(11) = 0
    dblPoints(12) = 10: dblPoints(13) = 0: dblPoints(14) = 0

    '' draw the entity
If ThisDrawing.ActiveSpace = acModelSpace Then
   Set objEnt = ThisDrawing.ModelSpace.AddSpline(dblPoints, dblBegin, dblEnd)
Else
   Set objEnt = ThisDrawing.PaperSpace.AddSpline(dblPoints, dblBegin, dblEnd)
End If
    objEnt.Update
End Sub
```

## The XLine Object

The XLine object represents a straight line that passes through two specified points and extends to infinity in both directions. You use the AddXline method to create a new XLine object:

```
Set XLineObject = Object.AddXline(FirstPoint, SecondPoint)
```

Table 8-11 provides a brief description of each argument.

*Table 8-11. AddXline Method Parameters*

| NAME | DATA TYPE | DESCRIPTION |
| --- | --- | --- |
| FirstPoint | Variant | A three-element array of doubles specifying a point through which the XLine object passes in WCS coordinates. |
| SecondPoint | Variant | A three-element array of doubles specifying a second point through which the XLine passes. This point simply determines the direction of the XLine. |

Figure 8-9 illustrates the Xline object.

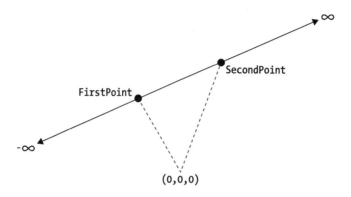

*Figure 8-9. The Xline object*

The following example illustrates how to implement the AddXline method:

```
Public Sub TestAddXline()
Dim varStart As Variant
Dim varEnd As Variant
Dim objEnt As AcadXline

On Error Resume Next
    '' get input from user
    With ThisDrawing.Utility
        varStart = .GetPoint(, vbCr & "Pick the start point: ")
        varEnd = .GetPoint(varStart, vbCr & "Indicate an angle: ")
    End With

    '' draw the entity
If ThisDrawing.ActiveSpace = acModelSpace Then
  Set objEnt = ThisDrawing.ModelSpace.AddXline(varStart, varEnd)
Else
  Set objEnt = ThisDrawing.PaperSpace.AddXline(varStart, varEnd)
End If
    objEnt.Update
End Sub
```

## Other Objects of Interest

The following sections describe some other objects of interest, starting with the Hatch object.

## The Hatch Object

The Hatch object represents an area filled with a pattern. The pattern may be associated with the area boundary (i.e., if the boundary changes, the pattern also changes appropriately) or the pattern may be independent of the area boundary. The read-only AssociativeHatch property determines whether or not the pattern is associated with the Hatch object. You set this property when you create the Hatch object, using the AddHatch method:

```
Set HatchObject = Object.AddHatch(PatternType, PatternName, Associativity)
```

Table 8-12 provides a brief description of each argument.

*Table 8-12. AddHatch Method Parameters*

| NAME | DATA TYPE | DESCRIPTION |
| --- | --- | --- |
| PatternType | Long | Specifies the type of pattern to use. It may take one of the three possible values given in Table 8-13. |
| PatternName | String | Specifies which hatch pattern to use from the .pat file. |
| Associativity | Boolean | Determines whether or not the hatch is associative. Set this parameter to True to create an associative hatch. |

Table 8-13 shows the three possible values for the PatternType parameter.

*Table 8-13. PatternType Parameter Values*

| CONSTANT | VALUE | DESCRIPTION |
| --- | --- | --- |
| AcHatchPatternTypeUserDefined | 0 | Allows you to define a pattern of lines using the current line type |
| AcHatchPatternTypePredefined | 1 | Uses a pattern name from those defined in the acad.pat file |
| AcHatchPatternTypeCustomDefined | 2 | Uses a pattern name from those defined in a .pat file other than the acad.pat file |

After you create the Hatch object, you must specify the boundary or loop using the AppendOuterLoop method. You must close and add this loop before any inner loops. You create any inner loops you may need one at a time using the AppendInnerLoop method.

**CAUTION**   *The documentation for the AddHatch method warns that you must call AppendOuterLoop immediately after you add the Hatch object; otherwise, AutoCAD will enter an unpredictable state.*

The following code gets a center point and radius from the user, and then creates some entities using these inputs. The new entities are then used to specify the inner and outer boundaries for a new Hatch object. The resulting Hatch object is shown in Figure 8-10.

```
Public Sub TestAddHatch()
Dim varCenter As Variant
Dim dblRadius As Double
Dim dblAngle As Double
Dim objEnt As AcadHatch
Dim varOuter() As AcadEntity
Dim varInner() As AcadEntity

On Error Resume Next
    '' get input from user
    With ThisDrawing.Utility
        varCenter = .GetPoint(, vbCr & "Pick the center point: ")
        dblRadius = .GetDistance(varCenter, vbCr & "Indicate the radius: ")
        dblAngle = .AngleToReal("180", acDegrees)
    End With

'' draw the entities    With ThisDrawing.ModelSpace

        '' draw the Outer loop (circle)
        ReDim varOuter(0)
        Set varOuter(0) = .AddCircle(varCenter, dblRadius)

        '' draw then Inner loop (semicircle)
        ReDim varInner(1)
        Set varInner(0) = .AddArc(varCenter, dblRadius * 0.5, 0, dblAngle)
```

```
        Set varInner(1) = .AddLine(varInner(0).StartPoint, _
                                   varInner(0).EndPoint)


        '' create the Hatch object
        Set objEnt = .AddHatch(acHatchPatternTypePreDefined, "ANSI31", True)

        '' append boundaries to the hatch
        objEnt.AppendOuterLoop varOuter
        objEnt.AppendInnerLoop varInner

        '' evaluate and display hatched boundaries
        objEnt.Evaluate
        objEnt.Update
    End With
End Sub
```

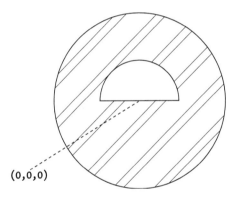

(0,0,0)

*Figure 8-10. The Hatch object*

As you can see, the AppendOuterLoop and AppendInnerLoop methods take as a parameter an array of objects forming a closed loop. The Evaluate method of the Hatch object evaluates the lines or fill for the hatch pattern.

**NOTE**   *In AutoCAD 2004,* Hatch *objects support a gradient fill display behavior. This in turn provides several new properties, such as* GradientAngle, GradientCentered, GradientColor1, *and* GradientColor2. *Consult the AutoCAD 2004 Customization Guide for more information about new* Hatch *object features.*

## The MText Object

The MText object represents a paragraph of alphanumeric characters that fits within a nonprinting bounding box. Each MText object is treated as a single object, regardless of the number of lines of text it contains. The bounding box remains an integral part of the entity, even though it isn't plotted or printed. MText objects use word wrap to break long lines into paragraphs.

You can create an MText entity using the AddMText method:

```
Set MTextObject = Object.AddMText(InsertionPoint, Width, TextString)
```

Table 8-14 provides a brief description of each argument.

*Table 8-14. AddMText Method Parameters*

| NAME | DATA TYPE | DESCRIPTION |
|------|-----------|-------------|
| InsertionPoint | Variant | A three-element array of doubles specifying the point at which the MText bounding box will be inserted with respect to the WCS |
| Width | Double | The width of the text block |
| TextString | String | The text displayed in the drawing space |

Figure 8-11 illustrates the MText object.

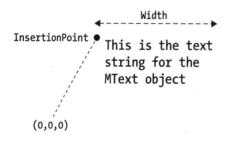

*Figure 8-11. The MText object*

The following example demonstrates the AddMText method:

```
Public Sub TestAddMText()
Dim varStart As Variant
Dim dblWidth As Double
Dim strText As String
Dim objEnt As AcadMText

On Error Resume Next
    '' get input from user
    With ThisDrawing.Utility
        varStart = .GetPoint(, vbCr & "Pick the start point: ")
        dblWidth = .GetDistance(varStart, vbCr & "Indicate the width: ")
        strText = .GetString(True, vbCr & "Enter the text: ")
    End With

    '' add font and size formatting
    strText = "\Fromand.shx;\H0.5;" & strText

    '' create the mtext

    Set objEnt = ThisDrawing.ModelSpace.AddMText(varStart, dblWidth, strText)
    objEnt.Update
End Sub
```

Rich text format (RTF) control codes aren't recognized in an MText entity. Text from other programs with embedded formatting will lose that formatting when you import it into an MText-style paragraph if you're working with AutoCAD 2000, 2000i, or 2002. Formatting is well preserved within AutoCAD 2004, however. You can paste Microsoft Word documents directly into AutoCAD 2002 as MText and maintain their original formatting.

AutoCAD 2000, 2000i, and 2002 exhibit odd behavior with respect to exploding block insertions that contain MText entities. In these versions, the nested MText entities are automatically exploded into individual Text entities when you use the VBA Explode method. This doesn't occur in AutoCAD 2004, however, and MText is preserved after the Explode method is executed.

## The Point Object

Point objects can act as nodes to which you can snap objects. You can specify a full 3-D WCS location for a point. You use the AddPoint method to create a new Point object, as follows:

```
Set PointObject = Object.AddPoint(PointPosition)
```

Table 8-15 provides a brief description of each argument.

*Table 8-15. AddPoint Method Parameter*

| NAME | DATA TYPE | DESCRIPTION |
| --- | --- | --- |
| PointPosition | Variant | A three-element array of doubles specifying the point's coordinates in WCS coordinates |

### Controlling How a Point Object Is Displayed

The appearance of Point objects is controlled by the system variables PDMODE and PDSIZE. The PDMODE variable specifies the figure used to represent a point. This variable may take a value from 0 to 4, as Figure 8-12 illustrates. A value of 1 means that nothing is displayed.

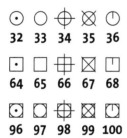

*Figure 8-12. The Point object*

You can optionally combine the PDMODE variable value with the number 32, 64, or 96, which represents a surrounding shape. Figure 8-13 shows the resulting possible combined symbols for a Point object.

⊙ ○ ⊕ ⊗ ◔
**32 33 34 35 36**

⊡ ☐ ⊞ ⊠ ⊓
**64 65 66 67 68**

⊡ ◻ ⊕ ⊠ ◎
**96 97 98 99 100**

*Figure 8-13. Various point styles*

The PDSIZE variable controls the size of the Point object figure. It has no effect if you set PDMODE to 0 or 1. You may set PDSIZE to a positive, negative, or zero value:

- A positive value specifies an absolute size for the point in drawing units.

- A negative value specifies the point symbol size as a percentage of the viewport area.

- A zero setting will generate the points at 5 percent of the height of the graphics area.

When you regenerate the drawing, AutoCAD recalculates the size of all points. So if you change PDMODE and PDSIZE, the appearance of existing points doesn't change until AutoCAD regenerates the drawing. You set the PDMODE and PDSIZE variables using the SetVariable method, which I discuss in Appendix C.

The following example illustrates how to use the PDMODE and PDSIZE variables and the AddPoint method:

```
Public Sub TestAddPoint()
Dim objEnt As AcadPoint
Dim varPick As Variant
Dim strType As String
Dim intType As Integer
Dim dblSize As Double

On Error Resume Next

    With ThisDrawing.Utility
        '' get the pdmode center type
        .InitializeUserInput 1, "Dot None Cross X Tick"
        strType = .GetKeyword(vbCr & "Center type [Dot/None/Cross/X/Tick]: ")
        If Err Then Exit Sub

        Select Case strType
            Case "Dot": intType = 0
            Case "None": intType = 1
            Case "Cross": intType = 2
            Case "X": intType = 3
            Case "Tick": intType = 4
        End Select
```

```
        '' get the pdmode surrounding type
        .InitializeUserInput 1, "Circle Square Both"
        strType = .GetKeyword(vbCr & "Outer type [Circle/Square/Both]: ")
        If Err Then Exit Sub

        Select Case strType
            Case "Circle": intType = intType + 32
            Case "Square": intType = intType + 64
            Case "Both": intType = intType + 96
        End Select

        '' get the pdsize
        .InitializeUserInput 1, ""
        dblSize = .GetDistance(, vbCr & "Enter a point size: ")
        If Err Then Exit Sub

        '' set the system varibles
        With ThisDrawing
        .SetVariable "PDMODE", intType
        .SetVariable "PDSIZE", dblSize
        End With
        '' now add points in a loop
        Do
            '' get user point for new vertex, use last pick as basepoint
            varPick = .GetPoint(, vbCr & "Pick a point <exit>: ")

            '' exit loop if no point picked
            If Err Then Exit Do

            '' add new vertex to pline at last offset

            ThisDrawing.ModelSpace.AddPoint varPick
        Loop
    End With
End Sub
```

## The Region Object

The Region object represents a bounded plane and may consist of Line, Arc, Circle, Elliptical Arc, LightweightPolyline, and Spline objects. To create a Region object from a set of drawing entities, use the AddRegion method as follows:

```
RegionArray = Object.AddRegion(ObjectsArray)
```

Table 8-16 provides a brief description of each argument.

*Table 8-16. AddRegion Method Parameter*

| NAME | DATA TYPE | DESCRIPTION |
|------|-----------|-------------|
| ObjectsArray | Array of objects | The objects used to make the region objects. These objects must form a closed area and must be coplanar. |

AddRegion returns an array of the Region objects created from the ObjectsArray parameter, as shown in Figure 8-14.

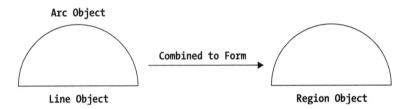

*Figure 8-14. Region objects*

The ObjectsArray may contain drawing objects that form more than one enclosed plane. For each enclosed plane, a Region object is formed and held in an array of Region objects. If two or more curves share end points, the region created may be arbitrary.

The following example demonstrates how to build and manipulate regions. The objEnts variable is an array of objects that forms two closed coplanar faces to be converted into Region objects. One region is a full circle and the other is a closed semicircle. Once the AddRegion method is executed, these two regions are held in the regions variable. Next, the code uses the Boolean method (detailed in Chapter 9) to subtract the semicircle from the larger full circle. Finally, the region is moved to a new location, showing that it's a single composite object.

```
Public Sub TestAddRegion()
Dim varCenter As Variant
Dim varMove As Variant
Dim dblRadius As Double
Dim dblAngle As Double
Dim varRegions As Variant
```

```
Dim objEnts() As AcadEntity

    On Error Resume Next
    '' get input from user
    With ThisDrawing.Utility
        varCenter = .GetPoint(, vbCr & "Pick the center point: ")
        dblRadius = .GetDistance(varCenter, vbCr & "Indicate the radius: ")
        dblAngle = .AngleToReal("180", acDegrees)
    End With

    '' draw the entities
    With ThisDrawing.ModelSpace

        '' draw the outer region (circle)
        ReDim objEnts(2)
        Set objEnts(0) = .AddCircle(varCenter, dblRadius)

        '' draw the inner region (semicircle)
        Set objEnts(1) = .AddArc(varCenter, dblRadius * 0.5, 0, dblAngle)
        Set objEnts(2) = .AddLine(objEnts(1).StartPoint, objEnts(1).EndPoint)

        '' create the regions
        varRegions = .AddRegion(objEnts)
    End With

    '' get new position from user
        varMove = ThisDrawing.Utility.GetPoint(varCenter, vbCr & _
                                          "Pick a new location: ")

    '' subtract the inner region from the outer
    varRegions(1).Boolean acSubtraction, varRegions(0)

    '' move the composite region to a new location
    varRegions(1).Move varCenter, varMove
End Sub
```

You may also explode individual regions by using the Explode method. Be aware that invoking the Region entity incurs a performance hit while AutoCAD loads the ACIS or ShapeManager solid-modeling engine, depending upon what version of AutoCAD you're working with.

## The Solid Object

The Solid object represents a 2-D polygon. You can create a polygon by specifying two points to define the first edge. The third point defines an edge back to the start point, not to the second point as you might imagine. Next, you have the option to define a fourth point in the same position as the third, which results in a triangular shape. Alternatively, you can specify a different fourth point to define a variety of shapes (e.g., a rectangle, a parallelogram, a trapezoid, a chevron, or a bow tie). Use the AddSolid method as follows:

```
Set SolidObject = Object.AddSolid(Point1, Point2, Point3, Point4)
```

Table 8-17 provides a brief description of each argument.

*Table 8-17. AddSolid Method Parameters*

| NAME | DATA TYPE | DESCRIPTION |
| --- | --- | --- |
| Point1 | Variant | A three-element array of doubles defining the start of the polygon's first side in WCS coordinates. |
| Point2 | Variant | A three-element array of doubles defining the end of the polygon's first side in WCS coordinates. |
| Point3 | Variant | A three-element array of doubles defining the end of the polygon's second side in WCS coordinates. This point is opposite Point1 on the second edge. |
| Point4 | Variant | A three-element array of doubles specifying the last point that defines the polygon's third and optionally fourth edges in WCS coordinates. It may be the same as Point3, in which case only three polygon edges are visible. |

If the FILLMODE system variable is set to 1, the shape will be shaded; otherwise, only the boundary lines are visible. The following example uses AddSolid with input from the user:

```
Public Sub TestAddSolid()
Dim varP1 As Variant
Dim varP2 As Variant
Dim varP3 As Variant
```

```
Dim varP4 As Variant
Dim objEnt As AcadSolid

On Error Resume Next
    '' ensure that solid fill is enabled
    ThisDrawing.SetVariable "FILLMODE", 1

    '' get input from user
    With ThisDrawing.Utility
        varP1 = .GetPoint(, vbCr & "Pick the start point: ")
        varP2 = .GetPoint(varP1, vbCr & "Pick the second point: ")
        varP3 = .GetPoint(varP1, vbCr & "Pick a point opposite the start: ")
        varP4 = .GetPoint(varP3, vbCr & "Pick the last point: ")
    End With

    '' draw the entity

    Set objEnt = ThisDrawing.ModelSpace.AddSolid(varP1, varP2, varP3, varP4)
    objEnt.Update
End Sub
```

## The Text Object

The Text object represents text on a drawing. It differs from the MText object in that it consists of only one line of text. It also lacks the embedded formatting capabilities of MText. The AddText method creates a new Text object:

```
Set TextObject = Object.AddText(TextString, InsertionPoint, Height)
```

Table 8-18 provides a brief description of each argument.

*Table 8-18. AddText Method Parameters*

| NAME | DATA TYPE | DESCRIPTION |
| --- | --- | --- |
| TextString | String | The text to be displayed in the drawing |
| InsertionPoint | Variant | A three-element array of doubles representing the text's position with respect to the WCS |
| Height | Double | A positive number indicating the text's height |

The following code example shows the `AddText` method in practice:

```
Public Sub TestAddText()
Dim varStart As Variant
Dim dblHeight As Double
Dim strText As String
Dim objEnt As AcadText

On Error Resume Next
    '' get input from user
    With ThisDrawing.Utility
        varStart = .GetPoint(, vbCr & "Pick the start point: ")
        dblHeight = .GetDistance(varStart, vbCr & "Indicate the height: ")
        strText = .GetString(True, vbCr & "Enter the text: ")
    End With


    '' create the text
If ThisDrawing.ActiveSpace = acModelSpace Then
  Set objEnt = ThisDrawing.ModelSpace.AddText(strText, varStart, dblHeight)
Else
  Set objEnt = ThisDrawing.PaperSpace.AddText(strText, varStart, dblHeight)
End If
    objEnt.Update
End Sub
```

## Summary

In this chapter you learned how to create a number of different 2-D drawing objects. In the next chapter you'll learn how to create a variety of 3-D objects.

# CHAPTER 9

# Creating 3-D Objects

IN CHAPTER 8 YOU LEARNED how to create simple 2-D drawing entities, such as
circles, lines, and text. AutoCAD also provides you with a number of methods to
programmatically create complex 3-D solid entities. Represented by the 3DSolid
object, each solid entity and the creation of this object in its various disguises
will form the basis of this chapter.

This chapter covers the following topics:

- 3-D primitives (the box, cone, cylinder, sphere, torus, and wedge objects)

- Elliptical cones and cylinders

- Extruded and revolved solids

- Manipulation of solids(slicing, checking interference, and spatial
  properties)

## The 3DSolid Object

The 3DSolid object represents a solid with a free-form surface. This means that
the solid may take virtually any shape. You may add a 3DSolid object to a drawing
or block by using one of the AddXXX methods I describe in this chapter.

Although you can do amazing things with the ActiveX solids and surfacing
features in AutoCAD, they don't provide all of the functionality that AutoCAD can
tap into. Some examples of this functionality include SOLIDEDIT operations such
as Shell, Imprint, Copy Faces, Taper Faces, Clean, and Check.

This limitation is due to the manner in which solids and surfaces are constructed and managed using an external modeling kernel. Up until AutoCAD 2002,
the solid modeling kernel was ACIS by Spatial (http://www.spatial.com). With
AutoCAD 2004, however, Autodesk has parted ways with ACIS and uses its own
modeling technology, ShapeManager, which was adapted from ACIS. Developing
applications that work with ACIS objects internally requires a separate developer's

license with Spatial. Autodesk is developing an API for ShapeManager, but so far it is built on ObjectARX only.

Methods are exposed by the ModelSpace, PaperSpace, and Block objects to create each of the 3-D solid objects. When I present the syntax for each method, I use the word "Object" to refer any of these objects. For example:

```
Set 3DSolidObject = Object.AddBox(BoxCenter, Length, Width, Height)
```

Because you may combine solids to form very sophisticated geometric shapes, they have no characteristic start or end points. Instead, you specify solids through a control point, the Centroid, that sits at the center of a bounding box. No matter how complex the solid becomes, the Centroid point can quickly be calculated. Many of the examples in this chapter demonstrate how to convert user input for each primitive, such as the corner of a box, into the Centroid point specification.

In the examples that follow, you'll change the angle at which the drawing is displayed so that you can view the newly created objects unambiguously. You achieve this by changing the Direction property of the active ViewPort object. You use the following function to consolidate this operation:

```
Sub SetViewpoint(Optional Zoom As Boolean = False, _
                 Optional X As Double = 1, _
                 Optional Y As Double = -2, _
                 Optional Z As Double = 1)

    Dim dblDirection(2) As Double
    dblDirection(0) = X:  dblDirection(1) = Y:  dblDirection(2) = Z

    With ThisDrawing
        .Preferences.ContourLinesPerSurface = 10    ' set surface countours
        .ActiveViewport.Direction = dblDirection     ' assign new direction
        .ActiveViewport = .ActiveViewport            ' force a viewportupdate
        If Zoom Then .Application.ZoomAll            ' zoomall if requested
    End With
End Sub
```

Notice that the ContourLinesPerSurface property of the drawing Preferences object is set to 10. This setting controls the number of surface lines AutoCAD shows on each surface. You can set a higher number with a resulting increase in surface lines.

## Creating Simple Solid Objects

This section demonstrates how to create the various 3-D solid objects.

### *The Box*

A box is a 3DSolid object with edges parallel to the axes of the WCS. You create it using the AddBox method:

```
Set 3DSolidObject = Object.AddBox(BoxCenter, Length, Width, Height)
```

Table 9-1 presents the AddBox method's parameters.

*Table 9-1. AddBox Method Parameters*

| NAME | DATA TYPE | DESCRIPTION |
|------|-----------|-------------|
| BoxCenter | Variant | A three-element array of doubles specifying the center of the box in WCS coordinates. |
| Length | Double | A positive value representing the length of the box. |
| Width | Double | A positive value representing the width of the box. |
| Height | Double | A positive value representing the height of the box. |

Figure 9-1 shows an example of a box in AutoCAD.

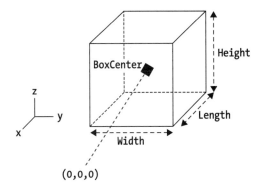

*Figure 9-1. Box*

The following code creates a box based on user input:

```
Public Sub TestAddBox()
      Dim varPick As Variant
      Dim dblLength As Double
      Dim dblWidth As Double
      Dim dblHeight As Double
      Dim dblCenter(2) As Double
      Dim objEnt As Acad3DSolid

      '' set the default viewpoint
      SetViewpoint Zoom:=True

      '' get input from user
      With ThisDrawing.Utility
          .InitializeUserInput 1
          varPick = .GetPoint(, vbCr & "Pick a corner point: ")
          .InitializeUserInput 1 + 2 + 4, ""
          dblLength = .GetDistance(varPick, vbCr & "Enter the X length: ")
          .InitializeUserInput 1 + 2 + 4, ""
          dblWidth = .GetDistance(varPick, vbCr & "Enter the Y width: ")
          .InitializeUserInput 1 + 2 + 4, ""
          dblHeight = .GetDistance(varPick, vbCr & "Enter the Z height: ")
      End With

      '' calculate center point from input
      dblCenter(0) = varPick(0) + (dblLength / 2)
      dblCenter(1) = varPick(1) + (dblWidth / 2)
      dblCenter(2) = varPick(2) + (dblHeight / 2)

      '' draw the entity
      Set objEnt = ThisDrawing.ModelSpace.AddBox(dblCenter, dblLength, _
                                            dblWidth, dblHeight)
      objEnt.Update
      ThisDrawing.SendCommand "_shade" & vbCr
End Sub
```

## The Cone

You create a 3DSolid object in the form of a cone using the AddCone method. The base of the cone is parallel with the XY plane of the WCS.

```
Set 3DSolidObject = Object.AddCone(ConeCenter, BaseRadius, Height)
```

Table 9-2 presents the AddCone method's parameters, and Figure 9-2 shows an example of a cone in AutoCAD.

*Table 9-2. AddCone Method Parameters*

| NAME | DATA TYPE | DESCRIPTION |
| --- | --- | --- |
| ConeCenter | Variant | A three-element array of doubles specifying the cone's center in WCS coordinates |
| BaseRadius | Double | A positive value representing the radius of the cone's circular base. |
| Height | Double | A positive value representing the cone's height |

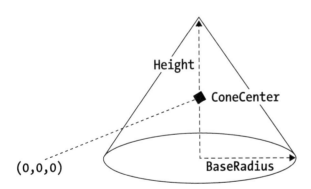

*Figure 9-2. Cone*

This example creates a cone based on user input:

```
Public Sub TestAddCone()
    Dim varPick As Variant
    Dim dblRadius As Double
    Dim dblHeight As Double
```

```
        Dim dblCenter(2) As Double
        Dim objEnt As Acad3DSolid

    '' set the default viewpoint
    SetViewpoint

    '' get input from user
    With ThisDrawing.Utility
        .InitializeUserInput 1
        varPick = .GetPoint(, vbCr & "Pick the base center point: ")
        .InitializeUserInput 1 + 2 + 4, ""
        dblRadius = .GetDistance(varPick, vbCr & "Enter the radius: ")
        .InitializeUserInput 1 + 2 + 4, ""
        dblHeight = .GetDistance(varPick, vbCr & "Enter the Z height: ")
    End With

    '' calculate center point from input
    dblCenter(0) = varPick(0)
    dblCenter(1) = varPick(1)
    dblCenter(2) = varPick(2) + (dblHeight / 2)

    '' draw the entity
    Set objEnt = ThisDrawing.ModelSpace.AddCone(dblCenter, dblRadius, _
                                                dblHeight)
    objEnt.Update

    ThisDrawing.SendCommand "_shade" & vbCr
End Sub
```

## *The Cylinder*

You add a cylinder to a drawing using the AddCylinder method. The base of the cylinder lies in a plane parallel to the WCS XY plane.

```
Set 3DSolidObject = Object.AddCylinder(CylinderCenter, Radius, Height)
```

Table 9-3 presents the AddCylinder method's parameters, and Figure 9-3 shows an example of a cylinder in AutoCAD.

*Table 9-3. AddCylinder Method Parameters*

| NAME | DATA TYPE | DESCRIPTION |
|------|-----------|-------------|
| `CylinderCenter` | Variant | A three-element array of doubles specifying the cylinder's center in WCS coordinates |
| `Radius` | Double | A positive value representing the radius of the cylinder's base |
| `Height` | Double | A positive value representing the cylinder's height |

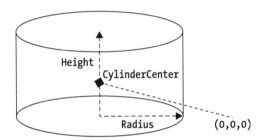

*Figure 9-3. Cylinder*

The following example creates a cylinder based on user input:

```
Public Sub TestAddCylinder()
    Dim varPick As Variant
    Dim dblRadius As Double
    Dim dblHeight As Double
    Dim dblCenter(2) As Double
    Dim objEnt As Acad3DSolid

    '' set the default viewpoint
    SetViewpoint

    '' get input from user
    With ThisDrawing.Utility
        .InitializeUserInput 1
        varPick = .GetPoint(, vbCr & "Pick the base center point: ")
        .InitializeUserInput 1 + 2 + 4, ""
```

```
        dblRadius = .GetDistance(varPick, vbCr & "Enter the radius: ")
        .InitializeUserInput 1 + 2 + 4, ""
        dblHeight = .GetDistance(varPick, vbCr & "Enter the Z height: ")
    End With

    '' calculate center point from input
    dblCenter(0) = varPick(0)
    dblCenter(1) = varPick(1)
    dblCenter(2) = varPick(2) + (dblHeight / 2)

    '' draw the entity
    Set objEnt = ThisDrawing.ModelSpace.AddCylinder(dblCenter, dblRadius, dblHeight)
    objEnt.Update

    ThisDrawing.SendCommand "_shade" & vbCr
End Sub
```

## *The Sphere*

You use the AddSphere method to create a 3DSolid object representing a sphere and to add it to a drawing:

```
Set 3DSolidObject = Object.AddSphere(SphereCenter, Radius)
```

Table 9-4 presents the AddSphere method's parameters, and Figure 9-4 shows an example of a sphere in AutoCAD.

*Table 9-4. AddSphere Method Parameters*

| NAME | DATA TYPE | DESCRIPTION |
|------|-----------|-------------|
| SphereCenter | Variant | A three-element array of doubles specifying the sphere's center in WCS coordinates |
| Radius | Double | A positive value representing the sphere's radius |

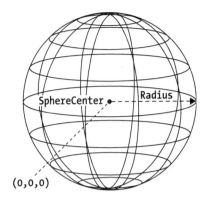

*Figure 9-4. Sphere*

This example creates a sphere based on user input:

```
Public Sub TestAddSphere()
     Dim varPick As Variant
     Dim dblRadius As Double
     Dim objEnt As Acad3DSolid

    '' set the default viewpoint
    SetViewpoint

    '' get input from user
    With ThisDrawing.Utility
        .InitializeUserInput 1
        varPick = .GetPoint(, vbCr & "Pick the center point: ")
        .InitializeUserInput 1 + 2 + 4, ""
        dblRadius = .GetDistance(varPick, vbCr & "Enter the radius: ")
    End With

    '' draw the entity
    Set objEnt = ThisDrawing.ModelSpace.AddSphere(varPick, dblRadius)
    objEnt.Update

    ThisDrawing.SendCommand "_shade" & vbCr
End Sub
```

## The Torus

Use the AddTorus method to create a torus and add it at a given point in a drawing, such that the ring lays flat in the XY plane:

```
Set 3DSolidObject = Object.AddTorus(TorusCenter, TorusRadius, TubeRadius)
```

Table 9-5 presents the AddTorus method's parameters, and Figure 9-5 shows an example of a torus in AutoCAD.

*Table 9-5. AddTorus Method Parameters*

| NAME | DATA TYPE | DESCRIPTION |
|------|-----------|-------------|
| TorusCenter | Variant | A three-element array of doubles specifying the point about which the torus is centered in WCS coordinates |
| TorusRadius | Double | A positive value representing the distance from the torus's center to the tube's center |
| TubeRadius | Double | A positive value representing the tube's radius |

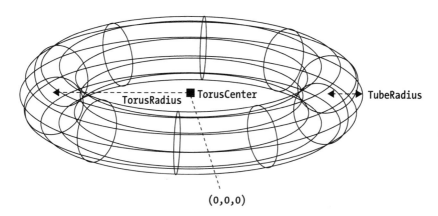

*Figure 9-5. Torus*

The following example creates a torus based on user input:

```
Public Sub TestAddTorus()
      Dim pntPick As Variant
      Dim pntRadius As Variant
      Dim dblRadius As Double
      Dim dblTube As Double
      Dim objEnt As Acad3DSolid
      Dim intI As Integer

    '' set the default viewpoint
    SetViewpoint

    '' get input from user
    With ThisDrawing.Utility
        .InitializeUserInput 1
        pntPick = .GetPoint(, vbCr & "Pick the center point: ")
        .InitializeUserInput 1
        pntRadius = .GetPoint(pntPick, vbCr & "Pick a radius point: ")
        .InitializeUserInput 1 + 2 + 4, ""
        dblTube = .GetDistance(pntRadius, vbCr & "Enter the tube radius: ")
    End With

    '' calculate radius from points
    For intI = 0 To 2
        dblRadius = dblRadius + (pntPick(intI) - pntRadius(intI)) ^ 2
    Next
    dblRadius = Sqr(dblRadius)

    '' draw the entity
    Set objEnt = ThisDrawing.ModelSpace.AddTorus(pntPick, dblRadius, dblTube)
    objEnt.Update

    ThisDrawing.SendCommand "_shade" & vbCr
End Sub
```

## The Wedge

The AddWedge method creates a wedge with edges parallel to the WCS axes:

```
Set 3DSolidObject = Object.AddWedge(FaceCenter, Length, Width, Height)
```

Table 9-6 presents the AddWedge method's parameters, and Figure 9-6 shows an example of a wedge in AutoCAD.

*Table 9-6. AddWedge Method Parameters*

| NAME | DATA TYPE | DESCRIPTION |
| --- | --- | --- |
| FaceCenter4 | Variant | A three-element array of doubles specifying the bounding box's center in WCS coordinates. This corresponds to the sloping face's center as well. |
| Length | Double | A positive value representing the wedge base's length (X-axis). |
| Width | Double | A positive value representing the wedge base's width (Y-axis). |
| Height | Double | A positive value representing the wedge base's height (Z-axis). |

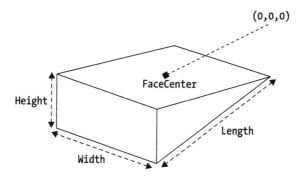

*Figure 9-6. Wedge*

This example creates a wedge based on user input:

```
Public Sub TestAddWedge()
    Dim varPick As Variant
    Dim dblLength As Double
    Dim dblWidth As Double
    Dim dblHeight As Double
    Dim dblCenter(2) As Double
    Dim objEnt As Acad3DSolid
```

```
'' set the default viewpoint
SetViewpoint

'' get input from user
With ThisDrawing.Utility
    .InitializeUserInput 1
    varPick = .GetPoint(, vbCr & "Pick a base corner point: ")
    .InitializeUserInput 1 + 2 + 4, ""
    dblLength = .GetDistance(varPick, vbCr & "Enter the base X length: ")
    .InitializeUserInput 1 + 2 + 4, ""
    dblWidth = .GetDistance(varPick, vbCr & "Enter the base Y width: ")
    .InitializeUserInput 1 + 2 + 4, ""
    dblHeight = .GetDistance(varPick, vbCr & "Enter the base Z height: ")
End With

'' calculate center point from input
dblCenter(0) = varPick(0) + (dblLength / 2)
dblCenter(1) = varPick(1) + (dblWidth / 2)
dblCenter(2) = varPick(2) + (dblHeight / 2)

'' draw the entity
Set objEnt = ThisDrawing.ModelSpace.AddWedge(dblCenter, dblLength, _
                                             dblWidth, dblHeight)

objEnt.Update

ThisDrawing.SendCommand "_shade" & vbCr
End Sub
```

# Creating Elliptical 3-D Objects

AutoCAD provides two methods for creating elliptical solids. The first creates an elliptical cone, and the second creates an elliptical cylinder.

## *The Elliptical Cone*

The AddEllipticalCone method creates a 3DSolid object in the form of an elliptical cone whose base lies flat on the WCS XY plane. The major axis of the ellipse may lie in either the X or Y direction.

```
Set 3DSolidObject = Object.AddEllipticalCone(ConeCenter, XLength, _
YLength, Height)
```

Table 9-7 presents the AddElliptical method's parameters, and Figure 9-7 shows an example of an elliptical cone in AutoCAD.

*Table 9-7. AddEllipticalCone Method Parameters*

| NAME | DATA TYPE | DESCRIPTION |
|---|---|---|
| ConeCenter | Variant | A three-element array of doubles specifying the center of the bounding box in WCS coordinates |
| XLength | Double | A positive value representing the length of the X-axis of the cone's elliptical base |
| YLength | Double | A positive value representing the length of the Y-axis of the cone's elliptical base |
| Height | Double | A positive value representing the cone's height |

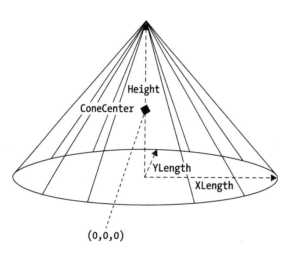

*Figure 9-7. Elliptical cone*

The following example creates an elliptical cone based on user input:

```
Public Sub TestAddEllipticalCone()
    Dim varPick As Variant
    Dim dblXAxis As Double
```

```
        Dim dblYAxis As Double
        Dim dblHeight As Double
        Dim dblCenter(2) As Double
        Dim objEnt As Acad3DSolid

    '' set the default viewpoint
    SetViewpoint

    '' get input from user
    With ThisDrawing.Utility
        .InitializeUserInput 1
        varPick = .GetPoint(, vbCr & "Pick a base center point: ")
        .InitializeUserInput 1 + 2 + 4, ""
        dblXAxis = .GetDistance(varPick, vbCr & "Enter the X eccentricity: ")
        .InitializeUserInput 1 + 2 + 4, ""
        dblYAxis = .GetDistance(varPick, vbCr & "Enter the Y eccentricity: ")
        .InitializeUserInput 1 + 2 + 4, ""
        dblHeight = .GetDistance(varPick, vbCr & "Enter the cone Z height: ")
    End With

    '' calculate center point from input
    dblCenter(0) = varPick(0)
    dblCenter(1) = varPick(1)
    dblCenter(2) = varPick(2) + (dblHeight / 2)

    '' draw the entity
    Set objEnt = ThisDrawing.ModelSpace.AddEllipticalCone(dblCenter, _
                                        dblXAxis, dblYAxis, dblHeight)

    objEnt.Update

    ThisDrawing.SendCommand "_shade" & vbCr
End Sub
```

## The Elliptical Cylinder

Use the AddEllipticalCylinder method to add a 3DSolid elliptical cylinder whose base lies parallel to the WCS XY plane. The major axis of the elliptical base lies either in the X or Y direction.

```
Set 3DSolidObject = Object.AddEllipticalCylinder _
(CylinderCenter, XLength, YLength, Height)
```

Table 9-8 presents the AddEllipticalCylinder method's parameters, and Figure 9-8 shows an example of an elliptical cylinder in AutoCAD.

*Table 9-8. AddEllipticalCylinder Method Parameters*

| NAME | DATA TYPE | DESCRIPTION |
|------|-----------|-------------|
| CylinderCenter | Variant | A three-element array of doubles specifying the center of the bounding box in WCS coordinates |
| XLength | Double | A positive value representing the length of the X-axis of the cylinder's elliptical base |
| YLength | Double | A positive value representing the length of the Y-axis of the cylinder's elliptical base |
| Height | Double | A positive value representing the cylinder's height |

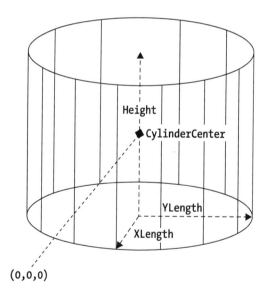

*Figure 9-8. Elliptical cylinder*

This example creates an elliptical cylinder based on user input:

```
Public Sub TestAddEllipticalCylinder()
    Dim varPick As Variant
    Dim dblXAxis As Double
    Dim dblYAxis As Double
    Dim dblHeight As Double
    Dim dblCenter(2) As Double
    Dim objEnt As Acad3DSolid

    '' set the default viewpoint
    SetViewpoint

    '' get input from user
    With ThisDrawing.Utility
        .InitializeUserInput 1
        varPick = .GetPoint(, vbCr & "Pick a base center point: ")
        .InitializeUserInput 1 + 2 + 4, ""
        dblXAxis = .GetDistance(varPick, vbCr & "Enter the X eccentricity: ")
        .InitializeUserInput 1 + 2 + 4, ""
        dblYAxis = .GetDistance(varPick, vbCr & "Enter the Y eccentricity: ")
        .InitializeUserInput 1 + 2 + 4, ""
        dblHeight = .GetDistance(varPick, vbCr & _
                                        "Enter the cylinder Z height: ")
    End With

    '' calculate center point from input
    dblCenter(0) = varPick(0)
    dblCenter(1) = varPick(1)
    dblCenter(2) = varPick(2) + (dblHeight / 2)

    '' draw the entity
    Set objEnt = ThisDrawing.ModelSpace.AddEllipticalCylinder(dblCenter, _
                                    dblXAxis, dblYAxis, dblHeight)
    objEnt.Update

    ThisDrawing.SendCommand "_shade" & vbCr
End Sub
```

## Creating Extruded and Revolved Objects

You create extruded and revolved solids by taking planar Region objects and adding thickness to them, either by extruding them along the Z-axis or by revolving them about an arbitrary axis. The newly created entities are 3DSolid objects.

## *The Extruded Solid*

You create this solid by extruding a planar region along its Z-axis. You may extrude the region in a positive or negative direction, and you may taper or expand it in the extrusion direction.

```
Set 3DSolidObject = Object.AddExtrudedSolid(Region, Height, TaperAngle)
```

Table 9-9 presents the AddExtrudedSolid method's parameters.

*Table 9-9. AddExtrudedSolid Method Parameters*

| NAME | DATA TYPE | DESCRIPTION |
| --- | --- | --- |
| Region | Region object | A closed planar region to be extruded. |
| Height | Double | A nonzero value representing the extrusion's height. If this value is positive, the region is extruded in the OCS Z-direction. If this value is negative, the region is extruded in the $-Z$ direction. |
| TaperAngle | Double | The angle of tapering or expansion of the extrusion given in radians. It must lie between $-90$ degrees and $+90$ degrees. Positive values taper in from the base, and negative values expand. |

In Figure 9-9 you can see that the Height parameter is positive as the region is extruded in the +Z direction, and the TaperAngle is negative as the object becomes wider as it's extruded.

AutoCAD won't create the extruded object if it intersects itself. In this event, AutoCAD will raise a run-time error. To avoid this possibility, you should be careful to choose the Height and TaperAngle parameters so that this doesn't occur.

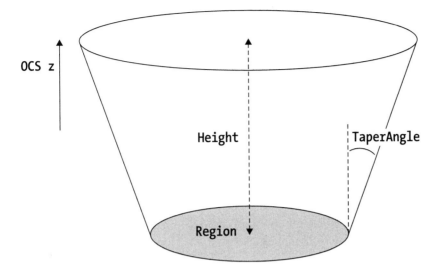

*Figure 9-9. Extruded solid*

The following example creates a circular region and extrudes it into a solid based on user input:

```
Public Sub TestAddExtrudedSolid()
    Dim varCenter As Variant
    Dim dblRadius As Double
    Dim dblHeight As Double
    Dim dblTaper As Double
    Dim strInput As String
    Dim varRegions As Variant
    Dim objEnts() As AcadEntity
    Dim objEnt As Acad3DSolid
    Dim varItem As Variant


On Error GoTo Done

    '' get input from user
    With ThisDrawing.Utility
        .InitializeUserInput 1
        varCenter = .GetPoint(, vbCr & "Pick the center point: ")
```

```
            .InitializeUserInput 1 + 2 + 4
            dblRadius = .GetDistance(varCenter, vbCr & "Indicate the radius: ")
            .InitializeUserInput 1 + 2 + 4
            dblHeight = .GetDistance(varCenter, vbCr & _
                                    "Enter the extrusion height: ")

            '' get the taper type
            .InitializeUserInput 1, "Expand Contract None"
            strInput = .GetKeyword(vbCr & _
                                    "Extrusion taper [Expand/Contract/None]: ")

            '' if none, taper = 0
            If strInput = "None" Then
                dblTaper = 0

            '' otherwise, get the taper angle
            Else
                .InitializeUserInput 1 + 2 + 4
                dblTaper = .GetReal("Enter the taper angle ( in degrees): ")
                dblTaper = .AngleToReal(CStr(dblTaper), acDegrees)


                '' if expanding, negate the angle
                If strInput = "Expand" Then dblTaper = -dblTaper
            End If
    End With

    '' draw the entities
    With ThisDrawing.ModelSpace

        '' draw the outer region (circle)
        ReDim objEnts(0)
        Set objEnts(0) = .AddCircle(varCenter, dblRadius)

        '' create the region
        varRegions = .AddRegion(objEnts)
        '' extruded the solid
        Set objEnt = .AddExtrudedSolid(varRegions(0), dblHeight, dblTaper)
```

```
        '' update the extruded solid
        objEnt.Update
    End With

Done:
    If Err Then MsgBox Err.Description

    '' delete the temporary geometry
    For Each varItem In objEnts
        varItem.Delete
    Next
    For Each varItem In varRegions
        varItem.Delete
    Next

    ThisDrawing.SendCommand "_shade" & vbCr
End Sub
```

## *The Extruded Solid Along a Path*

You use the AddExtrudedSolidAlongPath method to create a new 3DSolid object
that represents the extrusion of a closed planar region along a given path. This
path may take the form of a polyline, spline, circle, ellipse, or arc. The new solid
is extruded from the current location of the region using the translation of the
path to the region's Centroid.

```
Set 3DSolidObject = Object.AddExtrudedSolidAlongPath(Region, Path)
```

Table 9-10 presents the AddExtrudedSolidAlongPath method's parameters, and
Figure 9-10 shows an example of and extruded solid along a path.

*Table 9-10. AddExtrudedSolidAlongPath Method Parameters*

| NAME | DATA TYPE | DESCRIPTION |
|------|-----------|-------------|
| Region | Region object | A closed planar region to be extruded. |
| Path | Polyline, Spline, Circle, Ellipse, or Arc object | The path along which the plane region is to be extruded. This path can't lie in the same plane as the region to be extruded. |

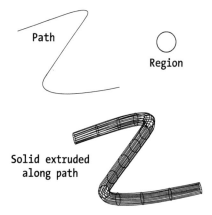

*Figure 9-10. Extruded solid along a path*

As with the extruded solid, the newly created object may not intersect itself. Therefore, you should avoid self-intersecting paths or those with sections of high curvature.

The following example extrudes a circular region into a solid along the path of a spline specified by the user:

```
Public Sub TestAddExtrudedSolidAlongPath()
      Dim objPath As AcadSpline
      Dim varPick As Variant
      Dim intI As Integer
      Dim dblCenter(2) As Double
      Dim dblRadius As Double
      Dim objCircle As AcadCircle
      Dim objEnts() As AcadEntity
      Dim objShape As Acad3DSolid
      Dim varRegions As Variant
      Dim varItem As Variant

   '' set default viewpoint
   SetViewpoint

   '' pick path and calculate shape points
   With ThisDrawing.Utility
```

```
        '' pick the path
On Error Resume Next
        .GetEntity objPath, varPick, "Pick a Spline for the path"
        If Err Then
            MsgBox "You did not pick a spline"
            Exit Sub
        End If
        objPath.Color = acGreen
        For intI = 0 To 2
            dblCenter(intI) = objPath.FitPoints(intI)
        Next
        .InitializeUserInput 1 + 2 + 4
        dblRadius = .GetDistance(dblCenter, vbCr & "Indicate the radius: ")

    End With



    '' draw the circular region, then extrude along path
    With ThisDrawing.ModelSpace

        '' draw the outer region (circle)
        ReDim objEnts(0)
        Set objCircle = .AddCircle(dblCenter, dblRadius)
        objCircle.Normal = objPath.StartTangent
        Set objEnts(0) = objCircle
        '' create the region
        varRegions = .AddRegion(objEnts)

        Set objShape = .AddExtrudedSolidAlongPath(varRegions(0), objPath)
        objShape.Color = acRed
    End With

    '' delete the temporary geometry
    For Each varItem In objEnts: varItem.Delete:  Next
    For Each varItem In varRegions:  varItem.Delete:  Next

    ThisDrawing.SendCommand "_shade" & vbCr
End Sub
```

## The Revolved Solid

You add a 3DSolid object representing a revolved solid, which you create by sweeping a planar region about an axis, to a drawing by using the AddRevolvedSolid method:

```
Set 3DSolidObject = Object.AddRevolvedSolid(Region, AxisPoint, _
AxisDirection, Angle)
```

Table 9-11 presents the AddRevolvedSolid method's parameters, and Figure 9-11 shows an example of a revolved solid in AutoCAD.

*Table 9-11. AddRevolvedSolid Method Parameters*

| NAME | DATA TYPE | DESCRIPTION |
|---|---|---|
| Region | Region object | A closed planar region to be revolved. |
| AxisPoint | Variant | A three-element array of doubles specifying the center of the axis of rotation in WCS coordinates. |
| AxisDirection | Variant | A three-element array of doubles specifying a directional vector for the axis of rotation |
| Angle | Double | The angle through which the region is swept, measured in radians. You determine the positive direction of rotation by applying the arbitrary axis algorithm to AxisDirection. |

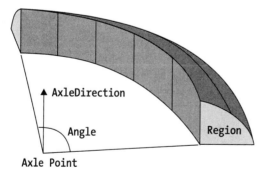

*Figure 9-11. Revolved solid*

The following example lets the user choose a closed region, which is then revolved into a solid based on user input:

```
Public Sub TestAddRevolvedSolid()
    Dim objShape As AcadLWPolyline
    Dim varPick As Variant
    Dim objEnt As AcadEntity
    Dim varPnt1 As Variant
    Dim dblOrigin(2) As Double
    Dim varVec As Variant
    Dim dblAngle As Double
    Dim objEnts() As AcadEntity
    Dim varRegions As Variant
    Dim varItem As Variant

    '' set default viewpoint
    SetViewpoint

    '' draw the shape and get rotation from user
    With ThisDrawing.Utility

        '' pick a shape
On Error Resume Next
        .GetEntity objShape, varPick, "pick a polyline shape"
        If Err Then
            MsgBox "You did not pick the correct type of shape"
            Exit Sub
        End If
On Error GoTo Done

        objShape.Closed = True

        '' add pline to region input array
        ReDim objEnts(0)
        Set objEnts(0) = objShape

        '' get the axis points
        .InitializeUserInput 1
        varPnt1 = .GetPoint(, vbLf & "Pick an origin of revolution: ")
        .InitializeUserInput 1
        varVec = .GetPoint(dblOrigin, vbLf & _
            "Indicate the axis of revolution: ")
```

```
            '' get the angle to revolve
            .InitializeUserInput 1
            dblAngle = .GetAngle(, vbLf & "Angle to revolve: ")
        End With

    '' make the region, then revolve it into a solid
    With ThisDrawing.ModelSpace

        '' make region from closed pline
        varRegions = .AddRegion(objEnts)

        '' revolve solid about axis
        Set objEnt = .AddRevolvedSolid(varRegions(0), varPnt1, varVec, _
                dblAngle)
        objEnt.Color = acRed
    End With

Done:
    If Err Then MsgBox Err.Description
    '' delete the temporary geometry
    For Each varItem In objEnts:  varItem.Delete:  Next
    If Not IsEmpty(varRegions) Then
        For Each varItem In varRegions:  varItem.Delete:  Next
    End If

    ThisDrawing.SendCommand "_shade" & vbCr
End Sub
```

# Editing Solids

You may combine and edit individual 3DSolid objects to form new, more complex 3DSolid objects. You may perform operations to combine solids, subtract one solid from another, and find the common intersection between solids. You can use other methods to create sections and slices of individual solids. In each of this section's examples, you call the ORBIT command so that the user can view the resultant solids from whatever angle desired.

## Boolean Operations

You perform the primary editing operations using the Boolean method (see Table 9-12 for parameter details). This method, whose name is derived from its algebraic nature, alters the solid according to the Operation parameter:

```
3DSolidObject.Boolean(Operation, SolidObject)
```

*Table 9-12. Boolean Method Parameters*

| NAME | DATA TYPE | DESCRIPTION |
| --- | --- | --- |
| Operation | Long | The type of operation that takes place. It must be one of the AcBooleanType constants: acUnion, acIntersection, or acSubtraction. |
| SolidObject | 3DSolid object | The object the Boolean operation is performed against. |

This method is destructive to the solid passed in the SolidObject parameter—that is, the 3DSolid object passed to this method is destroyed during the combination with the calling object.

 **NOTE**   *If you specify the* Intersection *operation and the object passed in the* SolidObject *parameter doesn't spatially intersect the calling object, both* 3DSolid *objects are destroyed.*

The following example combines selected solids using the Boolean operation specified. Try it out on some of the solids you created in the preceding examples.

```
Public Sub TestBoolean()
    Dim objFirst As Acad3DSolid
    Dim objSecond As Acad3DSolid
    Dim varPick As Variant
    Dim strOp As String

On Error Resume Next
    With ThisDrawing.Utility

        '' get first solid from user
        .GetEntity objFirst, varPick, vbCr & "Pick a solid to edit: "
        If Err Then
            MsgBox "That is not an Acad3DSolid"
            Exit Sub
        End If
```

```
         '' highlight entity
         objFirst.Highlight True
         objFirst.Update

         '' get second solid from user
         .GetEntity objSecond, varPick, vbCr & "Pick a solid to combine: "
         If Err Then
             MsgBox "That is not an Acad3DSolid"
             Exit Sub
         End If

         '' exit if they're the same
         If objFirst Is objSecond Then
             MsgBox "You must pick 2 different solids"
             Exit Sub
         End If

         '' highlight entity
         objSecond.Highlight True
         objSecond.Update

         '' get boolean operation
         .InitializeUserInput 1, "Intersect Subtract Union"
         strOp = .GetKeyword(vbCr & _
                             "Boolean operation [Intersect/Subtract/Union]: ")

         '' combine the solids
         Select Case strOp
         Case "Intersect": objFirst.Boolean acIntersection, objSecond
         Case "Subtract": objFirst.Boolean acSubtraction, objSecond
         Case "Union": objFirst.Boolean acUnion, objSecond
         End Select

         '' highlight entity
         objFirst.Highlight False
         objFirst.Update
    End With

    '' shade the view, and start the interactive orbit command
    ThisDrawing.SendCommand "_shade" & vbCr & "_orbit" & vbCr
End Sub
```

# Interference Operation

You can use another, nondestructive operation to deal with the common space shared by 3DSolid objects. The CheckInterference method (see Table 9-13 for parameter details) calculates the common space between the calling solid and a second object passed to it. It optionally creates and returns a new 3DSolid object.

```
[Set 3DSolidObject =] 3DSolidObject.CheckInterference(SolidObject, _
CreateInterferenceSolid)
```

*Table 9-13. CheckInterference Method Parameters*

| NAME | DATA TYPE | DESCRIPTION |
|------|-----------|-------------|
| SolidObject | 3DSolid object | The object that is checked against. |
| CreateInterferenceSolid | Boolean | Specifies whether a solid representing the interference of the two solids should be created. If it is set to True, the interference solid is created. |

The following example combines selected solids using this method. Compare its results to the Boolean operators used in the last example:

```
Public Sub TestInterference()
    Dim objFirst As Acad3DSolid
    Dim objSecond As Acad3DSolid
    Dim objNew As Acad3DSolid
    Dim varPick As Variant
    Dim varNewPnt As Variant

On Error Resume Next
    '' set default viewpoint
    SetViewpoint

    With ThisDrawing.Utility

        '' get first solid from user
        .GetEntity objFirst, varPick, vbCr & "Pick the first solid: "
```

```
If Err Then
    MsgBox "That is not an Acad3DSolid"
    Exit Sub
End If


'' highlight entity
objFirst.Highlight True
objFirst.Update


'' get second solid from user
.GetEntity objSecond, varPick, vbCr & "Pick the second solid: "
If Err Then
    MsgBox "That is not an Acad3DSolid"
    Exit Sub
End If


'' exit if they're the same
If objFirst Is objSecond Then
    MsgBox "You must pick 2 different solids"
    Exit Sub
End If


'' highlight entity
objSecond.Highlight True
objSecond.Update

'' combine the solids
Set objNew = objFirst.CheckInterference(objSecond, True)
If objNew Is Nothing Then
    MsgBox "Those solids don't intersect"
Else
    '' highlight new solid
    objNew.Highlight True
    objNew.Color = acWhite
    objNew.Update

    '' move new solid
    .InitializeUserInput 1
    varNewPnt = .GetPoint(varPick, vbCr & "Pick a new location: ")
    objNew.Move varPick, varNewPnt
End If
```

```
            '' dehighlight entities
            objFirst.Highlight False
            objFirst.Update
            objSecond.Highlight False
            objSecond.Update
        End With

        '' shade the view, and start the interactive orbit command
        ThisDrawing.SendCommand "_shade" & vbCr & "_orbit" & vbCr
    End Sub
```

## Slicing Solids

Use the SliceSolid method (see Table 9-14 for parameter details) to allow 3DSolid objects to be sliced by an arbitrary plane. This plane, defined by three WCS points, destructively cuts the solid into a front and optional back half. If the back half is desired, then this method returns a new 3DSolid object.

```
Set 3DSolidObject = 3DSolidObject.SliceSolid(PlanePoint1, _
PlanePoint2, PlanePoint3, Negative)
```

*Table 9-14. SliceSolid Method Parameters*

| NAME | DATA TYPE | DESCRIPTION |
| --- | --- | --- |
| PlanePoint1 | Variant | A three-element array of doubles specifying a point in the slice plane. |
| PlanePoint2 | Variant | A three-element array of doubles specifying another point in the slice plane. |
| PlanePoint3 | Variant | A three-element array of doubles specifying a third point in the slice plane. |
| Negative | Boolean | A parameter controlling the return of the slice on the negative side of the plane. If it is False, no object is returned, and the back half of the slice is discarded. If it is True, the method returns the back half. In both cases, the calling object retains the front half. |

The following example slices a selected solid and moves the new back half to another location. It might be quite difficult to choose three points that define a plane that slices through your selected object, but using overrides such as Near and Perpendicular should make this easier. Try it on some of the solids you created in the chapter's previous examples.

```
Public Sub TestSliceSolid()
        Dim objFirst As Acad3DSolid
        Dim objSecond As Acad3DSolid
        Dim objNew As Acad3DSolid
        Dim varPick As Variant
        Dim varPnt1 As Variant
        Dim varPnt2 As Variant
        Dim varPnt3 As Variant
        Dim strOp As String
        Dim blnOp As Boolean


On Error Resume Next
    With ThisDrawing.Utility

        '' get first solid from user
        .GetEntity objFirst, varPick, vbCr & "Pick a solid to slice: "
        If Err Then
            MsgBox "That is not a 3DSolid"
            Exit Sub
        End If

        '' highlight entity
        objFirst.Highlight True
        objFirst.Update

        .InitializeUserInput 1
        varPnt1 = .GetPoint(varPick, vbCr & "Pick first slice point: ")
        .InitializeUserInput 1
        varPnt2 = .GetPoint(varPnt1, vbCr & "Pick second slice point: ")
        .InitializeUserInput 1
        varPnt3 = .GetPoint(varPnt2, vbCr & "Pick last slice point: ")

        '' section the solid
        Set objNew = objFirst.SliceSolid(varPnt1, varPnt2, varPnt3, True)
        If objNew Is Nothing Then
            MsgBox "Couldn't slice using those points"
        Else
```

```
        '' highlight new solid
        objNew.Highlight False
        objNew.Color = objNew.Color + 1
        objNew.Update

        '' move section region to new location
        .InitializeUserInput 1
        varPnt2 = .GetPoint(varPnt1, vbCr & "Pick a new location: ")
        objNew.Move varPnt1, varPnt2
    End If
  End With

  '' shade the view
  ThisDrawing.SendCommand "_shade" & vbCr
End Sub
```

## Sectioning Solids

The SectionSolid method (see Table 9-15 for parameter details) creates a new Region object defined by the intersection of a 3DSolid object and an arbitrary plane. The plane is defined by three WCS points.

```
Set RegionObject = 3DSolidObject.SectionSolid (PlanePoint1, _
PlanePoint2, PlanePoint3)
```

*Table 9-15. SectionSolid Method Parameters*

| NAME | DATA TYPE | DESCRIPTION |
|---|---|---|
| PlanePoint1 | Variant | A three-element array of doubles specifying a point in the intersection plane |
| PlanePoint2 | Variant | A three-element array of doubles specifying another point in the intersection plane |
| PlanePoint3 | Variant | A three-element array of doubles specifying a third point in the intersection plane |

The following example sections a selected solid and moves the new region to another location. Remember to use object snap overrides such as Near and

Perpendicular when you define the section plane. Try it on some of the solids you created earlier in this chapter.

```
Public Sub TestSectionSolid()
        Dim objFirst As Acad3DSolid
        Dim objSecond As Acad3DSolid
        Dim objNew As AcadRegion
        Dim varPick As Variant
        Dim varPnt1 As Variant
        Dim varPnt2 As Variant
        Dim varPnt3 As Variant


On Error Resume Next

    With ThisDrawing.Utility
        '' get first solid from user
        .GetEntity objFirst, varPick, vbCr & "Pick a solid to section: "
        If Err Then
            MsgBox "That is not an Acad3DSolid"
            Exit Sub
        End If

        '' highlight entity
        objFirst.Highlight True
        objFirst.Update

        .InitializeUserInput 1
        varPnt1 = .GetPoint(varPick, vbCr & "Pick first section point: ")
        .InitializeUserInput 1
        varPnt2 = .GetPoint(varPnt1, vbCr & "Pick second section point: ")
        .InitializeUserInput 1
        varPnt3 = .GetPoint(varPnt2, vbCr & "Pick last section point: ")

        '' section the solid
        Set objNew = objFirst.SectionSolid(varPnt1, varPnt2, varPnt3)
        If objNew Is Nothing Then
            MsgBox "Couldn't section using those points"
        Else
            '' highlight new solid
            objNew.Highlight False
            objNew.Color = acWhite
            objNew.Update
```

```
          '' move section region to new location
          .InitializeUserInput 1
          varPnt2 = .GetPoint(varPnt1, vbCr & "Pick a new location: ")
          objNew.Move varPnt1, varPnt2
      End If


      '' dehighlight entities
      objFirst.Highlight False
      objFirst.Update
  End With


  '' shade the view
  ThisDrawing.SendCommand "_shade" & vbCr
End Sub
```

## Analyzing Solids: Mass Properties

Each 3DSolid object has a number of mass properties that you can use for analysis. These properties include the center of gravity, the total volume of the solid, the radii of gyration, the product of inertia, and the moment of inertia.

The following example displays the mass properties for a selected solid. Try it on one of the solids you created earlier in the chapter.

```
Public Sub TestMassProperties()
    Dim objEnt As Acad3DSolid
    Dim varPick As Variant
    Dim strMassProperties As String
    Dim varProperty As Variant
    Dim intI As Integer

On Error Resume Next
    '' let user pick a solid
    With ThisDrawing.Utility
        .GetEntity objEnt, varPick, vbCr & "Pick a solid: "
        If Err Then
            MsgBox "That is not an Acad3DSolid"
            Exit Sub
        End If
    End With
```

```
'' format mass properties
With objEnt
    strMassProperties = "Volume: "
    strMassProperties = strMassProperties & vbCr & "     " & .Volume
    strMassProperties = strMassProperties & vbCr & vbCr & _
                        "Center Of Gravity: "
    For Each varProperty In .Centroid
        strMassProperties = strMassProperties & vbCr & "     "_
                        & varProperty
    Next
    strMassProperties = strMassProperties & vbCr & vbCr & _
                        "Moment Of Inertia: "
    For Each varProperty In .MomentOfInertia
        strMassProperties = strMassProperties & vbCr & "     " & _
                        varProperty
    Next
    strMassProperties = strMassProperties & vbCr & vbCr & _
                        "Product Of Inertia: "
    For Each varProperty In .ProductOfInertia
        strMassProperties = strMassProperties & vbCr & "     " & _
                        varProperty
    Next
    strMassProperties = strMassProperties & vbCr & vbCr & _
                        "Principal Moments: "
    For Each varProperty In .PrincipalMoments
        strMassProperties = strMassProperties & vbCr & "     " & _
                        varProperty
    Next
    strMassProperties = strMassProperties & vbCr & vbCr & _
                        "Radii Of Gyration: "
    For Each varProperty In .RadiiOfGyration
        strMassProperties = strMassProperties & vbCr & "     " & _
                        varProperty
    Next
    strMassProperties = strMassProperties & vbCr & vbCr & _
                        "Principal Directions: "
    For intI = 0 To UBound(.PrincipalDirections) / 3
        strMassProperties = strMassProperties & vbCr & "     (" & _
                        .PrincipalDirections((intI - 1) * 3) & ", " & _
                        .PrincipalDirections((intI - 1) * 3 + 1) & "," & _
                        .PrincipalDirections((intI - 1) * 3 + 2) & ")"
    Next

End With
```

```
        '' highlight entity
        objEnt.Highlight True
        objEnt.Update

        '' display properties
        MsgBox strMassProperties, , "Mass Properties"

        '' dehighlight entity
        objEnt.Highlight False
        objEnt.Update
End Sub
```

## Summary

In this chapter you've learned how to create each of the simple solid primitives.
You've considered how you can use planar figures to create more free-form solid
entities by extruding and revolving regions. You've also examined how you can
combine existing solids to create sophisticated shapes, and how to section and
slice those shapes.

# CHAPTER 10

# Editing Objects

AutoCAD GIVES YOU PLENTY of methods and properties so you can edit drawing objects, which you'd normally have to do in the AutoCAD interface. By employing these methods and properties, you can adapt and combine editing tasks in macros and VBA applications as needed.

This chapter considers editing objects, first through their methods and then through their properties. Specifically, this chapter covers:

- Copying, deleting, exploding, highlighting, mirroring, moving, offsetting, rotating, and scaling objects

- Working with polar and rectangular arrays

- Changing the color, layer, linetype, and visibility of objects

Whenever you modify an object in your code, the changes to the drawing don't appear until you call the object's `Update` method, the `Application` object's `Update` method, or the `Document` object's `Regen` method. In some cases, AutoCAD updates the display when your macro or program is complete, but it is safest for your code to force the update. This chapter's examples use the modified object's `Update` method to update the drawing display:

```
DrawingObject.Update
```

## Editing with Methods

AutoCAD VBA editing methods edit differently from properties. Methods generally change an entity's the shape, size, and position or create a new entity based on the original. Properties, on the other hand, tend to change the appearance of the object boundary lines, which represent the objects on the screen or on the plotter.

Unlike Visual LISP, VBA provides no equivalent functions for (vlax-method-applicable-p) for making sure an object exposes a specific method. For this reason, for each object against which you want to invoke a method, be sure that the object supports the method you are using. Your best tools for this are error trapping and error handling.

## Copying Objects

Use the Copy method to copy an existing drawing object. The new object occupies the same position as the original object and is drawn on top of all other objects. This method has the following syntax:

```
Set DrawingObject = DrawingObject.Copy
```

The following code asks the user to pick a drawing object from the screen. It then copies the object and moves it to a point the user chooses.

```
Public Sub CopyObject()
      Dim objDrawingObject As AcadEntity
      Dim objCopiedObject As Object
      Dim varEntityPickedPoint As Variant
      Dim varCopyPoint As Variant

On Error Resume Next
    ThisDrawing.Utility.GetEntity objDrawingObject, varEntityPickedPoint, _
        "Pick an entity to copy: "
    If objDrawingObject Is Nothing Then
        MsgBox "You did not pick an object"
        Exit Sub
    End If

    'Copy the object
    Set objCopiedObject = objDrawingObject.Copy()
    varCopyPoint = ThisDrawing.Utility.GetPoint(, "Pick point to copy to: ")

    'put the object in its new position
    objCopiedObject.Move varEntityPickedPoint, varCopyPoint
    objCopiedObject.Update

End Sub
```

# Deleting Objects

To remove an object from a drawing, use the `Delete` method, which has the following simple syntax:

```
Object.Delete
```

Many AutoCAD objects expose this method. For full details, see Appendix A. The following example shows how to implement this method:

```
Public Sub DeleteObject()
    Dim objDrawingObject As AcadEntity
    Dim varEntityPickedPoint As Variant

On Error Resume Next
    ThisDrawing.Utility.GetEntity objDrawingObject, varEntityPickedPoint, _
    "Pick an entity to delete: "
    If objDrawingObject Is Nothing Then
        MsgBox "You did not pick an object."
        Exit Sub
    End If

    'delete the object
    objDrawingObject.Delete

End Sub
```

The Erase method is similar to the Delete method, except it erases only selectionset groups. You can't use it to delete objects.

# Exploding Objects

Use the `Explode` method to break a compound object into its subentities. It returns an array of objects that hold references to these subentities. This might mean breaking a block reference into its constituent drawing objects or a polyline into its individual straight-line polylines. Block insertions leave the original block object behind, and the resulting exploded set of entities is actually a copy of each original nested entity in the block insertion. To produce behavior similar to the AutoCAD EXPLODE command, also delete the original Block insertion entity. This method has the following syntax:

```
varObjectArray = Object.Explode
```

The 3DPoly, BlockRef, LightweightPolyline, MInsertBlock, PolygonMesh, Polyline, and Region objects expose this method.

This code example asks the user to choose a Region object. It then explodes the object and displays a message box that lists the types of the objects into which it was exploded.

```
Public Sub ExplodeRegion()
      Dim objDrawingObject As AcadEntity
      Dim varEntityPickedPoint As Variant

On Error Resume Next
    ThisDrawing.Utility.GetEntity objDrawingObject, varEntityPickedPoint, _
                               "Please pick a region object."
    If objDrawingObject Is Nothing Or _
       objDrawingObject.ObjectName <> "AcDbRegion" Then
       MsgBox "You did not choose a region object."
       Exit Sub
    End If

Dim varObjectArray As Variant
Dim strObjectTypes As String
Dim intCount As Integer

    varObjectArray = objDrawingObject.Explode
    strObjectTypes = "The region you chose has been exploded " & _
            "into the following: " & UBound(varObjectArray) + 1 & " objects:"
    For intCount = 0 To UBound(varObjectArray)
        strObjectTypes = strObjectTypes & vbCrLf & _
                          varObjectArray(intCount).ObjectName
    Next
    MsgBox strObjectTypes

End Sub
```

 **NOTE** *In AutoCAD versions before AutoCAD 2004, the Explode method exploded nested MText entities in Block insertions, resulting in individual Text entities. In AutoCAD 2004, the Explode method preserves nested MText entities as MText.*

## Highlighting Entities

Use the `Highlight` method to set whether an entity is highlighted in the drawing editor window. Changes to an entity's highlight become effective only when you update or regenerate the entity. You can apply this method to drawing entities and the `Group` and `SelectionSet` objects. This method has the following syntax:

```
Object.Highlight Highlighted
```

This method's Highlighted parameter, a `Boolean`, indicates whether to highlight the object (`True`) or not (`False`).

The following example illustrates the `Highlight` method in action. It asks the user to choose a selection of objects from the drawing area. It then highlights and un-highlights each of these objects.

```
Public Sub ToggleHighlight()
    Dim objSelectionSet As AcadSelectionSet
    Dim objDrawingObject As AcadEntity

    'choose a selection set name that you only use as temporary storage and
    'ensure that it does not currently exist
    On Error Resume Next
    ThisDrawing.SelectionSets("TempSSet").Delete
    Set objSelectionSet = ThisDrawing.SelectionSets.Add("TempSSet")

    'ask user to pick entities on the screen
    objSelectionSet.SelectOnScreen

    'change the highlight status of each entity selected
    For Each objDrawingObject In objSelectionSet
        objDrawingObject.Highlight True
        objDrawingObject.Update
        MsgBox "Notice that the entity is highlighted"
        objDrawingObject.Highlight (False)
        objDrawingObject.Update
        MsgBox "Notice that the entity is not highlighted"
    Next

    ` objSelectionSet.Delete

End Sub
```

## *Mirroring Objects*

Use the `Mirror` method to create an object that is the mirror image of an existing planar object. This method has the following syntax:

```
Set DrawingObject = DrawingObject.Mirror(Point1, Point2)
```

Table 10-1 explains this method's parameters.

*Table 10-1.* `Mirror` *method parameters*

| NAME | DATA TYPE | DESCRIPTION |
| --- | --- | --- |
| Point1 | Variant | A three-element array of doubles specifying the 3-D WCS coordinates of a point on the mirror axis. |
| Point2 | Variant | A three-element array of doubles specifying the 3-D WCS coordinates of a second point on the mirror axis. |

The following code lets the user choose a selection of objects and a mirror axis, and then mirrors the objects around that axis.

```
Public Sub MirrorObjects()
    Dim objSelectionSet As AcadSelectionSet
    Dim objDrawingObject As AcadEntity
    Dim objMirroredObject As AcadEntity
    Dim varPoint1 As Variant
    Dim varPoint2 As Variant

    ThisDrawing.SetVariable "MIRRTEXT", 0

    'choose a selection set name that you only use as temporary storage and
    'ensure that it does not currently exist
    On Error Resume Next
    ThisDrawing.SelectionSets("TempSSet").Delete
    Set objSelectionSet = ThisDrawing.SelectionSets.Add("TempSSet")

    'ask user to pick entities on the screen
    ThisDrawing.Utility.Prompt "Pick objects to be mirrored." & vbCrLf
    objSelectionSet.SelectOnScreen
```

```
'change the highlight status of each entity selected
    varPoint1 = ThisDrawing.Utility.GetPoint(, _
        "Select a point on the mirror axis")
    varPoint2 = ThisDrawing.Utility.GetPoint(varPoint1, _
        "Select a point on the mirror axis")

    For Each objDrawingObject In objSelectionSet
        Set objMirroredObject = objDrawingObject.Mirror(varPoint1, varPoint2)
        objMirroredObject.Update
    Next

    objSelectionSet.Delete

End Sub
```

Note that the MIRRTEXT system variable has been set to 0. This setting mirrors text objects to the appropriate place on the drawing, but does not mirror the text itself, as shown in Figure 10-1. The default value of MIRRTEXT in AutoCAD 2004 is 0, but it defaulted to 1 in earlier versions of AutoCAD. If you set MIRRTEXT to 1, the text gets mirrored just as any other object. See Figure 10-1.

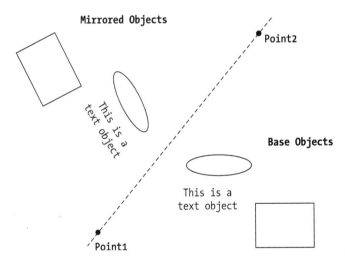

*Figure 10-1. Mirrored objects*

Use the `Mirror3D` method to reflect an object in a plane, where the new object lies outside the plane of the original object.

```
Set DrawingObject = DrawingObject.Mirror3D(PlanePoint1, PlanePoint2, PlanePoint3)
```

Table 10-2 explains this method's parameters.

*Table 10-2. `Mirror 3D` method parameters*

| NAME | DATA TYPE | DESCRIPTION |
|---|---|---|
| PlanePoint1 | Variant | A three-element array of doubles specifying the 3-D WCS coordinates of a point in the mirror plane. |
| PlanePoint2 | Variant | A three-element array of doubles specifying the 3-D WCS coordinates of a second point in the mirror plane. |
| PlanePoint3 | Variant | A three-element array of doubles specifying the 3-D WCS coordinates of a third point defining the mirror plane. |

Figure 10-2 shows an object reflected on a plane.

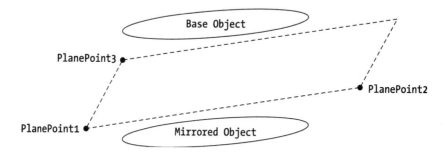

*Figure 10-2. A 3-D mirrored object*

The code below adds a new drawing object that reflects the base object around the WCS XY plane.

```
Public Sub MirrorObjectinXYplane()
    Dim objDrawingObject As AcadEntity
```

```
        Dim varEntityPickedPoint As Variant
        Dim objMirroredObject As AcadEntity
        Dim dblPlanePoint1(2) As Double
        Dim dblPlanePoint2(2) As Double
        Dim dblPlanePoint3(2) As Double

On Error Resume Next
    ThisDrawing.Utility.GetEntity objDrawingObject, varEntityPickedPoint, _
                                "Please an entity to reflect: "
    If objDrawingObject Is Nothing Then
        MsgBox "You did not choose an object"
        Exit Sub
    End If

    'set plane of reflection to be the XY plane
    dblPlanePoint2(0) = 1#
    dblPlanePoint3(1) = 1#

    objDrawingObject.Mirror3D dblPlanePoint1, dblPlanePoint2, dblPlanePoint3

End Sub
```

## Moving Objects

Use the Move method to perform three-dimensional translations on drawing objects. This method has the following syntax:

```
DrawingObject.Move Point1, Point2
```

Table 10-3 explains this method's parameters:

*Table 10-3. Move method parameters*

| NAME | DATA TYPE | DESCRIPTION |
|---|---|---|
| Point1 | Variant | A three-element array of doubles specifying the 3-D WCS coordinates of the translation vector's starting point. |
| Point2 | Variant | A three-element array of doubles specifying the 3-D WCS coordinates of the translation vector's ending point. |

Figure 10-3 shows an object moved from one place to another.

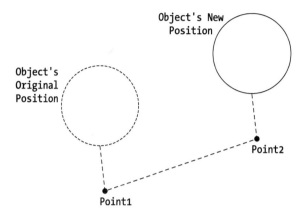

*Figure 10-3. A moved object*

The following example shows how to implement this method. The user first picks a selection of objects to be moved and specifies the translation vector on the screen.

```
Public Sub MoveObjects()
    Dim varPoint1 As Variant
    Dim varPoint2 As Variant
    Dim objSelectionSet As AcadSelectionSet
    Dim objDrawingObject As AcadEntity

    'choose a selection set name that you only use as temporary storage and
    'ensure that it does not currently exist
    On Error Resume Next
    ThisDrawing.SelectionSets("TempSSet").Delete
    Set objSelectionSet = ThisDrawing.SelectionSets.Add("TempSSet")

    'ask user to pick entities on the screen
    objSelectionSet.SelectOnScreen
```

```
varPoint1 = ThisDrawing.Utility.GetPoint(, vbCrLf _
    & "Base point of displacement: ")
varPoint2 = ThisDrawing.Utility.GetPoint(varPoint1, vbCrLf _
    & "Second point of displacement: ")

'move the selection of entities
For Each objDrawingObject In objSelectionSet
 objDrawingObject.Move varPoint1, varPoint2
 objDrawingObject.Update
Next

objSelectionSet.Delete

End Sub
```

## Offsetting Objects

The Offset method creates a new object with boundaries offset a specified distance from an existing object's boundaries. You can apply this method to the Arc, Circle, Ellipse, Line, LightweightPolyline, Polyline, Spline, and Xline objects. This method returns an array of the newly created object(s). Even though this array frequently contains only one object of the same type as the object from which it is offset, this is not always this case, as seen in the example below.

```
varObjectArray = Object.Offset(OffsetDistance)
```

This method has one parameter, OffsetDistance, a double. It's a non-zero number that indicates the offset's size and direction. Negative numbers mean that the offset makes the new object smaller than the original. If this has no meaning, as for a single straight line, a negative number positions the new object closer to the WCS origin.

In Figure 10-4, the center object is an Ellipse from which the two other objects have been offset. You can see that the new objects are not Ellipses as each point of each new object is the same distance from the original Ellipse. In these cases, the returned object is a Spline. In this example, the negative offset must be greater than –50.

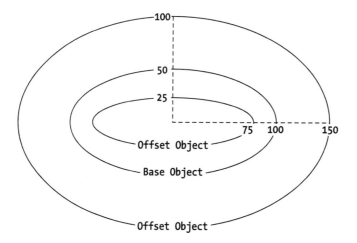

*Figure 10-4. Offset objects*

The following code sample creates the Ellipse and Splines in Figure 10-4 and shows the user a message box of the new objects' types.

```
Public Sub OffsetEllipse()
     Dim objEllipse As AcadEllipse
     Dim varObjectArray As Variant
     Dim dblCenter(2) As Double
     Dim dblMajor(2) As Double

     dblMajor(0) = 100#
     Set objEllipse = ThisDrawing.ModelSpace.AddEllipse(dblCenter, dblMajor, _
                                               0.5)

     varObjectArray = objEllipse.Offset(50)
     MsgBox "The offset object is a " & varObjectArray(0).ObjectName

     varObjectArray = objEllipse.Offset(-25)
     MsgBox "The offset object is a " & varObjectArray(0).ObjectName

End Sub
```

**NOTE** *For the sake of accuracy, when you consider that offsetting an* Ellipse *creates non-elliptical* Spline *entities, instead consider creating new* Ellipse *entities with calculated geometry. This produces accurate* Ellipse *entities instead of approximated elliptical* Splines. *The same is true for offsetting* Spline *or curve-fitted* Polyline *or* LightweightPolyline *entities.*

## Rotating Objects

Use the Rotate method to rotate a drawing object around a given point in the User Coordinate System's (UCS) XY plane. This method has the following syntax:

```
DrawingObject.Rotate BasePoint, RotationAngle
```

Table 10-4 explains this method's parameters:

*Table 10-4.* Rotate *method parameters*

| NAME | DATA TYPE | DESCRIPTION |
|------|-----------|-------------|
| BasePoint | Variant | A three-element array of doubles that specifies the 3-D WCS coordinates of the point through which the axis of rotation, parallel to the Z-axis of the UCS, passes. |
| RotationAngle | Double | The angle of rotation given in radians and measured counterclockwise from the UCS's X-axis. |

Figure 10-5 shows a rotated object.

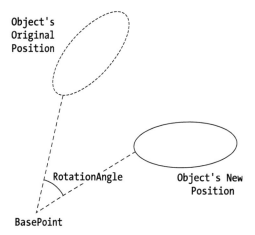

*Figure 10-5. A rotated object*

The following sample rotates an object based on user input.

```
Public Sub RotateObject()
    Dim objDrawingObject As AcadEntity
    Dim varEntityPickedPoint As Variant
    Dim varBasePoint As Variant
    Dim dblRotationAngle As Double


On Error Resume Next
    ThisDrawing.Utility.GetEntity objDrawingObject, varEntityPickedPoint, _
                                "Please pick an entity to rotate: "
    If objDrawingObject Is Nothing Then
        MsgBox "You did not choose an object."
        Exit Sub
    End If
    varBasePoint = ThisDrawing.Utility.GetPoint(, _
                "Enter a base point for the rotation.")
    dblRotationAngle = ThisDrawing.Utility.GetReal( _
                    "Enter the rotation angle in degrees: ")
```

```
'convert to radians
dblRotationAngle = ThisDrawing.Utility. _
                    AngleToReal(CStr(dblRotationAngle), acDegrees)

'Rotate the object
objDrawingObject.Rotate varBasePoint, dblRotationAngle
objDrawingObject.Update

End Sub
```

Use the Rotate3D method to perform a three-dimensional rotation of an object around an axis. This method has the following syntax:

```
DrawingObject.Rotate3D AxisPoint1, AxisPoint2, RotationAngle
```

Table 10-5 explains this method's parameters.

*Table 10-5. Rotate 3D method parameters*

| NAME | DATA TYPE | DESCRIPTION |
| --- | --- | --- |
| AxisPoint1 | Variant | A three-element array of doubles that specifies the 3-D WCS coordinates of a point through which the axis of rotation passes. |
| AxisPoint2 | Variant | A three-element array of doubles that specifies the 3-D WCS coordinates of a second point through which the axis of rotation passes. |
| RotationAngle | Double | The angle of rotation given in radians and measured counterclockwise about the specified axis. |

Figure 10-6 shows an object rotated around an axis.

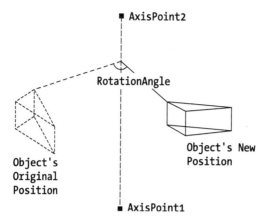

*Figure 10-6. An object rotated in 3-D*

The code example lets the user choose an object to rotate and the points that define the axis of rotation. It then rotates the object around that axis at an angle the user chooses.

```
Public Sub Rotate3DObject()
Dim objDrawingObject As AcadEntity
Dim varEntityPickedPoint As Variant
Dim objMirroredObject As AcadEntity
Dim varAxisPoint1 As Variant
Dim varAxisPoint2 As Variant
Dim dblRotationAxis As Double

On Error Resume Next
    ThisDrawing.Utility.GetEntity objDrawingObject, _
        varEntityPickedPoint, "Please an entity to rotate: "
    If objDrawingObject Is Nothing Then
        MsgBox "You did not choose an object"
        Exit Sub
    End If
```

```
'ask user for axis points and angle of rotation
varAxisPoint1 = ThisDrawing.Utility.GetPoint(, _
                            "Enter first point of axis of rotation: ")
varAxisPoint2 = ThisDrawing.Utility.GetPoint(, _
                            "Enter second point of axis of rotation: ")
dblRotationAxis = ThisDrawing.Utility.GetReal( _
                            "Enter angle of rotation in degrees")
'convert to radians
dblRotationAxis = ThisDrawing.Utility.AngleToReal(CStr(dblRotationAxis), _
                                        acDegrees)


objDrawingObject.Rotate3D varAxisPoint1, varAxisPoint2, dblRotationAxis

End Sub
```

## Scaling Objects

The ScaleEntity method scales a drawing object uniformly in all directions around a base point. This method has the following syntax:

```
DrawingObject.ScaleEntity BasePoint, ScaleFactor
```

Table 10-6 explains this method's parameters.

*Table 10-6. ScaleEntity method parameters*

| NAME | DATA TYPE | DESCRIPTION |
| --- | --- | --- |
| BasePoint | Variant | A three-element array of doubles that specifies the 3-D WCS coordinates of the scale's base point. |
| ScaleFactor | Double | A positive number that represents how much to scale the object relative to its current size. Each of the object's dimensions, measured from the base point, is multiplied by this parameter. A scale factor greater than 1 enlarges the object, while a scale factor less than 1 shrinks the object. |

Figure 10-7 shows a scaled object.

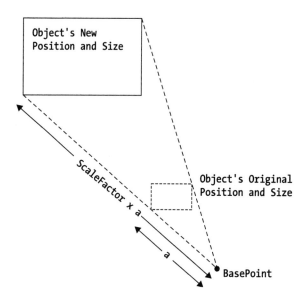

*Figure 10-7. A scaled object*

This example shows how to implement this method:

```
Public Sub ScaleObject()
    Dim objDrawingObject As AcadEntity
    Dim varEntityPickedPoint As Variant
    Dim varBasePoint As Variant
    Dim dblScaleFactor As Double

On Error Resume Next
    ThisDrawing.Utility.GetEntity objDrawingObject, varEntityPickedPoint, _
                            "Please pick an entity to scale: "
    If objDrawingObject Is Nothing Then
        MsgBox "You did not choose an object"
        Exit Sub
    End If

    varBasePoint = ThisDrawing.Utility.GetPoint(, _
                "Pick a base point for the scale:")
    dblScaleFactor = ThisDrawing.Utility.GetReal("Enter the scale factor: ")
```

```
        'Scale the object
        objDrawingObject.ScaleEntity varBasePoint, dblScaleFactor
        objDrawingObject.Update
End Sub
```

 **NOTE**    *There is no direct equivalent to the SCALE command's Reference option. AutoCAD performs those calculations for you. To mimic that functionality, you have to write the code that performs the calculations.*

# Object Arrays

Use the ArrayPolar and ArrayRectangular methods to create an array of objects based on an existing object. Both methods copy the base object into a regular pattern at a specified distance from one another.

## Creating a Polar Array of Objects

A polar array is a pattern of drawing objects lying on an arc's path. The ArrayPolar method creates a polar array, placing a specified number of objects over an angle. It returns an array of the new objects.

```
varObjectArray = DrawingObject.ArrayPolar (NumberofObjects, _
    AngleToFill, ArrayCenter)
```

Table 10-7 explains this method's parameters.

*Table 10-7. ArrayPolar method parameters*

| NAME | DATA TYPE | DESCRIPTION |
| --- | --- | --- |
| NumberofObjects | Long | The number of objects in the polar array. |
| AngleToFill | Double | A non-zero value representing the angle, measured counterclockwise in radians, over which the array path will extend. |
| ArrayCenter | Variant | A three-element array of doubles specifying the 3-D WCS coordinates of the arc's center. |

Always set the `NumberofObjects` parameter greater than 1. The original object is counted as an element of the polar array, even though this method doesn't return it in the object array. Consequently, the size of the object array is `NumberofObjects-1`. If you set `NumberofObjects` to 1, the method returns an empty array, but doesn't raise an error.

Figure 10-8 shows an ellipse arranged along an arc using the `ArrayPolar` method.

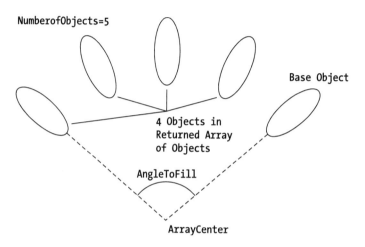

*Figure 10-8.* `ArrayPolar` *arrangement of ellipses*

The distance from the `ArrayCenter` to objects depends upon the object type. To specify the distance to the objects and the vector from which to measure the `AngleToFill`, use a circle or arc's center, a block or shape's insertion point, text's start point, or a line or trace's end point.

The following example shows how to implement this method. The objects returned in the array are red.

```
Public Sub CreatePolarArray()
    Dim objDrawingObject As AcadEntity
    Dim varEntityPickedPoint As Variant
    Dim varArrayCenter As Variant
    Dim lngNumberofObjects As Long
    Dim dblAngletoFill As Double
    Dim varPolarArray As Variant
    Dim intCount As Integer
```

```
On Error Resume Next
    ThisDrawing.Utility.GetEntity objDrawingObject, varEntityPickedPoint, _
                    "Please an entity to form the basis of a polar array"
    If objDrawingObject Is Nothing Then
        MsgBox "You did not choose an object"
        Exit Sub
    End If

    varArrayCenter = ThisDrawing.Utility.GetPoint(, _
                    "Pick the center of the array: ")
    lngNumberofObjects = ThisDrawing.Utility.GetInteger( _
                    "Enter total number of objects required in the array: ")
    dblAngletoFill = ThisDrawing.Utility.GetReal( _
            "Enter an angle (in degrees) over which the array should extend: ")
    dblAngletoFill = ThisDrawing.Utility.AngleToReal _
                    (CStr(dblAngletoFill), acDegrees)
    varPolarArray = objDrawingObject.ArrayPolar(lngNumberofObjects, _
                                    dblAngletoFill, varArrayCenter)

    For intCount = 0 To UBound(varPolarArray)
        varPolarArray(intCount).Color = acRed
        varPolarArray(intCount).Update
    Next

End Sub
```

 **NOTE**   *Unlike the AutoCAD ARRAY command, there is no ActiveX method available to control rotation of copied entities in polar arrays. You must handle that yourself through programming to rotate each copied entity appropriately along the array path's circumference.*

## Creating a Rectangular Array of Objects

A rectangular array is a grid pattern of drawing objects. This pattern may be two- or three-dimensional and you can construct it using the ArrayRectangular method. Just like the ArrayPolar method, this method returns an array of objects that hold a reference to the new drawing objects.

```
varObjectArray = DrawingObject.ArrayRectangular (NumberOfRows, _
NumberOfColumns, NumberOfLevels, DistBetweenRows, _
DistBetweenColumns, DistBetweenLevels)
```

Table 10-8 explains this methods parameters.

*Table 10-8. ArrayRectangular parameters*

| NAME | DATA TYPE | DESCRIPTION |
| --- | --- | --- |
| NumberofRows | Long | A positive number representing the number of rows in the rectangular array. If this parameter is set to 1, then NumberofColumns must be greater than 1. |
| NumberOfColumns | Long | A positive number representing the number of columns in the rectangular array. If this parameter is set to 1, then NumberofRows must be greater than 1. |
| NumberOfLevels | Long | A positive number representing the number of levels in a 3-D array. |
| DistBetweenRows | Double | The distance between the rows. If this parameter is positive, rows extend upwards from the base object; if negative they extend downwards. If set to zero, objects are placed on top of the base object. |
| DistBetweenColumns | Double | The distance between the columns. If this parameter is positive, rows extend upwards from the base object; if negative they extend downwards. If set to zero, objects are placed on top of the base object. |
| DistBetweenLevels | Double | The distance between the levels. If this parameter is positive, rows extend upwards from the base object; if negative they extend downwards. If set to zero, objects are placed on top of the base object. |

Figure 10-9 shows a two-dimensional rectangular array. A three-dimensional array is a simple extension of a two-dimensional array.

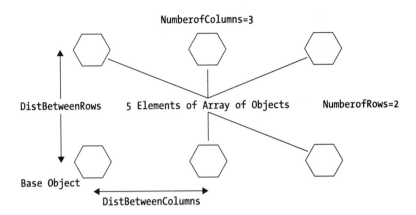

*Figure 10-9. Objects arranged with* ArrayRectangular

To create a two-dimensional array, set the NumberOfLevels parameters to 1, as shown the code example below. Again, the new objects are colored red.

```
Public Sub Create2DRectangularArray()
        Dim objDrawingObject As AcadEntity
        Dim varEntityPickedPoint As Variant
        Dim lngNoRows As Long
        Dim lngNoColumns As Long
        Dim dblDistRows As Long
        Dim dblDistCols As Long
        Dim varRectangularArray As Variant
        Dim intCount As Integer

On Error Resume Next
    ThisDrawing.Utility.GetEntity objDrawingObject, varEntityPickedPoint, _
            "Please pick an entity to form the basis of a rectangular array: "
    If objDrawingObject Is Nothing Then
        MsgBox "You did not choose an object"
        Exit Sub
    End If
```

```
        lngNoRows = ThisDrawing.Utility.GetInteger( _
                            "Enter the required number of rows: ")
        lngNoColumns = ThisDrawing.Utility.GetInteger( _
                            "Enter the required number of columns: ")
        dblDistRows = ThisDrawing.Utility.GetReal(_
                            "Enter the required distance between rows: ")
        dblDistCols = ThisDrawing.Utility.GetReal( _
                            "Enter the required distance between columns: ")


        varRectangularArray = objDrawingObject.ArrayRectangular(lngNoRows, _
                            lngNoColumns, 1, dblDistRows, dblDistCols, 0)
        For intCount = 0 To UBound(varRectangularArray)
            varRectangularArray(intCount).Color = acRed
            varRectangularArray(intCount).Update
        Next

End Sub
```

## Editing with Properties

Unlike the methods described above, you can use a drawing object's properties to modify the on-screen appearance of the lines that represent AutoCAD objects. The rest of this chapter covers some of the most commonly used properties.

### *Changing an Object's Color*

Use the Color property to read or set a drawing object's color. The Group and Layer objects also expose this property. Beginning with AutoCAD 2004, all objects have a new TrueColor property that supports the Color property. This new property uses RGB color values, Pantone color palettes, and color book values. This property has the following syntax:

```
Object.Color = lngColor
```

lngColor may be one of 257 colors, 9 of which are represented by the predefined AutoCAD AcColor constants detailed in Table 10-9.

*Table 10-9.* `AcColor contstants`

| CONSTANT | COLOR INDEX | COLOR |
|---|---|---|
| acByBlock | 0 | ByBlock |
| acRed | 1 | Red |
| acYellow | 2 | Yellow |
| acGreen | 3 | Green |
| acCyan | 4 | Cyan |
| acBlue | 5 | Blue |
| acMagenta | 6 | Magenta |
| acWhite | 7 | White/Black depending on the screen background color |
| acByLayer | 256 | ByLayer |

The following code changes the color of user-selected objects to green.

```
Public Sub ColorGreen()

    Dim objSelectionSet As AcadSelectionSet
    Dim objDrawingObject As AcadEntity

    'choose a selection set name that you only use as temporary storage and
    'ensure that it does not currently exist
    On Error Resume Next
    ThisDrawing.SelectionSets("TempSSet").Delete
    Set objSelectionSet = ThisDrawing.SelectionSets.Add("TempSSet")

    'ask user to pick entities on the screen
    objSelectionSet.SelectOnScreen

    For Each objDrawingObject In objSelectionSet
        objDrawingObject.Color = acGreen
        objDrawingObject.Update
    Next

    objSelectionSet.Delete

End Sub
```

## Changing an Object's TrueColor Property

AutoCAD 2004's TrueColor property lets you specify RGB color values, Pantone color palette values, and color book values. This is a vast improvement for users who need accurate color matching for precision rendering and presentation graphics. The following example shows how to create a new Line entity and assign it an RGB color value of 80, 100, 244. The figure below also shows how the new color palette options appear in AutoCAD 2004.

```
Sub Example_TrueColor()
    ' This example draws a line and returns the RGB values
    Dim color As AcadAcCmColor
    Set color = AcadApplication.GetInterfaceObject("AutoCAD.AcCmColor.16")
    Call color.SetRGB(80, 100, 244)

    Dim line As AcadLine
    Dim startPoint(0 To 2) As Double
    Dim endPoint(0 To 2) As Double

    startPoint(0) = 1#: startPoint(1) = 1#: startPoint(2) = 0#
    endPoint(0) = 5#: endPoint(1) = 5#: endPoint(2) = 0#

    Set line = ThisDrawing.ModelSpace.AddLine(startPoint, endPoint)
    ZoomAll

    line.TrueColor = color
    Dim retcolor As AcadAcCmColor
    Set retcolor = line.TrueColor

    MsgBox "Red = " & retcolor.Red & vbCrLf & _
    "Green = " & retcolor.Green & vbCrLf & _
    "Blue = " & retcolor.Blue
End Sub
```

The AutoCAD 2004 Developer's documentation gives more examples for using the TrueColor object.

## Changing an Object's Color Properties

The AcCmColor object represents colors. Use the AcCmColor object to set colors and perform other color-related operations on objects. This object belongs to the AutoCAD class AcadAcCmColor. Invoke this class using one of these two methods:

- GetInterfaceObject ("AutoCAD.AcCmColor.16")

- Dim col As New AcadAcCmColor

The object includes properties for colors, color names, color book names, and the color index. The following example shows how to invoke the SetColorBook method to use Pantone color books on a Circle entity.

```
Dim fColor As AcadAcCmColor
Set fColor = AcadApplication.GetInterfaceObject("AutoCAD.AcCmColor.16")
Call color.SetRGB(80, 100, 244)
Call fColor.SetColorBookColor("PANTONE Yellow", _
    "Pantone solid colors-uncoated.acb")
objCircle.TrueColor = fColor
```

The AutoCAD 2004 Developer's documentation gives more examples for using the AcCmColor object.

## Changing an Object's Layer

By changing a drawing or Group object's layer, any of the object's properties that are set to acByLayer change to reflect the new layer's attributes. Change an object's layer by setting its Layer property to the name of a different layer, as this syntax shows:

```
Object.Layer = strLayerName
```

The following code demonstrates the effects of changing a layer. It adds two circles to layer 0. The first circle is red, while the other circle's color is left at its default value of ByLayer. When the circles are moved to a new Layer, the first circle stays red, while the second adopts the new layer's color.

```
Public Sub ChangeLayer()
      Dim objNewLayer As AcadLayer
      Dim objCircle1 As AcadCircle
      Dim objCircle2 As AcadCircle
      Dim dblCenter1(2) As Double
```

```
      Dim dblCenter2(2) As Double
      dblCenter2(0) = 10#


'reference a layer called "New Layer" is it exists or
'add a new layer if it does not
Set objNewLayer = ThisDrawing.Layers.Add("New Layer")


objNewLayer.Color = acBlue


ThisDrawing.ActiveLayer = ThisDrawing.Layers("0")
Set objCircle1 = ThisDrawing.ModelSpace.AddCircle(dblCenter1, 10#)
Set objCircle2 = ThisDrawing.ModelSpace.AddCircle(dblCenter2, 10#)
objCircle1.Color = acRed
objCircle1.Update


objCircle1.Layer = "New Layer"
objCircle2.Layer = "New Layer"


End Sub
```

## Changing an Object's Linetype

To change the appearance of the lines that represent a drawing object on the screen, reset the object's Linetype property to the name of a Linetype object. This property also applies to the Group and Layer objects. This property has the following syntax:

```
Object.Linetype = strLinetypeName
```

This simple code sample sets an object's linetype to be continuous.

```
Public Sub ChangeLinetype()
    Dim objDrawingObject As AcadEntity
    Dim varEntityPickedPoint As Variant

On Error Resume Next
    ThisDrawing.Utility.GetEntity objDrawingObject, varEntityPickedPoint, _
                                "Please pick an object"
    If objDrawingObject Is Nothing Then
        MsgBox "You did not choose an object"
        Exit Sub
    End If
```

```
ThisDrawing.Utility.GetEntity objDrawingObject, varEntityPickedPoint, _
                                "Pick an entity to change linetype: "
objDrawingObject.Linetype = "Continuous"
objDrawingObject.Update

End Sub
```

---

**TIP**   *Always use strict error handling should someone assign a nonexistent linetype to an object. If you don't, your programs will crash. Chapter 6 covers* Linetype *objects in detail.*

---

## Changing an Object's Visibility

Use the Visible property to set whether a drawing object is visible or not. This method is also available to the Application, Group, and Toolbar objects, although for a group it is write-only. Set this property True to make an object visible and False to hide it. Making object invisible can be useful for performing complex entity creation or modification tasks. This property has the following syntax:

```
Object.Visible = blnVisible
```

The following example shows how to implement this method. It hides, and then makes visible, an object.

```
Public Sub ToggleVisibility()
    Dim objDrawingObject As AcadEntity
    Dim varEntityPickedPoint As Variant

On Error Resume Next
    ThisDrawing.Utility.GetEntity objDrawingObject, varEntityPickedPoint, _
                                "Choose an object to toggle visibility: "
    If objDrawingObject Is Nothing Then
        MsgBox "You did not choose an object"
        Exit Sub
    End If

  objDrawingObject.Visible = False
  objDrawingObject.Update
  MsgBox "The object was made invisible!"
```

```
objDrawingObject.Visible = True
objDrawingObject.Update
MsgBox "Now it is visible again!"

End Sub
```

 **NOTE**   *Other factors, such as whether the object's layer is frozen or turned off, can override this property.*

## The Update Method

This chapter and most of this book use the Update method extensively. It forces the AutoCAD graphics display engine to regenerate a specified object on the drawing screen. You need to do this often to accurately reflect changes made to objects.

## Summary

This chapter examined several methods and properties you use to edit drawing entities. The next chapter covers adding dimensions and annotations to AutoCAD drawings.

# CHAPTER 11

# Dimensions and Annotations

**ALTHOUGH AUTOCAD PROVIDES AN ENVIRONMENT** that allows users to make detailed and precise drawings, it's often necessary for users to incorporate further information. A typical user will add textual annotations and measurement annotations (dimensions) to a drawing for manufacturing, modeling, engineering, mapping, and surveying purposes, and to help clarify design intent. AutoCAD VBA provides a number of methods to help users create annotations and dimensions that they normally create through the AutoCAD application interface.

In this chapter you'll learn how to create dimensions and annotations and add them to your drawings. You'll also see how to set and use different text and dimension styles.

## Dimensions

You add dimension entities to drawings to show the dimension or size of different drawing elements. You can use them to measure angles, distances, and chords. In this section, you'll examine each of the seven different dimension objects in turn. First, however, you'll take a look at the DimStyle object, which you use to determine the appearance of dimensions, leaders, and geometric tolerances.

## *The DimStyle Object*

The DimStyle object represents a group of settings that determine the appearance of a dimension, tolerance, or leader. DimStyle objects are held in the DimStyles collection, and you may access them via the DimStyles collection's Item method.

To create a new DimStyle object through code, you need to use the Add method of the DimStyles collection:

```
Set DimStyleObject = DimStylesCollection.Add(DimStyleName)
```

Table 11-1 shows the Add method's parameter.

*Table 11-1. Add Method Parameter*

| NAME | DATA TYPE | DESCRIPTION |
| --- | --- | --- |
| DimStyleName | String | An identifying name for the new DimStyle object |

The following code shows how to add a new DimStyle object:

```
Dim objDimStyle As AcadDimStyle

Set objDimStyle = ThisDrawing.DimStyles.Add("NewDimStyle")
```

## Setting Dimension Styles

A DimStyle object that is newly created using the Add method inherits the dimension styles of the current active DimStyle object, regardless of any system variables settings that might be overriding the styles of the active DimStyle object. To set the styles for a DimStyle object, you need to set the system variables to reflect your required styles and then use the CopyFrom method explained in the next section.

### The CopyFrom Method

You use the CopyFrom method to copy to a DimStyle object a set of dimension styles from a dimension, tolerance, leader, document, or another DimStyle object.

```
DimStyleObject.CopyFrom SourceObject
```

The SourceObject parameter is the object whose dimension styles are copied. The styles copied depend upon the source object used, as shown in Table 11-2.

*Table 11-2. CopyFrom Method Parameters*

| OBJECT | STYLES COPIED |
| --- | --- |
| Dimension, Tolerance, Leader | The style for that object plus any object overrides |
| Document | The active dimension style settings for the drawing plus any drawing overrides |
| DimStyle | The style data from that dimension style but no drawing overrides |

The following code creates a new dimension style called NewDimStyle. This object inherits all the dimension style properties of the currently active dimension style, except that the color of dimension lines, extension lines, and dimension text is set to red, blue, and white, respectively.

```
Public Sub NewDimStyle
Dim objDimStyle As AcadDimStyle

    Set objDimStyle = ThisDrawing.DimStyles.Add("NewDimStyle")
    SetVariable "DIMCLRD", acRed
    SetVariable "DIMCLRE", acBlue
    SetVariable "DIMCLRT", acWhite
    SetVariable "DIMLWD ", acLnWtByLwDefault
    objDimStyle.CopyFrom ThisDrawing
End Sub
```

## Using Dimension Styles

You may associate a dimension style with a particular dimension object by setting its StyleName property, or you may set it to be the currently active style via the ActiveDimStyle property of the Document object. In the latter case, any objects created after the style is made active and not specifically associated with a different dimension style will adopt the style of the active DimStyle object.

**NOTE**  *No matter which property you use to set the dimension style for an object added to your drawing though code, the newly created object will not adopt any system variable overrides.*

### The StyleName Property

You use this property to set the dimension style associated with a dimension, tolerance, or leader. To set or change the DimStyle used, simply set or reset the value of this property.

```
Object.StyleName = DimStyleName
```

Table 11-3 shows the StyleName property's parameters.

*Table 11-3. StyleName Property Parameters*

| NAME | DATA TYPE | DESCRIPTION |
|------|-----------|-------------|
| Object | Dimension, Leader, or Tolerance object | The object to which the dimension style is linked |
| DimStyleName | String | The identifying name of the DimStyle object |

The following example asks the user to choose a dimension and changes the style of the dimension to one of the existing dimension styles. The StyleName property of the chosen object is then set appropriately.

```
Public Sub ChangeDimStyle()
Dim objDimension As AcadDimension
Dim varPickedPoint As Variant
Dim objDimStyle As AcadDimStyle
Dim strDimStyles As String
Dim strChosenDimStyle As String

On Error Resume Next
    ThisDrawing.Utility.GetEntity objDimension, varPickedPoint, _
                            "Pick a dimension whose style you wish to set"
    If objDimension Is Nothing Then
        MsgBox "You failed to pick a dimension object"
        Exit Sub
    End If

    For Each objDimStyle In ThisDrawing.DimStyles
        strDimStyles = strDimStyles & objDimStyle.Name & vbCrLf
    Next objDimStyle
    strChosenDimStyle = InputBox("Choose one of the following " & _
                        "Dimension styles to apply" & vbCrLf & strDimStyles)
    If strChosenDimStyle = "" Then Exit Sub

    objDimension.StyleName = strChosenDimStyle
End Sub
```

### The ActiveDimStyle Property

You use the `ActiveDimStyle` property to make a dimension style the default for any newly created dimension, tolerance, or leader objects. Unlike the `ActiveTextStyle` property, the `ActiveDimStyle` property doesn't affect any preexisting objects.

```
Set DocumentObject.ActiveDimStyle = DimStyleObject
```

Table 11-4 shows the `ActiveTextStyle` property's parameter.

*Table 11-4. ActiveDimStyle Property Parameter*

| NAME | DATA TYPE | DESCRIPTION |
|------|-----------|-------------|
| DimStyleObject | DimStyle object | The object holding the setting for the required dimension style |

The following code displays the current dimension style to the user and provides an opportunity for the user to change it:

```
Public Sub SetActiveDimStyle()
Dim strDimStyles As String
Dim strChosenDimStyle As String
Dim objDimStyle As AcadDimStyle

    For Each objDimStyle In ThisDrawing.DimStyles
        strDimStyles = strDimStyles & objDimStyle.Name & vbCrLf
    Next

    strChosenDimStyle = InputBox("Choose one of the following Dimension " & _
      styles:" & vbCr & vbCr & strDimStyles, "Existing Dimension style is: " _
      & ThisDrawing.ActiveDimStyle.Name, ThisDrawing.ActiveDimStyle.Name)
    If strChosenDimStyle = "" Then Exit Sub

On Error Resume Next
    ThisDrawing.ActiveDimStyle = ThisDrawing.DimStyles(strChosenDimStyle)
    If Err Then MsgBox "Dimension style was not recognized"
End Sub
```

## Creating Dimensions

Dimension objects are entities that provide information about distances and angles within an AutoCAD drawing. It makes sense, then, that just as for the drawing objects covered in Chapters 7 and 8, the AddDimXXX methods used to add dimensions to drawings are exposed by the ModelSpace, PaperSpace, and Block objects.

It's worth noting that not all properties of dimension entities are exposed through the ActiveX object model. For example, the dimension line control points of DimAligned objects are only available as DXF 13 and 14 codes. In addition, some dimension objects behave differently between AutoCAD 2002 and 2004, and I should emphasize that developers should research the changes in newer versions, especially with respect to dimensions and dimension styles.

### The Dim3PointAngular Object

The Dim3PointAngular object is used to display the angular distance between three points. You can use the AddDim3PointAngular method to add this type of dimension to a drawing.

```
Set Dim3PointAngularObject = _
Object.AddDim3PointAngular(VertexPoint, Point1, Point2, _
 TextPosition)
```

Table 11-5 shows the AddDim3PointAngular method's parameters.

*Table 11-5. AddDim3PointAngular Method Parameters*

| NAME | DATA TYPE | DESCRIPTION |
| --- | --- | --- |
| VertexPoint | Variant | A three-element array of doubles specifying the WCS position of the vertex whose angle is to be measured. |
| Point1 | Variant | A three-element array of doubles specifying the WCS position of one of the end points. |
| Point2 | Variant | A three-element array of doubles specifying the WCS position of the other end point. |
| TextPosition | Variant | A three-element array of doubles specifying the WCS position of the text displayed the angle size. |

Figure 11-1 depicts a three-point angular style dimension.

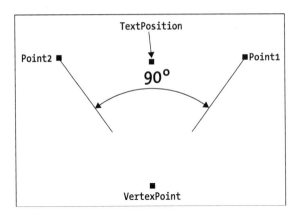

*Figure 11-1. Three-point angular dimension*

This code illustrates how to implement the AddDim3PointAngular method:

```
Public Sub Add3PointAngularDimension()
Dim varAngularVertex As Variant
Dim varFirstPoint As Variant
Dim varSecondPoint As Variant
Dim varTextLocation As Variant
Dim objDim3PointAngular As AcadDim3PointAngular

    'Define the dimension
    varAngularVertex = ThisDrawing.Utility.GetPoint(, _
                                            "Enter the center point: ")
    varFirstPoint = ThisDrawing.Utility.GetPoint(varAngularVertex, _
                                            "Select first point: ")
    varSecondPoint = ThisDrawing.Utility.GetPoint(varAngularVertex, _
                                            "Select second point: ")
    varTextLocation = ThisDrawing.Utility.GetPoint(varAngularVertex, _
                "Pick dimension text location: ")

    Set objDim3PointAngular = ThisDrawing.ModelSpace.AddDim3PointAngular( _
        varAngularVertex, varFirstPoint, varSecondPoint, varTextLocation)
    objDim3PointAngular.Update
End Sub
```

## The DimAligned Object

You use the DimAligned object to display the length of a line. Extension lines emanate at right angles from the ends of the line to be measured to the level of the dimension text. You use the AddDimAligned method to add this object to your drawing.

```
Set DimAlignedObject = Object.AddDimAligned(Point1, Point2, TextPosition)
```

Table 11-6 shows the AddDimAligned method's parameters.

*Table 11-6. AddDimAligned Method Parameters*

| NAME | DATA TYPE | DESCRIPTION |
|------|-----------|-------------|
| Point1 | Variant | A three-element array of doubles specifying the WCS position of one end of the line to be measured |
| Point2 | Variant | A three-element array of doubles specifying the WCS position of the other end of the line to be measured |
| TextPosition | Variant | A three-element array of doubles specifying the WCS position of the text to be displayed |

Figure 11-2 depicts an aligned style dimension.

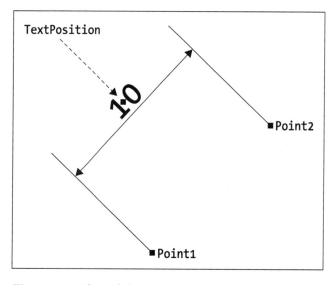

*Figure 11-2. Aligned dimension*

The following example asks the user to select the points that he or she would like to be dimensioned. It then uses the AddDimAligned method to add the dimension. Finally, the units are changed to engineering units.

```
Public Sub AddAlignedDimension()
Dim varFirstPoint As Variant
Dim varSecondPoint As Variant
Dim varTextLocation As Variant
Dim objDimAligned As AcadDimAligned
    'Define the dimension
    varFirstPoint = ThisDrawing.Utility.GetPoint(, "Select first point: ")
    varSecondPoint = ThisDrawing.Utility.GetPoint(varFirstPoint, _
                                        "Select second point: ")
    varTextLocation = ThisDrawing.Utility.GetPoint(, _
                                    "Pick dimension text location: ")


    'Create an aligned dimension
    Set objDimAligned = ThisDrawing.ModelSpace.AddDimAligned(varFirstPoint, _
                                        varSecondPoint, varTextLocation)
    objDimAligned.Update

    MsgBox "Now we will change to Engineering units format"
    objDimAligned.UnitsFormat = acDimLEngineering
    objDimAligned.Update
End Sub
```

## The DimAngular Object

The DimAngular object is much like the Dim3PointAngular object. It's designed to hold dimension text displaying the angle between two lines or spanned by an arc or circle. You use the AddDimAngular method to create a new DimAngular object.

```
Set DimAngularObject = Object.AddDimAngular(Vertex, Point1, Point2, TextPosition)
```

Table 11-7 shows the AddDimAngular method's parameters.

*Table 11-7. AddDimAngular Method Parameters*

| NAME | DATA TYPE | DESCRIPTION |
|------|-----------|-------------|
| Vertex | Variant | A three-element array of doubles specifying the WCS position of the vertex whose angle is to be measured. |
| Point1 | Variant | A three-element array of doubles specifying the WCS position of one of the end points. |
| Point2 | Variant | A three-element array of doubles specifying the WCS position of the other end point. |
| TextPosition | Variant | A three-element array of doubles specifying the WCS position of the text displaying the angle size. |

Figure 11-3 depicts an angular dimension for an arc.

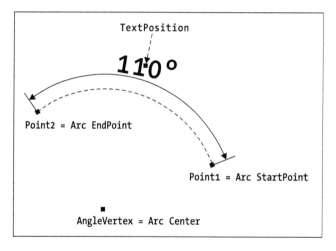

*Figure 11-3. Angular dimension for an arc*

The following code sample shows how to use the AddDimAngular method. Once you've added the new dimension, its units are changed to degrees, minutes, and seconds.

```
Public Sub AddAngularDimension()
Dim varAngularVertex As Variant
Dim varFirstPoint As Variant
Dim varSecondPoint As Variant
Dim varTextLocation As Variant
Dim objDimAngular As AcadDimAngular

    'Define the dimension
    varAngularVertex = ThisDrawing.Utility.GetPoint(, _
                                            "Enter the center point: ")
    varFirstPoint = ThisDrawing.Utility.GetPoint(varAngularVertex, _
                                            "Select first point: ")
    varSecondPoint = ThisDrawing.Utility.GetPoint(varAngularVertex, _
                                            "Select second point: ")
    varTextLocation = ThisDrawing.Utility.GetPoint(varAngularVertex, _
            "Pick dimension text location: ")

    'Create an angular dimension
    Set objDimAngular = ThisDrawing.ModelSpace.AddDimAngular( _
            varAngularVertex, varFirstPoint, varSecondPoint, varTextLocation)
    objDimAngular.AngleFormat = acGrads
    objDimAngular.Update
    MsgBox "Angle measured in GRADS"

    objDimAngular.AngleFormat = acDegreeMinuteSeconds
    objDimAngular.TextPrecision = acDimPrecisionFour
    objDimAngular.Update
    MsgBox "Angle measured in Degrees Minutes Seconds"
End Sub
```

## The DimDiametric Object

The DimDiametric object represents a dimension showing the length of a chord across a circle or arc. The AddDimDiametric method creates a new diametric dimension.

```
DimDiametricObject = Object.AddDimDiametric _
(ChordPoint1, ChordPoint2, LeaderLength)
```

Table 11-8 shows the `AddDimDiametric` method's parameters.

*Table 11-8. AddDimDiametric Method Parameters*

| NAME | DATA TYPE | DESCRIPTION |
|------|-----------|-------------|
| ChordPoint1 | Variant | A three-element array of doubles specifying the WCS position of one end of the chord to be measured |
| ChordPoint2 | Variant | A three-element array of doubles specifying the WCS position of the other end of the chord to be measured |
| LeaderLength | Double | The distance from ChordPoint1 to the dimension text |

Figure 11-4 depicts a diametric style dimension.

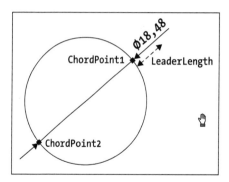

*Figure 11-4. Diametric dimension*

The following code sample adds a new diametric dimension. The object snap mode setting is changed so that the user can only select the diameter of his or her chosen circle. After the dimension has been added, this setting is returned to its original value.

```
Public Sub AddDiametricDimension()
Dim varFirstPoint As Variant
Dim varSecondPoint As Variant
Dim dblLeaderLength As Double
Dim objDimDiametric As AcadDimDiametric
Dim intOsmode As Integer
```

```
    'get original object snap settings
    intOsmode = ThisDrawing.GetVariable("osmode")
    ThisDrawing.SetVariable "osmode", 512 ' Near

    With ThisDrawing.Utility
        varFirstPoint = .GetPoint(, "Select first point on circle: ")
        ThisDrawing.SetVariable "osmode", 128 ' Per
        varSecondPoint = .GetPoint(varFirstPoint, _
                                "Select a point opposite the first: ")
        dblLeaderLength = .GetDistance(varFirstPoint, _
                                "Enter leader length from first point: ")
    End With

    Set objDimDiametric = ThisDrawing.ModelSpace.AddDimDiametric(_
                            varFirstPoint, varSecondPoint, dblLeaderLength)
    objDimDiametric.UnitsFormat = acDimLEngineering
    objDimDiametric.PrimaryUnitsPrecision = acDimPrecisionFive
    objDimDiametric.FractionFormat = acNotStacked
    objDimDiametric.Update

    'reinstate original object snap settings
    ThisDrawing.SetVariable "osmode", intOsmode
End Sub
```

## The DimOrdinate Object

The DimOrdinate object represents dimensioning text displaying the absolute value of the X or Y coordinate of a given point. You use the AddDimOrdinate method to create a new ordinate dimension.

```
Set DimOrdinateObject = Object.AddDimOrdinate(DefinitionPoint, _
LeaderEndPoint, UseXAxis)
```

Table 11-9 shows the AddDimOrdinate method's parameters.

*Table 11-9. AddDimOrdinate Method Parameters*

| NAME | DATA TYPE | DESCRIPTION |
|---|---|---|
| DefinitionPoint | Variant | A three-element array of doubles specifying, with respect to the WCS, the point whose projection onto the X- or Y-axis is to be measured. |
| LeaderEndPoint | Variant | A three-element array of doubles specifying the WCS position of the dimension text, placed at the end of an arrow. |
| UseXAxis | Boolean | Determines whether the DefinitionPoint is measured from the X- or Y-axis. If this is set to True, the X-axis is used as a reference. |

Figure 11-5 depicts a ordinate style dimension.

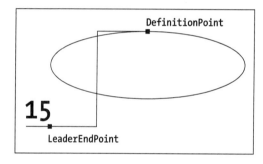

*Figure 11-5. Ordinate dimension*

The following example sets an ordinate dimension for either the X or Y direction:

```
Public Sub AddOrdinateDimension()
Dim varBasePoint As Variant
Dim varLeaderEndPoint As Variant
Dim blnUseXAxis As Boolean
Dim strKeywordList As String
Dim strAnswer As String
Dim objDimOrdinate As AcadDimOrdinate

    strKeywordList = "X Y"
    'Define the dimension
```

```
      varBasePoint = ThisDrawing.Utility.GetPoint(, _
                                    "Select ordinate dimension position: ")
    ThisDrawing.Utility.InitializeUserInput 1, strKeywordList
    strAnswer = ThisDrawing.Utility.GetKeyword("Along Which Axis? <X/Y>: ")

    If strAnswer = "X" Then
      varLeaderEndPoint = ThisDrawing.Utility.GetPoint(varBasePoint, _
                                    "Select X point for dimension text: ")
      blnUseXAxis = True
      Else
        varLeaderEndPoint = ThisDrawing.Utility.GetPoint(varBasePoint, _
                                    "Select Y point for dimension text: ")
        blnUseXAxis = False
    End If

    'Create an ordinate dimension
    Set objDimOrdinate = ThisDrawing.ModelSpace.AddDimOrdinate( _
                          varBasePoint, varLeaderEndPoint, blnUseXAxis)
    objDimOrdinate.TextSuffix = "units"
    objDimOrdinate.Update
End Sub
```

## The DimRadial Object

A radial dimension displays the length of the radius of a circle or arc. You create it using the AddDimRadial method.

```
Set DimRadialObject = Object.AddDimRadial (CenterPoint, ChordPoint, LeaderLength)
```

Table 11-10 shows the AddDimRadial method's parameters.

*Table 11-10. AddDimRadial Method Parameters*

| NAME | DATA TYPE | DESCRIPTION |
|---|---|---|
| CenterPoint | Variant | A three-element array of doubles specifying the WCS coordinates of the center of an arc or circle |
| ChordPoint | Variant | A three-element array of doubles holding the WCS coordinates of a point on the edge of the circle or arc at which an arrow and the text will be placed |
| LeaderLength | Double | The distance from the text to the ChordPoint |

Figure 11-6 depicts a radial style dimension.

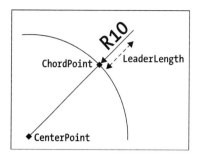

*Figure 11-6. Radial dimension*

The following example illustrates the AddDimRadial method by adding a radial dimension to a circle or arc picked by the user:

```
Public Sub AddRadialDimension()
Dim objUserPickedEntity As Object
Dim varEntityPickedPoint As Variant
Dim varEdgePoint As Variant
Dim dblLeaderLength As Double
Dim objDimRadial As AcadDimRadial
Dim intOsmode As Integer

    intOsmode = ThisDrawing.GetVariable("osmode")
    ThisDrawing.SetVariable "osmode", 512 ' Near

    'Define the dimension
    On Error Resume Next
    With ThisDrawing.Utility
        .GetEntity objUserPickedEntity, varEntityPickedPoint, _
                "Pick Arc or Circle:"
        If objUserPickedEntity Is Nothing Then
            MsgBox "You did not pick an entity"
            Exit Sub
        End If
        varEdgePoint = .GetPoint(objUserPickedEntity.Center, _
                                "Pick edge point")
        dblLeaderLength = .GetReal("Enter leader length from this point: ")
    End With
```

```
'Create the radial dimension
Set objDimRadial = ThisDrawing.ModelSpace.AddDimRadial( _
              objUserPickedEntity.Center, varEdgePoint, dblLeaderLength)
objDimRadial.ArrowheadType = acArrowArchTick
objDimRadial.Update
'reinstate original setting
ThisDrawing.SetVariable "osmode", intOsmode
End Sub
```

## The DimRotated Object

The DimRotated object measures the length of the projection of a line onto a direction specified by an angle from the X-axis.

```
Set DimRotatedObject = Object.AddDimRotated(Point1, Point2, _
DimLocationPoint, RotationAngle)
```

Table 11-11 shows the AddDimRotated method's parameters.

*Table 11-11. AddDimRotated Method Parameters*

| NAME | DATA TYPE | DESCRIPTION |
|------|-----------|-------------|
| Point1 | Variant | A three-element array of doubles specifying the WCS coordinates of one end of a line |
| Point2 | Variant | A three-element array of doubles specifying the WCS coordinates of the other end of a line |
| DimLocationPoint | Variant | A three-element array of doubles specifying the WCS coordinates of a point lying on the line of the arrow and text |
| RotationAngle | Double | The angle of projection measured in radians from the X-axis |

Figure 11-7 depicts a rotated style dimension.

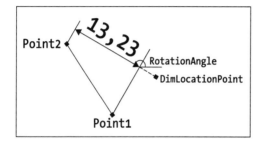

*Figure 11-7. Rotated dimension*

The following example illustrates how to add a rotated dimension at a position and angle chosen by the user:

```
Public Sub AddRotatedDimension()
Dim varFirstPoint As Variant
Dim varSecondPoint As Variant
Dim varTextLocation As Variant
Dim strRotationAngle As String
Dim objDimRotated As AcadDimRotated

    'Define the dimension
    With ThisDrawing.Utility
      varFirstPoint = .GetPoint(, "Select first point: ")
      varSecondPoint = .GetPoint(varFirstPoint, "Select second point: ")
      varTextLocation = .GetPoint(, "Pick dimension text location: ")
      strRotationAngle = .GetString(False, "Enter rotation angle in degrees")
    End With
    'Create a rotated dimension
    Set objDimRotated = ThisDrawing.ModelSpace.AddDimRotated(varFirstPoint, _
      varSecondPoint, varTextLocation, _
      ThisDrawing.Utility.AngleToReal(strRotationAngle, acDegrees))
    objDimRotated.DecimalSeparator = ","
    objDimRotated.Update
End Sub
```

## The Tolerance Object

The Tolerance object represents a geometric tolerance in a feature control frame. Tolerances are used to specify allowable deviations of orientation, location and so on, from the exact geometry of a drawing.

```
Set ToleranceObject = Object.AddTolerance(Text, _
InsertionPoint, TextDirection)
```

Table 11-12 shows the AddTolerance method's parameters.

*Table 11-12. AddTolerance Method Parameters*

| NAME | DATA TYPE | DESCRIPTION |
|---|---|---|
| Text | String | The text string to be displayed |
| InsertionPoint | Variant | A three-element array of doubles specifying the WCS point at which the tolerance is inserted |
| TextDirection | Variant | A three-element array of doubles specifying the three-dimensional vector for the direction of the tolerance text |

Figure 11-8 depicts a tolerance feature flag.

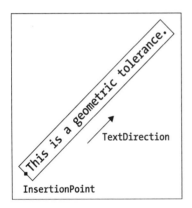

*Figure 11-8. Tolerance feature flag*

This code adds a Tolerance object to model space with the user-chosen text, position, and direction:

```
Public Sub CreateTolerance()
Dim strToleranceText As String
Dim varInsertionPoint As Variant
Dim varTextDirection As Variant
Dim intI As Integer
```

```
Dim objTolerance As AcadTolerance

strToleranceText = InputBox("Please enter the text for the tolerance")
varInsertionPoint = ThisDrawing.Utility.GetPoint(, _
                      "Please enter the insertion point for the tolerance")
varTextDirection = ThisDrawing.Utility.GetPoint(varInsertionPoint, _
                          "Please enter a direction for the tolerance")

For intI = 0 To 2
  varTextDirection(intI) = varTextDirection(intI) - varInsertionPoint(intI)
Next

Set objTolerance = ThisDrawing.ModelSpace.AddTolerance(strToleranceText, _
                      varInsertionPoint, varTextDirection)

End Sub
```

Table 11-13 shows the formatting codes for Tolerance symbols.

*Table 11-13. Formatting Codes for Tolerance Feature Flag Symbols*

| CODE | SYMBOL |
| --- | --- |
| {\Fgdt;a} | Angularity symbol (similar to <) |
| {\Fgdt;b} | Perpendicularity symbol (two perpendicular lines) |
| {\Fgdt;c} | Flatness symbol (parallelogram) |
| {\Fgdt;d} | Profile of a surface symbol (closed half-circle) |
| {\Fgdt;e} | Circularity or roundness symbol (single circle) |
| {\Fgdt;f} | Parallelism symbol (//) |
| {\Fgdt;g} | Cylindricity symbol (/O/) |
| {\Fgdt;h} | Circular runout symbol (/ with arrow at top end) |
| {\Fgdt;i} | Symmetry symbol (like a division sign) |
| {\Fgdt;j} | Positional symbol (circle with a cross in it) |
| {\Fgdt;k} | Profile of a line symbol (open half-circle) |
| {\Fgdt;l} | Least material condition symbol (circle with an *L* in it) |
| {\Fgdt;m} | Maximum material condition symbol (circle with an *M* in it) |

*Table 11-13. Formatting Codes for Tolerance Feature Flag Symbols, continued*

| CODE | SYMBOL |
| --- | --- |
| {\Fgdt;n} | Diameter symbol |
| {\Fgdt;o} | Square symbol |
| {\Fgdt;p} | Projected tolerance zone symbol (circle with a *P* in it) |
| {\Fgdt;q} | Centerline symbol |
| {\Fgdt;r} | Concentricity symbol (two concentric circles) |
| {\Fgdt;s} | Regardless of feature size (circle with an *S* in it) |
| {\Fgdt;t} | Total runout symbol (// with arrows at top of each slash) |
| {\Fgdt;u} | Straightness symbol (-) |
| {\Fgdt;v} | Counterbore symbol |
| {\Fgdt;w} | Countersink symbol |
| {\Fgdt;x} | Depth symbol |
| {\Fgdt;y} | Conical taper symbol |
| {\Fgdt;z} | Slope symbol |
| %%v | Used to create a vertical separation line between each symbol |

Tolerances are related to the dimension objects and so are influenced by several dimension system variables: DIMCLRD controls the color of the feature control frame, DIMCLRT controls the color of the tolerance text, DIMGAP controls the gap between the feature control frame and the text, DIMTXT controls the size of the tolerance text, and DIMTXTSTY controls the style of the tolerance text.

## Annotations

*Annotations* are simply explanatory text added to a drawing to clarify some aspect of that drawing. The AutoCAD objects you may use for this purpose are the Text and MText objects, and for blocks you may use the Attribute and AttributeReference objects (see Chapter 13 for more information). In addition, you can use the Tolerance object to add text, but it's more related to the dimension objects, so I cover it later in this chapter. The format and style of the text is controlled by the TextStyle object as well as a number of system variables. In this section you'll concentrate on the TextStyle object and how to set and use text styles.

## The TextStyle Object

A *text style* determines the appearance of any text you add to a drawing. TextStyle objects represent the settings for different styles and are held in the TextStyles collection. When you first create a drawing, this collection contains only one TextStyle object, named "Standard". You can read the settings for this object through code using the GetFont method and the Height, Width, ObliqueAngle, and TextGenerationFlag properties outlined in the following sections. Alternatively, you can view the settings in the Text Style dialog box, which you access through the Format ➤ Text Style menu of the AutoCAD interface.

Figure 11-9 shows the Text Style dialog box.

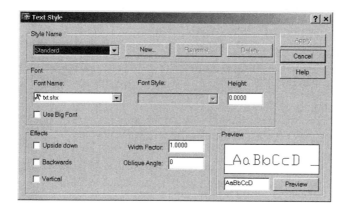

*Figure 11-9. The Text Style dialog box*

## Creating TextStyle Objects

By creating new TextStyle objects for different types of text or information, you can have at your fingertips all the text styles that you require for a drawing. To create a new TextStyle object, use the Add method as follows:

```
Set TextStyleObject = TextStylesCollection.Add(TextStyleName)
```

Table 11-14 shows the Add method's parameter.

*Table 11-14. Add Method Parameter*

| NAME | DATA TYPE | DESCRIPTION |
|------|-----------|-------------|
| TextStyleName | String | An identifying name for the new TextStyle object. |

If you try to add a TextStyle with the name of an existing TextStyle object, this method will return a reference to the existing object. The newly created object will have the same settings as the active TextStyle object.

## Retrieving and Setting Text Styles

Once you've created a new TextStyle object, you'll need to set its font settings. You may also want to modify or check the settings of an existing TextStyle object. You can do this through the SetFont and GetFont methods. In addition, you can use the font settings held within an .shx file through the FontFile and BigFontFile properties.

### The SetFont Method

You use the SetFont method to define the font for a TextStyle object. It sets the typeface, if text will be bold and/or italicized, and the character set and pitch and family definitions.

```
TextStyleObject.SetFont TypeFace, Bold, Italic, CharacterSet, PitchAndFamily
```

**NOTE** *Many TrueType fonts are licensed and aren't provided for public use without explicit permission. Be sure to comply with any licensing terms if you set a custom font, and package the font with your drawing files to send to customers.*

Table 11-15 shows the SetFont method's parameters.

*Table 11-15. SetFont Method Parameters*

| NAME | DATA TYPE | DESCRIPTION |
|---|---|---|
| TypeFace | String | The name of a font, for example "Times New Roman." If the TextStyle is determined by an .shx file, this parameter holds an empty string. |
| Bold | Boolean | Determines if the text will be boldface. If this value is set to True, the text will be bold. Otherwise, the text style isn't bold. |
| Italic | Boolean | Determines if the text will be italicized. If this value is set to True, the text will be italic. Otherwise, the text style isn't italic. |
| CharacterSet | Long | Specifies the character set for the font. Use the following constants in your application in the declaration section of your code:<br>×Public Const ANSI_CHARSET<br>= 0×Public Const DEFAULT_CHARSET<br>= 1×Public Const SYMBOL_CHARSET<br>= 2×Public Const SHIFTJIS_CHARSET<br>= 128×Public Const OEM_CHARSET = 255 |
| PitchAndFamily | Long | Specifies the pitch and family values for the font. The value is a combination of three different settings for pitch, family, and optionally the TrueType flag (only required when you're specifying a TrueType font). Use the following constants in your application in the declaration section of your code:<br>×' Pitch Values×Public Const DEFAULT_PITCH<br>= 0×Public Const FIXED_PITCH<br>= 1×Public Const VARIABLE_PITCH<br>= 2×' Family Values×Public Const FF_DONTCARE<br>= 0 ×Public Const FF_ROMAN<br>= 16 ×Public Const FF_SWISS<br>= 32 ×Public Const FF_MODERN<br>= 48×Public Const FF_SCRIPT<br>= 64 ×Public Const FF_DECORATIVE<br>= 80×' TrueType Flag×Public Const TMPF_TRUETYPE<br>= &H4 |

This example creates a new `TextStyle` object and sets its font style to bold Greek symbols:

```
Public Sub AddTextStyle
Dim objTextStyle As AcadTextStyle

    Set objTextStyle = ThisDrawing.TextStyles.Add("Bold Greek Symbols")
    objTextStyle.SetFont "Symbol", True, False, 0, 0
End Sub
```

### The GetFont Method

The `GetFont` method works in much the same way as the `SetFont` method, except it retrieves the font settings:

```
TextStyleObject.GetFont TypeFace, Bold, Italic, CharacterSet, PitchAndFamily
```

Table 11-16 shows the `GetFont` method's parameters.

*Table 11-16. GetFont Method Parameters*

| NAME | DATA TYPE | DESCRIPTION |
| --- | --- | --- |
| TypeFace | String | The name of a font, for example "Times New Roman." If the `TextStyle` is determined by a `.shx` file, this parameter holds an empty string. |
| Bold | Boolean | Determines if the text will be boldface. If this value is set to `True`, the text will be bold. Otherwise, the text style isn't bold. |
| Italic | Boolean | Determines if the text will be italicized. If this value is set to `True`, the text will be italic. Otherwise the text style isn't italic. |
| CharacterSet | Long | See Table 11-3 for a description of this parameter. |
| PitchAndFamily | Long | See Table 11-3 for a description of this parameter. |

The following example asks the user for the name of a text style and then presents him or her with the font settings:

```
Public Sub GetTextSettings()
Dim objTextStyle As AcadTextStyle
Dim strTextStyleName As String
Dim strTextStyles As String
Dim strTypeFace As String
Dim blnBold As Boolean
Dim blnItalic As Boolean
Dim lngCharacterSet As Long
Dim lngPitchandFamily As Long
Dim strText As String

    ' Get the name of each text style in the drawing
    For Each objTextStyle In ThisDrawing.TextStyles
        strTextStyles = strTextStyles & vbCr & objTextStyle.Name
    Next
    ' Ask the user to select the Text Style to look at
    strTextStyleName = InputBox("Please enter the name of the TextStyle " & _
                "whose setting you would like to see" & vbCr & _
                strTextStyles,"TextStyles", ThisDrawing.ActiveTextStyle.Name)
    ' Exit the program if the user input was cancelled or empty
    If strTextStyleName = "" Then Exit Sub

On Error Resume Next
    Set objTextStyle = ThisDrawing.TextStyles(strTextStyleName)
    ' Check for existence the text style
    If objTextStyle Is Nothing Then
        MsgBox "This text style does not exist"
        Exit Sub
    End If

    ' Get the Font properties
    objTextStyle.GetFont strTypeFace, blnBold, blnItalic, lngCharacterSet, _
                lngPitchandFamily
    ' Check for Type face
    If strTypeFace = "" Then   ' No True type
        MsgBox "Text Style: " & objTextStyle.Name & vbCr & _
                "Using file font: " & objTextStyle.fontFile, _
                vbInformation, "Text Style: " & objTextStyle.Name

    Else
        ' True Type font info
        strText = "The text style: " & strTextStyleName & " has " & vbCrLf & _
                "a " & strTypeFace & " type face"
```

```
        If blnBold Then strText = strText & vbCrLf & " and is bold"
        If blnItalic Then strText = strText & vbCrLf & " and is italicized"
        MsgBox strText & vbCr & "Using file font: " & objTextStyle.fontFile, _
                vbInformation, "Text Style: " & objTextStyle.Name
    End If
End Sub
```

### The FontFile Property

You use the FontFile property to set the TextStyle object to adopt the font style held in an .shx file, or vice versa.

```
TextStyleObject.FontFile = FontFileName
```

Table 11-17 shows the FontFile property's parameter.

*Table 11-17. FontFile Property Parameter*

| NAME | DATA TYPE | DESCRIPTION |
| --- | --- | --- |
| FontFileName | String | The path and file name of the required font file |

The following code sample sets the font file for a new TextStyle object named "Roman" to be the romand.shx file:

```
Public Sub SetFontFile
Dim objTextStyle As AcadTextStyle

    Set objTextStyle = ThisDrawing.TextStyles.Add("Roman")
    objTextStyle.fontFile = "romand.shx"
End Sub
```

To set or retrieve the font settings of an Asian-language big font file, use the BigFontFile property.

### Other TextStyle Properties

There are some other properties of a TextStyle object that you can use to set the way text appears: Height, Width, ObliqueAngle, and TextGenerationFlag.

The effects of setting the Height and Width properties are shown in Figure 11-10. The Height simply holds the height of uppercase text in the current drawing units. The Width, on the other hand, sets the character spacing and may lie in the range 0 < Width [ 100. A value of more than 1.0 expands the text; a value of less than 1.0 condenses it.

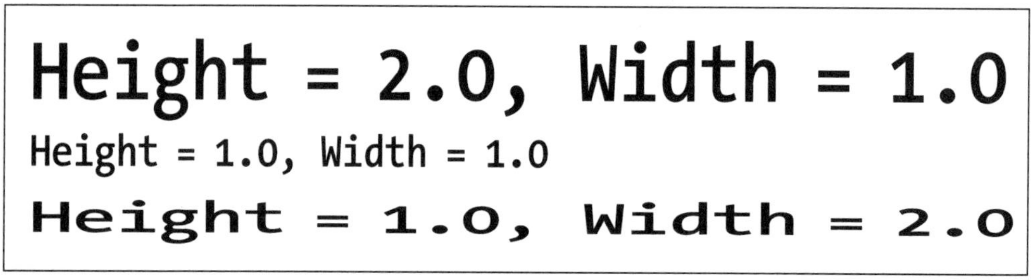

# Height = 2.0, Width = 1.0
Height = 1.0, Width = 1.0
## Height = 1.0, Width = 2.0

*Figure 11-10. Height variations example*

You can use the ObliqueAngle property to set the angle of slant of the text away from its vertical axis. You may set it to any value between –858 and 858, with a negative value indicating a slope to the left. The result of setting this property is shown in Figure 11-11.

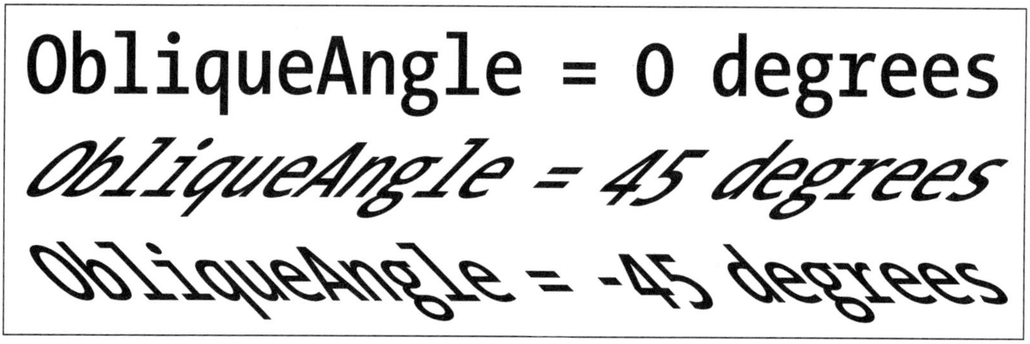

# ObliqueAngle = 0 degrees
*ObliqueAngle = 45 degrees*
*ObliqueAngle = -45 degrees*

*Figure 11-11. Oblique angle variations example*

Finally, the TextGenerationFlag property determines whether the text is written back to front and/or upside down. This property holds one or a combination of the acTextGeneration constants given in Table 11-18.

*Table 11-18. TextGeneration Constants*

| CONSTANT | VALUE | DESCRIPTION |
| --- | --- | --- |
| acTextFlagBackward | 2 | The letters of the text appear in reverse order. |
| acTextFlagUpsideDown | 4 | The text appears upside down. |

Figure 11-12 shows an example of each of the possible settings for the `TextGenerationFlag` property.

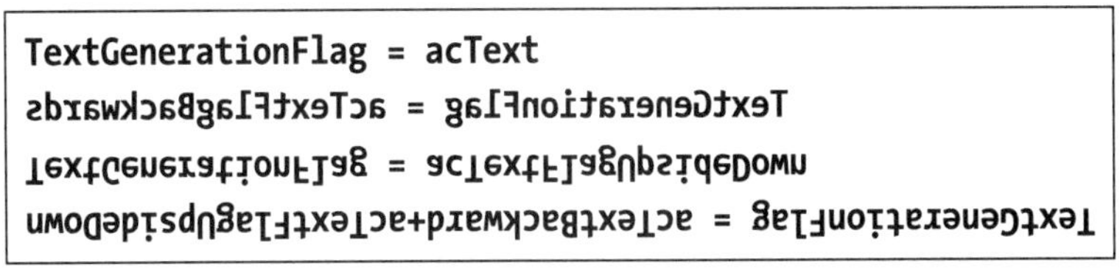

```
TextGenerationFlag = acText
TextGenerationFlag = acTextFlagBackwards
TextGenerationFlag = acTextFlagUpsideDown
TextGenerationFlag = acTextBackward+acTextFlagUpsideDown
```

*Figure 11-12. TextGenerationFlag variations example*

## Using a TextStyle

Once you've set up all the text fonts and formats for a `TextStyle` object, you'll probably want to use it. You have two ways to associate text to a particular style. The first way is to use the `StyleName` property, which sets the style for a particular object, and the second way is to make a `TextStyle` object active, using the `ActiveStyle` property of the `Document` object, and set the text style for newly created objects and any existing text objects that don't have their `StyleName` property set.

### The StyleName Property

You use this property to set the style used with an object. To set or change the `TextStyle` used with a `Text`, `MText`, `Attribute`, or `AttributeRef` object, simply set or reset the value of this property.

```
Object.StyleName = TextStyleName
```

Table 11-19 shows the `StyleName` property's parameters.

*Table 11-19. StyleName Property Parameters*

| NAME | DATA TYPE | DESCRIPTION |
| --- | --- | --- |
| Object | Text, MText, Attribute, or AttributeRef object | The object to which the text style is linked |
| TextStyleName | String | The identifying name of the TextStyle object |

This code changes all text in model space to adopt a user's chosen text style:

```
Public Sub ChangeTextStyle()
Dim strTextStyles As String
Dim objTextStyle As AcadTextStyle
Dim objLayer As AcadLayer
Dim strLayerName As String
Dim strStyleName As String
Dim objAcadObject As AcadObject

On Error Resume Next
    For Each objTextStyle In ThisDrawing.TextStyles
        strTextStyles = strTextStyles & vbCr & objTextStyle.Name
    Next
    strStyleName = InputBox("Enter name of style to apply:" & vbCr & _
            strTextStyles, "TextStyles", ThisDrawing.ActiveTextStyle.Name)
    Set objTextStyle = ThisDrawing.TextStyles(strStyleName)
    If objTextStyle Is Nothing Then
        MsgBox "Style does not exist"
        Exit Sub
    End If

    For Each objAcadObject In ThisDrawing.ModelSpace
        If objAcadObject.ObjectName = "AcDbMText" Or -
            objAcadObject.ObjectName = "AcDbText" Then
            objAcadObject.StyleName = strStyleName
            objAcadObject.Update
        End If
    Next
End Sub
```

### The ActiveTextStyle Property

You use the ActiveTextStyle property to make a text style the default for any newly created text and for any existing text that doesn't have a particular text style already associated with it.

```
Set DocumentObject.ActiveTextStyle = TextStyleObject
```

Table 11-20 shows the ActiveTextStyle property's parameter.

*Table 11-20. ActiveTextStyle Property Parameter*

| NAME | DATA TYPE | DESCRIPTION |
|------|-----------|-------------|
| TextStyleObject | TextStyle object | The object holding the setting for the required text style |

The following example sets the default text style based on user input:

```
Public Sub SetDefaultTextStyle()
Dim strTextStyles As String
Dim objTextStyle As AcadTextStyle
Dim strTextStyleName As String

    For Each objTextStyle In ThisDrawing.TextStyles
        strTextStyles = strTextStyles & vbCr & objTextStyle.Name
    Next
    strTextStyleName = InputBox("Enter name of style to apply:" & vbCr & _
            strTextStyles, "TextStyles", ThisDrawing.ActiveTextStyle.Name)
    If strTextStyleName = "" Then Exit Sub

On Error Resume Next
    Set objTextStyle = ThisDrawing.TextStyles(strTextStyleName)
    If objTextStyle Is Nothing Then
        MsgBox "This text style does not exist"
        Exit Sub
    End If

    ThisDrawing.ActiveTextStyle = objTextStyle
End Sub
```

## Adding Annotations

To add annotations through VBA code, you need to add a Text, MText, or AttributeReference object. You may add each of these objects to the model space, the paper space, or a block definition. Chapters 8 and 13 provide details of how to add these objects. At this point, it's worth mentioning the Leader object.

## The Leader Object

A Leader object consists of an arrowhead attached to a spline or straight-line segments. You can use this object to associate text with a drawing object. To add a Leader object to your drawing, use the AddLeader method.

```
Set LeaderObject = Object.AddLeader(PointsArray, Annotationtype, ArrowType)
```

Table 11-21 shows the AddLeader method's parameters.

*Table 11-21. AddLeader method parameters*

| NAME | DATA TYPE | DESCRIPTION |
| --- | --- | --- |
| PointsArray | Variant | A three-element array of doubles specifying the three dimensional WCS coordinates of the vertices of line segments or the fit points of a spline. |
| AnnotationType | Object | The annotation with which the leader is associated. This may by a Tolerance, MText, or BlockRef object or NULL. |
| ArrowType | Long | One of the AcLeaderType constants identifying the appearance of the leader. |

Figure 11-13 shows each of the AcLeaderType constants and its result.

The following example adds a straight-line leader with associated text to model space. The alignment of the text is set depending on the direction of the leader.

```
Public Sub CreateStraightLeaderWithNote()
Dim dblPoints(5) As Double
Dim varStartPoint As Variant
Dim varEndPoint As Variant
Dim intLeaderType As Integer
Dim objAcadLeader As AcadLeader
Dim objAcadMtext As AcadMText
Dim strMtext As String
Dim intI As Integer

    intLeaderType = acLineWithArrow
    varStartPoint = ThisDrawing.Utility.GetPoint(, _
                                        "Select leader start point: ")
    varEndPoint = ThisDrawing.Utility.GetPoint(varStartPoint, _
                                        "Select leader end point: ")
```

```
For intI = 0 To 2
  dblPoints(intI) = varStartPoint(intI)
  dblPoints(intI + 3) = varEndPoint(intI)
Next

strMtext = InputBox("Notes:", "Leader Notes")
If strMtext = "" Then Exit Sub
' Create the text for the leader
Set objAcadMtext = ThisDrawing.ModelSpace.AddMText(varEndPoint, _
Len(strMtext) * ThisDrawing.GetVariable("dimscale"), strMtext)
' Flip the alignment direction of the text
If varEndPoint(0) > varStartPoint(0) Then
    objAcadMtext.AttachmentPoint = acAttachmentPointMiddleLeft
Else
    objAcadMtext.AttachmentPoint = acAttachmentPointMiddleRight
End If
objAcadMtext.InsertionPoint = varEndPoint

'Create the leader object
Set objAcadLeader = ThisDrawing.ModelSpace.AddLeader(dblPoints, _
                                      objAcadMtext, intLeaderType)

objAcadLeader.Update
End Sub
```

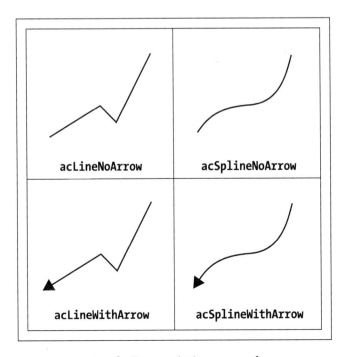

*Figure 11-13. LeaderType variations example*

## Summary

In this chapter you examined the AutoCAD VBA objects for creating textual and dimension annotations. You use these objects to clarify a drawing's purpose and display the size and orientation of drawing elements. You also looked in detail at how to set up text and dimension styles using the `TextStyle` and `DimStyle` objects.

CHAPTER 12

# Selection Sets
# and Groups

AUTOCAD ALLOWS USERS TO PERFORM many operations on arbitrary sets of
entities. The user builds these sets of entities either on an as-needed basis as
a *selection set* or more permanently as a *group*. Selection sets (also referred to
as PickSets) are transient and are destroyed when AutoCAD closes a drawing.
Groups, on the other hand, are stored persistently in the drawing file.

This chapter covers the following topics:

- Creating and manipulating selection sets and groups

- Filtering sets of entities using selection set filters

- Interacting with user by building dynamic selection sets

- Working with the PickFirst selection set

- Manipulating groups

## Selection Sets

A selection set is a temporary collection of drawing entities. With a selection set,
users can perform an operation such as move, copy, or delete on a number of
entities at once, rather than on one at a time.

Each AutoCAD drawing has a SelectionSets collection that contains
SelectionSet objects. You can create any number of selection sets by adding
new SelectionSet objects to the SelectionSets collection. Because selection sets
aren't persistent, and so disappear when the drawing is closed, the SelectionSets
collection will always be empty when a drawing is first opened or created.

## *Adding a SelectionSet Object*

Selection sets are usually added to the collection on an as-needed basis. You can create as many as you need, but they're typically transient—you create them on demand and then discard them. You use the Add method (see Table 12-1 for parameter details) of the SelectionSets collection to create a SelectionSet object.

```
Set SelectionSetObject = SelectionSetsCollection.Add(SelectionSetName)
```

*Table 12-1. Add Method Parameters*

| NAME | DATA TYPE | DESCRIPTION |
| --- | --- | --- |
| SelectionSetName | String | Name of the newly created selection set |

The Name parameter is simply used as a handle for the newly created selection set; it's never shown in the user interface. If a SelectionSet object already exists in the current drawing with that name, an exception is raised. You can use the Name parameter to retrieve the selection set during the same session in which it was created by using the Item method.

The following example attempts to add a selection set using a name obtained from the user:

```
Public Sub TestAddSelectionSet()
    Dim objSS As AcadSelectionSet
    Dim strName As String

On Error Resume Next
    '' get a name from user
    strName = InputBox("Enter a new selection set name: ")
    If "" = strName Then Exit Sub

    '' create it
    Set objSS = ThisDrawing.SelectionSets.Add(strName)

    '' check if it was created
    If objSS Is Nothing Then
        MsgBox "Unable to Add '" & strName & "'"
    Else
        MsgBox "Added selection set '" & objSS.Name & "'"
    End If
End Sub
```

Try adding a few selection sets. You'll access them again in the next example.

## Accessing and Iterating Selection Sets

As I mentioned previously, you access the SelectionSets collection via a Document object. In the following code, ThisDrawing is used as the active document:

```
Dim objSelections As AcadSelectionSets
Set objSelections = ThisDrawing.SelectionSets
```

To set a reference to an existing SelectionSet object, use the Item method of the SelectionSets collection:

```
Dim objSelection As AcadSelectionSet

Set objSelection = objSelections.Item(2)
Set objSelection = objSelections.Item("My SelectionSet")
```

The parameter of this method is either a number representing the position of the desired SelectionSet object within the SelectionSets collection or a string representing the name of the desired SelectionSet object. If you use an index number, it must be between 0 and SelectionSets.Count minus 1. The Count property returns the total number of SelectionSet objects in the collection.

As with other AutoCAD collections, Item is the default method for SelectionSets. This means that you may omit the method name and the parameter is passed straight to the SelectionSets reference. This is often preferred because it's simpler to type and read, but you should avoid using default methods as Microsoft is moving away from implicitness to explicitness in programming technologies such as .NET. The following code does the same thing as the earlier example using the default method to specify the SelectionSet object:

```
Dim objSelection As AcadSelectionSet

Set objSelection = objSelections(2)
Set objSelection = objSelections("My SelectionSet")
```

### Iterating the SelectionSets Collection

Situations will arise in which a programmer needs to step through each item in a collection one at a time—perhaps to check or alter some property of every element. Like all collections in VBA, SelectionSets has built-in support for iteration using a For ... Each loop.

The following example iterates the SelectionSets collection and displays the name of all the SelectionSet objects in a message box. Try it after running the previous TestAddSelectionSet example:

```
Public Sub ListSelectionSets()
    Dim objSS As AcadSelectionSet
    Dim strSSList As String

    For Each objSS In ThisDrawing.SelectionSets
        strSSList = strSSList & vbCr & objSS.Name
    Next
    MsgBox strSSList, , "List of Selection Sets"
End Sub
```

## Selecting Entities

Newly created SelectionSet objects are empty. A SelectionSet is populated either by adding an array of objects, which I describe how to do later in this chapter, or by using one of the SelectXXX methods I describe in this section. There are SelectXXX methods for obtaining entities by specific point, by window, by arbitrary fence or polygon, by dynamic user selection, and by filtering the entities using specific criteria.

### The Select Method

The Select method (see Table 12-2 for parameter details) is the basic way to add entities to SelectionSet objects. It allows you to select the previous selection set, the last visible entity, everything in the current space, or by rectangular region.

```
SelectionSetObject.Select Mode [, Point1, Point2] _
[, FilterCodes, FilterValues]
```

The Select method has several modes of operation specified by the Mode parameter. AutoCAD provides the following AcSelect enum constants for use with this parameter, as shown in Table 12-3.

*Table 12-2. Select Method Parameters*

| NAME | DATA TYPE | DESCRIPTION |
|---|---|---|
| Mode | Long | Determines the selection mode to be used. It must be one of the AcSelect constants described in Table 12-3. |
| Point1 | Variant | An optional three-element array of doubles indicating the first corner of a rectangular region. It must be used in conjunction with Point2. |
| Point2 | Variant | An optional three-element array of doubles indicating the other corner of a rectangular region. It must be used in conjunction with Point1. |
| FilterCodes | Variant | An optional array of integer entity selection filter codes. It must be used in conjunction with, and have the same length as, FilterValues. |
| FilterValues | Variant | An optional array of variant entity selection filter values. It must be used in conjunction with, and have the same length as, FilterCodes. |

*Table 12-3. Select Method Modes*

| CONSTANT | VALUE | DESCRIPTION |
|---|---|---|
| acSelectionSetWindow | 0 | Entities completely contained within a window specified by Point1 and Point2 are selected. |
| acSelectionSetCrossing | 1 | Entities contained or crossing over a window specified by Point1 and Point2 are selected. |
| acSelectionSetPrevious | 3 | Entities from the most recent selection set in the current space are selected. Point1 and Point2 aren't used. |
| acSelectionSetLast | 4 | The most recently created entity within the current viewport is selected. Point1 and Point2 aren't used. |
| acSelectionSetAll | 5 | All entities in the current space are selected. Point1 and Point2 aren't used. |

**NOTE** *The* Select *method is capable of selecting entities on all layers, even if a certain layer is frozen or locked.*

The following example creates a new selection set and then populates it based on user input. Try each of the modes to see how they differ.

```
Public Sub TestSelect()
      Dim objSS As AcadSelectionSet
      Dim varPnt1 As Variant
      Dim varPnt2 As Variant
      Dim strOpt As String
      Dim lngMode As Long

On Error GoTo Done
    With ThisDrawing.Utility

        '' get input for mode
        .InitializeUserInput 1, "Window Crossing Previous Last All"
        strOpt = .GetKeyword(vbCr & _
        "Select [Window/Crossing/Previous/Last/All]: ")

        '' convert keyword into mode
        Select Case strOpt
        Case "Window":   lngMode = acSelectionSetWindow
        Case "Crossing": lngMode = acSelectionSetCrossing
        Case "Previous": lngMode = acSelectionSetPrevious
        Case "Last":     lngMode = acSelectionSetLast
        Case "All":      lngMode = acSelectionSetAll
        End Select

        '' create a new selectionset
        Set objSS = ThisDrawing.SelectionSets.Add("TestSelectSS")

        '' if it's window or crossing, get the points
        If "Window" = strOpt Or "Crossing" = strOpt Then

            '' get first point
            .InitializeUserInput 1
            varPnt1 = .GetPoint(, vbCr & "Pick the first corner: ")
```

```
            '' get corner, using dashed lines if crossing
            .InitializeUserInput 1 + IIf("Crossing" = strOpt, 32, 0)
            varPnt2 = .GetCorner(varPnt1, vbCr & "Pick other corner: ")

            '' select entities using points
            objSS.Select lngMode, varPnt1, varPnt2
        Else

            '' select entities using mode
            objSS.Select lngMode
        End If

        '' highlight the selected entities
        objSS.Highlight True

        '' pause for the user
        .GetString False, vbCr & "Enter to continue"

        '' dehighlight the entities
        objSS.Highlight False

    End With

Done:

    '' if the selectionset was created, delete it
    If Not objSS Is Nothing Then
        objSS.Delete
    End If
End Sub
```

### Selection Set Filters

You use the optional FilterCodes and FilterValues parameters to filter the selection of entities based on some criteria. Common criteria include objects with a specific color or linetype, or objects on a particular layer.

The FilterCodes parameter is an array of integers that specifies the entity group codes to filter. Entity group codes are available for every entity property. See the AutoCAD DXF Reference for a complete listing of the available group codes. The FilterValues parameter is an array of variants that specifies the corresponding values for each entity group code present in the FilterCodes parameter. Because these two arrays have a one-to-one mapping, they must be of the same length.

The following example filters all the entities into a selection set based on a layer name entered by the user:

```
Public Sub TestSelectionSetFilter()
        Dim objSS As AcadSelectionSet
        Dim intCodes(0) As Integer
        Dim varCodeValues(0) As Variant
        Dim strName As String

On Error GoTo Done

    With ThisDrawing.Utility
        strName = .GetString(True, vbCr & "Layer name to filter: ")
        If "" = strName Then Exit Sub

        '' create a new selectionset
        Set objSS = ThisDrawing.SelectionSets.Add("TestSelectionSetFilter")

        '' set the code for layer
        intCodes(0) = 8

        '' set the value specified by user
        varCodeValues(0) = strName

        '' filter the objects
        objSS.Select acSelectionSetAll, , , intCodes, varCodeValues

        '' highlight the selected entities
        objSS.Highlight True

        '' pause for the user
        .Prompt vbCr & objSS.Count & " entities selected"
        .GetString False, vbLf & "Enter to continue "

        '' dehighlight the entities
        objSS.Highlight False
    End With

Done:

    '' if the selection was created, delete it
    If Not objSS Is Nothing Then
        objSS.Delete
    End If
End Sub
```

When multiple filter codes are specified, they're implicitly combined using a logical AND operator. You can explicitly control how codes contribute to the selection criteria by using *filter operators.* The filter operators are designated by a special group code of –4 and special string keywords for the values. You use filter operators in pairs surrounding a number of filter codes known as *operands.*

Table 12-4 lists the SelectionSet filter operators, their meaning, and the required number of operands that may be used.

*Table 12-4. SelectionSet Filter Operators*

| FILTER OPERATOR | START AND END VALUE | NUMBER OF OPERANDS | DESCRIPTION |
| --- | --- | --- | --- |
| "<AND" | ... <br> "AND>" | One or more | A logical AND of all the operands. If a criterion matches all of the operands, it will be included. This is the default for multiple criteria when no filter operators are specified. |
| "<OR" | ... <br> "OR>" | One or more | A logical OR of all the operands. If a criterion matches any of the operands, it will be included. |
| "<XOR" | ... <br> "XOR>" | Exactly two | A logical XOR of two operands. If a criterion matches one, but not the other, it will be included. |
| "<NOT" | ... <br> "NOT>" | Exactly one | A logical NOT of a single operand. If a criterion doesn't match the operand, it will be included. |

The following example uses filter operators to limit the selection to lines, arcs, and circles that are *not* on a specified layer:

```
Public Sub TestSelectionSetOperator()
    Dim objSS As AcadSelectionSet
    Dim intCodes() As Integer
    Dim varCodeValues As Variant
    Dim strName As String
```

```
On Error GoTo Done
    With ThisDrawing.Utility
        strName = .GetString(True, vbCr & "Layer name to exclude: ")
        If "" = strName Then Exit Sub

        '' create a new selectionset
        Set objSS = ThisDrawing.SelectionSets.Add("TestSelectionSetOperator")

        '' using 9 filters
        ReDim intCodes(9):  ReDim varCodeValues(9)

        '' set codes and values - indented for clarity
        intCodes(0) = -4:  varCodeValues(0) = "<and"
        intCodes(1) = -4:    varCodeValues(1) = "<or"
        intCodes(2) = 0:       varCodeValues(2) = "line"
        intCodes(3) = 0:       varCodeValues(3) = "arc"
        intCodes(4) = 0:       varCodeValues(4) = "circle"
        intCodes(5) = -4:    varCodeValues(5) = "or>"
        intCodes(6) = -4:    varCodeValues(6) = "<not"
        intCodes(7) = 8:       varCodeValues(7) = strName
        intCodes(8) = -4:    varCodeValues(8) = "not>"
        intCodes(9) = -4:  varCodeValues(9) = "and>"

        '' filter the objects
        objSS.Select acSelectionSetAll, , , intCodes, varCodeValues

        '' highlight the selected entities
        objSS.Highlight True

        '' pause for the user
        .Prompt vbCr & objSS.Count & " entities selected"
        .GetString False, vbLf & "Enter to continue "

        '' dehighlight the entities
        objSS.Highlight False
    End With

Done:

    '' if the selection was created, delete it
    If Not objSS Is Nothing Then
        objSS.Delete
    End If
End Sub
```

The group code values can contain wild card expressions if the code represents a string property. You can often use wild card expressions to make filter criteria more succinct. For example, the preceding filter took nine group codes to define. By using wild cards, you can reduce it to just two:

```
ReDim intCodes(1):  ReDim varCodeValues(1)
intCodes(0) = 0:  varCodeValues(0) = "line,arc,circle"
intCodes(1) = 8:  varCodeValues(1) = "~" & strName
```

See the AutoCAD 2004 Customization Guide for more details on wild card expressions.

## The SelectOnScreen Method

You use this method to obtain a selection of entities interactively from the user (see Table 12-5 for parameter details). A "Select objects:" prompt is shown at the command line, where all the standard selection set options such as Window, Crossing, and Last are available to the user for dynamic selection.

```
SelectionSetObject.SelectOnScreen [, FilterCodes, FilterValues]
```

*Table 12-5. SelectOnScreen Method Parameters*

| NAME | DATA TYPE | DESCRIPTION |
| --- | --- | --- |
| FilterCodes | Variant | An optional array of integer entity selection filter codes. This must be used in conjunction with, and have the same length as, FilterValues. |
| FilterValues | Variant | An optional array of variant entity selection filter values. This must be used in conjunction with, and have the same length as, FilterCodes. |

Like the Select method, SelectOnScreen can optionally filter the selected entities using criteria specified in the FilterCodes and FilterValues parameters. See the previous section for a full description of filtering.

The following example gets a selection of entities dynamically from the user:

```
Public Sub TestSelectOnScreen()
    Dim objSS As AcadSelectionSet

    On Error GoTo Done
    With ThisDrawing.Utility

        '' create a new selectionset
        Set objSS = ThisDrawing.SelectionSets.Add("TestSelectOnScreen")

        '' let user select entities interactively
        objSS.SelectOnScreen

        '' highlight the selected entities
        objSS.Highlight True

        '' pause for the user
        .Prompt vbCr & objSS.Count & " entities selected"
        .GetString False, vbLf & "Enter to continue "

        '' dehighlight the entities
        objSS.Highlight False

    End With

Done:

    '' if the selection was created, delete it
    If Not objSS Is Nothing Then
        objSS.Delete
    End If
End Sub
```

## *The SelectAtPoint Method*

The SelectAtPoint method (see Table 12-6 for parameter details) selects a single entity that passes through a specified point. Unlike most of the other Select*XXX* methods (except the acSelectionSetLast mode of Select), it selects only a single entity.

```
SelectionSet.SelectAtPoint Point [,FilterCodes, FilterValues]
```

*Table 12-6. SelectAtPoint Method Parameters*

| NAME | DATA TYPE | DESCRIPTION |
|---|---|---|
| Point | Variant | A three-element array of doubles indicating the point through which the selected entity must pass. |
| FilterCodes | Variant | An optional array of integer entity selection filter codes. This must be used in conjunction with, and have the same length as, FilterValues. |
| FilterValues | Variant | An optional array of variant entity selection filter values. This must be used in conjunction with, and have the same length as, FilterCodes. |

Like the other Select methods, SelectAtPoint can optionally filter the selected entities using criteria specified in the FilterCodes and FilterValues parameters. (This was covered earlier in the chapter.)

The following example selects an entity passing through a point chosen by the user:

```
Public Sub TestSelectAtPoint()
    Dim varPick As Variant
    Dim objSS As AcadSelectionSet

    On Error GoTo Done

    With ThisDrawing.Utility

        '' create a new selectionset
        Set objSS = ThisDrawing.SelectionSets.Add("TestSelectAtPoint")

        '' get a point of selection from the user
        varPick = .GetPoint(, vbCr & "Select entities at a point: ")

        '' let user select entities interactively
        objSS.SelectAtPoint varPick

        '' highlight the selected entities
        objSS.Highlight True

        '' pause for the user
        .Prompt vbCr & objSS.Count & " entities selected"
        .GetString False, vbLf & "Enter to continue "
```

```
'' dehighlight the entities
objSS.Highlight False

    End With

Done:

    '' if the selection was created, delete it
    If Not objSS Is Nothing Then
        objSS.Delete
    End If
End Sub
```

## The SelectByPolygon Method

This method (see Table 12-7 for parameter details) selects entities by using a boundary that may be either a closed polygon or an open figure called a *fence*. In the case of a closed polygon, you can further limit entities to only those lying completely within the polygon (Window-Polygon) or those that pass through the boundary as well (Crossing-Polygon).

```
SelectionSetObject.SelectByPolygon Mode, Vertices _
[, FilterType, FilterData]
```

*Table 12-7. SelectByPolygon Method Parameters*

| NAME | DATA TYPE | DESCRIPTION |
|------|-----------|-------------|
| Mode | Long | Determines the selection mode to be used. It must be one of the AcSelect constants described in Table 12-8. |
| Vertices | Variant | A required array of doubles specifying a list of 3-D vertex points in WCS coordinates. It's a simple array with a single dimension composed of alternating X, Y, and Z values (i.e., p1x, p1y, p1z, p2x, p2y, p2z, etc.). |
| FilterCodes | Variant | An optional array of integer entity selection filter codes. This must be used in conjunction with, and have the same length as, FilterValues. |
| FilterValues | Variant | An optional array of variant entity selection filter values. This must be used in conjunction with, and have the same length as, FilterCodes. |

The `SelectByPolygon` method has several modes of operation specified by the `Mode` parameter. AutoCAD provides the `AcSelect` constants listed in Table 12-8 for use with this parameter.

*Table 12-8. SelectByPolygon Method Modes*

| CONSTANT | VALUE | DESCRIPTION |
|---|---|---|
| acSelectionSetFence | 2 | Entities crossing a multisegment fence specified by `Vertices`. At least two vertices must be specified. |
| acSelectionSetWindowPolygon | 6 | Entities completely contained within a polygon specified by the `Vertices` are selected. At least three vertices must be specified. |
| acSelectionSetCrossingPolygon | 7 | Entities contained within or crossing a polygon specified by the `Vertices` are selected. At least three vertices must be specified. |

Like the other `Select` methods, `SelectByPolygon` can optionally filter the selected entities using criteria specified in the `FilterCodes` and `FilterValues` parameters. See the "Selection Set Filters" section for a full description of filtering.

The following example selects entities based on a user specified boundary and mode:

```
Public Sub TestSelectByPolygon()
    Dim objSS As AcadSelectionSet
    Dim strOpt As String
    Dim lngMode As Long
    Dim varPoints As Variant

    On Error GoTo Done
    With ThisDrawing.Utility

        '' create a new selectionset
        Set objSS = ThisDrawing.SelectionSets.Add("TestSelectByPolygon1")

        '' get the mode from the user
        .InitializeUserInput 1, "Fence Window Crossing"
        strOpt = .GetKeyword(vbCr & "Select by [Fence/Window/Crossing]: ")
```

```
'' convert keyword into mode
Select Case strOpt
        Case "Fence":    lngMode = acSelectionSetFence
        Case "Window":   lngMode = acSelectionSetWindowPolygon
        Case "Crossing": lngMode = acSelectionSetCrossingPolygon
End Select

'' let user digitize points
varPoints = InputPoints()

'' select entities using mode and points specified
objSS.SelectByPolygon lngMode, varPoints

'' highlight the selected entities
objSS.Highlight True

'' pause for the user
.Prompt vbCr & objSS.Count & " entities selected"
.GetString False, vbLf & "Enter to continue "

'' dehighlight the entities
objSS.Highlight False

      End With

Done:

'' if the selection was created, delete it
If Not objSS Is Nothing Then
    objSS.Delete
End If
End Sub
```

This example uses a helper function named InputPoints to obtain the boundary points. Here's the code for this function:

```
Function InputPoints() As Variant
    Dim varStartPoint As Variant
    Dim varNextPoint As Variant
    Dim varWCSPoint As Variant
    Dim lngLast As Long
    Dim dblPoints() As Double
```

```
    On Error Resume Next
  '' get first points from user
  With ThisDrawing.Utility
      .InitializeUserInput 1
      varStartPoint = .GetPoint(, vbLf & "Pick the start point: ")

      '' setup initial point
      ReDim dblPoints(2)
      dblPoints(0) = varStartPoint(0)
      dblPoints(1) = varStartPoint(1)
      dblPoints(2) = varStartPoint(2)
      varNextPoint = varStartPoint

      '' append vertexes in a loop
      Do
          '' translate picked point to UCS for basepoint below
          varWCSPoint = .TranslateCoordinates(varNextPoint, acWorld, _
                                              acUCS, True)

          '' get user point for new vertex, use last pick as basepoint
          varNextPoint = .GetPoint(varWCSPoint, vbCr & _
                                  "Pick another point <exit>: ")

          '' exit loop if no point picked
          If Err Then Exit Do

          '' get the upper bound
          lngLast = UBound(dblPoints)

          '' expand the array
          ReDim Preserve dblPoints(lngLast + 3)

          '' add the new point
          dblPoints(lngLast + 1) = varNextPoint(0)
          dblPoints(lngLast + 2) = varNextPoint(1)
          dblPoints(lngLast + 3) = varNextPoint(2)
      Loop
  End With

  '' return the points
  InputPoints = dblPoints
End Function
```

Figure 12-1 illustrates the results of the three selection options. The solid shapes represent AutoCAD drawing objects, and the dashed line represents the path of the selecting polygon.

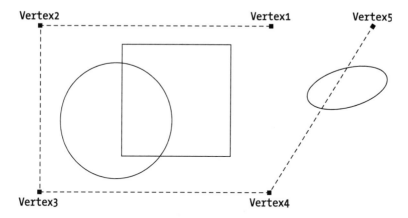

*Figure 12-1. TestSelectByPolygon example output*

The following parameters are used to define the area selected:

```
acSelectionSetFence: only the ellipse is selected
acSelectionSetWindowPolygon: the circle and square are both selected
acSelectionSetCrossingPolygon: all objects are selected
```

## Adding and Removing Items

You can add individual entities to and remove individual entities from a selection set by using the AddItem and RemoveItem methods (see Table 12-9 for parameter details). These methods take an array of entities as a parameter. Both methods will raise exceptions if for some reason they're unable to add or remove all the entities in the array.

```
SelectionSetObject.AddItem(Entities)
SelectionSetObject.RemoveItem(Entities)
```

*Table 12-9. AddItem and RemoveItem Method Parameters*

| NAME | DATA TYPE | DESCRIPTION |
|------|-----------|-------------|
| Entities | Array of AcadEntity objects | The entities to add to or remove from the selection set |

The following example adds and removes entities in a selection set until the user is satisfied with his or her choice:

```
Public Sub TestSelectAddRemoveClear()
    Dim objSS As AcadSelectionSet
    Dim objSStmp As AcadSelectionSet
    Dim strType As String
    Dim objEnts() As AcadEntity
    Dim intI As Integer

    On Error Resume Next

  With ThisDrawing.Utility
      '' create a new selectionset
      Set objSS = ThisDrawing.SelectionSets.Add("ssAddRemoveClear")
      If Err Then GoTo Done

      '' create a new temporary selection
      Set objSStmp = ThisDrawing.SelectionSets.Add("ssAddRemoveClearTmp")
      If Err Then GoTo Done

      '' loop until the user has finished
      Do
          '' clear any pending errors
          Err.Clear

          '' get input for type
          .InitializeUserInput 1, "Add Remove Clear Exit"
          strType = .GetKeyword(vbCr & "Select [Add/Remove/Clear/Exit]: ")

          '' branch based on input
          If "Exit" = strType Then

              '' exit if requested
              Exit Do
```

```
                ElseIf "Clear" = strType Then

                    '' dehighlight the main selection
                    objSS.Highlight False

                    '' clear the main set
                    objSS.Clear

            '' otherwise, we're adding/removing
            Else

                    '' clear the temporary selection
                    objSStmp.Clear

                    objSStmp.SelectOnScreen
                    '' highlight the temporary selection
                    objSStmp.Highlight True

                    '' convert temporary selection to array

                    '' resize the entity array to the selection size
                    ReDim objEnts(objSStmp.Count - 1)

                    '' copy entities from the selection to entity array
                    For intI = 0 To objSStmp.Count - 1
                        Set objEnts(intI) = objSStmp(intI)
                    Next

                    '' add/remove items from main selection using entity array
                    If "Add" = strType Then
                        objSS.AddItems objEnts
                    Else
                        objSS.RemoveItems objEnts
                    End If

                    '' dehighlight the temporary selection
                    objSStmp.Highlight False

                    '' highlight the main selection
                    objSS.Highlight True
            End If
        Loop
    End With
```

```
Done:

    '' if the selections were created, delete them
    If Not objSS Is Nothing Then

        '' dehighlight the entities
        objSS.Highlight False

        '' delete the main selection
        objSS.Delete
    End If

    If Not objSStmp Is Nothing Then

        '' delete the temporary selection
        objSStmp.Delete
    End If
End Sub
```

## The Clear, Delete, and Erase Methods

The remaining methods deal with clearing all entities from the selection, deleting the SelectionSet object itself, and erasing all the selected entities.

The Clear method simply clears the contents of a SelectionSet object. Entities that were in the selection are still present in the AutoCAD drawing—they're just no longer in the selection set.

```
SelectionSetObject.Clear
```

The Delete method deletes a SelectionSet object by removing it from the SelectionSets collection. Entities that were in the selection are still present in the AutoCAD drawing—the selection set is just deleted. Most of the examples in this chapter have used Delete after the program is complete.

```
SelectionSetObject.Delete
```

The Erase method erases the contents of a SelectionSet object from the AutoCAD drawing. Entities that were in the selection are immediately erased, but the SelectionSet object is still active and new entities may be added to it.

```
SelectionSetObject.Erase
```

The following example erases a selection of entities based on user input:

```
Public Sub TestSelectErase()
    Dim objSS As AcadSelectionSet

    On Error GoTo Done
    With ThisDrawing.Utility

        '' create a new selectionset
        Set objSS = ThisDrawing.SelectionSets.Add("TestSelectErase")

        '' let user select entities interactively
        objSS.SelectOnScreen

        '' highlight the selected entities
        objSS.Highlight True

        '' erase the selected entities
        objSS.Erase

        '' prove that the selection is empty (but still viable)
        .Prompt vbCr & objSS.Count & " entities selected"

    End With

Done:

    '' if the selection was created, delete it
    If Not objSS Is Nothing Then
        objSS.Delete
    End If
End Sub
```

## The PickFirstSelectionSet Property

AutoCAD allows users to select entities in either a verb-noun or a noun-verb manner. A verb-noun selection is one in which a command is issued first, followed by a selection of entities to work with. A noun-verb selection is one in which entities are selected first and then a command that uses them is issued. One of the benefits of noun-verb selection is that by performing only one selection, you can run multiple independent commands in sequence on the same set of entities.

The selection of entities built by the user when AutoCAD is idle at the command prompt is called the PickFirst selection set. This selection set is available via the read-only `PickfirstSelectionSet` property of each drawing object. A special `SelectionSet` named `PICKFIRST` is created by AutoCAD whenever the property is accessed. If the user does not preselect any entities, this selection set will be empty.

```
Set SelectionSetObject = DocumentObject.PickfirstSelectionSet
```

## The SelectionChanged Event

You can receive notification every time the user add entities to or removes entities from the PickFirst selection set by using the `SelectionChanged` event of each `Document` object. This event is fired any time the PickFirst selection set is altered. Chapter 4 discusses events in more detail.

To demonstrate that the `SelectionChanged` event is triggered, the following example, which you should place in the `ThisDrawing` module, tells the user how many objects are in the PickFirst selection set and then changes the highlight of the PickFirst selection set after .5 second. No doubt you'll find a more useful way to use this event.

```
Private Sub AcadDocument_SelectionChanged()
     Dim objSS As AcadSelectionSet
     Dim dblStart As Double

    '' get the pickfirst selection from drawing
    Set objSS = ThisDrawing.PickfirstSelectionSet

    '' highlight the selected entities
    objSS.Highlight True
    MsgBox "There are " & objSS.Count & " objects in selection set: " &
objSS.Name
    '' delay for 1/2 second
    dblStart = Timer
    Do While Timer < dblStart + 0.5
    Loop

    '' dehighlight the selected entities
    objSS.Highlight False
End Sub
```

## Groups

AutoCAD allows you to have a more permanent form of selection set called a *group*. Just like SelectionSet objects, Group objects associate an arbitrary set of entities into a collection that you can use all at once in many operations. You can associate entities with any number of groups, and you can have any number of entities in a single group.

By default, when an entity that belongs to a group is selected, all the other members of the group are automatically selected as well. The behavior is controlled by the PICKSTYLE system variable. See the AutoCAD User's Guide for details on other possible values for this variable.

Despite being collected into a group, entities that make up a group are still easily editable on an individual basis. This is in contrast to blocks in which, once entities are collected into a Block Definition and then inserted, the entities are quite difficult to edit individually. However, it's interesting to note that Group objects can have Xdata attached to them, and they have available nearly all the same default properties that other entities have, such as Color, Linetype, Lineweight, PlotStyle, Visible, and even TrueColor.

You normally create and edit groups through the Object Grouping dialog box (see Figure 12-2), which you can view by typing **GROUP** at the AutoCAD command prompt.

*Figure 12-2. The Object Grouping dialog box*

## Adding a Group Object

Just like with selection sets, you use the Add method of the collection to create a new Group object as detailed in Table 12-10.

```
Set GroupObject = GroupsCollection.Add(Name)
```

*Table 12-10. Add Method Parameters*

| NAME | DATA TYPE | DESCRIPTION |
| --- | --- | --- |
| Name | String | The name of the newly created group |

If you try to add a Group object with a name that is already being used, this method will return a reference to the existing object.

The following example attempts to add a group using a name obtained from the user:

```
Public Sub TestAddGroup()
    Dim objGroup As AcadGroup
    Dim strName As String

    On Error Resume Next
    '' get a name from user
    strName = InputBox("Enter a new group name: ")
    If "" = strName Then Exit Sub

    Set objGroup = ThisDrawing.Groups.Item(strName)
    '' create it
    If Not objGroup Is Nothing Then
        MsgBox "Group already exists"
        Exit Sub
    End If

    Set objGroup = ThisDrawing.Groups.Add(strName)

    '' check if it was created
    If objGroup Is Nothing Then
        MsgBox "Unable to Add '" & strName & "'"
```

```
        Else
            MsgBox "Added group '" & objGroup.Name & "'"
        End If
End Sub
```

## Accessing and Iterating Groups

The Groups collection is accessed via a Document object. In this code, ThisDrawing is used as the active document:

```
Dim objGroups As AcadGroups
Set objGroups = ThisDrawing.Groups
```

To set a reference to an existing Group object, use the Item method of the Groups collection:

```
Dim objGroup As AcadGroup

Set objGroup = objGroups.Item(2)
Set objGroup = objGroups.Item("My Group")
```

The parameter of this method is either a number representing the position of the desired Group object within the Groups collection or a string representing the name of the desired Group object. If you use an index number, it must be between 0 and N-1, in which N is the total number of groups in the collection.

Like other AutoCAD collections, Item is the default method for Groups. This means that the method name may be omitted, and the parameter passed straight to the Groups reference. Again, however, Microsoft guidelines recommend against using default methods and properties. You should always make a habit of invoking methods and accessing properties explicitly.

You may iterate through the Groups collection in the same way as you do the SelectionSets collection discussed at the beginning of this chapter.

```
Public Sub ListGroups()
    Dim objGroup As AcadGroup
    Dim strGroupList As String

    For Each objGroup In ThisDrawing.Groups
        strGroupList = strGroupList & vbCr & objGroup.Name
    Next
    MsgBox strGroupList, vbOKOnly, "List of Groups"
End Sub
```

# Adding and Removing Items

You can add individual entities to and remove individual entities from a group by using the AppendItem and RemoveItem methods (see Table 12-11 for parameter details). These methods take an array of entities as a parameter. Both methods raise exceptions if for some reason they're unable to append or remove all the entities in the array. So if you try to append three items and one of them is already a member of the group, an error is raised and none of the items will be appended.

```
GroupObject.AppendItem(Entities)
GroupObject.RemoveItem(Entities)
```

*Table 12-11. AppendItem and RemoveItem Method Parameters*

| NAME | DATA TYPE | DESCRIPTION |
| --- | --- | --- |
| Entities | Array of AcadEntity objects | The entities to append to or remove from the group |

 **NOTE**  *The* RemoveItem *method doesn't remove the entities from your drawing. It simply dissociates them from the* Group *object.*

The following example adds or removes entities in a selection set depending on the user's choice:

```
Public Sub TestGroupAppendRemove()
    Dim objSS As AcadSelectionSet
    Dim objGroup As AcadGroup
    Dim objEnts() As AcadEntity
    Dim strName As String
    Dim strOpt As String
    Dim intI As Integer

    On Error Resume Next
    '' set pickstyle to NOT select groups
    ThisDrawing.SetVariable "Pickstyle", 2
```

```
With ThisDrawing.Utility
    '' get group name from user
    strName = .GetString(True, vbCr & "Group name: ")
    If Err Or "" = strName Then GoTo Done

    '' get the existing group or add new one
    Set objGroup = ThisDrawing.Groups.Add(strName)

    '' pause for the user
    .Prompt vbCr & "Group contains: " & objGroup.Count & " entities" & _
            vbCrLf

    '' get input for mode
    .InitializeUserInput 1, "Append Remove"
    strOpt = .GetKeyword(vbCr & "Option [Append/Remove]: ")
    If Err Then GoTo Done

    '' create a new selectionset
    Set objSS = ThisDrawing.SelectionSets.Add("TestGroupAppendRemove")
    If Err Then GoTo Done

    '' get a selection set from user
    objSS.SelectOnScreen

    '' convert selection set to array
    '' resize the entity array to the selection size
    ReDim objEnts(objSS.Count - 1)

    '' copy entities from the selection to entity array
    For intI = 0 To objSS.Count - 1
        Set objEnts(intI) = objSS(intI)
    Next

    '' append or remove entities based on input
    If "Append" = strOpt Then
        objGroup.AppendItems objEnts
    Else
        objGroup.RemoveItems objEnts
    End If

    '' pause for the user
    .Prompt vbCr & "Group contains: " & objGroup.Count & " entities"
```

```
      '' dehighlight the entities
      objSS.Highlight False
   End With


Done:
   If Err Then MsgBox "Error occurred: " & Err.Description
   '' if the selection was created, delete it
   If Not objSS Is Nothing Then
      objSS.Delete
   End If
End Sub
```

## The Delete Method

The Delete method deletes a Group object by removing it from the Groups collection. Entities that were in the group are still present in the AutoCAD drawing; the Group object is just deleted. This is somewhat like exploding a block insertion, except that when the Group object has been eliminated, so has its name from the collection stack.

```
GroupObject.Delete
```

The following example deletes a group based on user input:

```
Public Sub TestGroupDelete()
      Dim objGroup As AcadGroup
      Dim strName As String

      On Error Resume Next
   With ThisDrawing.Utility

      strName = .GetString(True, vbCr & "Group name: ")
      If Err Or "" = strName Then Exit Sub

      '' get the existing group
      Set objGroup = ThisDrawing.Groups.Item(strName)
      If Err Then
         .Prompt vbCr & "Group does not exist "
         Exit Sub
      End If
```

```
        '' delete the group
        objGroup.Delete
        If Err Then
            .Prompt vbCr & "Error deleting group "
            Exit Sub
        End If

        '' pause for the user
        .Prompt vbCr & "Group deleted"
    End With
End Sub
```

## Summary

In this chapter you've seen how to build SelectionSet collections and SelectionSet objects, filter their content using specific criteria, allow the user to create dynamic selections, and handle PickFirst selections. You've also learned how to make Group objects for a more persistent type of entity association and manipulation capabilities.

CHAPTER 13

# Blocks, Attributes, and External References

**BLOCKS COLLECT ANY NUMBER** of AutoCAD entities into a single container object. Create a `BlockReference` object to insert the `Block` container object (also known as a *block definition*) model space, paper space, or another block definition. Because the `BlockReference` refers to the block definition's geometry, it is a very efficient means for managing drawing data:

- You can add, move, copy, and so on, the entity collection as a whole.

- You can create a library of commonly used geometry, ready for reuse.

- You can save memory by storing all block references in one block definition.

- You can make global changes by redefining the block definition at any time—all block references immediately reflect the changes.

Blocks differ from `Group` objects in several ways:

- They are more distinctly named and constructed.

- You can also use ObjectDBX to import and export them between drawings because they contain entity construct data, whereas `Group` objects only maintain a list of entities that belong to them.

- AutoCAD lets you create `Block` objects and programmatically add them to your drawing, much as users do through the AutoCAD user interface.

- There is neither a limit to the number of entities in a block definition, nor any limit to the number of block references.

When you define a block, you can use it as often as you need. You can create drawings faster because you don't have to create the individual objects in the block.

Attributes let you attach text to blocks. Like the blocks to which they are attached, attributes have both a definition and a reference. The `Attribute` object is the definition, and is associated with a `Block` object. This *attribute definition* is the template for creating `AttributeReference` objects associated with new `BlockReference` objects.

While the geometry for each `BlockReference` is identical, the associated `Attribute` objects may differ. You can make the `Attribute` visible, give it all the font characteristics of AutoCAD `Text` entities, or make it invisible if the text only stores data.

This chapter explains

- How to create and manipulate `Block` objects

- How to insert a `Block` object into an AutoCAD drawing

- How to work with external reference files

- How to create `Attribute` objects

- How to insert `Block` objects with attributes

## Blocks and Block References

The `Block` object represents a block definition, which contains a name and a set of entities. `Block` objects have two elements:

- A *block definition*, which is the abstract database structure that defines a `Block` object's entities.

- A *block reference* (or *block insertion*), which is the actual insertion in a drawing.

Changing a block definition also changes every block reference in the drawing. When you explode, modify, and recreate a block in a drawing, AutoCAD rebuilds the block definition in the drawing database. You can, however, directly modify the block definition database programmatically without having to do anything in the graphical interface.

There are three kinds of blocks:

**Simple block.** The most common type of block definition, the simple block is a collection of objects that form a single new Block object. You can populate simple blocks either with new geometric entities, by copying existing drawing objects into it, or by inserting another AutoCAD drawing into it. You create references to simple blocks with the InsertBlock method, which returns a new BlockReference object. You can control the insertion point, scales and rotation angle of this reference, or *instance*, in the drawing.

**Externally referenced block.** An *externally referenced* block is linked to another drawing file on disk. When someone makes changes to the drawing on disk, AutoCAD shows the changes the next time you generate the reference. Because the block definition is not in the current file, you can't modify its contents from the current drawing. You can get around this in the graphical environment using AutoCAD 2002/2004 commands like REFEDIT.

**Layout block.** A *layout* block contains the geometry associated with one of the Layout objects, which is represented as tabs at the bottom of the drawing window. You create layout blocks using the Layouts collection's Add method, which returns a new Layout object. You can use this object's Block property to access the layout block.

AutoCAD creates several layouts, which have the layout blocks listed in Table 13-1.

*Table 13-1. Created Layouts*

| LAYOUT NAME | PURPOSE |
| --- | --- |
| *MODEL_SPACE | The model space layout and corresponds to the ModelSpace collection. |
| *PAPER_SPACE | The active paper space layout and corresponds to the PaperSpace collection. |
| *PAPER_SPACE0 through *PAPER_SPACEn | The first through the last paper space layouts created. |

**NOTE**  *When a paper space layout becomes active it is renamed* *PAPER_SPACE.

Use the `IsLayout` and `IsXRef` properties to identify the block definition type. If both of these properties are `False`, then the `Block` object is a simple block.

Users usually create simple block definitions using the `Block Definition` dialog box. Use the `BLOCK` command to open it. Figure 13-1 shows this dialog box.

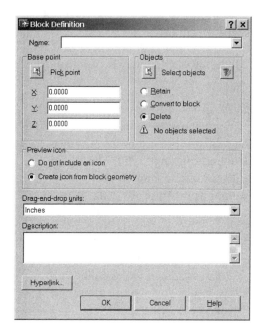

*Figure 13-1. The Block Definition dialog box*

All of the GUI's functionality is available in the `Block` object's properties and methods.

## Accessing Block Objects

AutoCAD `Document` objects have a `Blocks` collection that contains all of the drawing's `Block` definition objects. Access the `Blocks` collection with a `Document` object. The following code uses `ThisDrawing` as the active document:

```
Dim objBlocks As AcadBlocks
Set objBlocks = ThisDrawing.Blocks
MsgBox "There are " & objBlocks.Count & " Block objects"
```

To set a reference to an existing `Block` object, use the `Blocks` collection's `Item` method.

```
Dim objBlock As AcadBlock

Set objBlock = ThisDrawing.Blocks.Item(2)
Set objBlock = ThisDrawing.Blocks.Item("My Block")
```

As in other AutoCAD collections, `Item` is the default method for `Blocks`, so you can omit the method name and pass the parameter straight to the `Blocks` reference.

---

 **NOTE** *Even though this method is simpler to type and read, it goes against Microsoft programming guidelines and is no longer supported in the .NET and VSA programming environments.*

---

The following code does the same thing as the previous example, instead using the default method to specify the `Block` object:

```
Dim objBlock As AcadBlock

Set objBlock = ThisDrawing.Blocks(2)
Set objBlock = ThisDrawing.Blocks("My Block")
```

## Iterating the Blocks Collection

As in all Visual Basic collections, `Blocks` support iteration using a `For ... Each` loop. The following example iterates through the `Blocks` collection, displaying each `Block` name in a message box:

```
Public Sub ListBlocks()
Dim objBlock As AcadBlock
Dim strBlockList As String

    strBlockList = "List of blocks: "

    For Each objBlock In ThisDrawing.Blocks
        strBlockList = strBlockList & vbCr & objBlock.Name
    Next

    MsgBox strBlockList
End Sub
```

Figure 13-2 shows this code's result for a newly created drawing.

*Figure 13-2. Block code output*

Try adding a new layout to AutoCAD and then running this code again. It adds a new block. AutoCAD links these new Block objects to the different Layout objects, and hold the geometry of the various drawing layouts.

## Creating Blocks

You can create as many blocks as you need. You can create a simple block definition in two ways. The first uses the Blocks collection's Add method to create an empty Block object. You can then add entities to this new definition. The second uses the InsertBlock method of ModelSpace, PaperSpace or a Block object to both create a block definition and insert a block reference from an external drawing file.

### The Add Method

Use the Blocks collection's Add method to add a new Block object. The method takes a single string parameter—the new block's name. It returns a reference to the new Block object. If the parameter is not a valid block name, Add raises an exception. If you try to name a new block the same as an existing block, Add returns a reference to the existing Block object. This method has the following syntax:

```
Set BlockObject = BlocksCollection.Add(InsertionPoint, BlockName)
```

Table 13-2 explains this method's parameters.

When you create this object, it does not contain any entities. You can add them with the AddXXX methods discussed later in this chapter and in more detail in Chapters 8 and 9.

*Table 13-2. Add Method Parameters*

| NAME | DATA TYPE | DESCRIPTION |
|------|-----------|-------------|
| InsertionPoint | Variant | A three-element array of doubles that specify the block's insertion basepoint in WCS coordinates. |
| BlockName | String | The new Block object's name. |

The following example adds a simple block definition to the Blocks collection and adds a circle to it. The user can then insert the new block in the normal way.

```
Public Sub AddBlock()
Dim dblOrigin(2) As Double
Dim objBlock As AcadBlock
Dim strName As String

    '' get a name from user
    strName = InputBox("Enter a new block name: ")
    If "" = strName Then Exit Sub          ' exit if no old name

    '' set the origin point
    dblOrigin(0) = 0:  dblOrigin(1) = 0:   dblOrigin(2) = 0

    ''check if block already exists
On Error Resume Next
    Set objBlock = ThisDrawing.Blocks.Item(strName)
    If Not objBlock Is Nothing Then
        MsgBox "Block already exists"
        Exit Sub
    End If

    '' create the block
    Set objBlock = ThisDrawing.Blocks.Add(dblOrigin, strName)

    '' then add entities (circle)
    objBlock.AddCircle dblOrigin, 10

End Sub
```

### AddXXX Methods

Use the Add*XXX* methods to add drawing entities to a Block object, and therefore populate a new Block object. We've already seen a simple example of this in the AddBlock example earlier. Chapters 8 and 9 cover the Add*XXX* methods fully.

### CopyObject Method

Another way to populate a Block object with new entities is to use the Document object's CopyObject method to add duplicate entities. This method copies objects from one container to another. It also returns a variant array of the objects created during the copy. These new objects are exact duplicates, with the same relative positions, sizes, scales and properties. This method has the following syntax:

```
varCopies = Owner.CopyObjects(Objects [, NewOwner] [, IdMap])
```

Table 13-3 explains this method's parameters.

*Table 13-3. CopyObject Method Parameters*

| NAME | DATA TYPE | DESCRIPTION |
|------|-----------|-------------|
| Owner | Document, PaperSpace, ModelSpace or Block objects | The current containing owner of the objects to copy. |
| Objects | Variant | An array of objects to copy. The objects must all belong to the Owner object. |
| NewOwner | Variant | Optional. Specifies the objects' new owner of. If null, the objects are copied to the Owner object. This can also be another document object. |
| IdMap | Variant | Optional. An array that holds IDPair objects. |

The IdMap array is most useful for copying objects between databases or drawing files. The IDPair object describes how objects map from source to destination, including non-primary but referenced objects. A full description of the IDPair object and its use is beyond the scope of this chapter. You will not need this optional functionality when you create blocks.

The following example creates and populates a block definition by copying the specified entities into the block:

```
Public Sub TestCopyObjects()
Dim objSS As AcadSelectionSet
Dim varBase As Variant
Dim objBlock As AcadBlock
Dim strName As String
Dim strErase As String
Dim varEnt As Variant
Dim objSourceEnts() As Object
Dim varDestEnts As Variant
Dim dblOrigin(2) As Double
Dim intI As Integer


    'choose a selection set name that you only use as temporary storage and
    'ensure that it does not currently exist
On Error Resume Next
    ThisDrawing.SelectionSets.Item("TempSSet").Delete
    Set objSS = ThisDrawing.SelectionSets.Add("TempSSet")
    objSS.SelectOnScreen

    '' get the other user input
    With ThisDrawing.Utility
        .InitializeUserInput 1
        strName = .GetString(True, vbCr & "Enter a block name: ")
        .InitializeUserInput 1
        varBase = .GetPoint(, vbCr & "Pick a base point: ")
        .InitializeUserInput 1, "Yes No"
        strErase = .GetKeyword(vbCr & "Erase originals [Yes/No]? ")
    End With

    '' set WCS origin
    dblOrigin(0) = 0: dblOrigin(1) = 0: dblOrigin(2) = 0

    '' create the block
    Set objBlock = ThisDrawing.Blocks.Add(dblOrigin, strName)
```

```
'' put selected entities into an array for CopyObjects
ReDim objSourceEnts(objSS.Count - 1)
For intI = 0 To objSS.Count - 1
    Set objSourceEnts(intI) = objSS(intI)
Next

'' copy the entities into block
varDestEnts = ThisDrawing.CopyObjects(objSourceEnts, objBlock)

'' move copied entities so that basepoint becomes origin
For Each varEnt In varDestEnts
    varEnt.Move varBase, dblOrigin
Next

'' if requested, erase the originals
If strErase = "Yes" Then
    objSS.Erase
End If

'' we're done - prove that we did it
ThisDrawing.SendCommand "._-insert" & vbCr & strName & vbCr

'' clean up selection set
objSS.Delete
End Sub
```

**NOTE** *If you try to copy the container object to itself, it reproduces itself an infinite number of times. You can't execute this method at the same time you iterate through a collection. An iteration opens the work space as read only, while this method tries to perform a read/write operation. Complete any iteration before you call this method. The CopyObjects operation copies objects that the Objects parameter's primary objects own or reference.*

## Renaming a Block Object

To rename a block definition, assign a new string value to its Name property. Block references to the block definition are automatically adjusted. Take care to address other possible exceptions that may be thrown: invalid name, existing name, and so on.

**NOTE** *Renaming an AutoCAD-defined layout block or any anony-mous block, which is a block whose name begins with an asterisk (\*), may crash AutoCAD.*

The following example renames a `Block` definition based on user input:

```
Public Sub RenameBlock()
Dim strName As String
Dim objBlock As AcadBlock

On Error Resume Next                  ' handle exceptions inline
    strName = InputBox("Original Block name: ")
    If "" = strName Then Exit Sub          ' exit if no old name

    Set objBlock = ThisDrawing.Blocks.Item(strName)
    If objBlock Is Nothing Then            ' exit if not found
        MsgBox "Block '" & strName & "' not found"
        Exit Sub
    End If

    strName = InputBox("New Block name: ")
    If "" = strName Then Exit Sub          ' exit if no new name

    objBlock.Name = strName                ' try and change name
    If Err Then                            ' check if it worked
        MsgBox "Unable to rename block: " & vbCr & Err.Description
    Else
        MsgBox "Block renamed to '" & strName & "'"
    End If

End Sub
```

## Deleting a Block Object

The `Delete` method removes a `Block` object from the `Blocks` collection. This method takes no parameters and returns nothing. It has the following syntax:

```
BlockObject.Delete
```

You can delete a block whenever you choose—unless the block can't be deleted. You can't delete a block when:

**A BlockReference object references it.** If a `BlockReference` object references a block definition in model space, any paper space layout, or any other block definition, you can't delete it. There is no definitive way to tell which entities reference a specific block, short of exhaustively searching each of these collections. If you delete all references or make them reference a different block, you can then delete the block definition. Keep in mind that deleting a block object does not delete the block definition table entry. To completely remove a block definition, invoke a Purge operation on the document.

**It depends on an Xref.** You create a block that depends on Xref when you attach an activate an External Reference File. You don't need to delete these blocks, however, because they're simply duplications of the blocks in the external drawing. AutoCAD doesn't save them with the current drawing.

---

 **NOTE** *AutoCAD creates certain blocks for its own purposes, such as the special layout blocks created for each layout. Deleting an AutoCAD-defined layout block or any other block whose name begins with an asterisk (\*) can crash AutoCAD.*

---

The following example deletes a block based on user input. Try it on some blocks created with the `AddBlock` code sample. In general, whenever you delete a collection member, such a block definition, execute a Purge to clean up your drawing database. You'll see that you can't delete the block definition until you remove all the block references:

```
Public Sub DeleteBlock()
Dim strName As String
Dim objBlock As AcadBlock

On Error Resume Next                    ' handle exceptions inline
    strName = InputBox("Block name to delete: ")
    If "" = strName Then Exit Sub            ' exit if no old name

    Set objBlock = ThisDrawing.Blocks.Item(strName)
    If objBlock Is Nothing Then              ' exit if not found
        MsgBox "Block '" & strName & "' not found"
        Exit Sub
```

```
        End If

        objBlock.Delete                      ' try to delete it
        If Err Then                          ' check if it worked
            MsgBox "Unable to delete Block: " & vbCr & Err.Description
        Else
            MsgBox "Block '" & strName & "' deleted"
        End If
End Sub
```

### The InsertBlock Method

The InsertBlock method of ModelSpace, PaperSpace, and Block objects serves two purposes. Its first purpose, which this chapter discusses in detail later, is to create a BlockReference object. Its second purpose is to create a block definition from a drawing file on disk. When you give it an external file name, InsertBlock imports the external drawing, creating a new Block object with the drawing's contents and inserting that file as a block reference.

**NOTE**   *This operation imports any other blocks defined in the external drawing file.*

## Defining and Manipulating Blocks

After you define a block, you can use a number of methods to change the block's composition, select objects from the block, and break the block down into its parts.

### The Item Method

Use the Item method to access the objects in the block definition object. This method has the following syntax:

```
Set objEntity = BlockObject.Item(Index)
```

This method has one parameter, Index, an Integer that gives the element's position in the Block collection object.

Because the Item method is the Block object's default method, you can omit and use the following syntax. But it's best to avoid this in favor of using explicit references to all properties and methods, since Microsoft programming technologies are dropping this feature to gain performance, security and consistency. For example, .NET and VSA no longer let you use default methods and properties.

```
Set objEntity = BlockObject(Index)
```

## The InsertBlock Method

Use the InsertBlock method to add a BlockReference object to a drawing or to nest a block in another Block object. This can be either a block in the Blocks collection or an external drawing file. In either case, this method returns a BlockReference object. The PaperSpace, ModelSpace, and Block objects expose this method.

```
Set BlockReferenceObject = Object.InsertBlock(InsertionPoint, BlockName, _
Xscale, Yscale, ZScale, RotationAngle)
```

Table 13-4 explains this method's parameters.

*Table 13-4. InsertBlock Method Parameters*

| NAME | DATA TYPE | DESCRIPTION |
| --- | --- | --- |
| InsertionPoint | Variant | A three-element array of doubles that specifies the 3D WCS coordinates where the block will be inserted into the Object. |
| BlockName | String | The name of a Block object in the Blocks collection or the path and file name of an AutoCAD drawing file to import. |
| Xscale | Double | A scaling factor for the block's X direction. It may not be 0. Negative numbers mirror the insertion on this axis. |
| Yscale | Double | A scaling factor for the block's Y direction. It may not be 0. Negative numbers mirror the insertion on this axis. |
| Zscale | Double | A scaling factor for the block's Z direction. It may not be 0. Negative numbers mirror the insertion on this axis. |
| RotationAngle | Double | The rotation angle relative to the WCS X-axis, expressed in radians. |

The following example creates a block reference based on user input:

```
Public Sub TestInsertBlock()
Dim strName As String
Dim varInsertionPoint As Variant
Dim dblX As Double
Dim dblY As Double
Dim dblZ As Double
Dim dblRotation As Double

    '' get input from user
    With ThisDrawing.Utility
        .InitializeUserInput 1
        strName = .GetString(True, vbCr & "Block or file name: ")
        .InitializeUserInput 1
        varInsertionPoint = .GetPoint(, vbCr & "Pick the insert point: ")
        .InitializeUserInput 1 + 2
        dblX = .GetDistance(varInsertionPoint, vbCr & "X scale: ")
        .InitializeUserInput 1 + 2
        dblY = .GetDistance(varInsertionPoint, vbCr & "Y scale: ")
        .InitializeUserInput 1 + 2
        dblZ = .GetDistance(varInsertionPoint, vbCr & "Z scale: ")
        .InitializeUserInput 1
        dblRotation = .GetAngle(varInsertionPoint, vbCr & "Rotation angle: ")
    End With

    '' create the object
On Error Resume Next

    ThisDrawing.ModelSpace.InsertBlock varInsertionPoint, strName, dblX, _
                                    dblY, dblZ, dblRotation
    If Err Then MsgBox "Unable to insert this block."

End Sub
```

Try it with the name of a block in the current drawing and with an external file name (including the .dwg file extension).

To give the user with a more friendly way to input the path and file name, you can build a GUI with a UserForm and use a Windows CommonDialog control. This control is not available on the UserForm toolbox, but you can add it by right-clicking the toolbox, selecting Additional Controls, and checking the Microsoft Common Dialog Control, Version 6.0 option. See Figure 13-3.

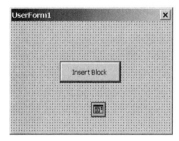

*Figure 13-3. Example UserForm*

If you add a Command Button named cmdInsertBlock and a CommonDialog control named dlgOpenFile to a UserForm, as shown in Figure 13-3, you could use the following code to see the familiar Open dialog box (see Figure 13-4) when you choose a drawing file.

```
Private Sub CommandButton1_Click()
    Dim objBlockRef As AcadBlockReference
    Dim varInsertionPoint As Variant
    Dim dblX As Double
    Dim dblY As Double
    Dim dblZ As Double
    Dim dblRotation As Double

    '' get input from user
    dlgOpenFile.Filter = "AutoCAD Blocks (*.DWG) | *.dwg"
    dlgOpenFile.InitDir = Application.Path      dlgOpenFile.ShowOpen

    If dlgOpenFile.FileName = "" Then Exit Sub
    Me.Hide
    With ThisDrawing.Utility
        .InitializeUserInput 1
        varInsertionPoint = .GetPoint(, vbCr & "Pick the insert point: ")
        .InitializeUserInput 1 + 2
        dblX = .GetDistance(varInsertionPoint, vbCr & "X scale: ")
        .InitializeUserInput 1 + 2
        dblY = .GetDistance(varInsertionPoint, vbCr & "Y scale: ")
        .InitializeUserInput 1 + 2
        dblZ = .GetDistance(varInsertionPoint, vbCr & "Z scale: ")
        .InitializeUserInput 1
        dblRotation = .GetAngle(varInsertionPoint, vbCr & "Rotation angle: ")
    End With
```

```
    '' create the object
On Error Resume Next
    Set objBlockRef = ThisDrawing.ModelSpace.InsertBlock(varInsertionPoint,
dlgOpenFile.FileName, dblX, _
        dblY, dblZ, dblRotation)

    If Err Then
        MsgBox "Unable to insert this block"
        Exit Sub
    End If
    objBlockRef.Update
    Me.Show
End Sub
```

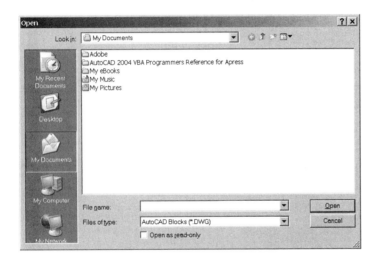

*Figure 13-4. The Open dialog box*

To control the displayed file types, set the CommonDialog control's Filter property. You must hide the form before you can access the AutoCAD interface, because AutoCAD 2000 VBA UserForms are modal.

## Deleting a Block Reference

As with any other entity, use the Delete method to delete block references. This method removes only the BlockReference object, not the Block definition object. This method has the following syntax:

```
BlockReferenceObject.Delete
```

## The Explode Method

The BlockReference object exposes the Explode method, which breaks down the block reference into its geometry. It returns an array of the block reference's objects. You can then select, move, copy, and so on, each entity individually. This method has the following syntax:

```
varArray = BlockReferenceObject.Explode
```

**NOTE**   *This method actually creates a new copy of the block defini-tion's entities and leaves the original unexploded block reference. If you don't want the reference, you must delete it yourself.*

**NOTE**   *In versions of AutoCAD before 2004, the* Explode *method explodes even nested* MText *objects into individual* Text *objects. The* Explode *method in AutoCAD 2004 leaves nested* MText *objects intact.*

The following example explodes a block reference and moves the resulting entities to a new location:

```
Public Sub TestExplode()
    Dim objBRef As AcadBlockReference
    Dim varPick As Variant
    Dim varNew As Variant
    Dim varEnts As Variant
    Dim intI As Integer

On Error Resume Next
    '' get an entity and new point from user
    With ThisDrawing.Utility
        .GetEntity objBRef, varPick, vbCr & "Pick a block reference: "
        If Err Then Exit Sub
        varNew = .GetPoint(varPick, vbCr & "Pick a new location: ")
        If Err Then Exit Sub
    End With
```

```
'' explode the blockref
varEnts = objBRef.Explode
If Err Then
    MsgBox "Error has occurred: " & Err.Description
    Exit Sub
End If

'' move resulting entities to new location
For intI = 0 To UBound(varEnts)
    varEnts(intI).Move varPick, varNew
Next
End Sub
```

## The WBlock Method

This method's name means *write block*. This Document object method saves a SelectionSet object's contents to disk as a new drawing file. You can import this file into other drawings as a block definition using InsertBlock as described earlier. The WBlock method returns nothing, but has the following syntax:

```
DocumentObject.WBlock FileName, SelectionSet
```

Table 13-5 explains this method's parameters.

*Table 13-5. WBlock Method Parameters*

| NAME | DATA TYPE | DESCRIPTION |
| --- | --- | --- |
| FileName | String | The new drawing file's name. If you don't specify an extension, the method uses .dwg. |
| SelectionSet | SelectionSet object | A selection set containing the entities to write to the new file. |

The method uses the selected entities' WCS origin as the base point for the drawing file. You may wish to relocate the entities before you use WBlock so that the new drawing has a meaningful base point.

The following example asks the user for a selection set of entities, a filename, and a base point to use as the new file origin. It then moves the entities to the

WCS origin using the selected base point. Next, it writes the entities to file using the WBlock method. Finally, it moves the entities back to their original location.

```
Public Sub TestWBlock()
Dim objSS As AcadSelectionSet
Dim varBase As Variant
Dim dblOrigin(2) As Double
Dim objEnt As AcadEntity
Dim strFilename As String

    'choose a selection set name that you only use as temporary storage and
    'ensure that it does not currently exist
On Error Resume Next
    ThisDrawing.SelectionSets("TempSSet").Delete
    Set objSS = ThisDrawing.SelectionSets.Add("TempSSet")
    objSS.SelectOnScreen

    With ThisDrawing.Utility
        .InitializeUserInput 1
        strFilename = .GetString(True, vbCr & "Enter a filename: ")
        .InitializeUserInput 1
        varBase = .GetPoint(, vbCr & "Pick a base point: ")
    End With

    '' WCS origin
    dblOrigin(0) = 0: dblOrigin(1) = 0: dblOrigin(2) = 0

    '' move selection to the origin
    For Each objEnt In objSS
        objEnt.Move varBase, dblOrigin
    Next

    '' wblock selection to filename
    ThisDrawing.Wblock strFilename, objSS

    '' move selection back
    For Each objEnt In objSS
        objEnt.Move dblOrigin, varBase
    Next

    '' clean up selection set
    objSS.Delete
End Sub
```

## Using MInsertBlock Objects

An `MInsertBlock` object contains a planar array of block references in rows and columns. This section tells how to add and modify `MInsertBlock` objects.

The `AddMInsertBlock` method works much like `InsertBlock`, except that the resulting entity is an `MInsertBlock` object. Just like `InsertBlock`, this method lets you specify new entity's insertion point, scale, and rotation angle. It has additional parameters for the arrayed rows and columns. The method has this syntax:

```
Set MInsertBlockObject = Object.AddMInsertBlock(InsertionPoint, BlockName, _
XScale, YScale, ZScale, RotationAngle, Rows, Columns, RowSpacing, _
ColumnSpacing)
```

Table 13-6 explains this method's parameters.

*Table 13-6. AddMInsertBlock Method Parameters*

| NAME | DATA TYPE | DESCRIPTION |
|------|-----------|-------------|
| InsertionPoint | Variant | A three-element array of doubles that specifies the 3D WCS coordinates where the Xref will be inserted into the Object. |
| BlockName | String | The name of a Block object in the Blocks collection, or the path and file name for an AutoCAD drawing file to import. |
| Xscale | Double | A scaling factor for the Xref's X direction. It may not be 0. Negative numbers mirror the insertion on this axis. |
| Yscale | Double | A scaling factor for the Xref's Y direction. It may not be 0. Negative numbers mirror the insertion on this axis. |
| Zscale | Double | A scaling factor for the Xref's Z direction. It may not be 0. Negative numbers mirror the insertion on this axis. |
| RotationAngle | Double | The rotation angle relative to the WCS X-axis, expressed in radians. |
| Rows | Long | A positive number that sets the number of rows. |
| Columns | Long | A positive number that sets the number of columns. |

*continues*

*Table 13-6. AddMInsertBlock Method Parameters, continued*

| NAME | DATA TYPE | DESCRIPTION |
|---|---|---|
| RowSpacing | Double | A nonzero number that specifies the spacing of rows in the array. A negative number creates rows in a negative X direction. |
| ColumnSpacing | Double | A nonzero number that specifies the spacing of columns in the array. A negative number creates columns in a negative Y direction. |

The following example creates a `MInsertBlock` based on user input:

```
Public Sub TestAddMInsertBlock()
Dim strName As String
Dim varInsertionPoint As Variant
Dim dblX As Double
Dim dblY As Double
Dim dblZ As Double
Dim dR As Double
Dim lngNRows As Long
Dim lngNCols As Long
Dim dblSRows As Double
Dim dblSCols As Double

    '' get input from user
    With ThisDrawing.Utility
        .InitializeUserInput 1
        strName = .GetString(True, vbCr & "Block or file name: ")
        .InitializeUserInput 1
        varInsertionPoint = .GetPoint(, vbCr & "Pick the insert point: ")
        .InitializeUserInput 1 + 2
        dblX = .GetDistance(varInsertionPoint, vbCr & "X scale: ")
        .InitializeUserInput 1 + 2
        dblY = .GetDistance(varInsertionPoint, vbCr & "Y scale: ")
        .InitializeUserInput 1 + 2
        dblZ = .GetDistance(varInsertionPoint, vbCr & "Z scale: ")
        .InitializeUserInput 1
        dR = .GetAngle(varInsertionPoint, vbCr & "Rotation angle: ")
        .InitializeUserInput 1 + 2 + 4
        lngNRows = .GetInteger(vbCr & "Number of rows: ")
```

```
        .InitializeUserInput 1 + 2 + 4
        lngNCols = .GetInteger(vbCr & "Number of columns: ")
        .InitializeUserInput 1 + 2
        dblSRows = .GetDistance(varInsertionPoint, vbCr & "Row spacing: ")
        .InitializeUserInput 1 + 2
        dblSCols = .GetDistance(varInsertionPoint, vbCr & "Column spacing: ")
    End With


    '' create the object
    ThisDrawing.ModelSpace.AddMInsertBlock varInsertionPoint, strName, _
                dblX, dblY, dblZ, dR, lngNRows, lngNCols, dblSRows, dblSCols
End Sub
```

While the `MInsertBlock` object is similar to a `BlockReference`, because it's an array, it has these extra properties: Row, Column, RowSpacing, and ColumnSpacing.

The following example adjusts an `MInsertBlock` object's array properties. Try it on the object the last example created.

```
Public Sub TestEditobjMInsertBlock()
Dim objMInsert As AcadMInsertBlock
Dim varPick As Variant
Dim lngNRows As Long
Dim lngNCols As Long
Dim dblSRows As Double
Dim dblSCols As Double


On Error Resume Next
    '' get an entity and input from user
    With ThisDrawing.Utility
        .GetEntity objMInsert, varPick, vbCr & "Pick an MInsert: "
        If objMInsert Is Nothing Then
            MsgBox "You did not choose an MInsertBlock object"
            Exit Sub
        End If
        .InitializeUserInput 1 + 2 + 4
        lngNRows = .GetInteger(vbCr & "Number of rows: ")
        .InitializeUserInput 1 + 2 + 4
        lngNCols = .GetInteger(vbCr & "Number of columns: ")
        .InitializeUserInput 1 + 2
        dblSRows = .GetDistance(varPick, vbCr & "Row spacing: ")
        .InitializeUserInput 1 + 2
        dblSCols = .GetDistance(varPick, vbCr & "Column spacing: ")
    End With
```

```
'' update the objMInsert
With objMInsert
    .Rows = lngNRows
    .Columns = lngNCols
    .RowSpacing = dblSRows
    .ColumnSpacing = dblSCols
    .Update
End With
End Sub
```

## External References

External references, or *Xrefs*, are blocks that are not permanently loaded into the current drawing file. Instead, Xrefs refer to an external drawing file for their geometry (hence their name).

External references share many properties and methods with simple blocks, and for many purposes you can treat them as simple blocks. But sometimes you might also need to use external references' special capabilities. This section explains the following Xref methods:

- Attaching and detaching

- Loading and unloading

- Binding

### Attaching External References

The `AttachExternalReference` method works much like `InsertBlock`, except that the resulting entity is an external reference instead of a block reference. Just like `InsertBlock`, the `PaperSpace`, `ModelSpace`, and `Block` objects expose this method and let you specify the insertion point, scale, and rotation angle in the drawing.

```
Set ExternalReferenceObject = Object.AttachExternalReference(FileName, _
BlockName, InsertionPoint, Xscale, Yscale, Zscale, RotationAngle, Overlay)
```

Table 13-7 explains this method's parameters.

*Table 13-7. AttachExternalReference Method Parameters*

| NAME | DATA TYPE | DESCRIPTION |
|---|---|---|
| FileName | String | The external AutoCAD drawing file's name. You must specify the .dwg extension. Optionally, you can specify a path to the file. If you don't, AutoCAD tries to find the file in the system search path. |
| BlockName | String | A name for the internal Block object that will point to the external drawing file. |
| InsertionPoint | Variant | A three-element array of doubles that specifies the 3D WCS coordinates where the Xref will be inserted into the Object. |
| Xscale | Double | A non-zero number representing the scaling factor for the Xref's X direction. Negative numbers mirror the insertion on this axis. |
| Yscale | Double | A non-zero number representing the scaling factor for the Xref's Y direction. Negative numbers mirror the insertion on this axis. |
| Zscale | Double | A non-zero number representing the scaling factor for the Xref's Z direction. Negative numbers mirror the insertion on this axis. |
| RotationAngle | Double | The rotation angle relative to the WCS X-axis, expressed in radians. |
| Overlay | Boolean | Controls how the Xref is attached. If True, the Xref is brought in as an overlay. Overlay external references aren't visible if the current drawing is attached as an Xref to another drawing. In this way, overlay Xrefs can reduce the need to detach Xrefs before sharing drawings. If this parameter is False, the Xref is an attachment. |

The following example creates an Xref based on user input:

```
Public Sub TestAttachExternalReference()
Dim strPath As String
Dim strName As String
Dim varInsertionPoint As Variant
```

```
Dim dblX As Double
Dim dblY As Double
Dim dblZ As Double
Dim dblRotation As Double
Dim strInput As String
Dim blnOver As Boolean

    '' get input from user
    With ThisDrawing.Utility
        .InitializeUserInput 1
        strPath = .GetString(True, vbCr & "External file name: ")
        .InitializeUserInput 1
        strName = .GetString(True, vbCr & "Block name to create: ")
        .InitializeUserInput 1
        varInsertionPoint = .GetPoint(, vbCr & "Pick the insert point: ")
        .InitializeUserInput 1 + 2
        dblX = .GetDistance(varInsertionPoint, vbCr & "X scale: ")
        .InitializeUserInput 1 + 2
        dblY = .GetDistance(varInsertionPoint, vbCr & "Y scale: ")
        .InitializeUserInput 1 + 2
        dblZ = .GetDistance(varInsertionPoint, vbCr & "Z scale: ")
        .InitializeUserInput 1
        dblRotation = .GetAngle(varInsertionPoint, vbCr & "Rotation angle: ")
        .InitializeUserInput 1, "Attach Overlay"
        strInput = .GetKeyword(vbCr & "Type [Attach/Overlay]: ")
        blnOver = IIf("Overlay" = strInput, True, False)
    End With

    '' create the object
    ThisDrawing.ModelSpace.AttachExternalReference strPath, strName, _
                    varInsertionPoint, dblX, dblY, dblZ, dblRotation, blnOver

End Sub
```

## Detaching External References

You can detach an external reference from the current drawing using the Block
object's Detach method. It has this syntax:

```
BlockObject.Detach
```

**NOTE** *You detach an Xref's block definition, the method removes all associated ExternalReference objects from the drawing too. This includes linetypes, textstyles, dimstyles, nested block definitions, and layers.*

## Unloading External References

You can also unload external references without detaching them from the current drawing. Use the Block object's Unload method. It has this syntax:

```
BlockObject.Unload
```

Though not visible, unloaded Xrefs are still associated with the current drawing. To regenerate them, reload them.

## Reloading External References

Use the Block object's Reload method to reload an external reference whenever you want, even if the Xref is already loaded. Reload an already-loaded Xref when you modify the underlying drawing and then want to update the in-memory copy in the current drawing. This method has the following syntax:

```
BlockObject.Reload
```

The following example demonstrates the Detach, Reload, and Unload methods using an external reference:

```
Public Sub TestExternalReference()
Dim strName As String
Dim strOpt As String
Dim objBlock As AcadBlock

On Error Resume Next    '' get input from user
    With ThisDrawing.Utility
        '' get the block name
        .InitializeUserInput 1
        strName = .GetString(True, vbCr & "External reference name: ")
        If Err Then Exit Sub
```

```
            '' get the block definition
            Set objBlock = ThisDrawing.Blocks.Item(strName)

            '' exit if not found
            If Err Then
                MsgBox "Unable to get block " & strName
                Exit Sub
            End If

            '' exit if not an xref
            If Not objBlock.IsXRef Then
                MsgBox "That is not an external reference"
                Exit Sub
            End If

            '' get the operation
            .InitializeUserInput 1, "Detach Reload Unload"
            strOpt = .GetKeyword(vbCr & "Option [Detach/Reload/Unload]: ")
            If Err Then Exit Sub

            '' perform operation requested
            If strOpt = "Detach" Then
                objBlock.Detach
            ElseIf strOpt = "Reload" Then
                objBlock.Reload
            Else
                objBlock.Unload
            End If
    End With
End Sub
```

## Binding External References

Use the Block object's Bind method to convert external references to simple blocks. This operation builds an internal copy of the external drawing file in much the same way the InsertBlock method does using an external filename. Instead of referring to the external drawing database, Bind converts any former ExternalReference objects to simple block references. This method has the following syntax:

```
BlockObject.Bind(Merge)
```

This method has one parameter, `Merge`, a Boolean. When it's `True`, the method merges dependent symbol table entries in the external file with the current drawings entries. When it's `False`, the method prefixes them to avoid collision with any other entry name in the current drawing. The prefix has the form `BlockName$X$EntryName`, where

- `BlockName` is the block definition name for the current drawing's external reference

- `X` is an automatically generated integer that makes the name unique in the current drawing

- `EntryName` is the name of the symbol table entry in the externally referenced drawing file.

**NOTE**  *If* Merge *is set to* True *and an entry is already present in the current drawing, the method maps the external entry to the current drawing entry. This is identical behavior to inserting block definitions that contain duplicate layers, linetypes, or textstyles in the current drawing.*

The following example binds the specified external reference using either style:

```
Public Sub TestBind()
Dim strName As String
Dim strOpt As String
Dim objBlock As AcadBlock

On Error Resume Next

    '' get input from user
    With ThisDrawing.Utility

        '' get the block name
        .InitializeUserInput 1
        strName = .GetString(True, vbCr & "External reference name: ")
        If Err Then Exit Sub

        '' get the block definition
        Set objBlock = ThisDrawing.Blocks.Item(strName)
```

```
            '' exit if not found
            If Err Then
                MsgBox "Unable to get block " & strName
                Exit Sub
            End If

            '' exit if not an xref
            If Not objBlock.IsXRef Then
                MsgBox "That is not an external reference"
                Exit Sub
            End If

            '' get the option
            .InitializeUserInput 1, "Prefix Merge"
            strOpt = .GetKeyword(vbCr & "Dependent entries [Prefix/Merge]: ")
            If Err Then Exit Sub

            '' perform the bind, using option entered
            objBlock.Bind ("Merge" = strOpt)
        End With
    End Sub
```

# Attributes

Attributes let you attach text to blocks. Each attribute has an identifier called the Tag, a prompt string called the Prompt, and a string field of user data called the Value. You can make this text either visible with all the font characteristics of standard AutoCAD text entities, or invisible if the text is used to store data.

---

 **NOTE**   *When a user inserts a block that contains attributes, AutoCAD asks the user to enter attribute values. See the AutoCAD User's Guide for an explanation of system variables that change this default behavior.*

---

## Creating Attributes

Like the blocks to which they are attached, attributes have both a definition and a reference. The Attribute object is the definition, and it's associated with a Block object. This *attribute definition* provides the template for creating AttributeReference objects associated with new BlockReference objects.

## The AddAttribute Method

Use the AddAttribute method of a PaperSpace, ModelSpace, or Block object to create a new Attribute object. This attribute definition specifies the corresponding AttributeReference's characteristics. The most important characteristics are passed as parameters to this method, including the Prompt to display when inserting a block, the Tag used to identify the attribute, and a default Value to assign the attribute. This method has the following syntax:

```
Set AttributeObject = Object.AddAttribute(Height, Mode, Prompt, _
InsertionPoint, Tag, Value)
```

Table 13-8 explains this method's attributes.

*Table 13-8. AddAttribute Method Parameters*

| NAME | DATA TYPE | DESCRIPTION |
| --- | --- | --- |
| Height | Double | The attribute definition's text size in the current drawing units. |
| Mode | Long | How the Attribute object behaves when a block containing this attribute definition is inserted. Table 13-9 lists this parameter's values. |
| Prompt | String | The method displays this prompt when a block containing this attribute definition is inserted. If null, the method displays the Tag instead. |
| InsertionPoint | Variant | A three-element array of doubles that specify the attribute's location in the block or drawing. It is a 3-D WCS coordinate. |
| Tag | String | An identifier used to access a specific attribute. It may contain any characters except spaces and exclamation points. AutoCAD converts it to uppercase. |
| Value | String | The attribute's default value. |

AutoCAD provides several AcAttributeMode constants for the Mode parameter, which you can specify in any combination. Table 13-9 lists these values.

*Table 13-9. Mode Parameter Values*

| CONSTANT | VALUE | DESCRIPTION |
|---|---|---|
| acAttributeModeNormal | 0 | The default mode, in which none of the other modes are applied. |
| acAttributeModeInvisible | 1 | When the block is inserted, the attribute's values aren't visible. The ATTDISP system variable overrides this mode setting. |
| acAttributeModeConstant | 2 | Each inserted block's attribute values are fixed. AutoCAD does not prompt for the attribute. |
| acAttributeModeVerify | 4 | When you insert the block, AutoCAD asks you to verify that the attribute value is correct. |
| acAttributeModePreset | 8 | AutoCAD inserts the block with its default attribute values. You can't edit these values. |

The user can establish a preferred global mode for new attributes. The AFLAGS system variable stores this preferred global mode. You can access and set it using the GetVariable and SetVariable methods, which Appendix C discusses.

The following example creates a simple block containing an attribute of each type, and then interactively inserts it:

```
Public Sub TestAddAttribute()
    Dim dblOrigin(2) As Double
    Dim dblEnt(2) As Double
    Dim dblHeight As Double
    Dim lngMode As Long
    Dim strTag As String
    Dim strPrompt As String
    Dim strValue As String
    Dim objBlock As AcadBlock
    Dim objEnt As AcadEntity

    '' create the block
    dblOrigin(0) = 0:  dblOrigin(1) = 0:  dblOrigin(2) = 0
    Set objBlock = ThisDrawing.Blocks.Add(dblOrigin, "Affirmations")
```

```
'' delete existing entities (in case we've run before)
For Each objEnt In objBlock
    objEnt.Delete
Next


'' create an ellipse in the block
dblEnt(0) = 4:  dblEnt(1) = 0:  dblEnt(2) = 0
objBlock.AddEllipse dblOrigin, dblEnt, 0.5


'' set the height for all attributes
dblHeight = 0.25
dblEnt(0) = -1.5:  dblEnt(1) = 0:  dblEnt(2) = 0


'' create a regular attribute
lngMode = acAttributeModeNormal
strTag = "Regular"
strPrompt = "Enter a value"
strValue = "I'm regular"
dblEnt(1) = 1
objBlock.AddAttribute dblHeight, lngMode, strPrompt, dblEnt, strTag, _
                        strValue


'' create an invisible attribute
lngMode = acAttributeModeInvisible
strTag = "Invisible"
strPrompt = "Enter a hidden value"
strValue = "I'm invisible"
dblEnt(1) = 0.5
objBlock.AddAttribute dblHeight, lngMode, strPrompt, dblEnt, strTag, _
                        strValue


'' create a constant attribute
lngMode = acAttributeModeConstant
strTag = "Constant"
strPrompt = "Don't bother"
strValue = "I'm set"
dblEnt(1) = 0
objBlock.AddAttribute dblHeight, lngMode, strPrompt, dblEnt, strTag, _
                        strValue
```

```
'' create a verify attribute
lngMode = acAttributeModeVerify
strTag = "Verify"
strPrompt = "Enter an important value"
strValue = "I'm important"
dblEnt(1) = -0.5
objBlock.AddAttribute dblHeight, lngMode, strPrompt, dblEnt, strTag, _
                      strValue


'' create a preset attribute
lngMode = acAttributeModePreset
strTag = "Preset"
strPrompt = "No question"
strValue = "I've got values"
dblEnt(1) = -1
objBlock.AddAttribute dblHeight, lngMode, strPrompt, dblEnt, strTag, _
                      strValue


'' now insert block interactively using sendcommand
ThisDrawing.SendCommand "._-insert" & vbCr & "Affirmations" & vbCr
End Sub
```

Neither constant nor preset attributes prompt for values. The verify attribute prompt repeats. Only four attributes are visible in the drawing, as shown in Figure 13-5. The invisible attribute is present but hidden.

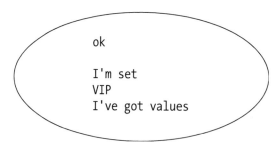

*Figure 13-5. Code output*

If, after you perform an insertion, you run the DDATTE command to review these values in the Edit Attributes dialog, four of them are editable. The constant attribute is not available, but you can change both the invisible and the preset values. See Figure 13-6.

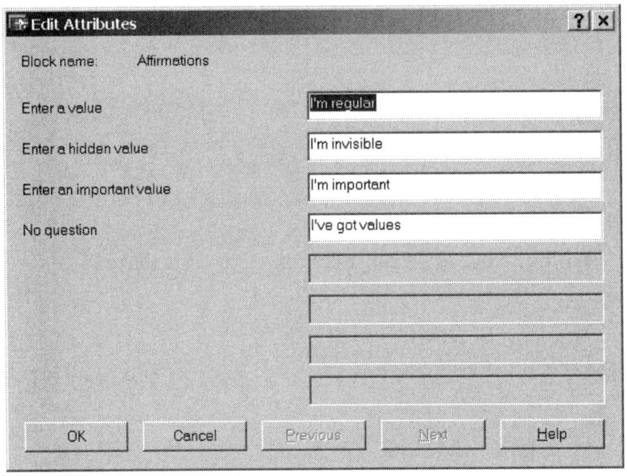

*Figure 13-6. Edit attributes*

## Manipulating Attribute References

Although the BlockReference has identical geometry, each block reference's
AttributeReference objects may have different values .

Access these attribute references using the GetAttributes method.

### The GetAttributes Method

Use the GetAttributes method of a BlockReference or MInsertBlock object to
retrieve any associated AttributeReference objects. It returns an array,
varAttributeRefs, that contains all the non-constant attributes. This method has
the following syntax:

```
varAttributeRefs = Object.GetAttributes()
```

The following example uses the debug window to display information about
each AttributeRef object associated with a block reference. Try it on an attrib-
uted block, such as the one created in the last example.

```
Public Sub TestGetAttributes()
Dim varPick As Variant
Dim objEnt As AcadEntity
Dim objBRef As AcadBlockReference
Dim varAttribs As Variant
```

```
    Dim strAttribs As String
    Dim intI As Integer

On Error Resume Next
    With ThisDrawing.Utility

        '' get an entity from user
        .GetEntity objEnt, varPick, vbCr & "Pick a block with attributes: "
        If Err Then Exit Sub

        '' cast it to a blockref
        Set objBRef = objEnt

        '' exit if not a block
        If objBRef Is Nothing Then
            .Prompt vbCr & "That wasn't a block."
            Exit Sub
        End If

        '' exit if it has no attributes
        If Not objBRef.HasAttributes Then
            .Prompt vbCr & "That block doesn't have attributes."
            Exit Sub
        End If

        '' get the attributerefs
        varAttribs = objBRef.GetAttributes

        '' show some information about each
        strAttribs = "Block Name: " & objBRef.Name & vbCrLf
        For intI = LBound(varAttribs) To UBound(varAttribs)
            strAttribs = strAttribs & " Tag(" & intI & "): " & _
            varAttribs(intI).TagString & vbTab & "  Value(" & intI & "): " & _
            varAttribs(intI).TextString & vbCrLf
        Next

    End With
    MsgBox strAttribs

End Sub
```

## The GetConstantAttributes Method

Use the GetConstantAttributes method of a BlockReference or MInsertBlock object to retrieve associated constant Attribute objects. This method has the following syntax:

```
varAttributes = Object.GetConstantAttributes()
```

It returns an array, varAttributes, that contains the constant attributes.

The following example uses the Debug window to display information about each constant Attribute object associated with a block reference. Try it on a block that has constant attributes, such as the one created earlier:

```
Public Sub TestGetConstantAttributes()
Dim varPick As Variant
Dim objEnt As AcadEntity
Dim objBRef As AcadBlockReference
Dim varAttribs As Variant
Dim strAttribs As String
Dim intI As Integer

    On Error Resume Next
    With ThisDrawing.Utility

        '' get an entity from user
        .GetEntity objEnt, varPick, vbCr & _
                "Pick a block with constant attributes: "
        If Err Then Exit Sub

        '' cast it to a blockref
        Set objBRef = objEnt

        '' exit if not a block
        If objBRef Is Nothing Then
            .Prompt vbCr & "That wasn't a block."
            Exit Sub
        End If

        '' exit if it has no attributes
        If Not objBRef.HasAttributes Then
            .Prompt vbCr & "That block doesn't have attributes."
            Exit Sub
        End If
```

```
          '' get the constant attributes
          varAttribs = objBRef.GetConstantAttributes

          '' show some information about each
          strAttribs = "Block Name: " & objBRef.Name & vbCrLf
          For intI = LBound(varAttribs) To UBound(varAttribs)
              strAttribs = strAttribs & " Tag(" & intI & "): " & _
              varAttribs(intI).TagString & vbTab & "Value(" & intI & "): " & _
              varAttribs(intI).TextString
          Next

      End With
      MsgBox strAttribs
  End Sub
```

## *Iterating Attribute Definitions*

The BlockReference object exposes methods to retrieve its associated
AttributeReference and Attribute objects. Unfortunately, similar functionality is
not available for a Block object's attribute definitions. You can see this when you
modify a block insertion in a drawing that contains multiple insertions of the
same block. If it contains Attributes and you change the ATDEF location or properties and redefine the block, the other insertions do not update their display
properties in unison with the changed insertion.

Use the following function to obtain a collection of attributes from a block.
The collection uses the TagString as its key so it can quickly find specific attributes.

```
Function GetAttributes(objBlock As AcadBlock) As Collection
Dim objEnt As AcadEntity
Dim objAttribute As AcadAttribute
Dim coll As New Collection

    '' iterate the block
    For Each objEnt In objBlock

        '' if it's an attribute
        If objEnt.ObjectName = "AcDbAttributeDefinition" Then

            '' cast to an attribute
            Set objAttribute = objEnt
```

```
            '' add attribute to the collection
            coll.Add objAttribute, objAttribute.TagString
        End If
    Next


    '' return collection
    Set GetAttributes = coll
End Function
```

This example uses the GetAttributes function to display information about attributes created in earlier example code:

```
Public Sub DemoGetAttributes()
Dim objAttribs As Collection
Dim objAttrib As AcadAttribute
Dim objBlock As AcadBlock
Dim strAttribs As String

    '' get the block
    Set objBlock = ThisDrawing.Blocks.Item("Affirmations")

    '' get the attributes
    Set objAttribs = GetAttributes(objBlock)

    '' show some information about each

    For Each objAttrib In objAttribs
        strAttribs = objAttrib.TagString & vbCrLf
        strAttribs = strAttribs & "Tag: " & objAttrib.TagString & vbCrLf & _
            "Prompt: " & objAttrib.PromptString & vbCrLf & " Value: " & _
                objAttrib.TextString & vbCrLf & "  Mode: " & _
                objAttrib.Mode
        MsgBox strAttribs
    Next

    '' find specific attribute by TagString
    Set objAttrib = objAttribs.Item("PRESET")

    '' prove that we have the right one
    strAttribs = "Tag: " & objAttrib.TagString & vbCrLf & "Prompt: " & _
      objAttrib.PromptString & vbCrLf & "Value: " & objAttrib.TextString & _
      vbCrLf & "Mode: " & objAttrib.Mode
    MsgBox strAttribs
End Sub
```

## *Inserting Blocks with Attributes*

Depending on the setting of the ATTREQ system variable, AutoCAD can automatically handle retrieving and setting attribute values a user inputs. But if you use the InsertBlock method to insert a block reference, you are responsible for setting attribute values.

The following example inserts a block and sets several attribute values by locating the appropriate Tags. It uses the "Affirmations" block defined in an earlier example.

```
Public Sub TestInsertAndSetAttributes()
Dim objBRef As AcadBlockReference
Dim varAttribRef As Variant
Dim varInsertionPoint As Variant
Dim dblX As Double
Dim dblY As Double
Dim dblZ As Double
Dim dblRotation As Double

    '' get block input from user
    With ThisDrawing.Utility
        .InitializeUserInput 1
        varInsertionPoint = .GetPoint(, vbCr & "Pick the insert point: ")
        .InitializeUserInput 1 + 2
        dblX = .GetDistance(varInsertionPoint, vbCr & "X scale: ")
        .InitializeUserInput 1 + 2
        dblY = .GetDistance(varInsertionPoint, vbCr & "Y scale: ")
        .InitializeUserInput 1 + 2
        dblZ = .GetDistance(varInsertionPoint, vbCr & "Z scale: ")
        .InitializeUserInput 1
        dblRotation = .GetAngle(varInsertionPoint, vbCr & "Rotation angle: ")
    End With

    '' insert the block
    Set objBRef = ThisDrawing.ModelSpace.InsertBlock(varInsertionPoint, _
                            "Affirmations", dblX, dblY, dblZ, dblRotation)

    '' interate the attributerefs
    For Each varAttribRef In objBRef.GetAttributes
```

```
    '' change specific values based on Tag
    Select Case varAttribRef.TagString
    Case "Regular":
        varAttribRef.TextString = "I have new values"
    Case "Invisible":
        varAttribRef.TextString = "I'm still invisible"
    Case "Verify":
        varAttribRef.TextString = "No verification needed"
    Case "Preset":
        varAttribRef.TextString = "I can be changed"
    End Select
  Next

End Sub
```

Notice that AutoCAD lets attribute references be changed freely, even if the attribute definition specifies that a value is preset or should be verified. You can decide to handle attribute modes in any way you want.

## Summary

This chapter explained how to create and manipulate blocks and external references. These objects give you many ways to efficiently store, manage, share and use common graphic data. This chapter also explained how to associate text with graphics using attributes. Because every block's attribute reference values are unique, they provide a simple form of non-graphic data storage right inside the AutoCAD drawing.

# CHAPTER 14

# Views and Viewports

A *VIEW* IS A NAMED VIEWPOINT CONFIGURATION in model space. A View object contains spatial references to the point of view, the target of view, and other parameters. A user can name and save a view in their drawing and reuse it later. AutoCAD VBA provides methods and properties that let you create, set and delete views.

A *viewport*, on the other hand, is a bounded area that displays some part of model or paper space. There are two viewport objects: the Viewport object for model space and the PViewport object for paper space, used for plotting.

This chapter covers these topics:

- Creating, setting, and deleting views

- Creating model-space viewports

- Creating paper-space viewports

## Views

AutoCAD VBA uses a View object to represent a view. When you create a new drawing, no views are set up. All the views that you save in a drawing become members of the Views collection. The following code iterates through the Views collection and displays the names of saved views.

```
Public Sub DisplayViews()
    Dim objView As AcadView
    Dim strViewNames As String

    If ThisDrawing.Views.Count > 0 Then
        For Each objView In ThisDrawing.Views
            strViewNames = strViewNames & objView.Name & vbCrLf
        Next
        MsgBox "The following views are saved for this drawing:" & vbCrLf _
                & strViewNames
```

```
    Else
        MsgBox "There are no saved View objects in the Views collection."
    End If

End Sub
```

Figure 14-1 shows this code's output. This is equivalent to the views displayed in the View dialog box's Named View tab (Figure 14-2).

*Figure 14-1. List of views in a drawing*

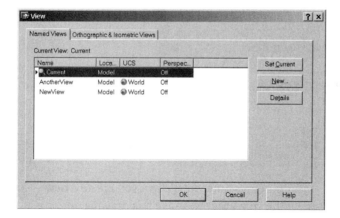

*Figure 14-2. The View dialog box's Named View tab*

The view named Current is not saved and is not part of the Views collection. Also, the Views collection is not imported into other drawings when you insert one drawing into another.

## Creating a View

To create a new view in the Views collection, use the Add method. It has the following syntax:

```
Set ViewObject = ViewsCollection.Add(ViewName)
```

This method has one parameter, `ViewName`, a String. It contains the new `View` object's name.

After you add a `View` object to the `Views` collection, set the view's properties. The `Center`, `Target`, and `Direction` properties determine the drawing's viewing angle. Table 14-1 describes these properties.

*Table 14-1. View Properties*

| PROPERTY | DESCRIPTION |
| --- | --- |
| Center | The view's center. A 2-D coordinate. |
| Target | The vector from the view's `Center` to its `Target` is the view's line of sight. A 3-D WCS coordinate. |
| Direction | The vector from which the drawing is viewed. A 3-D coordinate. |

The `Height` and `Width` properties have no effect on the viewport. They only determine the view's visible portion in the viewport.

Use the following code to add a view to a drawing. It takes its settings from the active viewport, so the user must set the view they want on screen and then use this macro to create a named view for that setup.

```
Public Sub AddView()
    Dim objView As AcadView
    Dim objActViewPort As AcadViewport
    Dim strNewViewName As String
    Dim varCenterPoint As Variant
    Dim dblPoint(1) As Double

    strNewViewName = InputBox("Enter name for new view: ")
    If strNewViewName = "" Then Exit Sub

    On Error Resume Next
    Set objView = ThisDrawing.Views.Item(strNewViewName)
    If objView Is Nothing Then
        Set objView = ThisDrawing.Views.Add(strNewViewName)
        ThisDrawing.ActiveSpace = acModelSpace

        varCenterPoint = ThisDrawing.GetVariable("VIEWCTR")
        dblPoint(0) = varCenterPoint(0): dblPoint(1) = varCenterPoint(1)

        Set objActViewPort = ThisDrawing.ActiveViewport

        'Current view info. is stored in the new AcadView object
```

```
    With objView
        .Center = dblPoint
        .Direction = ThisDrawing.GetVariable("VIEWDIR")
        .Height = objActViewPort.Height
        .Target = objActViewPort.Target
        .Width = objActViewPort.Width
    End With

        MsgBox "A new view called " & objView.Name & _
                " has been added to the Views collection."
    Else
        MsgBox "This view already exists."
    End If

End Sub
```

The VIEWCTR and VIEWDIR system variables hold center and direction information. Appendix C lists all system variables.

## Setting a View as Current

After you create a view, you'll probably want to use it. Use a Viewport object's SetView method set one of the View objects as the current view. This method has the following syntax:

```
ViewportObject.SetView ViewObject
```

The parameter ViewObject is a reference to a View object, not the View object's name. The following code asks the user to enter a new view to use. If this view exists in the Views collection, the code sets it as the current view.

```
Public Sub SetView()
Dim objView As AcadView
Dim objActViewPort As AcadViewport
Dim strViewName As String

    ThisDrawing.ActiveSpace = acModelSpace
    Set objActViewPort = ThisDrawing.ActiveViewport
    'Redefine the current ViewPort with the View info
    strViewName = InputBox("Enter the view you require.")

    If strViewName = "" Then Exit Sub
```

```
    On Error Resume Next
    Set objView = ThisDrawing.Views.Item(strViewName)
    If Not objView Is Nothing Then
        objActViewPort.SetView objView
        ThisDrawing.ActiveViewport = objActViewPort
    Else
        MsgBox "View was not recognized."
    End If

End Sub
```

## Deleting a View

When you finish using a view, you can delete it. Use the Delete method as follows:

```
ViewObject.Delete
```

This example illustrates how to implement this method.

```
Public Sub DeleteView()
Dim objView As AcadView
Dim strViewName As String
Dim strExistingViewNames As String

    For Each objView In ThisDrawing.Views
        strExistingViewNames = strExistingViewNames & objView.Name & vbCrLf
    Next

    strViewName = InputBox("Existing Views: " & vbCrLf & _
                        strExistingViewNames & vbCrLf & _
                        "Enter the view you wish to delete from the list.")
    If strViewName = "" Then Exit Sub

    On Error Resume Next
    Set objView = ThisDrawing.Views.Item(strViewName)
    If Not objView Is Nothing Then
        objView.Delete
    Else
        MsgBox "View was not recognized."
    End If

End Sub
```

## Viewports

Viewports are windowed views of your drawing in model and paper space. The `ActiveSpace` property determines which type of viewport is in use.

You construct paper-space and model-space viewports differently. The rest of this chapter explains these two approaches.

## *The Model-Space Viewport*

Model-space viewports give you a number of windows in which to view and edit your model. The `MAXACTVP` system variable controls the maximum number of active viewports, and it's initially set to 64. Remember, though, that each new viewport adversely affects performance, so keep the number of active viewports to a minimum.

The following code shows how to create a model-space viewport. The paragraphs after the code explain this reasonably involved procedure.

```
Public Sub CreateViewport()
Dim objViewPort As AcadViewport
Dim objCurrentViewport As AcadViewport
Dim varLowerLeft As Variant
Dim dblViewDirection(2) As Double
Dim strViewPortName As String

    strViewPortName = InputBox("Enter a name for the new viewport.")
    'user cancelled
    If strViewPortName = "" Then Exit Sub
    'check if viewport already exists
    On Error Resume Next
    Set objViewPort = ThisDrawing.Viewports.Item(strViewPortName)
    If Not objViewPort Is Nothing Then
        MsgBox "Viewport already exists"
        Exit Sub
    End If

    'Create a new viewport
    Set objViewPort = ThisDrawing.Viewports.Add(strViewPortName)

    'Split the screen viewport into 4 windows
    objViewPort.Split acViewport4
```

```
    For Each objCurrentViewport In ThisDrawing.Viewports
        If objCurrentViewport.LowerLeftCorner(0) = 0 Then
            If objCurrentViewport.LowerLeftCorner(1) = 0 Then
                'this takes care of Top view
                dblViewDirection(0) = 0: dblViewDirection(1) = 0: _
                                        dblViewDirection(2) = 1
                objCurrentViewport.Direction = dblViewDirection
            Else
                'this takes care of Front view
                dblViewDirection(0) = 0: dblViewDirection(1) = -1: _
                                        dblViewDirection(2) = 0
                objCurrentViewport.Direction = dblViewDirection
            End If
        End If
        If objCurrentViewport.LowerLeftCorner(0) = 0.5 Then
            If objCurrentViewport.LowerLeftCorner(1) = 0 Then
                'this takes care of the Right view
                dblViewDirection(0) = 1: dblViewDirection(1) = 0: _
                                        dblViewDirection(2) = 0
                objCurrentViewport.Direction = dblViewDirection
            Else
                'this takes care of the Isometric view
                dblViewDirection(0) = 1: dblViewDirection(1) = -1: _
                                        dblViewDirection(2) = 1
                objCurrentViewport.Direction = dblViewDirection
            End If
        End If
    Next
    'make viewport active to see effects of changes
    ThisDrawing.ActiveViewport = objViewPort

End Sub
```

First, use the Viewports collection's Add method to create a new viewport. This method has the following syntax:

```
Set ViewportObject = ViewportsCollection.Add(ViewportName)
```

This method has one parameter, ViewportName, a String, that contains the new Viewport object's name.

Here's how the example code implements this method:

```
'Create a new viewport
Set objViewPort = ThisDrawing.Viewports.Add(strViewPortName)
```

Next, the code uses the `Split` method to create the windows in the viewport.

```
ViewportObject.Split NumberOfWindows
```

The `NumberOfWindows` parameter must be one of the AutoCAD `AcViewportSplitType` constants in Table 14-2.

*Table 14-2. AcViewportSplitType Constants*

| CONSTANT | VALUE | DESCRIPTION |
|---|---|---|
| acViewport2Horizontal | 0 | Splits the viewport horizontally into two equal sections. |
| acViewport2Vertical | 1 | Splits the viewport vertically into two equal sections. |
| acViewport3Left | 2 | Splits the viewport into two vertical halves. The left half is split horizontally into two equal sections. |
| acViewport3Right | 3 | Splits the viewport into two vertical halves. The right half is split horizontally into two equal sections. |
| acViewport3Horizontal | 4 | Splits the viewport horizontally into three equal sections. |
| acViewport3Vertical | 5 | Splits the viewport vertically into three equal sections. |
| acViewport3Above | 6 | Splits the viewport into two horizontal halves. The top half is a single viewport. The bottom half is split horizontally into two equal sections. |
| acViewport3Below | 7 | Splits the viewport into two horizontal halves. The bottom half is a single viewport. The top half is split horizontally into two equal sections. |
| acViewport4 | 8 | Splits the viewport horizontally and vertically into four equal sections. |

The following example shows how the code sample implements this method. For the effects of this method to become apparent, reset the viewport as the active viewport. You can reset the active viewport at the very end of the code, when it's time to view the changes.

```
'Split the screen viewport into 4 windows
objViewPort.Split acViewport4
```

> **NOTE** *Although the code calls the* Split *method, the changes don't appear until the* ActiveViewport *property makes the viewport active. You have to do this even if the viewport was active before the call to* Split. *A viewport does not have to be active for this method to work, but you must reset it to active or you won't see the method's results.*

You can identify each viewport using either the LowerLeftCorner or the UpperRightCorner properties, each of which holds a two-element array of doubles. Figure 14-3 applies to the code sample using acViewport4.

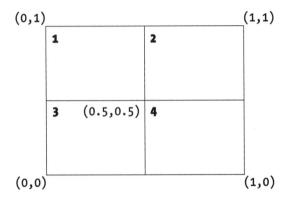

*Figure 14-3. Viewports*

Table 14-3 indicate's the coordinates used to create the viewports as shown in Figure 14-3.

*Table 14-3. Viewport Coordinates*

| VIEWPORT | LOWERLEFTCORNER PROPERTY | UPPERRIGHTCORNER PROPERTY |
|---|---|---|
| 1 | (0, 0.5) | (0.5, 1) |
| 2 | (0.5, 0.5) | (1, 1) |
| 3 | (0, 0) | (0.5, 0.5) |
| 4 | (0.5, 0) | (1, 0.5) |

The following code shows how this section's example code uses the LowerLeftCorner property to identify the viewports.

```
For Each objCurrentViewport In ThisDrawing.Viewports
   If objCurrentViewport.LowerLeftCorner(0) = 0 Then
     If objCurrentViewport.LowerLeftCorner(1) = 0 Then
        'this takes care of Top view
        dblViewDirection(0) = 0: dblViewDirection(1) = 0: _
dblViewDirection(2) = 1
        objCurrentViewport.Direction = dblViewDirection
     Else
        'this takes care of Front view
        dblViewDirection(0) = 0: dblViewDirection(1) = -1: _
        dblViewDirection(2) = 0
        objCurrentViewport.Direction = dblViewDirection
     End If
   End If
   If objCurrentViewport.LowerLeftCorner(0) = 0.5 Then
     If objCurrentViewport.LowerLeftCorner(1) = 0 Then
        'this takes care of the Right view
        dblViewDirection(0) = 1: dblViewDirection(1) = 0: _
                    dblViewDirection(2) = 0
        objCurrentViewport.Direction = dblViewDirection
     Else
        'this takes care of the Isometric view
        dblViewDirection(0) = 1: dblViewDirection(1) = -1: _
dblViewDirection(2) = 1
        objCurrentViewport.Direction = dblViewDirection
     End If
   End If
Next
```

Set the Direction property for each viewport. This property has the following syntax:

```
ViewportObject.Direction = ViewDirection
```

ViewDirection is three-element array of doubles that specifies the direction from which the drawing is viewed for that viewport.

Users typically have a Top, Front, Right, and maybe an Isometric view of their drawing. Each of these views has a specific set of points relative to an imaginary target point at (0, 0, 0), which defines the direction of view. Table 14-4 lists the standard views and their Direction properties.

*Table 14-4. Views and Their Direction Properties*

| VIEW | DIRECTION | VIEW | DIRECTION |
|------|-----------|------|-----------|
| Top | (0, 0, 1) | Bottom | (0, 0, -1) |
| Front | (0, -1, 0) | Back | (0, 1, 0) |
| Left | (-1, 0, 0) | Right | (1, 0, 0) |
| North East | (1, 1, 1) | North West | (-1, 1, 1) |
| South East | (1, -1, 1) | South West | (-1, -1, 1) |

In this section's example, the following code sets the Top view's Direction property:

```
'this takes care of the Top view
dblViewDirection(0) = 0: dblViewDirection(1) = 0: dblViewDirection(2) = 1
objCurrentViewport.Direction = dblViewDirection
```

When you finish setting up the viewports, reset the viewport to be the active viewport to see the effects of your changes. Here's how to set the active viewport in code using the ActiveViewport property:

```
ThisDrawing.ActiveViewport = ViewportObject
```

At the end of the macro, use the following code to see the code's effects:

```
ThisDrawing.ActiveViewport = objViewPort
```

Figure 14-4 shows the result of running this macro on a drawing.

That may have seemed like a lot of work, but it's really not as difficult as it looks. Experimentation is your greatest ally when dealing with viewports. Remember to use the LowerLeftCorner and UpperRightCorner properties to determine which window you are dealing with.

You must activate a viewport before you can change it. To tell which viewport is active, look for the viewport with the bold border. Also, only the active viewport contains the crosshair cursor. When you finish making changes, reset the viewport to see them.

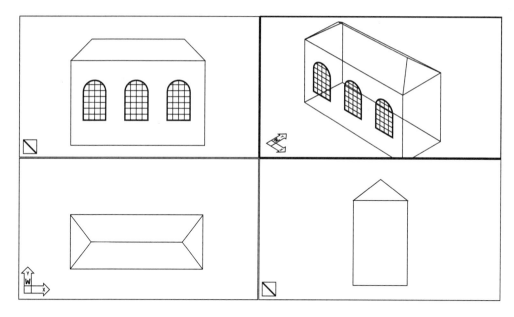

*Figure 14-4. Four-viewport view*

## The Paper-Space Viewport

Paper-space viewports, represented by PViewport objects, are created for plotting purposes using the AddPViewport method as follows:

```
Set PViewportObject = _ PaperSpaceCollection.AddPViewport(CenterPoint, _
Width, Height)
```

Table 14-5 explains this method's parameters.

*Table 14-5. AddPViewport Method Parameters*

| NAME | DATA TYPE | DESCRIPTION |
| --- | --- | --- |
| CenterPoint | Variant | A three-element array of doubles that specifies the viewport's center coordinates. |
| Width | Double | A positive number that specifies the viewport's width. |
| Height | Double | A positive number that specifies the viewport's height. |

There is currently no programmatic means to quickly create, select, or manipulate polygonal PViewports, since they are made up of LwPolyline entities with additional information to relate the LwPolyline to the Pviewport.

The following example shows how to set up four different viewports for paper space. It's quite a long section of code, so the paragraphs that follow split it up into more manageable chunks and explain each step.

```
Public Sub CreatePViewports()
    Dim objTopVPort As AcadPViewport
    Dim objFrontVPort As AcadPViewport
    Dim objRightVPort As AcadPViewport
    Dim objIsoMetricVPort As AcadPViewport
    Dim objLayout As AcadLayout
    Dim objAcadObject As AcadObject
    Dim dblPoint(2) As Double
    Dim dblViewDirection(2) As Double
    Dim dblOrigin(1) As Double
    Dim dblHeight As Double
    Dim dblWidth As Double
    Dim varMarginLL As Variant
    Dim varMarginUR As Variant

    ThisDrawing.ActiveSpace = acPaperSpace

    Set objLayout = ThisDrawing.ActiveLayout
    dblOrigin(0) = 0: dblOrigin(1) = 0

    objLayout.PlotOrigin = dblOrigin
    If objLayout.PlotRotation = ac0degrees Or objLayout.PlotRotation = _
                                    ac180degrees Then
        objLayout.GetPaperSize dblWidth, dblHeight
    Else
        objLayout.GetPaperSize dblHeight, dblWidth
    End If

    objLayout.GetPaperMargins varMarginLL, varMarginUR

    dblWidth = dblWidth - (varMarginUR(0) + varMarginLL(0))
    dblHeight = dblHeight - (varMarginUR(1) + varMarginLL(1))
    dblWidth = dblWidth / 2#
    dblHeight = dblHeight / 2#
```

```
'Clear the layout of old PViewports
For Each objAcadObject In ThisDrawing.PaperSpace
    If TypeName(objAcadObject) = "IAcadPViewport" Then
    objAcadObject.Delete
    End If
Next

'create Top Viewport
dblPoint(0) = dblWidth - dblWidth * 0.5 '25
dblPoint(1) = dblHeight - dblHeight * 0.5 '75
dblPoint(2) = 0#

Set objTopVPort = ThisDrawing.PaperSpace.AddPViewport(dblPoint, _
                                            dblWidth, dblHeight)

'need to set view direction
dblViewDirection(0) = 0
dblViewDirection(1) = 0
dblViewDirection(2) = 1
objTopVPort.Direction = dblViewDirection

objTopVPort.Display acOn
ThisDrawing.MSpace = True

ThisDrawing.ActivePViewport = objTopVPort
ThisDrawing.Application.ZoomExtents
ThisDrawing.Application.ZoomScaled 0.5, acZoomScaledRelativePSpace

'create Front Viewport
dblPoint(0) = dblWidth - dblWidth * 0.5
dblPoint(1) = dblHeight + dblHeight * 0.5
dblPoint(2) = 0

Set objFrontVPort = ThisDrawing.PaperSpace.AddPViewport(dblPoint, _
                                            dblWidth, dblHeight)

'need to set view direction
dblViewDirection(0) = 0
dblViewDirection(1) = -1
dblViewDirection(2) = 0
objFrontVPort.Direction = dblViewDirection
```

```
objFrontVPort.Display acOn
ThisDrawing.MSpace = True

ThisDrawing.ActivePViewport = objFrontVPort
ThisDrawing.Application.ZoomExtents
ThisDrawing.Application.ZoomScaled 0.5, acZoomScaledRelativePSpace

'create Right Viewport
dblPoint(0) = dblWidth + dblWidth * 0.5
dblPoint(1) = dblHeight - dblHeight * 0.5
dblPoint(2) = 0

Set objRightVPort = ThisDrawing.PaperSpace.AddPViewport(dblPoint, _
                                                  dblWidth, dblHeight)


'need to set view direction
dblViewDirection(0) = 1
dblViewDirection(1) = 0
dblViewDirection(2) = 0
objRightVPort.Direction = dblViewDirection

objRightVPort.Display acOn
ThisDrawing.MSpace = True

ThisDrawing.ActivePViewport = objRightVPort
ThisDrawing.Application.ZoomExtents
ThisDrawing.Application.ZoomScaled 0.5, acZoomScaledRelativePSpace

'create Isometric Viewport
dblPoint(0) = dblWidth + dblWidth * 0.5
dblPoint(1) = dblHeight + dblHeight * 0.5
dblPoint(2) = 0

Set objIsoMetricVPort = ThisDrawing.PaperSpace.AddPViewport(dblPoint, _
                                                  dblWidth, dblHeight)


'need to set view direction
dblViewDirection(0) = 1
dblViewDirection(1) = -1
dblViewDirection(2) = 1
objIsoMetricVPort.Direction = dblViewDirection
```

```
        objIsoMetricVPort.Display acOn
        ThisDrawing.MSpace = True

        ThisDrawing.ActivePViewport = objIsoMetricVPort
        ThisDrawing.Application.ZoomExtents
        ThisDrawing.Application.ZoomScaled 0.5, acZoomScaledRelativePSpace

        'make paper space active again and we're almost done
        ThisDrawing.ActiveSpace = acPaperSpace
        ThisDrawing.Application.ZoomExtents

        'regen in all viewports
        ThisDrawing.Regen acAllViewports
End Sub
```

First, this code sets the active space to be paper space and uses the active Layout object's GetPaperSize method to find the paper's size. Because the viewports need to stay inside the plottable area, the code finds out the margins' size. It uses the GetPaperMargins method, which returns two two-element arrays that hold the offset of the lower-left and upper-right plot area from the lower-left and upper-right paper corners.

```
ThisDrawing.ActiveSpace = acPaperSpace

Set objLayout = ThisDrawing.ActiveLayout
dblOrigin(0) = 0: dblOrigin(1) = 0

objLayout.PlotOrigin = dblOrigin
If objLayout.PlotRotation = ac0degrees Or objLayout.PlotRotation = _
                                    ac180degrees Then
    objLayout.GetPaperSize dblWidth, dblHeight
Else
    objLayout.GetPaperSize dblHeight, dblWidth
End If

objLayout.GetPaperMargins varMarginLL, varMarginUR

dblWidth = dblWidth - (varMarginUR(0) + varMarginLL(0))
dblHeight = dblHeight - (varMarginUR(1) + varMarginLL(1))
dblWidth = dblWidth / 2#
dblHeight = dblHeight / 2#
```

Figure 14-5 shows a template of a viewport labeled with the different parameters to create.

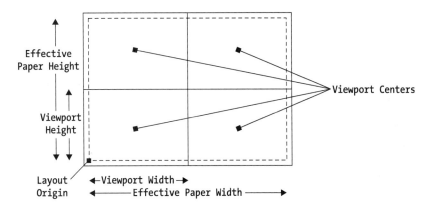

*Figure 14-5. Viewport parameters*

The code then halves the width and height dimensions to use as each viewpoint's size. It also uses this information to calculate each viewport's center.

The code then ensures that no old viewports exist, since they'd overlap or interfere with our new viewport.

```
'Clear the layout of old PViewports
For Each objAcadObject In ThisDrawing.PaperSpace
    If TypeName(objAcadObject) = "IAcadPViewport" Then
        objAcadObject.Delete
    End If
Next
```

Now the code creates the viewports. The code is similar for each viewport. Here's how it creates the Front viewport:

```
'create Front Viewport
dblPoint(0) = dblWidth - dblWidth * 0.5
dblPoint(1) = dblHeight + dblHeight * 0.5
dblPoint(2) = 0

Set objFrontVPort = ThisDrawing.PaperSpace.AddPViewport(dblPoint, _
                                              dblWidth, dblHeight)
```

Next, the code sets the viewport's viewpoint with the Direction property, as follows:

```
'need to set view direction
dblViewDirection(0) = 0
dblViewDirection(1) = -1
dblViewDirection(2) = 0

objFrontVPort.Direction = dblViewDirection
```

Next, the code sets what the viewport displays using the Display method to enable the viewport display and then setting the MSpace method to allow editing of model space from a floating paper-space viewport. Finally, the code sets the drawing to fill the viewport by scaling it to half its size relative to paper-space units.

```
objFrontVPort.Display acOn

ThisDrawing.MSpace = True

ThisDrawing.ActivePViewport = objFrontVPort
ThisDrawing.Application.ZoomExtents
ThisDrawing.Application.ZoomScaled 0.5, acZoomScaledRelativePSpace
```

After the code sets up all the viewports, the only thing left for it to do is regenerate the drawing to see all of the changes.

```
'regen in all viewports
ThisDrawing.Regen acAllViewports
```

Figure 14-6 shows this code's result.

AutoCAD gives you a number of properties to control the viewport's view. You can also control the layer on which the viewport is created and the linetype used to create the viewport. For full details, see Appendix A.

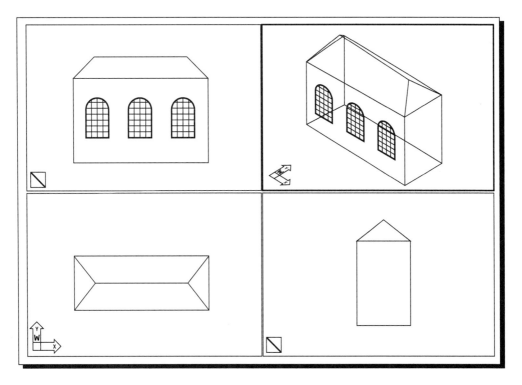

*Figure 14-6. Four-viewport view*

## Summary

This chapter showed you how to name, define, and save a view for use later. AutoCAD provides methods and properties that let you create, set, and delete views. Viewports are bounded areas that display a specific view of your drawing in model space and paper space. This chapter examined the processes of creating both model-space and paper-space viewports.

# CHAPTER 15

# Layout and Plot Configurations

BEING ABLE TO DRAW ON THE SCREEN is great, but eventually you'll want a hardcopy printout of your design. For most businesses, this is a requirement as part of the customer deliverable product. AutoCAD provides a number of methods to create through code plots of your drawing that the user normally generates using the AutoCAD Plot dialog box interface.

This chapter covers the following topics:

- Examining the Plot and PlotConfiguration objects

- Previewing and plotting a drawing

- Understanding the Layouts collection and the Layout object

- Controlling plot parameters

## The Plot Object

The Plot object consists of a number of methods and properties that are used to plot layouts. The Layout object (discussed later in the chapter) holds the plot settings and visual properties of a model space or paper space block. You access the Plot object via the Document object using the following syntax:

```
Set PlotObject = DocumentObject.Plot
```

To declare and set a reference to the Plot object for the currently active drawing, you might use this code:

```
Dim objPlot As AcadPlot

Set objPlot = ThisDrawing.Plot
```

Through the methods and properties of the Plot object, you can display a plot preview, plot to a plotting device or to a file, and employ batch-mode plotting. A detailed discussion of batch-mode plotting falls outside the scope of this book, but Appendix A covers the relevant properties and methods.

## Plotting Your Drawing

This section details the various means used to plot your drawings.

### The DisplayPlotPreview Method

Generally, it's a good idea to preview your drawing before you actually print it out. AutoCAD provides a means of previewing the active layout of your drawing using the DisplayPlotPreview method. This method displays the Plot Preview box, which must be dismissed by the user rather than through code. The drawing for which the DisplayPlotPreview method is invoked will become the active drawing and will remain so even after you've dismissed the Plot Preview box.

```
PlotObject.DisplayPlotPreview Preview
```

Table 15-1 shows the DisplayPlotPreview property's parameters.

*Table 15-1. DisplayPlotPreview Property Parameters*

| NAME | DATA TYPE | DESCRIPTION |
| --- | --- | --- |
| Preview | Long | This determines the kind of preview used. It must be one of the AcPreviewMode constants described in Table 15-2. |

There are two types of preview: partial and full. The full preview takes longer to perform, as it requires a regeneration of the drawing, although no optimization or vector sorting takes place.

Table 15-2 shows the Preview type's constants.

*Table 15-2. Preview Type Constants*

| CONSTANT | VALUE | DESCRIPTION |
| --- | --- | --- |
| acPartialPreview | 0 | This type of preview shows the effective plot area relative to the paper size. |
| acFullPreview | 1 | This type of preview displays the drawing on screen, as it will appear when plotted. |

The following code allows the user to decide the type of plot preview:

```
Public Sub PlotPreview()
    If MsgBox("A preview of your drawing will be displayed." & _
            "Would you like to see a full preview?", vbYesNo) = vbYes Then
        ThisDrawing.Plot.DisplayPlotPreview acFullPreview
    Else
        ThisDrawing.Plot.DisplayPlotPreview acPartialPreview
    End If
End Sub
```

Figure 15-1 depicts the two different types of plot previews.

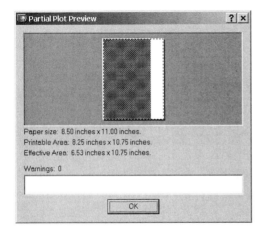

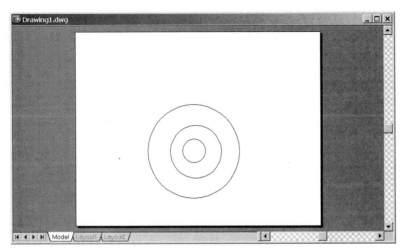

*Figure 15-1. Partial versus full plot preview*

## Plotting with Layouts

Layout configurations that you create to control plot settings and visual proper-ties of model or paper space geometry are held in the `Layouts` collection. ActiveX layouts differ from their AutoCAD user interface counterparts by splitting the standard AutoCAD layout into two objects: a `Layout` object containing the visual properties and plot settings as they would appear in the standard AutoCAD interface and a `Block` object containing the geometry.

You access the `Layouts` collection via the `Document` object using the following syntax:

```
Set LayoutsCollection = DocumentObject.Layouts
```

To declare and set a reference to the `Layouts` object for the currently active drawing, you might use this code:

```
Dim objLayouts As AcadLayouts

Set objLayouts = ThisDrawing.Layouts
```

A `Layout` object has only one `Block` object associated with it and you access it via the `Block` property. Similarly, the one layout is associated with a `Block` object and you can access it through the `Layout` property.

You can access a `Layout` object using the `Item` method of the `Layouts` collec-tion or you can reference the active layout through the `ActiveLayout` property of the `Document` object:

```
Set LayoutObject = DocumentObject.ActiveLayout
```

You can use many of the properties and methods of the `Layout` object to con-trol plotting features such as plot rotation and scale. These properties are also exposed by the `PlotConfiguration` object and are covered later in this chapter.

## The SetLayoutsToPlot Method

You use the `SetLayoutsToPlot` method to specify the layout or layouts that you want to plot. You'll normally use this method prior to a call to the `PlotToDevice` or `PlotToFile` method to override the default plotting of the active layout. After you've called either of these plotting methods, the default returns to the active layout.

```
PlotObject.SetLayoutsToPlot(Layouts)
```

Table 15-3 shows the SetLayoutsToPlot method's parameters.

*Table 15-3. SetLayoutsToPlot Method Parameters*

| NAME | DATA TYPE | DESCRIPTION |
| --- | --- | --- |
| Layouts | Variant | An array of string names identifying the layouts to plot. If this list is Null, this method is effectively useless and the default layout to plot will remain as the active layout. |

The following code plots the layouts specified by the user:

```
Public Sub PlotLayouts()
Dim objLayout As AcadLayout
Dim strLayoutList() As String
Dim intCount As Integer
Dim objPlot As AcadPlot

    intCount = -1
    For Each objLayout In ThisDrawing.Layouts
      If MsgBox("Do you wish to plot the layout: " _
                & objLayout.Name, vbYesNo) = vbYes Then
        intCount = intCount + 1
        ReDim Preserve strLayoutList(intCount)
          strLayoutList(intCount) = objLayout.Name
      End If
    Next objLayout

    Set objPlot = ThisDrawing.Plot
    objPlot.SetLayoutsToPlot strLayoutList
    objPlot.PlotToDevice
End Sub
```

## The PlotToDevice Method

You may print or plot a layout of the active drawing to a file by any device connected to your system using the PlotToDevice method. This method plots using the current configuration or using configuration settings held in a PC3 file. You can specify the device through the ConfigName property for the Layout or PlotConfiguration objects. This method returns a value of True if the plot was successful; otherwise, it returns False.

By default, this method will print the currently active layout. If you want to print a different selection of layouts, you need to call the SetLayoutsToPlot method, described previously, to specify the required layouts.

```
blnPlotSuccessful = PlotObject.PlotToDevice [PlotConfiguration]
```

Table 15-4 shows the PlotToDevice method's parameters.

*Table 15-4. PlotToDevice Method Parameters*

| NAME | DATA TYPE | DESCRIPTION |
|------|-----------|-------------|
| PlotConfiguration | String | This optional parameter specifies the full path and file name of a PC3 file to use instead of the current configuration. If the file isn't found, AutoCAD will search the printer configuration path for the file. If this parameter isn't provided or is invalid, the current configuration will be used. |

You can look at the available printers using the Options dialog box inside AutoCAD, as shown in Figure 15-2. Located on the Plotting tab are all the available printer device names. Unfortunately, AutoCAD doesn't provide a means to see this list programmatically.

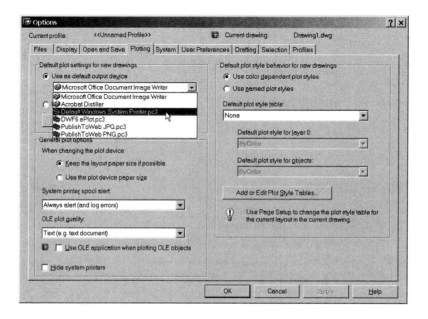

*Figure 15-2. The Options dialog box*

## The *PlotToFile* Method

This method works in a similar way to the PlotToDevice method except that it plots layouts of the active drawing to a specified file. The default layout to be plotted is the active layout, but this may be overridden by the SetLayoutsToPlot method given earlier in this chapter. This method returns a Boolean indicating whether the plot to file was successful. A value of True indicates success.

```
blnPlotSuccessful = PlotObject.PlotToFile _
(PlotFile [, PlotConfiguration])
```

Table 15-5 shows the PlotToFile method's parameters.

*Table 15-5. PlotToFile Method Parameters*

| NAME | DATA TYPE | DESCRIPTION |
| --- | --- | --- |
| PlotFile | String | The name of the file that the layout or layouts is plotted to. When you're plotting multiple layouts, it's possible for the file name for each plot to be generated from the drawing and layout names. This automatic generation of plot file names will occur if a path but no file name is supplied. Otherwise, the last layout specified will be plotted to the file name provided. |
| PlotConfiguration | String | This optional parameter specifies the full path and file name of a PC3 file to use instead of the current configuration. If the file isn't found, AutoCAD will search the printer configuration path for the file. If this parameter isn't provided or is invalid, the current configuration will be used. |

It isn't necessary to provide an extension for the plot file. However, if an extension isn't provided, then the generated extension depends upon the default extension for the driver or device specified in the PlotConfiguration parameter. If a file extension is provided, it will be overwritten for certain raster output drivers that replace user-provided extensions with .gif.

Some plot configurations will invoke a plot to file indirectly, such as Adobe Acrobat PDF or the newer Microsoft Office 2003 Document Imaging (MDI) output. For example, a PC3 configuration like this will still work with PlotToDevice, but it will then hand the request to the Adobe rendering service to produce the PDF output or the MDI rendering service for producing MDI or TIFF documents.

## Plot Configurations

When you plot a drawing, its appearance depends upon the *plot configuration* you use. AutoCAD provides the PlotConfiguration object to hold the settings for a particular configuration. A plot configuration is similar to a layout, as it contains the same plot information and its corresponding AutoCAD objects expose almost identical properties and methods. However, a PlotConfiguration object isn't associated with any Block Definition, and so consists of a collection of plot settings that you may use with any geometry.

### PlotConfiguration Objects

You can have as many PlotConfiguration objects as you need, identified by a name and held in the PlotConfigurations collection. You access this collection through the Document object as follows:

```
Set PlotConfigurationsCollection = DocumentObject.PlotConfigurations
```

A PlotConfiguration object belongs either to model space or paper space (layouts) only, but not both. Additionally, when you import a PlotConfiguration object by way of a PageSetup import (by command or programmatically), it will only apply and attach to the appropriate working space from which it's related to in the source drawing. To create a new PlotConfiguration object, you use the Add method, which for the PlotConfigurations collection takes the syntax shown here:

```
Set PlotConfigurationObject = PlotConfigurationsCollection.Add(Name[, ModelType])
```

Table 15-6 shows the Add method's parameters.

*Table 15-6. Add Method Parameters*

| NAME | DATA TYPE | DESCRIPTION |
| --- | --- | --- |
| Name | String | The identifying name of the new PlotConfiguration object. |
| ModelType | Boolean | An optional parameter that determines which layouts the plot configuration may apply to. If this is set to True, the configuration applies only to model space; otherwise, it applies to all layouts. The default is False. |

To create a new PlotConfiguration object named PlotConfig1 that applies only to model space, you could use the following code:

```
Public Sub AddPConfig()
Dim objPlotConfigs As AcadPlotConfigurations
Dim objPlotConfig As AcadPlotConfiguration

  Set objPlotConfigs = ThisDrawing.PlotConfigurations
  Set objPlotConfig = objPlotConfigs.Add("PlotConfig1", True)

End Sub
```

You use each of the properties and methods discussed in the sections that follow to determine the appearance of a plot. They're exposed by both the PlotConfiguration and the Layout objects, although for a Layout object they apply only to the individual layout. Remember, a Layout object defines a specific view of your drawing geometry for plotting, whereas a PlotConfiguration object is generic and not associated with any particular view or drawing view layout. Effectively, they both achieve the same result but with the capability to use completely different input data.

When I present the syntax of each method or property in the sections that follow, the word "object" represents both the PlotConfiguration and Layout objects.

## The PlotType Property

You use this property to read or set how much of a drawing or layout is plotted. Modifications to this property only come into effect after the drawing is regenerated.

```
Object.PlotType = lngPlotType
```

The PlotType property holds one of the AcPlotType constants listed in Table 15-7.

*Table 15-7. AcPlotType Constants*

| CONSTANT | VALUE | DESCRIPTION |
| --- | --- | --- |
| acDisplay | 0 | Everything within the current display is printed. |
| acExtents | 1 | Everything within the extents of the currently selected space is printed. |
| acLimits | 2 | Everything within the limits of the current space is printed. |
| acView | 3 | The view named by the ViewToPlot property is printed. You must call the ViewToPlot property before you can set PlotType to acView. |
| acWindow | 4 | Everything in the window specified by the SetWindowToPlot method is printed. You must call the SetWindowToPlot method before you can set the PlotType to acWindow. |
| acLayout | 5 | Everything within the margins of the specified paper size is printed. The origin is calculated from the (0,0) coordinate location of the layout. This option doesn't apply to model space. |

## The ViewToPlot Property

AutoCAD allows you to plot a previously named view by setting the ViewToPlot property to the name of the view you want to use. For this to have an effect, it's then necessary to set the PlotType property of the Layout or PlotConfiguration object to acView. You supply the view name as a string.

```
Object.ViewToPlot = strViewName
```

I discuss how to manipulate views through code in Chapter 14. To view the currently available views through the AutoCAD user interface, navigate to the View dialog box via the View ➤ Named Views menu. Figure 15-3 shows the View dialog box.

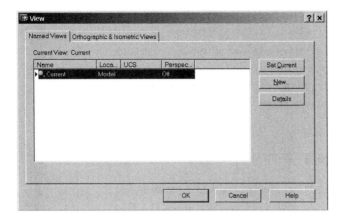

*Figure 15-3. The View dialog box*

The following code example sets the view to be plotted based on user input and then plots that view to file:

```
Public Sub PlotView()
Dim intCount As Integer
Dim strViewToPlot As String
Dim objView As AcadView
Dim strFilename As String

    strViewToPlot = InputBox("Enter name of view to plot: ", "Plot View")

On Error Resume Next
    Set objView = ThisDrawing.Views(strViewToPlot)
    If objView Is Nothing Then
        MsgBox "This view does not exist"
        Exit Sub
    End If

    strFilename = InputBox("Enter a filename to plot to")
    If strFilename = "" Then Exit Sub

    'set view to plot
    ThisDrawing.ModelSpace.Layout.ViewToPlot = strViewToPlot
    ThisDrawing.ModelSpace.Layout.PlotType = acView

    'Initiate the plot
    ThisDrawing.Plot.PlotToFile strFilename
End Sub
```

## The SetWindowToPlot Method

AutoCAD allows you to plot part of a layout within a rectangular window by using the SetWindowToPlot method to set the coordinates defining the lower-left and upper-right coordinates of the window. For this method to have an effect, it's necessary to set the PlotType property of the Layout or PlotConfiguration object to acWindow.

Object.SetWindowToPlot(LowerLeftCorner, UpperRightCorner)

Table 15-8 shows the SetWindowToPlot method's parameters.

*Table 15-8. SetWindowToPlot Method Parameters*

| NAME | DATA TYPE | DESCRIPTION |
|------|-----------|-------------|
| LowerLeftCorner | Variant | A two-element array of doubles specifying in paper units the X and Y values, measured from the origin, for the lower-left corner of the window to be plotted |
| UpperRightCorner | Variant | A two-element array of doubles specifying in paper units the X and Y values, measured from the origin, for the upper-right corner of the window to be plotted |

The following example illustrates how to implement this method by retrieving a window to plot from the user and then plotting that part of the drawing to file:

```
Public Sub PlotWindow()
Dim varLowerLeftCorner As Variant
Dim varUpperRightCorner As Variant
Dim dblLowerLeftCorner(1) As Double
Dim dblUpperRightCorner(1) As Double
Dim intCount As Integer
Dim strFilename As String

    'set the plot type
    varLowerLeftCorner = ThisDrawing.Utility.GetPoint(, _
                                "Select lower-left corner of window: ")
```

```
varUpperRightCorner = ThisDrawing.Utility.GetCorner(varLowerLeftCorner, _
                            "Select upper-right corner of window: ")
For intCount = 0 To 1
    dblLowerLeftCorner(intCount) = CDbl(varLowerLeftCorner(intCount))
    dblUpperRightCorner(intCount) = CDbl(varUpperRightCorner(intCount))
Next intCount
ThisDrawing.ActiveLayout.SetWindowToPlot dblLowerLeftCorner, _
                                    dblUpperRightCorner

ThisDrawing.ActiveLayout.PlotType = acWindow
'initiate the plot
strFilename = InputBox("Enter a filename to plot to")
If strFilename = "" Then Exit Sub

ThisDrawing.Plot.PlotToFile strFilename

End Sub
```

## Controlling Plot Parameters

A number of parameters are normally set using the Plot dialog box shown in Figure 15-4. AutoCAD provides a means to control these settings programmatically. In this section I cover the options that are most commonly modified.

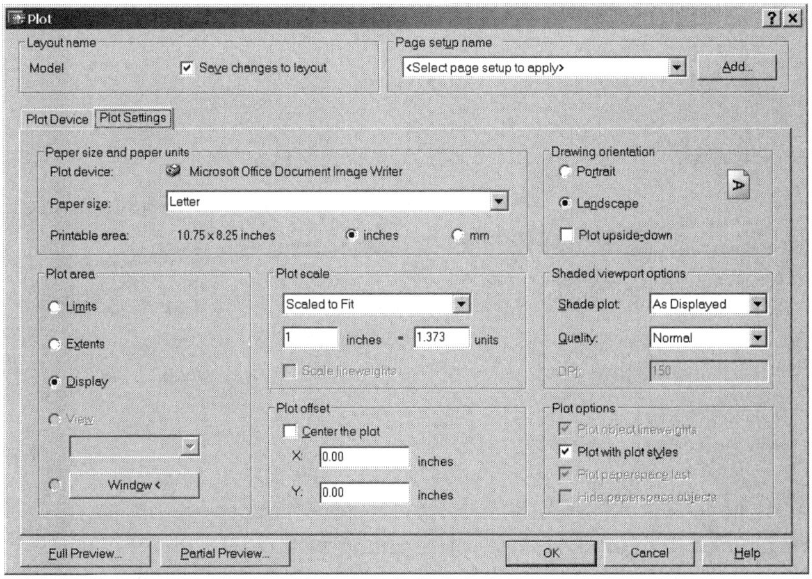

*Figure 15-4. The Plot dialog box*

All the methods and properties for controlling the plot parameters are available to both the PlotConfiguration and Layout objects. Consequently, when I present the syntax in the following sections, I use the word "object" to denote either object.

### The CanonicalMediaName Property

You can read or set the paper size to be used when plotting using the CanonicalMediaName property of the Layout or PlotConfiguration object. You specify the paper size by a name given as a string, and changes to this property won't take effect until the drawing has been regenerated.

```
Object.CanonicalMediaName = strPaperSize
```

This code snippet shows how to read the current setting of the paper size for the active layout of a drawing:

```
Public Sub PaperSizeNames()
    MsgBox "The paper size for the active layout is " & _
            ThisDrawing.ActiveLayout.CanonicalMediaName
End Sub
```

The result of this code may be similar to that shown in Figure 15-5.

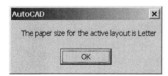

*Figure 15-5. PaperSizeNames output*

### The GetCanonicalMediaNames Method

You can use the GetCanonicalMediaNames method to retrieve the names of the available paper sizes for a specified plot device. The return value for this method is an array of strings holding the names of the available paper sizes.

```
varPaperSizeNames = Object.GetCanonicalMediaNames()
```

It's advisable to call the RefreshPlotDeviceInfo method before you use this method for the first time or each time you're changing the default plot device. This ensures that the plot, paper size names, and plot style table information accurately reflect the current system state.

### The GetPaperSize Method

Although you can read the `CanonicalMediaName` property to find out the name of
the paper size to be used, you may want to know the actual width and height
dimensions. The `GetPaperSize` method retrieves the width and height of the configured paper, given in the current paper units.

```
Object.GetPaperSize Width, Height
```

Table 15-9 shows the `GetPaperSize` method's parameters.

*Table 15-9. GetPaperSize Method Parameters*

| NAME | DATA TYPE | DESCRIPTION |
| --- | --- | --- |
| Width | Double | The width of the paper in units specified by the `PaperUnits` property of the layout or plot configuration |
| Height | Double | The height of the paper in units specified by the `PaperUnits` property of the layout or plot configuration |

The following code example incorporates the property and methods associated with the paper size. First, the available paper sizes for the current layout are
retrieved and displayed to the user. If the user then enters one of these in an
input box, the dimensions of the chosen paper size display.

```
Public Sub PaperSize()
Dim varPaperSizeNames As Variant
Dim strPaperSizeNames As String
Dim intCount As Integer
Dim strChoosenPaperSize As String

    varPaperSizeNames = ThisDrawing.ActiveLayout.GetCanonicalMediaNames
    strPaperSizeNames = "These are the paper sizes available:" & vbCrLf
    For intCount = 0 To UBound(varPaperSizeNames)
        strPaperSizeNames = strPaperSizeNames & _
                varPaperSizeNames(intCount) & ", "
    Next intCount
    strPaperSizeNames = strPaperSizeNames & vbCrLf & " Please choose one."

    strChoosenPaperSize = InputBox(strPaperSizeNames, "Pick a paper size")
```

```
    For intCount = 0 To UBound(varPaperSizeNames)
        If StrComp(strChoosenPaperSize, varPaperSizeNames(intCount), 1) = 0 _
            Then GoTo DisplaySize
    Next intCount
    MsgBox "You did not enter a valid paper size name."
    Exit Sub

DisplaySize:
Dim dblPaperWidth As Double
Dim dblPaperHeight As Double
Dim lngPaperUnits As Long
Dim strPaperUnits As String

    ThisDrawing.ActiveLayout.GetPaperSize dblPaperWidth, dblPaperHeight
    lngPaperUnits = ThisDrawing.ActiveLayout.PaperUnits
    Select Case lngPaperUnits
        Case 0
            strPaperUnits = "inches"
        Case 1
        strPaperUnits = "millimeters"
    End Select

    MsgBox dblPaperWidth & " by " & dblPaperHeight & " " & strPaperUnits
End Sub
```

## The Plot Scale

You normally draw an AutoCAD drawing in units that reflect the true size of the
object being represented. Therefore, when you print your drawing you'll probably need to scale the plot so that it fits comfortably onto the paper. There are two
types of plot scales, and both give the ratio of the plot size to drawing size. The
first is the *standard scale* and it's set to one of AutoCAD's predefined scales. The
second, *custom scale,* can be set to any value.

### The StandardScale Property

You can use the StandardScale property to set the plot scale to one of the predefined AutoCAD scales.

```
Object.StandardScale = lngAcPlotScale
```

This must be one of the `AcPlotScale` constants detailed in Table 15-10.

*Table 15-10. AcPlotScale Constants*

| CONSTANT | VALUE | DESCRIPTION | CONSTANT | VALUE | DESCRIPTION |
|---|---|---|---|---|---|
| acScaleToFit | 0 | Scale to Fit | ac1_1 | 16 | 1:1 |
| ac1_128in_1ft | 1 | 1/128" : 1' | ac1_2 | 17 | 1:2 |
| ac1_64in_1ft | 2 | 1/64" : 1' | ac1_4 | 18 | 1:4 |
| ac1_32in_1ft | 3 | 1/32" : 1' | ac1_8 | 19 | 1:8 |
| ac1_16in_1ft | 4 | 1/16" : 1' | ac1_10 | 20 | 1:10 |
| ac3_32in_1ft | 5 | 3/32" : 1' | ac1_16 | 21 | 1:16 |
| ac1_8in_1ft | 6 | 1/8" : 1' | ac1_20 | 22 | 1:20 |
| ac3_16in_1ft | 7 | 3/16" : 1' | ac1_30 | 23 | 1:30 |
| ac1_4in_1ft | 8 | 1/4" : 1' | ac1_40 | 24 | 1:40 |
| ac3_8in_1ft | 9 | 3/8" : 1' | ac1_50 | 25 | 1:50 |
| ac1_2in_1ft | 10 | 1/2" : 1' | ac1_100 | 26 | 1:100 |
| ac3_4in_1ft | 11 | 3/4" : 1' | ac2_1 | 27 | 2:1 |
| ac1in_1ft | 12 | 1" : 1' | ac4_1 | 28 | 4:1 |
| ac3in_1ft | 13 | 3" : 1' | ac8_1 | 29 | 8:1 |
| ac6in_1ft | 14 | 6" : 1' | ac10_1 | 30 | 10:1 |
| ac1ft_1ft | 15 | 1' : 1' | ac100_1 | 31 | 100:1 |

### The GetCustomScale Method

You use this method to examine the scale for a layout or plot configuration.

```
Object.GetCustomScale(Numerator, Denominator)
```

Table 15-11 shows the `GetCustomScale` method's parameters.

*Table 15-11. GetCustomScale Method Parameters*

| NAME | DATA TYPE | DESCRIPTION |
|------|-----------|-------------|
| Numerator | Double | The numerator in the scale ratio. This value represents the number of inches or millimeters for the plot. The unit of measurement is held in the PaperUnits parameter. |
| Denominator | Double | The denominator in the scale ratio. This value represents the number of drawing units used to scale to the measurement given in the numerator. |

You can use the following code to retrieve the scales used in each of the layouts of your drawing:

```
Public Sub GetScales()
Dim objLayout As AcadLayout
Dim dblNumerator As Double
Dim dblDenominator As Double

    For Each objLayout In ThisDrawing.Layouts
        'Get custom scale information
        objLayout.GetCustomScale dblNumerator, dblDenominator
        If objLayout.PaperUnits = acInches Then
            MsgBox "The scale of " & objLayout.Name & _
                    " is " & dblNumerator & " inches = " & _
                    dblDenominator & " Drawing Units"
        ElseIf objLayout.PaperUnits = acMillimeters Then
            MsgBox "The scale of " & objLayout.Name & _
                    " is " & dblNumerator & " millimeters = " & _
                    dblDenominator & " Drawing Units"
        Else
        MsgBox "The scale of " & objLayout.Name & " is " & _
                dblNumerator & " pixels = " & dblDenominator & _
                " Drawing Units"
        End If
    Next
End Sub
```

### The SetCustomScale Method

This method works in a similar way to the GetCustomScale described previously, except it sets the plot scale. Any changes you make through this method become effective only after the drawing has been regenerated.

```
Object.SetCustomScale(Numerator, Denominator)
```

Table 15-12 shows the SetCustomScale method's parameters.

*Table 15-12. SetCustomScale Method Parameters*

| NAME | DATA TYPE | DESCRIPTION |
| --- | --- | --- |
| Numerator | Double | A positive value representing the number of inches or millimeters of the plot. The unit of measurement is held in the PaperUnits parameter. |
| Denominator | Double | A positive value representing the number of drawing units for the drawing that will be scaled to the measurement given in the numerator. |

### The UseStandardScale Property

You use this property to read or set whether a plot should use a standard or custom scale. It holds a Boolean value that is set to True if a standard scale is in use or False if a custom plot scale is in use.

```
Object.UseStandardScale = blnStandardScale
```

The following code sample employs the UseStandardScale property to retrieve the type of scale used for each layout and displays that information to the user:

```
Public Sub UseStandardScale()
Dim objLayout As AcadLayout

    For Each objLayout In ThisDrawing.Layouts
        If objLayout.UseStandardScale Then
            MsgBox "The scale of " & objLayout.Name & " is a Standard scale"
        Else
            MsgBox "The scale of " & objLayout.Name & " is a Custom scale"
        End If
    Next
End Sub
```

## The PlotRotation Property

If you want to plot a layout at an angle other than the default of 08, then you'll need to specify the angle of rotation using the PlotRotation property. This property allows you to select predefined angles of 08, 908, 1808, and 2708, measured counterclockwise in the XY plane from the X-axis of the WCS. Changes to the PlotRotation property won't take effect until the drawing has been regenerated.

```
Object.PlotRotation = lngAcPlotRotation
```

Any of the AcPlotRotation constants shown in Table 15-13 is an acceptable value for this property.

*Table 15-13. AcPlotRotation Constants*

| CONSTANT | VALUE | DESCRIPTION |
|---|---|---|
| ac0degrees | 0 | The layout and plot have the same orientation. |
| ac90degrees | 1 | The plot is rotated by an angle of 908 from the layout. |
| ac180degrees | 2 | The plot is rotated by an angle of 1808 from the layout. |
| ac270degrees | 3 | The plot is rotated by an angle of 2708 from the layout. |

In the following code sample, the user is asked at which angle he or she would like to preview the active layout. The preview then displays, and finally the PlotRotation property returns to its original value.

```
Public Sub PlotAngle()
Dim strPlotAngle As String
Dim lngStoreAngle As Long

    lngStoreAngle = ThisDrawing.ActiveLayout.PlotRotation
    strPlotAngle = InputBox("For a plot preview please enter the angle" & _
                "(in degrees: 0, 90, 180 or 270) that you would like" & _
                " your layout plotted at", , "0")

    Select Case strPlotAngle
      Case "0"
          ThisDrawing.ActiveLayout.PlotRotation = ac0degrees
      Case "90"
          ThisDrawing.ActiveLayout.PlotRotation = ac90degrees
```

```
    Case "180"
        ThisDrawing.ActiveLayout.PlotRotation = ac180degrees
      Case "270"
        ThisDrawing.ActiveLayout.PlotRotation = ac270degrees
      Case Else
        MsgBox "You entered an invalid value"
        Exit Sub
    End Select
    ThisDrawing.Regen acActiveViewport
    ThisDrawing.Plot.DisplayPlotPreview acFullPreview
    ThisDrawing.ActiveLayout.PlotRotation = lngStoreAngle
    ThisDrawing.Regen acActiveViewport
End Sub
```

## Summary

In this chapter you explored several topics specific to plotting. This is one area in which AutoCAD 2000 and higher versions are vastly different from previous versions. In AutoCAD 2000 and higher, Autodesk added a lot of plotting power, and when you're programming your plotting applications, the use of plot configuration files can reduce the amount of hard coding required by taking advantage of the features built into the AutoCAD product. Some differences exist between AutoCAD 2000, 2000i, 2002, and 2004 as far as programmatic capabilities with respect to plotting and plot configuration management, so you should be sure to refer to the appropriate documentation for your platform.

CHAPTER 16

# Controlling Menus and Toolbars

AUTOCAD 2000 AND HIGHER GIVES YOU the ability to control the menus and toolbars programmatically. You can manipulate existing menus or create new entries using the objects exposed by the AutoCAD object model. Although you can't create a completely new menu structure programmatically, you can make changes to the existing menus.

This chapter covers the following topics in detail:

- Loading, saving, and unloading menu groups

- Assigning accelerator keys

- Manipulating the menu bar

- Creating and editing menus

- Creating and editing toolbars

- Floating and docking toolbars

Figure 16-1 shows the Select Menu File dialog box.

I start this chapter with the MenuGroups collection because it's the parent object of the MenuGroup object, which in turn is the parent object of the ToolBars and PopupMenus collections. The MenuBar collection holds all the PopupMenu objects that are currently displayed in the AutoCAD menu bar.

**NOTE** *This chapter's content is specific to AutoCAD 2000 or later. The previous object models didn't expose any objects to deal with menus and toolbars.*

*Figure 16-1. The Select Menu File dialog box*

## The MenuGroups Collection

The menus loaded into the current session of AutoCAD are contained in the MenuGroups collection. These menus, grouped into MenuGroup objects, may or may not be visible on the menu bar, but they're all still contained within this collection. Each MenuGroup object provides access to the toolbars and pop-up menus available within an AutoCAD session.

### Loading Menu Groups

You can use the Load method of the MenuGroups collection to load a new menu group contained in a menu file (.mnc, .mns, or .mnu) into an AutoCAD session.

```
Set MenuGroupObject = MenuGroupsCollection.Load (MenuFileName [,BaseMenu])
```

Table 16-1 shows the Load method's parameters.

*Table 16-1. Load Method Parameters*

| NAME | DATA TYPE | DESCRIPTION |
|---|---|---|
| MenuFileName | String | The path and file name of the menu file to be loaded. |
| BaseMenu | Boolean | This optional parameter determines whether the menu group is loaded as a base or partial menu. If it's set to True, then the menu group is loaded as a base menu. Otherwise, the menu group is loaded as a partial menu. The default is False. |

Using the Load method with the BaseMenu parameter set to True equates to executing the MENU command inside the AutoCAD application and selecting a file through the Select Menu File dialog box (or executing the MENULOAD command and checking the Replace All option in the Menu Customization dialog box, as shown in Figure 16-2). The newly loaded menu file becomes the only loaded menu group and completely replaces the previous menu bar.

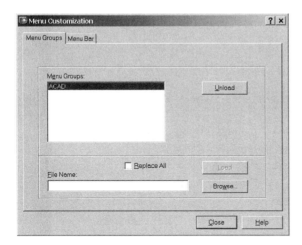

*Figure 16-2. The Menu Customization dialog box*

Alternatively, using the Load method with the BaseMenu parameter set to False equates to executing the MENULOAD command inside the AutoCAD application and selecting a file through the Menu Customization dialog box. The menu group is loaded in addition to the already existing menu groups.

To find out what type of menu groups are loaded into an AutoCAD session, you can examine the Type property for each MenuGroup object.

```
lngMenuGroupType = MenuGroupObject.Type
```

This read-only property holds one of the AcMenuGroupType constants listed in Table 16-2.

*Table 16-2. AcMenuGroupType Constants*

| CONSTANT | VALUE | DESCRIPTION |
|----------|-------|-------------|
| AcBaseMenuGroup | 0 | The menu group is a base menu group. |
| AcPartialMenuGroup | 1 | The menu group is a partial menu group. |

The following code displays a list of all the currently loaded menu groups and their types:

```
Public Sub ListMenuGroups()
Dim objMenuGroup As AcadMenuGroup
Dim strMenuGroupNames As String

    strMenuGroupNames = "The following menu groups are currently loaded, "

    For Each objMenuGroup In Application.MenuGroups
        If objMenuGroup.Type = acBaseMenuGroup Then
            strMenuGroupNames = strMenuGroupNames & vbCrLf & _
                                objMenuGroup.Name & ": Base menu"
        Else
            strMenuGroupNames = strMenuGroupNames & vbCrLf & _
                                objMenuGroup.Name & ": Partial menu"
        End If
    Next
    MsgBox strMenuGroupNames

End Sub
```

For my setup, this code yielded the result shown in Figure 16-3.

*Figure 16-3. ListMenuGroups() code output*

Note that the MenuGroups collection doesn't expose an Add method, so you can't create brand-new menu groups through code. However, you can make a copy of an .mns file to a new file name and then load and edit it as you require. You can also write a new .mnu or .mns file and load it entirely from VBA. It's usually best to work with partial menus and avoid modifying or replacing the AutoCAD menu system entirely, for two main reasons:

- You don't want to upset your users (customers) by changing the familiar menu system entirely.

- Keeping your menus separate avoids the possibility of an AutoCAD service pack wiping out your hard work.

Until you feel confident with the material covered in this chapter, you should make a copy of an existing menu group file, unload the original, and load and use this copy to try out the code in this chapter. You can then unload the copy and reload the original to restore your original AutoCAD menu structure.

 **NOTE** *You can't edit image tile menu items, screen menus, or tablet menus programmatically. However, you can load and unload these menu types using AutoCAD VBA.*

## The MenuGroup Object

Once you've loaded a menu group, its corresponding MenuGroup object is added to the MenuGroups collection. A MenuGroup object contains two collections, PopupMenus and Toolbars. All the menus within a menu group are members of the PopupMenus collection, and all the toolbars are members of the Toolbars collection. You access these two collections via the Menus and Toolbars properties of the MenuGroup object with the following syntax:

```
Set PopupMenusCollection = MenuGroupObject.Menus

Set ToolbarsCollection = MenuGroupObject.Toolbars
```

The following code sample sets a reference to the MenuGroup object representing the ACAD menu group if it's loaded into the current session. It then displays a list of each of the menus and toolbars that make up this menu group. Here I used the NameNoMneumonic property of the menus to display their names rather than the Name property because I didn't want to show all the accelerator or hot keys.

```
Public Sub ListMenusAndToolbars()
Dim objMenuGroup As AcadMenuGroup
Dim objPopupMenu As AcadPopupMenu
Dim objToolBar As AcadToolbar
Dim strMenusAndToolbars As String

    On Error Resume Next
    Set objMenuGroup = ThisDrawing.Application.MenuGroups.Item("ACAD")
    If objMenuGroup Is Nothing Then
        MsgBox "ACAD menu group is not loaded"
        Exit Sub
    End If

    strMenusAndToolbars = _
            "The ACAD menu group comprises the following menus: " & vbCrLf
    For Each objPopupMenu In objMenuGroup.Menus
        strMenusAndToolbars = strMenusAndToolbars & _
                            objPopupMenu.NameNoMnemonic & ", "
    Next

    strMenusAndToolbars = strMenusAndToolbars & vbCrLf & vbCrLf & _
                        " and the following toolbars: " & vbCrLf

    For Each objToolBar In objMenuGroup.Toolbars
        strMenusAndToolbars = strMenusAndToolbars & objToolBar.Name & ", "
    Next
    MsgBox strMenusAndToolbars

End Sub
```

The result of this code is shown in Figure 16-4. As you can see, the File, Edit, and View menus belong to this group, as well as the Draw, Modify, and Dimension toolbars. Note that many of these menus and toolbars aren't normally visible when you use the AutoCAD interface.

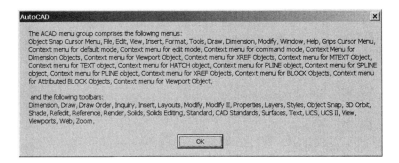

*Figure 16-4. Loaded menu group*

## Saving Menu Groups

You have two methods for saving a menu group: Save and SaveAs. As you would expect, the first saves the menu group to the file it's already associated with, and the second allows you to save the menu group under a new name.

```
MenuGroupObject.Save MenuFileType
```

```
MenuGroupObject.SaveAs FileName, MenuFileType
```

Table 16-3 shows the SaveAs method's parameters.

*Table 16-3. SaveAs Method Parameters*

| NAME | DATA TYPE | DESCRIPTION |
| --- | --- | --- |
| MenuFileType | Long | Determines whether the menu group is saved as a source or compiled file. It must take one of the AcMenuFileType constants in Table 16-4. |
| FileName | String | The full path and file name for the file to save to. The menu group then adopts this new name. |

Table 16-4 presents the AcMenuFileType constants.

*Table 16-4. AcMenuFileType Constants*

| CONSTANT | VALUE | DESCRIPTION |
| --- | --- | --- |
| acMenuFileCompiled | 0 | A compiled menu file (.mnc extension) |
| acMenuFileSource | 1 | A source menu file (.mns extension) |

You can use this code to take a compiled menu and save it as an .mns file, ensuring that the user doesn't overwrite the ACAD menu group file:

```
Public Sub SaveMenuGroupAsSource()
Dim strMenuGroup As String
Dim strSaveto As String
Dim objMenuGroup As AcadMenuGroup

    strMenuGroup = InputBox("Enter the name of the menu group you" & _
                            " wish to save")
    If strMenuGroup = "" Then Exit Sub

On Error Resume Next
    Set objMenuGroup = ThisDrawing.Application.MenuGroups.Item(strMenuGroup)

    If objMenuGroup Is Nothing Then
        MsgBox "The menu group was not recognized"
        Exit Sub
    End If

    strSaveto = InputBox("Enter the filename to save" & strMenuGroup & " to")
    If UCase(strSaveto) = "ACAD" Then
        MsgBox "You should not overwrite the ACAD file"
        Exit Sub
    End If

    objMenuGroup.SaveAs strSaveto, acMenuFileSource

End Sub
```

## Unloading Menu Groups

If you're sure that you no longer require a menu group, you can unload it from the AutoCAD session using the Unload method, which is the programmatic counterpart to using the MENULOAD or MENUUNLOAD commands.

`MenuGroupObject.Unload`

When you unload a menu group, any references that you've set up through code to the menus and toolbars contained in that group become invalid. It's wise, therefore, to release all such references before you use this method.

## Accelerator Keys

You can include accelerator keys in the name of a menu or menu item. You achieve this by placing an ampersand (&) before the character you want to be the accelerator key. For example, setting a menu name to "&File" causes it to appear as File and allows it to be quickly accessed by pressing Alt+F.

## Changing the Menu Bar

As I pointed out earlier, AutoCAD 2000 allows you to completely replace the current menu bar with a new menu group by loading it as the base menu. The individual menus that the menu bar displays are contained in the MenuBar collection. You can add, rearrange, and remove menus from a menu group from the menu bar, and it's such modification of the menu bar that you'll consider next.

### Adding Menus to the Menu Bar

There are two ways to add a new menu to the menu bar. The first uses the InsertInMenuBar method of the PopupMenu object to be inserted. When a menu not displayed on the AutoCAD menu bar is added to the menu bar, its OnMenuBar property changes from False to True.

`PopupMenuObject.InsertInMenuBar(Index)`

Table 16-5 shows the `InsertInMenuBar` method's parameters.

*Table 16-5. InsertInMenuBar Method Parameters*

| NAME | DATA TYPE | DESCRIPTION |
| --- | --- | --- |
| Index | Variant | The position within the menu bar where the pop-up menu will be added. It can be either an integer between 0 and N, where N is the number of objects in the menu bar, or a string giving the name of an existing menu (including & accelerator key character) that the new item will be placed directly before. If the menu specified by the index doesn't exist, then the new menu is added at the end of the menu bar. |

This example places a user-named menu at the beginning of the menu bar:

```
Public Sub InsertMenu1()
Dim objMenuGroup As AcadMenuGroup
Dim strMenuGroupNames As String
Dim strChosenMenuGroup As String
Dim objMenu As AcadPopupMenu
Dim strMenuNames As String
Dim strChosenMenu As String

    strMenuGroupNames = "Choose one of the loaded menu groups: " & vbCrLf
    For Each objMenuGroup In ThisDrawing.Application.MenuGroups
        strMenuGroupNames = strMenuGroupNames & objMenuGroup.Name & vbCrLf
    Next objMenuGroup

    strChosenMenuGroup = InputBox(strMenuGroupNames, "Choose a menu group")
    If strChosenMenuGroup = "" Then Exit Sub

    On Error Resume Next
    Set objMenuGroup =
ThisDrawing.Application.MenuGroups.Item(strChosenMenuGroup)
    If objMenuGroup Is Nothing Then
        MsgBox "The menu group you chose does not exist"
        Exit Sub
    End If

    strMenuNames = "Choose a menu to add to the menu bar:" & vbCrLf
```

```
    For Each objMenu In objMenuGroup.Menus
        strMenuNames = strMenuNames & objMenu.Name & vbCrLf
    Next objMenu


    strChosenMenu = InputBox(strMenuNames, "Choose a menu")
    If strChosenMenu = "" Then Exit Sub


    ' check if menu is already on menu bar
    Set objMenu = ThisDrawing.Application.MenuBar.Item(strChosenMenu)
    If Not objMenu Is Nothing Then
        MsgBox "This menu is already present on the menu bar"
        Exit Sub
    End If
    Set objMenu = objMenuGroup.Menus.Item(strChosenMenu)
    If objMenu Is Nothing Then
        MsgBox "The menu you chose does not exist"
        Exit Sub
    End If



    objMenu.InsertInMenuBar 0

End Sub
```

This example places a user-named menu just before an existing menu chosen by the user:

```
Public Sub InsertMenu2()
Dim objMenuGroup As AcadMenuGroup
Dim strMenuGroupNames As String
Dim strChosenMenuGroup As String
Dim objMenu As AcadPopupMenu
Dim strMenuNames As String
Dim strChosenMenu As String
Dim strMenuPosition As String

    strMenuGroupNames = "Choose one of the loaded menu groups: " & vbCrLf
    For Each objMenuGroup In ThisDrawing.Application.MenuGroups
        strMenuGroupNames = strMenuGroupNames & objMenuGroup.Name & vbCrLf
    Next

    strChosenMenuGroup = InputBox(strMenuGroupNames, "Choose a menu group")
    If strChosenMenuGroup = "" Then Exit Sub
```

```
    On Error Resume Next
    Set objMenuGroup =
ThisDrawing.Application.MenuGroups.Item(strChosenMenuGroup)
    If objMenuGroup Is Nothing Then
        MsgBox "The menu group you chose does not exist"
        Exit Sub
    End If

    strMenuNames = "Choose a menu to add to the menu bar:" & vbCrLf
    For Each objMenu In objMenuGroup.Menus
        strMenuNames = strMenuNames & objMenu.Name & vbCrLf
    Next

    strChosenMenu = InputBox(strMenuNames, "Choose a menu")
    If strChosenMenu = "" Then Exit Sub

    Set objMenu = objMenuGroup.Menus.Item(strChosenMenu)
    If objMenu Is Nothing Then
        MsgBox "The menu you chose does not exist"
        Exit Sub
    End If

    strMenuPosition = InputBox("Enter name of menu you wish to place it" & _
                            " before (including accelerator keys)")

    objMenu.InsertInMenuBar strMenuPosition

End Sub
```

Figure 16-5 shows the result of adding the "Context menu for Viewport Object" menu of the Viewport menu group before the Draw menu of the ACAD menu group. Note that if the existing menu on the menu bar wasn't recognized, then the new menu will be placed at the end of the menu bar.

*Figure 16-5. Menu indices*

The second way to add a menu to the menu bar employs the InsertMenuInMenuBar method of a PopupMenus collection.

```
PopupMenusCollection.InsertMenuInMenuBar MenuName, Index
```

Table 16-6 shows the InsertMenuInMenuBar method's parameters.

*Table 16-6. InsertMenuInMenuBar Method Parameters*

| NAME | DATA TYPE | DESCRIPTION |
| --- | --- | --- |
| MenuName | String | The identifying name of the pop-up menu to be added to the menu bar. |
| Index | Variant | The position within the menu bar where the pop-up menu will be added. It can be either an integer between 0 and N, where N is the number of objects in the menu bar, or a string giving the name of an existing menu (including the & accelerator key character) that the new item will be placed directly before. If the menu specified by the index doesn't exist, then the new menu is added at the end of the menu bar. |

The following example again adds a user-chosen menu to the menu bar. If the menu that the user has chosen isn't recognized, no error is raised and it's simply not added to the menu bar.

```
Public Sub InsertMenu3()
Dim objMenuGroup As AcadMenuGroup
Dim strMenuGroupNames As String
Dim strChosenMenuGroup As String
Dim objMenu As AcadPopupMenu
Dim strMenuNames As String
Dim strChosenMenu As String
Dim strMenuPosition As String

    strMenuGroupNames = "Choose one of the loaded menu groups: " & vbCrLf
    For Each objMenuGroup In ThisDrawing.Application.MenuGroups
        strMenuGroupNames = strMenuGroupNames & objMenuGroup.Name & vbCrLf
    Next

    strChosenMenuGroup = InputBox(strMenuGroupNames, "Choose a menu group")
    If strChosenMenuGroup = "" Then Exit Sub
```

```
        On Error Resume Next
        Set objMenuGroup =
ThisDrawing.Application.MenuGroups.Item(strChosenMenuGroup)
        If objMenuGroup Is Nothing Then
            MsgBox "The menu group you chose does not exist"
            Exit Sub
        End If

        strMenuNames = "Choose a menu to add to the menu bar:" & vbCrLf
        For Each objMenu In objMenuGroup.Menus
            strMenuNames = strMenuNames & objMenu.Name & vbCrLf
        Next

        strChosenMenu = InputBox(strMenuNames, "Choose a menu")
        If strChosenMenu = "" Then Exit Sub

        strMenuPosition = InputBox("Enter name of menu you wish to place it" & _
                                   " before (including accelerator keys)")

        objMenuGroup.Menus.InsertMenuInMenuBar strChosenMenu, strMenuPosition
End Sub
```

You can use the specified position and order in which menus are added to menu bar to arrange/rearrange the menus that make up your menu bar.

## Removing Menus

Just as with adding menus to the menu bar, you have two ways to remove them: the RemoveFromMenuBar method of a PopupMenu object and the RemoveMenuFromMenuBar method of a PopupMenus collection. The first method takes the following simple syntax:

```
PopupMenuObject.RemoveFromMenuBar
```

This code iterates through the menus on the menu bar and removes those that the user specifies:

```
Sub RemoveMenus()
Dim objMenu As AcadPopupMenu
```

```
    For Each objMenu In ThisDrawing.Application.MenuBar
        If MsgBox("Remove " & objMenu.Name & "?", vbYesNo) = vbYes Then
            objMenu.RemoveFromMenuBar
    Next

End Sub
```

When you use the second method, you need to specify which menu you
want to remove:

```
PopupMenusCollection.RemoveMenuFromMenuBar Index
```

Table 16-7 shows the `RemoveMenuFromMenuBar` method's parameters.

*Table 16-7. RemoveMenuFromMenuBar Method Parameters*

| NAME | DATA TYPE | DESCRIPTION |
| --- | --- | --- |
| Index | Variant | The position within the menu bar of the menu to be removed. It can be either an integer between 0 and N-1, where N is the number of objects in the menu bar, or a string giving the name of the menu (including the & accelerator key character). If the menu specified by the index doesn't exist, then this method does nothing. |

To allow the user to choose a menu to remove, you use this code:

```
Public Sub RemoveMenu()
Dim objMenuGroup As AcadMenuGroup
Dim strMenuGroupNames As String
Dim strChosenMenuGroup As String
Dim strOnMenuBar As String
Dim objMenu As AcadPopupMenu
Dim strChosenMenu As String

    strMenuGroupNames = "Choose one of the loaded menu groups: " & vbCrLf
    For Each objMenuGroup In ThisDrawing.Application.MenuGroups
        strMenuGroupNames = strMenuGroupNames & objMenuGroup.Name & vbCrLf
    Next

    strChosenMenuGroup = InputBox(strMenuGroupNames, "Choose a menu group")
    If strChosenMenuGroup = "" Then Exit Sub
```

```
      On Error Resume Next
      Set objMenuGroup = _
ThisDrawing.Application.MenuGroups.Item(strChosenMenuGroup)
      If objMenuGroup Is Nothing Then
          MsgBox "The menu group you chose does not exist"
          Exit Sub
      End If


      strOnMenuBar = "the following menus with the " & objMenuGroup.Name & _
                 " menu group are displayed in the menu bar." & vbCrLf
      For Each objMenu In objMenuGroup.Menus
          If objMenu.OnMenuBar = True Then
              strOnMenuBar = strOnMenuBar & objMenu.Name & vbCrLf
      Next
      strOnMenuBar = strOnMenuBar & "Please choose a menu to remove"

      strChosenMenu = InputBox(strOnMenuBar)

      objMenuGroup.Menus.RemoveMenuFromMenuBar strChosenMenu

End Sub
```

 **NOTE** *Removed menus are still available in their designated menu group even though they're no longer visible to the user.*

## Editing Menus

Programmatically, you can create and customize two types of menus: *pull-down* and *shortcut* menus. You access pull-down menus via the AutoCAD menu bar, and you access shortcut menus by pressing *Shift* and clicking with the right mouse button. Both types of menus are displayed as cascading style menus.

Pull-down style menu structures are limited to 999 items and shortcut style menu structures are limited to 499 items. These limits include everything in the menu structure. AutoCAD will ignore any menu items beyond these limits. Figure 16-6 reveals how the numbering of menu items works. You can see that the separators count as menu items.

If the space available on the graphics screen is less than that required to display the menu structure, it will be truncated to fit within the available space, and arrows will be placed at the top and bottom to allow navigation of the menu, as shown in Figure 16-7.

*Figure 16-6. A menu bar*

*Figure 16-7. A custom menu*

## Creating New Menus

You can add a new menu, represented by a PopupMenu object, to a PopupMenus collection using the Add method.

```
Set PopupMenuObject = PopupMenusCollection.Add(MenuName)
```

Table 16-8 shows the Add method's parameters.

*Table 16-8. Add Method Parameters*

| NAME | DATA TYPE | DESCRIPTION |
|------|-----------|-------------|
| MenuName | String | The identifying name of the newly created PopupMenu object |

The MenuName parameter may be a simple string such as VBATestMenu or one containing special characters such as an ampersand (&) character placed before a character specifying it as the accelerator key. By setting the menu name to &VBATestMenu it will appear as VBATestMenu in the menu bar and you can view it by pressing Alt+V. For a complete list of special codes, please see the AutoCAD Customization Guide.

The following example illustrates how to create a new menu and add it to the menu bar with the heading "Apress," and define a shortcut for the "r" character within it:

```
Public Sub CreateApressMenu1()
Dim objMenus As AcadPopupMenus
Dim objMyMenu As AcadPopupMenu
Dim strNewMenuName As String

    Set objMenus = ThisDrawing.Application.MenuGroups.Item(0).Menus

    On Error Resume Next
    Set objMyMenu = objMenus.Item("Apr&ess")
    If Not objMyMenu Is Nothing Then
        MsgBox "Menu already exists"
        Exit Sub
    End If

    Set objMyMenu = objMenus.Add("Ap&ress")

    objMyMenu.InsertInMenuBar ThisDrawing.Application.MenuBar.Count

End Sub
```

Note that the Apress menu has an accelerator key of "r". This character is underlined and the menu, and you may view it by pressing Alt+R. You'll find that pressing this key combination doesn't do much yet, because the menu you've created is empty. Next you'll look at how to add items to a menu.

## Adding New Menu Items

You can add a new item, represented by a PopupMenuItem object, to a menu through the AddMenuItem method of the PopupMenu object.

```
Set PopupMenuItemObject = PopupMenuObject.AddMenuItem(Index, Label, Macro)
```

Table 16-9 shows the AddMenuItem method's parameters.

*Table 16-9. AddMenuItem Method Parameters*

| NAME | DATA TYPE | DESCRIPTION |
|------|-----------|-------------|
| Index | Variant | The position within the menu that the pop-up menu item will be added. It can either be an integer between 0 and N, where N is the number of objects in the menu, or a string giving the name of an existing menu item (including the & accelerator key character) that the new item will be placed directly before. If the menu item specified by the index doesn't exist, then the new menu item is added at the end of the menu. |
| Label | String | A label for the menu item. The label may contain DIESEL string expressions, which conditionally change the label each time it's displayed. Labels also identify the accelerator keys. |
| Macro | String | A string that will be written to the AutoCAD command prompt when the menu item is clicked. |

You can't change the Index value of the menu item once it has been created through the Index property, as it's read-only. To rearrange menu items, you must first delete a menu item and add it again at the position you want it within the menu structure.

The following example code adds a menu item to the Apress menu. I've included a very simple macro to demonstrate how the Macro parameter works. In this case, you can call a macro that you've written yourself by using the -VBARUN command described in Chapter 1. Note that you need to leave a space at the end of the macro name so that AutoCAD knows the end of the command has been reached.

```
Public Sub CreateApressMenu2()
Dim objMenus As AcadPopupMenus
Dim objMyMenu As AcadPopupMenu
Dim strNewMenuName As String
Dim objMyMenuItem As AcadPopupMenuItem

    Set objMenus = ThisDrawing.Application.MenuGroups.Item(0).Menus

    On Error Resume Next
    Set objMyMenu = objMenus.Item("Ap&ress")
    If objMyMenu Is Nothing Then
        Set objMyMenu = objMenus.Add("Ap&ress")
    End If
```

```
'Check if the Menu is displayed on the MenuBar
If Not objMyMenu.OnMenuBar Then
'Display the menu on the menu bar
    objMyMenu.InsertInMenuBar ThisDrawing.Application.MenuBar.Count
End If
Set objMyMenuItem = objMyMenu.AddMenuItem(0, "Add &Circle", _
    "-vbarun AddCircle ")
objMyMenuItem.HelpString = "This adds a circle at the origin"

End Sub
Public Sub AddCircle()
Dim dblCenter(2) As Double
  If ThisDrawing.ActiveSpace = acModelSpace Then
    ThisDrawing.ModelSpace.AddCircle dblCenter, 2
  Else
    ThisDrawing.PaperSpace.AddCircle dblCenter, 2
  End If
End Sub
```

You can see from the preceding code that it's possible to set the HelpString property of a PopupMenuIem object so that text, which provides information about what the menu item does, appears in the AutoCAD status line. If you hover your mouse over the newly created menu item, you'll see the phrase "This adds a circle at the origin" in the AutoCAD status line. This property is also exposed by the Toolbar and ToolbarItem objects.

## Adding Separators

You can use the AddSeparator method to add a separator to your menu structure or to a toolbar. This method takes a single parameter and returns either a PopupMenuItem or ToolbarItem object. Here's the syntax for adding a separator to a menu:

```
Set PopupMenuItemObject = PopupMenuObject.AddSeparator(Index)
```

Table 16-10 shows the AddSeparator method's parameter.

**NOTE** *You can't have adjacent separators or a separator at the beginning of a menu or toolbar.*

*Table 16-10. AddSeparator Method Parameter*

| NAME | DATA TYPE | DESCRIPTION |
|------|-----------|-------------|
| Index | Variant | The position within the menu where the separator will be added. It can either be an integer between 0 and N, where N is the number of objects in the menu, or a string giving the name of an existing menu item (including the & accelerator key character) that the separator will be placed directly before. If the menu item specified by the index doesn't exist, then the separator is placed at the end of the menu. |

## Creating Cascading Submenus

You can create cascading submenus by adding a submenu to an existing menu via the AddSubMenu method. This new cascading menu is blank, and you can modify it in precisely the same way as any other PopupMenu object.

```
Set PopupMenuObject = PopupMenuObject.AddSubMenu(Index, Label)
```

Table 16-11 shows the AddSubMenu method's parameters.

*Table 16-11. AddSubMenu Method Parameters*

| NAME | DATA TYPE | DESCRIPTION |
|------|-----------|-------------|
| Index | Variant | The position within the menu that the submenu will be added. It can either be an integer between 0 and N, where N is the number of objects in the menu, or a string giving the name of an existing menu item (including the & accelerator key character) that the submenu will be placed directly before. If the menu item specified by the index doesn't exist, then the submenu is placed at the end of the menu. |
| Label | String | A label for the menu item. The label may contain DIESEL string expressions, which conditionally change the label each time it's displayed. Labels also identify the accelerator keys. |

The following example illustrates how to create a complete cascading menu structure:

```
Public Sub CreateSubMenus()
Dim objMenus As AcadPopupMenus
'main menu definition
Dim objMenuCreates As AcadPopupMenu
'submenu definitions
Dim objMenuLine As AcadPopupMenuItem
Dim objMenuRectangle As AcadPopupMenuItem
Dim objSubMenuCircle As AcadPopupMenu
Dim objSubMenuCenterRadius As AcadPopupMenuItem
Dim objSubMenuCenterDiameter As AcadPopupMenuItem
Dim objSubMenuText As AcadPopupMenu
Dim objSubMenuMulti As AcadPopupMenuItem
Dim objSubMenuSingle As AcadPopupMenuItem
Dim strEscEsc As String

    Set objMenus = ThisDrawing.Application.MenuGroups.Item(0).Menus

    'Create the new main menu
    On Error Resume Next
    Set objMenuCreates = objMenus.Item("Creates")
    If objMenuCreates Is Nothing Then Set objMenuCreates = _
        objMenus.Add("Creates")

    strEscEsc = Chr(27) & Chr(27) & Chr(95)
    'Add a menu items to the new main menu
    If objMenuCreates("Rectangle") Is Nothing Then
        Set objMenuRectangle = _
        objMenuCreates.AddMenuItem(objMenuCreates.Count, "Rectangle", _
                strEscEsc & "rectang ")
    If objMenuCreates("Line") Is Nothing Then
        Set objMenuLine = objMenuCreates.AddMenuItem(objMenuCreates.Count, _
                "Line", strEscEsc & "line ")

    'create the circle submenu
    If objMenuCreates("Circle") Is Nothing Then
      Set objSubMenuCircle = objMenuCreates.AddSubMenu(objMenuCreates.Count, _
                "Circle")
        Set objSubMenuCenterRadius = objSubMenuCircle.AddMenuItem( _
          objSubMenuCircle.Count, "Center, Radius", strEscEsc & "circle ")
```

```
            Set objSubMenuCenterDiameter = objSubMenuCircle.AddMenuItem( _
                objSubMenuCircle.Count, "Center, Diameter", _
                                strEscEsc & "circle \d ")
        End If


        'create the text submenu
        If objMenuCreates("Text") Is Nothing Then
            Set objSubMenuText = objMenuCreates.AddSubMenu(objMenuCreates.Count, _
                    "Text")
            Set objSubMenuMulti = objSubMenuText.AddMenuItem( _
                objSubMenuText.Count, "MultiLine Text", strEscEsc & "mtext ")
            Set objSubMenuSingle = objSubMenuText.AddMenuItem( _
                objSubMenuText.Count, "SingleLine Text", strEscEsc & "dtext ")
        End If


        'Display the menu on the menu bar
        If objMenuCreates.OnMenuBar = False Then objMenuCreates.InsertInMenuBar _
                (ThisDrawing.Application.MenuBar.Count)

End Sub
```

Figure 16-8 shows the result of this code.

*Figure 16-8. A cascading menu*


## Deleting Menu Items

To delete a menu item from a PopupMenu object, you simply use the Delete method:

```
PopupMenuItemObject.Delete
```

You can use the following macro to delete menus on the menu bar. The user specifies which menu they want to delete. The code then iterates through the menu items in that menu and the user is asked if he or she wants to delete each item.

```
Public Sub DeleteMenu()
Dim objMenu As AcadPopupMenu
Dim objMenuItem As AcadPopupMenuItem
Dim strDeleteMenuName As String
Dim strMenuName As String

    strDeleteMenuName = InputBox("Enter name of Menu to remove: ")
    If strDeleteMenuName = "" Then Exit Sub

On Error Resume Next
    Set objMenu = ThisDrawing.Application.MenuBar.Item(strDeleteMenuName)
    If objMenu Is Nothing Then
        MsgBox "Menu is not on the menu bar"
        Exit Sub
    End If

    For Each objMenuItem In objMenu
        strMenuName = objMenuItem.Caption
        If strMenuName = "" Then strMenuName = "Separator"

        If MsgBox("Delete " & strMenuName, vbYesNo, _
                "Confirm deletion of a MenuItem") = _
            vbYes Then
             objMenuItem.Delete
        End If
    Next

End Sub
```

## Adding Menu Items to the Shortcut Menu

The shortcut menu accessed by pressing *Shift* and right-clicking is a menu within the AutoCAD base menu group. The Boolean ShortcutMenu property of a PopupMenu object is set to True if the menu is a shortcut menu. You can add menu items to the shortcut menu in precisely the same way as you do to a drop-down menu, as I discussed earlier in this chapter. The following code sample adds a Zoom Extents menu item to the shortcut menu:

```
Public Sub AddMenuItemToShortcutMenu()
Dim objMenuGroup As AcadMenuGroup
Dim objShortcutMenu As AcadPopupMenu
Dim objMenuItem As AcadPopupMenu

    'only need the ACAD menugroup
    Set objMenuGroup = ThisDrawing.Application.MenuGroups.Item("ACAD")
    'find the shortcut menu
    For Each objMenuItem In objMenuGroup.Menus
        If objMenuItem.ShortcutMenu = True Then
            Set objShortcutMenu = objMenuItem
        End If
    Next


    'Add menu item to the shortcut menu
    objShortcutMenu.AddMenuItem "", "&Zoom &Extents", "_zoom e "
End Sub
```

# Editing Toolbars

All the toolbars that belong to a MenuGroup object loaded in the current session of AutoCAD are contained within its Toolbars collection. These toolbars may or may not be visible in the AutoCAD interface. The code in "The MenuGroup Object" section shows how to display a list of all toolbars that are loaded. In the following sections, you'll learn how to create, edit, and delete AutoCAD toolbars.

## Creating New Toolbars

You can create and add a new Toolbar object to the Toolbars collection through the Add method, which returns a reference to the new Toolbar object.

```
Set ToolbarObject = ToolbarsCollection.Add(ToolbarName)
```

Table 16-12 shows the Add method's parameter.

*Table 16-12. Add Method Parameter*

| NAME | DATA TYPE | DESCRIPTION |
|------|-----------|-------------|
| ToolbarName | String | The identifying name of the newly created Toolbar object |

The following example illustrates how to create a new toolbar in the AutoCAD collection. A check is in place to ensure that a toolbar of the same name doesn't already exist, as this would cause an error to be raised.

```
Public Sub AddNewToolbar()
Dim strTBName As String
Dim objToolbar As AcadToolbar

    strTBName = InputBox("Please enter name for new toolbar")
    If strTBName = "" Then Exit Sub

On Error Resume Next
    Set objToolbar = ThisDrawing.Application.MenuGroups.Item("ACAD"). _
                    Toolbars.Item(strTBName)
    If Not objToolbar Is Nothing Then
        MsgBox "This toolbar already exists"
    Else
        ThisDrawing.Application.MenuGroups.Item("ACAD").Toolbars.Add strTBName
    End If

End Sub
```

As you can see from Figure 16-9, the newly created toolbar, which becomes visible after creation, will be empty, so the next thing that you'll want to do is add some toolbar buttons.

*Figure 16-9. A new toolbar*

## Adding Toolbar Buttons

A toolbar button is represented by a ToolbarItem object. You can use the AddToolbarButton method to add a new toolbar item at a specified position within a toolbar.

```
Set ToolbarItemObject = ToolbarObject.AddToolbarButton(Index, ButtonName, _
HelpString, Macro[, FlyoutButton])
```

Table 16-13 shows the AddToolbarButton method's parameters.

*Table 16-13. AddToolbarButton Method Parameters*

| NAME | DATA TYPE | DESCRIPTION |
|---|---|---|
| Index | Variant | The position within the toolbar that the toolbar button will be added. It can either be an integer between 0 and N, where N is the number of objects in the menu, or a string giving the name of an existing toolbar button that the button will be placed directly before. If the button specified by the index doesn't exist, then the new button is placed at the end of the toolbar. |
| ButtonName | String | An identifying name for the new toolbar button. It's displayed when the user hovers over the button. It must consist of only alphanumeric characters, dashes (-), and underscores (_). |
| HelpString | String | A string that appears in the AutoCAD status line when a user highlights a toolbar item for selection. |
| Macro | String | A string that is written to the AutoCAD command prompt when the menu item is clicked. |
| FlyoutButton | Boolean | An optional parameter that determines whether the new button will be a flyout button. You use a flyout button to nest a set of buttons under a single toolbar button. Set this to True to create a flyout button. The default is False. |

Once you've created the toolbar button, you can't change the Index value of the toolbar button using the Index property. To do this, you must first delete the toolbar button and the add it again in the position within the toolbar structure that you require.

The following example illustrates how to use the AddToolbarButton method by creating a toolbar with same functionality as the cascading menu that you created earlier in the chapter:

```
Public Sub CreateNewToolbars()
Dim objMenuGroup As AcadMenuGroup
Dim objToolbars As AcadToolbars
Dim objToolbar0 As AcadToolbar
Dim objToolbar1 As AcadToolbar
Dim objToolbar2 As AcadToolbar
Dim objToolBarCircle As AcadToolbarItem
```

```
Dim objToolBarText As AcadToolbarItem
Dim strEscEsc As String

  Set objMenuGroup = ThisDrawing.Application.MenuGroups.Item(0)
  Set objToolbars = objMenuGroup.Toolbars

  'Create three new toolbars
On Error Resume Next
  Set objToolbar0 = objToolbars.Item("Custom Toolbar Create")
  If Not objToolbar0 Is Nothing Then
      MsgBox "The 'Custom Toolbar Create' already exists"
      Exit Sub
  End If

  Set objToolbar0 = objToolbars.Add("Custom Toolbar Create")
  Set objToolbar1 = objToolbars.Add("Circle")
  Set objToolbar2 = objToolbars.Add("Text")

  'Add a toolbar item to the new toolbar
  objToolbar0.AddToolbarButton objToolbar0.Count, "Line", _
      "Draw a line", strEscEsc & "line "
  objToolbar0.AddToolbarButton objToolbar0.Count, "Rectangle", _
      "Draw a rectangle", strEscEsc & "rectang "

  'create the circle flyout toolbar button
  Set objToolBarCircle = objToolbar0.AddToolbarButton(objToolbar0.Count, _
      "Circle", "Draw a circle", "Circle", True)
  'create the circle flyout toolbar
  objToolbar1.AddToolbarButton objToolbar1.Count, "Center, Radius", _
      "Draw circle using Center point and radius", strEscEsc & "circle "
  objToolbar1.AddToolbarButton objToolbar1.Count, "Center, Diameter", _
      "Draw circle using Center point and diameter", strEscEsc & "circle \d "

  'create the text submenu
  Set objToolBarText = objToolbar0.AddToolbarButton(objToolbar0.Count, _
      "Text", "Create text strings", "Text", True)
  'create the text flyout toolbar
  objToolbar2.AddToolbarButton objToolbar2.Count, "MultiLine Text", _
      "Create multi-text", strEscEsc & "mtext "
  objToolbar2.AddToolbarButton objToolbar2.Count, "SingleLine Text", _
      "Create single-line text", strEscEsc & "dtext "
```

```
    objToolBarCircle.AttachToolbarToFlyout objMenuGroup.Name, objToolbar1.Name
    objToolBarText.AttachToolbarToFlyout objMenuGroup.Name, objToolbar2.Name

    objToolbar0.Visible = True
    objToolbar1.Visible = False
    objToolbar2.Visible = False
End Sub
```

In Figure 16-10 you can see the newly created toolbars. Note the `ButtonName` and `HelpString` text displayed as the tooltip and in the status line of AutoCAD. In addition, you can see that flyout buttons have a small black triangle in the lower-right corner.

*Figure 16-10. New toolbars*

The default icon when you add a toolbar button through code is the ballooned question mark. You'll now look at how to set the icons to your choice of image.

## Defining the Toolbar Button Image

To set and retrieve the bitmaps of the icons associated with a toolbar button, you can use the `SetBitmaps` and `GetBitmaps` methods. Both methods have similar syntax and require two parameters (see Table 16-14), one for each of the two icons (small and large).

```
ToolbarItemObject.SetBitmaps SmallIconName, LargeIconName

ToolbarItemobject.GetBitmaps SmallIconName, LargeIconName
```

*Table 16-14. SetBitmaps and GetBitmaps Method Parameters*

| NAME | DATA TYPE | DESCRIPTION |
|------|-----------|-------------|
| SmallIconName | String | The path and file name for the small bitmap (16×15 pixels) |
| LargeIconName | String | The path and file name for the small bitmap (24×22 pixels) |

The following code example sets the small and large icons for the Line button of the toolbar you just created with the previous code. Note that here I'm using bitmaps that I created and stored in the My Documents folder so, if you want to try this code out, you'll need to change the path and file information to suitable files on your machine.

```
Public Sub SetIcons(strIconSmall As String, strIconLarge As String)
Dim objToolBarItem As AcadToolbarItem
    Set objToolBarItem = ThisDrawing.Application.MenuGroups(0).Toolbars(_
                                         "Custom Toolbar Create")("Line")

    objToolBarItem.SetBitmaps strIconSmall, _
                        strIconLarge

End Sub
```

**NOTE** *Autodesk has sought Microsoft Windows XP logo certification from Microsoft for the entire AutoCAD 2004 product line and beyond. One of the requirements of this logo certification involves toolbar icon graphics. If you intend to develop software for marketing, you should seriously investigate these requirements if you want to produce products that coincide with the base platform (AutoCAD) on which they're used. Refer to the MSDN website at* http://msdn.microsoft.com *for more information.*

## Adding Separators

You can use the AddSeparator method to add a separator to your menu structure or to a toolbar. This method takes a single parameter and returns either a PopupMenuItem or ToolbarItem object. Here's the syntax for adding a separator to a toolbar:

```
Set ToolbarItemObject = ToolbarObject.AddSeparator(Index)
```

Table 16-15 shows the AddSeparator method's parameter.

*Table 16-15. AddSeparator Method Parameter*

| NAME | DATA TYPE | DESCRIPTION |
|------|-----------|-------------|
| Index | Variant | The position within the toolbar that the separator will be added. It can either be an integer between 0 and N, where N is the number of objects in the toolbar collection, or a string giving the name of an existing toolbar item (including the & accelerator key character) that the separator will be placed directly before. If the toolbar item specified by the index doesn't exist, then the separator is placed at the end of the menu. |

**NOTE**   *You can't have adjacent separators or a separator at the beginning of a menu or toolbar.*

## Floating and Docking Toolbars

Toolbars may either float onscreen or be docked to an edge of the AutoCAD drawing window. You use the `Float` method to float a toolbar at a specified point on the screen. This point may lie outside the AutoCAD window.

```
ToolbarObject.Float Top, Left, NumberOfRows
```

Table 16-16 shows the `Float` method's parameters.

*Table 16-16. Float Method Parameters*

| NAME | DATA TYPE | DESCRIPTION |
|------|-----------|-------------|
| Top | Long | The position of the top edge of the toolbar from the top of the screen given in pixels. |
| Left | Long | The position of the left side of the toolbar from the left edge of the screen given in pixels. |
| NumberOfRows | Long | The number of rows that the toolbar buttons should be distributed over. If this is set to more than the number of buttons on the toolbar, this parameter will be ignored. |

This code sample shows how to use the `Float` method by floating the AutoCAD Draw toolbar to the top left of the screen:

```
Public Sub FloatDrawToolbar()
Dim objToolBarDraw As AcadToolbar

    Set objToolBarDraw =

ThisDrawing.Application.MenuGroups.Item("ACAD").Toolbars.Item("Draw")
    objToolBarDraw.Float 0, 0, 3

End Sub
```

Figure 16-11 shows the floating toolbar.

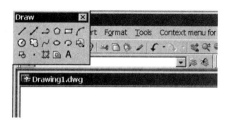

*Figure 16-11. Floating toolbar*

Note that the toolbar lies outside the AutoCAD window and is split over three rows.

To dock a toolbar, use the `Dock` method:

```
ToolbarObject.Dock DockStatus
```

Table 16-17 shows the `Dock` method's parameter.

*Table 16-17. Dock Method Parameter*

| NAME | DATA TYPE | DESCRIPTION |
| --- | --- | --- |
| DockStatus | Long | This specifies which edge of the window to dock to. It must be one of the `AcToolbarDockStatus` constants presented in Table 16-18. |

Table 16-18 contains the `AcToolbarDockStatus` constants.

*Table 16-18. AcToolbarDockStatus Constants*

| CONSTANT | VALUE | DESCRIPTION |
|---|---|---|
| acToolbarDockTop | 0 | Toolbar is docked to the top of the drawing window |
| acToolbarDockBottom | 1 | Toolbar is docked to the bottom of the drawing window. |
| acToolbarDockLeft | 2 | Toolbar is docked to the left side of the drawing window |
| acToolbarDockRight | 3 | Toolbar is docked to the right side of the drawing window |

This time the AutoCAD Draw toolbar is docked to the bottom of the drawing window:

```
Public Sub DockDrawToolbar()
Dim objToolBarDraw As AcadToolbar

    Set objToolBarDraw =

ThisDrawing.Application.MenuGroups.Item("ACAD").Toolbars.Item("Draw")
    objToolBarDraw.Dock acToolbarDockBottom

End Sub
```

Figure 16-12 shows the docked toolbar.

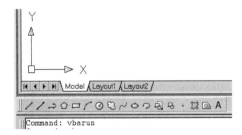

*Figure 16-12. Docked toolbar*

## Deleting Toolbars and Toolbar Buttons

You can delete both toolbars and toolbar buttons with the Delete method:

```
ToolbarObject.Delete
```

```
ToolbarItemObject.Delete
```

## Summary

You've covered a lot of material in this chapter. The part of the AutoCAD object model that represents the menu and toolbar structure is quite complicated. I hope the information in this chapter has provided you with a sound basis for modifying menus and toolbars. You may have noticed that I didn't discuss the new Tool Palettes feature in AutoCAD 2004. This is because it isn't part of the menu object model, nor does it provide an exposed API within AutoCAD, because it's maintained as external XML documents. For details of every property and method of the menu structure objects, please consult Appendix A.

# CHAPTER 17

# Drawing Security

AutoCAD 2004 INTRODUCES TWO NEW FEATURES aimed at providing security to
drawing files: Digital Signatures and Password Protection. You can access and
manipulate both features from the command prompt, a GUI interface, or programmatically. The command interface is SECURITYOPTIONS, which displays a
dialog form for configuring Digital Signature and Password Locking options,
as shown in Figure 17-1.

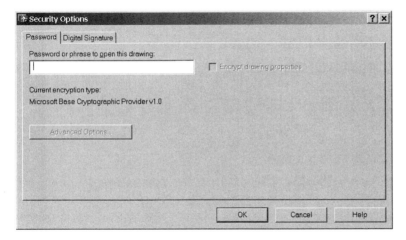

*Figure 17-1. Digital Signature and Password Locking options*

## Digital Signatures

To support the Digital Signatures features from a programming standpoint,
Autodesk added a new object called SecurityParams. This object allows you to set
various security options, including drawing and properties encryption, digital
signature, and a timestamp. A number of different options are available that provide varying levels of security, as presented in this chapter. Although it isn't
possible to provide extensive details about cryptography, further details are
available on the MSDN website (http://msdn.microsoft.com).

 The new Digital Signatures API features in AutoCAD 2004 are provided
through the SecurityParams object. To attach a digital signature to a document

of any kind, you first need a digital ID from a certificate authority such as
VeriSign. There are ways to generate your own "self-signed" certificates, but
they're intended for internal use, not for use by your customers. Your digital
signature is valid as long as the drawing isn't changed. Anyone receiving your
drawing can validate it to see that it really came from you. If your drawing has
an invalid signature, the recipient can easily tell that it was changed after you
attached the digital signature.

The following example illustrates using the properties of the SecurityParams
object to save and encrypt a drawing file:

```
Public Sub SaveWithEncryption()
Dim oSecurity As New AcadSecurityParams
    With oSecurity
        .Action = AcadSecurityParamsType.ACADSECURITYPARAMS_ENCRYPT_DATA
        .Algorithm = AcadSecurityParamsConstants.ACADSECURITYPARAMS_ALGID_RC4
        .Comment = "Add comment to drawing"
        .Issuer = "Your Company Name"
        .KeyLength = 40
        'AutoCAD converts all passwords to uppercase before applying them
        .Password = UCase("br549")
        .ProviderName = "Microsoft Base Cryptographic Provider v1.0"
        .ProviderType = 1
        .SerialNumber = "BR549"
        .Subject = "The Flying DeLorean"
        .TimeServer = "NIST(time.nist.gov)"
    End With

    ThisDrawing.SaveAs "C:\MyDrawing.dwg", , oSecurity
End Sub
```

## The Action Property

The Action property is the heart of the SecurityParams object (and, of course, the
Password property, which is pretty straightforward).

When specifying values for the Action property, you must specify one or
more of the constants in Table 17-1 for drawing encryption, drawing properties
encryption, a digital signature, or a timestamp.

*Table 17-1. Action Property Constants*

| CONSTANT | VALUE |
| --- | --- |
| ACADSECURITYPARAMS_ENCRYPT_DATA | 0x00000001 |
| ACADSECURITYPARAMS_ENCRYPT_PROPS | 0x00000002 |
| ACADSECURITYPARAMS_SIGN_DATA | 0x00000010 |
| ACADSECURITYPARAMS_ADD_TIMESTAMP | 0x00000020 |

Each constant represents a security-related operation. When you use the Action property, at some point in the set of operations you must set the Action property to either the ACADSECURITYPARAMS_ENCRYPT_DATA constant, the ACADSECURITYPARAMS_SIGN_DATA constant, or both.

To specify multiple security-related operations, add the constants representing the operations. The following example shows how to sign a drawing and use a timestamp:

```
ACADSECURITYPARAMS_SIGN_DATA + ACADSECURITYPARAMS_ADD_TIMESTAMP
```

 **NOTE** *You can only specify* AcadSecurityParamsConstants.ACAD-SECURITYPARAMS_ALGID_RC4 *for the* Algorithm *property. Any other value will generate an error.*

## The Algorithm Property

The Algorithm property specifies the identifier of the encryption algorithm to be used in signing the drawing file:

```
object.Algorithm
```

Table 17-2 shows the Algorithm property's parameters.

*Table 17-2. Algorithm Property Parameters*

| NAME | RETURNS | DESCRIPTION |
| --- | --- | --- |
| object | SecurityParams | The object or objects this property applies to |
| Algorithm | Long; AcadSecurityParamsConstants enum; read-write | Specify only the following constant: ACADSECURITYPARAMS_ALGID_RC4_ 0x00006801 |

Here's an example of setting the Algorithm property:

```
Dim sp As New AcadSecurityParams
sp.Algorithm = AcadSecurityParamsConstants.ACADSECURITYPARAMS_ALGID_RC4
```

## The Issuer Property

The Issuer property specifies the name of the issuer of the digital certificate. The Put option requires one parameter, Issuer, which is a string value.

```
object.Issuer
```

Table 17-3 shows the Issuer property's parameters.

*Table 17-3. Issuer Property Parameters*

| NAME | RETURNS | DESCRIPTION |
| --- | --- | --- |
| object | SecurityParams | The object or objects this property applies to |
| Issuer | String; read-write | The issuer name of the digital certificate |

Here's an example of setting the Issuer property:

```
Dim sp As New AcadSecurityParams
sp.Issuer = "Personal Freemail RSA 2000.8.30"
```

## The ProviderName Property

This property specifies the name of the provider of the digital certificate.

`object.ProviderName`

Table 17-4 shows the `ProviderName` property's parameters.

*Table 17-4. ProviderName Property Parameters*

| NAME | RETURNS | DESCRIPTION |
| --- | --- | --- |
| object | SecurityParams | The object or objects this property applies to |
| ProviderName | String; read-write | The encryption provider name |

More information about cryptography providers is available on MSDN.

## The SerialNumber Property

The `SerialNumber` property specifies the serial number identifier for the digital certificate. It uses the following options:

`object.SerialNumber`

Table 17-5 shows the `SerialNumber` property's parameters.

*Table 17-5. SerialNumber Property Parameters*

| NAME | RETURNS | DESCRIPTION |
| --- | --- | --- |
| object | SecurityParams | The object or objects this property applies to |
| SerialNumber | String; read-write | The serial number of the digital certificate |

Here's an example of setting the SerialNumber property:

```
Dim sp As New AcadSecurityParams
sp.SerialNumber = "073848"
```

## The Subject Property

This property specifies a subject string name value of the digital certificate:

```
object.Subject
```

Table 17-6 shows the Subject property's parameters.

*Table 17-6. Subject Property Parameters*

| NAME | RETURNS | DESCRIPTION |
| --- | --- | --- |
| object | SecurityParams | The object or objects this property applies to |
| Subject | String; read-write | The subject name of the digital certificate |

## The TimeServer Property

The TimeServer property specifies the name of the time server to be used for a digital signature. If you don't set this property, the time from the local machine is used as the timestamp for the digital signature.

```
object.TimeServer
```

Table 17-7 shows the TimeServer property's parameters.

*Table 17-7. TimeServer Property Parameters*

| NAME | RETURNS | DESCRIPTION |
| --- | --- | --- |
| object | SecurityParams | The object or objects this property applies to |
| TimeServer | String; read-write | The name of the time server to be used for a digital signature |

Here's an example of setting the `TimeServer` property:

```
Dim sp As New AcadSecurityParams
sp.TimeServer = "NIST(time.nist.gov)"
```

# Password Protection

Probably one of the most controversial security features added to AutoCAD 2004 is Password Protection. Basically, this feature allows a user to lock a drawing file with a password to prevent unwanted people from opening and viewing or modifying it. It's an all-or-nothing feature in that the drawing is either completely locked or completely unlocked; there's no intermediate locking capability (such as locking layers or permitting viewing but not modification or printing, as is possible with products such as Adobe Acrobat).

To quote Autodesk:

*"When you password-protect a drawing, you encrypt the drawing, altering it with a secret code. A password-protected or encrypted drawing can only be opened by someone who knows the correct password."*

And additionally:

*"Warning! If you lose the password, it is not recoverable. Before you add a password, you should create a backup that is not protected with a password."*

Password Protection can be disabled during installation and is quite often handled this way at the vast majority of sites with large numbers of users.

If you decide to employ this feature, you should know that it is indeed very secure. In addition to setting a unique password, you can configure additional options for the encryption method. From the GUI interface, you must enter a default password in the password entry box in order to access the Advanced Options button, which opens the Advanced Options form shown in Figure 17-2. There are quite a few options available.

From a programmatic aspect, the same object model applies to password locking (aka encryption) as with the signing of drawings via digital certificates. In fact, it uses the same `SecurityParams` object to provide the interface to saving an encrypted drawing. The following example shows how to save an encrypted drawing file using this object.

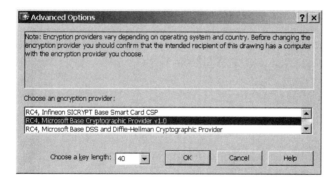

*Figure 17-2. The Advanced Options dialog box*

It's worth noting that AutoCAD converts the password string value to upper-case before storing it in the drawing. The result is a case-insensitive password entry match when you attempt to open the drawing.

```
Sub SaveLockedDrawing()
  ' This example encrypts and saves a file.
  Dim acadApp As New AcadApplication
  Dim sp As New AcadSecurityParams

  acadApp.Visible = True
  sp.Action = AcadSecurityParamsType.ACADSECURITYPARAMS_ENCRYPT_DATA
  sp.Algorithm =   AcadSecurityParamsConstants.ACADSECURITYPARAMS_ALGID_RC4
  sp.KeyLength = 40
  sp.Password = UCase("unique-password)
  sp.ProviderName = "Microsoft Base Cryptographic Provider v1.0"
  sp.ProviderType = 1
  acadApp.ActiveDocument.SaveAs "C:\LockedDrawing1.dwg", , sp
End Sub
```

## Summary

This chapter covered the two most important security features provided in AutoCAD 2004: Digital Signatures and Password Protection. Though these features impose serious consideration of potential risks, they offer obvious security benefits to users who need such protection for their work.

# CHAPTER 18

# Using the Windows API

THIS CHAPTER TELLS YOU HOW to take advantage of the Windows API. This isn't a definitive guide to the Windows API, but it gives you enough information to get you started, including common examples such as the Open and SaveAs common dialogs.

## Declarations

You must declare every Windows API function that you use, *period*. Unlike in VBA, the Windows API includes no type library against which to resolve your function calls. So for them to be resolved—and you must resolve all function calls—you have to declare each one before you use it. This line of code shows how to declare a function call:

```
Public Declare Function SetForegroundWindow Lib "user32.dll" _
   (ByVal hwnd As Long) As Long
```

The syntax breakdown is as follows:

```
[Scope] Declare Function <FunctionName> Lib <DLL Filename String> _
   (List of Parameters) As <DataType>
```

The easiest way to get the declaration is to use the API Viewer as shown in Figure 18-1.

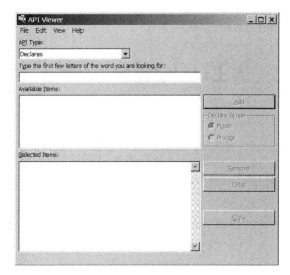

*Figure 18-1. API Viewer dialog box*

## Windows Data Structures

A data structure is a collection of related information that is accessible through a single variable name. Data structures are widely used in the C and, to some extent, the C++ languages, but *classes* have replaced them in modern programming practices. Classes let you define functions that work on the class's data, letting you hide variables and functionality from the outside world. On the other hand, data structures are nothing more than data structures. But you're in luck because the Windows API has a ton of data structures, as the following code demonstrates:

```
Public Type POINTS
  x As Integer
  y As Integer
End Type
```

## DLL to Visual Basic Calling Conventions

To call DLL function procedures from Visual Basic, convert the C syntax that documents them into valid Declare statements Visual Basic can call these procedures using the right parameter data type declarations.

You must convert the C data types into Visual Basic data types. Also, specify whether the calling convention is ByVal (by value) or ByRef (by reference).

Table 18-1 illustrates the conversions for 32-bit Windows C-language data types to Visual Basic.

*Table 18-1. C vs. Visual Basic Data Type Declarations*

| C LANGUAGE DATA TYPE | DECLARE IN VISUAL BASIC AS | CALL WITH |
|---|---|---|
| ATOM | ByVal *variable* As Integer | An expression that evaluates to an Integer |
| BOOL | ByVal *variable* As Long | An expression that evaluates to a Long |
| BYTE | ByVal *variable* As Byte | An expression that evaluates to a Byte |
| CHAR | ByVal *variable* As Byte | An expression that evaluates to a Byte |
| COLORREF | ByVal *variable* As Long | An expression that evaluates to a Long |
| DWORD | ByVal *variable* As Long | An expression that evaluates to a Long |
| HWND, HDC, HMENU, etc. (Windows handles) | ByVal *variable* As Long | An expression that evaluates to a Long |
| INT, UINT | ByVal *variable* As Long | An expression that evaluates to a Long |
| LONG | ByVal *variable* As Long | An expression that evaluates to a Long |
| LPARAM | ByVal *variable* As Long | An expression that evaluates to a Long |
| LPDWORD | *variable* As Long | An expression that evaluates to a Long |
| LPINT, LPUINT | *variable* As Long | An expression that evaluates to a Long |
| LPRECT | *variable* As type | Any variable of that user-defined type |
| LPSTR, LPCSTR | ByVal *variable* As String | An expression that evaluates to a String |

*continues*

*Table 18-1. C vs. Visual Basic Data Type Declarations, continued*

| C LANGUAGE DATA TYPE | DECLARE IN VISUAL BASIC AS | CALL WITH |
|---|---|---|
| LPVOID | *variable* As Any | Any variable (use ByVal when passing a string) |
| LPWORD | *variable* As Integer | An expression that evaluates to an Integer |
| LRESULT | ByVal *variable* As Long | An expression that evaluates to a Long |
| NULL | As Any or ByVal *variable* As Long | ByVal Nothing or ByVal 0& or vbNullString |
| SHORT | ByVal *variable* As Integer | An expression that evaluates to an Integer |
| VOID | Sub procedure | Not applicable |
| WORD | ByVal *variable* As Integer | An expression that evaluates to an Integer |
| WPARAM | ByVal *variable* As Long | An expression that evaluates to a Long |

## Specifying the Library

Visual Basic uses the Declare statement's Lib clause to find the .dll file that contains the procedures. When you declare a function that uses one of the core Windows API libraries, specify the file name extension .dll.

 **TIP** *For consistency, get into the habit of specifying this extension all the time, because you'll need to specify it for noncore API libraries that you use.*

Here's how to use the Lib clause:

```
Public Declare Function SetForegroundWindow Lib "user32.dll" _
    (ByVal hwnd As Long) As Long
```

For noncore API libraries, you can specify a path in the `Lib` clause. If you don't specify a path, then Visual Basic searches for the file in the following order:

1. Directory containing the `.exe` file

2. Current directory

3. Windows system directory (usually C:\Windows\System)

4. Windows directory (usually C:\Windows)

5. Path environment variable

# The Major Windows DLLs

Table 18-2 lists the most commonly used libraries of Windows API functions.

*Table 18-2. Common Windows API Libraries*

| FILE NAME | DESCRIPTION |
| --- | --- |
| Advapi32.dll | Advanced API services library supporting numerous APIs, including many security and registry calls |
| Comdlg32.dll | Common dialog API library |
| Gdi32.dll | Graphics Device Interface API library |
| Kernel32.dll | Core Windows 32-bit base API support |
| Lz32.dll | 32-bit compression routines |
| Mpr.dll | Multiple Provider Router library |
| Netapi32.dll | 32-bit Network API library |
| Shell32.dll | 32-bit Shell API library |
| User32.dll | Library for user interface routines |
| Version.dll | Version library |
| Winmm.dll | Windows multimedia library |
| Winspool.drv | Print spooler interface that contains print-spooler API calls |

## Working with Windows API Procedures That Use Strings

The Declare statement's Alias clause is required when you call Windows API procedures that use strings to specify the correct character set. There are actually two formats for procedures that contain strings: ANSI and Unicode.

For example, the SetWindowText function does not really exist. Instead, you use two separate functions depending on whether you use ANSI or Unicode. The following code illustrates the ANSI version:

```
Private Declare Function SetWindowText Lib "user32" Alias _
"SetWindowTextA" (ByVal hwnd As Long, ByVal lpString As String) _
As Long
```

The string that follows the Alias clause must be the procedure's true, case-sensitive name.

Specify the ANSI version of functions in Visual Basic because only Windows NT supports the Unicode versions. Use Unicode only when you're certain your application will run on Windows NT.

## Passing Arguments by Value or by Reference

By default, Visual Basic passes arguments by reference. Instead of passing the actual value of the argument, it passes a 32-bit address specifying the value's location. The ByRef keyword is not required, but it's a good idea to specify the exact method of passing the argument to make your code more readable.

**NOTE**  *This is no longer true with VB .NET or any of the .NET languages, which default to* ByValue *arguments.*

Many DLL procedures expect you to pass an argument by value. The function expects to receive the actual value instead of its memory location. If you pass the argument to the function using ByRef, the function receives information that it has no idea how to handle.

To pass an argument by value, place the ByVal keyword in front of the Declare statement's argument declaration. The InvertRect procedure accepts its first argument by value and its second by reference, as the following example shows:

```
Declare Function InvertRect Lib "user32" Alias "InvertRectA" _
(ByVal hdc As Long, lpRect As RECT) As Long
```

**NOTE** *When you look at DLL procedure documentation that uses C language syntax, remember that C passes all arguments except arrays by value.*

## Learning by Example

The best way to learn the Windows API is to follow other programmers' examples and try different situations on your own. So this section gives you examples of using the Windows API. These examples illustrate some of the most common Windows API functions that AutoCAD developers use, and should give you enough information to pursue using Windows API functions in your own application development.

### OpenFile Common Control Dialog Replacement for VBA

Using the OpenFile common control dialog adds a look of consistency to your application. The OpenFile dialog is part of the comdlg32.dll library of Windows API routines and is easily accessed. The following example illustrates using these routines to request a drawing file to open.

```
Private Declare Function GetOpenFileName Lib "comdlg32.dll" Alias _
"GetOpenFileNameA" (pOpenfilename As OPENFILENAME) As Long
Private Type OPENFILENAME
   lStructSize As Long
   hwndOwner As Long
   hInstance As Long
   lpstrFilter As String
   lpstrCustomFilter As String
   nMaxCustFilter As Long
   nFilterIndex As Long
   lpstrFile As String
   nMaxFile As Long
   lpstrFileTitle As String
   nMaxFileTitle As Long
   lpstrInitialDir As String
   lpstrTitle As String
   flags As Long
   nFileOffset As Integer
   nFileExtension As Integer
```

```
        lpstrDefExt As String
        lCustData As Long
        lpfnHook As Long
        lpTemplateName As String
    End Type

    Public Function ShowOpen(Filter As String, _
                             InitialDir As String, _
                             DialogTitle As String) As String

    Dim OFName As OPENFILENAME

        'Set the structure size
        OFName.lStructSize = Len(OFName)
        'Set the owner window
        OFName.hwndOwner = 0
        'Set the filter
        OFName.lpstrFilter = Filter
        'Set the maximum number of chars
        OFName.nMaxFile = 255
        'Create a buffer
        OFName.lpstrFile = Space(254)
        'Create a buffer
        OFName.lpstrFileTitle = Space$(254)
        'Set the maximum number of chars
        OFName.nMaxFileTitle = 255
        'Set the initial directory
        OFName.lpstrInitialDir = InitialDir
        'Set the dialog title
        OFName.lpstrTitle = DialogTitle
        'no extra flags
        OFName.flags = 0
        'Show the 'Open File' dialog
        If GetOpenFileName(OFName) Then
           ShowOpen = Trim(OFName.lpstrFile)

        Else
           ShowOpen = ""
      End If
    End Function
```

The following sample code illustrates using the ShowOpen routine, which returns the selected file name as a string.

```
Dim Filter As String
Dim InitialDir As String
Dim DialogTitle As String

  Filter = "Drawing Files (*.dwg)" + Chr$(0) + "*.dwg" + Chr$(0) + _
    "All Files (*.*)" + Chr$(0) + "*.*" + Chr$(0)
  InitialDir = "C:\Program Files\AutoCAD 2004\Sample"
  DialogTitle = "Open a DWG file"

  Label1.Caption = ShowOpen(Filter, InitialDir, DialogTitle)
```

The Filter parameter is a string that details which file types, by extension, to display when the OpenFile dialog box appears. The InitialDir parameter specifies which directory to display by default. To give a name to your OpenFile dialog box, use the DialogTitle parameter.

With each of these parameters defined, executing this code results in the OpenFile dialog box shown in Figure 18-2.

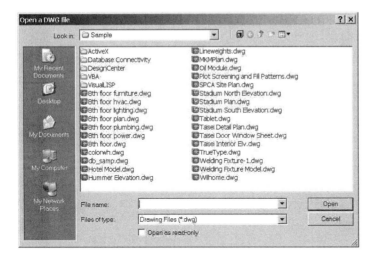

*Figure 18-2. Open File dialog box example*

## SaveAsFile Common Control Dialog Replacement for VBA

Using the SaveAsFile common control dialog adds a look of consistency to your application. The SaveAsFile dialog is part of the comdlg32.dll library of Windows API routines and is easily accessed. The following example shows this using these routines to save a drawing file.

```
Private Declare Function GetSaveFileName Lib "comdlg32.dll" Alias _
"GetSaveFileNameA" (pOpenfilename As OPENFILENAME) As Long

Private Type OPENFILENAME
    lStructSize As Long
    hwndOwner As Long
    hInstance As Long
    lpstrFilter As String
    lpstrCustomFilter As String
    nMaxCustFilter As Long
    nFilterIndex As Long
    lpstrFile As String
    nMaxFile As Long
    lpstrFileTitle As String
    nMaxFileTitle As Long
    lpstrInitialDir As String
    lpstrTitle As String
    flags As Long
    nFileOffset As Integer
    nFileExtension As Integer
    lpstrDefExt As String
    lCustData As Long
    lpfnHook As Long
    lpTemplateName As String
End Type

Public Function ShowSave(Filter As String, _
                         InitialDir As String, _
                         DialogTitle As String) As String

Dim OFName As OPENFILENAME

    'Set the structure size
    OFName.lStructSize = Len(OFName)
    'Set the owner window
    OFName.hwndOwner = 0
    'Set the filter
    OFName.lpstrFilter = Filter
    'Set the maximum number of chars
    OFName.nMaxFile = 255
```

```
'Create a buffer
OFName.lpstrFile = Space(254)
'Create a buffer
OFName.lpstrFileTitle = Space$(254)
'Set the maximum number of chars
OFName.nMaxFileTitle = 255
'Set the initial directory
OFName.lpstrInitialDir = InitialDir
'Set the dialog title
OFName.lpstrTitle = DialogTitle
'no extra flags
OFName.flags = 0
'Show the 'SaveAs File' dialog
If GetSaveFileName(OFName) Then
   ShowSave = Trim(OFName.lpstrFile)

   Else
      ShowSave = ""
   End If
End Function
```

The following sample code shows the ShowSave routine:

```
Dim Filter As String
Dim InitialDir As String
Dim DialogTitle As String

  Filter = "Drawing Files (*.dwg)" + Chr$(0) + "*.dwg" + Chr$(0) + _
    "All Files (*.*)" + Chr$(0) + "*.*" + Chr$(0)
  InitialDir = "C:\Program Files\AutoCAD 2004\Sample"
  DialogTitle = "Save DWG as file"

  Label1.Caption = ShowSave(Filter, InitialDir, DialogTitle)
```

The Filter parameter is a string that details which file types, by extension, to display when the SaveAsFile dialog box appears. The InitialDir parameter specifies which directory to display by default. To give a name to your SaveAsFile dialog box, use the DialogTitle parameter.

With each of these parameters defined, executing this code opens the SaveAsFile dialog box shown in Figure 18-3.

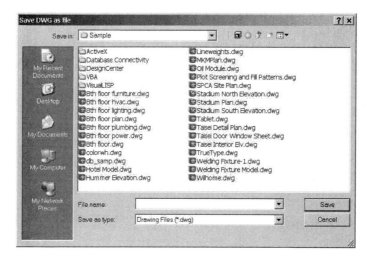

*Figure 18-3. Save As File dialog box example*

## Retrieving the Status of the CapsLock, NumLock, and ScrollLock Keys

Sometimes, you need to know the status of the Caps Lock, Num Lock, or Scroll Lock keys. Visual Basic doesn't directly let you do this, but the Windows API does. The following example shows how to do it:

```
Private Const VK_CAPITAL = &H14
Private Const VK_NUMLOCK = &H90
Private Const VK_SCROLL = &H91


Private Type KeyboardBytes
   kbByte(0 To 255) As Byte
End Type

Private Declare Function GetKeyState Lib "user32" (ByVal nVirtKey As Long) _
   As Long
Private Declare Function GetKeyboardState Lib "user32" (kbArray As KeyboardBytes) _
   As Long
Private Declare Function SetKeyboardState Lib "user32" (kbArray As KeyboardBytes) _
   As Long


Dim kbArray As KeyboardBytes
```

This example implements these routines. This first example uses the key passed to it in the vkKey parameter to turn that key on.

```
Public Sub TurnOn(vkKey As Long)
   'Get the keyboard state
   GetKeyboardState kbArray
   'Change a key
   kbArray.kbByte(vkKey) = 1
   'Set the keyboard state
   SetKeyboardState kbArray
End Sub
```

This example does the opposite of the TurnOn routine. It uses the key passed to it in the vkKey parameter to turn off that key.

```
Public Sub TurnOff(vkKey As Long)
   'Get the keyboard state
   GetKeyboardState kbArray
   'change a key
   kbArray.kbByte(vkKey) = 0
   'set the keyboard state
   SetKeyboardState kbArray
End Sub
```

This final example gets the status of the key passed in the vkKey parameter and returns True is the key is on or False if it's off.

```
Public Function GetKeyStatus(vkKey As Long) As Boolean
   'Get the keyboard state
   GetKeyboardState kbArray
   'change a key
   GetKeyStatus = kbArray.kbByte(vkKey)
End Function
```

Using these routines helps you enforce the case users input. If you need everything entered to be all capital letters, these routines ensure that you get only uppercase.

Don't be frightened by the verbosity of these code examples. The power implied here is with respect to reuse. If you put this code to work, you'll quickly realize the benefit of encapsulating this code in class modules, which you can reuse many times with minimal coding. You can easily create custom dialog forms or other adapted features and make them basic class items from which you can draw.

## Summary

This short chapter presented an enormous amount of information. The best way for you to really be proficient at accessing the Windows API is through trial and error. This chapter did present some useful routines that should help get you started writing robust applications using the Windows API.

# CHAPTER 19

# Connecting to External Applications

IN THIS CHAPTER YOU'LL LEARN the basics of connecting to applications external to AutoCAD such as Microsoft Excel and Word. Once connected, you'll see how to create basic documents and populate those external documents with information you control from within AutoCAD.

This chapter is intended to be an introduction on how to connect and perform basic functions with external applications. It doesn't present in-depth coverage of all the tasks that you could accomplish, as there are numerous books dedicated to the subject of customization for these products.

At the end of this chapter, you'll examine how to connect to a database created in Microsoft Access, which is the typical way AutoCAD developers use and manipulate database files.

## Making the Connection

Most applications you connect to will have similar connection methods. First, you'll need to include the necessary references in the programming environment, as illustrated in Figure 19-1.

Next, you will need a routine that

- Checks for a running instance of the application

- Has additional code to actually start an instance of the application if it is not already running

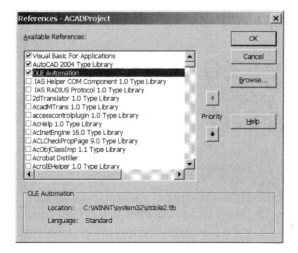

*Figure 19-1. The References dialog box*

The following example illustrates starting Microsoft Excel programmatically:

```
Public Sub StartExcel(App As Excel.Application, Visible As Boolean)
    'handle errors inline
    On Error Resume Next
    Set App = GetObject(, "Excel.Application")  'depends on application
    'check to see if application is running
    If Err Then
        'no, application will need to be started
        Err.Clear
        Set App = CreateObject("Excel.Application")  'depends on application
        'check to see if application was started
        If Err Then
            'no, application could not be started - exit
            Exit Sub
        End If
    End If
    'set the application visibility
    App.Visible = Visible
End Sub
```

**NOTE**  *Depending on the version of Excel you're using (especially if you have multiple versions installed), you should make a habit of requesting type libraries by explicit version name (e.g., "Excel.Application.11"). In fact, AutoCAD 2004 requires you to reference the application object using "AutoCAD.Application.16" (which isn't necessary within AutoCAD 2004 VBA because the* Application *object is always present).*

Here's how you can use this routine to ensure an instance of Excel is running before doing anything else:

```
Public Sub Start()
Dim oExcel As Excel.Application
   'attempt to start Excel
   StartExcel oExcel, True

   If Not oExcel Is Nothing Then
     MsgBox "Success"

     Else
       MsgBox "Could not start Excel, exiting ...", vbCritical
       Exit Sub
   End If
End Sub
```

In these examples, there are two applications you can start with a slight modification to code listed, as shown in Table 19-1. The acceptable variations are listed in Table 19-2.

*Table 19-1. Application Class Identification*

| APPLICATION | CLASS IDENTIFICATION |
|---|---|
| Excel | Excel.Application.*x* (where *x* is the product version index) |
| Word | Word.Application.*x* (where *x* is the product version index) |

*Table 19-2. Microsoft Product Versions*

| PRODUCT | VERSION | EXAMPLE |
| --- | --- | --- |
| Office 95 | 7 | Word.Application.7 |
| Office 97 | 8 | Excel.Application.8 |
| Office 2000 | 9 | Word.Application.9 |
| Office XP | 10 | Powerpoint.Application.10 |
| Office 2003 | 11 | Outlook.Application.11 |

## Connecting to Microsoft Excel

Now that you have a connection to Microsoft Excel, you're going to learn how to create a new workbook and worksheet. Then, you'll write and read values from the cells of a worksheet. Finally, you'll save the worksheet and close Excel.

### Creating a New Workbook

To create a workbook, declare a variable of the Excel.Workbook object data type. Then using the Add method of the Excel application object, add a new workbook as in the following example:

```
Dim Workbook As Excel.Workbook
Set Workbook = App.Workbooks.Add
```

### Creating a New Worksheet

To create a worksheet, declare a variable of the Excel.WorkSheet object data type. Then use the Add method of the WorkSheets collection object to create a new worksheet, as illustrated in the following example:

```
Dim WorkSheet As Excel.WorkSheet
Set WorkSheet = App.Worksheets.Add
```

## Accessing a Worksheet

To access a worksheet, declare a variable of the Excel.WorkSheet object data type. Then assign the Worksheets collection object of the Workbook object to the newly declared variable as in the following example:

```
Dim WorkSheet As Excel.WorkSheet
Set WorkSheet = App.Worksheets(1)
```

## Writing and Reading Cells

Using the WorkSheet object, you may assign values to Cells, as shown in the following example:

```
With WorkSheet
    .Cells(1, 1).Value = 1: .Cells(1, 2).Value = 2
    .Cells(2, 1).Value = 1.5: .Cells(2, 2).Value = 3
    .Cells(3, 1).Value = "Text 1": .Cells(3, 2).Value = "Text 2"
End With
```

**NOTE** *Items such as the row and column indexes start at 1, not 0.*

Reading the values contained in Cells is the reverse of writing them, as the following example illustrates:

```
With WorkSheet
    MsgBox .Cells(1, 1).Value & ", " & .Cells(1, 2).Value
    MsgBox .Cells(2, 1).Value & ", " & .Cells(2, 2).Value
    MsgBox .Cells(3, 1).Value & ", " & .Cells(3, 2).Value
End With
```

## Saving and Exiting Excel

Using the Close method of the Workbook object, you can close the workbook. The first parameter of the Close method determines whether the workbook should be saved or not. You supply the second parameter, a file name, if the first parameter is True as in the following example:

```
Workbook.Close True, "C:\Test.xls"
```

Once you've completed your work with the Excel application, use the Quit method of the Excel application object to properly close the application:

```
App.Quit
```

## Connecting to Microsoft Word

This section presents the code necessary to connect to Microsoft Word programmatically.

### Creating a New Document

To create a document, declare of a variable of the Word.Document object data type. Then use the Add method of the Documents collection object to add a new document, as shown here:

```
Dim oDocument As Word.Document
Set oDocument = App.Documents.Add
```

### Adding Text to the Document

To add text to your document, simply set the Text property of the Content Range object of the document, as in the following example:

```
oDocument.Content.Text = "This is some sample text"
```

### Setting Page Orientation

You make the page orientation either portrait or landscape by setting the Orientation property of the PageSetup object for the document using this:

```
oDocument.PageSetup.Orientation = wdOrientPortrait
```

or this:

```
oDocument.PageSetup.Orientation = wdOrientLandscape
```

## Setting Margins

Set the margins for your document by setting the LeftMargin, RightMargin, TopMargin, or BottomMargin property of the PageSetup object for the document, as shown in the following example:

```
oDocument.PageSetup.LeftMargin = InchesToPoints(0.5)
oDocument.PageSetup.RightMargin = InchesToPoints(0.5)
oDocument.PageSetup.TopMargin = InchesToPoints(0.5)
oDocument.PageSetup.BottomMargin = InchesToPoints(0.5)
```

**NOTE**   *The value supplied to the XXXMargin properties must be in points. If you want to supply the values in inches (as in the example) you'll need to convert the values to points using the built-in VBA function* InchesToPoints.

## Setting the Document Header and Footer

You can set the document's header and/or footer by setting the Text property of the Headers and/or Footers collection object like this:

```
oDocument.Sections(1).Headers(wdHeaderFooterPrimary)
.Range.Text = "This is Header text"
```

or this:

```
oDocument.Sections(1).Headers(wdHeaderFooterPrimary) _
.Range.Text = "This is Header text"
```

## Saving and Exiting Word

Use the SaveAs method of the Document object to save your document:

```
oDocument.SaveAs "Sample"
```

To close your document, use the Close method of the Documents collection object:

```
oWord.Documents("Sample.doc").Close True
```

Finally, use the `Quit` method of the `Word.Application` object to actually close the Word application, as shown here:

```
oWord.Quit
```

## Connecting to a Microsoft Access Database

Most AutoCAD developers use Microsoft Access to create the database structure file, and then they use the Microsoft ActiveX Data Objects (ADO) library through VBA to access the `.mdb` file created by Access. You can use the same approach (and quite often the same code) to work with other data sources, such as Microsoft SQL Server, Oracle, DB2, and even Microsoft Exchange. This section details the steps necessary to connect to and access the data contained in a database file in a Microsoft Access application. Please refer to the same database file to follow along with these examples.

### Connecting to a Database File

First, you need to add a reference to the Microsoft ActiveX Data Objects library, as shown in Figure 19-2.

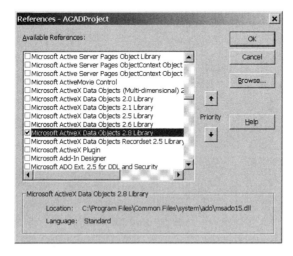

*Figure 19-2. Microsoft ActiveX Data Objects library reference*

Next, you need to establish a Connection object similar to the following example:

```
Dim oAccess As New ADODB.Connection

oAccess.Open "Provider=Microsoft.Jet.OLEDB.4.0;" & _
             "Data Source=" & "C:\AutoCAD-VBA.mdb" & ";"
```

**NOTE**  *The example database for this exercise was created in Microsoft Access 2000. If you want to use a different file format database, such as Access 97 or 2002, you'll need to change the* Provider *string appropriately or use an ODBC data source name (DSN) to provide the interface connection directives.*

## Retrieving a Set of Records

The ability to retrieve the records stored in a database file is essential. The following example illustrates how to retrieve all the records from a table called Layers and displays each record in a typical MsgBox:

```
'retrieve records from the Layers table
Dim oRecordset As New ADODB.Recordset

oRecordset.Open "Select * From Layers", oAccess, adOpenKeyset

With oRecordset
  Do While Not .EOF
    MsgBox !LayerName & ", Color is " & !color
    .MoveNext
  Loop
  .Close
End With
```

## Writing Values to the Database File

Another essential operation you'll need is the ability to perform writing data to a table within the database file. The following example iterates through the Layers collection object and writes each layer's name and color value to the Layers table:

```
Dim oLayer As AcadLayer

oRecordset.Open "Select * From Layers", oAccess, adOpenKeyset, _ adLockOptimistic

For Each oLayer In ThisDrawing.Layers
  With oRecordset
    .AddNew
    !LayerName = oLayer.Name
    !Color = oLayer.Color
    .Update
  End With
Next oLayer

oRecordset.Close
```

## Closing the Connection

Once you've finished using the connection to a database file, you should always close the database connection, as shown in the following example:

```
oAccess.Close
```

You can go even further and create new databases, and then build the tables and queries within them using ADO and ADOX features. You can find a full reference of the ADO and ADOX objects, properties, methods, and events on the Microsoft MSDN website (http://msdn.microsoft.com) or Microsoft's Data Access Technologies website (http://www.microsoft.com/data).

**TIP**  *One of the most often overlooked time-savers for this type of programming (working with external applications) is the Macro Recorder feature. You can save an enormous amount of time and frustration trying to figure out the specifics of performing a task in Excel by just doing the task while recording it and then opening the results. Quite often, you can copy and paste the results directly into the AutoCAD VBA editor with minor modifications and be on your way. This is true with any VBA-enabled product that has the Macro Recorder feature, including Microsoft Visio, PowerPoint, and Outlook.*

## Working with Other Databases

Although Microsoft Access is a very popular database, it is by no means the only one you will encounter. Many companies, especially larger firms, rely on larger-scale database systems such as Oracle, SQL Server, and DB2. These products provide much more power and reliability than desktop databases such as Access, dBASE, and FoxPro. You should be aware of the differences you'll commonly encounter when you move data from one place to another, and between different database environments.

For example, the data type aspects can vary widely and you should *never* assume data types are consistent between such products as Microsoft Access, Microsoft SQL Server, DB2, and Oracle. For example, when you convert databases in Access 2000 to SQL Server 2000, memo fields are converted into ntext or nvarchar fields, which are very different. Other common differences relate to date and time values, currency, and special fields such as Pictures, Hyperlinks, and BLOBs (binary large objects).

## Connectivity Automation Objects

The dbConnect feature added in AutoCAD 2000 provides a powerful means for linking drawing entities to external data sources such as Excel spreadsheets, Access databases, and other ODBC data sources. It also provides a means for automatically labeling entities using Leader callouts with special control over the text labeling that is driven directly by linked values in the external data source.

This functionality is provided through a special API called Connectivity Automation Objects, or CAO. CAO is a very simple, compact object model, with a small set of objects, properties, methods, and so on (compared to AutoCAD, anyway). It exposes all of the power and capability of dbConnect to developers, from within and from outside of AutoCAD. Like most ActiveX features in AutoCAD, you can employ CAO from VBA within AutoCAD or from VBA in an external application.

## Advanced Database Issues

Don't be lulled into thinking that because you feel comfortable with the AutoCAD drawing "database" environment, you can translate it quickly into the world of database development. The differences are staggering. Although many similarities exist, you'll encounter numerous issues in database development that aren't present in AutoCAD. For example, referential integrity, normalization, indexing, views, and job scheduling are all common in mainstream database development. And although these topics may seem unimportant or remote to you as an

AutoCAD developer, they're crucial to database developers and the work they do every day.

If you aren't a seasoned database developer, it often helps to partner with one while you're learning the ropes with database programming. Although you can certainly learn database development skills, it's truly a world unto its own. Finally, before you begin building a large, complex database application with AutoCAD, consult an experienced database developer to make sure you don't reinvent the wheel or waste precious time building a solution that would have been easier or more robust if it were instead developed on the database end.

## Working with Services and Other APIs

Like applications, services are processes that run within the operating system–protected namespaces. Unlike applications, though, services normally don't provide a graphical interface and are instead intended for under-the-hood purposes such as monitoring, logging, reacting, or protecting other system resources. Many services are very useful for making sure the overall environment is known.

One service you might be interested in using is the Active Directory Service Interfaces (ADSI) object for accessing Active Directory Services on a Windows 2000 or 2003 network. An example of a commonly used API is the FileSystemObject (FSO), which is used by many applications to create, edit, read, and delete files, as well as perform file system operations on drives, folders, and so forth.

To find out the drive type and file system in use on the C: drive, for example, you could access the FSO Drive object for "C:" and then query its DriveType and FileSystem properties:

```
Function ShowDriveType(drvpath)
    Dim fso, d, dt
    Set fso = CreateObject("Scripting.FileSystemObject")
    Set d = fso.GetDrive(drvpath)
    Select Case d.DriveType
        Case 0: dt = "Unknown"
        Case 1: dt = "Removable"
        Case 2: dt = "Fixed"
        Case 3: dt = "Network"
        Case 4: dt = "CD-ROM"
        Case 5: dt = "RAM Disk"
    End Select
    ShowDriveType = dt
End Function
```

```
Function ShowFileSystemType(drvspec)
    Dim fso,d
    Set fso = CreateObject("Scripting.FileSystemObject")
    Set d = fso.GetDrive(drvspec)
    ShowFileSystemType = d.FileSystem
End Function


MsgBox "C: Drive Type is " & ShowDriveType("C")
MsgBox "C: File System is " & ShowFileSystemType("C")
```

The ADSI object is built into Windows 2000 and Windows XP Professional, and also corresponding server versions of these products. It provides an API for interfacing with directory services such as Lightweight Directory Access Protocol (LDAP) and Active Directory. A common task might be to retrieve a list of all the users, groups, or computers on your domain. To do this, you could invoke the ADSI interface to the WinNT object, as shown here:

```
Sub ShowAllComputers()
  Dim adsDomain
  Set adsDomain = GetObject("WinNT://MyDomainName")
  For each objMember in adsDomain
    If objMember.Class = "Computer" Then
      Debug.Print objMember.Name & ": " & objMember.Description & vbCrLf
    End If
  Next
  Set adsDomain = Nothing
End Sub
```

You might have noticed in the preceding code that GetObject is used instead of CreateObject. This is because a true "service" is always available through the GetObject interface and doesn't require instantiation to obtain an instance.

The FileSystemObject, ADSI, and LanManServer API references are all published on the MSDN website, along with many other useful APIs and services such as WMI/WBEM, CDO/CDONTS, LDAP, Windows Script Host (WSH), and many more.

## Summary

This chapter briefly touched upon the capabilities provided to you through VBA for working with external applications; it's by no means exhaustive. You can interface with an almost limitless number of external applications, services, and processes from within AutoCAD VBA. The more you look and experiment, the more you'll be amazed at what you can do.

# APPENDIX A

# AutoCAD Object Summary

THIS APPENDIX CONTAINS A REFERENCE to the full AutoCAD object model. The first part of the appendix provides information on properties, methods, and events that are common to a number of the AutoCAD objects. The second and major part of the appendix is devoted to listing and explaining the methods, properties, and events of each object and collection in alphabetical order.

## AutoCAD Collections

The AutoCAD object model has the following collections:

| | |
|---|---|
| AcadBlock | AcadPaperSpace |
| AcadBlocks | AcadPlotConfigurations |
| AcadDictionaries | AcadPopupMenu |
| AcadDimStyles | AcadPopupMenus |
| AcadDocuments | AcadRegisteredApplications |
| AcadGroup | AcadSelectionSet |
| AcadGroups | AcadSelectionSets |
| AcadHyperlinks | AcadTextStyles |
| AcadLayers | AcadToolbar |
| AcadLayouts | AcadToolbars |
| AcadLinetypes | AcadUCSs |
| AcadMenuBar | AcadViewports |
| AcadMenuGroups | AcadViews |
| AcadModelSpace | |

### Common Collection Methods

All the collections in the AutoCAD object model support the Item method, which is used to select an item from the collection.

| NAME | RETURNS | DESCRIPTION |
| --- | --- | --- |
| Item | Object | Returns the object at the given index in the collection. Parameter: Index As Variant (Integer or String). If the Index value is a String, it must match an existing object's name. |

### Common Collection Property

All collections in the AutoCAD object model support the following property.

| NAME | RETURNS | DESCRIPTION |
| --- | --- | --- |
| Count | Long | Gets the number of items in the collection |

## The Application Property

There is just one property common to all the objects in the AutoCAD object model: the Application property.

| NAME | RETURNS | DESCRIPTION |
| --- | --- | --- |
| Application | AcadApplication | Gets the AcadApplication object, which represents the application's frame controls and path settings and provides the means to navigate down the object hierarchy. This property's value is read-only. |

## The AcadObject Object

This object represents methods and properties common to the following objects:

| | |
|---|---|
| Acad3DFace | AcadExternalReference |
| Acad3DPoly | AcadGroup |
| Acad3DSolid | AcadGroups |
| AcadArc | AcadHatch |
| AcadAttribute | AcadLayer |
| AcadAttributeReference | AcadLayers |
| AcadBlock | AcadLayout |
| AcadBlockReference | AcadLayouts |
| AcadBlocks | AcadLeader |
| AcadCircle | AcadLWPolyLine |
| AcadDictionaries | AcadLine |
| AcadDictionary | AcadLinetype |
| AcadDim3PointAngular | AcadLinetypes |
| AcadDimAligned | AcadMInsertBlock |
| AcadDimAngular | AcadMLine |
| AcadDimDiametric | AcadModelSpace |
| AcadDimOrdinate | AcadMText |
| AcadDimRadial | AcadPaperSpace |
| AcadDimRotated | AcadPlotConfiguration |
| AcadDimStyle | AcadPlotConfigurations |
| AcadDimStyles | AcadPoint |
| AcadEllipse | AcadPolyfaceMesh |

| | |
|---|---|
| AcadPolygonMesh | AcadTextStyles |
| AcadPolyline | AcadTolerance |
| AcadRasterImage | AcadTrace |
| AcadRay | AcadUCS |
| AcadRegion | AcadUCSs |
| AcadRegisteredApplication | AcadView |
| AcadRegisteredApplications | AcadViews |
| AcadShape | AcadViewport |
| AcadSolid | AcadViewports |
| AcadSpline | AcadXLine |
| AcadText | AcadXRecord |
| AcadTextStyle | |

## Common AcadObject Methods

The following table presents common AcadObject methods.

| NAME | DESCRIPTION |
|---|---|
| Delete | Deletes a specified object. If an object in a collection is deleted, all the remaining items are reassigned a new index based on the current count. Note that you can't delete collections, so you can't use this method for collections without creating an error. |
| GetExtensionDictionary | Returns AcadDictionary and gets the extension dictionary associated with an object. If an object doesn't have an extension dictionary, this method will create one for that object and return it. |

| NAME | DESCRIPTION |
|------|-------------|
| GetXData | Gets the extended data (XData), that is, instance-specific data, associated with an object. A NULL string value for the AppName parameter will return all the data attached to the object, regardless of the application that created it. Supplying an application name will return only the data that was created by the specified application. Parameters: AppName_As_String, XDataType As_Variant (array of Integers), and XDataValue_As Variant (array of Variants). |
| SetXData | Sets the extended data (XData)that is, instance-specific dataassociated with an object. Parameters: XDataType_As_Variant (array of Integers) and XDataValue_As_Variant (array of Variants). |

## Common AcadObject Properties

The following table presents common AcadObject properties.

| NAME | RETURNS | DESCRIPTION |
|------|---------|-------------|
| Application | Object | Gets the Application object. This property's value is read-only. The Application object represents the application's frame controls and path settings and provides the means to navigate down the object hierarchy. |
| Document | Object | Gets the document or drawing in which the object belongs. This property's value is read-only. |
| Handle | String | Gets the handle of an object. This property's value is read-only. An object ID and a handle are the two ways of referencing an object. A handle stays the same in a drawing for the lifetime of the object. |

| NAME | RETURNS | DESCRIPTION |
| --- | --- | --- |
| HasExtensionDictionary | Boolean | Determines if the object has an extension dictionary associated with it. This property's value is read-only. |
| ObjectID | Integer | Gets the object ID of the object. This property's value is read-only. You can use an object ID or a handle to reference an object. It's better to use a handle unless you plan to work with certain ObjectARX functions that require an object ID. |
| ObjectName | String | Gets the AutoCAD class name of the object. This property's value is read-only. |
| OwnerID | Integer | Gets the object ID of the owner (i.e., the parent object). This property's value is read-only. |

## Common AcadObject Event

Apart from the AcadApplication and AcadDocument objects, which expose a variety of events, AutoCAD provides only one other event, the Modified event. This event is common to all the objects listed previously. When coding in VBA, you must provide an event handler for all objects enabled for the Modified event; otherwise, your application may crash. No events are fired while a modal dialog box is displayed.

| EVENT | DESCRIPTION |
| --- | --- |
| Modified | Triggered whenever an object is modified. Note that setting the value of a property even if that value remains unchanged is considered to be a modification. Parameter: Entity As AcadEntity, the object in the drawing that is modified. The AcadEntity object is covered in the next section. |

# The AcadEntity Object

The AcadEntity object represents a generic object that exposes all the methods and properties common to a set of AutoCAD objects known as the Drawing Objects. These objects, which define all the different drawing capabilities, from drawing planar and solid objects, to inserting text and hyperlinks, to linking external documents, are listed here:

| | |
|---|---|
| Acad3DFace | AcadLine |
| Acad3DPoly | AcadMInsertBlock |
| Acad3DSolid | AcadMLine |
| AcadArc | AcadMText |
| AcadAttribute | AcadPoint |
| AcadAttributeRef | AcadPolyfaceMesh |
| AcadBlockReference | AcadPolygonMesh |
| AcadCircle | AcadPolyline |
| AcadDim3PointAngular | AcadPViewport |
| AcadDimAligned | AcadRasterImage |
| AcadDimAngular | AcadRay |
| AcadDimDiametric | AcadRegion |
| AcadDimOrdinate | AcadShape |
| AcadDimRadial | AcadSolid |
| AcadDimRotated | AcadSpline |
| AcadEllipse | AcadText |
| AcadExternalReference | AcadTolerance |
| AcadHatch | AcadTrace |
| AcadLeader | AcadXline |
| AcadLWPolyline | |

## Common AcadEntity Methods

In addition to the methods inherited from the AcadObject object, the AcadEntity object supports the following methods.

| NAME | RETURNS | DESCRIPTION |
|------|---------|-------------|
| ArrayPolar | Variant | Creates an array of selected objects in a polar pattern. The distance is determined from the array's center point to a reference point on the last object selected, which in turn depends on the type of object previously selected. AutoCAD uses the center point of a circle or arc, the insertion point of a block or shape, the start point of text, and one end point of a line or trace. Note that you can't use this method for the AcadAttributeReference object. Note also that you can't use this method while iterating through a collection. Parameters: NumberOfObjects As Integer, AngleToFill As Double, and CenterPoint As Variant.

The NumberOfObjects parameter specifies the number of objects to be created in the polar array. This must be a positive integer greater than 1.

The AngleToFill parameter specifies the angle to fill in radians. A positive value indicates counterclockwise rotation. This parameter can't be equal to 0.

The CenterPoint parameter specifies the 3-D WCS coordinates specifying the center point for the polar array. |

| NAME | RETURNS | DESCRIPTION |
|------|---------|-------------|
| ArrayRectangular | Variant | Creates an array of selected objects in a rectangular pattern. AutoCAD builds the rectangular array along a baseline defined by the current snap rotation angle, which is 0 by default. Note that you can't use this method for the `AcadAttributeReference` object. Note also that you can't use this method while iterating through a collection. Parameters: `NumberOfRows As Integer`, `NumberOfColumns As Integer`, `NumberOfLevels As Integer`, `DistBetweenRows As Double`, `DistBetweenCols As Double`, and `DistBetweenLevels As Double`.<br><br>The `NumberOfRows` parameter specifies the number of rows in the rectangular array. This must be a positive number. If `NumberOfColumns` is 1, then `NumberOfRows` must be greater than 1.<br><br>The `NumberOfColumns` parameter specifies the number of rows in the rectangular array. This must be a positive number. If `NumberOfRows` is 1, then `NumberOfColumns` must be greater than 1.<br><br>The `NumberOfLevels` parameter specifies the number of levels in a 3-D array.<br><br>The `DistBetweenRows` parameter specifies the distance between the rows. If positive, rows are added upward from the base entity; otherwise, they're added downward.<br><br>The `DistBetweenCols` parameter specifies the distance between the columns. If positive, columns are added to the right of the base entity; otherwise, they're added to the left.<br><br>The `DistBetweenLevels` parameter specifies the distance between the array levels. |

| NAME | RETURNS | DESCRIPTION |
|------|---------|-------------|
| CopyObject | | Duplicates the given object to the same location. Note that you can't use this method for the `AcadAttributeReference` object. Note also that you can't use this method while iterating through a collection. |
| GetBoundingBox | | Gets two points of a box enclosing the specified object. Parameters: `MinPoint As Variant` and `MaxPoint As Variant` (both of these are three-element arrays of Doubles). |
| Highlight | | Sets the highlight status for the given object or for all objects in a given selection set. Note that you'll see the changes only once the drawing is updated. Parameter: `HighlightFlag As Boolean`. |
| IntersectWith | Variant | Returns the points at which one object intersects another object in the drawing as an array of Doubles. The object supplied as the parameter can be any drawing object. However, this method isn't supported by the `AcadPolygonMesh` and `AcadPViewport` objects. Parameters: `IntersectObject As Object` and `option As AcExtendOption`. For a list of the values of the `AcExtendOption` enumerated type, see Appendix B. |
| MirrorObject | | Creates a mirror image copy of a planar object around an axis, defined by two points. This method places the reflected image into the drawing and retains the original object. To remove the original object, use the `Delete` method. To manage the reflection properties of text objects, use the `MIRRTEXT` system variable. Note that you can't use this method for the `AcadAttributeReference` object. Note also that you can't use this method while iterating through a collection. Parameters: `Point1 As Variant` and `Point2 As Variant`. |

| NAME | RETURNS | DESCRIPTION |
|------|---------|-------------|
| Mirror3D | Object | Creates a mirror image copy of a planar object reflected in a plane, defined by three points. AutoCAD checks to see if the object to be copied owns any other object. If it does, it performs a copy on those objects as well. The process continues until all owned objects have been copied. Note that you can't use this method for the AcadAttributeReference object. Note also that you can't use this method while iterating through a collection. Parameters: Point1 As Variant, Point2 As Variant, and Point3 As Variant. |
| Move | | Moves an object along a vector, defined by two points. Parameters: FromPoint As Variant and ToPoint As Variant. |
| Rotate | | Rotates an object around a base point. Parameters: BasePoint As Variant and RotationAngle As Double. The RotationAngle parameter should be specified in radians. |
| Rotate3D | | Rotates an object around an axis in 3-D space, defined by two points, which become the axis of rotation. Parameters: Point1 As Variant, Point2 As Variant, and RotationAngle As Double. The RotationAngle parameter should be in radians. |
| ScaleEntity | | Scales an object equally in the X, Y, and Z directions. Parameters: BasePoint As Variant and ScaleFactor As Double.<br><br>The BasePoint parameter is a set of 3-D WCS coordinates and is the only common point in the original and scaled system.<br><br>The ScaleFactor parameter determines the level of scaling. A value greater than 1 enlarges the object. A value between 0 and 1 shrinks the object. The scale factor must be greater than 0. |

| NAME | RETURNS | DESCRIPTION |
|------|---------|-------------|
| TransformBy | | Moves, scales, and rotates an object given a 4×4 transformation matrix. See the AutoCAD documentation for more information. Parameter: TransformationMatrix As Variant (a 4×4 array of Doubles). |
| Update | | Updates the object to the drawing screen. |

## Common AcadEntity Properties

In addition to the properties inherited from the AcadObject, the AcadEntity object supports the following properties.

| NAME | RETURNS | DESCRIPTION |
|------|---------|-------------|
| Color | AcColor | Gets or sets the color of an entity. For a list of possible values for the AcColor enumerated type, see Appendix B. |
| EntityName | String | Gets the class name of the object. Retained for backward compatibility onlyuse the VBA TypeName function instead. This property's value is read-only. |
| EntityType | AcEntityName | Gets the entity type of the object. Retained for backward compatibility onlyuse the VBA TypeOf keyword instead. This property's value is read-only. For a list of the values for the AcEntityName enumerated type, see Appendix B. |
| Hyperlinks | AcadHyperlinks | Gets the AcadHyperlinks collection for an entity. This property's value is read-only. |
| Layer | String | Gets or sets the layer for an entity. |
| Linetype | String | Gets or sets the linetype of an entity. |
| LinetypeScale | Double | Gets or sets the linetype scale of an entity. The default value is 1.0. |

| NAME | RETURNS | DESCRIPTION |
|------|---------|-------------|
| Lineweight | AcLineWeight | Gets or sets the lineweight of an individual entity or the default lineweight for the drawing. For a list of possible values for the AcLineWeight enumerated type, see Appendix B. |
| PlotStyleName | String | Gets or sets the object's plot style name. |
| TrueColor | AcCmColor | Gets or sets the RGB color index, color name, or Pantone color book settings |
| Visible | Boolean | Specifies whether or not the object (or application) is visible. |

 **NOTE** *Because this object inherits from* AcadObject, *it supports the* Modified *event.*

## *AcadDimension Object*

The AcadDimension object represents a generic object with a set of properties that are common to the seven dimension objects, namely the following:

AcadDim3PointAngular

AcadDimAligned

AcadDimAngular

AcadDimDiametric

AcadDimOrdinate

AcadDimRadial

AcadDimRotated

In addition, it inherits all the methods and properties of the AcadEntity and AcadObject objects.

## *Common AcadDimension Properties*

The AcadDimension object inherits all the properties of the AcadEntity and AcadObject objects, as well as the common Application property. It also supports the following properties.

| NAME | RETURNS | DESCRIPTION |
|------|---------|-------------|
| DecimalSeparator | String | Gets or sets the character used as the decimal separator for dimension values. The initial value for this property is the period (.), though any character will be accepted as a valid value for this property. Use this property only when the UnitsFormat property is set to acDimDecimal. This property overrides the value of the DIMSEP system variable. |
| Normal | Variant | Gets or sets the 3-D (Z-axis) normal unit vector for the dimension object. |
| Rotation | Double | Gets or sets the rotation angle (in radians) for the dimension line, relative to the X-axis with positive values going counterclockwise when viewed along the Z-axis toward the origin. |
| ScaleFactor | Double | Gets or sets the object's relative X scale factor. The initial value for this property is 1.0000. |
| StyleName | String | Gets or sets the name of the object's style. Use the AcadDimStyle object to change the attributes of a given dimension style. The name given must already be defined in the drawing. |
| SuppressLeadingZeros, SuppressTrailingZeros | Boolean | Gets or sets whether leading/trailing zeros are suppressed in the object's values. It overrides the value of the DIMZIN system variable. The initial value for both these properties is False. |

| NAME | RETURNS | DESCRIPTION |
|------|---------|-------------|
| TextColor | AcColor | Gets or sets the color of the text. Use a color index number from 0 to 256 or one of the constants listed here: acByBlock (where AutoCAD draws objects in the default color) or acByLayer (where AutoCAD draws objects in the color specified for the layer). For a list of possible values for the AcColor enumerated type, see Appendix B. |
| TextGap | Double | Gets or sets the distance between the text and the dimension line when the dimension line is broken to make room for the text. A negative value creates basic dimensioningthat is, dimension text with a box around it. This property overrides the value of the DIMGAP system variable. |
| TextHeight | Double | Gets or sets the height of the text. The initial value for this property is 0.1800. |
| TextMovement | AcDimTextMovement | Gets or sets how text is drawn when it's moved. The initial value for this property is acMoveTextNoLeader. For a list of possible values for the AcDimTextMovement enumerated type, see Appendix B. |
| TextOverride | String | Gets or sets the text string, which has a maximum length of 256 characters. The user string replaces the calculated dimension value. You can revert to the calculated dimension value by setting the text to a NULL string (""). You can append or prefix text to the primary dimension value by using a closed set of brackets (<>) to represent the value. The primary dimension value will replace the brackets when the string is displayed. |
| TextPosition | Variant | Gets or sets the position of the text as a set of WCS coordinates. |

| NAME | RETURNS | DESCRIPTION |
|------|---------|-------------|
| TextPrefix | String | Gets or sets the prefix of the dimension value. The initial value for this property is NULL. To turn off an established prefix, set this property equal to a single period. |
| TextRotation | Double | Gets or sets the angle of the text in radians. The valid range is 0 to 6.28. |
| TextStyle | String | Gets or sets the style of the text. The initial value for this property is STANDARD. |
| TextSuffix | String | Gets or sets the suffix of the dimension value. The initial value for this property is NULL. To turn off an established suffix, set this property equal to a single period. |
| ToleranceDisplay | AcDimToleranceMethod | Gets or sets whether the tolerances are displayed with the text. It overrides the value of the DIMTOL system variable. The initial value for this property is acTolNone. For a list of possible values for the AcDimToleranceMethod enumerated type, see Appendix B. |
| ToleranceHeightScale | Double | Gets or sets the scale factor of the height of the text for the tolerance values relative to the object's general text height. The initial value for this property is 1.0000. This property is only available when the ToleranceDisplay property is set to any value other than acTolNone. |
| ToleranceJustification | AcDimToleranceJustify | Get or sets the vertical justification of tolerance values relative to that of the object's general text. The initial value for this property is acTolMiddle. This property is only available when the ToleranceDisplay property is set to any value other than acTolNone. For a list of possible values for the AcDimToleranceJustify enumerated type, see Appendix B. |

| NAME | RETURNS | DESCRIPTION |
|------|---------|-------------|
| ToleranceLowerLimit | Double | Gets or sets the minimum tolerance for text. The initial value for this property is 0.0000. This property is only available when the ToleranceDisplay property is set to acTolDeviation or acTolLimits. |
| TolerancePrecision | AcDimPrecision | Gets or sets the precision of tolerance values in the primary dimensions. This property isn't available when ToleranceDisplay is set to acTolNone. For a list of possible values for the AcDimPrecision enumerated type, see Appendix B. |
| ToleranceSuppressLeadingZeros | Boolean | Gets or sets whether leading zeros in tolerance values are suppressed. It overrides the value of the DIMTZIN system variable. The initial value for this property is False. |
| ToleranceSuppressTrailingZeros | Boolean | Gets or sets whether trailing zeros in tolerance values are suppressed. It overrides the value of the DIMTZIN system variable. The initial value for this property is False. |
| ToleranceUpperLimit | Double | Gets or sets the maximum tolerance for text. The initial value for this property is 0.0000. This property is only available when the ToleranceDisplay property is set to acTolSymmetrical, acTolDeviation, or acTolLimits. |
| VerticalTextPosition | AcDimVertical-Justification | Gets or sets the vertical position of the text relative to the dimension line. It overrides the value of the DIMTAD system variable. The initial value for this property is acVertCentered. For a list of possible values for the AcDimVerticalJustification enumerated type, see Appendix B. |

> **NOTE** *Because this object inherits from* AcadObject, *it supports the* Modified *event.*

## AutoCAD Object Reference

The following section details the remaining AutoCAD object model objects derived from the base class objects detailed earlier in this appendix.

## *Acad3DFace Object*

The Acad3DFace object represents a 3-D triangle or a quadrilateral plane section. You create it using the Add3DFace method of the AcadBlock, AcadModelSpace, or AcadPaperSpace object. You can specify different Z coordinates for each corner point of a Acad3DFace object, and you can build solid objects by joining 3-D faces together (e.g., a cube consists of six 3-D faces joined together). You control which edges of the face are visible through the SetInvisibleEdge method, which allows accurate modeling of objects with holes.

### *Acad3DFace Object Methods*

The Acad3DFace object inherits all the methods of the AcadEntity and AcadObject objects. It also supports the following methods.

| NAME | RETURNS | DESCRIPTION |
| --- | --- | --- |
| GetInvisibleEdge | Boolean | Gets the visibility setting for an edge of a Acad3DFace object at a given index. It's True if the edge is invisible and False otherwise. Parameter: Index As Integer. |
| SetInvisibleEdge | | Sets the visibility state of an edge at a given index. To see any changes in visibility, the drawing must be regenerated. Parameters: Index As Integer and State As Boolean. The Index parameter must be in the range 0 to 3. Set the State parameter to True for an invisible edge and False otherwise. |

## *Acad3DFace Object Properties*

The Acad3DFace object inherits all the properties of the AcadEntity and AcadObject objects, as well as the common Application property. It also supports the following properties.

| NAME | RETURNS | DESCRIPTION |
| --- | --- | --- |
| Coordinate | Variant | Gets or sets the coordinate of a single vertex in the object. This will replace the specified vertex of the object. Use standard array-handling techniques to process the values contained in this property. It returns a three-element array of Doubles containing 3-D coordinates in WCS. Note that the Z coordinate will default to 0 on the active UCS. Parameter: Index As Integer (the index in the zero-based array of vertices for the vertex you want to set or query). |
| Coordinates | Variant | Gets or sets the coordinates for each vertex in the object. This will replace any existing coordinates for the specified object. Use standard array-handling techniques to process the coordinates contained in this property. Note that you can't change the number of coordinates in the object by using this property, you can only change the location of existing coordinates. It returns a three-element array of Doubles containing 3-D coordinates in WCS. Note also that he Z coordinate will always default to 0 on the active UCS. |
| VisibilityEdge1 | Boolean | Gets or sets whether edge 1 is visible. For this property and the three that follow, True means the edge is visible and False means the edge isn't visible. |
| VisibilityEdge2 | Boolean | Gets or sets whether edge 2 is visible. |
| VisibilityEdge3 | Boolean | Gets or sets whether edge 3 is visible. |
| VisibilityEdge4 | Boolean | Gets or sets whether edge 4 is visible. In the case of a triangle, this property will still return a value, because a triangle is defined as a quadrilateral in which point 3 is equal to point 4. |

**NOTE** *Because this object inherits from* AcadObject, *it supports the* Modified *event.*

## *Acad3DPolyline Object*

The Acad3DPolyline object represents a 3-D polyline of straight-line segments. You create it using the Add3DPoly method of the AcadBlock, AcadModelSpace, or AcadPaperSpace object.

### *Acad3DPolyline Object Methods*

The Acad3DPolyline object inherits all the methods of the AcadEntity and AcadObject objects. It also supports the following methods.

| NAME | RETURNS | DESCRIPTION |
| --- | --- | --- |
| AppendVertex | | Appends a vertex to the polyline, which is an array of 3-D coordinates. Parameter: vertex_As_Variant (a three-element array of Doubles). |
| Explode | Variant | Explodes the polyline into its constituent lines and returns them as an array of Objects. |

### *Acad3DPolyline Object Properties*

The Acad3DPolyline object inherits all the properties of the AcadEntity and AcadObject objects, as well as the common Application property. It also supports the following properties.

| NAME | RETURNS | DESCRIPTION |
| --- | --- | --- |
| Closed | Boolean | Gets or sets whether the polyline is closed (True) or open (False). |

| NAME | RETURNS | DESCRIPTION |
|------|---------|-------------|
| Coordinate | Variant | Gets or sets the coordinate of a single vertex in the object. This will replace the specified existing vertex of the object. Use standard array-handling techniques to process the values contained in this property. It returns a Variant (three-element array of Doubles). These coordinates can be converted to and from other coordinate systems using the TranslateCoordinates method. Parameter: Index As Integer (the index in the zero-based array for the vertex you want to set or query). |
| Coordinates | Variant | Gets or sets the coordinates for each vertex in the object. This will replace any existing coordinates for the specified object. Use standard array-handling techniques to process the coordinates contained in this property. When you set the coordinates for a polyline, if you supply fewer coordinates than the object currently possesses, the polyline will be truncated. Any fit points applying to the truncated vertices will also be truncated. If you supply more coordinates than the object currently possesses, the extra vertices will be appended to the polyline. It returns the vertex points as a Variant (a three-element array of Doubles) containing the X, Y, and Z coordinates for the vertices in WCS. These coordinates can be converted to and from other coordinate systems using the TranslateCoordinates method. |
| Type | Ac3DPolylineType | Gets or sets the type of the 3-D polyline. You can use this property to convert a 3-D polyline into a spline. For a list of the values of the Ac3DPolylineType enumerated type, see Appendix B. |

**NOTE** *Because this object inherits from* AcadObject, *it supports the* Modified *event.*

## Acad3DSolid Object

The Acad3DSolid object represents a solid object with free-form surface support. You don't create general Acad3DSolid objects, as there's no Add3DSolid method supported by the AcadBlock, AcadModelSpace, and AcadPaperSpace objects. Instead, you use this object to represent a whole series of 3-D shapes for which no specific AutoCAD object exists: boxes, cones, cylinders, spheres, wedges, tori (donuts), and others. You can then combine these shapes to create more complex solids by joining or subtracting them or finding their intersecting (overlapping) volume. You can also create solids by sweeping a 2-D object along a path or revolving it about an axis.

To create an Acad3DSolid object, use one of the following methods, all of which are common to the AcadBlock, AcadModelSpace, and AcadPaperSpace objects:

AddBox

AddCone

AddCylinder

AddEllipticalCone

AddEllipticalCylinder

AddExtrudedSolid

AddExtrudedSolidAlongPath

AddRevolvedSolid

AddSphere

AddTorus

AddWedge

See the section on the AcadBlock object for more details on each of these.

## Acad3DSolid Object Methods

The Acad3DSolid object inherits all the methods of the AcadEntity and AcadObject objects. It also supports the following methods.

| NAME | RETURNS | DESCRIPTION |
|------|---------|-------------|
| Boolean | | Performs a destructive operation returning the union, intersection, or subtraction between the object and another Acad3DSolid or AcadRegion object. Parameters: Operation As AcBooleanType and SolidObject_As Acad3DSolid. For a list of possible values for the AcBooleanType enumerated type, see Appendix B. |
| CheckInterference | Acad3DSolid | Checks for interference between the object and another Acad3DSolid object and creates an object representing the interference if required. Parameters: Object As Acad3DSolid and CreateInterferenceSolid As Boolean. The second parameter is True if an interference solid is required and False otherwise. |
| SectionSolid | AcadRegion | Creates an AcadRegion object representing the intersection of the object with the plane containing the specified points. Parameters: Point1 As Variant, Point2 As Variant, and Point3 As Variant. |
| SliceSolid | Acad3DSolid | Creates an Acad3DSolid object representing the portion of the object on one side of the plane containing the specified points. Parameters: Point1 As Variant, Point2 As Variant, Point3 As Variant, and Negative As Boolean. The fourth parameter determines if the resulting solid should be returned on the negative side of the plane, which is True if this is the case and False otherwise. The original Acad3DSolid object retains the positive side of the slice. |

## Acad3DSolid Object Properties

The Acad3DSolid object inherits all the properties of the AcadEntity and AcadObject objects, as well as the common Application property. It also supports the following properties.

| NAME | RETURNS | DESCRIPTION |
|------|---------|-------------|
| Centroid | Variant | Gets the center of area or mass for a solid as a 2-D coordinate. It returns a two-element array of Doubles. This property is read-only. |
| MomentOfInertia | Variant | Gets the moment of inertia for the solid as a 3-D coordinate. It returns a three-element array of Doubles. This property is read-only. |
| PrincipalDirections | Variant | Gets the principal directions of the solid as X, Y, and Z coordinates calculated on the current coordinate system. This property is read-only. |
| PrincipalMoments | Variant | Gets the principal moments property of the solid as X, Y, and Z coordinates calculated on the current coordinate system. This property's value is read-only. |
| ProductOfInertia | Variant | Gets the product of inertia of the solid as X, Y, and Z coordinates calculated on the current coordinate system. This property's value is read-only. |
| RadiiOfGyration | Variant | Gets the radius of gyration of the solid as X, Y, and Z coordinates calculated on the current coordinate system. This property's value is read-only. |
| Volume | Double | Gets the object's volume. This property's value is read-only. |

**NOTE** *Because this object inherits from* AcadObject, *it supports the* Modified *event.*

# AcadApplication Object

The AcadApplication object represents an instance of the AutoCAD application and is accessed in VBA by using ThisDrawing.Application. The AcadApplication object is also the global object for the ActiveX interface, and all methods and properties are available in the global namespace. The object supports 19 methods, which control the loading or listing of the currently loaded external applications and interface objects, and 20 properties, which reflect the properties of the main application window. In addition, there are over 20 events associated with the AcadApplication object.

## AcadApplication Object Methods

The AcadApplication object supports the following methods.

| NAME | RETURNS | DESCRIPTION |
|------|---------|-------------|
| Eval | | Executes a line of VBA code without the need to create a macro. Parameter: Expression As String. |
| GetAcadState | AcadState | Returns an AcadState object that will monitor the state of the AutoCAD application from other applications. |
| GetInterfaceObject | Object | Loads a program ID into AutoCAD as an in-process server. Although the object will be loaded into AutoCAD, it won't show up in its type library. The object will have its own type library. This method lets you connect to an ActiveX Automation server. Parameter: ProgID As String. |
| ListARX | Variant | Returns the currently loaded AutoCAD ARX applications as an array. It returns empty if none are loaded. |
| LoadARX | | Loads an AutoCAD ARX application. Parameter: Name As String. |
| LoadDVB | | Loads an AutoCAD VBA project file. Parameter: Name As String. |

| NAME | RETURNS | DESCRIPTION |
|---|---|---|
| Quit | | Closes the drawing file and the AutoCAD application. If AutoCAD is in the middle of a command, an error message will be generated. If the modified document hasn't been saved, a prompt message will be generated. |
| RunMacro | | Runs a VBA macro. Parameter: `MacroPath As String`. If the full path name isn't specified, AutoCAD will use its search path to find the macro or search all currently loaded projects. Syntax: `RunMacro "MyProject.Module1"`. |
| UnloadARX | | Unloads an unlocked AutoCAD ARX application. Parameter: `Name As String`. Don't attempt to unload the file `acadvba.arx`. |
| UnloadDVB | | Unloads an AutoCAD VBA project file. Parameter: `Name As String`. |
| Update | | Updates the screen. |
| ZoomAll | | Zooms the current active model space or paper space viewport to display the entire drawing. For a 2-D view, AutoCAD displays the whole drawing or the current extent, whichever is greater. For a 3-D view, this method is equivalent to `ZoomExtents`. |
| ZoomCenter | | Zooms the current active model space or paper space viewport as specified by the parameters. Parameters: `Center As Variant` and `Magnify As Double`. |
| ZoomExtents | | Zooms the current active model space or paper space viewport to the extent of the drawing. |
| ZoomPickWindow | | Zooms the current active model space or paper space viewport to a window defined by points picked on the screen. |
| ZoomPrevious | | Zooms the current active model space or paper space viewport to its previous state. |

| NAME | RETURNS | DESCRIPTION |
|------|---------|-------------|
| ZoomScaled | | Zooms the current active model space or paper space viewport to the specified scale factor. Parameters: `Scale As Double` and `ScaleType As AcZoomScaleType`. For the values of the second parameter, see Appendix B. |
| ZoomWindow | | Zooms the current active model space or paper space viewport as specified by the parameters. Parameters: `LowerLeft As Variant` and `UpperRight As Variant`. Parameters are three-element arrays of Doubles specifying WCS coordinates. |

## AcadApplication Object Properties

The `AcadApplication` object supports the following properties.

| NAME | RETURNS | DESCRIPTION |
|------|---------|-------------|
| ActiveDocument | AcadDocument | Gets or sets a reference to the active document. |
| Application | AcadApplication | Gets the `AcadApplication` object, which represents the application's frame controls and path settings, and provides the means to navigate down the object hierarchy. |
| Caption | String | Gets the text seen by the user in the window caption bar. This property is read-only. Note that if the caption is modified using Win32 API function `SetWindowText`, the caption property will return the modified caption text. |
| Documents | AcadDocuments | Gets the `Documents` collection. This property is read-only. |
| FullName | String | Gets the full name, including the path, of the application. This property's value is read-only. |

| NAME | RETURNS | DESCRIPTION |
|------|---------|-------------|
| Height | Integer | Gets or sets the height of the application window in pixels. |
| LocaleID | Long | Gets the regional settings for the session as defined by the Windows 95 or Windows NT operating systems. This property's value is read-only. |
| MenuBar | AcadMenuBar | Gets the AcadMenuBar object for the session. This property's value is read-only. |
| MenuGroups | AcadMenuGroups | Gets the MenuGroups collection for the session. |
| Name | String | Gets the name of the application. This property's value is read-only. |
| Path | String | Gets the path of the application without the file name. This property's value is read-only. |
| Preferences | AcadPreferences | Gets the application's AcadPreferences object. This property's value is read-only. |
| StatusID | Boolean | Gets the current active status of the viewport. It's True if the specified viewport is active and False otherwise. This property's value is read-only. Parameter: VportObj As AcadViewport. |
| VBE | VBAIDE | Gets the VBAIDE extensibility object. This isn't available if the acadvba.arx application hasn't been loaded. This property's value is read-only. |
| Version | String | Gets the version of the AutoCAD application. This property's value is read-only. For AutoCAD 2000, the value is 15.0. |
| Visible | Boolean | Gets or sets whether the application is visible. |
| Width | Integer | Gets or sets the width of the application window in pixels. |

| NAME | RETURNS | DESCRIPTION |
|------|---------|-------------|
| WindowLeft | Integer | Gets or sets the distance between the left edge of the application window and the left edge of the screen in pixels. This distance will establish the X coordinate of the upper-left corner (0,0) of the application. |
| WindowState | AcWindowState | Gets or sets the state of the application window. Possible values are acMin (minimized), acMax (maximized), or acNorm (normal). |
| WindowTop | Integer | Gets or sets the distance between the top of the application window and the top of the screen in pixels. This distance will establish the Y coordinate of the upper-left corner (0,0) of the application. |

## AcadApplication Object Events

The following events are triggered during various stages in the lifetime of the AcadApplication object. Note that no events will be fired while a modal dialog box is displayed.

| EVENT | DESCRIPTION |
|-------|-------------|
| AppActivate | Occurs before the main application window is activated. |
| AppDeactivate | Occurs before the main application window is deactivated. |
| ARXLoaded | Occurs after an ObjectARX application is loaded. Parameter: FullPathName As String. |
| ARXUnloaded | Occurs after an ObjectARX application is unloaded. Parameter: FullPathName As String. |
| BeginCommand | Occurs after a command is issued but before it is completed. Parameter: CommandName As String. |
| BeginFileDrop | Occurs when a file is dropped on the main application window. Parameters: FileName As String and Cancel As Boolean. If Cancel is set to True, this aborts the loading of the drawing, LISP file, or ARX file; otherwise, loading is allowed to continue. |

| EVENT | DESCRIPTION |
|---|---|
| BeginLISP | Occurs after a request to evaluate a LISP expression is received. Parameter: FirstLine As String. FirstLine won't have any case conversion of the alpha characters. |
| BeginModal | Occurs before a modal dialog box is displayed. You should never issue a message box from within an event handler for the BeginModal event. |
| BeginOpen | Occurs after a request to open an existing drawing is received. Parameter: Filename As String. |
| BeginPlot | Occurs after a request to print a drawing is received. Parameter: DrawingName As String. |
| BeginQuit | Occurs just before the session ends. Parameter: Cancel As Boolean. |
| BeginSave | Occurs after a request to save a drawing is received. Parameter: Filename As String. |
| EndCommand | Occurs after a command is completed. Parameter: CommandName As String. |
| EndLISP | Occurs after a LISP expression is executed. |
| EndModal | Occurs after a modal dialog box is dismissed. |
| EndOpen | Occurs after an existing drawing is opened. Parameter: Filename As String. |
| EndPlot | Occurs after a document is sent to the printer. Parameter: DrawingName As String. |
| EndSave | Occurs after a drawing is saved. Parameter: Filename As String. |
| LISPCancelled | Occurs when the evaluation of a LISP expression is canceled. |
| NewDrawing | Occurs before a drawing is created. |
| SysVarChanged | Occurs when the value of a system variable is changed. Parameters: SysVarName As String and NewVal As Variant. |
| WindowChanged | Occurs when the application window is changed. Parameter: WindowState As Integer (acMin, acMax, or acNorm). |
| WindowMovedOrResized | Occurs after one document window is moved or resized. Parameters: HWNDFrame As Long and Moved As Boolean. If Moved is set to True, the window was moved; otherwise, it was resized. |

# AcadArc Object

The AcadArc object represents a circular arc, which is always drawn counter-clockwise from the start point to the end point. The StartPoint and EndPoint properties of an arc are calculated through the StartAngle, EndAngle, and Radius properties. The AcadArc object is created using the AddArc method of the AcadBlock, AcadModelSpace, or AcadPaperSpace objects.

## AcadArc Object Methods

The AcadArc object inherits all the methods of the AcadEntity and AcadObject objects. It also supports the following method.

| NAME | RETURNS | DESCRIPTION |
| --- | --- | --- |
| Offset | Variant | Creates a new arc by offsetting the current arc by a specified distance, which must be a nonzero number. If the offset is positive, a concentric arc with a larger radius is created. If the offset is negative, a smaller arc is created. The return value isn't an arc but a Variant, which is an array of Objects. Parameter: Distance As Double. |

## AcadArc Object Properties

The AcadArc object inherits all the properties of the AcadEntity and AcadObject objects, as well as the common Application property. It also supports the following properties.

| NAME | RETURNS | DESCRIPTION |
| --- | --- | --- |
| ArcLength | Double | Gets the length of the arc. This property's value is read-only. |
| Area | Double | Gets the enclosed area of the arc. This property's value is read-only. |
| Center | Variant | Gets or sets the center of the arc as an array of the Doubles. |
| EndAngle | Double | Gets or sets the end angle of the arc in radians. |

| NAME | RETURNS | DESCRIPTION |
|---|---|---|
| EndPoint | Variant | Gets the end point of the arc as an array of three Doubles. This property's value is read-only. |
| Normal | Variant | Gets or sets the 3-D (Z-axis) normal unit vector for the arc. |
| Radius | Double | Gets or sets the radius of the arc. |
| StartAngle | Double | Gets or sets the start angle of the arc in radians. |
| StartPoint | Variant | Gets the start point of the arc as an array of three Doubles. This property's value is read-only. |
| Thickness | Double | Gets or sets the distance the AcadArc object is extruded above or below its elevation, in a Z-axis direction. The default is 0.0. |
| TotalAngle | Double | Gets the total angle of the arc in radians. This property's value is read-only. |

**NOTE**  *Because this object inherits from* AcadObject, *it supports the* Modified *event.*

## AcadAttribute Object

The AcadAttribute object represents an object appearing as a text string that describes the characteristics of an attribute reference, or in other words an attribute definition. You create it using the AddAttribute method of the AcadBlock, AcadModelSpace, or AcadPaperSpace objects.

### AcadAttribute Object Methods

The AcadAttribute object inherits all the methods of the AcadEntity and AcadObject objects. It supports no other methods.

## *AcadAttribute Object Properties*

The AcadAttribute object inherits all the properties of the AcadEntity and AcadObject objects, as well as the common Application property. It also supports the following properties.

| NAME | RETURNS | DESCRIPTION |
| --- | --- | --- |
| Alignment | AcAlignment | Gets or sets the horizontal and vertical alignments of the attribute. For a list of the values for the AcAlignment enumeration, see Appendix B. |
| Backward | Boolean | Gets or sets whether the text is backward. |
| Constant | Boolean | Gets or sets whether the attribute has the same value in every occurrence. AutoCAD doesn't prompt for a value of constant attributes. |
| FieldLength | Integer | Gets or sets the field length of the attribute. |
| Height | Double | Gets or sets the height of the attribute. |
| HorizontalAlignment | AcHorizontalAlignment | Gets or sets the horizontal alignment of the attribute. |
| InsertionPoint | Variant | Gets the insertion point of the attribute. |
| Invisible | Boolean | Gets or sets whether the attribute is invisible. An invisible attribute will not be displayed or plotted. This property's value is read-only. |

| NAME | RETURNS | DESCRIPTION |
|------|---------|-------------|
| Mode | Integer | Gets or sets the mode of the attribute definition. Values: acAttributeModeNormal, acAttributeModeInvisible, acAttributeModeConstant, acAttributeModeVerify, or acAttributeModePreset. |
| Normal | Variant | Gets or sets the 3-D (Z-axis) normal unit vector for the attribute. |
| ObliqueAngle | Double | Gets or sets the oblique angle of the attribute and is measured from the vertical axis. The units are radians within the range of –85 to +85 degrees. A positive value denotes a lean toward the right. |
| Preset | Boolean | Gets or sets whether the attribute is preset or not. A preset attribute sets the attribute to its default value when the user inserts the block. |
| PromptString | String | Gets or sets the prompt string for the attribute that appears when a block containing this attribute is inserted. The default for this string is the TagString property. |
| Rotation | Double | Gets or sets the rotation angle (in radians) for the attribute, relative to the X-axis, with positive values going counterclockwise when viewed along the Z-axis toward the origin. |
| ScaleFactor | Double | Gets or sets the scale factor for the attribute. It must be positive. A scale factor greater than 1 enlarges the object. A scale factor between 0 and 1 shrinks the object. The initial value for this property is 1.0. |
| StyleName | String | Gets or sets the name of the style used with the object, the default being the current style. |
| TagString | String | Gets or sets the tag string, which identifies each occurrence of the attribute. The tag string identifies each occurrence of the attribute and may contain any characters other than spaces and exclamation marks. Lowercase letters are changed to uppercase. |

| NAME | RETURNS | DESCRIPTION |
|------|---------|-------------|
| TextAlignmentPoint | Variant | Gets or sets the alignment point for text, returning a three-element array of Doubles. This property's value is read-only when the Alignment property is set to acAlignmentLeft. |
| TextGenerationFlag | AcTextGenerationFlag | Gets or sets the attribute text generation flag. Values: acTextFlagBackward and acTextFlagUpsideDown. The values can be combined. |
| TextString | String | Gets or sets the text string for the attribute. |
| Thickness | Double | Gets or sets the distance the Attribute object is extruded above or below its elevation, in a Z-axis direction. The default is 0.0. |
| UpsideDown | Boolean | Specifies whether or not the text is upside down. |
| Verify | Boolean | Specifies whether or not the user is prompted for verification when inserting the block. |
| VerticalAlignment | AcVerticalAlignment | Gets or sets the vertical alignment of the attribute. For a list of possible values for the AcVerticalAlignment enumeration, see Appendix B. |

**NOTE**   *Because this object inherits from* AcadObject, *it supports the* Modified *event.*

## AcadAttributeReference Object

The AcadAttributeReference object represents an object containing text that links to a block or to an instance of the AcadAtribute object. These objects can't be directly created but are added to a drawing when a block containing an attribute definition is inserted. This is achieved by calling the InsertBlock method, which is common to the AcadBlock, AcadModelSpace, and AcadPaperSpace objects. The GetAttributes method of the AcadBlockReference object returns an array of all attribute references attached to the inserted block.

### AcadAttributeReference Object Methods

The AcadAttributeReference object inherits all the methods of the AcadEntity and AcadObject objects. It supports no other methods.

### AcadAttributeReference Object Properties

The AcadAttributeReference object inherits all the properties of the AcadEntity and AcadObject objects, as well as the common Application property. It also supports all the other properties supported by the AcadAttribute object *except* for Mode, Preset, PromptString, and Verify. It supports no other properties.

**NOTE**  *Because this object inherits from* AcadObject, *it supports the* Modified *event.*

## AcadBlock Object

The AcadBlock object represents a block definition containing a name and a set of objects. There's no limit to the number of objects a block can contain. There are three kinds of block: a simple block, an XRef block, and a layout block. Blocks are discussed in Chapter 12.

## AcadBlock Object Methods

In addition to the methods inherited from the AcadObject object, the AcadBlock object supports the following methods.

| NAME | RETURNS | DESCRIPTION |
| --- | --- | --- |
| Add3DFace | Acad3DFace | Creates an Acad3DFace object using the four vertices. If the last parameter is omitted, a three-sided face is created. Points must be entered in a clockwise or counterclockwise order to create the object. Parameters: Point1 As Variant, Point2 As Variant, Point3 As Variant, and Point4 As Variant. |
| Add3DMesh | AcadPolygonMesh | Creates a free-form AcadPolygonMesh object representing an M×N free-form mesh from the given array of coordinates. Parameters: M As Integer, N As Integer, and PointsMatrix As Variant.<br><br>The size of the mesh in both the M and N directions is limited to between 2 and 256.<br><br>The PointsMatrix parameter is a 3×M×N array of 3-D WCS coordinates. All the coordinates for row M must be supplied before any vertices for row M+1. |
| Add3DPoly | Acad3DPolyline | Creates an Acad3DPolyline object from the given array of 3-D WCS coordinates. The polyline will be created according to the order of the coordinates in the array. Parameter: PointsArray As Variant. |
| AddArc | AcadArc | Creates an AcadArc object as specified by the parameters. Parameters: Center As Variant (an array of three Doubles representing 3-D WCS coordinates), Radius As Double, StartAngle As Double, and EndAngle As Double. The start and end angles must be in radians. If StartAngle is greater than EndAngle, a clockwise arc is created. |
| AddAttribute | AcadAttribute | Creates an AcadAttribute object as specified by the parameters. Parameters: Height As Double, Mode As AcAttributeMode, Prompt As String, InsertionPoint As Variant (an array of three Doubles representing 3-D WCS coordinates), Tag As String, and Value As String. For the values of the Mode parameter, see Appendix B. |

| NAME | RETURNS | DESCRIPTION |
| --- | --- | --- |
| AddBox | Acad3DSolid | Creates an Acad3DSolid object representing a solid box with center at the given origin and with edges parallel to the axes of the WCS. Parameters: Origin As Variant (an array of three Doubles as 3-D WCS coordinates), Length As Double, Width As Double, and Height As Double. |
| AddCircle | AcadCircle | Creates an AcadCircle object as specified by the parameters. Parameters: Center As Variant (an array of three Doubles representing 3-D WCS coordinates) and Radius As Double. |
| AddCone | Acad3DSolid | Creates an Acad3DSolid object representing a solid cone with base on the XY plane of the WCS. Parameters: Center As Variant (an array of three Doubles representing 3-D WCS coordinates), BaseRadius As Double, and Height As Double. |
| AddCustomObject | Object | Creates a custom object. Parameter: ClassName As String. ClassName must be an ARX file prior to the call. |
| AddCylinder | Acad3DSolid | Creates an Acad3DSolid object representing a cylinder whose base is on the XY plane of the WCS. Parameters: Center As Variant (an array of three Doubles representing 3-D WCS coordinates), Radius As Double, and Height As Double. |
| AddDim3PointAngular | AcadDim3PointAngular | Creates an AcadDim3PointAngular object as specified by the parameters. Parameters: AngleVertex As Variant, FirstEndPoint As Variant, SecondEndPoint As Variant, and TextPoint As Variant. All four parameters are arrays of three Doubles representing 3-D WCS coordinates. |

| NAME | RETURNS | DESCRIPTION |
|------|---------|-------------|
| AddDimAligned | AcadDimAligned | Creates an AcadDimAligned object as specified by the parameters. Parameters: `ExtLine1Point As Variant`, `ExtLine2Point As Variant`, and `TextPosition As Variant`. All three parameters are arrays of three Doubles representing 3-D WCS coordinates. |
| AddDimAngular | AcadDimAngular | Creates an `AcadDimAngular` object representing the angular dimension for an arc, two lines, or a circle. Parameters: `AngleVertex As Variant`, `FirstEndPoint As Variant`, `SecondEndPoint As Variant`, and `TextPoint As Variant`. All four parameters are arrays of three Doubles representing 3-D WCS coordinates. |
| AddDimDiametric | AcadDimDiametric | Creates a diametric dimension for a circle or arc given the two points on the diameter and the length of the leader line. Parameters: `ChordPoint As Variant`, `FarChordPoint As Variant`, and `LeaderLength As Double`. The first two parameters are arrays of three Doubles representing 3-D WCS coordinates. |
| AddDimOrdinate | AcadDimOrdinate | Creates an ordinate dimension given the definition point and leader end point. Parameters: `DefinitionPoint As Variant`, `LeaderEndPoint As Variant`, and `UseXAxis As Integer`. The first two parameters are arrays of three Doubles representing 3-D WCS coordinates. |
| AddDimRadial | AcadDimRadial | Creates a radial dimension for the selected object at the given location. Parameters: `Center As Variant`, `ChordPoint As Variant`, and `LeaderLength As Double`. The first two parameters are arrays of three Doubles representing 3-D WCS coordinates. |
| AddDimRotated | AcadDimRotated | Creates an `AcadDimRotated` object as specified by the parameters. Parameters: `ExtLine1Point As Variant`, `ExtLine2Point As Variant`, `DimLineLocation As Variant`, and `RotationAngle As Double`. The first three parameters are arrays of three Doubles representing 3-D WCS coordinates. |

| NAME | RETURNS | DESCRIPTION |
|---|---|---|
| AddEllipse | AcadEllipse | Creates an `AcadEllipse` object representing an ellipse in the XY plane of the WCS as specified by the parameters. Parameters: `Center As Variant`, `MajorAxis As Variant`, and `RadiusRatio As Double`. The first two parameters are arrays of three Doubles representing 3-D WCS coordinates. |
| AddEllipticalCone | Acad3DSolid | Creates an `Acad3DSolid` object representing an elliptical cone in the XY plane of the WCS given the center, major radius, minor radius, and height. Parameters: `Center As Variant` (an array of three Doubles representing 3-D WCS coordinates), `MajorRadius As Double`, `MinorRadius As Double`, and `Height As Double`. |
| AddEllipticalCylinder | Acad3DSolid | Creates an `Acad3DSolid` object representing an elliptical cylinder as specified by the parameters with its base in the XY plane. Parameters: `Center As Variant` (an array of three Doubles representing 3-D WCS coordinates), `MajorRadius As Double`, `MinorRadius As Double`, and `Height As Double`. |
| AddExtrudedSolid | Acad3DSolid | Creates an `Acad3DSolid` object representing an extruded solid as specified by the parameters. Parameters: `Profile As AcadRegion`, `Height As Double`, and `TaperAngle As Double`.<br><br>The `Height` parameter specifies the height of the extrusion along the Z-axis of the object's coordinate system.<br><br>The `TaperAngle` parameter must be provided in radians. The range of the taper angle is from −90 to +90 degrees. Positive angles taper in from the base; negative angles taper out. The default angle, 0, extrudes a 2-D object perpendicular to its plane. Only 2-D planar regions can be extruded. |

| NAME | RETURNS | DESCRIPTION |
|------|---------|-------------|
| AddExtrudedSolidAlongPath | Acad3DSolid | Creates an `Acad3DSolid` object representing an extruded solid, given the profile and an extrusion path. Only 2-D planar regions can be extruded and the path shouldn't lie on the same plane as the profile, nor should it have areas of high curvature. Parameters: `Profile As AcadRegion` and `Path As Object`. |
| AddHatch | AcadHatch | Creates an `AcadHatch` object as specified by the parameters. Parameters: `PatternType As AcPatternType`, `PatternName As String`, and `Associativity As Boolean`.<br><br>For a list of possible values for the `AcPatternType` enumerated type, see Appendix B.<br><br>The `Associativity` parameter is `True` if the hatch is to be associative and `False` otherwise. Don't forget to create the outer boundary for the hatch and to append it using `Obj.AppendOuterLoop(outerLoop)`, in which `Obj` is the newly created hatch and `outerLoop` is an array of drawing objects forming the hatch boundary. (See the section on the `AcadHatch` object for details.) |
| AddLeader | AcadLeader | Creates an `AcadLeader` object as specified by the parameters. Parameters: `PointsArray As Variant`, `Annotation As AcadEntity`, and `Type As AcLeaderType`.<br><br>The `PointsArray` parameter must be an array of 3-D WCS coordinates (Doubles) and has a minimum of two points (six elements).<br><br>The `Annotation` parameter must be an `AcadTolerance`, `AcadMText`, or `AcadBlockReference` object or `NULL`.<br><br>See Appendix B for the values of the `AcLeaderType` enumeration. |

| NAME | RETURNS | DESCRIPTION |
|------|---------|-------------|
| AddLightWeightPolyline | AcadLWPolyline | Creates an AcadLWPolyline object as specified by the parameter. Parameter: VerticesList As Variant. VerticesList is an array of 2-D OCS coordinates specifying the vertices of the polyline. A minimum of two vertices or four elements is required. Conversion between OCS and WCS can be achieved using the TranslateCoordinates method (see the section on the AcadUtility object for details). Arcs are added to vertices using the SetBulge method (see the section on the AcadLWPolyline object for details). |
| AddLine | AcadLine | Creates an AcadLine object representing a line passing through the given points. Parameters: StartPoint As Variant and EndPoint As Variant. Both parameters are arrays of three Doubles representing 3-D WCS coordinates. |
| AddMInsertBlock | AcadMInsertBlock | Inserts an array of AcadBlockReferences from an original block definition of a given Name, as specified by the parameters. Parameters: InsertionPoint As Variant, Name As String, Xscale As Double, Yscale As Double, Zscale As Double, Rotation As Double, NumRows As Integer, NumColumns As Integer, RowSpacing As Integer, and ColumnSpacing As Integer. The InsertionPoint parameter is a set of 3-D WCS coordinates. The rotation angle is in radians. |
| AddMLine | AcadMLine | Creates an AcadMLine representing a set of lines passing through the points specified in the parameter. Parameter: VertexList As Variant. VertexList is an array of the 3-D WCS coordinates specifying the vertices for the multiline. |

| NAME | RETURNS | DESCRIPTION |
|------|---------|-------------|
| AddMText | AcadMText | Creates an AcadMText object as specified by the parameters. Parameters: InsertionPoint As Variant, Width As Double, and Text As String. The InsertionPoint parameter is a set of 3-D WCS coordinates. |
| AddPoint | AcadPoint | Creates an AcadPoint object as specified by the 3-D WCS coordinates specified. Parameter: Point As Variant. |
| AddPolyfaceMesh | AcadPolyfaceMesh | Creates an AcadPolyfaceMesh object from a list of vertices. Parameters: VertexList As Variant and FaceList As Variant.<br><br>VertexList is an array of 3-D WCS coordinates used to create the polyface mesh vertices. At least four points (12 elements) are required for constructing a polyface mesh object.<br><br>FaceList is an array of integers representing the vertex numbers for each face. Faces are defined in groups of four vertex index values. |
| AddPolyline | AcadPolyline | Creates an AcadPolyline object from a list of vertices. An array of OCS coordinates used to create the polyline vertices. At least two points (six values) are required to form a polyline. Parameter: VerticesList As Variant.<br><br>Conversion between OCS and WCS can be achieved using the TranslateCoordinates method (see the section on the AcadUtility object for details).<br><br>Arcs are added to vertices using the SetBulge method (see the section on the AcadPolyline object for details). |

| NAME | RETURNS | DESCRIPTION |
|------|---------|-------------|
| AddRaster | AcadRasterImage | Creates an AcadRasterImage object based on the given image file. Parameters: ImageFileName As String, InsertionPoint As Variant, ScaleFactor As Double, and RotationAngle As Double. |
| | | The InsertionPoint parameter is a set of 3-D WCS coordinates. |
| | | The default value for the ScaleFactor parameter is 1. |
| | | The RotationAngle is in radians. |
| AddRay | AcadRay | Creates an AcadRay object representing a ray passing through two points. Parameters: Point1 As Variant and Point2 As Variant. Both parameters are arrays of three Doubles representing 3-D WCS coordinates. |
| AddRegion | Variant | Creates a region from an array of AcadEntity objects. The array must consist of AcadLine, AcadArc, AcadCircle, AcadEllipse, AcadLWPolyline, and AcadSpline objects, which must form a closed coplanar region. Parameter: ObjectList As Variant. |
| AddRevolvedSolid | Acad3DSolid | Creates an Acad3DSolid object representing a revolved solid as specified by the parameters. Parameters: Profile As AcadRegion, AxisPoint As Variant, AxisDir As Variant, and Angle As Double. |
| | | The AxisPoint parameter specifies the start point of the axis of revolution and is defined with an array of 3-D WCS coordinates. |
| | | The AxisDir parameter specifies the direction of the axis of revolution. |
| | | The Angle parameter is the angle of revolution in radians. Enter **6.28** for a full circle revolution. |

| NAME | RETURNS | DESCRIPTION |
|------|---------|-------------|
| AddShape | AcadShape | Creates an AcadShape object based on a template identified by name, at the given insertion point, scale factor, and rotation. Parameters: Name As String, InsertionPoint As Variant, ScaleFactor As Double, and RotationAngle As Double. The InsertionPoint parameter is a set of 3-D WCS coordinates. |
| AddSolid | AcadSolid | Creates an AcadSolid object representing a 2-D solid polygon. The first two points define one edge of the polygon. For a four-sided solid, the third point is defined to be diagonally opposite from the second point. If the third and fourth points are equal, then a triangle is created. The AcadSolid is filled when the FILLMODE system variable is set to 1. Parameters: Point1 As Variant, Point2 As Variant, Point3 As Variant, and Point4 As Variant. |
| AddSphere | Acad3DSolid | Creates an Acad3DSolid object representing a sphere as specified by the parameters. Parameters: Center As Variant (an array of three Doubles representing 3-D WCS coordinates) and Radius As Double. |
| AddSpline | AcadSpline | Creates an AcadSpline object as specified by the parameters, the first one being an array of 3-D WCS coordinates defining the spline curve. The StartTangent and EndTangent parameters specify the tangents (a 3-D vector) at the two ends of the spline. At least two points (six elements) are required for constructing an AcadSpline object. Parameters: PointsArray As Variant, StartTangent As Variant, and EndTangent As Variant. |
| AddText | AcadText | Creates an AcadText object representing a single line of text. Parameters: TextString As String, InsertionPoint As Variant, and Height As Double. The InsertionPoint parameter is a set of 3-D WCS coordinates. |
| AddTolerance | AcadTolerance | Creates an AcadTolerance object from the supplied parameters, the second one being a set of 3-D WCS coordinates and the last a 3-D vector. Parameters: Text As String, InsertionPoint As Variant, and Direction As Variant. |

| NAME | RETURNS | DESCRIPTION |
|------|---------|-------------|
| AddTorus | Acad3DSolid | Creates an Acad3DSolid object representing a torus from the parameters. Parameters: Center As Variant, TorusRadius As Double, and TubeRadius As Double. The first parameter is a set of 3-D WCS coordinates, and the values for both radii must be positive. |
| AddTrace | AcadTrace | Creates an AcadTrace object from an array of points. Parameter: PointsArray As Variant (an array of three Doubles representing 3-D WCS coordinates). |
| AddWedge | Acad3DSolid | Creates an Acad3DSolid object representing a wedge with edges parallel to the axes given the length, width, and height. Parameters: Center As Variant (an array of three Doubles representing 3-D WCS coordinates), Length As Double, Width As Double, and Height As Double. |
| AddXline | AcadXline | Creates an AcadXline object representing an infinite line passing through the given points. Parameters: Point1 As Variant and Point2 As Variant. Both parameters are arrays of three Doubles representing 3-D WCS coordinates. The width and fill mode are set using the TRACEWID and FILLMODE system variables. |
| AttachExternal-Reference | AcadExternal-Reference | Attaches an AcadExternalReference (XRef) object to the AcadBlock, given the full path name of the external drawing, the name of the XRef, and other parameters. Note that attached AcadExternalReference objects can be nested. Parameters: PathName As String, Name As String, InsertionPoint As Variant, Xscale As Double, Yscale As Double, Zscale As Double, Rotation As Double, and Overlay As Boolean.<br><br>The InsertionPoint parameter is a set of 3-D WCS coordinates.<br><br>The Rotation parameter specifies the angle of rotation of the XRef, in radians.<br><br>The Overlay parameter specifies whether or not the XRef is to be an overlay (True) or an attachment (False). An overlaid XRef will be ignored when the container drawing is referenced at its turn. |

| NAME | RETURNS | DESCRIPTION |
|------|---------|-------------|
| Bind | | Binds an `AcadExternalReference` (XRef) object as a nested block, complete with all its named dependent symbols (dimension styles, linetypes, etc.). This operation makes the XRef a permanent part of the drawing and not an externally referenced file. Named objects from the XRef can be used in the current drawing. Parameter: `PrefixName As Boolean`. |
| | | If this parameter is `True`, then the symbols named in the XRef are prefixed with `<blockname>$x$`, where x is an integer that is automatically incremented to avoid overriding existing block functions. If this parameter is `False`, no prefix is used. If there is a clash of names, AutoCAD uses the symbols already defined in the drawing. |
| Detach | | Detaches an `AcadExternalReference` (XRef) object from the block, including all copies of the XRef and the definition itself. |
| InsertBlock | `AcadBlockReference` | Inserts an `AcadBlockReference` object representing a file or a block that has been defined in the current drawing. Parameters: `InsertionPoint As Variant`, `Name As String`, `Xscale As Double`, `Yscale As Double`, `Zscale As Double`, and `Rotation As Double`. The `InsertionPoint` parameter is a set of 3-D WCS coordinates. If the `Name` is a file name, include any path information necessary for AutoCAD to find the file and the `.dwg` extension. |
| Item | `AcadEntity` | Gets the member object at a given index in the block. Parameter: `Index As Variant` (String or Integer). |

| NAME | RETURNS | DESCRIPTION |
| --- | --- | --- |
| Reload | | Reloads the most recently saved version of the external reference (XRef) or an unloaded XRef. |
| Unload | | Unloads an external reference (XRef). This means that the drawing opens faster and uses less memory. The XRef and its table of symbols don't appear in the drawing. |

## AcadBlock Object Properties

In addition to the properties inherited from the AcadEntity object and the common Application property, the AcadBlock object supports the following properties.

| NAME | RETURNS | DESCRIPTION |
| --- | --- | --- |
| Count | Integer | Gets the number of items in the block. This property is read-only. |
| IsLayout | Boolean | Determines whether or not the block is a layout block. This property's value is read-only. If the values for IsLayout and IsXRef are both False, then the block is a simple block. |
| IsXRef | Boolean | Determines whether or not the block is an XRef block. This property's value is read-only. |
| Layout | AcadLayout | Gets the plot settings (AcadLayout object) for the block. This property's value is read-only. |
| Name | String | Gets the name of the block. |
| Origin | Variant | Gets or sets the origin of the block in WCS coordinates. |
| XRefDatabase | AcadDatabase | Gets the AcadDatabase object that defines the contents of the block. Only available if the IsXRef property for the block is True. This property's value is read-only. |

**NOTE** *Because this object inherits from* AcadObject, *it supports the* Modified *event.*

# AcadBlockReference Object

The AcadBlockReference object represents an instance of a block definition inserted into a drawing. The creation of a new block definition is done automatically when an external block file is inserted with the InsertBlock method. To add or delete items from the block reference, you may first use the Explode method to break it into its component objects (subentities). However, the block definition still remains in the drawing's block symbol table with all its constituents.

## AcadBlockReference Object Methods

The AcadBlockReference object inherits all the methods of the AcadEntity and AcadObject objects. It also supports the following methods.

| NAME | RETURNS | DESCRIPTION |
| --- | --- | --- |
| Explode | Variant | Explodes the block and returns the subentities as an array of Objects |
| GetAttributes | Variant | Returns an array of editable attribute references attached to the block reference, only if the HasAttributes property is set to True |
| GetConstantAttributes | Variant | Returns an array of constant attributes for the block |

## AcadBlockReference Object Properties

The AcadBlockReference object inherits all the properties of the AcadEntity and AcadObject objects, as well as the common Application property. It also supports the following properties.

| NAME | RETURNS | DESCRIPTION |
|------|---------|-------------|
| HasAttributes | Boolean | Specifies if the block has any attributes in it. This property's value is read-only. |
| InsertionPoint | Variant | Gets or sets an insertion point in the block as a set of 3-D WCS coordinates. It returns a three-element array of Doubles. |
| Name | String | Gets or sets the name of the block. |
| Normal | Variant | Gets or sets the 3-D (Z-axis) normal unit vector for the block. |
| Rotation | Double | Gets or sets the rotation angle (in radians) for the block, relative to the X-axis with positive values going counterclockwise when viewed along the Z-axis toward the origin. |
| XScaleFactor | Double | Gets or sets the X scale factor for the block. |
| YScaleFactor | Double | Gets or sets the Y scale factor for the block |
| ZScaleFactor | Double | Gets or sets the Z scale factor for the block. |

**NOTE** *Because this object inherits from* AcadObject, *it supports the* Modified *event.*

## *AcadBlocks Collection*

The AcadBlocks collection contains all of the blocks in the drawing. The collection contains two special collections, one for model space entities, the AcadModelSpace collection, and the other for paper space entities, the AcadPaperSpace collection. Although the AcadBlocks collection inherits a Delete method, you can't actually delete the collection. There's no limit to the number of blocks you can create in your drawing. However, there can be only one instance of the AcadBlocks collection predefined for each drawing. You can make multiple references to it by using the Blocks property of the AcadDocument object.

## *AcadBlocks Collection Methods*

In addition to the methods inherited from the AcadObject object, the AcadBlocks collection supports the following methods.

| NAME | RETURNS | DESCRIPTION |
|------|---------|-------------|
| Add | AcadBlock | Creates an AcadBlock object and adds it to the collection. Parameters: InsertionPoint As Variant and Name As String. The InsertionPoint parameter is a set of 3-D WCS coordinates that specify where the AcadBlock object will be added. Once the AcadBlock has been created, you can add subentities to it. |
| Item | AcadBlock | Returns the object at the given index in the collection. Parameter: Index As Variant (Integer or String). If the Index value is a String, it must match an existing block definition. |

## *AcadBlocks Collection Properties*

The AcadBlocks collection supports the Count property, the common Application property, and those properties inherited from the AcadObject object. It supports no other properties.

**NOTE** *Because this collection inherits from* AcadObject, *it supports the* Modified *event.*

# *AcadCircle Object*

The AcadCircle object represents a full circle. It is created using the AddCircle method of the AcadBlock, AcadModelSpace, or AcadPaperSpace object.

## AcadCircle Object Methods

The AcadCircle object inherits all the methods of the AcadEntity and AcadObject objects. It also supports the following method.

| NAME | RETURNS | DESCRIPTION |
| --- | --- | --- |
| Offset | Variant | Creates a new circle by offsetting the current circle by a specified distance, which must be nonzero. If the offset is positive, a larger circle is created with the same origin. If the offset is negative, a smaller circle is created. Parameter: Distance_As_Double. |

## AcadCircle Object Properties

The AcadCircle object inherits all the properties of the AcadEntity and AcadObject objects, as well as the common Application property. It also supports the following properties.

| NAME | RETURNS | DESCRIPTION |
| --- | --- | --- |
| Area | Double | Gets the area of the circle in square drawing units. This property's value is read-only. |
| Center | Variant | Gets or sets the center of the circle as a set of 3-D coordinates. |
| Circumference | Double | Gets or sets the circumference of the circle. |
| Diameter | Double | Gets or sets the diameter of the circle. |
| Normal | Variant | Gets or sets the 3-D (Z-axis) normal unit vector for the object. |
| Radius | Double | Gets or sets the radius of the circle. |
| Thickness | Double | Gets or sets the distance the AcadCircle object is extruded above or below its elevation, in a Z-axis direction. The default is 0.0. |

**NOTE** *Because this object inherits from* AcadObject, *it supports the* Modified *event.*

# AcadDatabase Object

The AcadDatabase object represents the contents of an external reference (XRef) block. This object provides access to the contents of an external reference block. It's only available on blocks whose IsXRef property is equal to True.

## AcadDatabase Object Methods

The AcadDatabase object supports the following methods. These are identical to three of the methods supported by the AcadDocument object, except they act upon the contents of an XRef block, not the active document.

| NAME | RETURNS | DESCRIPTION |
|------|---------|-------------|
| CopyObjects | Variant | Duplicates an object along with other objects owned and referenced by it. This is called *deep cloning*. Parameters: Objects As Variant, [Owner As Variant], and [IDPairs As Variant]. |
| | | The Objects parameter is array of primary objects to be copied. They must all have the same owner. |
| | | The Owner parameter is the new owner for the copied objects. If unspecified, the original owner is assumed. |
| | | The IDPairs parameter gives information on what happened during the copy and translation process. Input is an empty Variant. Output is an array of AcadIDPair objects. |
| | | You can't execute this method while simultaneously iterating through a collection. |
| HandleToObject | Object | Returns the object that corresponds to the given handle. The object must be in the current XRef drawing. Parameter: Handle As String. A handle is persistent. It can be stored for reuse with this method for the lifetime of the object |
| ObjectIDToObject | Object | Returns the object that corresponds to the given object ID. The object must be in the current XRef drawing. Parameter: ObjectID As Integer. An object ID isn't persistent. Its lifetime is limited to a drawing session. |

## AcadDatabase Object Properties

As well as the common `Application` property, the `AcadDatabase` object supports the following properties. These are identical to the corresponding properties of the `AcadDocument` object, except they refer to the contents of an XRef block, not the active document.

| NAME | RETURNS | DESCRIPTION |
|---|---|---|
| Blocks | AcadBlocks | Gets the `AcadBlocks` collection for the XRef drawing. This property's value is read-only. |
| Dictionaries | AcadDictionaries | Gets the `AcadDictionaries` collection for the XRef drawing. This property's value is read-only. |
| DimStyles | AcadDimStyles | Gets the `AcadDimStyles` collection for the XRef drawing. This property's value is read-only. |
| ElevationModelSpace | Double | Gets or sets the elevation setting in the model space. The current elevation is the Z value that is used whenever a 3-D point is expected but only the X and Y values are supplied. |
| ElevationPaperSpace | Double | Gets or sets the elevation setting in the paper space. The current elevation is the Z value that is used whenever a 3-D point is expected but only the X and Y values are supplied. |
| Groups | AcadGroups | Gets the `AcadGroups` collection for the XRef drawing. This property's value is read-only. |
| Layers | AcadLayers | Gets the `AcadLayers` collection for the XRef drawing. This property's value is read-only. |
| Layouts | AcadLayouts | Gets the `AcadLayouts` collection for the XRef drawing. This property's value is read-only. |
| Limits | Variant | Gets or sets the XRef drawing limits in the XY plane. Two sets of WCS coordinates specify the lower-left (`LIMMIN`) and upper-right corners (`LIMMAX`) of the plane. |
| Linetypes | AcadLineTypes | Gets the `AcadLinetypes` collection for the XRef drawing. This property's value is read-only. |

| NAME | RETURNS | DESCRIPTION |
|------|---------|-------------|
| ModelSpace | AcadModelSpace | Gets the AcadModelSpace collection for the XRef drawing. This property's value is read-only. |
| PaperSpace | AcadPaperSpace | Gets the AcadPaperSpace collection for the XRef drawing. This property's value is read-only. |
| PlotConfigurations | AcadPlotConfigurations | Gets the AcadPlotConfigurations collection for the XRef drawing. This property's value is read-only. |
| Preferences | AcadDatabasePreferences | Gets the AcadPreferences object for the XRef drawing. The AcadPreferences object holds the options from the Options dialog box that resides in the Registry. Options that reside in the drawing can be found through the AcadDatabasePreferences object. This property's value is read-only. |
| RegisteredApplications | AcadRegisteredApplications | Gets the AcadRegisteredApplications collection for the XRef drawing. This property's value is read-only. |
| TextStyles | AcadTextStyles | Gets the AcadTextStyles collection for the XRef drawing. This property's value is read-only. |
| UserCoordinateSystems | AcadUCSs | Gets the AcadUCSs collection for the XRef drawing. This property's value is read-only. |
| Viewports | AcadViewports | Gets the AcadViewports collection for the XRef drawing. This property's value is read-only. |
| Views | AcadViews | Gets the AcadViews collection for the XRef drawing. This property's value is read-only. |

# AcadDatabasePreferences Object

The AcadDatabasePreferences object specifies the current AutoCAD drawing-specific settings, that is, all the options from the Options dialog box that reside in a drawing. (Options that reside in the Registry can be found through the main AcadPreferences object.) This object has no methods.

## AcadDatabasePreferences Object Properties

As well as the common Application property, the AcadDatabasePreferences object supports the following properties.

| NAME | RETURNS | DESCRIPTION |
| --- | --- | --- |
| AllowLongSymbolNames | Boolean | Determines if symbol names are extended (True) or restricted (False). ("Symbol names" refers to the names of nongraphical objects such as linetypes and layers.) Extended symbol names can be up to 255 characters and can use any symbol not reserved by Microsoft or AutoCAD, in addition to the letters, numerals, and the space. This is the default. Restricted symbol names can only be up to 31 letters long and are restricted to the letters and numerals, the underscore (_), dollar ($), and hyphen (-). The value for this property is stored in the EXTNAMES system variable. |
| ContourLinesPerSurface | Integer | Gets or sets the number of contour lines per surface on an object. The valid range is 0 to 2047. The number is stored in the ISOLINES system variable. |
| DisplaySilhouette | Boolean | Determines whether silhouette curves of solid objects are displayed in wireframe mode: True for silhouette curves and False for isolines (default). The value is stored in the DISPSILH system variable. |

| NAME | RETURNS | DESCRIPTION |
|------|---------|-------------|
| Lineweight | AcLineWeight | Gets or sets the default lineweight for the drawing. For a list of possible values for the AcLineWeight enumerated type, see Appendix B. |
| LineweightDisplay | Boolean | Determines whether or not lineweights are displayed in the model space. True is the default. This property is read/write. |
| MaxActiveViewports | Integer | Gets or sets the maximum number of active viewports. The range is 2 to 48. The value of is stored in the MAXACTVP system variable. |
| ObjectSortByPlotting | Boolean | Specifies whether or not objects are sorted by their plotting order. True is the default. The values of this property and the five that follow are stored in the SORTENTS system variable. Note that setting these additional ObjectSortBy... properties to True slows your application. |
| ObjectSortByPSOutput | Boolean | Specifies whether or not objects are sorted by their PostScript output order. True is the default. |
| ObjectSortByRedraws | Boolean | Specifies whether or not objects are sorted by their redraw order. False is the default. |
| ObjectSortByRegens | Boolean | Specifies whether or not objects are sorted by their regeneration order. False is the default. |
| ObjectSortBySelection | Boolean | Specifies whether or not drawing objects are sorted by object selection. False is the default. |
| ObjectSortBySnap | Boolean | Gets or sets whether drawing objects are sorted by object snap. False is the default. |

| NAME | RETURNS | DESCRIPTION |
|---|---|---|
| OLELaunch | Boolean | Specifies whether or not the parent application is launched when OLE objects are plotted. The value of this property is stored in the OLESTARTUP system variable. The initial value of this property is False. This gives a high-quality plot, but at the cost of speed. |
| RenderSmoothness | Double | Gets or sets the smoothness of shaded, rendered, and hidden line–removed objects. The value of this property is stored in the FACETRES system variable. The initial value for this property is 0.5. Values less than or equal to 1 increase performance. |
| SegmentPerPolyline | Integer | Gets or sets the number of line segments for each polyline curve. The value of this property is stored in the SPLINESEGS system variable. The initial value is 8. |
| SolidFill | Boolean | Specifies whether or not multilines, traces, solids, hatches, and wide polylines are filled in. The value of this property is stored in the FILLMODE system variable. The default value is True. |
| TextFrameDisplay | Boolean | Specifies whether or not the frames for text objects are displayed rather than the text itself. The value of this property is stored in the QTEXTMODE system variable. The default is False. |
| XRefEdit | Boolean | Determines if the current drawing can be edited in place while being referenced by another user. The value of this property is stored in the XEDIT system variable. The default is True. |
| XRefLayerVisibility | Boolean | Specifies whether or not Xref-dependent layers are visible and whether nested XRef path changes are saved. If True, XRef-dependent layer changes made in the current drawing take precedence (default). If False, the layer table as stored in the reference drawing (XRef) takes precedence. The value of this property is stored in the VISRETAIN system variable. |

# AcadDictionaries Collection

The AcadDictionaries collection contains all the dictionaries in the drawing. Although this collection inherits a Delete method, you can't actually delete it. If you need to delete a specific dictionary, use the Delete method found in the AcadDictionary object. There's no limit to the number of dictionaries you can create in your drawing. However, there can be only one instance of the AcadDictionaries collection, which is predefined for each drawing. You can make multiple references to it by using the Dictionaries property.

## AcadDictionaries Collection Methods

In addition to the methods inherited from the AcadObject object, the AcadDictionaries collection supports the following methods.

| NAME | RETURNS | DESCRIPTION |
|------|---------|-------------|
| Add | AcadDictionary | Creates a member object and adds it to the collection. Parameter: Name As String. |
| Item | AcadObject | Gets the member object at a given index in a collection. Parameter: Index As Variant (an Integer or a String). If the value for Index is a String, it must match an existing object name in the collection. |

## AcadDictionaries Collection Properties

The AcadDictionaries collection supports the Count property, the common Application property, and the properties inherited from the AcadObject object. It supports no other properties.

**NOTE** *Because this collection inherits from* AcadObject, *it supports the* Modified *event.*

## AcadDictionary Object

The AcadDictionary object represents a container object for storing and retrieving objects, with associated string keywords by which they are referenced. A dictionary can contain any type of object, including other dictionaries. You can create new dictionaries, add entries to an existing dictionary, and get the keyword for a given object or the object for a given keyword. You can change the object associated with a given keyword or rename the keyword for a given object. However, it doesn't perform type checking of entries.

Note that this object doesn't represent the spell-checking dictionary, which is specified in the AcadPreferences object.

### AcadDictionary Object Methods

In addition to the methods inherited from the AcadObject object, the AcadDictionary object supports the following properties.

| NAME | RETURNS | DESCRIPTION |
| --- | --- | --- |
| AddObject | AcadObject | Adds an object to a named dictionary. Note that an entry replaces one already existing with the same name. Parameters: Keyword As String and ObjectName As String. |
| | | The first parameter is the keyword to be listed in the dictionary for this object. The second parameter is the name of the object to be stored. The ARX application defining the object must first be loaded with the LoadArx method. |
| AddXRecord | AcadXRecord | Creates an XRecord object in any dictionary. Parameter: Keyword As String. |
| GetName | String | Gets the keyword of an object in a dictionary. The parameter is the object's name. Parameter: Object As AcadObject. |
| GetObject | AcadObject | Gets the object in a dictionary, given the keyword for the object. Parameter: Name As String. |
| Item | AcadObject | Gets the member object at a given index in the dictionary. Parameter: Index As Variant (Integer or String). If the value for Index is a String, it must match an existing object name in the collection. |

| NAME | RETURNS | DESCRIPTION |
|---|---|---|
| Remove | AcadObject | Removes a named object from the dictionary, given its keyword. Parameter: `Name As String`. |
| Rename | | Renames the keyword of an item in the dictionary. Parameters: `OldName As String` and `NewName As String`. |
| Replace | | Replaces an item in the dictionary by a given item. This changes the object but retains the keyword. Parameters: `OldName As String` and `Obj As AcadObject`. |

## AcadDictionary Object Properties

In addition to the properties inherited from the `AcadObject` object and the common `Application` property, the `AcadDictionary` object supports the following properties.

| NAME | RETURNS | DESCRIPTION |
|---|---|---|
| Count | Integer | Gets the number of items in the dictionary. This property's value is read-only. |
| Name | String | Gets or sets the name of the dictionary. |

**NOTE** *Because this object inherits from* `AcadObject`, *it supports the* `Modified` *event.*

## AcadDim3PointAngular Object

The `AcadDim3PointAngular` object represents a dimension of the angular distance defined by three points. When creating a three-point angular dimension, AutoCAD draws the dimension line arc between the extension lines, which are drawn from the angle end points to the intersection of the dimension line arc. AutoCAD uses the location of the dimension line arc to choose between the minor and major angles specified by the angle vertex and extension lines. To create a three-point angular dimension, use the AddDim3PointAngular method of the AcadBlock, AcadModelSpace, or AcadPaperSpace object.

## AcadDim3PointAngular Object Methods

The AcadDim3PointAngular object inherits all the methods of the AcadEntity and AcadObject objects. It supports no other methods.

## AcadDim3PointAngular Object Properties

The AcadDim3PointAngular object inherits all the properties of the AcadEntity object, the AcadObject object, and the AcadDimension object, as well as the common Application property. It also supports the following properties.

| NAME | RETURNS | DESCRIPTION |
|---|---|---|
| AngleFormat | AcAngleUnits | Gets or sets the unit format for angles. The initial value is acDegrees. For the values of the AcAngleUnit enumerated type, see Appendix B. |
| AngleVertex | Variant | Gets or sets a 3-D set of coordinates representing the vertex. |
| Arrowhead1Block, Arrowhead2Block | String | Gets or sets the block used as the custom arrowhead at the first/second end of the dimension line. It overrides the value of the DIMBLK1 or DIMBLK2 system variable. |
| Arrowhead1Type, Arrowhead2Type | AcDimArrowhead Type | Gets or sets the type of arrowhead at the first/second end of the dimension line. For the values of the AcDimArrowheadType enumerated type, see Appendix B. |
| ArrowheadSize | Double | Gets or sets the size of the dimension line arrowheads, leader line arrowheads, and hook lines. The initial value for this property is 0.1800. |

| NAME | RETURNS | DESCRIPTION |
|------|---------|-------------|
| DimensionLineColor | AcColor | Gets or sets the color of the dimension lines. Use a color index number from 0 to 256, or one of the constants listed here: acByBlock (where AutoCAD draws objects in the default color) or acByLayer (where AutoCAD draws objects in the color specified for the layer). For a list of possible values for the AcColor enumerated type, see Appendix B. |
| DimensionLineWeight | AcLineWeight | Gets or sets the lineweight of the dimension lines. It overrides the value of the DIMLWD system variable. For a list of possible values for the AcLineWeight enumerated type, see Appendix B. |
| DimLine1Suppress, DimLine2Suppress | Boolean | Gets or sets whether or not the first/second dimension line is suppressed. It overrides the value of the DIMSD1 or DIMSD2 system variable. The initial value for this property is False. When this property is set to True, the display of the dimension line and arrowhead between the first extension line and the text is suppressed. |
| DimLineInside | Boolean | Gets or sets whether or not the dimension lines are only displayed inside the extension lines. It overrides the value of the DIMSOXD system variable. The initial value for this property is False. |
| ExtensionLineColor | AcColor | Gets or sets the color of the extension lines. Use a color index number from 0 to 256, or one of the constants listed here: acByBlock (where AutoCAD draws objects in the default color), acByLayer (where AutoCAD draws objects in the color specified for the layer), or the AcColor enumerated type (see Appendix B). It overrides the value of the DIMCLRE system variable. |

| NAME | RETURNS | DESCRIPTION |
|------|---------|-------------|
| ExtensionLineExtend | Double | Gets or sets the distance that the extension line extends beyond the dimension line. It overrides the value of the DIMEXE system variable. The initial value for this property is 0.1800. |
| ExtensionLineOffset | Double | Gets or sets the distance that the extension lines are offset from the origin points. It overrides the value of the DIMEXO system variable. The initial value for this property is 0.0625. |
| ExtensionLineWeight | AcLineWeight | Gets or sets the lineweight of the extension lines. It overrides the value of the DIMLWE system variable. For a list of possible values for the AcLineWeight enumerated type, see Appendix B. |
| ExtLine1EndPoint, ExtLine2EndPoint | Variant | Gets or sets the end point of the first/second extension line. |
| ExtLine1Suppress, ExtLine2Suppress | Boolean | Gets or sets whether the first/second extension line is suppressed. It overrides the value of the DIMSE1 or DIMSE2 system variable. The initial value for this property is False. |
| Fit | AcDimFit | Gets or sets whether text and arrowheads are placed inside or outside extension lines given the availability of space between the extension lines. This property sets priorities for moving text and arrowheads when space isn't available to fit both within the extension lines. It overrides the value of the DIMAFIT system variable. The initial value for this property is acBestFit. For a list of the possible values, see Appendix B. |

| NAME | RETURNS | DESCRIPTION |
|---|---|---|
| ForceLineInside | Boolean | Gets or sets whether or not a dimension line is drawn between the extension lines when the text is outside the extension lines. It overrides the value of the DIMTOFL system variable. The initial value for this property is False. |
| HorizontalText-Position | AcDimHorizontal-Justification | Gets or sets the horizontal position of the text. For a list of possible values for the AcDimHorizontalJustification enumerated type, see Appendix B. |
| Measurement | Double | Gets the measurement for the dimension. For angular dimensions, this property overrides the value for the DIMAUNIT system variable. This property's value is read-only. |
| TextInside | Boolean | Gets or sets whether the text appears inside the extension lines. It overrides the value of DIMTIX system variable. The initial value for this property is True. If False, AutoCAD places it inside if there is room. |
| TextInsideAlign, TextOutsideAlign | Boolean | Gets or sets the position of any text inside/outside the extension lines. The values for these properties override the values of the DIMTIH or DIMTOH system variable, respectively. The initial value for this property is True. The TextInsideAlign property is only available when the TextInside property is set to True. |
| TextPrecision | AcDimPrecision | Gets or sets the precision of the text. For the possible values for the AcDimPrecision enumerated type, see Appendix B. |

**NOTE** *Because this object inherits from* AcadObject, *it supports the* Modified *event.*

# AcadDimAligned Object

The AcadDimAligned object represents a linear dimension, measuring the distance between two points, that's displayed parallel to the points being measured. In aligned dimensions, the dimension line is parallel to the extension line origins. The extension line origins are specified using the ExtLine1Point and ExtLine2Point properties. The AcadDimAligned object is created using the AddDimAligned method of the AcadBlock, AcadModelSpace, or AcadPaperSpace objects.

## AcadDimAligned Object Methods

The AcadDimAligned object inherits all the methods of the AcadEntity and AcadObject objects. It supports no other methods.

## AcadDimAligned Object Properties

The AcadDimAligned object inherits all the properties of the AcadEntity object, the AcadObject object, and the AcadDimension object, as well as the common Application property. It also supports the following properties.

| NAME | RETURNS | DESCRIPTION |
| --- | --- | --- |
| AltRoundDistance | Double | Gets or sets the rounding of alternative units, if the AltUnits property is turned on. This property, and the two that follow, all override the value of the DIMALTZ system variable. |
| AltSuppressLeadingZeros | Boolean | Gets or sets whether leading zeros in alternative dimension values are suppressed. The initial value for this property is False. |
| AltSuppressTrailingZeros | Boolean | Gets or sets whether trailing zeros in alternative dimension values are suppressed. The initial value for this property is False. |
| AltSuppressZeroFeet, AltSuppressZeroInches | Boolean | Gets or sets whether a zero foot/inches measurement is suppressed in alternative dimension values. Both properties change the value of the DIMALTZ system variable. The initial value for this property is False. |

| NAME | RETURNS | DESCRIPTION |
| --- | --- | --- |
| AltTextPrefix, AltTextSuffix | String | Gets or sets a prefix/suffix for the alternative dimension measurement. Both properties override the value of the DIMAPOST system variable. The initial value for this property is a NULL string. To turn off an established prefix, set this property equal to a single period (.). |
| AltTolerancePrecision | AcDimPrecision | Gets or sets the precision of tolerance values in alternative dimensions. The initial value for this property is acDimPrecisionTwo. This property is only available when the ToleranceDisplay property is set to any value other than acTolNone, and it overrides the value of the DIMTDEC system variable. For a list of the values for the AcDimPrecision enumerated type, see Appendix B. |
| AltTolerance-SuppressLeadingZeros | Boolean | Gets or sets whether leading zeros are suppressed in alternative dimension values. This property, and the three that follow, all override the DIMALTTZ system variable. The initial value for this property is False. |
| AltTolerance-SuppressTrailingZeros | Boolean | Gets or sets whether trailing zeros are suppressed in alternative dimension values. The initial value for this property is False. |
| AltTolerance-SuppressZeroFeet | Boolean | Gets or sets whether a zero foot measurement is suppressed in alternative tolerance values. The initial value for this property is False. |
| AltTolerance-SuppressZeroInches | Boolean | Gets or sets whether a zero inch measurement is suppressed in alternative tolerance values. The initial value for this property is False. |
| AltUnits | Boolean | Gets or sets whether or not alternative units dimensioning is enabled. It overrides the value of the DIMALT system variable. |
| AltUnitsFormat | AcDimUnits | Gets or sets the units format for alternative units. The initial value for this property is acDimDecimal. It overrides the value of the DIMALTU system variable. For a list of possible values for the AcDimUnits enumerated type, see Appendix B. |

| NAME | RETURNS | DESCRIPTION |
|------|---------|-------------|
| AltUnitsPrecision | AcDimPrecision | Gets or sets the number of decimal places in alternative units. It overrides the value of the DIMALTD system variable. For a list of possible values for the AcDimPrecision enumerated type, see Appendix B. |
| AltUnitsScale | Double | Gets or sets the scale factor for alternative units. If the AltUnits property is turned on, this property multiplies linear dimensions by a factor to produce a value in an alternate system of measurement. The initial value represents the number of millimeters in an inch. It overrides the value of the DIMALTF system variable. |
| Arrowhead1Block, Arrowhead2Block | String | Gets or sets the block used as the custom arrowhead at the first/second end of the dimension line. It overrides the value of the DIMBLK1 or DIMBLK2 system variable. |
| Arrowhead1Type, Arrowhead2Type | AcDimArrowheadType | Gets or sets the type of arrowhead at the first/second end of the dimension line. For a list of possible values for the AcDimArrowheadType enumerated type, see Appendix B. |
| ArrowheadSize | Double | Gets or sets the size of the dimension line arrowheads, leader line arrowheads, and hook lines. It overrides the value of the DIMASZ system variable. The initial value for this property is 0.1800. |
| DimensionLineColor | AcColor | Gets or sets the color of the dimension lines. Use a color index number from 0 to 256, or one of the constants listed here: acByBlock (where AutoCAD draws objects in the default color) or acByLayer (where AutoCAD draws objects in the color specified for the layer). For a list of possible values for the AcColor enumerated type, see Appendix B. |

| NAME | RETURNS | DESCRIPTION |
|------|---------|-------------|
| DimensionLineExtend | Double | Gets or sets the distance the dimension line extends beyond the extension line when oblique strokes rather than arrowheads are used. It overrides the value of the DIMDLE system variable. The initial value for this property is 0.0000. |
| DimensionLineWeight | AcLineWeight | Gets or sets the lineweight of the dimension lines. It overrides the value of the DIMLWD system variable. For a list of possible values for the AcLineWeight enumerated type, see Appendix B. |
| DimLine1Suppress, DimLine2Suppress | Boolean | Gets or sets whether or not the first/second dimension line is suppressed. It overrides the value of the DIMSD1 or DIMSD2 system variable. The initial value for this property is False. When this property is set to True, the display of the dimension line and arrowhead between the first extension line and the text is suppressed. |
| DimLineInside | Boolean | Gets or sets whether or not the dimension lines are only displayed inside the extension lines. It overrides the value of the DIMSOXD system variable. The initial value for this property is False. |
| ExtensionLineColor | AcColor | Gets or sets the color of the extension lines. Use a color index number from 0 to 256, or one of the constants listed here: acByBlock (where AutoCAD draws objects in the default color), acByLayer (where AutoCAD draws objects in the color specified for the layer), or the AcColor enumerated type (see Appendix B). It overrides the value of the DIMCLRE system variable. |
| ExtensionLineExtend | Double | Gets or sets the distance that the extension line extends beyond the dimension line. It overrides the value of the DIMEXE system variable. The initial value for this property is 0.1800. |
| ExtensionLineOffset | Double | Gets or sets the distance that the extension lines are offset from the origin points. It overrides the value of the DIMEXO system variable. The initial value for this property is 0.0625. |

| NAME | RETURNS | DESCRIPTION |
| --- | --- | --- |
| ExtensionLineWeight | AcLineWeight | Gets or sets the lineweight of the extension lines. It overrides the value of the DIMLWE system variable. For a list of possible values for the AcLineWeight enumerated type, see Appendix B. |
| ExtLine1EndPoint, ExtLine2EndPoint | Variant | Gets or sets the end point of the first/second extension line. |
| ExtLine1Suppress, ExtLine2Suppress | Boolean | Gets or sets whether the first/second extension line is suppressed. It overrides the value of the DIMSE1 or DIMSE2 system variables. The initial value for this property is False. |
| Fit | AcDimFit | Gets or sets whether text and arrowheads are placed inside or outside extension lines given the availability of space between the extension lines. This property sets priorities for moving text and arrowheads when space isn't available to fit both within the extension lines. It overrides the value of the DIMAFIT system variable. The initial value for this property is acBestFit. For a list of the possible values, see Appendix B. |
| ForceLineInside | Boolean | Gets or sets whether or not a dimension line is drawn between the extension lines when the text is outside the extension lines. It overrides the value of the DIMTOFL system variable. The initial value for this property is False. |
| FractionFormat | AcDimFractionType | Gets or sets the formats of fractional values. It overrides the value of the DIMFRAC system variable. This property is used when the UnitsFormat property is set to acDimLArchitectural or acDimLFractional. Possible values: acHorizontal, acDiagonal, and acNotStacked. |

| NAME | RETURNS | DESCRIPTION |
| --- | --- | --- |
| HorizontalTextPosition | AcDimHorizontal-Justification | Gets or sets the horizontal position of the text. It overrides the value of the DIMJUST system variable. For a list of possible values for the AcDimHorizontalJustification enumerated type, see Appendix B. |
| LinearScaleFactor | Double | Gets or sets the global scale factor for linear dimensioning measurements. It overrides the value of the DIMLFAC system variable. The initial value for this property is 1.0000. When LinearScaleFactor is assigned a negative value, the factor is only applied in paper space. |
| Measurement | Double | Gets the measurement for the dimension. This property overrides the value for the DIMLUNIT system variable. This property's value is read-only. |
| PrimaryUnitsPrecision | AcDimPrecision | Gets or sets the number of decimal places displayed for the primary units. For a list of possible values for the AcDimPrecision enumerated type, see Appendix B. |
| RoundDistance | Double | Gets or sets the rounding of units. It overrides the value of the DIMRND system variable. |
| SuppressZeroFeet | Boolean | Gets or sets whether a zero foot measurement is suppressed. It overrides the value of the DIMZIN system variable. The initial value for this property is False. |

| NAME | RETURNS | DESCRIPTION |
|------|---------|-------------|
| SuppressZeroInches | Boolean | Gets or sets whether a zero inch measurement is suppressed. It overrides the value of the DIMZIN system variable. The initial value for this property is False. |
| TextInside | Boolean | Gets or sets whether the text appears inside the extension lines. It overrides the value of DIMTIX system variable. The initial value for this property is True. If False, AutoCAD places it inside if there is room. |
| TextInsideAlign, TextOutsideAlign | Boolean | Gets or sets the position of any text inside/outside the extension lines. The values for these properties override the values of the DIMTIH or DIMTOH system variable, respectively. The initial value for this property is True. The TextInsideAlign property is only available when the TextInside property is set to True. |
| Tolerance-SuppressZeroFeet | Boolean | Gets or sets whether a zero foot measurement is suppressed in tolerance values. It overrides the value of the DIMZIN system variable. The initial value for this property is False. |
| Tolerance-SuppressZeroInches | Boolean | Gets or sets whether a zero inch measurement is suppressed in tolerance values. It overrides the value of the DIMZIN system variable. The initial value for this property is False. |
| UnitsFormat | AcDimLUnits | Gets or sets the unit format. The initial value for this property is acDimLDecimal, in which the format specified by the DecimalSeparator and PrimaryUnitsPrecision properties will be used to format the decimal value. For a list of possible values for the AcDimLUnits enumerated type, see Appendix B. |

**NOTE** *Because this object inherits from* AcadObject, *it supports the* Modified *event.*

# AcadDimAngular Object

The AcadDimAngular object represents a dimension of the angular distance between two lines or the angle of a circular arc. If you need extension lines, they'll be added automatically. The end points provided will be used as origin points for the extension lines. The AcadDimAngular object is created using the AddDimAngular method of the AcadBlock, AcadModelSpace, or AcadPaperSpace object.

## AcadDimAngular Object Methods

The AcadDimAngular object inherits all the methods of the AcadEntity and AcadObject objects. It supports no other methods.

## AcadDimAngular Object Properties

The AcadDimAngular object inherits all the properties of the AcadEntity object, the AcadObject object, and the AcadDimension object, as well as the common Application property. It also supports all the other properties supported by the AcadDim3PointAngular object *except* for the AngleVertex property. This object, however, has the following two extra properties.

| NAME | RETURNS | DESCRIPTION |
|---|---|---|
| ExtLine1StartPoint, ExtLine2StartPoint | Variant | Gets or sets the start point of the first/second extension line. |

 **NOTE** *Because this object inherits from* AcadObject, *it supports the* Modified *event.*

# AcadDimDiametric Object

The AcadDimDiametric object represents a dimension of the diameter of a circle or arc. The position of the text, set in the TextPosition property, determines the location of the dimension line. The AcadDimDiametric object is created using the AddDimDiametric method of the AcadBlock, AcadModelSpace, or AcadPaperSpace object.

## AcadDimDiametric Object Methods

The AcadDimDiametric object inherits all the properties of the AcadEntity and AcadObject objects. It supports no other methods.

## AcadDimDiametric Object Properties

The AcadDimDiametric object supports all the properties inherited from the AcadEntity object, the AcadObject object, and the AcadDimension object, as well as the common Application property. It also supports the following properties.

| NAME | RETURNS | DESCRIPTION |
| --- | --- | --- |
| AltRoundDistance | Double | Gets or sets the rounding of alternative units if the AltUnits property is turned on. This property and the two that follow override the value of the DIMALTZ system variable. |
| AltSuppressLeadingZeros | Boolean | Gets or sets whether leading zeros in alternative dimension values are suppressed. The initial value for this property is False. |
| AltSuppressTrailingZeros | Boolean | Gets or sets whether trailing zeros in alternative dimension values are suppressed. The initial value for this property is False. |
| AltSuppressZeroFeet, AltSuppressZeroInches | Boolean | Gets or sets whether a zero foot/inches measurement is suppressed in alternative dimension values. Both properties change the value of the DIMALTZ system variable. The initial value for this property is False. |
| AltTextPrefix, AltTextSuffix | String | Gets or sets a prefix/suffix for the alternative dimension measurement. Both properties override the value of the DIMAPOST system variable. The initial value for this property is a NULL string. To turn off an established prefix, set this property equal to a single period (.). |

| NAME | RETURNS | DESCRIPTION |
|------|---------|-------------|
| AltTolerancePrecision | AcDimPrecision | Gets or sets the precision of tolerance values in alternative dimensions. The initial value for this property is acDimPrecisionTwo. This property is only available when the ToleranceDisplay property is set to any value other than acTolNone, and it overrides the value of the DIMTDEC system variable. For a list of the values for the AcDimPrecision enumerated type, see Appendix B. |
| AltToleranceSuppress-LeadingZeros | Boolean | Gets or sets whether leading zeros are suppressed in alternative dimension values. This property and the three that follow override the DIMALTTZ system variable. The initial value for this property is False. |
| AltToleranceSuppress-TrailingZeros | Boolean | Gets or sets whether trailing zeros are suppressed in alternative dimension values. The initial value for this property is False. |
| AltToleranceSuppress-ZeroFeet | Boolean | Gets or sets whether a zero foot measurement is suppressed in alternative tolerance values. The initial value for this property is False. |
| AltToleranceSuppress-ZeroInches | Boolean | Gets or sets whether a zero inch measurement is suppressed in alternative tolerance values. The initial value for this property is False. |
| AltUnits | Boolean | Gets or sets whether or not alternative units dimensioning is enabled. It overrides the value of the DIMALT system variable. |
| AltUnitsFormat | AcDimUnits | Gets or sets the units format for alternative units. The initial value for this property is acDimDecimal. It overrides the value of the DIMALTU system variable. For a list of possible values for the AcDimUnits enumerated type, see Appendix B. |

| NAME | RETURNS | DESCRIPTION |
|---|---|---|
| AltUnitsPrecision | AcDimPrecision | Gets or sets the number of decimal places in alternative units. It overrides the value of the DIMALTD system variable. For a list of possible values for the AcDimPrecision enumerated type, see Appendix B. |
| AltUnitsScale | Double | Gets or sets the scale factor for alternative units. If the AltUnits property is turned on, this property multiplies linear dimensions by a factor to produce a value in an alternate system of measurement. The initial value represents the number of millimeters in an inch. It overrides the value of the DIMALTF system variable. |
| Arrowhead1Block, Arrowhead2Block | String | Gets or sets the block used as the custom arrowhead at the first/second end of the dimension line. It overrides the value of the DIMBLK1 or DIMBLK2 system variable. |
| Arrowhead1Type, Arrowhead2Type | AcDimArrowheadType | Gets or sets the type of arrowhead at the first/second end of the dimension line. For a list of possible values for the AcDimArrowheadType enumerated type, see Appendix B. |
| ArrowheadSize | Double | Gets or sets the size of the dimension line arrowheads, leader line arrowheads, and hook lines. It overrides the value of the DIMASZ system variable. The initial value for this property is 0.1800. |
| CenterMarkSize | Double | Gets or sets the size of the center mark. It overrides the value of the DIMCEN system variable. The initial value for this property is 0.0900. This property isn't available if the CenterType property is set to acCenterNone. |
| CenterType | AcDimCenterType | Gets or sets the type of the center mark. The center mark is visible only if you place the dimension line outside the circle or arc. It overrides the value of the DIMCEN system variable. For a list of possible values for the AcDimCenterType enumerated type, see Appendix B. |

| NAME | RETURNS | DESCRIPTION |
|------|---------|-------------|
| DimensionLineColor | AcColor | Gets or sets the color of the dimension lines. Use a color index number from 0 to 256 or one of the constants listed here: acByBlock (where AutoCAD draws objects in the default color) or acByLayer (where AutoCAD draws objects in the color specified for the layer). For a list of possible values for the AcColor enumerated type, see Appendix B. |
| DimensionLineWeight | AcLineWeight | Gets or sets the lineweight of the dimension lines. It overrides the value of the DIMLWD system variable. For a list of possible values for the AcLineWeight enumerated type, see Appendix B. |
| DimLine1Suppress, DimLine2Suppress | Boolean | Gets or sets whether or not the first/second dimension line is suppressed. It overrides the value of the DIMSD1 or DIMSD2 system variable. The initial value for this property is False. When this property is set to True, the display of the dimension line and arrowhead between the first extension line and the text is suppressed. |
| Fit | AcDimFit | Gets or sets whether text and arrowheads are placed inside or outside extension lines given the availability of space between the extension lines. This property sets priorities for moving text and arrowheads when space isn't available to fit both within the extension lines. It overrides the value of the DIMAFIT system variable. The initial value for this property is acBestFit. For a list of the possible values, see Appendix B. |
| ForceLineInside | Boolean | Gets or sets whether or not a dimension line is drawn between the extension lines when the text is outside the extension lines. It overrides the value of the DIMTOFL system variable. The initial value for this property is False. |

| NAME | RETURNS | DESCRIPTION |
|------|---------|-------------|
| FractionFormat | AcDimFractionType | Gets or sets the formats of fractional values. It overrides the value of the DIMFRAC system variable. This property is used when the UnitsFormat property is set to acDimLArchitectural or acDimLFractional. Possible values: acHorizontal, acDiagonal, and acNotStacked. |
| HorizontalTextPosition | AcDimHorizontal-Justification | Gets or sets the horizontal position of the text. For a list of possible values for the AcDimHorizontalJustification enumerated type, see Appendix B. |
| LeaderLength | Double | Sets the length of the leader. This property is write-only; it's used when the object is created and isn't stored. |
| LinearScaleFactor | Double | Gets or sets the global scale factor for linear dimensioning measurements. It overrides the value of the DIMLFAC system variable. The initial value for this property is 1.0000. When LinearScaleFactor is assigned a negative value, the factor is only applied in paper space. |
| Measurement | Double | Gets the measurement for the dimension. This property overrides the value for the DIMLUNIT system variable. This property's value is read-only. |
| PrimaryUnitsPrecision | AcDimPrecision | Gets or sets the number of decimal places displayed for the primary units. For a list of possible values for the AcDimPrecision enumerated type, see Appendix B. |
| RoundDistance | Double | Gets or sets the rounding of units. It overrides the value of the DIMRND system variable. |
| SuppressZeroFeet | Boolean | Gets or sets whether a zero foot measurement is suppressed. It overrides the value of the DIMZIN system variable. The initial value for this property is False. |

| NAME | RETURNS | DESCRIPTION |
|---|---|---|
| SuppressZeroInches | Boolean | Gets or sets whether a zero inch measurement is suppressed. It overrides the value of the DIMZIN system variable. The initial value for this property is False. |
| TextInside | Boolean | Gets or sets whether the text appears inside the extension lines. It overrides the value of DIMTIX system variable. The initial value for this property is True. If False, AutoCAD places it inside if there's room. |
| TextInsideAlign, TextOutsideAlign | Boolean | Gets or sets the position of any text inside/outside the extension lines. The values for these properties override the values of the DIMTIH and DIMTOH system variables, respectively. The initial value for this property is True. The TextInsideAlign property is only available when the TextInside property is set to True. |
| ToleranceSuppress-ZeroFeet | Boolean | Gets or sets whether a zero foot measurement is suppressed in tolerance values. It overrides the value of the DIMZIN system variable. The initial value for this property is False. |
| ToleranceSuppress-ZeroInches | Boolean | Gets or sets whether a zero inch measurement is suppressed in tolerance values. It overrides the value of the DIMZIN system variable. The initial value for this property is False. |
| UnitsFormat | AcDimLUnits | Gets or sets the unit format. The initial value for this property is acDimLDecimal, where the format specified by the DecimalSeparator and PrimaryUnitsPrecision properties will be used to format the decimal value. For a list of possible values for the AcDimLUnits enumerated type, see Appendix B. |

> **NOTE** *Because this object inherits from* AcadObject, *it supports the* Modified *event.*

## AcadDimOrdinate Object

The AcadDimOrdinate object represents a dimension of the absolute X or Y position of a point from the origin. Ordinate dimensions display the X or Y UCS coordinate of an object along with a simple leader line. The absolute value of the coordinate is used according to the prevailing standards for ordinate dimensions. To change the extension lines of an ordinate dimension, change the Rotation property and/or the TextPosition property. The extension lines will be recalculated to fit the new requirements. The AcadDimOrdinate object is created using the AddDimOrdinate method of the AcadBlock, AcadModelSpace, or AcadPaperSpace object.

### AcadDimOrdinate Object Methods

The AcadDimOrdinate object inherits all the methods of the AcadEntity and AcadObject objects. It supports no other methods.

### AcadDimOrdinate Object Properties

The AcadDimOrdinate object inherits all the properties of the AcadEntity object, the AcadObject object, and the AcadDimension object, as well as the common Application property. It also supports the following properties.

| NAME | RETURNS | DESCRIPTION |
|---|---|---|
| AltRoundDistance | Double | Gets or sets the rounding of alternative units if the AltUnits property is turned on. This property and the two that follow override the value of the DIMALTZ system variable. |
| AltSuppressLeadingZeros | Boolean | Gets or sets whether leading zeros in alternative dimension values are suppressed. The initial value for this property is False. |

| NAME | RETURNS | DESCRIPTION |
|------|---------|-------------|
| AltSuppressTrailingZeros | Boolean | Gets or sets whether trailing zeros in alternative dimension values are suppressed. The initial value for this property is False. |
| AltSuppressZeroFeet, AltSuppressZeroInches | Boolean | Gets or sets whether a zero foot/inches measurement is suppressed in alternative dimension values. Both properties change the value of the DIMALTZ system variable. The initial value for this property is False. |
| AltTextPrefix, AltTextSuffix | String | Gets or sets a prefix/suffix for the alternative dimension measurement. Both properties override the value of the DIMAPOST system variable. The initial value for this property is a NULL string. To turn off an established prefix, set this property equal to a single period (.). |
| AltTolerancePrecision | AcDimPrecision | Gets or sets the precision of tolerance values in alternative dimensions. The initial value for this property is acDimPrecisionTwo. This property is only available when the ToleranceDisplay property is set to any value other than acTolNone, and it overrides the value of the DIMTDEC system variable. For a list of the values for the AcDimPrecision enumerated type, see Appendix B. |
| AltToleranceSuppress-LeadingZeros | Boolean | Gets or sets whether leading zeros are suppressed in alternative dimension values. This property and the three that follow override the DIMALTTZ system variable. The initial value for this property is False. |
| AltToleranceSuppress-TrailingZeros | Boolean | Gets or sets whether trailing zeros are suppressed in alternative dimension values. The initial value for this property is False. |
| AltToleranceSuppress-ZeroFeet | Boolean | Gets or sets whether a zero foot measurement is suppressed in alternative tolerance values. The initial value for this property is False. |

| NAME | RETURNS | DESCRIPTION |
|------|---------|-------------|
| AltToleranceSuppress-ZeroInches | Boolean | Gets or sets whether a zero inch measurement is suppressed in alternative tolerance values. The initial value for this property is False. |
| AltUnits | Boolean | Gets or sets whether or not alternative units dimensioning is enabled. It overrides the value of the DIMALT system variable. |
| AltUnitsFormat | AcDimUnits | Gets or sets the units format for alternative units. The initial value for this property is acDimDecimal. It overrides the value of the DIMALTU system variable. For a list of possible values for the AcDimUnits enumerated type, see Appendix B. |
| AltUnitsPrecision | AcDimPrecision | Gets or sets the number of decimal places in alternative units. It overrides the value of the DIMALTD system variable. For a list of possible values for the AcDimPrecision enumerated type, see Appendix B. |
| AltUnitsScale | Double | Gets or sets the scale factor for alternative units. If the AltUnits property is turned on, this property multiplies linear dimensions by a factor to produce a value in an alternate system of measurement. The initial value represents the number of millimeters in an inch. It overrides the value of the DIMALTF system variable. |
| ArrowheadSize | Double | Gets or sets the size of the dimension line arrowheads, leader line arrowheads, and hook lines. It overrides the value of the DIMASZ system variable. The initial value for this property is 0.1800. |
| ExtensionLineColor | AcColor | Gets or sets the color of the extension lines. Use a color index number from 0 to 256 or one of the constants listed here: acByBlock (where AutoCAD draws objects in the default color), acByLayer (where AutoCAD draws objects in the color specified for the layer), or the AcColor enumerated type (see the AcadEntity object in Appendix B). It overrides the value of the DIMCLRE system variable. |

| NAME | RETURNS | DESCRIPTION |
|------|---------|-------------|
| ExtensionLineOffset | Double | Gets or sets the distance that the extension lines are offset from the origin points. It overrides the value of the DIMEXO system variable. The initial value for this property is 0.0625. |
| ExtensionLineWeight | AcLineWeight | Gets or sets the lineweight of the extension lines. It overrides the value of the DIMLWE system variable. For a list of possible values for the AcLineWeight enumerated type, see Appendix B. |
| FractionFormat | AcDimFractionType | Gets or sets the formats of fractional values. It overrides the value of the DIMFRAC system variable. This property is used when the UnitsFormat property is set to acDimLArchitectural or acDimLFractional. Possible values: acHorizontal, acDiagonal, and acNotStacked. |
| LinearScaleFactor | Double | Gets or sets the global scale factor for linear dimensioning measurements. It overrides the value of the DIMLFAC system variable. The initial value for this property is 1.0000. When LinearScaleFactor is assigned a negative value, the factor is only applied in paper space. |
| Measurement | Double | Gets the measurement for the dimension. This property overrides the value for the DIMLUNIT system variable. This property's value is read-only. |
| PrimaryUnitsPrecision | AcDimPrecision | Gets or sets the number of decimal places displayed for the primary units. For a list of possible values for the AcDimPrecision enumerated type, see Appendix B. |
| RoundDistance | Double | Gets or sets the rounding of units. It overrides the value of the DIMRND system variable. |
| SuppressZeroFeet | Boolean | Gets or sets whether a zero foot measurement is suppressed. It overrides the value of the DIMZIN system variable. The initial value for this property is False. |

| NAME | RETURNS | DESCRIPTION |
|---|---|---|
| SuppressZeroInches | Boolean | Gets or sets whether a zero inch measurement is suppressed. It overrides the value of the DIMZIN system variable. The initial value for this property is False. |
| TextInside | Boolean | Gets or sets whether the text appears inside the extension lines. It overrides the value of DIMTIX system variable. The initial value for this property is True. If False, AutoCAD places it inside if there's room. |
| TextInsideAlign, TextOutsideAlign | Boolean | Gets or sets the position of any text inside/outside the extension lines. The values for these properties override the values of the DIMTIH and DIMTOH system variables, respectively. The initial value for this property is True. The TextInsideAlign property is only available when the TextInside property is set to True. |
| ToleranceSuppress-ZeroFeet | Boolean | Gets or sets whether a zero foot measurement is suppressed in tolerance values. It overrides the value of the DIMZIN system variable. The initial value for this property is False. |
| ToleranceSuppress-ZeroInches | Boolean | Gets or sets whether a zero inch measurement is suppressed in tolerance values. It overrides the value of the DIMZIN system variable. The initial value for this property is False. |
| UnitsFormat | AcDimLUnits | Gets or sets the unit format. The initial value for this property is acDimLDecimal, where the format specified by the DecimalSeparator and PrimaryUnitsPrecision properties will be used to format the decimal value. For a list of possible values for the AcDimLUnits enumerated type, see Appendix B. |

**NOTE** *Because this object inherits from* AcadObject, *it supports the* Modified *event.*

## AcadDimRadial Object

The AcadDimRadial object represents a dimension of the radius of a circle or arc. The position of the text, set in the TextPosition property, determines the location of the dimension line. The AcadDimRadial object is created using the AddDimRadial method of the AcadBlock, AcadModelSpace, or AcadPaperSpace object.

### AcadDimRadial Object Methods

The AcadDimRadial object inherits all the methods of the AcadEntity and AcadObject objects. It supports no other methods.

### AcadDimRadial Object Properties

The AcadDimRadial object inherits all the properties of the AcadEntity object, the AcadObject object, and the AcadDimension object, as well as the common Application property. It also supports the following properties.

| NAME | RETURNS | DESCRIPTION |
| --- | --- | --- |
| AltRoundDistance | Double | Gets or sets the rounding of alternative units if the AltUnits property is turned on. This property and the two that follow override the value of the DIMALTZ system variable. |
| AltSuppressLeadingZeros | Boolean | Gets or sets whether leading zeros in alternative dimension values are suppressed. The initial value for this property is False. |
| AltSuppressTrailingZeros | Boolean | Gets or sets whether trailing zeros in alternative dimension values are suppressed. The initial value for this property is False. |
| AltSuppressZeroFeet, AltSuppressZeroInches | Boolean | Gets or sets whether a zero foot/inches measurement is suppressed in alternative dimension values. Both properties change the value of the DIMALTZ system variable. The initial value for this property is False. |

| NAME | RETURNS | DESCRIPTION |
|------|---------|-------------|
| AltTextPrefix, AltTextSuffix | String | Gets or sets a prefix/suffix for the alternative dimension measurement. Both properties override the value of the DIMAPOST system variable. The initial value for this property is a NULL string. To turn off an established prefix, set this property equal to a single period (.). |
| AltTolerancePrecision | AcDimPrecision | Gets or sets the precision of tolerance values in alternative dimensions. The initial value for this property is acDimPrecisionTwo. This property is only available when the ToleranceDisplay property is set to any value other than acTolNone, and it overrides the value of the DIMTDEC system variable. For a list of the values for the AcDimPrecision enumerated type, see Appendix B. |
| AltToleranceSuppress-LeadingZeros | Boolean | Gets or sets whether leading zeros are suppressed in alternative dimension values. This property and the three that follow override the DIMALTTZ system variable. The initial value for this property is False. |
| AltToleranceSuppress-TrailingZeros | Boolean | Gets or sets whether trailing zeros are suppressed in alternative dimension values. The initial value for this property is False. |
| AltToleranceSuppress-ZeroFeet | Boolean | Gets or sets whether a zero foot measurement is suppressed in alternative tolerance values. The initial value for this property is False. |
| AltToleranceSuppress-ZeroInches | Boolean | Gets or sets whether a zero inch measurement is suppressed in alternative tolerance values. The initial value for this property is False. |
| AltUnits | Boolean | Gets or sets whether or not alternative units dimensioning is enabled. It overrides the value of the DIMALT system variable. |

| NAME | RETURNS | DESCRIPTION |
|------|---------|-------------|
| AltUnitsFormat | AcDimUnits | Gets or sets the units format for alternative units. The initial value for this property is acDimDecimal. It overrides the value of the DIMALTU system variable. For a list of possible values for the AcDimUnits enumerated type, see Appendix B. |
| AltUnitsPrecision | AcDimPrecision | Gets or sets the number of decimal places in alternative units. It overrides the value of the DIMALTD system variable. For a list of possible values for the AcDimPrecision enumerated type, see Appendix B. |
| AltUnitsScale | Double | Gets or sets the scale factor for alternative units. If the AltUnits property is turned on, this property multiplies linear dimensions by a factor to produce a value in an alternate system of measurement. The initial value represents the number of millimeters in an inch. It overrides the value of the DIMALTF system variable. |
| ArrowheadBlock | String | Gets or sets the block used as the custom arrowhead. |
| ArrowheadSize | Double | Gets or sets the size of the dimension line arrowheads, leader line arrowheads, and hook lines. It overrides the value of the DIMASZ system variable. The initial value for this property is 0.1800. |
| ArrowheadType | AcDimArrowheadType | Gets or sets the type of the arrowhead. It overrides the value of the DIMLDRBLK system variable. For a list of possible values for the AcDimArrowheadType enumerated type, see Appendix B. |
| CenterMarkSize | Double | Gets or sets the size of the center mark. The initial value for this property is 0.0900. This property isn't available if the CenterType property is set to acCenterNone. |

| NAME | RETURNS | DESCRIPTION |
|------|---------|-------------|
| CenterType | AcDimCenterType | Gets or sets the type of the center mark. The center mark is visible only if you place the dimension line outside the circle or arc. It overrides the value of the DIMCEN system variable. For a list of possible values for the AcDimCenterType enumerated type, see Appendix B. |
| DimensionLineColor | AcColor | Gets or sets the color of the dimension lines. Use a color index number from 0 to 256 or one of the constants listed here: acByBlock (where AutoCAD draws objects in the default color) or acByLayer (where AutoCAD draws objects in the color specified for the layer). For a list of possible values for the AcColor enumerated type, see Appendix B. |
| DimensionLineWeight | AcLineWeight | Gets or sets the lineweight of the dimension lines. It overrides the value of the DIMLWD system variable. For a list of possible values for the AcLineWeight enumerated type, see Appendix B. |
| DimLineSuppress | Boolean | Specifies whether or not the dimension line is suppressed. It overrides the value of the DIMSD2 system variable. The initial value for this property is False. When this property is set to True, the display of the dimension line and arrowhead between the extension line and the text is suppressed. |
| Fit | AcDimFit | Gets or sets whether text and arrowheads are placed inside or outside extension lines given the availability of space between the extension lines. This property sets priorities for moving text and arrowheads when space isn't available to fit both within the extension lines. It overrides the value of the DIMAFIT system variable. The initial value for this property is acBestFit. For a list of the possible values, see Appendix B. |

| NAME | RETURNS | DESCRIPTION |
|---|---|---|
| ForceLineInside | Boolean | Gets or sets whether or not a dimension line is drawn between the extension lines when the text is outside the extension lines. It overrides the value of the DIMTOFL system variable. The initial value for this property is False. |
| FractionFormat | AcDimFractionType | Gets or sets the formats of fractional values. It overrides the value of the DIMFRAC system variable. This property is used when the UnitsFormat property is set to acDimLArchitectural or acDimLFractional. Possible values: acHorizontal, acDiagonal, and acNotStacked. |
| HorizontalTextPosition | AcDimHorizontal-Justification | Gets or sets the horizontal position of the text. For a list of possible values for the AcDimHorizontalJustification enumerated type, see Appendix B. |
| LeaderLength | Double | Sets the length of the leader. This property is write-only; it's used when the object is created and isn't stored. |
| LinearScaleFactor | Double | Gets or sets the global scale factor for linear dimensioning measurements. It overrides the value of the DIMLFAC system variable. The initial value for this property is 1.0000. When LinearScaleFactor is assigned a negative value, the factor is only applied in paper space. |
| Measurement | Double | Gets the measurement for the dimension. This property overrides the value for the DIMLUNIT system variable. This property's value is read-only. |
| PrimaryUnitsPrecision | AcDimPrecision | Gets or sets the number of decimal places displayed for the primary units. For a list of possible values for the AcDimPrecision enumerated type, see Appendix B. |
| RoundDistance | Double | Gets or sets the rounding of units. It overrides the value of the DIMRND system variable. |

| NAME | RETURNS | DESCRIPTION |
|------|---------|-------------|
| SuppressZeroFeet | Boolean | Gets or sets whether a zero foot measurement is suppressed. It overrides the value of the DIMZIN system variable. The initial value for this property is False. |
| SuppressZeroInches | Boolean | Gets or sets whether a zero inch measurement is suppressed. It overrides the value of the DIMZIN system variable. The initial value for this property is False. |
| TextInside | Boolean | Gets or sets whether the text appears inside the extension lines. It overrides the value of the DIMTIX system variable. The initial value for this property is True. If False, AutoCAD places it inside if there's room. |
| TextInsideAlign, TextOutsideAlign | Boolean | Gets or sets the position of any text inside/outside the extension lines. The values for these properties override the values of the DIMTIH and DIMTOH system variables, respectively. The initial value for this property is True. The TextInsideAlign property is only available when the TextInside property is set to True. |
| ToleranceSuppressZeroFeet | Boolean | Gets or sets whether a zero foot measurement is suppressed in tolerance values. It overrides the value of the DIMZIN system variable. The initial value for this property is False. |
| ToleranceSuppress-ZeroInches | Boolean | Gets or sets whether a zero inch measurement is suppressed in tolerance values. It overrides the value of the DIMZIN system variable. The initial value for this property is False. |
| UnitsFormat | AcDimLUnits | Gets or sets the unit format. The initial value for this property is acDimLDecimal, where the format specified by the DecimalSeparator and PrimaryUnitsPrecision properties will be used to format the decimal value. For a list of possible values for the AcDimLUnits enumerated type, see Appendix B. |

**NOTE** *Because this object inherits from* AcadObject, *it supports the* Modified *event.*

## AcadDimRotated Object

The AcadDimRotated object represents a dimension that measures the distance between two points and is displayed at a given rotation. To change the extension lines of a rotated dimension, change the Rotation property and/or the TextPosition property. The extension lines will be recalculated to fit the new requirements. The AcadDimRotated object is created using the AddCircle method of the AcadBlock, AcadModelSpace, or AcadPaperSpace object.

### AcadDimRotated Object Methods

The AcadDimRotated object inherits all the methods of the AcadEntity and AcadObject objects. It supports no other methods.

### AcadDimRotated Object Properties

The AcadDimRadial object inherits all the properties of the AcadEntity object, the AcadObject object, and the AcadDimension object, as well as the common Application property. It also supports the following properties.

| NAME | RETURNS | DESCRIPTION |
| --- | --- | --- |
| AltRoundDistance | Double | Gets or sets the rounding of alternative units if the AltUnits property is turned on. This property and the two that follow override the value of the DIMALTZ system variable. |
| AltSuppressLeadingZeros | Boolean | Gets or sets whether leading zeros in alternative dimension values are suppressed. The initial value for this property is False. |
| AltSuppressTrailingZeros | Boolean | Gets or sets whether trailing zeros in alternative dimension values are suppressed. The initial value for this property is False. |

| NAME | RETURNS | DESCRIPTION |
|------|---------|-------------|
| AltSuppressZeroFeet, AltSuppressZeroInches | Boolean | Gets or sets whether a zero foot/inches measurement is suppressed in alternative dimension values. Both properties change the value of the DIMALTZ system variable. The initial value for this property is False. |
| AltTextPrefix, AltTextSuffix | String | Gets or sets a prefix/suffix for the alternative dimension measurement. Both properties override the value of the DIMAPOST system variable. The initial value for this property is a NULL string. To turn off an established prefix, set this property equal to a single period (.). |
| AltTolerancePrecision | AcDimPrecision | Gets or sets the precision of tolerance values in alternative dimensions. The initial value for this property is acDimPrecisionTwo. This property is only available when the ToleranceDisplay property is set to any value other than acTolNone, and it overrides the value of the DIMTDEC system variable. For a list of the values for the AcDimPrecision enumerated type, see Appendix B. |
| AltToleranceSuppress-LeadingZeros | Boolean | Gets or sets whether leading zeros are suppressed in alternative dimension values. This property and the three that follow override the DIMALTTZ system variable. The initial value for this property is False. |
| AltToleranceSuppress-TrailingZeros | Boolean | Gets or sets whether trailing zeros are suppressed in alternative dimension values. The initial value for this property is False. |
| AltToleranceSuppress-ZeroFeet | Boolean | Gets or sets whether a zero foot measurement is suppressed in alternative tolerance values. The initial value for this property is False. |
| AltToleranceSuppress-ZeroInches | Boolean | Gets or sets whether a zero inch measurement is suppressed in alternative tolerance values. The initial value for this property is False. |
| AltUnits | Boolean | Gets or sets whether or not alternative units dimensioning is enabled. It overrides the value of the DIMALT system variable. |

| NAME | RETURNS | DESCRIPTION |
|------|---------|-------------|
| AltUnitsFormat | AcDimUnits | Gets or sets the units format for alternative units. The initial value for this property is acDimDecimal. It overrides the value of the DIMALTU system variable. For a list of possible values for the AcDimUnits enumerated type, see Appendix B. |
| AltUnitsPrecision | AcDimPrecision | Gets or sets the number of decimal places in alternative units. It overrides the value of the DIMALTD system variable. For a list of possible values for the AcDimPrecision enumerated type, see Appendix B. |
| AltUnitsScale | Double | Gets or sets the scale factor for alternative units. If the AltUnits property is turned on, this property multiplies linear dimensions by a factor to produce a value in an alternate system of measurement. The initial value represents the number of millimeters in an inch. It overrides the value of the DIMALTF system variable. |
| Arrowhead1Block, Arrowhead2Block | String | Gets or sets the block used as the custom arrowhead at the first/second end of the dimension line. It overrides the value of the DIMBLK1 or DIMBLK2 system variable. |
| Arrowhead1Type, Arrowhead2Type | AcDimArrowheadType | Gets or sets the type of arrowhead at the first/second end of the dimension line. For a list of possible values for the AcDimArrowheadType enumerated type, see Appendix B. |
| ArrowheadSize | Double | Gets or sets the size of the dimension line arrowheads, leader line arrowheads, and hook lines. It overrides the value of the DIMASZ system variable. The initial value for this property is 0.1800. |

| NAME | RETURNS | DESCRIPTION |
|------|---------|-------------|
| DimensionLineColor | AcColor | Gets or sets the color of the dimension lines. Use a color index number from 0 to 256 or one of the constants listed here: acByBlock (where AutoCAD draws objects in the default color) or acByLayer (where AutoCAD draws objects in the color specified for the layer). For a list of possible values for the AcColor enumerated type, see Appendix B. |
| DimensionLineExtend | Double | Gets or sets the distance the dimension line extends beyond the extension line when oblique strokes rather than arrowheads are used. It overrides the value of the DIMDLE system variable. The initial value for this property is 0.0000. |
| DimensionLineWeight | AcLineWeight | Gets or sets the lineweight of the dimension lines. It overrides the value of the DIMLWD system variable. For a list of possible values for the AcLineWeight enumerated type, see Appendix B. |
| DimLine1Suppress, DimLine2Suppress | Boolean | Gets or sets whether or not the first/second dimension line is suppressed. It overrides the value of the DIMSD1 or DIMSD2 system variable. The initial value for this property is False. When this property is set to True, the display of the dimension line and arrowhead between the first extension line and the text is suppressed. |
| DimLineInside | Boolean | Gets or sets whether or not the dimension lines are only displayed inside the extension lines. It overrides the value of the DIMSOXD system variable. The initial value for this property is False. |

| NAME | RETURNS | DESCRIPTION |
| --- | --- | --- |
| ExtensionLineColor | AcColor | Gets or sets the color of the extension lines. Use a color index number from 0 to 256 or one of the constants listed here: acByBlock (where AutoCAD draws objects in the default color), acByLayer (where AutoCAD draws objects in the color specified for the layer), or the AcColor enumerated type (see Appendix B). It overrides the value of the DIMCLRE system variable. |
| ExtensionLineExtend | Double | Gets or sets the distance that the extension line extends beyond the dimension line. It overrides the value of the DIMEXE system variable. The initial value for this property is 0.1800. |
| ExtensionLineOffset | Double | Gets or sets the distance that the extension lines are offset from the origin points. It overrides the value of the DIMEXO system variable. The initial value for this property is 0.0625. |
| ExtensionLineWeight | AcLineWeight | Gets or sets the lineweight of the extension lines. It overrides the value of the DIMLWE system variable. For a list of possible values for the AcLineWeight enumerated type, see Appendix B. |
| ExtLine1Suppress, ExtLine2Suppress | Boolean | Gets or sets whether or not the first/second extension line is suppressed. It overrides the value of the DIMSE1 or DIMSE2 system variables. The initial value for this property is False. |
| Fit | AcDimFit | Gets or sets whether text and arrowheads are placed inside or outside extension lines given the availability of space between the extension lines. This property sets priorities for moving text and arrowheads when space isn't available to fit both within the extension lines. It overrides the value of the DIMAFIT system variable. The initial value for this property is acBestFit. For a list of the possible values, see Appendix B. |

| NAME | RETURNS | DESCRIPTION |
|------|---------|-------------|
| ForceLineInside | Boolean | Gets or sets whether or not a dimension line is drawn between the extension lines when the text is outside the extension lines. It overrides the value of the DIMTOFL system variable. The initial value for this property is False. |
| FractionFormat | AcDimFractionType | Gets or sets the formats of fractional values. It overrides the value of the DIMFRAC system variable. This property is used when the UnitsFormat property is set to acDimLArchitectural or acDimLFractional. Possible values: acHorizontal, acDiagonal, and acNotStacked. |
| HorizontalTextPosition | AcDimHorizontal-Justification | Gets or sets the horizontal position of the text. It overrides the value of the DIMJUST system variable. For a list of possible values for the AcDimHorizontalJustification enumerated type, see Appendix B. |
| LinearScaleFactor | Double | Gets or sets the global scale factor for linear dimensioning measurements. It overrides the value of the DIMLFAC system variable. The initial value for this property is 1.0000. When LinearScaleFactor is assigned a negative value, the factor is only applied in paper space. |
| Measurement | Double | Gets the measurement for the dimension. This property overrides the value for the DIMLUNIT system variable. This property's value is read-only. |
| PrimaryUnitsPrecision | AcDimPrecision | Gets or sets the number of decimal places displayed for the primary units. For a list of possible values for the AcDimPrecision enumerated type, see Appendix B. |
| RoundDistance | Double | Gets or sets the rounding of units. It overrides the value of the DIMRND system variable. |

| NAME | RETURNS | DESCRIPTION |
|------|---------|-------------|
| SuppressZeroFeet | Boolean | Gets or sets whether a zero foot measurement is suppressed. It overrides the value of the DIMZIN system variable. The initial value for this property is False. |
| SuppressZeroInches | Boolean | Gets or sets whether a zero inch measurement is suppressed. It overrides the value of the DIMZIN system variable. The initial value for this property is False. |
| TextInside | Boolean | Gets or sets whether the text appears inside the extension lines. It overrides the value of DIMTIX system variable. The initial value for this property is True. If False, AutoCAD places it inside if there's room. |
| TextInsideAlign, TextOutsideAlign | Boolean | Gets or sets the position of any text inside/outside the extension lines. The values for these properties override the values of the DIMTIH and DIMTOH system variables, respectively. The initial value for this property is True. The TextInsideAlign property is only available when the TextInside property is set to True. |
| ToleranceSuppressZeroFeet | Boolean | Gets or sets whether a zero foot measurement is suppressed in tolerance values. It overrides the value of the DIMZIN system variable. The initial value for this property is False. |
| ToleranceSuppress-ZeroInches | Boolean | Gets or sets whether a zero inch measurement is suppressed in tolerance values. It overrides the value of the DIMZIN system variable. The initial value for this property is False. |
| UnitsFormat | AcDimLUnits | Gets or sets the unit format. The initial value for this property is acDimLDecimal, where the format specified by the DecimalSeparator and PrimaryUnitsPrecision properties will be used to format the decimal value. For a list of possible values for the AcDimLUnits enumerated type, see Appendix B. |

**NOTE** *Because this object inherits from* AcadObject, *it supports the* Modified *event.*

## AcadDimStyle Object

The AcadDimStyle object represents a group of dimension settings, which determine the appearance of new dimensions created in the drawing. It is created by the Add method of the AcadDimStyles collection and is activated through the ActiveDimStyle property of the Document object. To change the style of a dimension, use the StyleName property found on the dimension. To control the settings of the current document overrides, use the dimensioning system variables.

When you change a dimensioning system variable, you aren't changing the active dimension style itself. Rather, you're setting a document override for the dimension style, which means that all newly created dimensions will still be created with the active dimension style. They won't reflect the overrides from the system variables until the active dimension style is updated. To change the settings of any dimension style, use the CopyFrom method. Dimensions created via ActiveX use the active dimension style only. To apply the system overrides for dimensions created by ActiveX, use the CopyFrom method to copy the dimension style from the document to the active dimension style.

### AcadDimStyle Object Methods

In addition to the methods inherited from the AcadObject object, the AcadDimStyle object supports the following method.

| NAME | DESCRIPTION |
| --- | --- |
| CopyFrom | Copies the dimension style data from a source object, which can be a document, dimension, or another dimension style. Parameter: StyleSource As Object. |
| | If StyleSource is an AcadDocument object, this method copies the active dimension style settings for the drawing plus any drawing overrides. If it's a dimension, an AcadTolerance object, or an AcadLeader object, this method copies the style for that object plus any object overrides. If StyleSource is an AcadDimStyle object, then the style data from that dimension style is copied. |

### AcadDimStyle Object Properties

In addition to the properties inherited from the AcadObject object and the common Application property, the AcadDimStyle object supports the following property.

| NAME | RETURNS | DESCRIPTION |
| --- | --- | --- |
| Name | String | Gets or sets the object's name |

 **NOTE** *Because this object inherits from* AcadObject, *it supports the* Modified *event.*

## AcadDimStyles Collection

The AcadDimStyles collection contains all the dimension styles in the drawing. Although this collection inherits a Delete method, you can't actually delete it. If you need to delete a specific dimension style, use the Delete method found in the AcadDimStyle object. There's no limit to the number of dimension styles you can create in your drawing. However, there can be only one instance of the AcadDimStyles collection, which is predefined for each drawing. You can make multiple references to it by using the DimStyles property.

### AcadDimStyles Collection Methods

In addition to the methods inherited from the AcadObject object, the AcadDimStyles collection supports the following methods.

| NAME | RETURNS | DESCRIPTION |
| --- | --- | --- |
| Add | AcadDimStyle | Creates an AcadDimStyle object and adds it to the collection. Parameter: Name As String. |
| Item | AcadDimStyle | Gets the member object at a given index in the collection. Parameter: Index As Variant (Integer or String). If the Index value is a String, it must match an existing style definition. |

## AcadDimStyles Collection Properties

The AcadDimStyles collection supports the Count property, the common Application property, and the properties inherited from the AcadObject object. It supports no other properties.

 **NOTE** *Because this collection inherits from* AcadObject, *it supports the* Modified *event.*

## AcadDocument Object

The AcadDocument object represents an AutoCAD drawing. The active document can be accessed using ThisDrawing in VBA and the ActiveDocument property of the AcadApplication object in Visual Basic.

Certain objects in the drawing establish the format, location, or style that new objects will adopt. These include the AcadDimStyle, AcadTextStyle, AcadLinetype, AcadViewport, and AcadLayer objects. A drawing may contain many objects of these types, but only one can be active at a time. The AcadDocument object also contains a link property to all the collections, all of which are created when the document is created. You can thus iterate through every object in the drawing.

You control the model space and paper space settings from the AcadDocument object by using its ActiveSpace property, its MSpace property, and the Display method of the AcadPViewport object. By default, a drawing is opened in the model space with the tiled viewport setting.

Changes to most active objects will appear immediately. However, several objects must be reset for changes to appear: the active text style, the active UCS, and the active viewport. These are reset using the ActiveTextStyle, ActiveUCS, and ActiveViewport properties, respectively. An example syntax for resetting the active viewport is as follows:

```
ThisDrawing.ActiveViewport = modifiedViewportObj
```

## AcadDocument Object Methods

The AcadDocument object supports the following methods.

| NAME | RETURNS | DESCRIPTION |
| --- | --- | --- |
| Activate | | Makes the specified drawing active. |
| AuditInfo | | Evaluates the drawing's integrity. For every error detected, AutoCAD provides a description of the error and recommends corrective action. Parameter: FixError As Boolean. If the parameter is set to True, AutoCAD should attempt to fix any errors. |
| Close | | Closes the specified drawing. If no drawing is specified, the drawing is only closed if it already has a valid file name or wasn't modified. Parameters: SaveChanges As Boolean and FileName As String. If the first parameter is set to True, changes are saved. The second parameter specifies the name to assign to the drawing. |
| | | The document will be closed and no error will occur if the drawing hasn't been modified or if the first parameter is set to False. The document will be saved and closed if the first parameter is set to True (the default value) and the drawing was previously saved or was opened from an existing drawing file. In any other case, a valid name has to be specified. |
| CopyObjects | Variant | Copies objects, their child objects and so on recursively (deep cloning). Parameters: Objects As Variant, [Owner As Variant], and [IDPairs As Variant]. For more information on this method, see the AcadDatabaseObject section. |
| EndUndoMark | | Marks the end of a block of operations. See also the StartUndoMark method. |

| NAME | RETURNS | DESCRIPTION |
|------|---------|-------------|
| Export | | Exports the drawing to a `.wmf`, `.sat`, `.eps`, `.dxf`, or `.bmp` format. Parameters: `FileName As String`, `Extension As String`, and `SelectionSet As AcadSelectionSet`. |
| | | When exporting to `wmf`, `.sat`, or `.bmp` format, a nonempty selection set must be provided. For the `.sat` format only `AcadRegion` and `Acad3DSolid` objects can be exported. When exporting to `.eps` and `.dxf` formats, the selection set is ignored and the entire drawing is exported. |
| GetVariable | Variant | Returns the current setting of an AutoCAD system variable. For a list of all the AutoCAD system variables and their types, please refer to Appendix C. Parameter: `Name As String`. |
| HandleToObject | Object | Returns the object that corresponds to a handle. This method can only return objects in the current document. Parameter: `Handle As String`. A handle is persistent. It can be stored for reuse with this method for the lifetime of the object. |
| Import | Object | Imports a drawing in `.wmf`, `.sat`, `.eps`, or `.dxf` format. In the case of importing a `.wmf` file, an `AcadBlockReference` object is returned. In all other cases, the return value is `NULL`. Parameters: `FileName As String`, `InsertionPoint As Variant`, and `ScaleFactor As Double`. |
| LoadShapeFile | | Loads an `.shx` (shape) file. This method makes all the shapes in the shape file available to the current drawing. Parameter: `FullName As String`. |
| New | AcadDocument | Creates a new document in SDI mode. It's good practice to immediately save the new document with a valid file name. This will simplify later use of the save and close methods. Parameter: `TemplateFileName As String`. |

| NAME | RETURNS | DESCRIPTION |
| --- | --- | --- |
| ObjectIDToObject | Object | Returns the object that corresponds to an object ID. This method can only return objects in the current document. Parameter: ID As Long. An object ID isn't persistent. Its lifetime is limited to a drawing session. |
| Open | | Opens an existing .dwg (drawing) file when working in SDI mode. The file becomes the active document. Parameters: Name As String and [ReadOnly As Boolean]. The Name parameter is an existing file name including the path or the valid URL address of the drawing to open. The second parameter is True if the drawing is to be read-only and False otherwise (the default). |
| PurgeAll | | Removes all unused named references from the document. Deleted objects remain in the document until they're purged using this method. |
| Regen | | Regenerates the entire drawing and updates the screen coordinates and view resolution for all objects. Parameter: WhichViewports As AcRegenType (acActiveViewport or acAllViewports). |
| Save | | Saves the document. When the user is saving to a secure URL, a dialog box will prompt the user for the necessary password information. Message boxes may also appear if the user hasn't suppressed this activity in the browser. |
| SaveAs | | Saves the document as specified by the parameters. Parameters: FileName As String and FileType As AcMenuFileType. For a list of possible values for the AcMenuFileType enumeration, see Appendix B. |

| NAME | RETURNS | DESCRIPTION |
| --- | --- | --- |
| SendCommand | | Sends a command string from a VB or VBA application to the document to be processed. If the drawing specified isn't active, it will be made active. This method processes any AutoCAD command-line function, including LISP expressions. This method is generally synchronous. Only when responding to user interaction or when called from an event handler will commands be processed asynchronously. You should never use this method to issue a command for which there is an ActiveX method available. Instead, use the LoadDVB method. Parameter: Command As String. |
| SetVariable | | Sets the value of an AutoCAD system variable. For a list of all AutoCAD system variables and their types, please refer to Appendix C. Parameters: Name As String and Value As Variant. |
| StartUndoMark | | Marks the beginning of a block of operations that will be treated as a unique operation in an Undo command. Unfortunately, the Undo command hasn't been wrapped for VBA but is available synchronously using the SendCommand method. |
| WBlock | | Creates a new drawing file from the selection set. Parameter: FileName As String and SelectionSet As AcadSelectionSet. |

**NOTE** *The insertion point isn't specified. If it isn't already at the origin, each object within the selection set will have to be copied and moved before a call to* WBlock.

## AcadDocument Object Properties

As well as the common `Application` property, the `AcadDocument` object supports the following properties.

| NAME | RETURNS | DESCRIPTION |
|------|---------|-------------|
| Active | Boolean | Specifies whether or not the document is active. This property's value is read-only. |
| ActiveDimStyle | AcadDimStyle | Gets or sets the active dimension style. This style will be applied to all newly created dimensions. |
| ActiveLayer | AcadLayer | Gets or sets the active layer. New objects are placed on the active layer as they're created. |
| ActiveLayout | AcadLayout | Gets or sets the active layout. |
| ActiveLinetype | AcadLinetype | Gets or sets the active linetype. The specified linetype must already exist in the drawing. |
| ActivePViewport | AcadPViewport | Gets or sets the active paper space viewport. A viewport must be set active using this property before you can see any changes to it. |
| ActiveSelectionSet | AcadSelectionSet | Gets or sets the active selection set. |
| ActiveSpace | AcActiveSpace | Gets or sets whether the paper space or the model space is active. The value is stored in the TILEMODE system variable. For model space and floating viewports, this value is set to acPaperSpace. Even though you have the ability to edit the model, when the MSpace property is set to True, you're still technically in paper space. Values for AcActiveSpace: acModelSpace or acPaperSpace. |
| ActiveTextStyle | AcadTextStyle | Gets or sets the active text style. New text added to the drawing will adopt this text style. Existing text that has no distinct text style specified will adopt the new style. Note that a call to the Regen method is necessary to see any changes. |
| ActiveUCS | AcadUCS | Gets or sets the active UCS. Changes made to the current active UCS will become visible only after that UCS is reset as the active UCS. |

| NAME | RETURNS | DESCRIPTION |
|------|---------|-------------|
| ActiveViewport | AcadViewport | Gets or sets the active viewport. Changes made to the current active viewport will become visible only after you reset the viewport as the active viewport. |
| Blocks | AcadBlocks | Gets the drawing's blocks collection. This property's value is read-only. |
| Database | AcadDatabase | Gets the database to which the document belongs. This property's value is read-only. |
| Dictionaries | AcadDictionaries | Gets the document's dictionaries collection. This property's value is read-only. |
| DimStyles | AcadDimStyles | Gets the document's dimension styles collection. This property's value is read-only. |
| ElevationModelSpace | Double | Gets or sets the elevation setting for the model space. The current elevation is the Z value that is used whenever a 3-D point is expected but only the X and Y values are supplied. |
| ElevationPaperSpace | Double | Gets or sets the elevation setting for the paper space. The current elevation is the Z value that is used whenever a 3-D point is expected but only the X and Y values are supplied. |
| FullName | String | Gets the document's name including the path. It returns a null string for a new drawing. This property's value is read-only. |
| Groups | AcadGroups | Gets the document's groups collection. This property's value is read-only. |
| HWND | Long | Gets the window handle of the document's window frame. This property's value is read-only. |
| Layers | AcadLayers | Gets the document's layers collection. |
| Layouts | AcadLayouts | Gets the document's layouts collection. |

| NAME | RETURNS | DESCRIPTION |
|---|---|---|
| Limits | Variant | Gets or sets the document's drawing limits as an array of four Double numbers: the X and Y coordinates of the lower-left limit and the second pair of values define the X and Y coordinates of the upper-right limit. You can't specify limits for the Z-axis. |
| Linetypes | AcadLinetypes | Gets the document's linetypes collection. This property's value is read-only. |
| ModelSpace | AcadModelSpace | Gets the document's model space object. This property's value is read-only. |
| MSpace | Boolean | Specifies whether or not it is possible to edit the model from the floating paper space viewports. |
| Name | String | Gets the document's name, but not the path. It returns a null string for a new drawing. This property's value is read-only. |
| ObjectSnapMode | Boolean | Specifies whether the document's snap mode is on or off. True indicates that it is on. |
| PaperSpace | AcadPaperSpace | Gets the document's paper space object. This property's value is read-only. |
| Path | String | Gets the document's path, but not the file name. This property's value is read-only. |
| PickfirstSelectionSet | AcadSelectionSet | Gets the PickFirst selection set. This property's value is read-only. |
| Plot | AcadPlot | Gets the document's AcadPlot object. This property's value is read-only. |
| PlotConfigurations | AcadPlot-Configurations | Gets the document's plot configurations collection. This property's value is read-only. |
| Preferences | AcadPreferences | Gets the document's AcadPreferences object. This property's value is read-only. |
| ReadOnly | Boolean | Specifies whether or not the document is read-only. This property's value is read-only. |
| RegisteredApplications | AcadRegistered-Applications | Gets the document's registered applications collection. This property's value is read-only. |

| NAME | RETURNS | DESCRIPTION |
|---|---|---|
| Saved | Boolean | Specifies whether or not the document has any unsaved changes. It's True if there are no unsaved changes and False if there are. This property's value is read-only. |
| SelectionSets | AcadSelectionSets | Gets the document's selection set collection. This property's value is read-only. |
| TextStyles | AcadTextStyles | Gets the document's text styles collection. This property's value is read-only. |
| UserCoordinateSystems | AcadUCSs | Gets the document's UCSs collection. This property's value is read-only. |
| Utility | AcadUtility | Gets the document's AcadUtility object. This property's value is read-only. |
| Viewports | AcadViewports | Gets the document's viewports collection. This property's value is read-only. |
| Views | AcadViews | Gets the document's views collection. This property's value is read-only. |
| WindowState | AcWindowState | Gets or sets the state of the document window. Values: acMin, acMax, and acNorm. |
| WindowTitle | String | Gets the title of the document window, which will be the same as for the Name property for a saved document. This property's value is read-only. |

## AcadDocument Object Events

The following events are triggered during various stages in the lifetime of the AcadDocument object. Note that no events will be fired while a modal dialog box is displayed.

| EVENT | DESCRIPTION |
|---|---|
| Activate | Occurs when the document window is activated. |
| BeginClose | Occurs after a request to close a drawing is received. |

| EVENT | DESCRIPTION |
|---|---|
| BeginCommand | Occurs after a command is issued but before it's initiated. Parameter: Command As String. |
| BeginDoubleClick | Occurs after the user double-clicks anywhere in the drawing. Parameter: PickPoint As Variant (array of WCS coordinates). |
| BeginLISP | Occurs after a request to evaluate a LISP expression is received. Parameter: FirstLine As String. FirstLine won't have any case conversion of the alpha characters. |
| BeginPlot | Occurs after a request to print a drawing is received. Parameter: DrawingName As String. |
| BeginRightClick | Occurs after the user right-clicks anywhere in the drawing window. Parameter: PickPoint As Variant. |
| BeginSave | Occurs after a request to save a drawing is received. Parameter: FileName As String. |
| BeginShortcutMenuCommand | Occurs after the user right-clicks in the drawing window, but before the menu is in command mode. Parameters: ShortcutMenu As AcadPopupMenu and Command As String. |
| BeginShortcutMenuDefault | Occurs after the user right-clicks in the drawing window but before the menu is in default mode. Parameter: ShortcutMenu As AcadPopupMenu. |
| BeginShortcutMenuEdit | Occurs after the user right-clicks in the drawing window but before the menu is in edit mode. Parameters: ShortcutMenu As AcadPopupMenu and SelectionSet As AcadSelectionSet. |
| BeginShortcutMenuGrip | Occurs after the user right-clicks in the drawing window but before the menu is in grip mode. Parameter: ShortcutMenu As AcadPopupMenu. |
| BeginShortcutMenuOSnap | Occurs after the user right-clicks in the drawing window but before the menu is in osnap mode. Parameter: ShortcutMenu As AcadPopupMenu. |
| Deactivate | Occurs when the drawing window is deactivated. |
| EndCommand | Occurs after a command is executed. Parameter: CommandName As String. |
| EndLISP | Occurs after a LISP expression is evaluated. |
| EndPlot | Occurs after a document is sent to the printer. Parameter: DrawingName As String. |

| EVENT | DESCRIPTION |
|---|---|
| EndSave | Occurs after a drawing has been saved. Parameter: FileName As String. |
| EndShortcutMenu | Occurs after a shortcut menu appears. Use this event to perform any cleanup work on the shortcut menu. Parameter: ShortcutMenu As AcadPopupMenu. |
| LayoutSwitched | Occurs after the user changes the layout. Parameter: LayoutName As String. |
| LISPCancelled | Occurs when the evaluation of a LISP expression is canceled. |
| ObjectAdded | Occurs after an object is added to the drawing. Parameter: Entity As AcadEntity. |
| ObjectErased | Occurs after an object is erased from the drawing. Parameter: ObjectID As Long. |
| ObjectModified | Occurs after an object in the drawing is modified. Parameter: Entity As AcadEntity. |
| SelectionChanged | Occurs when the current PickFirst selection set changes. |
| WindowChanged | Occurs when the drawing or document window is changed. Parameter: WindowState As acMin or acMax or acNorm. This event (and the one that follows) is helpful when implementing floating palettes, toolbars, or modeless dialog boxes that track with the application or document window. The VB or ObjectARX application can use the HWNDFrame parameter to get the coordinates of the window, convert those coordinates to either screen or parent coordinates, and use this information to position other windows. |
| WindowMovedOrResized | Occurs after the drawing or document window is moved or resized. Parameters: HWNDFrame As Long and Moved As Boolean. If Moved is set to True, the window was moved; otherwise, it was resized. |

## AcadDocuments Collection

The AcadDocuments collection contains all AutoCAD drawings open in the current session. To add a new member to the collection, use the Add or Open method. To select a specific document, use the Item method. To close all the documents, use the Close method similar to the one found in the AcadDocument object. To close all documents, use the Close method found in this collection. There's no limit to the number of documents you can create in your drawing. However, there can be only one instance of the AcadDocuments collection, which is predefined for each application. You can make multiple references to it by using the Documents property or the AcadDocuments object.

## AcadDocuments Collection Methods

The AcadDocuments collection supports these four methods.

| NAME | RETURNS | DESCRIPTION |
|------|---------|-------------|
| Add | AcadDocument | Creates an AcadDocument object and adds it to the collection. Optional parameter: Name As String. This method should not be called when AutoCAD runs in SDI mode. |
| Close | | Closes all open drawings in MDI mode. Note that you can't call this method while in SDI mode. Use the Close method of the AcadDocument object. |
| Item | AcadDocument | Returns the object at the given index in the collection. Parameter: Index As Variant (Integer or String). If the Index value is a String, it must match an existing document in the collection. |
| Open | | Opens an existing .dwg (drawing) file in MDI mode. The document then becomes the active document. When the user is accessing a secure URL, a dialog box will be posted that prompts the user for the necessary password information. Message boxes may also appear if the user hasn't suppressed this activity in the browser. Parameters: Name As String and [ReadOnly As Boolean]. The second parameter specifies whether or not the drawing is read-only. |

### AcadDocuments Collection Properties

The AcadDocuments collection supports the common Application property and the Count property but no other properties.

# AcadEllipse Object

The AcadEllipse object represents an elliptical arc or full ellipse, drawing a true ellipse, not a polyline approximation. It is created using the AddEllipse method of the AcadBlock, AcadModelSpace, or AcadPaperSpace object.

### AcadEllipse Object Methods

The AcadEllipse object inherits all the methods of the AcadEntity and AcadObject objects. It also supports the following method.

| NAME | RETURNS | DESCRIPTION |
| --- | --- | --- |
| Offset | Variant | Creates a new ellipse by offsetting the current ellipse by a specified distance, which must be nonzero. If the offset is positive, a larger ellipse is created with the same origin. If the offset is negative, a smaller ellipse is created. Parameter: Distance As Double. |

### AcadEllipse Object Properties

The AcadEllipse object inherits all the properties of the AcadEntity and AcadObject objects, as well as the common Application property. It also supports the following properties.

| NAME | RETURNS | DESCRIPTION |
| --- | --- | --- |
| Area | Double | Gets the area of the ellipse. This property's value is read-only. |
| Center | Variant | Gets or sets the center of the ellipse as an array of the Doubles. |

| NAME | RETURNS | DESCRIPTION |
|------|---------|-------------|
| EndAngle | Double | Gets or sets the end angle of the ellipse in radians. Use 6.28 radians to specify a closed ellipse. |
| EndParameter | Double | Gets or sets the end parameter for an ellipse. The valid range is 0 to 2*PI. |
| EndPoint | Variant | Gets the 3-D coordinates of the end point of the ellipse. This property's value is read-only. |
| MajorAxis | Variant | Gets or sets the direction of the major (i.e., longer) axis of the ellipse as a 3-D vector. The vector originates at the ellipse center. |
| MajorRadius | Double | Gets or sets the length of the major (i.e., longer) axis of the ellipse. |
| MinorAxis | Variant | Gets the direction of the minor (i.e., shorter) axis of the ellipse as a 3-D vector. This property's value is read-only. |
| MinorRadius | Double | Gets or sets the length of the minor (i.e., shorter) axis of the ellipse. |
| Normal | Variant | Gets or sets the 3-D (Z-axis) normal unit vector for the ellipse. |
| RadiusRatio | Double | Gets or sets the major to minor axis ratio of an ellipse. A value of 1.0 denotes a circle. |
| StartAngle | Double | Gets or sets the start angle of the ellipse in radians. Use 6.28 radians to specify a closed ellipse. |
| StartParameter | Double | Gets or sets the start parameter for an ellipse. The valid range is 0 to 2*PI. |
| StartPoint | Variant | Gets the X, Y, Z coordinate of the start point of the ellipse. This property's value is read-only. |

**NOTE** *Because this object inherits from* AcadObject, *it supports the* Modified *event.*

## AcadExternalReference Object

The AcadExternalReference object represents an instance of an external reference (XRef) inserted into a drawing (i.e., where a second drawing is linked into the current drawing). It differs from the AcadBlockReference object in the following respect. If a block is inserted into a drawing, its definition and all associated geometry are stored in the current drawing database and aren't updated if the original drawing changes. However, when you insert a drawing as an XRef, changes are updated in the externally referenced file. Like a block reference, an XRef is displayed in the current drawing as a single object. However, it doesn't significantly increase the file size of the current drawing and can't be exploded. The AcadExternalReference object is created using the AttachExternalReference method of the AcadBlock, AcadModelSpace, or AcadPaperSpace object. Note that many methods and properties of the AcadBlock and AcadDatabase objects are specific to XRefs.

### AcadExternalReference Object Methods

The AcadExternalReference object inherits all the methods of the AcadEntity and AcadObject objects. It also supports the following method.

| NAME | RETURNS | DESCRIPTION |
| --- | --- | --- |
| GetConstantAttributes | Variant | Returns an array of constant attributes for the external reference |

### AcadExternalReference Object Properties

The AcadExternalReference object inherits all the properties of the AcadEntity and AcadObject objects, as well as the common Application property. It also supports the following properties.

| NAME | RETURNS | DESCRIPTION |
|------|---------|-------------|
| HasAttributes | Boolean | Specifies whether or not the external reference has any attributes. This property's value is read-only. |
| InsertionPoint | Variant | Gets or sets the insertion point for the external reference as a set of 3-D WCS coordinates. It returns a three-element array of Doubles. |
| Name | String | Gets or sets the name of the external reference. |
| Normal | Variant | Gets or sets the 3-D (Z-axis) normal unit vector for the external reference. |
| Path | String | Gets or sets the path of the external reference. This doesn't include the file name. |
| Rotation | Double | Specifies the rotation angle (in radians) for the block, relative to the X-axis with positive values going counterclockwise when viewed along the Z-axis toward the origin. |
| XScaleFactor | Double | Gets or sets the X scale factor for the block. |
| YScaleFactor | Double | Gets or sets the Y scale factor for the block. |
| ZScaleFactor | Double | Gets or sets the Z scale factor for the block. |

**NOTE** *Because this object inherits from* AcadObject, *it supports the* Modified *event.*

## AcadFileDependency Object

The AcadFileDependency object describes an entry in the File Dependency List. The files on which a drawing file depends are in its File Dependency List, which is the AcadFileDependencies collection object. This object has no methods, but it supports the following properties.

| NAME | RETURNS | DESCRIPTION |
|------|---------|-------------|
| AffectsGraphics | Boolean | If True, affects; if False, doesn't affect. |
| Feature | String | Feature name (e.g., "Acad:Xref"). |
| FileName | String | File name of current file. |
| FileSize | Long | File size in bytes. This property's value is read-only. |
| FingerprintGUID | String | The GUID fingerprint of the file. |
| FoundPath | String | Alternate path found in (if any). |
| FullFileName | String | Saved full file name. |
| IsModified | Boolean | If True, modified; if False, not modified. |
| ReferenceCount | Long | Current item count of reference. |
| TimeStamp | Long | Current time/date in seconds since 1/1/1980. |
| VersionGUID | String | GUID version stamp. |

## AcadFileDependencies Object

The AcadFileDependencies object creates, updates, retrieves, and removes items in the File Dependency List. The File Dependency List is a list of the files on which the drawing file depends. You can perform operations on the File Dependency List using the FileDependencies collection.

### AcadFileDependencies Object Methods

In addition to the methods inherited from the AcadDocument object, the following methods are available.

| NAME | RETURNS | DESCRIPTION |
|------|---------|-------------|
| CreateEntry | Long | An index into the File Dependency List |
| IndexOf | Long | The index of an entry in the File Dependency List |
| RemoveEntry | | Removes an entry from the File Dependency List |
| UpdateEntry | | Updates an entry in the File Dependency List |

# *AcadGroup Object*

The AcadGroup object represents a named AcadSelectionSet object. It is created using the Add method of the AcadGroups collection and can be accessed by the Item method of the AcadGroups collection. See the AcadSelectionSet object for more information on selection sets.

## *AcadGroup Object Methods*

In addition to the methods inherited from the AcadObject object, the AcadGroup object supports the following methods.

| NAME | RETURNS | DESCRIPTION |
|---|---|---|
| AppendItems | | Appends one or more entities to the specified group. Parameter: Objects As Variant. |
| Highlight | | Determines whether or not the objects in a given group are to be highlighted. Parameter: HighlightFlag As Boolean. |
| Item | AcadEntity | Gets the member object at a given index in a group. Parameter: Index As Variant (Integer or String). If the Index value is a String, it must match an existing object name in the collection. |
| RemoveItems | | Removes specified items from the group. Note that items removed from a group remain in the drawing; they're no longer associated with the group. Parameter: Objects As Variant. |
| Update | | Updates the object to the drawing screen. |

## *AcadGroup Object Properties*

In addition to the properties inherited from the AcadObject object, the AcadGroup object supports the following properties.

| NAME | RETURNS | DESCRIPTION |
|------|---------|-------------|
| Color | AcColor | Gets or sets the color of the group object. Use a color index number from 0 to 256 or one of the constants listed here: acByBlock (where AutoCAD draws objects in the default color) or acByLayer (where AutoCAD draws objects in the color specified for the layer). For a list of possible values for the AcColor enumerated type, see Appendix B. |
| Count | Integer | Gets the number of items in the group. This property's value is read-only. |
| Layer | String | Gets or sets the layer for the group. |
| Linetype | String | Gets or sets the linetype of the group. |
| LinetypeScale | Double | Gets or sets the linetype scale of the group. The default value is 1.0. |
| Lineweight | AcLineWeight | Gets or sets the lineweight of the group. For a list of possible values for the AcLineWeight enumerated type, see Appendix B. |
| Name | String | Gets or sets the name of the group. |
| PlotStyleName | String | Gets or sets the group's plot style name. |
| Visible | Boolean | Specifies whether or not the group is visible. |

**NOTE** *Because this object inherits from* AcadObject, *it supports the* Modified *event.*

## AcadGroups Collection

The AcadGroups collection contains all the groups in the drawing. Although this collection inherits a Delete method, you can't actually delete it. If you need to delete a specific group, use the Delete method found in the AcadGroup object. There is no limit to the number of groups you can create in your drawing. However, there can be only one instance of the AcadGroups collection, which is predefined for each drawing. You can make multiple references to it by using the Groups property.

### AcadGroups Collection Methods

In addition to the methods inherited from the AcadObject object, the AcadGroups collection supports the following methods.

| NAME | RETURNS | DESCRIPTION |
| --- | --- | --- |
| Add | AcadGroup | Creates a member object and adds it to the collection. Parameter: Name As String. |
| Item | AcadGroup | Gets the member object at a given index in a group. Parameter: Index As Variant (an Integer or a String). If the Index value is a String, it must match an existing group in the collection. |

### AcadGroups Collection Properties

The AcadGroups collection supports the Count property, the common Application property, and the properties inherited from the AcadObject object. It supports no other properties.

**NOTE**   *Because this collection inherits from* AcadObject, *it supports the* Modified *event.*

## AcadHatch Object

The AcadHatch object represents an area fill consisting of a pattern of lines. It is created using the AddHatch method of the AcadBlock, AcadModelSpace, or AcadPaperSpace object. After creating the hatch, what you must do next is add the outer loop using the AppendOuterLoop method. You have to do this for the hatch to be a valid AutoCAD object; otherwise, AutoCAD will enter an unpredictable state. Once you've successfully created the outer loop, you can add any inner loops using the AppendInnerLoop method or any other operation carried out on the hatch.

## AcadHatch Object Methods

In addition to the methods inherited from the AcadObject object, the AcadHatch object supports the following methods.

| NAME | DESCRIPTION |
| --- | --- |
| AppendInnerLoop | Appends an inner loop to the hatch. You must add the outer loop before you can add any inner loop. Parameter: ObjectArray As Variant. |
| | The parameter is an array of objects forming a closed boundary, which can consist of one or more objects. If more than one object is used, their end points must coincide for the loop to be created properly. The loop may contain the following types of objects: AcadLine, AcadPolyline, AcadCircle, AcadEllipse, AcadSpline, or AcadRegion. It's important that the object array used in the call to AppendInnerLoop forms a closed boundary. |
| AppendOuterLoop | Appends an outer loop to the hatch. The outer loop must be closed and must be created before any inner loops can be added. Parameter: ObjectArray As Variant. |
| | For a description of the parameter, see the AppendInnerLoop method. It's important that the object array used in the call to AppendOuterLoop forms a closed boundary. |
| Evaluate | Evaluates the hatch lines or solid fill using the specified hatch pattern. For regular hatch patterns, this method performs intersection calculations between pattern definition lines and hatch boundary curves to form hatch lines. For solid fill hatch patterns, this method performs triangulation of the hatch area and fills in the triangular meshes with the given color. AutoCAD may not succeed in evaluating an AcadHatch object when either the inner or outer loop is too small for the hatch patterns and will return an ambiguous output error. |
| GetLoopAt | Gets the objects used to define a loop at the given index of the hatch. Parameters: Index As Integer and ObjectArray As Variant. The Index parameter can take any value from 0 (the index for the outer loop) to the index of the last loop created with AppendInnerLoop. The second parameter is an object or an array of objects that makes up the loop. |

| NAME | DESCRIPTION |
|------|-------------|
| InsertLoopAt | Inserts a loop at a given index of a hatch. Parameters: Index As Integer, LoopType As AcLoopType, and ObjectArray As Variant. Values for the AcLoopType enumeration are given in Appendix B. For a description of the third parameter, see the AppendInnerLoop method. |
| SetPattern | Sets the pattern type and name of the hatch. Note that the integer value for the pattern type is supplied. Parameters: PatternType As AcPatternType and PatternName As String. See the AcPatternType enumeration table in Appendix B. |

## AcadHatch Object Properties

In addition to the properties inherited from the AcadEntity object, the AcadObject object, and the common Application property, the AcadHatch object supports the following properties.

| NAME | RETURNS | DESCRIPTION |
|------|---------|-------------|
| AssociativeHatch | Boolean | Specifies if the hatch is associative or not. An associative hatch is updated when its boundaries are modified. |
| Elevation | Double | Gets or sets the current elevation of the hatch object. |
| Gradient1 | AcCmColor | Gets or sets the start color of the gradient. It must be one of the constants acColorMethodByACI or acColorMethodByBlock. |
| Gradient2 | AcCmColor | Gets or sets the end color of the gradient. It must be one of the constants acColorMethodByACI or acColorMethodByBlock. |
| GradientCentered | Boolean | Gets or sets whether the gradient is centered. |

| NAME | RETURNS | DESCRIPTION |
|------|---------|-------------|
| GradientName | String | Gets or sets the pattern name. The pattern name for the gradient may be LINEAR, CYLINDER, INVCYLINDER, SPHERICAL, HEMISPHERICAL, CURVED, INVSPHERICAL, INVHEMISPHERICAL, or INVCURVED. |
| HatchObjectType | AcHatchObjectType enum | Gets or sets the hatch object type to be hatch, classic or gradient. The default value of this property is 0, acHatchObject, which creates a classic hatch.<br><br>If the value of this property is 1, acGradientObject, a gradient is created by the AddHatch method for hatch creation. If a gradient is created, then PatternType should be AcGradientPatternType and PatternName should contain a gradient pattern name of LINEAR, CYLINDER, INVCYLINDER, SPHERICAL, HEMISPHERICAL, CURVED, INVSPHERICAL, INVHEMISPHERICAL, or INVCURVED. |
| HatchStyle | AcHatchStyle | Gets or sets the hatch style. For a list of possible values for the AcHatchStyle enumerated type, see Appendix B. |
| ISOPenWidth | AcISOPenWidth | Gets or sets the ISO pen width of an ISO hatch pattern. For a list of possible values for the AcISOPenWidth enumerated type, see Appendix B. When you query a hatch and receive a value of acPenWidthUnk, use the PatternScale property to obtain the nonstandard value. Setting the pen width of any hatch to acPenWidthUnk has no effect. |
| Normal | Variant | Gets or sets the 3-D (Z-axis) normal unit vector for the hatch object. |
| NumberOfLoops | Integer | Gets the number of loops in the hatch boundary. This property's value is read-only. |
| PatternAngle | Double | Gets or sets the angle of the hatch pattern in radians. The valid range is 0 to 6.28. The value is stored in the HPANG system variable. |

| NAME | RETURNS | DESCRIPTION |
|------|---------|-------------|
| PatternDouble | Boolean | Specifies whether or not the user-defined hatch is double-hatched. The value of this property is stored in the HPDOUBLE system variable. If the PatternType property is set to acHatchPatternTypePreDefined or acHatchPatternTypeCustomDefined, this property isn't used. |
| PatternName | String | Gets or sets the pattern name of the hatch, which can be up to 34 characters long but can't have spaces (by default). To remove the default setting, enter a period (.), and a NULL string is returned. If the PatternType property is set to acHatchPatternTypePreDefined, then this property refers to the name of a hatch pattern in acad.pat. If the PatternType property is set to acHatchPatternTypeCustomDefined, then this property refers to the name of a hatch pattern in a custom .pat file. If the PatternType property is set to acHatchPatternTypeUserDefined, then this property isn't used. The value of this property is stored in the HPNAME system variable. This property's value is read-only. |
| PatternScale | Double | Gets or sets the hatch pattern scale. The value of this property must not be zero and it is stored in the HPSCALE system variable. If the PatternType property is set to acHatchPatternTypeUserDefined, then this property isn't used. |
| PatternSpace | Double | Gets or sets the user-defined hatch pattern spacing. This value is also controlled by the HPSPACE system variable. If the PatternType property is set to acHatchPatternTypePreDefined or acHatchPatternTypeCustomDefined, then this property isn't used. |
| PatternType | AcPatternType | Gets the pattern type of the hatch. For a list of possible values for the AcPatternType enumerated type, see Appendix B. This property's value is read-only. |

**NOTE** *Because this object inherits from* AcadObject, *it supports the* Modified *event.*

## AcadHyperlink Object

The AcadHyperlink object represents a URL and URL description, which is stored within the XData of the object's corresponding entity and not in the drawing itself. This means that a hyperlink object is created every time a URL is requested and the name and description is read from the XData. In this manner, it's similar to the AcadUtility object. You should take care not to create multiple hyperlink objects referencing the same URL. If one such object is updated, the others won't be.

### AcadHyperlink Object Method

The AcadHyperlink object doesn't inherit from AcadEntity or AcadObject. It supports only a single method.

| NAME | DESCRIPTION |
| --- | --- |
| Delete | Deletes a specified hyperlink object |

### AcadHyperlink Object Properties

In addition to the common Application property, the AcadHyperlink object supports the following properties.

| NAME | RETURNS | DESCRIPTION |
| --- | --- | --- |
| URL | String | Gets or sets the URL for the hyperlink object. The file pointed to by the URL can be stored locally on a network drive or on an Internet connection. |

| NAME | RETURNS | DESCRIPTION |
|------|---------|-------------|
| URLDescription | String | Gets or sets the URL description for the hyperlink object. This is useful if the URL name itself isn't very helpful in identifying the contents of the file. |
| URLNamedLocation | String | Gets or sets the named location for the hyperlink object. This can be another AutoCAD drawing or a completely different application, such as a word processing program. If you specify a named view to jump to in an AutoCAD drawing, AutoCAD restores that view when the hyperlink is opened. |

## AcadHyperlinks Collection

The AcadHyperlinks collection contains all the hyperlinks for a given entity. To add a new member to the collection, use the Add method. To select a specific hyperlink, use the Item method. It is accessed via the Hyperlinks property on all AcadEntity objects.

### AcadHyperlinks Collection Methods

The AcadHyperlinks collection doesn't inherit from AcadObject. It supports the following methods.

| NAME | RETURNS | DESCRIPTION |
|------|---------|-------------|
| Add | AcadHyperlink | Creates a named AcadHyperlink object and adds it to the collection. Parameters: Name As String, [Description As Variant], and [NamedLocation As Variant]. |
| Item | AcadHyperlink | Gets the member object at a given index in a collection, group, or selection set. Parameter: Index As Integer (An Integer of a String). If the value for Index is a String, it must match an existing object name in the collection. |

### AcadHyperlinks Collection Properties

The AcadHyperlinks collection supports the common Application and Count properties. It supports no other properties.

## AcadIDPair Object

The AcadIDPair object is a transient object used as an optional parameter in the CopyObjects method of the AcadDatabase and AcadDocument objects. It contains the object IDs of both the source and destination objects. See the AcadDatabase object for more details. The CopyObjects method populates the AcadIDPair object with the object IDs of the source objects and the newly copied objects, thus creating a map between all the objects copied and created. This object also contains information about the copy and translation process.

Note that this object is used for advanced cloning functions. General users should avoid using this optional functionality.

The AcadIDPair object has no methods.

### AcadIDPair Object Properties

The AcadIDPair object supports the common Application property and the following properties.

| NAME | RETURNS | DESCRIPTION |
| --- | --- | --- |
| IsCloned | Boolean | Determines if the source object in a CopyObjects operation has been cloned. This property's value is read-only. |
| IsOwnerXlated | Boolean | Determines if the owning object in a CopyObjects operation has been translated. This property's value is read-only. |
| IsPrimary | Boolean | Determines if the source object in a CopyObjects operation was part of the primary set of objects being copied or if it was simply owned by a member in the primary set. This property's value is read-only. |
| Key | Integer | The object ID of the source object in the CopyObjects operation. This property's value is read-only. |
| Value | Integer | The object ID of the newly created cloned object in the CopyObjects operation. This property's value is read-only. |

# AcadLayer Object

The AcadLayer object represents a logical grouping of data, similar to transparent acetate overlays on a drawing. It is created using the Add method of the AcadLayers collection and can be accessed by the Item method of the AcadLayers collection. All new objects are added to the active layer. To make a layer active, use the ActiveLayer property of the Document object.

## AcadLayer Object Methods

The AcadLayer object supports the methods inherited from the AcadObject object and no other methods. Note that layer 0 can't be deleted and layer DEFPOINTS shouldn't. This restriction applies also to layers referenced in a block definition.

## AcadLayer Object Properties

In addition to the properties inherited from the AcadObject object, and the common Application property, the AcadLayer object supports the following properties.

| NAME | RETURNS | DESCRIPTION |
|---|---|---|
| Color | AcColor | Gets or sets the color of the layer object, which will determine the acByLayer color of the entities on the specific layer. Use a color index number from 0 to 256 or the AcColor enumeration (see Appendix B). |
| Freeze | Boolean | Specifies the freeze status of a layer: True if frozen, False if thawed. Freezing layers makes them invisible and excludes them from regeneration and plotting. Thawing a layer enables these capabilities. You can't freeze the active layer or make a frozen layer active. |
| LayerOn | Boolean | Specifies whether a layer is on or off. Layers that are "off" aren't displayed or plotted, though they're regenerated when the drawing is regenerated. |
| Linetype | String | Gets or sets the linetype for the layer. The default linetype for any new entity will become the linetype of the layer (ByLayer). |

| NAME | RETURNS | DESCRIPTION |
|------|---------|-------------|
| Lineweight | AcLineWeight | Gets or sets the lineweight for the layer. For a list of possible values for the AcLineWeight enumerated type, see Appendix B. |
| Lock | Boolean | Specifies whether or not a layer is locked. You can't edit objects on a locked layer, though they're still visible if the layer is on and thawed. You can activate locked layers and add objects to them, apply snap modes, freeze and turn them off, and change their associated colors. |
| Name | String | Gets or sets the name of the layer. Layer 0 can't be renamed. Layer DEFPOINTS is used for dimensioning shouldn't be renamed either. |
| PlotStyleName | String | Gets or sets the layer's plot style name. |
| Plottable | Boolean | Specifies whether or not the layer is plottable. |
| ViewportDefault | Boolean | Specifies whether or not the layer is to be frozen in new viewports. |

 **NOTE** *Because this object inherits from* AcadObject, *it supports the* Modified *event.*

## *AcadLayers Collection*

The AcadLayers collection contains all the layers in the drawing. Although this collection inherits a Delete method, you can't actually delete this collection. If you need to delete a specific layer, use the Delete method found in the AcadLayer object. There is no limit to the number of layers you can create in your drawing. However, there can be only one instance of the AcadLayers collection, which is predefined for each drawing. You can make multiple references to it by using the Layers property.

## AcadLayers Collection Methods

In addition to the methods inherited from the AcadObject object, the AcadLayers collection supports the following methods.

| NAME | RETURNS | DESCRIPTION |
|------|---------|-------------|
| Add | AcadLayer | Creates a member object and adds it to the collection. Parameter: Name As String. |
| Item | AcadLayer | Gets the member object at a given index in a collection, group, or selection set. Parameter: Index As Variant (an Integer or a String). If the Index value is a String, it must match an existing object name in the collection. |

## AcadLayers Collection Properties

The AcadLayers collection supports the Count property, the common Application property, and the properties inherited from the AcadObject object. It supports no other properties.

**NOTE** *Because this object inherits from* AcadObject, *it supports the* Modified *event.*

# AcadLayout and AcadPlotConfiguration Objects

The AcadLayout object contains the plot settings and visual properties of a model space or paper space block, as displayed in the AutoCAD user interface. Each AcadLayout object is associated with a single AcadBlock object, which can be accessed through the Block property. Alternatively, the AcadLayout object can be accessed through the Item property of the AcadLayouts collection, the Layout property of the AcadBlock (when IsLayout is set to True), the AcadModelSpace and AcadPaperSpace objects, or the ActiveLayout property of the Document object.

The `AcadPlotConfiguration` object is similar to the `AcadLayout` object in that it contains the same plot settings and visual properties. The difference between the two is as follows. Whereas a layout is only defined for a particular block, a plot configuration isn't specific to any one block; it's a named collection of plot settings that can be applied to any geometry.

As the two objects are all but identical, I present their methods and properties together.

## AcadLayout and AcadPlotConfiguration Objects: Methods

The `AcadLayout` and `AcadPlotConfiguration` objects support all the methods inherited from the `AcadObject` object. They also support the following methods.

| NAME | RETURNS | DESCRIPTION |
|---|---|---|
| CopyFrom | | Copies the settings from the given plot configuration. Parameter: `PlotConfig As AcadPlotConfiguration`. This method is specific to the `AcadPlotConfiguration` object. |
| GetCanonicalMediaNames | Variant | Returns all available canonical media names for the specified plot device. You should call `RefreshPlotDeviceInfo` before calling this method. This method returns the names as an array of strings. |
| GetCustomScale | | Gets the custom scale for a layout or plot configuration, in millimeters or inches, depending on the value of the `PaperUnits` property. Parameters: `Numerator As Double` and `Denominator As Double`. |
| GetLocaleMediaName | String | Given a canonical media name, this method returns the localized version of the canonical media name. Parameter: `Name As String`. |
| GetPaperMargins | | Gets the margins offsets for the layout or plot configuration, the units of which depend on the values of the `PaperUnits` property. The print origin is offset from the edge of the paper by the values returned by this method. Parameters: `LowerLeft As Variant` and `UpperRight As Variant`. (Both parameters are two-element arrays of Doubles.) |

| NAME | RETURNS | DESCRIPTION |
| --- | --- | --- |
| GetPaperSize | | Gets the width and height of the configured paper using the values specified by the PaperUnits property. Parameters: Width As Double and Height As Double. |
| GetPlotDeviceNames | Variant | Returns all available plot device names. You should call RefreshPlotDeviceInfo before calling this method. This method returns the names as an array of strings. |
| GetPlotStyleTableNames | Variant | Returns all available plot style table names. You should call RefreshPlotDeviceInfo before calling this method. This method returns the names as an array of strings. |
| GetWindowToPlot | | Gets the coordinates that define the portion of the layout to plot, the units of which depend on the values of the PaperUnits property. The coordinates of the window are taken from the origin. For these coordinates to be used for the plot, the PlotType property must be set to acWindows. Parameters: LowerLeft As Variant and UpperRight As Variant. (Both parameters are two-element arrays of Doubles.) |
| RefreshPlotDeviceInfo | | Updates the plot, canonical media, and plot style table information to reflect the current system state. You should call this method once before calling the GetCanonicalMediaNames, GetPlotDeviceNames, or GetPlotStyleTableNames method. |
| SetCustomScale | | Sets the custom scale for a layout or plot configuration, in millimeters or inches depending on the value of the PaperUnits property. Parameters: Numerator As Double and Denominator As Double. Note that the parameters must be greater than zero. |
| SetWindowToPlot | | Sets the coordinates that define the portion of the layout to plot, the units of which depend on the values of the PaperUnits property. The coordinates of the window are taken from the origin. For these coordinates that can be used for the plot, the PlotType property must be set to acWindows. Parameters: LowerLeft As Variant and UpperRight As Variant. |

## *AcadLayout and AcadPlotConfiguration Objects:Properties*

The AcadLayout and AcadPlotConfiguration objects inherit all the properties inherited from the AcadObject object, as well as the common Application property. They also support the following properties.

| NAME | RETURNS | DESCRIPTION |
| --- | --- | --- |
| Block | AcadBlock | This property is specific to the AcadLayout object. It gets the block associated with the layout. This property's value is read-only. |
| CanonicalMediaName | String | Gets or sets the name of the media that specifies the paper size. Note that changes to this property won't be visible until the drawing is regenerated. |
| CenterPlot | Boolean | Specifies whether or not there is centering of the plot on the media. Note that changes to this property won't be visible until the drawing is regenerated. Note also that this property can't be set to True if the PlotType property is set to acLayout. |
| ConfigName | String | Gets or sets the name of the PC3 file or print device to be used by the layout or plot configuration. Note that this property only takes the file name for the configuration file. Use the PrinterConfigPath property to specify the path for printer configuration files. |
| ModelType | Boolean | Specifies whether the plot configuration applies only to model space or to all layouts. If True, it applies only to the model space layout; if False, it applies to all layouts. This property's value is read-only. |
| Name | String | Gets or sets the name of the object. |
| PaperUnits | AcPlotPaperUnits | Gets or sets the units for the display of the layout or plot configuration in the user interface. Note that changes to this property won't be visible until the drawing is regenerated. Possible values for the AcPlotPaperUnits enumeration are acInches, acMillimeters, and acPixels. |

| NAME | RETURNS | DESCRIPTION |
|------|---------|-------------|
| PlotHidden | Boolean | Specifies whether or not objects in the paper space are to be hidden during a plot. This is True if objects are to be hidden and False otherwise. Note that this property does *not* affect objects inside floating model space viewports. |
| PlotOrigin | Variant | Gets or sets the origin of the UCS, block, layout, or raster image in WCS coordinates. It returns a two-element array of Doubles representing the XY coordinates of the origin. The origin is offset from the media edge by the paper margin and is given in millimeters. Note that changes to this property won't be visible until the drawing is regenerated. |
| PlotRotation | AcPlotRotation | Gets or sets the rotation angle for the layout or plot configuration relative to the X-axis, with positive values going counterclockwise when viewed along the Z-axis toward the origin. Note that changes to this property won't be visible until the drawing is regenerated. Possible values for the AcPlotRotation enumeration are ac0degrees, ac90degrees, ac180degrees, and ac270degrees. |
| PlotType | AcPlotType | Gets or sets the type of layout or plot configuration. Note that changes to this property won't be visible until the drawing is regenerated. Note also that the ViewToPlot property or SetWindowToPlot method needs to be called before you can set the PlotType to acView or acWindow, respectively. For a list of possible values for the AcPlotType enumerated type, see Appendix B. |
| PlotViewportBorders | Boolean | Specifies whether or not the viewport borders are to be plotted. |

| NAME | RETURNS | DESCRIPTION |
|------|---------|-------------|
| PlotViewportsFirst | Boolean | Specifies whether all geometry in paper space viewports is plotted first rather than the geometry in the paper space. This is True if geometry in the paper space viewports is plotted first and False otherwise. |
| PlotWithLineweights | Boolean | Specifies whether objects are plotted with the lineweights assigned from a plot style or from a drawing file. This is True if the plot uses the lineweights assigned from a plot style and False otherwise. |
| PlotWithPlotStyles | Boolean | Specifies whether objects are plotted with the plot configuration assigned from a plot style or from a drawing file. This is True if the plot uses the plot configuration assigned from a plot style and False otherwise. |
| ScaleLineweights | Boolean | Specifies whether or not the lineweight is scaled with the rest of the geometry when a layout is printed. The value of this property is stored in the LWSCALE system variable. Note that this property is disabled for the model space layout. |
| ShowPlotStyles | Boolean | Specifies if plot styles are to be used in the plot (True) or use the plot styles assigned to objects in the drawing (False). |
| StandardScale | AcPlotScale | Gets or sets the standard scale for the layout, viewport, or plot configuration. For a list of possible values for the AcPlotScale enumerated type, see Appendix B. |
| StyleSheet | String | Gets or sets the name of the style sheet for the layout or plot configuration. |
| TabOrder | Integer | Gets or sets the tab order of a layout. Controls the order in which the layouts are displayed in the tab control. The tab order should be unique and sequential among all layouts in the database. The model space tab must have a tab order of 0. Paper space tabs must have a tab order of 1 or greater. This applies to the AcadLayout object only. |

| NAME | RETURNS | DESCRIPTION |
|------|---------|-------------|
| UseStandardScale | Boolean | Specifies whether the plot is to use a standard or custom scale. This is True if the standard scale is to be used and False otherwise. See the SetCustomScale method. |
| ViewToPlot | String | Gets or sets the name of the view to be plotted. Note that the PlotType property for the layout or plot configuration has to be set to acView. |

**NOTE**   *Because these objects inherit from* AcadObject, *they both support the* Modified *event.*

## AcadLayouts and AcadPlotConfigurations Collections

The AcadLayouts collection contains all the AcadLayout objects in the drawing. It is accessed by the Layouts property of the Document object. It is created when the document is created and can't be deleted (even though the collection inherits a Delete method from AcadObject). To remove a layout definition, use the Delete method of the AcadLayout object.

The AcadPlotConfigurations collection is similar to the AcadLayouts collection, except it contains all the AcadPlotConfiguration objects for a project. Whereas a layout is specific to a particular block, a plot configuration contains a named collection of plot settings that can be applied to any geometry. Once again, this collection inherits a Delete method that you can't use. To remove a plot configuration, use the Delete method of the AcadPlotConfiguration object.

As the two collections are all but identical, I present their methods and properties together.

### AcadLayouts and AcadPlotConfigurations Collections: Methods

The AcadLayouts and AcadPlotConfigurations collections support all the methods inherited from the AcadObject object. They also support the following methods.

| NAME | RETURNS | DESCRIPTION |
|------|---------|-------------|
| Add | AcadLayout or AcadPlot Configuration | Creates a named member object and adds it to the appropriate collection. Parameter: Name As String. Additional optional parameter (for the AcadPlotConfigurations collection only): ModelType As Variant (this is True if the plot configuration applies to a model space tab and False otherwise). |
| Item | AcadLayout or AcadPlot-Configuration | Gets the member object at a given index in a collection. Parameter: Index As Variant (an Integer or a String). If the Index value is a String, it must match an existing object name in the collection. |

### *AcadLayouts and AcadPlotConfigurations Collections: Properties*

The AcadLayouts and AcadPlotConfigurations collections support all the properties inherited from the AcadObject object, the Count property, and the common Application property. They support no other properties.

**NOTE** *Because these collections inherit from* AcadObject, *they both support the* Modified *event.*

## *AcadLeader Object*

A *leader line* is an object that can be composed of an arrowhead attached to either splines or a straight-line segments. In addition, a short horizontal line (*hook line*) connects descriptive text and/or feature control frames to the leader line. The AcadLeader object specifies such a complex leader line, and the Leader property of the AcadDimDiametric and AcadDimRadial objects specifies a simple leader line.

The AcadLeader object is created using the AddLeader method of the AcadBlock, AcadModelSpace, or AcadPaperSpace object. Any annotation attached to the leader line is defined in the Annotation property of the AcadLeader object.

## AcadLeader Object Methods

The AcadLeader object inherits all the methods of the AcadEntity and AcadObject objects. It also supports the following method.

| NAME | DESCRIPTION |
|------|-------------|
| Evaluate | Evaluates the relative position of the leader line to its associated annotation and updates the leader line's geometry if necessary |

## AcadLeader Object Properties

The AcadLeader object inherits all the properties of the AcadEntity and AcadObject objects, as well as the common Application property. It also supports the following properties.

| NAME | RETURNS | DESCRIPTION |
|------|---------|-------------|
| Annotation | AcadEntity | Gets or sets the annotation object for a leader, which can be a tolerance object, a multiline text object, or a block reference. Note that setting the Annotation property to a new annotation object modifies the drawing but returns an invalid input error. |
| ArrowheadBlock | String | Gets or sets the name of the block to use as the custom arrowhead for a leader line. |
| ArrowheadSize | Double | Gets or sets the size of the leader line arrowheads and hook lines. The initial value for this property is 0.1800. |
| ArrowheadType | AcDimArrowheadType | Gets or sets the type of arrowhead used for the leader line. The initial value for this property is acArrowDefault. Note that if you use the ArrowheadBlock property to specify a block to use as a custom arrowhead, this property will be set to acArrowUserDefined. For a list of possible values for the AcDimArrowheadType enumerated type, see Appendix B. |

| NAME | RETURNS | DESCRIPTION |
|---|---|---|
| Coordinate | Variant | Gets or sets the coordinate of a single vertex in the object. This will replace the existing vertex for the specified object. Use standard array-handling techniques to process the values contained in this property. It returns a three-element array of Doubles containing 3-D coordinates in WCS. Note that the Z coordinate will default to 0 on the active UCS. Parameter: Index As Integer (the index in the zero-based array for the vertex you want to set or query). |
| Coordinates | Variant | Gets or sets the coordinates for each vertex in the object. This will replace any existing coordinates for the specified object. Use standard array-handling techniques to process the coordinates contained in this property. Note that you can't change the number of coordinates in the object by using this property, you can only change the location of existing coordinates. It returns a three-element array of Doubles containing 3-D coordinates in WCS. Note also that the Z coordinate will always default to 0 on the active UCS. |
| DimensionLineColor | AcColor | Gets or sets the color of the leader object. Use a color index number from 0 to 256 or one of the constants listed here: acByBlock (where AutoCAD draws objects in the default color), acByLayer (where AutoCAD draws objects in the color specified for the layer), or the AcColor enumeration (see Appendix B). This property overrides the value of the DIMCLRD system variable for the given leader object. |
| DimensionLineWeight | AcLineWeight | Gets or sets the lineweight for the leader lines. See Appendix B for a list of the values of the AcLineWeight enumeration. |

| NAME | RETURNS | DESCRIPTION |
|---|---|---|
| Normal | Variant | Gets or sets the 3-D (Z-axis) normal unit vector for the leader line. |
| ScaleFactor | Double | Gets or sets the scale factor for the object. It has to be a value greater than 0.0. A scale factor greater than 1 enlarges the hook line. A scale factor between 0 and 1 shrinks the hook line. The initial value for this property is 1.0000. This property overrides the DIMSCALE system variable. |
| StyleName | String | Gets or sets the name of the style used with the object, the default being the current style. Use the TextStyle object to change the attributes of a given text style. Note that the name given must already be defined in the drawing. |
| TextGap | Double | Gets or sets the gap between the annotation and a hook line on a leader object. |
| Type | AcLeaderType | Gets or sets type of a leader line. For a list of possible values for the AcLeaderType enumerated type, see Appendix B. |
| VerticalTextPosition | AcDimVertical-Justification | Gets or sets the vertical position of text in relation to the leader line. This property overrides the value of the DIMTAD system variable for the given dimension, leader, or tolerance object. The initial value for this property is acVertCentered. (For a list of the values of the AcDimVerticalJustification enumerated type, see Appendix B.) |

**NOTE**   *Because this object inherits from* AcadObject, *it supports the* Modified *event.*

## AcadLine Object

The AcadLine object represents a single line segment. In AutoCAD, lines can be one segment or a series of connected segments, but each is a separate AcadLine object. You use this object if you want to edit individual segments. If, however, you need to draw a series of line segments as a single object, use the AcadLWPolyline object. The AcadLine object is created using the AddLine method of the AcadBlock, AcadModelSpace, or AcadPaperSpace object.

### AcadLine Object Methods

The AcadLine object inherits all the methods of the AcadEntity and AcadObject objects. It also supports the following method.

| NAME | RETURNS | DESCRIPTION |
| --- | --- | --- |
| Offset | Variant | Creates a new line by offsetting the current line by a specified distance, which can be positive or negative but can't be zero. If the offset is negative, this means that the line is drawn closer to the WCS origin. Parameter: Distance As Double. |

### AcadLine Object Properties

The AcadLine object inherits all the properties of the AcadEntity and AcadObject objects, as well as the common Application property. It also supports the following properties.

| NAME | RETURNS | DESCRIPTION |
| --- | --- | --- |
| Angle | Double | Gets the angle of the line in degrees, starting at the X-axis and proceeding counterclockwise. This property's value is read-only. |
| Delta | Variant | Gets the delta of the line. It returns a three-element array of Doubles representing the deltaX, deltaY, and deltaZ values for the line. This property's value is read-only. |

| NAME | RETURNS | DESCRIPTION |
|---|---|---|
| EndPoint | Variant | Gets or sets a set of 3-D coordinates representing the end point of the line. |
| Length | Double | Gets the length of the line. This property's value is read-only. |
| Normal | Variant | Gets or sets the 3-D (Z-axis) normal unit vector for the line object. |
| StartPoint | Variant | Gets or sets the set of 3-D WCS coordinates representing the start point for the line. |
| Thickness | Double | Gets or sets the distance the AcadLine object is extruded above or below its elevation, in a Z-axis direction. The default is 0.0. |

**NOTE** *Because this object inherits from* AcadObject, *it supports the* Modified *event.*

## *AcadLineType Object*

The AcadLineType object contains line definitions or components consisting of combinations of dashes, dots, spaces, text, and shapes. You can only create default linetypes programmatically using the Add method of the AcadLinetypes collection. However, you can load an existing linetype definition to your drawing by using the Load method of the AcadLinetypes collection. Although there is no limit to the number of linetypes defined in any one drawing, only one can be active at any one time. New objects are created using the linetype specified for the active layer. If no such linetype exists for the active layer, new objects are created with the active linetype. Linetypes are activated using the ActiveLinetype property.

### *AcadLineType Object Methods*

The AcadLineType object inherits all the methods of the AcadObject object. It supports no other methods.

### AcadLineType Object Properties

The AcadLineType object inherits all the properties of the AcadObject object, as well as the common Application property. It also supports the following properties.

| NAME | RETURNS | DESCRIPTION |
| --- | --- | --- |
| Description | String | Gets or sets a text description of the linetype object. This can be up to 47 characters long and can contain text or a series of characters to represent the linetype pattern itself (using underscores, dots, dashes, and spaces). |
| Name | String | Gets or sets the name of the linetype definition. |

**NOTE** *Because this object inherits from* AcadObject, *it supports the* Modified *event.*

## AcadLineTypes Collection

The AcadLinetypes collection contains all the linetypes defined for a drawing. You use the Add method to add a new linetype definition to the collection, and you can select a particular linetype using the Item method. You can load an existing linetype definition using the Load method. The collection also inherits a Delete method from AcadObject, but you can't use it, as the collection can't be deleted. To remove a linetype, use the Delete method of the AcadLinetype object. There is no limit to the number of linetypes you can create in your drawing. However, there can be only one instance of the AcadLinetypes collection, which is predefined for each drawing. You can make multiple references to it by using the Linetypes property.

### AcadLineTypes Collection Methods

The AcadLineTypes collection inherits all the methods of the AcadObject object. It also supports the following methods.

| NAME | RETURNS | DESCRIPTION |
|------|---------|-------------|
| Add | AcadLineType | Creates a named AcadLinetype object and adds it to the collection. Parameter: Name As String. |
| Item | AcadLineType | Gets the AcadLinetype object at a given index in the collection. Parameter: Index As Variant (an Integer or a String). If the Index value is a String, it must match an existing linetype definition. |
| Load | | Loads a definition of a named linetype from a library (.lin) file. Parameters: Name As String and FileName As String. |

### AcadLineTypes Collection Properties

The AcadLineTypes collection inherits all the properties of the AcadObject object, and supports the Count property and the common Application property. It supports no other properties.

**NOTE** *Because this collection inherits from* AcadObject, *it supports the* Modified *event.*

## AcadLWPolyline Object

The AcadLWPolyline object represents a 2-D line of adjustable width that's composed of line and arc segments. It's created using the AddLWPolyline method of the AcadBlock, AcadModelSpace, or AcadPaperSpace object.

## *AcadLWPolyline Object Methods*

The AcadLWPolyline object inherits all the methods of the AcadEntity and
AcadObject objects. It also supports the following methods.

| NAME | RETURNS | DESCRIPTION |
| --- | --- | --- |
| AddVertex | | Adds a vertex to the lightweight polyline, a vertex being the end point for a new line segment. See the SetBulge method for creating an arc. Each vertex is added to a three-element array of Doubles. Parameters: Index_As_Integer and Vertex_As_Variant. (Index refers to the position in the array where the new vertex is added. Vertex refers to the 3-D OCS coordinates where the vertex is to be created.) |
| Explode | Variant | Explodes the lightweight polyline and returns the subentities as an array of Objects (AcadLine and AcadArc). |
| GetBulge | Double | Returns the bulge value at a given index of the lightweight polyline. A bulge is the tangent of 1/4 of the included angle for the arc between the selected vertex and the next vertex in the polyline's vertex list. A negative bulge value indicates that the arc goes clockwise from the selected vertex to the next vertex. A bulge of 0 indicates a straight segment, and a bulge of 1 is a semicircle. Parameter: Index_As_Integer. |
| GetWidth | | Returns segment width at a given index of the lightweight polyline. Parameters: Index_As Integer, StartWidth_As_Double, and EndWidth_As Double. |
| Offset | Variant | Creates a new lightweight polyline by offsetting the existing polyline by a given distance, which must be nonzero. If the offset is negative, this means that the line is drawn closer to the WCS origin. Parameter: Distance As Double. |

| NAME | RETURNS | DESCRIPTION |
|------|---------|-------------|
| SetBulge | | Sets the vertex bulge of the lightweight polyline at a given index. See GetBulge for the definition of a bulge. Parameters: Index As Integer and bulge As Double. |
| SetWidth | | Sets the segment width of the lightweight polyline for a given index. Parameters: Index As Integer, StartWidth As Double, and EndWidth As Double. |

## AcadLWPolyline Object Properties

The AcadLWPolyline object inherits all the properties of the AcadEntity and AcadObject objects, as well as the common Application property. It also supports the following properties.

| NAME | RETURNS | DESCRIPTION |
|------|---------|-------------|
| Area | Double | Gets the area of a lightweight polyline in square drawing units. The area is computed as though a straight line connects the start and end points. This property's value is read-only. |
| Closed | Boolean | Specifies whether the lightweight polyline is closed (True) or open (False). Open is the default. |
| ConstantWidth | Double | Gets or sets a global width for all segments in a lightweight polyline. |
| Coordinate | Variant | Gets or sets the coordinate of a single vertex in the object. This will replace any existing vertices for the specified object. Use standard array-handling techniques to process the values contained in this property. This returns a two-element array of Doubles containing 2-D coordinates in OCS. These coordinates can be converted to and from other coordinate systems using the TranslateCoordinates method. Parameter: Index As Integer (the index in the zero-based array of vertices for the vertex you want to set or query). |

| NAME | RETURNS | DESCRIPTION |
|------|---------|-------------|
| Coordinates | Variant | Gets or sets the coordinates for each vertex in the object. This will replace any existing coordinates for the specified object. Use standard array-handling techniques to process the coordinates contained in this property. Note that you can't change the number of coordinates in the object by using this property, you can only change the location of existing coordinates. This returns the array point as a two-element array of Doubles containing 2-D points in OCS. These coordinates can be converted to and from other coordinate systems using the `TranslateCoordinates` method. |
| Elevation | Double | Gets or sets the current elevation of the lightweight polyline. |
| LinetypeGeneration | Boolean | Specifies the linetype generation of a lightweight polyline. If this is set to `True`, the linetype is generated in a continuous pattern through the polyline vertices; if it's set to `False`, the linetype is generated starting and ending with a dash at each polyline vertex. |
| Normal | Variant | Gets or sets the 3-D (Z-axis) normal unit vector for the lightweight polyline. |
| Thickness | Double | Gets or sets the distance the `AcadLWPolyline` object is extruded above or below its elevation, in a Z-axis direction. The default is 0.0. |

**NOTE** *Because this object inherits from* `AcadObject`, *it supports the* `Modified` *event.*

## *AcadMenuBar Collection*

The AcadMenuBar collection contains all the AcadPopupMenu objects displayed on the current AutoCAD menu bar. Any menu from a currently loaded menu group can be displayed on the menu bar. To display a menu on the menu bar, use the InsertInMenuBar method found on the AcadPopupMenu object. To remove a menu from the current menu bar, use the RemoveFromMenuBar method also found on the AcadPopupMenu object.

### *AcadMenuBar Collection Methods*

Just one method is supported.

| NAME | RETURNS | DESCRIPTION |
| --- | --- | --- |
| Item | Object | Returns the object at the specified index in the collection. Parameter: Index As Variant (Integer or String). If the Index value is a String, it must match an existing object name in the collection. |

### *AcadMenuBar Collection Properties*

As well as the common Application and Count properties, the AcadMenuBar collection supports the following property.

| NAME | RETURNS | DESCRIPTION |
| --- | --- | --- |
| Parent | AcadApplication | Returns the parent of the AcadMenuBar collection. This property's value is read-only. |

## AcadMenuGroup Object

The AcadMenuGroup object represents an AutoCAD menu group, which contains menus and toolbars, some or all of which may be currently displayed in AutoCAD. Each menu group contains an AcadPopupMenus collection and an AcadToolbars collection. The former collection contains all the menus within the menu group and can be accessed through the Menus property. The latter contains all the toolbars within the menu group and can be accessed through the Toolbars property. Menu groups are loaded into the AutoCAD session using the Load method, which adds the menu group to the AcadMenuGroups collection.

You can't create new menu groups. However, you can load an existing menu file containing a menu group and save it again with a new menu group name and to new menu file. The menus and toolbars thus become available for editing.

### AcadMenuGroup Object Methods

Three methods are supported by the AcadMenuGroup object.

| NAME | DESCRIPTION |
| --- | --- |
| Save | Saves the menu group. Note that certain changes to the appearance of the AutoCAD user interface, such as changing system colors, will cause the menus and toolbars to be reloaded from the menu file. Be certain to save changes to your menu group often, using the Save method, to avoid losing your customizations. Parameter: MenuFileType As AcMenuFileType. For a list of possible values for the AcMenuFileType enumerated type, see Appendix B. |
| SaveAs | Saves the menu group and gives it the specified name using the full path and file name, or valid URL address, for the file. The active menu group takes on the new name. Parameters: FileName As String and MenuFileType As AcMenuFileType. |
| Unload | Unloads the menu group. When a menu group is unloaded from the drawing, any references to the menus and toolbars within that group become invalid. Always delete or set to NULL any references to toolbars and menus before unloading. |

## AcadMenuGroup Object Properties

As well as the common Application property, the AcadMenuGroup object supports the following properties.

| NAME | RETURNS | DESCRIPTION |
|---|---|---|
| MenuFileName | String | Gets the name of the file in which the menu group is located. This property's value is read-only. |
| Menus | AcadPopupMenus | Gets the AcadPopupMenus collection for the menu group. |
| Name | String | Gets the name of the menu group. The name is limited to 32 characters and can't contain spaces or punctuation marks. This property's value is read-only. |
| Parent | AcadMenuGroups | Gets the parent of the AcadMenuGroup object. This property's value is read-only. |
| Toolbars | AcadToolbars | Gets the AcadToolbars collection for the menu group. |
| Type | AcMenuGroupType | Gets the type of the menu group. This property's value is read-only. The possible values for the AcMenuGroupType enumeration are acBaseMenuGroup and acPartialMenuGroup. |

## AcadMenuGroups Collection

The AcadMenuGroups collection contains all of the AcadMenuGroup objects, from which you can get a reference to all pop-up menus and toolbars loaded in the current AutoCAD session. To load a new menu group from a file into this collection, use the Load method. Note that you can't create new menu groups. However, you can load an existing menu group and save it out again with a new name and to new menu file. The menus and toolbars thus become available for editing. To unload a menu group from this collection, use the Unload method found on the AcadMenuGroup object.

## *AcadMenuGroups Collection Methods*

Three methods are supported by the AcadMenuGroups object.

| NAME | RETURNS | DESCRIPTION |
|------|---------|-------------|
| Item | AcadMenuGroup | Returns the object at the given index in the collection. Parameter: Index As Variant (Integer or String). If the Index value is a String, it must match an existing object name in the collection. |
| Load | AcadMenuGroup | Loads a menu group from a menu file. Parameters: MenuFileName As String and [BaseMenu As Variant]. The MenuFileName should have an .mnc, .mns, or .mnu extension. If the BaseMenu parameter is set to True, then the menu group will be loaded as a base menu, similar to the AutoCAD MENU command. If this parameter is omitted, the menu group will be loaded as a partial menu, similar to the AutoCAD MENULOAD command. |

## *AcadMenuGroups Collection Properties*

As well as the common Application property and the Count property, the AcadMenuGroups collection supports the following property.

| NAME | RETURNS | DESCRIPTION |
|------|---------|-------------|
| Parent | AcadApplication | Gets the parent of the collection. This property's value is read-only. |

# *AcadMInsertBlock Object*

The AcadMInsertBlock object represents a rectangular array of block references. It is created using the AddMInsertBlock method of the AcadBlock, AcadModelSpace, or AcadPaperSpace object.

## *AcadMInsertBlock Object Methods*

The `AcadMInsertBlock` object inherits all the methods of the `AcadEntity` and `AcadObject` objects. It also supports the following methods.

| NAME | RETURNS | DESCRIPTION |
| --- | --- | --- |
| Explode | Variant | Explodes the block and returns the subentities as an array of `AcadBlockReference` objects. |
| GetAttributes | Variant | Returns an array of editable attribute references attached to the multiple block reference. After you edit one `AcadAttribute` object and update the `AcadMInsertBlock` object, changes will appear in each nested blocks because there's only one set of attribute references for the multiple inserted blocks. |
| GetConstantAttributes | Variant | Returns an array of constant attributes for the multiple block. |

## *AcadMInsertBlock Object Properties*

The `AcadMInsertBlock` object inherits all the properties of the `AcadEntity` and `AcadObject` objects, as well as the common `Application` property. It also supports the following properties.

| NAME | RETURNS | DESCRIPTION |
| --- | --- | --- |
| Columns | Integer | Gets or sets the number of columns in a block array. |
| ColumnSpacing | Double | Gets or sets the spacing of the columns in a block array. |
| HasAttributes | Boolean | Indicates whether the block has any attributes in it. This property's value is read-only. |
| InsertionPoint | Variant | Represents an insertion point in the block as a set of 3-D WCS coordinates. It returns a three-element array of Doubles. |

| NAME | RETURNS | DESCRIPTION |
| --- | --- | --- |
| Name | String | Gets or sets the name of the multiple block, which is identical to the name of the block used in the AddMInsertBlock method. |
| Normal | Variant | Gets or sets the 3-D (Z-axis) normal unit vector for the block. |
| Rotation | Double | Gets or sets the rotation angle (in radians) for the block relative to the X-axis, with positive values going counterclockwise when viewed along the Z-axis toward the origin. |
| Rows | Integer | Gets or sets the number of rows in a block array. |
| RowSpacing | Double | Gets or sets the spacing of the rows in a block array. |
| XScaleFactor | Double | Gets or sets the X scale factor for the block. |
| YScaleFactor | Double | Gets or sets the Y scale factor for the block. |
| ZScaleFactor | Double | Gets or sets the Z scale factor for the block. |

**NOTE** *Because this object inherits from* AcadObject, *it supports the* Modified *event.*

## AcadMLine Object

The AcadMLine object represents multiple parallel lines. One AcadMLine object can comprise up to 16 lines. The object is created using the AddMLine method of the AcadBlock, AcadModelSpace, or AcadPaperSpace object.

### AcadMLine Object Methods

The AcadMLine object inherits all the methods of the AcadEntity and AcadObject objects. It supports no other methods.

## AcadMLine Object Properties

The AcadMLine object inherits all the properties of the AcadEntity and AcadObject objects, as well as the common Application property. It also supports the following properties.

| NAME | RETURNS | DESCRIPTION |
|------|---------|-------------|
| Coordinates | Variant | Gets or sets the coordinates for each vertex in the object. This will replace any existing coordinates for the specified object. Use standard array-handling techniques to process the coordinates contained in this property. Note that you can't change the number of coordinates in the object by using this property, you can only change the location of existing coordinates. Returns a three-element array of Doubles containing 3-D coordinates in WCS. Note also that the Z coordinate will always default to 0 on the active UCS. |
| StyleName | String | Gets the MLine style name. This property's value is read-only. |

**NOTE** *Because this object inherits from* AcadObject, *it supports the* Modified *event.*

## AcadModelSpace Collection

The AcadModelSpace collection contains all the objects in model space. It is similar to the AcadBlock object, and it supports exactly the same methods and properties. Moreover, objects contained in this collection can also be found in the blocks collection in a special block called *MODEL_SPACEthat is to say, both the block named *MODEL_SPACE and the AcadModelSpace collection actually point to the same data. The AcadModelSpace collection was created to provide a faster and easier means of accessing the data in model space. There is a single AcadModelSpace collection provided in the drawing. The collection can't be created or deleted. To add objects to the collection, you use the same Add* methods presented under the AcadBlock object.

Use model space for drafting and design work, and to create 2-D drawings or 3-D models.

## Methods and Properties

The AcadModelSpace collection supports all the methods and properties supported by the AcadBlock object, as well as the common Application property. See the AcadBlock object for more details.

> **NOTE** *Because this collection inherits from* AcadObject, *it supports the* Modified *event.*

# AcadMText Object

The AcadMText object represents a paragraph of alphanumeric characters that fits within a nonprinting text boundary. Each AcadMText object is a single object regardless of the number of lines it contains, and AutoCAD uses word wrap to break long lines into paragraphs. Text can be imported into an AcadMText object, but all embedded formatting will be lost. The text boundary definition specifies the width and alignment of the paragraph, and although it isn't plotted or printed, it remains part of the object's framework. AcadMText objects are created using the AddMText method of the AcadBlock, AcadModelSpace, or AcadPaperSpace object.

## AcadMText Object Methods

The AcadMText object inherits all the methods of the AcadEntity and AcadObject objects. It supports no other methods.

## AcadMText Object Properties

The AcadMText object inherits all the properties of the AcadEntity and AcadObject objects, as well as the common Application property. It also supports the following properties.

| NAME | RETURNS | DESCRIPTION |
|---|---|---|
| AttachmentPoint | AcAttachmentPoint | Gets or sets the attachment point for an AcadMText object. The option selected determines both the text justification and text spill in relation to the text boundary. When the property is changed, the position of the existing bounding box doesn't change. The text is simply rejustified within the bounding box. For a list of possible values for the AcAttachmentPoint enumerated type, see Appendix B. |
| DrawingDirection | AcDrawingDirection | Gets or sets the direction in which the MText paragraph is to be read. Possible values for the AcDrawingDirection enumeration are acLeftToRight and acTopToBottom. (Three other values are reserved for future use: acRightToLeft, acBottomToTop, and acByStyle.) |
| Height | Double | Sets the height of uppercase text, measured in the current units. This property is used as a scale factor for both the height and width of the text. \H also indicates a height change. |
| InsertionPoint | Variant | Sets the insertion point for the text and specifies the location for a corner of the text boundary. The AttachmentPoint property specifies which corner of the text boundary is to be positioned at this insertion point. |
| LineSpacingFactor | Double | Gets or sets the relative line spacing factor for the AcadMText object, defined as the vertical distance between the baseline of one text line and the baseline of the next text line. It's set as a multiple of single line spacing and should have a value between 2.5 and 4.0. |
| LineSpacingStyle | AcLineSpacingStyle | Gets or sets the line spacing style for the AcadMText object. For a list of possible values for the AcLineSpacingStyle enumerated type, see Appendix B. |
| Normal | Variant | Gets or sets the 3-D (Z-axis) normal unit vector for the AcadMText object. |

| NAME | RETURNS | DESCRIPTION |
|------|---------|-------------|
| Rotation | Double | Gets or sets the rotation angle (in radians) for MText relative to the X-axis, with positive values going counterclockwise when viewed along the Z-axis toward the origin. |
| StyleName | String | Gets or sets the name of the style used with the object, the default being the current style. Use the TextStyle object to change the attribute of a given text style. Note that the name given must already be defined in the drawing. |
| TextString | String | Gets or sets the text string for the entity. The text string may contain format codesfor example, you can underline text, add a line over text, and create stacked text. |
| Width | Double | Gets or sets the width of the text boundary in the current units. AutoCAD wraps the text within the text boundary; therefore, the width must be a positive number large enough to accommodate the text. If the width isn't large enough, the text may be difficult to read or may not be visible at all. \W also indicates a width change |

**NOTE** *Because this object inherits from* AcadObject, *it supports the* Modified *event.*

## AcadPaperSpace Collection

The AcadPaperSpace collection contains all the objects in paper space layout, and if a new paper space is made active, the data in this collection will be changed to reflect the data in the new active layout. It is similar to the AcadBlock object, and it supports exactly the same methods and properties, with just one additional method. Moreover, objects contained in this collection can also be found in the blocks collection in a special block called *PAPER_SPACE that is to say, both the block named *PAPER_SPACE and the AcadPaperSpace collection actually point to the same data. The AcadPaperSpace collection was created to provide a faster and easier means of accessing the data in the active paper space layout.

Paper space layouts are used for creating a finished layout for printing or plotting the drawing and not doing drafting or design work, which is carried out in the model space. Although both 2-D and 3-D objects can exist in paper space, commands that render a 3-D viewpoint are disabled. The AcadPaperSpace collection can't be created or deleted.

Use paper space to create a finished layout of a drawing for printing or plotting.

## AcadPaperSpace Collection Methods

The AcadPaperSpace collection inherits all the methods of the AcadBlock and AcadModelSpace collections. It also supports the following method.

| NAME | RETURNS | DESCRIPTION |
| --- | --- | --- |
| AddPViewport | AcadPViewport | Adds a paper space viewport, given the coordinates for the center of the viewport, its height, and its width. Parameters: Center As Variant, Width As Double, and Height As Double. |

## AcadPaperSpace Collection Properties

The AcadPaperSpace collection inherits all the properties of the AcadBlock and AcadModelSpace collections, as well as the common Application property. It supports no other properties.

**NOTE** *Because this collection inherits from* AcadObject, *it supports the* Modified *event.*

## AcadPlot Object

The AcadPlot object represents the set of methods and properties used for plotting specified layouts. You can display a plot preview, plot to a file or plot to a device, or batch-plot several plot commands. You can set the number of copies of the drawing to be plotted and specify quiet error mode, such that the plot session will be uninterrupted.

However, it should be noted that you can't create a configured plotter (PC3) file using ActiveX. To create a PC3 file, use the Add-a-Plotter wizard in AutoCAD. For more information on PC3 files, see "Plotter-Specific Configuration Information" in the AutoCAD documentation.

### AcadPlot Object Methods

The AcadPlot object supports the following methods.

| NAME | RETURNS | DESCRIPTION |
| --- | --- | --- |
| DisplayPlotPreview | | Displays the plot preview dialog box for the active layout. Parameter: Preview As AcPreviewMode. For a description of possible values for the AcPreviewMode enumerated type, see Appendix B. Note that there's no hourglass indicating the regeneration process and that the user needs to dismiss the preview for this method to return. Any VBA UserForm should be hidden during a plot preview. |
| PlotToDevice | Boolean | Plots a layout to a device and returns whether or not the plot was successfully sent. Parameter: plotConfig As String. The full path and file name of the PC3 file to use instead of the current configuration. If this parameter isn't provided, the current configuration will be used. A dialog window will indicate the printing progress. Any VBA UserForm should be hidden during a PlotToDevice operation. |

| NAME | RETURNS | DESCRIPTION |
|------|---------|-------------|
| PlotToFile | Boolean | Plots a layout to a file and returns whether or not the plot was successfully sent. Parameters: PlotFile As String and [PlotConfig As String]. PlotFile specifies the name of the file to plot the active layout to. When you plot multiple layouts, the file name for each plot will be generated from the drawing and layout names. A dialog window will indicate the printing progress. Any VBA UserForm should be hidden during a PlotToFile operation. PlotConfig specifies the full path and file name of the PC3 file to use instead of the current configuration. If this parameter isn't provided, the current configuration will be used. |
| SetLayoutsToPlot | | Sets the layout or layouts to be plotted. If you want a layout other than the active layout to be plotted, you must call this method. Parameter: LayoutList As Variant (an array of layout objects). If the LayoutList parameter is NULL or this method isn't called at all, the active layout is sent to the plot. Note that a call to this method has to precede each layout plotting in an iteration. Before you enter a batch operation, you have to specify the number of layouts to plot using the StartBatchMode method. |
| StartBatchMode | | Invokes batch mode printing. This method allows the plot progress dialog box to show the progress of batch plots. This remains active until the batch is completed. Parameter: EntryCount As Long. The EntryCount parameter specifies the number of calls to either the PlotToFile method or PlotToDevice method that must follow the StartBatchMode method. |

### AcadPlot Object Properties

As well as the common `Application` property, the `AcadPlot` object supports the following properties.

| NAME | RETURNS | DESCRIPTION |
| --- | --- | --- |
| QuietErrorMode | Boolean | Specifies whether or not quiet error mode is enabled. Quiet error mode logs all plot-related error messages into a log file. This is essential for certain plotting applications, such as batch plotting, that require uninterrupted application execution. When the quiet error mode is disabled, errors during printing are displayed in alert boxes. |
| NumberOfCopies | Long | Gets or sets the number of copies to be plotted. |
| BatchPlotProgress | Boolean | Specifies whether or not the batch plot is in progress. Setting this property to `False` terminates the batch plot. This can be achieved programmatically or by clicking the *Cancel* button in the progress dialog box. |

## AcadPlotConfiguration Object

See the `AcadLayout` object.

## AcadPlotConfigurations Collection

See the `AcadLayouts` collection.

## AcadPoint Object

The `AcadPoint` object represents a point marker on a drawing appearing as a dot, square, circle, X, tick, or plus sign, or as any combination of these. You can specify a full 3-D location for a point. However, the current elevation is assumed if you supply two coordinates. Points can also act as nodes onto which you can snap objects. The Coordinates property provides an array that can be used in any method requiring a point as an input parameter. AcadPoint objects are created using the AddPoint method of the AcadBlock, AcadModelSpace, or AcadPaperSpace object.

The PDMODE and PDSIZE system variables control the appearance of point objects. The values for PDMODE are as follows:

| | |
|---|---|
| 0 | Draws point as a dot (·) |
| 1 | No symbol drawn |
| 2 | Draws point as a plus (+) |
| 3 | Draws point as a cross (x) |
| 4 | Draws point as a vertical dash (') |

You can add 32, 64, or 96 to any of the preceding values to specify a shape to draw around the point in addition to the point symbol itself. The values represent a circle, a square, and a circle within a square, repectively.

The PDSIZE variable controls the size of the point symbols for PDMODE values 2 and 4. A setting of 0 generates the point at 5 percent of the graphics area height. A positive value specifies an absolute size for the point figures; a negative value is interpreted as a percentage of the viewport size.

Any changes to the points (PDMODE or PDSIZE) are displayed when the drawing is regenerated.

## AcadPoint Object Methods

The AcadPoint object inherits all the methods of the AcadEntity and AcadObject objects. It supports no other methods.

## AcadPoint Object Properties

The AcadPoint object inherits all the properties of the AcadEntity and AcadObject objects, as well as the common Application property. It also supports the following properties.

| NAME | RETURNS | DESCRIPTION |
|------|---------|-------------|
| Coordinates | Variant | Gets or sets the coordinates. It returns a three-element array of Doubles containing 3-D coordinates in WCS. |
| Normal | Variant | Gets or sets the 3-D (Z-axis) normal unit vector for the mesh. |
| Thickness | Double | Gets or sets the distance an AcadPoint object is extruded above or below its elevation, in a Z-axis direction. The default is 0.0. |

**NOTE**  *Because this object inherits from* AcadObject, *it supports the* Modified *event.*

## AcadPolyfaceMesh Object

The AcadPolyfaceMesh object represents a 3-D polyface mesh. It is created using the AddPolyfaceMesh method of the AcadBlock, AcadModelSpace, or AcadPaperSpace object.

### AcadPolyfaceMesh Object Methods

The AcadPolyfaceMesh object inherits all the methods of the AcadEntity and AcadObject objects. It supports no other methods.

### AcadPolyfaceMesh Object Properties

The AcadPolyfaceMesh object inherits all the properties of the AcadEntity and AcadObject objects, as well as the common Application property. It also supports the following properties.

| NAME | RETURNS | DESCRIPTION |
|------|---------|-------------|
| Coordinate | Variant | Gets or sets the coordinate of a single vertex in the object. This will replace an existing vertex for the specified object. Use standard array-handling techniques to process the values contained in this property. It returns a three-element array of Doubles containing 3-D coordinates in WCS. Note that the Z coordinate will default to 0 on the active UCS. Parameter: Index As Integer (the index in the zero-based array of vertices for the vertex you want to set or query). |
| Coordinates | Variant | Gets or sets the coordinates for each vertex in the object. This will replace any existing coordinates for the specified object. Use standard array-handling techniques to process the coordinates contained in this property. Note that you can't change the number of coordinates in the object by using this property, you can only change the location of existing coordinates. It returns a three-element array of Doubles containing 3-D coordinates in WCS. Note that the Z coordinate will always default to 0 on the active UCS. |
| NumberOfFaces | Integer | Gets the number of faces in the mesh. This property's value is read-only. |
| NumberOfVertices | Integer | Gets the number of vertices in the mesh. This property's value is read-only. |

**NOTE**  *Because this object inherits from* AcadObject, *it supports the* Modified *event.*

## AcadPolygonMesh Object

The AcadPolygonMesh object simulates the geometric representation of a mesh laid out on a 3-D surface. It is specified as an M×N mesh, where M represents the number of vertices in a row of the mesh and N represents the number of vertices in a column. A mesh can be open or closed in either or both the M and N directions. A mesh that is closed in a particular direction is considered to be continuous from the last row or column on to the first row or column. If it is open, it is treated as discontinuous between the last row and the first row. The AcadPolygonMesh object is created using the AddPolygonMesh method of the AcadBlock, AcadModelSpace, or AcadPaperSpace object.

### AcadPolygonMesh Object Methods

The AcadPolygonMesh object inherits all the methods of the AcadEntity and AcadObject objects. It also supports the following methods.

| NAME | RETURNS | DESCRIPTION |
| --- | --- | --- |
| AppendVertex | | Appends a vertex to the polygon mesh, which is an array of 3-D WCS coordinates specifying the appended row of vertices. Note that appending a vertex is the equivalent of adding an extra row to the polygon mesh matrix. Parameter: Vertex As Variant (a 3×M array of Doubles). Note that an array of the wrong size will result in an error, because a polygon mesh is a regular M×N matrix. |
| Explode | Variant | Explodes the polygon mesh and returns the subentities as an array of Objects (Acad3DFace objects). |

### AcadPolygonMesh Object Properties

The AcadPolygonMesh object inherits all the properties of the AcadEntity and AcadObject objects, as well as the common Application property. It also supports the following properties.

| NAME | RETURNS | DESCRIPTION |
| --- | --- | --- |
| Coordinate | Variant | Gets or sets the coordinate of a single vertex in the object. This will replace an existing vertex for the specified object. Use standard array-handling techniques to process the values contained in this property. For simple polylines, this property specifies simple vertices. For splines or curve-fit polylines, this property specifies control point vertices. It returns a three-element array of Doubles containing 3-D coordinates in WCS. Note that the Z coordinate will default to 0 on the active UCS. Parameter: Index As Integer (the index in the zero-based array of vertices for the vertex you want to set or query). |
| Coordinates | Variant | Gets or sets the coordinates for each vertex in the object. This will replace any existing coordinates for the specified object. Use standard array-handling techniques to process the coordinates contained in this property. For simple polylines, this property specifies simple vertices. For splines or curve-fit polylines, this property specifies control point vertices. Note that you can't change the number of coordinates in the object by using this property, you can only change the location of existing coordinates. It returns a 3×M×N-element array of Doubles containing 3-D coordinates in WCS. |
| MClose | Boolean | Specifies if the polygon mesh is closed in the M direction. The document has to be regenerated for the changes to appear. |

| NAME | RETURNS | DESCRIPTION |
|------|---------|-------------|
| MDensity | Integer | Gets or sets the smooth surface density of a polygon mesh in the M direction, the value of which is an integer between 2 and 255. The initial value for this property is derived from the value in the SURFU system variable plus 1. The M surface density is the number of vertices in the M direction for AcadPolygonMesh objects of the following types: acQuadSurfaceMesh, acCubicSurfaceMesh, and acBezierSurfaceMesh. |
| MVertexCount | Integer | Gets the vertex count in the M direction of the polygon mesh. This property's value is read-only. This is the number of vertices that will be used to make up an M row in the polygon mesh if the Type property is acSimpleMesh. For any other polygon mesh type, the MDensity value will be used as the row size. Note that you can't change the number of vertices for a simple mesh. This property is necessary when appending new vertices. |
| NClose | Boolean | Specifies if the polygon mesh is closed in the N direction. The document has to be regenerated for the changes to appear. |
| NDensity | Integer | Gets or sets the smooth surface density of a polygon mesh in the N direction, the value of which is an integer between 2 and 255. The initial value for this property is derived from the value in the SURFV system variable plus 1. The N surface density is the number of vertices in the N direction for AcadPolygonMesh objects of the following types: acQuadSurfaceMesh, acCubicSurfaceMesh, and acBezierSurfaceMesh. |

| NAME | RETURNS | DESCRIPTION |
|------|---------|-------------|
| NVertexCount | Integer | Gets the vertex count in the N direction of the polygon mesh. This property's value is read-only. This is the number of vertices that will be used to make up an N row in the polygon mesh if the Type property is acSimpleMesh. For any other polygon mesh type, the MDensity value will be used as the row size. Note that you can't change the number of vertices for a simple mesh. |
| Type | AcPolymeshType | Gets or sets type of a polygon mesh object. For a list of possible values for the AcPolymeshType enumerated type, see Appendix B. |

**NOTE**   *Because this object inherits from* AcadObject, *it supports the* Modified *event.*

## AcadPolyline Object

The AcadPolyline object represents a 2-D line of adjustable width or a 3-D line or mesh of nonadjustable width composed of line and arc segments. Use the AcadLWPolyline object to create polylines with an optimized format that saves memory and disk space. The AcadPolyline object is created using the AddPolyline method of the AcadBlock, AcadModelSpace, or AcadPaperSpace object.

### AcadPolyline Object Methods

The AcadPolyline object inherits all the methods of the AcadEntity and AcadObject objects. It also supports the following methods.

| NAME | RETURNS | DESCRIPTION |
|---|---|---|
| AppendVertex | | Appends a vertex to the polyline, which is an array of 3-D coordinates. The X and Y coordinates are given in OCS; the Z coordinate is ignored. Parameter: vertex As Variant (a three-element array of doubles). |
| Explode | Variant | Explodes the polyline and returns the subentities as an array of Objects (AcadLine and AcadArc). |
| GetBulge | Double | Returns the vertex bulge value at a given index of the polyline. A bulge is the tangent of 1/4 of the included angle for the arc between the selected vertex and the next vertex in the polyline's vertex list. A negative bulge value indicates that the arc goes clockwise from the selected vertex to the next vertex. A bulge of 0 indicates a straight segment, and a bulge of 1 is a semicircle. Note that this method will fail if the polyline Type property isn't acSimplePoly. Parameter: Index As Integer. |
| GetWidth | | Returns segment width at a given index of the polyline. Parameters: Index As Integer, StartWidth As Double, and EndWidth As Double. |
| Offset | Variant | Creates a new polyline by offsetting the polyline by a given distance, which must be nonzero. If the offset is negative, this means that the line is drawn closer to the WCS origin. Parameter: Distance As Double. |
| SetBulge | | Sets the vertex bulge of the polyline at a given index. See GetBulge for the definition of a bulge. Note that this method will fail if the polyline Type property isn't acSimplePoly. Parameters: Index As Integer and bulge As Double. |
| SetWidth | | Sets the segment width of the polyline for a given index. Parameters: Index As Integer, StartWidth As Double, and EndWidth As Double. |

## *AcadPolyline Object Properties*

The AcadPolyline object inherits all the properties of the AcadEntity and
AcadObject objects, as well as the common Application property. It also supports
the following properties.

| NAME | RETURNS | DESCRIPTION |
|------|---------|-------------|
| Area | Double | Gets the area of the polyline in square drawing units. The area is computed as though a straight line connects the start and end points. This property's value is read-only. |
| Closed | Boolean | Specifies whether the polyline is closed (True) or open (False). Open is the default. |
| ConstantWidth | Double | Gets or sets a global width for all segments in a polyline. |
| Coordinate | Variant | Gets or sets the coordinate of a single vertex in the object. This will replace an existing vertex for the specified object. Use standard array-handling techniques to process the values contained in this property. For simple polylines, this property specifies simple vertices. For splines or curve-fit polylines, this property specifies control point vertices. It returns a three-element array of Doubles containing 3-D coordinates in OCS (the Z coordinate is ignored). These coordinates can be converted to and from other coordinate systems using the TranslateCoordinates method. Parameter: Index As Integer (the index in the zero-based array of vertices for the vertex you want to set or query). |

| NAME | RETURNS | DESCRIPTION |
|------|---------|-------------|
| Coordinates | Variant | Gets or sets the coordinates for each vertex in the object. This will replace any existing coordinates for the specified object. Use standard array-handling techniques to process the coordinates contained in this property. For simple polylines, this property specifies simple vertices. For splines or curve-fit polylines, this property specifies control point vertices. Note that you can't change the number of coordinates in the object by using this property, you can only change the location of existing coordinates. It returns the array point as a three-element array of Doubles containing 3-D points in OCS (the Z coordinate is ignored). These coordinates can be converted to and from other coordinate systems using the `TranslateCoordinates` method. |
| Elevation | Double | Gets or sets the current elevation of the polyline. |
| LinetypeGeneration | Boolean | Specifies the linetype generation of a polyline. If it's set to `True`, the linetype is generated in a continuous pattern through the polyline vertices; if it's set to `False`, the linetype is generated starting and ending with a dash at each polyline vertex. |
| Normal | Variant | Gets or sets the 3-D (Z-axis) normal unit vector for the polyline. |
| Thickness | Double | Gets or sets the distance an `AcadPolyline` object is extruded above or below its elevation, in a Z-axis direction. The default is 0.0. |
| Type | AcPolylineType | Gets or sets type of a polyline object. For a list of possible values for the `AcPolylineType` enumerated type, see Appendix B. |

**NOTE** *Because this object inherits from* AcadObject, *it supports the* Modified *event.*

## AcadPopupMenu Object

The AcadPopupMenu object represents an AutoCAD cascading menu of which there are two types: pull-down menus, which are accessed from the AutoCAD menu bar, and shortcut menus, which are accessed by pressing *Shift* and right-clicking. A pop-up menu is a collection of menu items that includes AcadPopMenuItems, separators, and submenus, which can be added to the collection using the AddMenuItem, AddSeparator, and AddSubmenu methods.

To create a new pull-down menu, use the Add method to add a new AcadPopupMenu object to the AcadPopupMenus collection, and then add the menu to the menu bar using the InsertInMenuBar method. To create a new shortcut menu, you must first delete any existing shortcut menu, as there can be only one shortcut menu per menu group. If there is no other shortcut menu in a menu group, you can then add a menu with the label POP0, which will be recognized as the new shortcut menu. This label will tell AutoCAD that you want to create a cursor menu. Consult the AcadPreferenceUser object for the list of properties to customize the shortcut menu.

### AcadPopupMenu Object Methods

The AcadPopupMenu object supports the following methods.

| NAME | RETURNS | DESCRIPTION |
| --- | --- | --- |
| AddMenuItem | AcadPopupMenuItem | Adds an item to the pop-up menu. Parameters: Index As Variant (Integer or String), Label As String, and Macro As String. |
| | | The Index parameter for this property and the four that follow must be between 0 and N minus 1 (if it's an Integer), where N is the number of objects in the pop-up menu. The new item will be added immediately before the specified index location. To add the new menu item to the end of a menu, set the index to be greater than N. If a String is specified and the indexed item doesn't exist, then the new menu item is added at the end of the menu. |
| | | The Label parameter may contain DIESEL string expressions. Labels also identify the accelerator keys (keyboard key sequences) that correspond to the menu item by placing an ampersand (&) in front of the accelerator character. |

| NAME | RETURNS | DESCRIPTION |
| --- | --- | --- |
| AddSeparator | AcadPopupMenuItem | Adds a separator to the pop-up menu. The first item in a menu can't be a separator. You can't add a separator immediately next to another separator. Parameter: Index As Variant (Integer or String). |
| AddSubmenu | AcadPopupMenu | Adds a submenu to the pop-up menu. Parameters: Index As Variant (Integer or String) and Label As String. |
| | | The Label parameter may contain DIESEL string expressions. Labels also identify the accelerator keys (keyboard key sequences) that correspond to the menu item by placing an ampersand (&) in front of the accelerator character. |
| InsertInMenuBar | | Inserts the pop-up menu into the menu bar at the location specified by the index. Parameter: Index As Variant. |
| Item | AcadPopupMenuItem | Returns the member of the collection specified by the index. Parameter: Index As Variant (Integer or String). If the Index value is a String, it must match an existing object name in the collection. To determine if the returned item is a menu item, a separator, or a submenu, use the Type property of the returned AcadPopupMenuItem object. |
| RemoveFromMenuBar | | Removes the pop-up menu from the menu bar. |

## AcadPopupMenu Object Properties

As well as the common Application property and the Count property, the AcadPopupMenu object supports the following properties.

| NAME | RETURNS | DESCRIPTION |
|------|---------|-------------|
| Name | String | Gets or sets the name of the AcadPopupMenu object. |
| NameNoMnemonic | String | Gets the name of the menu without the underscore mnemonic. |
| OnMenuBar | Boolean | Specifies whether or not the menu is on the menu bar. This property's value is read-only. |
| Parent | Object | Gets the parent of the AcadPopupMenu object. This property's value is read-only. The valid object types are AcadMenuBar and AcadPopupMenus. |
| ShortcutMenu | Boolean | Specifies whether or not the menu is a shortcut menu. |
| TagString | String | Gets the menu's tag string, which can consist of alphanumeric and underscore (_) characters. This string uniquely identifies the item within a given menu file. This string is automatically assigned when the object is created and is used internally by AutoCAD for toolbar and menu identification. This property's value is read-only. |

## AcadPopupMenuItem Object

The AcadPopupMenuItem object represents a single menu item on an AutoCAD pull-down menu. There are three types: a simple menu item, a separator, and a submenu item. They are created using the AddMenuItem, AddSeparator, or AddSubmenu method of the AcadPopupMenu object.

Simple menu items have an index, a label, a tag, and a macro. The index is the position on the menu where the individual menu item is located. The label is a string that defines the content and formatting of the menu item as it appears to the user. The tag is a string consisting of alphanumeric and underscore (_) characters, which uniquely identifies the menu item within a given menu. The macro is a series of commands that execute specific actions when a menu item is selected.

Separators have only an index, which specifies where on the menu the separator is to appear. Submenu items have an index, a label, and a tag, but no macro. Instead, they have an entire `AcadPopupMenu` object associated with them, which appears when the user selects the submenu item. To find an `AcadPopupMenu` object associated with a submenu item, use the `SubMenu` property.

### AcadPopupMenuItem Object Methods

The `AcadPopupMenuItem` object supports a single method.

| NAME | DESCRIPTION |
| --- | --- |
| Delete | Deletes the item from the menu |

### AcadPopupMenuItem Object Properties

As well as the common `Application` property, the `AcadPopupMenuItem` object supports the following properties.

| NAME | RETURNS | DESCRIPTION |
| --- | --- | --- |
| Caption | String | Gets the text seen by the user for the menu item. This property is derived from the `Label` property by removing any `DIESEL` string expressions. This property's value is read-only. |
| Check | Boolean | Specifies the check status for the menu item (the tick to the left of the menu item caption). |
| Enable | Boolean | Specifies whether or not the item is enabled (grayed out). |
| EndSubMenuLevel | Integer | Gets or sets the last item in a submenu. The default value for this property is 0, specifying that this menu item isn't the last item in the submenu. A value of 1 indicates that this item is the last item in a submenu. A value of 2 indicates that this item is the last item of a submenu and also of its parent menu. This value should be incremented for each parent menu for which this item terminates. |

| NAME | RETURNS | DESCRIPTION |
|------|---------|-------------|
| HelpString | String | Gets or sets the help string for the menu item, which appears in the AutoCAD status line when a user highlights a menu item. |
| Index | Integer | Gets the index for the menu item. The first position in the index is 0. This property's value is read-only. |
| Label | String | Gets or sets the content and formatting of the menu item as they appear to the user. |
| Macro | String | Gets or sets the name of the macro associated with the menu item. |
| Parent | AcadPopupMenu | Gets the parent of the object. This property's value is read-only. |
| SubMenu | AcadPopupMenu | Gets the submenu, if the item is associated with one. This information can be obtained from the object Type property. This property's value is read-only. |
| TagString | String | Gets or sets the item's tag string, which can consist of alphanumeric and underscore (_) characters. This string uniquely identifies the item within a given menu file. This string is automatically assigned when the object is created and is used internally by AutoCAD for toolbar and menu identification. |
| Type | AcMenuItemType | Gets the item's type. This property's value is read-only. Possible values for the AcMenuItemType enumeration are acMenuItem, acMenuSeparator, and acMenuSubMenu. |

## AcadPopupMenus Collection

The AcadPopupMenus collection contains all the AcadPopupMenu objects loaded in the menu group, some or all of which may be currently displayed in AutoCAD. To load an existing menu into the current session, use the Load method of the AcadMenuGroups collection. To access this collection, use the Menus property on the specific AcadMenuGroup. To create a new menu, use the Add method. To display a

menu on the AutoCAD menu bar, use the `InsertMenuInMenuBar` method. To
remove a menu from the menu bar, use the `RemoveMenuFromMenuBar` method.

## AcadPopupMenus Collection Methods

The `AcadPopupMenus` collection supports four methods.

| NAME | RETURNS | DESCRIPTION |
|---|---|---|
| Add | AcadPopupMenu | Creates an `AcadPopupMenu` object and adds it to the collection. Parameter: `Name As String`. |
| InsertMenuInMenuBar | | Inserts a menu into the menu bar immediately before the position specified by the index. Parameters: `MenuName As String` and `Index As Variant` (Integer or String). If the `Index` is an Integer, it must be between 0 and N minus 1, where N is the number of pop-up menus in the menu bar. If the `Index` is a String, the name of the pop-up menu must contain any underscore (_) that appears in the menu. This method is equivalent to the `InsertInMenuBar` method of the `AcadPopupMenu` object. |
| Item | AcadPopupMenu | Returns the item in the collection specified by the index. Parameter: `Index As Variant` (Integer or String). |
| RemoveMenuFromMenuBar | | Removes the menu specified by the index from the menu bar. Parameter: `Index As Variant` (Integer or String). If the `Index` is an Integer, it must be between 0 and N minus 1, where N is the number of pop-up menus in the menu bar. If it is a `String`, the name of the pop-up menu must contain any underscore (_) that appears in the menu, which corresponds to the `TagString` property of the `AcadPopupMenu` object. |

### AcadPopupMenus Collection Properties

As well as the common `Application` property, the `AcadPopupMenus` collection supports the following property.

| NAME | DESCRIPTION |
| --- | --- |
| ParentAcadMenuGroup | Gets the collection's parent object. This property's value is read-only. |

# AcadPreferences Object

The `AcadPreferences` object specifies the current AutoCAD setting, holding all the options from the Options dialog box that reside in the registry. Consult this dialog box from the Tools menu for a list of all the current settings, most of them being accessed using the `AcadPreferences` object. Options that reside in the drawing can be found through the `AcadDatabasePreferences` object. The `AcadPreferences` object can be referenced from the `Preferences` property on the `AcadApplication` object. The `AcadPreferences` object has no methods.

### AcadPreferences Object Properties

In addition to the common `Application` property, the `AcadPreferences` object supports the following properties.

| NAME | RETURNS | DESCRIPTION |
| --- | --- | --- |
| Drafting | AcadPreferences-Drafting | Gets the `AcadPreferencesDrafting` object for the application. This property's value is read-only. |
| Display | AcadPreferences-Display | Gets the `AcadPreferencesDisplay` object for the application. This property's value is read-only. |
| Files | AcadPreferences-Files | Gets the `AcadPreferencesFiles` object for the application. This property's value is read-only. |

| NAME | RETURNS | DESCRIPTION |
|---|---|---|
| OpenSave | AcadPreferences-OpenSave | Gets the AcadPreferencesOpenSave object for the application. This property's value is read-only. |
| Output | AcadPreferences-Output | Gets the AcadPreferencesOutput object for the application. This property's value is read-only. |
| Profiles | AcadPreferences-Profiles | Gets the AcadPreferencesProfiles object for the application. This property's value is read-only. |
| Selection | AcadPreferences-Selection | Gets the AcadPreferencesSelection object for the application. This property's value is read-only. |
| System | AcadPreferences-System | Gets the AcadPreferencesSystem object for the application. This property's value is read-only. |
| User | AcadPreferences-User | Gets the AcadPreferencesUser object for the application. This property's value is read-only. |

## AcadPreferencesDisplay Object

The AcadPreferencesDisplay object contains the options from the Display tab on the Options dialog box. The object has no methods.

### AcadPreferencesDisplay Object Properties

In addition to the common Application property, the AcadPreferencesDisplay object supports the following properties.

| NAME | RETURNS | DESCRIPTION |
|---|---|---|
| AutoTrackingVecColor | VBA.ColorConstants | Gets or sets the color of the autotracking vector. The default color for this property is vbWhite. Possible values: any member of VBA.ColorConstants. |
| CursorSize | Integer | Gets or sets the size of the crosshairs as a percentage of the size of the screen. The default value for this property is 5 percent. The allowable range is 1 to 100 percent of the total screen. At 100 percent, the ends of the crosshairs aren't visible. The value for this property is stored in the CURSORSIZE system variable. |
| DisplayLayoutTabs | Boolean | Specifies whether or not the Model and Layout tabs appear in the drawing editor. True is the initial value. |
| DisplayScreenMenu | Boolean | Specifies whether or not the screen menu appears on the right side of the drawing window. False is the initial value. |
| DisplayScrollBars | Boolean | Specifies whether or not there are scrollbars at the bottom and right sides of the drawing window. False is the initial value. |
| DockedVisibleLines | Integer | Gets or sets the number of lines of text visible in the command window. The initial value for this property is 3. Note that while it's still available, this property has no effect in AutoCAD 2004 products. |
| GraphicsWinLayout-BackgrndColor | VBA.ColorConstants | Gets or sets the background color of the paper space layouts. The initial value for this property is a color halfway between the Windows standard background color and the Windows standard active button color. Possible values: any member of VBA.ColorConstants. |

| NAME | RETURNS | DESCRIPTION |
|------|---------|-------------|
| GraphicsWinModel-BackgrndColor | VBA.ColorConstants | Gets or sets the background color of the model space window. The default color for this property is vbBlack. Possible values: any member of VBA.ColorConstants. |
| HistoryLines | Integer | Gets or sets the number of lines of text from the text window kept in the memory. The initial value is 400. |
| ImageFrameHighlight | Boolean | Specifies how the raster image is displayed when the image is selected. If True, only the raster image is displayed. If False, the raster image content is displayed. The value for this property is stored in the IMAGEHLT system variable. |
| LayoutCreateViewport | Boolean | Specifies whether or not a viewport is automatically created for each new layout. True is the initial value. |
| LayoutCrosshairColor | VBA.ColorConstants | Gets or sets the color of the crosshairs and text in paper space layouts. The initial value for this property is the Windows standard text color. Possible values: any member of VBA.ColorConstants. |
| LayoutDisplayMargins | Boolean | Specifies whether or not margins are displayed in layouts. True is the initial value. |
| LayoutDisplayPaper | Boolean | Specifies whether or not the paper background is displayed in layouts. True is the initial value. |
| LayoutDisplayPaperShadow | Boolean | Specifies whether or not the paper back-ground shadow is displayed in layouts. True is the initial value. |
| LayoutShowPlotSetup | Boolean | Specifies whether or not the plot setup dialog box is displayed when a new layout is created. True is the initial value. |
| MaxAutoCADWindow | Boolean | Specifies whether or not AutoCAD occupies the entire screen at the start of the session. |

| NAME | RETURNS | DESCRIPTION |
|------|---------|-------------|
| ModelCrosshairColor | VBA.ColorConstants | Gets or sets the color of the crosshairs and of the text for the model space. The initial value of this property is vbWhite. Possible values: any member of VBA.ColorConstants. |
| ShowRasterImage | Boolean | Specifies how raster images are displayed during real-time pan and zooms. If True, the image content is displayed. If False, only the image outline is displayed (the default). If the dragging display is turned on and you enable ShowRasterImage, a copy of the image moves with the cursor as you reposition the original image. The value for this property is stored in the RTDISPLAY system variable. |
| TextFontSize | Integer | Gets or sets the font size for new text. The initial value for this property is 10. |
| TextFont | String | Gets or sets the font for new text. The initial value for this property is Courier. |
| TextFontStyle | AcTextFontStyle | Gets or sets the font style for new text. For a list of possible values for the AcTextFontStyle enumerated type, see Appendix B. |
| TextWinBackgrndColor | VBA.ColorConstants | Gets or sets the text window's background color. The default color for this property is the Windows standard window color. Possible values: any member of VBA.ColorConstants. |
| TextWinTextColor | VBA.ColorConstants | Gets or sets the text window's text color. The default color for this property is the Windows standard window text color. Possible values: any member of VBA.ColorConstants. |
| TrueColorImages | Boolean | Gets or sets how the colors in raster images and render images are displayed. If True, the highest possible color resolution is used. If False, palette colors are used (the default). |
| XrefFadeIntensity | Long | Gets or sets the percentage of fade for external references. The value must be between 1 and 90. The default value is 50. |

## AcadPreferencesDrafting Object

The AcadPreferencesDrafting object contains the options from the Drafting tab on the Options dialog box. The object has no methods.

### AcadPreferencesDrafting Object Properties

In addition to the common Application property, the AcadPreferencesDrafting object supports the following properties.

| NAME | RETURNS | DESCRIPTION |
| --- | --- | --- |
| AlignmentPointAcquisition | AcAlignmentPoint-Acquisition | Gets or sets how autoalignment points are acquired. For a list of possible values for the AcAlignmentPointAcquisition enumerated type, see Appendix B. |
| AutoSnapAperture | Boolean | Specifies whether or not the autosnap aperture is displayed in the center of the crosshairs when you snap to an object. This option is available only when the autosnap marker, magnet, or tooltip is enabled. The value for this property is stored in the APBOX system variable. The initial value for this property is True. |
| AutoSnapApertureSize | Long | Gets or sets whether the size of the autosnap aperture in pixels. This option is available only when the autosnap marker, magnet, or tooltip is enabled. The value for this property is stored in the APERTURE system variable. The initial value is 10. |
| AutoSnapMagnet | Boolean | Specifies whether or not the autosnap magnet is enabled. The value for this property is stored in the AUTOSNAP system variable. True is the initial value. |
| AutoSnapMarker | Boolean | Specifies whether or not the autosnap marker is enabled. The value for this property is stored in the AUTOSNAP system variable. True is the initial value. |

| NAME | RETURNS | DESCRIPTION |
|------|---------|-------------|
| AutoSnapMarkerColor | AcColor | Gets or sets the autosnap marker's color. For a list of possible values for the AcColor enumerated type, see Appendix B. |
| AutoSnapMarkerSize | Long | Gets or sets the autosnap marker's size in pixels. The value must be between 1 and 20. |
| AutoSnapToolTip | Boolean | Specifies whether or not the autosnap tooltips are enabled. The value for this property is stored in the AUTOSNAP system variable. True is the initial value. |
| AutoTrackToolTip | Boolean | Specifies whether or not the autotrack tooltips are displayed. When it's enabled, the user sees a tooltip whenever the cursor is over an alignment path. When it's disabled, the tooltip doesn't appear. The value for this property is stored in the AUTOSNAP system variable. True is the initial value. |
| FullScreenTrackingVector | Boolean | Specifies whether or not full-screen tracking vectors are displayed. The value for this property is stored in the TRACKPATH system variable. True is the initial value. |
| PolarTrackingVector | Boolean | Specifies whether or not polar tracking vectors are displayed. The value for this property is stored in the TRACKPATH system variable. True is the initial value. |

## AcadPreferencesFiles Object

The AcadPreferencesFiles object contains the options from the Files tab on the Options dialog box.

## AcadPreferencesFiles Object Methods

The AcadPreferencesFiles object supports just two methods.

| NAME | RETURNS | DESCRIPTION |
| --- | --- | --- |
| GetProjectFilePath | String | Returns the directory where external reference files are sought. This name is also controlled by the PROJECTNAME system variable. Parameter: ProjectName As String. |
| SetProjectFilePath | | Sets the directory where external reference files are sought. This name is also controlled by the PROJECTNAME system variable. Parameters: ProjectName As String and ProjectFilePath As String. |

## AcadPreferencesFiles Object Properties

In addition to the common Application property, the AcadPreferencesFiles object supports the following properties.

| NAME | RETURNS | DESCRIPTION |
| --- | --- | --- |
| AltFontFile | String | Gets or sets the location of the font file used if the original font can't be located and an alternative font isn't specified in the font-mapping file. |
| AltTabletMenuFile | String | Gets or sets the path for an alternative menu to swap with the AutoCAD standard tablet menu. This property is only applicable if you use a digitizer. |
| AutoSavePath | String | Gets or sets the path for the file that is created if automatic saving is enabled with the AutoSaveInterval property of the AcadPreferencesOpenSave object. The value for this property is stored in the SAVEFILEPATH system variable. |

| NAME | RETURNS | DESCRIPTION |
|------|---------|-------------|
| ConfigFile | String | Gets the location of the configuration file where information about the hardware device driver is stored. This value is read-only and can only be changed using the /c command-line switch, which is added to the acad.exe command line at startup. |
| CustomDictionary | String | Gets or sets the custom dictionary for the AutoCAD session. This property contains its drive, path, and file name. |
| DefaultInternetURL | String | Gets or sets the default Internet address. The value for this property is stored in the INETLOCATION system variable. |
| DriversPath | String | Gets or sets the directory where to look for ADI device drivers for the video display, pointing devices, printers, and plotters. Specify a drive letter and path for each path. Separate multiple directory listing with a semicolon (;). |
| FontFileMap | String | Gets or sets the location of the file that defines how fonts are converted if they can't be located. |
| HelpFilePath | String | Gets or sets the location of the AutoCAD help file. This property specifies its drive, path, and file name. |
| LicenseServer | String | Gets a list of client license servers available to the network license manager program. The value for this property is stored in the ACADSERVER environment variable. This property's value is read-only. |
| LogFilePath | String | Gets or sets the location of the log file. The value for this property is stored in the LOGFILEPATH system variable. Use the LogFileOn property of the AcadPreferencesOpenSave object to enable or disable log file capabilities. |
| MainDictionary | String | Gets or sets the dictionary used for spell checking. |

| NAME | RETURNS | DESCRIPTION |
|------|---------|-------------|
| MenuFile | String | Gets or sets the location of the menu file for the AutoCAD session. This property contains the drive, path, and file name for an .mnu, .mns, or .mnc file. |
| ObjectARXPath | String | Gets or sets the location for ObjectARX applications. |
| PostScriptPrologFile | String | Gets or sets a name for a customized prolog section in the acad.psf file. The value for this property is stored in the PSPROLOG system variable. |
| PrinterConfigPath | String | Gets or sets the location of the printer configuration files. A semicolon is used to separate multiple directories but shouldn't be used at the end of the string. |
| PrinterDescPath | String | Gets or sets the location of the printer description files. A semicolon is used to separate multiple directories but shouldn't be used at the end of the string. |
| PrinterStyleSheetPath | String | Gets or sets the location of the printer style sheet files. A semicolon is used to separate multiple directories but shouldn't be used at the end of the string. |
| PrintFile | String | Gets or sets an alternative name for the temporary plot file. The default is the name of the drawing followed by the extension .plt. |
| PrintSpoolerPath | String | Gets or sets the directory of the print spool files. The plot is written to this location. |
| PrintSpoolExecutable | String | Gets or sets the application used for print spooling including the drive, the path, and the application name of the print spooling executable used with autospool. |
| SupportPath | String | Gets or sets the directories to look for support files (support, fonts, help, and bonus files). A semicolon is used to separate multiple directories but shouldn't be used at the end of the string. |
| TempFilePath | String | Gets or sets the directory used to store temporary files. |
| TemplateDWGPath | String | Gets or sets the path for the template files used by the startup wizards. |

| NAME | RETURNS | DESCRIPTION |
|------|---------|-------------|
| TempXRefPath | String | Gets or sets the location of the external reference files. This location is used for the copy of the external reference if you choose acEnableWithCopy demand loading on the XRefDemandLoad property of the AcadPreferencesOpenSave object. |
| TextEditor | String | Gets or sets the name of the text editor for the MTEXT command. |
| TextureMapPath | String | Gets or sets the directory where to look for rendering texture maps. Multiple paths can be entered by using a semicolon (;) to paths. |
| WorkspacePath | String | Gets or sets the path for the database workspace file. |

## *AcadPreferencesOpenSave Object*

The AcadPreferencesOpenSave object contains the options from the Open and Save tab on the Options dialog box. The object has no methods.

### *AcadPreferencesOpenSave Object Properties*

In addition to the common Application property, the AcadPreferencesOpenSave object supports the following properties.

| NAME | RETURNS | DESCRIPTION |
|------|---------|-------------|
| AutoEdit | Boolean | Specifies whether or not an audit should be performed after a DXFIN or DXBIN interchange command is rendered. |
| AutoSaveInterval | Integer | Gets or sets an interval for automatic saving. The value must be between 0 and 600. A value of 0 indicates that no automatic saving is required. The timer starts as soon as you make a change to a drawing. It is reset and restarted whenever the drawing is saved. The value for this property is stored in the SAVETIME system variable. The initial setting for this property is 120. |

| NAME | RETURNS | DESCRIPTION |
|------|---------|-------------|
| CreateBackup | Boolean | Specifies whether or not a backup file is used. The value of this property is stored in the ISAVEBAK system variable. True is the initial value. |
| DemandLoadARXApp | AcARXDemandLoad | Gets and sets when a third-party application is loaded if a drawing contains custom objects created in that application. The value for this property is stored in the DEMANDLOAD system variable. For a list of possible values for the AcARXDemandLoad enumerated type, see Appendix B. |
| FullCRCValidation | Boolean | Specifies whether or not a cyclic redundancy check (CRC) should be performed whenever an object is read into the drawing. False is the initial value. If your drawings are being corrupted and you suspect a hardware problem or an AutoCAD error, set this property to True. |
| IncrementalSavePercent | Integer | Gets or sets the wasted space allowed in a file as a percentage. When the specified percentage is reached, a full save occurs instead of an incremental save. Full saves eliminate wasted space. If this property is 0, every save is a full save. Incremental saves increase the size of the drawing, but full saves take longer. The value of this property is stored in the ISAVEPERCENT system variable. The initial value of this property is 50. Autodesk recommends a setting of zero (0) when problems occur during file saves in network environments. |
| LogFileOn | Boolean | Specifies whether or not the contents of the text window are written to a log file. The value for this property is stored in the LOGFILEMODE system variable. True is the initial value. |

| NAME | RETURNS | DESCRIPTION |
|------|---------|-------------|
| MRUNumber | Long | Gets the number of most recently used files appearing in the File menu. The default value for this property is 4. This property's value is read-only. |
| ProxyImage | AcProxyImage | Gets or sets how objects are displayed in a drawing that has been created in a third-party application. Possible values for the AcProxyImage enumeration are acProxyNotShow, acProxyShow (default), and acProxyBoundingBox. |
| SaveAsType | AcSaveAsType | Gets or sets the drawing type the drawing is saved as. The initial value for this property is ac2004_DWG. For a list of possible values for the AcSaveAsType enumerated type, see Appendix B. |
| SavePreviewThumbnail | Boolean | Specifies whether or not .bmp preview images are saved with the drawing. The value for this property is saved in the RASTERPREVIEW system variable. True is the initial value. |
| ShowProxyDialogBox | Boolean | Specifies whether or not a warning message is displayed when a drawing that contains custom objects is opened. The value of this property is stored in the PROXYNOTICE system variable. True is the initial value. |
| TempFileExtension | String | Gets or sets the extension for temporary files. The string can contain up to three characters. The default value is "ac$". |
| XrefDemandLoad | AcXRefDemandLoad | Gets or sets demand loading of external references. The value for this property is stored in the XLOADCTL system variable. Demand loading improves performance by loading only the parts of the referenced drawing needed to regenerate the current drawing. The initial value for this property is acDemandLoadEnabled. For a list of possible values for the AcXRefDemandLoad enumerated type, see Appendix B. |

## AcadPreferencesOutput Object

The AcadPreferencesOutput object contains the options from the Output tab on the Options dialog box. The object has no methods.

### AcadPreferencesOutput Object Properties

As well as the common Application property, the AcadPreferencesOutput object supports the following properties.

| NAME | RETURNS | DESCRIPTION |
| --- | --- | --- |
| DefaultOutputDevice | String | Gets or sets the default output device for new layouts and model space. If there are no devices on the system, "None" will be returned. |
| DefaultPlotStyleForLayer | String | Gets or sets the default plot style for new drawings or for drawings created with earlier releases that haven't been saved in AutoCAD 2000 format. This property is only available when PlotPolicy is set to acPolicyNamed. The initial value of this property is "Normal". The value for this property is stored in the DEFLPLSTYLE system variable. |
| DefaultPlotStyleForObjects | String | Gets or sets the default plot style name for newly created objects. This property is only available if PlotPolicy is set to acPolicyNamed. The initial value is "ByLayer". The value for this property is stored in the DEFPLSTYLE system variable. |
| OLEQuality | AcOleQuality | Gets or sets the plot quality of OLE objects. The initial value is acOQText. The value for this property is stored in the OLEQUALITY system variable. Possible values for the AcOleQuality enumeration are acOQLineArt, acOQText (default), acOQGraphics, acOQPhoto, and acOQHighPhoto. |

| NAME | RETURNS | DESCRIPTION |
|------|---------|-------------|
| PlotLegacy | Boolean | Gets or sets whether legacy plot scripts can run. The value for this property is stored in the PLOTLEGACY system variable. The initial value is False. |
| PlotPolicy | AcPlotPolicy | Gets or sets whether an object's color property is associated with its plot style name when a new drawing is created. The value for this property is stored in the PSTYLEPOLICY system variable. The initial value for this property is acPolicyNamed. For a list of possible values for the AcPlotPolicy enumerated type, see Appendix B. |
| PrinterPaperSizeAlert | Boolean | Specifies whether or not the user is alerted when a layout is configured with a paper size that is different from the default setting for the PC3 file. The value for this property is stored in the PAPERALERT system variable. The initial value is True. |
| PrinterSpoolAlert | AcPrinterSpoolAlert | Gets or sets whether the user is alerted when output needs to be spooled through a system printer due to a conflict with an I/O port. The value for this property is stored in the PSPOOLALERT system variable. The initial value is acPrinterAlwaysAlert. For a list of possible values for the AcPrinterSpoolAlert enumerated type, see Appendix B. |
| UseLastPlotSettings | Boolean | Specifies whether or not the settings of the last successful plot are applied. |

## *AcadPreferencesProfiles Object*

The AcadPreferencesProfiles object contains the options from the Profiles tab on the Options dialog box.

## AcadPreferencesProfiles Object Methods

This object supports the following methods.

| NAME | DESCRIPTION |
|------|-------------|
| CopyProfile | Copies a profile in the registry. Parameters: oldProfileName As String and newProfileName As String. |
| DeleteProfile | Deletes a profile from the registry. Parameter: ProfileName As String. |
| ExportProfile | Exports a profile to a file so that other users can use it. Parameters: Profile As String and RegFile As String. The extension of the RegFile should be .arg. |
| GetAllProfileNames | Gets all profiles available to the system. Parameter: PNames As Variant. |
| ImportProfile | Imports a profile from a file created by another user. Parameters: Profile As String, RegFile As String, and IncludePathInfo As Boolean. The imported registry file specified by the RegFile parameter should have an .arg extension. The IncludePathInfo parameter is True if the path information in the registry file will be preserved and False otherwise. |
| RenameProfile | Renames a profile. Parameters: OrigProfileName As String and NewProfileName As String. |
| ResetProfile | Resets the value in a profile to its default values. The specified profile must be the currently active profile. Parameter: Profile As String. |

## AcadPreferencesProfiles Object Properties

As well as the common Application property, the AcadPreferencesProfiles object supports the following property.

| NAME | RETURNS | DESCRIPTION |
|---|---|---|
| ActiveProfile | String | Gets or sets the active profile for the session. The available profile names are returned by the GetAllProfileNames method. |

## AcadPreferencesSelection Object

The AcadPreferencesSelection object contains the options from the Selection tab on the Options dialog box. The object has no methods.

### AcadPreferencesSelection Object Properties

As well as the common Application property, the AcadPreferencesSelection object supports the following properties.

| NAME | RETURNS | DESCRIPTION |
|---|---|---|
| DisplayGrips | Boolean | Specifies whether or not selection set grips are displayed for the stretch, move, rotate, scale, and mirror grip modes. The value for this property is stored in the GRIPS system variable. The initial value is True. |
| DisplayGripsWithinBlocks | Boolean | Specifies whether or not grips are assigned within blocks. The value for this property is stored in the GRIPBLOCK system variable. The initial value is False. |
| GripColorSelected | AcColor | Gets or sets the color of selected grips. The value for this property is stored in the GRIPHOT system variable. The initial value is acRed. For a list of possible values for the AcColor enumerated type, see Appendix B. |
| GripColorUnselected | AcColor | Gets or sets the color of grips that aren't selected. The value for this property is stored in the GRIPCOLOR system variable. The initial value is acBlue. For a list of possible values for the AcColor enumerated type, see Appendix B. |

| NAME | RETURNS | DESCRIPTION |
|------|---------|-------------|
| GripSize | Long | Gets or sets the size of grips in pixels. The value for this property is stored in the GRIPSIZE system variable. The value may be between 1 and 255, but a size greater than 20 isn't recommended. The initial value is 3. |
| PickAdd | Boolean | Specifies whether or not objects are added to the selection set by using the Shift key. The value for this property is stored in the PICKADD system variable. The initial value is False. |
| PickAuto | Boolean | Specifies whether or not windowing is automatic at the select objects prompt. The value for this property is stored in the PICKAUTO system variable. The initial value is True. |
| PickBoxSize | Long | Gets or sets the size of the object selection target. The value for this property is stored in the PICKBOX system variable. The initial value is 3. |
| PickDrag | Boolean | Specifies how a selection window is drawn. The value for this property is stored in the PICKDRAG system variable. If True, the selection window is drawn by dragging. If False, the selection window is drawn by clicking the corners. The initial value is False. |
| PickFirst | Boolean | Specifies whether or not objects are selected before a command is issued. The value for this property is stored in the PICKFIRST system variable. The initial value is True. |
| PickGroup | Boolean | Specifies whether or not picking an object in a group selects the entire group. The initial value is False. |

**NOTE** *The* GRIPHOVER *system variable added in AutoCAD 2004 isn't exposed through ActiveX in any API.*

## *AcadPreferencesSystem Object*

The AcadPreferencesSystem object contains the options from the System tab on the Options dialog box. The object has no methods.

### *AcadPreferencesSystem Object Properties*

As well as the common Application property, the AcadPreferencesSystem object supports the following properties.

| NAME | RETURNS | DESCRIPTION |
|------|---------|-------------|
| BeepOnError | Boolean | Specifies whether or not an invalid entry causes an alarm to beep. The initial value is False. |
| DisplayOLEScale | Boolean | Specifies whether or not the OLE scaling dialog box is displayed when an OLE object is inserted into a drawing. The initial value is True. |
| EnableStartupDialog | Boolean | Specifies whether or not the startup dialog box is displayed at the beginning of the session. The initial value is True. |
| LoadAcadLspInAllDocuments | Boolean | Specifies when acad.lsp is loaded. The value for this property is stored in the ACADLSPASDOC system variable. If True, it's loaded with each drawing. If False, it's loaded at startup. |
| ShowWarningMessages | Boolean | Specifies whether or not all dialog boxes with a "Don't display this warning again" check box are displayed again. The initial value is False. |
| SingleDocumentMode | Boolean | Specifies whether or not AutoCAD runs in single-document mode rather than in multiple-document mode. The value for this property is stored in the SDI system variable. The initial is False. |
| StoreSQLIndex | Boolean | Specifies whether or not the SQL index is stored in the drawing. The initial value is True. |
| TablesReadOnly | Boolean | Specifies whether or not database tables are opened in read-only mode rather than read-write mode. The initial value is False. |

## *AcadPreferencesUser Object*

The AcadPreferencesUser object contains the options from the User tab on the Options dialog box. The object has no methods.

### *AcadPreferencesUser Object Properties*

As well as the common Application property, the AcadPreferencesUser object supports the following properties.

| NAME | RETURNS | DESCRIPTION |
| --- | --- | --- |
| ADCInsertUnits-DefaultSource | AcInsertUnits | Gets or sets the units that are automatically used for objects in the AutoCAD Design Center for a source drawing without assigned insert units. The value of this property is stored in the INSUNITSDEFSOURCE system variable. The initial value is acInsertUnitsUnitless. For a list of possible values for the AcInsertUnits enumerated type, see Appendix B. |
| ADCInsertUnits-DefaultTarget | AcInsertUnits | Gets or sets the units that are automatically used for objects in the AutoCAD Design Center for a target drawing without assigned insert units. The value of this property is stored in the INSUNITSDEFTARGET system variable. The initial value is acInsertUnitsUnitless. For a list of possible values for the AcInsertUnits enumerated type, see Appendix B. |
| HyperlinkDisplayCursor | Boolean | Specifies whether or not the hyperlink cursor and shortcut menu are displayed. When it's enabled, the user sees a small bitmap (just below and to the right of the crosshairs) whenever the cursor is over an object that contains a hyperlink. The initial value is True. |

| NAME | RETURNS | DESCRIPTION |
|------|---------|-------------|
| HyperlinkDisplayTooltip | Boolean | Specifies whether or not the hyperlink tooltips are displayed. When it's enabled, the user sees a tooltip whenever the cursor is over an object that contains a hyperlink. This property is automatically disabled when the HyperlinkDisplayCursor property is disabled. The initial value is True. |
| KeyboardAccelerator | AcKeyboard-Accelerator | Gets or sets the keyboard used. The initial value is acPreferenceCustom. For a list of possible values for the AcKeyboardAccelerator enumerated type, see Appendix B. |
| KeyboardPriority | AcKeyboard Priority | Gets or sets the response to the input of coordinate data. The value of this property is stored in the OSNAPCOORD system variable. The initial value is acKeyboardEntryExceptScripts. For a list of possible values for the AcKeyboardPriority enumerated type, see Appendix B. |
| SCMCommandMode | AcDrawingArea-SCMCommand | Gets or sets the right-click functionality in the drawing area while in command mode (that is, while a command is currently in progress). The value of this property (and the three that follow) is stored in the SHORTCUTMENU system variable. This property can only be set when the ShortcutMenuDisplay property is set to True. The initial value is acEnableSCMOptions. For a list of possible values for the AcDrawingArea-SCMCommand enumerated type, see Appendix B. |

| NAME | RETURNS | DESCRIPTION |
|------|---------|-------------|
| SCMDefaultMode | AcDrawingArea-SCMDefault | Gets or sets the right-click functionality in the drawing area while in default mode (that is, while no objects are selected and no commands are in progress). This property can only be set when the ShortcutMenuDisplay property is set to True. The initial value is acSCM. The initial value is acEnableSCMOptions. For a list of possible values for the AcDrawingAreaSCMDefault enumerated type, see Appendix B. |
| SCMEditMode | AcDrawingArea-SCMEdit | Gets or sets the right-click functionality in the drawing area while in edit mode (that is, while one or more objects are selected and no commands are in progress). This property can only be set when the ShortcutMenuDisplay property is set to True. The initial value is acEdSCM. For a list of possible values for the AcDrawingAreaSCMEdit enumerated type, see Appendix B. |
| ShortCutMenuDisplay | Boolean | Specifies whether or not right-clicking in the drawing area displays a shortcut. If False, a right-click will be interpreted as an *Enter.* The initial value is True. |

## *AcadPViewport Object*

The AcadPViewport object represents rectangular objects created in paper space that display views. The functionality of this object is slightly different from what is used in the AutoCAD user interface. In ActiveX Automation, the ActiveSpace property (of the Document object) is used to control the TILEMODE system variable. Also, the MSpace property (also of the Document object) is the equivalent of both AutoCAD's MSPACE and PSPACE commands. In addition, the ActiveX Automation user is required to use the Display method before setting the MSpace property to

acOn. It's good practice to activate the display using the `Display` method for at
least one `AcadPViewport` object before setting the `MSpace` property, or else the latter will throw an exception.

The `AcadPViewport` object is created using the `AddPViewport` method of the
`AcadPaperSpace` object.

## *AcadPViewport Object Methods*

The `AcadPViewport` object inherits all the methods of the `AcadEntity` and
`AcadObject` objects. It also supports the following methods.

| NAME | DESCRIPTION |
|------|-------------|
| Display | Determines whether viewport is on or off. The display control must be on before the `MSpace` property can be used to activate the model space editing capabilities. Use the `ViewportOn` property to determine if a paper space viewport display has already been turned on with this method. Parameter: `Status As Boolean`. |
| GetGridSpacing | Gets the grid spacing for the viewport. Parameters: `XSpacing As Double` and `YSpacing As Double`. |
| GetSnapSpacing | Gets the snap spacing for the viewport. Parameters: `XSpacing As Double` and `YSpacing As Double`. |
| SetGridSpacing | Sets the grid spacing for the viewport. Parameters: `XSpacing As Double` and `YSpacing As Double`. |
| SetSnapSpacing | Sets the snap spacing for the viewport. Parameters: `XSpacing As Double` and `YSpacing As Double`. |

## *AcadPViewport Object Properties*

The `AcadPViewport` object inherits all the properties of the `AcadEntity` and
`AcadObject` objects, as well as the common `Application` property. It also supports
the following properties.

| NAME | RETURNS | DESCRIPTION |
|------|---------|-------------|
| ArcSmoothness | Integer | Gets or sets the smoothness of circles, arcs, and ellipses. The initial value for this property is 100. The higher the number, the smoother the object, but AutoCAD needs longer to regenerate it. Performance can be improved by setting this property to a low value for drawing and increasing the value for rendering. The valid range is 1 to 20,000. |
| Center | Variant | Gets or sets the center of the viewport as a set of 2-D coordinates (as Doubles). The default center is (0,0). |
| Clipped | Boolean | Determines whether or not the viewport has been clipped. This property's value is read-only. |
| CustomScale | Double | Gets or sets the custom scale factor for the viewport. To set the viewport to a custom scale, first set the StandardScale property to acVpCustomScale, and then use this property to define the custom scale value. |
| Direction | Variant | Gets or sets the viewing direction for a 3-D visualization of the drawing. This property puts the viewer in a position to look at the drawing as if looking back at the origin (0, 0, 0) from a specified point in space. It's similar to AutoCAD's VPOINT command. It returns a three-element array of Doubles. |
| DisplayLocked | Boolean | Determines whether or not the viewport is locked, that is, whether it can or can't be modified (scaled, rotated, or moved). It's True if it is locked and False otherwise. |

| NAME | RETURNS | DESCRIPTION |
|------|---------|-------------|
| GridOn | Boolean | Specifies the status of the viewport grid. It's True if it's on and False otherwise. The value of this property is stored in the GRIDMODE system variable. Note that the grid is used only for visual reference. It isn't plotted and it isn't considered part of the drawing. The grid origin is set by the SnapBasePoint method. When you turn the grid on or off on a viewport, the visibility of the grid won't change until the viewport is made active or is reset (using the ActiveViewport property). |
| Height | Double | Use to set the height of the viewport, which is the Y-axis measurement of the viewport frame. The height also determines the magnification parameter in a ZoomCenter. |
| LensLength | Double | Gets or sets the lens length (in millimeters) used in perspective viewing, the value of which is stored in the LENSLENGTH system variable. |
| RemoveHiddenLines | Boolean | Specifies whether or not hidden lines are to be plotted on a paper space viewport. |
| SnapBasePoint | Variant | Gets or sets the snap base point for the viewport, the value of which is stored in the SNAPBASE system variable. The snap base point can't be changed for the active paper space viewport. Any changes to this property aren't reflected in the display until the drawing is regenerated. |
| SnapOn | Boolean | Specifies the status of snap mode. The value of this property is stored in the SNAPMODE system variable and its style is changed using the SNAPSTYLE system variable. This property activates snap mode using the current snap grid resolution, rotation, and style. Note that the snap grid is invisible. Use the GridOn property to activate a separate visible grid. |

| NAME | RETURNS | DESCRIPTION |
|------|---------|-------------|
| SnapRotationAngle | Double | Gets or sets the snap rotation angle (in radians) of the viewport relative to the current UCS, the value of which is stored in the SNAPANG system variable. Changes to this property aren't reflected in the drawing until it's updated. The valid range is 0 to 6.28. |
| StandardScale | AcViewportScale | Gets or sets the standard scale for the viewport. Changes to this property won't be visible until the drawing is regenerated. For a list of possible values for the AcViewportScale enumerated type, see Appendix B. |
| StyleSheet | String | Gets or sets the named style sheet for the viewport. |
| Target | Variant | Gets or sets the target point for the viewport as a set of 3-D WCS coordinates representing the target point. The line of sight is drawn from the center to the target point. It returns a three-element array of Doubles. |
| TwistAngle | Double | Gets or sets the twist angle (in radians) for the viewport. This method twists or tilts the view around the line of sight, measured counterclockwise. |
| UCSIconAtOrigin | Boolean | Specifies whether or not the UCS icon is displayed at the origin. |
| UCSIconOn | Boolean | Specifies whether or not the UCS icon is on. |
| UCSPerViewport | Boolean | Specifies whether or not the UCS is saved with the viewport. |
| ViewportOn | Boolean | Specifies the display status of the viewport. This property is set by the Display method. |
| Width | Double | Sets the width of the viewport, which is the X-axis measurement of the viewport frame. |

**NOTE**   *Because this object inherits from* AcadObject, *it supports the* Modified *event. There is no direct programmatic means to create or manipulate polygonal* PViewport *objects.*

## AcadRasterImage Object

The AcadRasterImage object represents an image consisting of a rectangular grid, or raster, of small squares or dots known as *pixels*. It is created using the AddRaster method of the AcadBlock, AcadModelSpace, or AcadPaperSpace object.

### AcadRasterImage Constant Methods

The AcadRasterImage object inherits all the methods of the AcadEntity and AcadObject objects. It also supports the following method.

| NAME | DESCRIPTION |
| --- | --- |
| ClipBoundary | Sets the clipping boundary for a raster image as an array of 2-D WCS coordinates. This must be a closed and visible polygon or rectangle completely contained within the boundaries of the image. You can use this method to define a region of an image for display or plotting. Multiple instances of the same image can have different boundaries. Parameter: Boundary_As_Variant (an array of two-element array of Doubles). |

### AcadRasterImage Constant Properties

The AcadRasterImage object inherits all the properties of the AcadEntity and AcadObject objects, as well as the common Application property. It also supports the following properties.

| NAME | RETURNS | DESCRIPTION |
| --- | --- | --- |
| Brightness | Integer | Gets or sets the current brightness value of an image, with values between 0 and 100. The default is 50. You adject this value to darken or lighten an image. Note that you can't use this property with bitonal images. |
| ClippingEnabled | Boolean | Enables or disables the clipping boundary, defined with the ClipBoundary method. |

| NAME | RETURNS | DESCRIPTION |
| --- | --- | --- |
| Contrast | Integer | Gets or sets the current contrast value of an image, with values between 0 and 100. The default is 50. You adject this value to make a dull image clearer. Note that you can't use this property with bitonal images. |
| Fade | Integer | Gets or sets the current fade value of an image, with values of 0 to 100. You adjust this value to make vectors easier to see over images and to create a watermark effect in your plotted output. Note that you can't use this property with bitonal images. |
| Height | Double | Gets the height of the raster image in pixels. This property's value is read-only. |
| ImageFile | String | Gets or sets the full path and file name of the raster image file. This property can be used to load a new raster image into an existing raster entity. |
| ImageHeight | Double | Gets or sets the height of the raster image in current units. For uniform stretching/ shrinking of the image, use the ScaleFactor property. |
| ImageVisibility | Boolean | Specifies if image visibility is on or off. Image redrawing speed is increased by turning off image visibility. Hidden images aren't displayed or plotted only the image boundary. Images can be hidden regardless of the current viewport coordinate system or when it isn't aligned with the current viewport coordinate system. |
| ImageWidth | Double | Gets or sets the width of the raster image in current units. For uniform stretching/ shrinking of the image, use the ScaleFactor property. |
| Name | String | Gets or sets the name of the raster object, but not its path (see the ImageFile property). |

| NAME | RETURNS | DESCRIPTION |
|---|---|---|
| Origin | Variant | Gets or sets the origin of the raster image in WCS coordinates, relative to the lower-left corner. Returned an array of Doubles. |
| Rotation | Double | Gets or sets the rotation angle (in radians) for the object, relative to the X-axis of the object's WCS with positive angles going counterclockwise when viewed down from the Z-axis toward the origin. |
| ScaleFactor | Double | Gets or sets the scale factor for the object. It has to be a value greater than 0. A scale factor greater than 1 enlarges the object. A scale factor between 0 and 1 shrinks the object. The initial value for this property is 1.0000. |
| ShowRotation | Boolean | Determines whether or not a raster image is displayed at the value of its Rotation property. |
| Transparency | Boolean | Specifies if the transparency for a particular bitonal image is on or off. Attached bitonal images inherit current layer settings for background and foreground color. In addition to the modifications you can make to any attached image, you can modify bitonal images by turning the transparency of the background on and off. Note that bitonal images and bitonal image boundaries are always the same color. |
| Width | Double | Gets the width of the raster image in pixels. This property's value is read-only. |

**NOTE**   *Because this object inherits from* AcadObject, *it supports the* Modified *event.*

## *AcadRay Object*

The AcadRay object represents a semi-infinite line and is commonly used as a construction line. A ray has a finite starting point and extends to infinity. The AcadRay object is created using the AddRay method of the AcadBlock, AcadModelSpace, or AcadPaperSpace object.

### *AcadRay Object Methods*

The AcadRay object inherits all the methods of the AcadEntity and AcadObject objects. It supports no other methods.

### *AcadRay Object Properties*

The AcadRay object inherits all the properties of the AcadEntity and AcadObject objects, as well as the common Application property. It also supports the following properties.

| NAME | RETURNS | DESCRIPTION |
| --- | --- | --- |
| BasePoint | Variant | Gets or sets the point through which the ray passes. It returns a set of 3-D coordinates as a three-element array of Doubles. |
| DirectionVector | Variant | Gets or sets the direction for the ray through a vector. It returns a three-element array of Doubles. |
| SecondPoint | Variant | Gets or sets the second point of the ray. It returns a set of 3-D WCS coordinates as a three-element array of Doubles. Note that you can't set the second point of a ray equal to its base point. |

**NOTE** *Because this object inherits from* AcadObject, *it supports the* Modified *event.*

# AcadRegion Object

The AcadRegion object represents a bounded planar face consisting of lines, circles, arcs, elliptical arcs, and spline curves. All objects in the region retain their layer, linetype, and color. AutoCAD deletes the original objects after converting them to regions and doesn't hatch the regions by default. The AcadRegion object is created using the AddRegion method of the AcadBlock, AcadModelSpace, or AcadPaperSpace object. Regions are mostly used as loops for AcadHatch objects to calculate the area of a composite figure or to find its Centroid and other physical characteristics.

## AcadRegion Object Methods

The AcadRegion object inherits all the methods of the AcadEntity and AcadObject objects. It also supports the following methods.

| NAME | RETURNS | DESCRIPTION |
| --- | --- | --- |
| Boolean | | Performs a Boolean operation against another region, allowing you to create composite regions from the intersection, union, or subtraction of one region from another. Parameters: Operation As AcBooleanType and Object As AcadRegion. For a list of AcBooleanType constants, see Appendix B. |
| Explode | Variant | Explodes the region and returns the subentities as an array of Objects. The individual loops of the regions are converted to lines, circular or elliptical arcs, or spline curves. |

## AcadRegion Object Properties

The AcadRegion object inherits all the properties of the AcadEntity and AcadObject objects, as well as the common Application property. It also supports the following properties.

| NAME | RETURNS | DESCRIPTION |
|------|---------|-------------|
| Area | Double | Gets the enclosed area of a region, which equals the combined area for all the objects in the region. The area of the object is specified in square drawing units. This property's value is read-only. |
| Centroid | Variant | Gets the center of area or mass for a region or solid as a 2-D coordinate. It returns as a two-element array of Doubles. This property's value is read-only. |
| MomentOfInertia | Variant | Gets the moment of inertia for the region as a 3-D coordinate. It returns as a three-element array of Doubles. This property's value is read-only. |
| Normal | Variant | Gets the 3-D (Z-axis) normal unit vector for the region. This property's value is read-only. |
| Perimeter | Double | Gets the total length of the inner and outer region loops in drawing units. This property's value is read-only. |
| PrincipalDirections | Variant | Gets the principal directions of the region as X, Y, and Z coordinates calculated on the current coordinate system. This property's value is read-only. |
| PrincipalMoments | Variant | Gets the principal moments property of the region as X, Y, and Z coordinates calculated on the current coordinate system. This property's value is read-only. |
| ProductOfInertia | Double | Gets the product of inertia of the region, as X, Y, and Z coordinates calculated on the current coordinate system. This property's value is read-only. |
| RadiiOfGyration | Variant | Gets the radius of gyration of the region, as X, Y, and Z coordinates calculated on the current coordinate system. This property's value is read-only. |

**NOTE** *Because this object inherits from* AcadObject, *it supports the* Modified *event.*

# AcadRegisteredApplication Object

The AcadRegisteredApplication object represents an external application that has been added to the drawing. To be recognized by AutoCAD, an application must register the name or names that it uses. This only happens once per drawing. These application names are then saved along with the extended data (XData) of each entity that uses them. Every instance of extended data referenced in a drawing must have its application registered in the drawing. Each AcadRegisteredApplication object is created using the Add method of the AcadRegisteredApplications collection and can be accessed using the Item method of the AcadRegisteredApplications collection.

## AcadRegisteredApplication Object Methods

The AcadRegisteredApplication object inherits all the methods of the AcadObject object. It supports no other methods.

## AcadRegisteredApplication Object Properties

The AcadRegisteredApplication object inherits all the properties of the AcadObject object, as well as the common Application property. It also supports the following property.

| NAME | RETURNS | DESCRIPTION |
|------|---------|-------------|
| Name | String | Gets or sets the name of the registered application |

**NOTE** *Because this object inherits from* AcadObject, *it supports the* Modified *event.*

## AcadRegisteredApplications Collection

The AcadRegisteredApplications collection contains a collection of all registered applications in the drawing. To add a new member to the collection, use the Add method. To select a specific registered application, use the Item method. Although this collection inherits a Delete method, you can't actually delete this collection. If you need to delete a specific registered application, use the Delete method found in the AcadRegisteredApplication object. There is no limit to the number of registered applications you can create in your drawing. However, there can be only one instance of the AcadRegisteredApplications collection, which is predefined for each drawing. You can make multiple references to it by using the RegisteredApplications property.

### AcadRegisteredApplications Collection Methods

The AcadRegisteredApplications collection inherits all the methods of the AcadObject object. It also supports the following methods.

| NAME | RETURNS | DESCRIPTION |
| --- | --- | --- |
| Add | AcadRegistered-Application | Creates a member object and adds it to the collection. Parameter: Name As String. |
| Item | AcadRegistered-Application | Gets the member object at a given index in a collection. Parameter: Index As Variant (an Integer or a String). If the Index value is a String, it must match an existing object name in the collection. |

### AcadRegisteredApplications Collection Properties

The AcadRegisteredApplications collection inherits all the properties of the AcadObject object, the Count property, and the common Application property. It supports no other properties.

**NOTE** *Because this collection inherits from* AcadObject, *it supports the* Modified *event.*

## *AcadSelectionSet Object*

The AcadSelectionSet object represents a group of one or more AutoCAD objects specified for processing as a single unit. It is created by the Add method of the AcadSelectionSets collections and can be accessed by the Item method of the AcadSelectionSets collection. There are four methods that can be used to remove selection sets or their contents: Clear, RemoveItems, Erase, and Delete.

### *AcadSelectionSet Object Methods*

The AcadSelectionSet object supports the following methods. Note that it does not inherit from AcadObject.

| NAME | RETURNS | DESCRIPTION |
| --- | --- | --- |
| AddItems | | Adds an object or objects to the selection set. Parameter: Items As Variant. The parameter must be an array containing a unique or multiple objects. |
| Clear | | The Clear method removes all the items from the selection set. The objects still exist, but they no longer reside in the selection set. |
| Delete | | The Delete method deletes a selection set object, but not the objects that were contained within it. The key (Name) is removed from the collection and is available for further use. |
| Erase | | The Erase method deletes all items in a selection set. The selection set still exists but the objects removed do not. |
| Highlight | | Sets the highlight status for all objects in the selection set. Once the highlight flag for an object has been set, a call to the Update or Regen method is required to view the change. Parameter: HighlightFlag As Boolean. The parameter is True if the object is highlighted and False otherwise. |

| NAME | RETURNS | DESCRIPTION |
|------|---------|-------------|
| Item | Object | Gets the member of the selection set specified by the index. Parameter: Index As Variant (Integer or String). If the Index value is a String, it must match an existing object name in the collection. |
| RemoveItems | | The RemoveItems method removes one or more items from a selection set. These objects still exist but they no longer reside in the selection set. Parameter: Objects As Variant. The parameter must be an array containing a unique or multiple objects. |
| Select | | Adds objects to the selection set. Parameters: Mode As AcSelect, [Point1 As Variant, Point2 As Variant], and [FilterType As Integer, FilterData As Variant]. For a list of possible values for the AcSelect enumeration (the Mode parameter), see Appendix B. The second and third parameters are three-element arrays of Doubles representing 3-D WCS coordinates. For this method and the three that follow, FilterType is a DXF group code specifying the type of filter to use. FilterData is the value to filter on. All four Select methods support the filtering mechanism. |
| SelectAtPoint | | Adds an object containing a point to the selection set. Parameters: Point As Variant and [FilterType As Integer, FilterData As Variant]. Point is a three-element array of Doubles representing 3-D WCS coordinates. |
| SelectByPolygon | | Adds any objects inside a polygon to the selection set. Parameters: Mode As AcSelect, PointsList As Variant, and [FilterType As Integer, FilterData As Variant]. For a list of possible values for the AcSelect enumeration (the Mode parameter), see Appendix B. PointsList is a three-element array of Doubles representing 3-D WCS coordinates. |

| NAME | RETURNS | DESCRIPTION |
|------|---------|-------------|
| SelectOnScreen | | Prompts the user to select an object from the screen. Parameters: [FilterType As Integer, FilterData As Variant]. |
| Update | | Updates the selection set. |

### AcadSelectionSet Object Properties

As well as the common Application property, the AcadSelectionSet object supports the following properties.

| NAME | RETURNS | DESCRIPTION |
|------|---------|-------------|
| Count | Integer | Gets the number of items in the selection set. |
| Name | String | Gets name of the selection set. This property's value is read-only. |

# AcadSelectionSets Collection

The AcadSelectionSets collection contains all of the selection sets in the drawing. To add a new member to the collection, use the Add method. To select a specific selection set, use the Item method. To delete a specific selection set, use the Delete method of the AcadSelectionSet object. AutoCAD allows you up to 128 selection sets objects. However, there can be only one instance of the AcadSelectionSets collection, which is predefined for each drawing. You can make multiple references to it by using the SelectionSets property of the AcadDocument object.

### AcadSelectionSets Collection Methods

The AcadSelectionSets collection supports just two methods. Note that it does not inherit from AcadObject.

| NAME | RETURNS | DESCRIPTION |
|------|---------|-------------|
| Add | AcadSelectionSet | Creates an AcadSelectionSet object and adds it to the collection. Parameter: Name As String. |
| Item | AcadSelectionSet | Returns the member of the collection specified by the index. Parameter: Index As Variant (Integer or String). If the Index value is a String, it must match an existing object name in the collection. |

### AcadSelectionSets Collection Properties

The AcadSelectionSets collection supports the Application property and the Count property, but no others.

## AcadShape Object

The AcadShape object represents an object comprising lines, arcs and circles defined in an .shx file. Note that before inserting a shape, you must load the file containing the desired shape file, using the LoadShapeFile method. The AcadShape object is created using the AddShape method of the AcadBlock, AcadModelSpace, or AcadPaperSpace object.

### AcadShape Object Methods

The AcadShape object inherits all the methods of the AcadEntity and AcadObject objects. It supports no other methods.

### AcadShape Object Properties

The AcadShape object inherits all the properties of the AcadEntity and AcadObject objects, as well as the common Application property. It also supports the following properties.

| NAME | RETURNS | DESCRIPTION |
|---|---|---|
| Height | Double | Sets the height of the shape object in drawing units. |
| InsertionPoint | Variant | Gets or sets the insertion point for a shape as a set of 3-D WCS coordinates. It returns a three-element array of Doubles. |
| Name | String | Gets or sets the name of the object. |
| Normal | Variant | Gets or sets the 3-D (Z-axis) normal unit vector for the shape object. |
| ObliqueAngle | Double | Gets or sets the oblique angle of the attribute and is measured from the vertical axis. The units are radians within the range of –85 to +85 degrees. A positive value denotes a lean toward the right. |
| Rotation | Double | Gets or sets the rotation angle (in radians) for the shape, relative to the X-axis with positive values going counterclockwise when viewed along the Z-axis toward the origin. |
| ScaleFactor | Double | Gets or sets the scale factor for the object. It has to be a value greater than 0.0. A scale factor greater than 1 enlarges the object. A scale factor between 0 and 1 shrinks the object. The initial value for this property is 1.0000. |
| Thickness | Double | Gets or sets the distance the AcadShape object is extruded above or below its elevation, in a Z-axis direction. The default is 0.0. |

**NOTE** *Because this object inherits from* AcadObject, *it supports the* Modified *event.*

## *AcadSolid Object*

The `AcadShape` object represents a solid-filled polygon. Solid objects are only filled when the `FILLMODE` system variable is on, which can be set or queried by the `SetVariable` and `GetVariable` methods. The `AcadSolid` object is created using the `AddSolid` method of the `AcadBlock`, `AcadModelSpace`, or `AcadPaperSpace` object.

### *AcadSolid Object Methods*

The `AcadSolid` object inherits all the methods of the `AcadEntity` and `AcadObject` objects. It supports no other methods.

### *AcadSolid Object Properties*

The `AcadSolid` object inherits all the properties of the `AcadEntity` and `AcadObject` objects, as well as the common `Application` property. It also supports the following properties.

| NAME | RETURNS | DESCRIPTION |
|------|---------|-------------|
| Coordinate | Variant | Gets or sets the coordinate of a single vertex in the object. This will replace an existing vertex for the specified object. Use standard array-handling techniques to process the values contained in this property. It returns a three-element array of Doubles containing 3-D coordinates in WCS. Note that the Z coordinate will default to 0 on the active UCS. Parameter: Index As Integer (the index in the zero-based array of vertices for the vertex you want to set or query). |
| Coordinates | Variant | Gets or sets the coordinates for each vertex in the object. This will replace any existing coordinates for the specified object. Use standard array-handling techniques to process the coordinates contained in this property. Note that you can't change the number of coordinates in the object by using this property, you can only change the location of existing coordinates. It returns a three-element array of Doubles containing 3-D coordinates in WCS. |

| NAME | RETURNS | DESCRIPTION |
|------|---------|-------------|
| Normal | Variant | Gets or sets the 3-D (Z-axis) normal unit vector for the solid object. |
| Thickness | Double | Gets or sets the distance the AcadSolidobject is extruded above or below its elevation, in a Z-axis direction. The default is 0.0. |

**NOTE**   *Because this object inherits from* AcadObject, *it supports the* Modified *event.*

## AcadSpline Object

A *spline* is a smooth curve passing through a given set of points. AutoCAD uses a particular type of spline known as a nonuniform rational B-spline (NURBS) curve, which produces a smooth curve between control points. Splines are useful for creating irregularly shaped curvesfor example, drawing contour lines for geographic information system applications or automobile design. Splines are created by specifying coordinate points and can form a closed loop if the start and end points and tangents are coincident. You can also alter the spline-fitting tolerance. *Fit tolerance* refers to how closely the spline fits the set of given coordinates. The lower the tolerance, the more closely the spline fits the points. *Zero tolerance* means that the spline passes through all the points.

The AcadSpline object represents a NURBS curve and is created using the AddSpline method of the AcadBlock, AcadModelSpace, or AcadPaperSpace object.

### AcadSpline Object Methods

The AcadSpline object inherits all the methods of the AcadEntity and AcadObject objects. It also supports the following methods.

| NAME | RETURNS | DESCRIPTION |
|------|---------|-------------|
| AddFitPoint | | Adds the fit point (a set of 3-D WCS coordinates) to the spline at a given index. If the index is negative, then the point is added to the beginning of the spline. If the index exceeds the maximum value of the index, then the point is added to the end of the spline. The fit point is added to the spline and is refitted through the new set of points. The changes can only be viewed if the drawing is regenerated. Parameters: Index As Integer and FitPoint As Variant. |
| DeleteFitPoint | | Deletes the fit point of the spline at a given index, which must be a positive integer between 0 and N minus 1, where N is the total number of fit points for the spline. The fit point is removed and the spline refitted through the remaining points. There must be at least three fit points in the spline for this method to succeed. The changes can only be viewed if the drawing is regenerated. Parameter: Index As Integer. |
| ElevateOrder | | Elevates the order of the spline. The range of values is one above the current order (which is the value of the Degree property plus 1) to a maximum of 26. When a spline is elevated, it is converted from an interpolated (fit) spline to a control point spline. Note that, once elevated, the spline order can't be reduced. The StartTangent and EndTangent properties are no longer used or accessible, the spline being editable by the mean of its control points. Parameter: Order As Integer. |
| GetControlPoint | Variant | Returns the 3-D WCS coordinates of the control point of the spline at a given index as an array of Doubles. Control points fine-tune a spline definition by adding weight to a portion of the spline curve. Parameter: Index As Integer. |

| NAME | RETURNS | DESCRIPTION |
|------|---------|-------------|
| GetFitPoint | Variant | Returns the 3-D WCS coordinates of the fit point of the spline at a given index as an array of Doubles. Parameter: Index As Integer. |
| GetWeight | Double | Returns the weight of the spline at a given control point index. Parameter: Index As Integer. |
| Offset | Variant | Creates a new spline by offsetting the current spline by a specified distance, which must be nonzero. If the offset is negative, this means that the spline is drawn closer to the WCS origin. Parameter: Distance As Double. |
| PurgeFitData | | Purges the fit data of the spline. |
| Reverse | | Reverses the direction of the spline. |
| SetControlPoint | | Sets the indexed control point of the spline at a specified point. Parameters: Index As Integer and ControlPoint As Variant. |
| SetFitPoint | | Sets the indexed fit point of the spline at a specified point. Parameters: Index As Integer and FitPoint As Variant. |
| SetWeight | | Sets the weight of the spline for a given control point index. Parameters: Index As Integer and Weight As Double. |

## AcadSpline Object Properties

The AcadSpline object inherits all the properties of the AcadEntity and AcadObject objects, as well as the common Application property. It also supports the following properties.

| NAME | RETURNS | DESCRIPTION |
|------|---------|-------------|
| Area | Double | Gets the enclosed area of the spline in square drawing units. The area is computed as though a straight line connects the start and end points. This property's value is read-only. |
| Closed | Boolean | Determines whether or not the spline is closed. When you close a spline, you make it tangent-continuous at both ends. If the spline's start and end points are already the same, closing the spline makes it tangent-continuous at both points. When you open a closed spline, if the start and end points were the same before the close, this property returns the spline to its original state. The start and end points remain the same but lose their tangent continuity. If the spline's start and end points were not the same before the close, opening the spline returns it to its original state and removes tangent continuity. This property's value is read-only. |
| ControlPoints | Variant | Gets or sets the control points of a spline storing the 3-D WCS coordinates as an array of Doubles. Control points fine-tune a spline definition by adding weight or density to a portion of the spline curve. |
| Degree | Integer | Gets the degree of the spline's polynomial representation. The return value must be in the range 1 to 25. This property's value is read-only. To set a higher value for the degree, use the ElevateOrder method. The higher the degree is, the higher the control points are. |
| EndTangent | Variant | Gets or sets the end tangent of the spline as a directional vector. This property is inaccessible to control points. |
| FitPoints | Variant | Gets or sets the fit points of a spline, which define the path of the spline. |

| NAME | RETURNS | DESCRIPTION |
|------|---------|-------------|
| FitTolerance | Double | Refits the spline to the existing points with new tolerance values. If this value is 0, the spline passes through all fit points. A value greater than zero allows the curve to pass through the fit points within the specified tolerance. |
| IsPeriodic | Boolean | Determines whether or not the given spline is periodic. This property's value is read-only. |
| IsPlanar | Boolean | Determines whether or not the spline is planar. This property's value is read-only. |
| IsRational | Boolean | Determines whether or not the given spline is rational. This property's value is read-only. |
| Knots | Variant | Gets the knot vector for a spline. |
| NumberOfControlPoints | Integer | Gets the number of control points of the spline. This property's value is read-only. |
| NumberOfFitPoints | Integer | Gets the number of fit points of the spline. This property's value is read-only. |
| StartTangent | Variant | Gets or sets the start tangent for the spline as a directional vector. This property is inaccessible to control points for an elevated spline. |
| Weights | Variant | Gets the weight vector for spline. |

**NOTE** *Because this object inherits from* AcadObject, *it supports the* Modified *event.*

## AcadState Object

The AcadState object is a special object for use in monitoring the state of AutoCAD from out-of-process applications. It is a transient object that is returned from the GetAcadState method of the AcadApplication object and is used to check for AutoCAD quiescence from out-of-process applications. This object has no methods.

### AcadState Object Properties

Other than the common Application property, the AcadState object supports just one property.

| NAME | RETURNS | DESCRIPTION |
|------|---------|-------------|
| IsQuiescent | Boolean | Returns True if AutoCAD is idle and False if AutoCAD is busy. This property's value is read-only. |

# AcadText Object

The AcadText object represents a single line of alphanumeric characters. This object differs from the AcadMText object in that it creates only a single line of text, whereas the AcadMText object creates a paragraph of text. The AcadText object is created using the AddText method of the AcadBlock, AcadModelSpace, or AcadPaperSpace object.

### AcadText Object Methods

The AcadText object inherits all the methods of the AcadEntity and AcadObject objects. It supports no other methods.

### AcadText Object Properties

The AcadText object inherits all the properties of the AcadEntity and AcadObject objects, as well as the common Application property. It also supports the following properties.

| NAME | RETURNS | DESCRIPTION |
|------|---------|-------------|
| Alignment | AcAlignment | Gets or sets both the vertical and horizontal alignments for the text. For a full list of the values of the AcAlignment enumerated type, see Appendix B. See also the InsertPoint and TextAlignmentPoint properties. |
| Backward | Boolean | Specifies the direction of text. True is for backward; False is for forward. |

| NAME | RETURNS | DESCRIPTION |
| --- | --- | --- |
| Height | Double | Use to set the height of uppercase text, measured in the current units. This property is used as a scale factor for both the height and width of the text. |
| HorizontalAlignment | AcHorizontal-Alignment | Gets or sets the horizontal alignment for the text. For a full list of the values of the AcHorizontalAlignment enumerated type, see Appendix B. See also the InsertPoint and TextAlignmentPoint properties |
| InsertionPoint | Variant | Gets or sets the insertion point for text. This property's value is read-only except for text whose Alignment property is set to acAlignmentLeft, acAlignmentAligned, or acAlignmentFit. To position text whose justification is other than left, aligned, or fit, use the TextAlignmentPoint property. Also, text with the HorizontalAlignment property set to acHorizontalAlignmentLeft, acHorizontalAlignmentAligned, or acHorizontalAlignmentFit uses this property to position the text. All other settings for HorizontalAlignment use the TextAlignmentPoint property. |
| Normal | Variant | Gets or sets the 3-D (Z-axis) normal unit vector for the text object. |
| ObliqueAngle | Double | Gets or sets the oblique angle of the attribute, and is measured from the vertical axis. The units are radians within the range of –85 to +85 degrees. A positive value denotes a lean toward the right. |
| Rotation | Double | Gets or sets the rotation angle (in radians) for the text object, relative to the X-axis with positive values going counterclockwise when viewed along the Z-axis toward the origin. The rotation angle is read-only for text whose Alignment property is set to acAlignmentAligned or acAlignmentFit. |

| NAME | RETURNS | DESCRIPTION |
|------|---------|-------------|
| ScaleFactor | Double | Gets or sets the scale factor for the object. It has to be a value greater than 0.0. A scale factor greater than 1 enlarges the object. A scale factor between 0 and 1 shrinks the object. The initial value for this property is 1.0000. |
| StyleName | String | Gets or sets the name of the style used with the object, the default being the current style. Use the TextStyle object to change the attribute of a given text style. Note that the name given must already be defined in the drawing. |
| TextAlignmentPoint | Variant | Gets or sets the alignment point for text, returning a three-element array of Doubles. If the Alignment property is set to acAlignmentLeft, this property will be reset to (0,0,0) and will become read-only. Also, you can't use this property to position text with the HorizontalAlignment property set to acHorizontalAlignmentLeft. In both cases, use the InsertPoint property. |
| TextGenerationFlag | AcTextGeneration-Flag | Gets or sets the attribute text generation flag. Possible values: acTextFlagBackward and acTextFlagUpsideDown. |
| TextString | String | Gets or sets the text string for the entity. |
| Thickness | Double | Gets or sets the distance the AcadText object is extruded above or below its elevation, in a Z-axis direction. The default is 0.0. |
| UpsideDown | Boolean | Specifies the direction of text. True is for upside down; False is for the right way up. |
| VerticalAlignment | AcVerticalAlignment | Gets or sets vertical alignment for the text. For a list of the values of the AcVerticalAlignment enumerated type, see Appendix B. |

**NOTE**  *Because this object inherits from* AcadObject, *it supports the* Modified *event.*

## AcadTextStyle Object

The AcadTextStyle object represents a named, saved collection of settings that determine the appearance of text characters. The ActiveTextStyle property sets the active text style, which is used to format new text created in the drawing and also existing text that has no individual text style specified. If changes are made to the active text style, the new AcadTextStyle object must be reset as the active text style, and the drawing must be regenerated for the changes to appear. To specify a distinct individual text style for an object so that it won't change along with the active text style, use the StyleName property for that particular object.

### AcadTextStyle Object Methods

The AcadTextStyle object inherits all the methods of the AcadObject object. It also supports the following methods.

| NAME | DESCRIPTION |
| --- | --- |
| GetFont | Gets the definition data of the font for the text style. Parameters: TypeFace As String, Bold As Boolean, Italic As Boolean, Charset As Integer, and PitchAndFamily As Integer. The TypeFace parameter specifies the font name of the text style. The Bold parameter is set to True for text to be bold. The Italic parameter is set to True for text to be italic. The Charset parameter specifies the character set for the font. The default value is 1. The PitchAndFamily parameter combines several constants (by a Boolean OR operation) to give the pitch and family values for the font. The default value is 0. A full list of constants can be found in the win32api.txt file supplied with the Visual Basic IDE. |
| SetFont | Sets the definition data of the font for the text style. Parameters: TypeFace As String, Bold As Boolean, Italic As Boolean, Charset As Integer, and PitchAndFamily As Integer. |

## *AcadTextStyle Object Properties*

The AcadTextStyle object inherits all the properties of the AcadObject object, as well as the common Application property. It also supports the following properties.

| NAME | RETURNS | DESCRIPTION |
| --- | --- | --- |
| BigFontFile | String | Gets or sets the name of the Asian language big font file associated with the text or attribute. The only valid file type is .shx, and the property can't be set to NULL or contain an empty string. |
| FontFile | String | Gets or sets the primary font file path and name. Fonts define the shapes of the text characters that make up each character set. Note that once this property has been set, you have to regenerate the drawing to see the changes to the text. |
| Height | Double | Sets the height of the text in current units. |
| LastHeight | Double | Gets or sets the last text height value used. |
| Name | String | Gets the name of the object. This property's value is read-only. |
| ObliqueAngle | Double | Gets or sets the oblique angle of the attribute and is measured from the vertical axis. The units are radians within the range of –85 to +85 degrees. A positive value denotes a lean toward the right. |
| TextGenerationFlag | Integer | Gets or sets the attribute text generation flag. Possible values are acTextFlagBackward and acTextFlagUpsideDown. |
| Width | Double | Gets or sets the width of the text boundary and sets the character spacing. Entering a value of less than 1.0 condenses the text. Entering a value of greater than 1.0 expands it. The maximum value is 100. |

**NOTE** *Because this object inherits from* AcadObject, *it supports the* Modified *event.*

## *AcadTextStyles Collection*

The AcadTextStyles collection contains all the text styles in the drawing. To add a new member to the collection, use the Add method. To select a specific text style, use the Item method. Although this collection inherits a Delete method, you can't actually delete this collection. If you need to delete a specific text style, use the Delete method found in the AcadTextStyle object. There is no limit to the number of text styles you can create in your drawing. However, there can be only one instance of the AcadTextStyles collection, which is predefined for each drawing. You can make multiple references to it by using the TextStyles property.

### *AcadTextStyles Collection Methods*

The AcadTextStyles collection inherits all the methods of the AcadObject object. It also supports the following methods.

| NAME | RETURNS | DESCRIPTION |
|------|---------|-------------|
| Add | AcadTextStyle | Creates a member object and adds it to the collection. Parameter: Name As String. |
| Item | AcadTextStyle | Gets the member object at a given index in a collection. Parameter: Index As Variant (an Integer or a String). If the Index value is a String, it must match an existing text style definition. |

### AcadTextStyles Collection Properties

The AcadTextStyles collection inherits all the properties of the AcadObject object, the Count property, and the common Application property. It supports no other properties.

 **NOTE**  *Because this collection inherits from* AcadObject, *it supports the* Modified *event.*

# AcadTolerance Object

The AcadTolerance object represents a geometric tolerance contained in a feature control frame. Tolerances are influenced by several system variables, which can be set and queried using the SetVariable and GetVariable methods. The color of the feature control frame is controlled by DIMCLRD. The color of the tolerance text is controlled by DIMCLRT. The gap between the feature control frame and the text is controlled by DIMGAP. The size of the tolerance text is controlled by DIMTXT. Finally, the style of the tolerance text is controlled by DIMTXTSTY.

The AcadTolerance object is created using the AddTolerance method of the AcadBlock, AcadModelSpace, or AcadPaperSpace objects.

### AcadTolerance Object Methods

The AcadTolerance object inherits all the methods of the AcadEntity and AcadObject objects. It supports no other methods.

### AcadTolerance Object Properties

The AcadTolerance object inherits all the properties of the AcadEntity and AcadObject objects, as well as the common Application property. It also supports the following properties.

| NAME | RETURNS | DESCRIPTION |
|------|---------|-------------|
| Arrowhead1Type | AcDimArrowheadType | Gets or sets the type of arrowhead for the tolerance object. It overrides the value of the DIMBLK1 system variable. For the values of the AcDimArrowheadType enumerated type, see Appendix B. |
| DecimalSeparator | String | Gets or sets the character used as the decimal separator in tolerance values. The initial value for this property is the period (.), though any character will be accepted as a valid value for this property. It overrides the value of the DIMSEP system variable. |
| DimensionLineColor | AcColor | Gets or sets the color of the tolerance object. Use a color index number from 0 to 256 or one of the constants listed here: acByBlock (where AutoCAD draws objects in the default color) or acByLayer (where AutoCAD draws objects in the color specified for the layer). For a list of possible values for the AcColor enumerated type, see Appendix B. This property overrides the value of the DIMCLRD system variable for the given object. |
| DirectionVector | Variant | Gets or sets the direction for the tolerance through a vector. It returns a three-element array of Doubles. |
| FractionFormat | AcDimFractionType | Gets or sets the formats of fractional values. It overrides the value of the DIMFRAC system variable. Possible values are acHorizontal, acDiagonal, and acNotStacked. |
| InsertionPoint | Variant | Represents an insertion point in the tolerance object as a set of 3-D WCS coordinates. It returns a three-element array of Doubles. |

| NAME | RETURNS | DESCRIPTION |
|---|---|---|
| Normal | Variant | Gets or sets the 3-D (Z-axis) normal unit vector for the tolerance object. |
| PrimaryUnitsPrecision | AcDimPrecision | Gets or sets the number of decimal places displayed for the primary units. For a list of possible values for the AcDimPrecision enumerated type, see Appendix B. |
| ScaleFactor | Double | Gets or sets the scale factor for the object. It has to be a value greater than 0.0. A scale factor greater than 1 enlarges the object. A scale factor between 0 and 1 shrinks the object. The initial value for this property is 1.0000. This property overrides the DIMSCALE system variable. |
| StyleName | String | Gets or sets the name of the style used with the object, the default being the current style. Use the TextStyle object to change the attribute of a given text style. Note that the name given must already be defined in the drawing. |
| TextColor | AcColor | Gets or sets the color of the tolerance text. Use a color index number from 0 to 256 or one of the constants listed here: acByBlock (where AutoCAD draws objects in the default color), acByLayer (where AutoCAD draws objects in the color specified for the layer), and the AcColor enumerated type (see Appendix B). This property overrides the value of the DIMCLRD system variable for the given object. |

| NAME | RETURNS | DESCRIPTION |
|------|---------|-------------|
| TextHeight | Double | Gets or sets the height for the tolerance text, the value of which overrides the value of the DIMTXT system variable. This property is ignored if the current text style has a fixed text height. The initial value is 0.1800. |
| TextString | String | Gets or sets the text string for the entity. |
| TextStyle | String | Gets or sets the text style for the tolerance text, the value of which overrides the value of the DIMTXSTY system variable. The initial value is STANDARD. |

**NOTE** *Because this object inherits from* AcadObject, *it supports the* Modified *event.*

## AcadToolbar Object

The AcadToolbar object represents an AutoCAD toolbar, which provides access to frequently used or custom commands, settings, and macros. You can add tools to or remove tools from the AutoCAD default toolbars and reposition them. You can also create your own toolbars.

You create a new toolbar with the Add method. AddToolbarButton inserts a new button to the toolbar, and AddSeparator adds a separator. Use the ToolbarItem object to add functionality to the toolbar button or to create flyout toolbar buttons. You can change the position of toolbars by docking them along the top, bottom, or sides of the AutoCAD screen, or you can float toolbars anywhere on the screen.

## AcadToolbar Object Methods

The AcadToolbar object supports the following methods.

| NAME | RETURNS | DESCRIPTION |
|------|---------|-------------|
| AddToolbarButton | AcadToolbarItem | Adds an item to the toolbar immediately before the position specified by the index. To associate a toolbar to a flyout button, use the AttachToolbarToFlyout method on the returned AcadToolbarItem object. Note that to add a button to a toolbar, it has to be visible. Parameters: Index As Variant (Integer or String), Name As String, HelpString As String, Macro As String, and [FlyoutButton As Variant]. |
| | | The Index parameter for this property, and the one that follows, must be between 0 and N minus 1 (if it is an Integer), where N is the number of objects in the pop-up menu. The new item will be added immediately before the specified index location. To add the new menu item to the end of a menu, set the index to be greater than N. If a String is specified and the indexed item doesn't exist, then the new menu item is added at the end of the menu. |
| | | The Name must be composed of alphanumeric characters with no punctuation other than a dash (-) or an underscore (_). This will show up as the tooltip. |
| | | The FlyoutButton parameter is a Boolean variable determining whether the new button is to be a flyout button (True) or not (False). False is the default value returned if this option is ignored. |

| NAME | RETURNS | DESCRIPTION |
|------|---------|-------------|
| AddSeparator | AcadToolbarItem | Adds a separator to the toolbar immediately before the position specified by the index. The first item in a menu can't be a separator. You can't add a separator immediately next to another separator. Parameter: Index As Variant (Integer or String). |
| Delete | | Deletes an item from the toolbar. Note that the item must have no Index parameter. |
| Dock | | Docks the toolbar to its owning frame window. Parameter: Side As AcToolbarDockStatus. For a list of possible values for the AcToolbarDockStatus enumeration, see Appendix B. |
| Float | | Floats the toolbar. Parameters: Top As Integer, Left As Integer, and NumberFloatRows As Integer. The Top and Left parameters specify the pixel location for the top and left edges of the toolbar, respectively, and are screen coordinates. Get the position of the document window to float in the drawing limits. The NumberFloatRows parameter designates the number of rows to create in the horizontal toolbar. The buttons on the toolbar will be distributed automatically across the number of rows designated. |
| Item | AcadToolbarItem | Returns the item from the collection specified by the index. Parameter: Index As Variant (Integer or String). If the Index value is a String, it must match an existing object name in the collection. |

## AcadToolbar Object Properties

As well as the common `Application` property and the `Count` property, the `AcadToolbar` object supports the following properties.

| NAME | RETURNS | DESCRIPTION |
|------|---------|-------------|
| DockStatus | AcToolbarDockStatus | Gets whether and where the toolbar is docked. This property's value is read-only. For a list of possible values for the AcToolbarDockStatus enumerated type, see Appendix B. |
| FloatingRows | Integer | Gets or sets the number of rows if the toolbar is floating. |
| Height | Integer | Gets the height of the toolbar. This property's value is read-only. |
| HelpString | String | Gets or sets the toolbar's help string. |
| LargeButtons | Boolean | Specifies whether or not the toolbar buttons are large. This property's value is read-only. |
| Left | Integer | Gets or sets the position in pixels of left edge of the toolbar from the left side of the screen. |
| Name | String | Gets or sets the toolbar's name. |
| Parent | AcadToolbars | Gets the object to which the toolbar object belongs. This property's value is read-only. |
| TagString | String | Gets the menu's tag string, which can consist of alphanumeric and underscore (_) characters. This string uniquely identifies the item within a given menu file. This string is automatically assigned when the object is created and is used internally by AutoCAD for toolbar and menu identification. This property's value is read-only. |
| Top | Integer | Gets or sets the position in pixels of the top edge of the toolbar from the top of the screen. |
| Visible | Boolean | Specifies whether or not the toolbar is visible. |
| Width | Double | Gets the width of the toolbar. This property's value is read-only. |

# AcadToolbarItem Object

The AcadToolbarItem object represents a single button or separator on an AutoCAD toolbar. A toolbar button can contain a macro to be executed when it is selected by the user, or it can contain a nested toolbar called a flyout. Separators can't contain macros or flyouts. The Macro property is used to add or change the button's associated macro.

## AcadToolbarItem Object Methods

The AcadToolbarItem object supports the following methods.

| NAME | DESCRIPTION |
| --- | --- |
| AttachToolbarToFlyout | Attaches the toolbar to a toolbar button defined as a flyout. To create a new button as a flyout, you must first use the AddToolbarButton method of the AcadToolbar object with the FlyoutButton parameter set to True. Only then can you attach the toolbar to the flyout using this method. Parameters: MenuGroupName As String and ToolbarName As String. |
| Delete | Deletes a specified toolbar item. Note that you can only add or remove toolbar items when the toolbar is visible. |
| GetBitmaps | Gets the large and small bitmaps used as icons for the toolbar item. Parameters: SmallIconName As String and LargeIconName As String. The parameters require both the path and file name of the bitmaps. |
| SetBitmaps | Sets the large (24×22 pixels) and small (15×16 pixels) bitmaps used as icons for the toolbar item. Parameters: SmallIconName As String and LargeIconName As String. The parameters require both the path and file name of the bitmaps. |

## AcadToolbarItem Object Properties

As well as the common Application property, the AcadToolbarItem object supports the following properties.

| NAME | RETURNS | DESCRIPTION |
|------|---------|-------------|
| Flyout | AcadToolbar | Gets the toolbar associated with the item, if it's a flyout toolbar item. This property's value is read-only. |
| HelpString | String | Gets or sets the help string for the menu item, which appears in the AutoCAD status line when a user highlights a menu item. |
| Index | Integer | Gets the index for the menu item. The first position in the index is 0. This property's value is read-only. |
| Macro | String | Gets or sets the macro associated with the toolbar item. |
| Name | String | Gets or sets the name of the toolbar item. |
| Parent | AcadToolbar | Gets the parent object of the toolbar item. This property's value is read-only. |
| TagString | String | Gets the menu's tag string, which can consist of alphanumeric and underscore (_) characters. This string uniquely identifies the item within a given menu file. This string is automatically assigned when the object is created and is used internally by AutoCAD for toolbar and menu identification. |
| Type | AcToolbarItemType | Gets the toolbar item's type. This property's value is read-only. Possible values for the AcToolbarItemType enumeration are acToolbarButton, acToolbarFlyout, and acToolbarControl. |

## AcadToolbars Collection

The AcadToolbars collection contains all the toolbars loaded in the current AutoCAD session, some or all of which may be currently displayed in AutoCAD. To load an existing toolbar into the current session, load the menu group that contains the toolbar using the Load method of the AcadMenuGroups collection. To display large buttons for all toolbars, set the LargeButtons property to True.

## AcadToolbars Collection Methods

The AcadToolbars collection supports just two methods.

| NAME | RETURNS | DESCRIPTION |
|------|---------|-------------|
| Add | AcadToolbar | Creates an AcadToolbar object and adds it to the collection. Parameter: Name As String. |
| Item | AcadToolbar | Returns the member of the collection specified by the index. Parameter: Index As Variant. |

## AcadToolbars Collection Properties

As well as the common Application property and the Count property, the AcadToolbars collection supports the following properties.

| NAME | RETURNS | DESCRIPTION |
|------|---------|-------------|
| LargeButtons | Boolean | Specifies whether or not the displayed toolbar buttons are large. |
| ParentAcadMenuGroup | | Gets the collection's parent object. This property's value is read-only. |

# AcadTrace Object

The AcadTrace object represents a 2-D solid line of specified width. The end points of a trace are always positioned on the centerline and are cut square. AutoCAD automatically calculates the correct bevels when connecting adjacent trace segments. Traces are solid-filled when the fill mode is on. Otherwise, only the outline of the trace appears. The fill mode uses the system variable FILLMODE, which is set using the SetVariable method and queried using the GetVariable method. The system variable TRACEWID stores the current width used for an AcadTrace object.

The AcadTrace object is created using the AddTrace method of the AcadBlock, AcadModelSpace, or AcadPaperSpace object.

## AcadTrace Object Methods

The AcadTrace object inherits all the methods of the AcadEntity and AcadObject objects. It supports no other methods.

## AcadTrace Object Properties

The AcadTrace object inherits all the properties of the AcadEntity and AcadObject objects, as well as the common Application property. It also supports the following properties.

| NAME | RETURNS | DESCRIPTION |
| --- | --- | --- |
| Coordinate | Variant | Gets or sets the coordinate of a single vertex in the object. This will replace an existing vertex for the specified object. Use standard array-handling techniques to process the values contained in this property. It returns a three-element array of Doubles containing 3-D coordinates in WCS. Note that the Z coordinate will default to 0 on the active UCS. Parameter: Index As Integer (the index in the zero-based array of vertices for the vertex you want to set or query). |
| Coordinates | Variant | Gets or sets the coordinates for each vertex in the object. This will replace any existing coordinates for the specified object. Use standard array-handling techniques to process the coordinates contained in this property. Note that you can't change the number of coordinates in the object by using this property, you can only change the location of existing coordinates. It returns a three-element array of Doubles containing 3-D coordinates in WCS. Note that the Z coordinate will always default to 0 on the active UCS. |

| NAME | RETURNS | DESCRIPTION |
|------|---------|-------------|
| Normal | Variant | Gets or sets the 3-D (Z-axis) normal unit vector for the trace object. |
| Thickness | Double | Gets or sets the distance the AcadTrace object is extruded above or below its elevation, in a Z-axis direction. The default is 0.0. |

**NOTE** *Because this object inherits from* AcadObject, *it supports the* Modified *event.*

## AcadUCS Object

The AcadUCS object represents a User-defined Coordinate System (UCS) that determines the orientation of the X-, Y-, and Z-axes in 3-D space. With this object you can change the location of the origin and the orientation of the XY plane and the Z-axis, and the resulting UCS definition can be orientated anywhere within the 3-D layout. Many UCSs can be defined as required for each drawing. The GetUCSMatrix method returns the transformation matrix for a given UCS. To turn on the UCS icon for a given viewport, use the UCSIconOn property of the AcadPViewport and AcadViewport objects. Note that all coordinates in ActiveX Automation are entered in the WCS.

The AcadUCS object is created by the Add method of the AcadUCSs collection and accessed by the Item method of the AcadUCSs collection. UCSs can also be activated using the ActiveUCS property of the Document object. If any changes are made to the active UCS, the new UCS object must be reset as the active UCS for the changes to appear.

### AcadUCS Object Methods

The AcadUCS object inherits all the methods of the AcadObject object. It also supports the following method.

| NAME | RETURNS | DESCRIPTION |
|---|---|---|
| GetUCSMatrix | Variant | Gets the transformation matrix consisting of UCS coordinate system data. It returns a 4×4 array of Doubles. This matrix is the passed as a parameter to the TransformBy method of a drawing object to apply a given UCS to that object. |

## AcadUCS Object Properties

The AcadUCS object inherits all the properties of the AcadObject object and the common Application property. It also supports the following properties.

| NAME | RETURNS | DESCRIPTION |
|---|---|---|
| Name | String | Gets or sets the name of the UCS object. |
| Origin | Variant | Gets or sets the origin of the UCS object in WCS coordinates, relative to the lower-left corner. It returns an array of Doubles. |
| XVector | Variant | Gets or sets the X direction of the given UCS. It returns a three-element array of Doubles, which is stored in the UCSXDIR system variable. If the X vector value is changed on the active UCS, you must reset the active UCS to see the change. |
| YVector | Variant | Gets or sets the Y direction of the given UCS. It returns a three-element array of Doubles, which is stored in the UCSYDIR system variable. If the Y vector value is changed on the active UCS, you must reset the active UCS to see the change. |

**NOTE** *Because this object inherits from* AcadObject, *it supports the* Modified *event.*

## AcadUCSs Collection

The AcadUCSs collection contains all the UCS definitions in the drawing. To add a new member to the collection, use the Add method. To select a specific UCS definition, use the Item method. Although this collection inherits a Delete method, you can't actually delete this collection. If you need to delete a specific UCS definition, use the Delete method found in the AcadUCS object. There is no limit to the number of UCS definitions you can create in your drawing. However, there can be only one instance of the AcadUCSs collection, which is predefined for each drawing. You can make multiple references to it by using the UserCoordinateSystems property.

### AcadUCSs Collection Methods

The AcadUCSs collection inherits all the methods of the AcadObject object. It also supports the following methods.

| NAME | RETURNS | DESCRIPTION |
| --- | --- | --- |
| Add | AcadUCS | Creates a member object and adds it to the collection. Parameters: Origin As Variant, XAxisPoint As Variant, YAxisPoint As Variant, and Name As String. The Origin parameter specifies where the UCS is to be added. The XAxisPoint parameter specifies a point on the positive X-axis of the UCS. The YAxisPoint parameter specifies a point on the positive Y-axis of the UCS. (The Z-axis follows by applying the right-hand rule.) These coordinates are all 3-D in WCS. Note that XAxisPoint and YAxisPoint together can't specify the same location as the Origin. The Name parameter specifies the name of the UCS to add to the collection. |
| Item | AcadUCS | Gets the member object at a given index in a collection. Parameter: Index As Variant (an Integer or a String). If the Index value is a String, it must match an existing object name in the collection. |

### AcadUCSs Collection Properties

The AcadUCSs collection inherits all the properties of the AcadObject object, the Count property, and the common Application property. It supports no other properties.

**NOTE** *Because this collection inherits from* AcadObject, *it supports the* Modified *event.*

## AcadUtility Object

The AcadUtility object represents a series of methods provided for utility purposes.

### AcadUtility Object Methods

The following methods are supported.

| NAME | RETURNS | DESCRIPTION |
|------|---------|-------------|
| AngleFromXAxis | Double | Returns the angle (in radians) of a line passing through two points from the X-axis. Parameters: Point1 As Variant and Point2 As Variant. The parameters are three-element arrays of Doubles. |
| AngleToReal | Double | Converts an angle as a string to a real number (Double). Parameters: Angle As String and Unit As AcAngleUnits. For the possible values of the AcAngleUnits enumerated type, see Appendix B. |

| NAME | RETURNS | DESCRIPTION |
|------|---------|-------------|
| AngleToString | String | Converts an angle from a real number (Double) to a string. Parameters: Angle As Double, Unit As AcAngleUnits, and Precision As Integer. For the possible values of the AcAngleUnits enumerated type, see Appendix B. The range of values for the third parameter is 0 to 8. |
| CreateTypedArray | | Creates an array that contains the values specified by the parameters. The resulting array can be passed into any AutoCAD method or property that accepts an array of numbers. Parameters: VarArr As Variant, Type As (Visual Basic Constant), Value1 As Type, [Value2 As Type], ..., and [ValueN As Type]. The values for Type are vbBoolean, vbInteger, vbLong, vbSingle, and vbDouble. |
| DistanceToReal | Double | Converts a distance from a string to a real number (Double). Parameters: Distance As String and Unit As AcUnits. For the possible values of the AcUnits enumerated type, see Appendix B. |
| GetAngle | Double | Asks the user to input an angle and then returns its value, taking into account the value in the ANGBASE system variable. The value of the angle returned is expressed in radians. The direction of angular increase is always counterclockwise. Parameters: [Point As Variant] and [Prompt As String]. The Point parameter in this method and the two that follow specifies 3-D WCS coordinates. The Prompt parameter in this method and the methods that follow specifies text string used to prompt the user for input. |

| NAME | RETURNS | DESCRIPTION |
| --- | --- | --- |
| GetCorner | Variant | Asks the user to input the corner of a rectangle and returns the point as an array of three Doubles. Note that a call to GetCorner will frequently follow a call to GetPoint, the first point selected being used as the first parameter for the GetCorner method. Parameters: Point As Variant and [Prompt As String]. |
| GetDistance | Variant | Asks the user to input a linear distance from the keyboard or by specifying two locations on the graphics screen, and returns it as a Double number or as an array of Double numbers. Parameters: [Point As Variant] and [Prompt As String]. |
| GetEntity | | Asks the user to select a drawing object by picking a point on the screen. The object is then placed in the first parameter. Parameters: Object As Object, PickedPoint As Variant, and [Prompt As String]. The PickedPoint parameter specifies 3-D WCS coordinates. |
| GetInput | String | Asks the user to input text and returns it. A call to this method must follow a call to a user-input function returning the error description "User input is a keyword". The input must be no longer than 511 characters. |
| GetInteger | Integer | Asks the user to input an integer and returns it. The AutoCAD user can enter any short) integer in the range of –32,768 to +32,767. Parameter: [Prompt As String]. |

| NAME | RETURNS | DESCRIPTION |
|------|---------|-------------|
| GetKeyword | String | Asks the user to input a keyword and returns it. The keyword must be no longer than 511 characters. If the user doesn't enter anything but presses the *Enter* key, this method returns an empty string. This method can only be used if `InitializeUserInput` is called first. Parameter: [`Prompt As String`]. |
| GetOrientation | Double | Asks the user to input an angle and then returns its value in radians without regard to the values stored in the `ANGBASE` system variable. The 0 angle employed by this method is always to the right (east). Parameters: [`Point As Variant`] and [`Prompt As String`]. The `Point` parameter specifies 3-D WCS coordinates. |
| GetPoint | Variant | Asks the user to choose a point and returns it. Parameters: [`Point As Variant`] and [`Prompt As String`]. The `Point` parameter and the return value specify 3-D WCS coordinates. |
| GetReal | Double | Asks the user to input a real (Double) number and returns it. Parameter: [`Prompt As String`]. |
| GetRemoteFile | | Downloads the specified file from a URL. Parameters: `URL As String`, `LocalFile As String`, and `IgnoreCache As Boolean`. The third parameter specifies whether or not to download the file, even if it has already been transferred earlier in this session. |
| GetString | String | Asks the user to input a string and returns it. Parameters: `HasSpaces As Boolean` and [`Prompt As String`]. `HasSpaces` determines whether or not the return string can contain spaces. If `True`, the string can contain spaces but terminated by a carriage return only. If `False`, the string can't contain spaces. It can be terminated by a carriage return or a space. |

| NAME | RETURNS | DESCRIPTION |
|------|---------|-------------|
| GetSubEntity | | Asks the user to select a drawing object by specifying the object and the selected in the first two parameters. Parameters: Object As Object, PickedPoint As Variant, TransMatrix As Variant, ContextData As Variant, and [Prompt As String]. |
| | | The PickedPoint parameter specifies 3-D WCS coordinates. |
| | | The TransMatrix parameter represents the translation matrix applied to this entity. |
| | | The Variant parameter is a 4×4 array of Doubles. |
| | | The ContextData parameter is an array of Longs, containing the object IDs for any nested objects in the selected object. More specifically, this argument returns an array holding the object ID(s) of the subentity's container block references. The first array element is the object ID of the block reference containing the picked entity. The last array element is the object ID of the block reference inserted directly in the drawing. The array of object IDs is therefore ordered from the most deeply nested block reference that contains the subentity to the object ID of the block reference that would have been picked with the GetEntity function. If the picked entity isn't a subentity (i.e., it isn't nested in a block reference), then the GetSubEntity function returns an empty array for the ContextData parameter. |
| InitializeUserInput | | Initializes the GetKeyword method. Parameter: Bits As Integer and [Keyword As String]. For the values for the Bits parameter and their explanations, see the following table. The second parameter specifies the keywords, delimited by spaces, that the GetKeyword method will recognize. This method must be called before GetKeyword. |

| NAME | RETURNS | DESCRIPTION |
|------|---------|-------------|
| IsRemoteFile | Boolean | Returns whether or not the specified file was downloaded from a remote location. This method is the inverse of the IsURL method and provides a mapping from a local file to the corresponding URL that the file was downloaded from. Parameters: LocalFile As String and URL As String. |
| IsURL | Boolean | Returns whether or not a string is a valid URL for the application. The default functionality of this method for AutoCAD supports the FTP, HTTP, HTTPS, and FILE protocols. Parameter: URL As String. |
| LaunchBrowserDialog | Boolean | Runs the web browser dialog box that allows the user to navigate to any URL and select a URL. It returns whether or not the operation was successful. Parameters: SelectedURL As String, DialogTitle As String, OpenButtonCaption As String, StartPageURL As String, RegistryRootKey As String, and OpenButtonAlwaysEnabled As Boolean. |
| | | The first four parameters specify the selected URL, the title to be displayed for the browser dialog box, the caption for the OK/Open button, and the URL that the web browser should use as its start page, respectively. |
| | | The fifth parameter is used to specify where in the registry persistent web browser dialog box information is stored. Input an empty string to disregard this functionality. |
| | | The sixth parameter determines whether the user can select HTML links in addition to downloadable file. If True, the Open button is enabled, allowing a file or link to be selected. If False, the Open button is disabled and is only enabled when the user selects a file for download. |
| PolarPoint | Variant | Returns a point at the specified angle (in radians) and distance (in current units) from the specified point. Parameters: Point As Variant, Angle As Double, and Distance As Double. The value for Point and the return value are both 3-D WCS coordinates. |

| NAME | RETURNS | DESCRIPTION |
|---|---|---|
| Prompt | | Sends a message to the command line. Parameter: `Message As String`. |
| PutRemoteFile | | Puts a local file at the location specified by a URL. This method is designed to complement `GetRemoteFile` method. When accessing a secure URL, a dialog box will be posted prompting the user for the necessary password information. Message boxes may also appear if the user hasn't suppressed this activity in the browser. Parameter: `URL As String`. |
| RealToString | String | Converts a real number into a properly formatted string. Parameters: `Value As Double`, `Unit As AcUnits`, and `Precision As Integer`. For a list of possible values for the `AcUnits` enumerated type, see Appendix B. The range of values for the third parameter is 0 to 8. |
| TranslateCoordinates | Variant | Changes a point from one coordinate system to another. You can't directly translate a set of coordinates from one OCS to another OCS. If you want to do this, you must first translate the OCS coordinates to WCS and then change these coordinates to the second OCS. Parameters: `OriginalPoint As Variant`, `From As AcCoordinateSystem`, `To As AcCoordinateSystem`, `Disp As Boolean`, and `[OCSNormal As Variant]`.<br><br>`OriginalPoint` specifies the original 3-D WCS coordinates to be translated. This parameter can be treated as a point or a displacement vector depending on the value of `Disp`.<br><br>For a list of possible values for the `AcCoordinateSystem` enumeration (the `From` and `To` parameters), see Appendix B.<br><br>`Disp` is a displacement vector flag. If `True`, `OriginalPoint` is treated as a displacement vector. Otherwise it is treated as a point.<br><br>The optional last parameter represents the normal for the OCS. |

## AcadUtility Object Properties

The AcadUtility object inherits the common Application property. It supports no other properties.

# AcadView Object

The AcadView object represents a graphical representation of a 2-D drawing or 3-D model from a specific location (viewpoint) in space. The line of sight is drawn from the viewpoint, represented by the Center property, to the target point. The Height and Width properties crop the view to fit into the viewport.

## AcadView Object Methods

The AcadView object inherits all the methods of the AcadObject object. It supports no other methods.

## AcadView Object Properties

The AcadView object inherits all the properties of the AcadObject object, as well as the common Application property. It also supports the following properties.

| NAME | RETURNS | DESCRIPTION |
| --- | --- | --- |
| Center | Variant | Gets or sets the center of the view as a set of 2-D coordinates (as Doubles). The default center is (0,0). |
| Direction | Variant | Gets or sets the viewing direction for a 3-D visualization of the drawing. This property puts the viewer in a position to look at the drawing as if looking back at the origin (0, 0, 0) from a specified point in space. It is similar to AutoCAD's VPOINT command. It returns a three-element array of Doubles. |
| Height | Double | Gets or sets the height of the view, which is the Y-axis measurement of the area within a viewport that is used to display the model. |
| Name | String | Gets or sets the name of the view. |

| NAME | RETURNS | DESCRIPTION |
|---|---|---|
| Target | Variant | Gets or sets the target point for the view as a set of 3-D WCS coordinates representing the target point. The line of sight is drawn from the center to the target point. It returns a three-element array of Doubles. |
| Width | Double | Gets or sets the width of the view, which is the X-axis measurement of the area within a viewport that is used to display the model. |

**NOTE** *Because this object inherits from* AcadObject, *it supports the* Modified *event.*

## AcadViewport Object

The AcadViewport object represents a bounded area that displays some portion of a drawing's model space. It can be activated using the ActiveViewport property of the Document object. The ActiveSpace property, which is equivalent to the TILEMODE system variable, determines the type of viewport used. Changes to the view can only be made while the viewport is active and any changes made can only be seen once the viewport has been reactivated.

### AcadViewport Object Methods

The AcadViewport object inherits all the methods of the AcadObject object. It also supports the following methods.

| NAME | DESCRIPTION |
|---|---|
| GetGridSpacing | Gets the grid spacing for the viewport. Parameters: XSpacing As Double and YSpacing As Double. |
| GetSnapSpacing | Gets the snap spacing for the viewport. Parameters: XSpacing As Double and YSpacing As Double. |

| NAME | DESCRIPTION |
|------|-------------|
| SetGridSpacing | Sets the grid spacing for the viewport. Parameters: XSpacing As Double and YSpacing As Double. |
| SetSnapSpacing | Sets the snap spacing for the viewport. Parameters: XSpacing As Double and YSpacing As Double. |
| SetView | Sets the view in a viewport to a saved view in the AcadViews collection. Parameter: View_As_AcadView. |
| Split | Splits a viewport into the given number of views. Parameter: NumWins_As_AcViewportSplitType. For a list of possible values for the AcViewportSplitType enumerated type, see Appendix B. |

## *AcadViewport Object Properties*

The AcadViewport object inherits all the properties of the AcadObject object, as well as the common Application property. It also supports the following properties. Note that many of these properties are identical to those of the AcadPViewport object. See the AcadPViewport object for more details for the ArcSmoothness, Center, Direction, GridOn, SnapBasePoint, SnapOn, and SnapRotationAngle properties.

| NAME | RETURNS | DESCRIPTION |
|------|---------|-------------|
| ArcSmoothness | Integer | Gets or sets the smoothness of circles, arcs, and ellipses. The valid range of values is from 1 to 20000. The initial value for this property is 100. |
| Center | Variant | Gets or sets the center of the viewport as a set of 2-D coordinates (as Doubles). The default center is (0,0). |
| Direction | Variant | Gets or sets the viewing direction for a 3-D visualization of the drawing. This property puts the viewer in a position to look at the drawing as if looking back at the origin (0, 0, 0) from a specified point in space. |
| GridOn | Boolean | Specifies the status of the viewport grid. The value of this property is stored in the GRIDMODE system variable. |

| NAME | RETURNS | DESCRIPTION |
|------|---------|-------------|
| Height | Double | Gets or sets the height of the viewport, which is the Y-axis measurement of the area within a viewport that is used to display the model. |
| LowerLeftCorner | Variant | Gets the lower-left corner of the current active viewport, which with the UpperRightCorner property represents the graphic placement of the viewport on the display. It returns a set of 2-D coordinates as an array of Doubles. This property's value is read-only. |
| Name | String | Gets or sets the name of the viewport. |
| OrthoOn | Boolean | Specifies status of the Ortho mode for the viewport. You can use Ortho mode to restrict the cursor to the horizontal or vertical axis, which helps you draw parallel lines or move objects. |
| SnapBasePoint | Variant | Gets or sets the snap base point for the viewport, the value of which is stored in the SNAPBASE system variable. The snap base point can't be changed for the active paper space viewport. Any changes to this property aren't reflected in the display until the drawing is regenerated. |
| SnapOn | Boolean | Specifies the status of snap mode. The value of this property is stored in the SNAPMODE system variable. |
| SnapRotationAngle | Double | Gets or sets the snap rotation angle (in radians) of the viewport relative to the current UCS. The value of this property is stored in the SNAPANG system variable. The valid range is 0 to 6.28. |
| Target | Variant | Gets or sets the target point for the viewport as a set of 3-D WCS coordinates representing the target point. The line of sight is drawn from the center to the target point. It returns a three-element array of Doubles. |

| NAME | RETURNS | DESCRIPTION |
| --- | --- | --- |
| UCSIconAtOrigin | Boolean | Specifies whether or not the UCS icon is displayed at the origin, or at the WCS coordinate defined by the UCSORG system variable. |
| UCSIconOn | Boolean | Specifies whether or not the UCS icon is on. |
| UpperRightCorner | Variant | Gets the upper-right corner of the current active viewport, which with the LowerLeftCorner property represents the graphic placement of the viewport on the display. It returns a set of 2-D coordinates as an array of Doubles. This property's value is read-only. |
| Width | Double | Gets or sets the width of the viewport, which is the X-axis measurement of the area within a viewport that is used to display the model. |

**NOTE** *Because this object inherits from* AcadObject, *it supports the* Modified *event. There is no programmatic means to directly create or manipulate polygonal viewports.*

## AcadViewports Collection

The AcadViewports collection contains all the viewports in the drawing. Although this collection inherits a Delete method, you can't actually delete this collection. If you need to delete a specific viewport, use the DeleteConfiguration method or the Delete method of the AcadViewport object. The number of viewports you can have active at one time is controlled by the MAXACTVP system variable. However, there can be only one instance of the AcadViewports collection, which is predefined for each drawing. You can make multiple references to it by using the Viewports property of the Document object.

### AcadViewports Collection Methods

The AcadViewports collection inherits all the methods of the AcadObject object. It also supports the following methods.

| NAME | RETURNS | DESCRIPTION |
|------|---------|-------------|
| Add | AcadViewport | Creates a member object and adds it to the collection. Parameter: Name As String. |
| DeleteConfiguration | | Deletes a viewport configuration, which consists of a single viewport that has been split using the Split method. Once a viewport has been split, the resulting viewports are considered a viewport configuration and have the same name as the original viewport before the split. Parameter: Name As String. |
| Item | AcadViewport | Gets the member object at a given index in a collection. Parameter: Index As Variant (an Integer or a String). If the Index value is a String, it must match an existing viewport in the collection. |

## *AcadViewports Collection Properties*

The AcadViewports collection inherits all the properties of the AcadObject object, the Count property, and the common Application property. It supports no other properties.

 **NOTE**  *Because this collection inherits from* AcadObject, *it supports the* Modified *event.*

# *AcadViews Collection*

The AcadViews collection contains all the views in the drawing. Although this collection inherits a Delete method, you can't actually delete this collection. If you need to delete a specific view, use the Delete method of the AcadView object. There is no limit to the number of views you can create in your drawing. However, there can be only one instance of the AcadViews collection, which is predefined for each drawing. You can make multiple references to it by using the Views property of the Document object.

### AcadViews Collection Methods

The AcadViews collection inherits all the methods of the AcadObject object. It supports no other methods.

### AcadViews Collection Properties

The AcadViews collection inherits all the properties of the AcadObject object, the Count property, and the common Application property. It supports no other properties.

 **NOTE** *Because this collection inherits from* AcadObject, *it supports the* Modified *event.*

# AcadXline Object

The AcadXline object represents a construction line that is infinite in both directions, unlike the AcadRay object, which is infinite in only one direction. It is created using the AddXline method of the AcadBlock, AcadModelSpace, or AcadPaperSpace object.

### AcadXline Object Methods

The AcadXline inherits all the methods of the AcadEntity and AcadObject objects. It also supports the following method.

| NAME | RETURNS | DESCRIPTION |
| --- | --- | --- |
| Offset | Variant | Creates a new line by offsetting the current Xline by a specified distance, which can be positive or negative but can't be zero. If the offset is negative, this means that the line is drawn closer to the WCS origin. Parameter: Distance As Double. |

## AcadXline Object Properties

The AcadXline object inherits all the properties of the AcadEntity and AcadObject objects, as well as the common Application property. It also supports the following properties.

| NAME | RETURNS | DESCRIPTION |
| --- | --- | --- |
| BasePoint | Variant | Gets or sets the point through which the Xline passes. It returns a set of 3-D coordinates as a three-element array of Doubles. |
| DirectionVector | Variant | Gets or sets the direction for the Xline through a vector. It returns a three-element array of Doubles. |
| SecondPoint | Variant | Gets or sets a second point on the Xline. It returns a set of 3-D WCS coordinates as a three-element array of Doubles. |

**NOTE** *Because this object inherits from* AcadObject, *it supports the* Modified *event.*

# AcadXRecord Object

The AcadXRecord object is used to store and manage arbitrary data. XRecords are similar in concept to XData but are not limited by size or order. They use standard AutoCAD group codes, the values of which are all below 1000, which means in addition to all the normally used data types, XRecords are capable of storing object IDs, allowing ownership of many other objects. For a list of supported group codes, see the AutoCAD documentation.

XRecord objects are saved with the drawing and can be directly accessed by other OBJECTARX and LISP programs. For this reason, you should take care when storing security information in XRecords. XRecords are created using the AddXRecord method of the Dictionary object and accessed programmatically through the Item method of the Dictionary object. The only basic operations that can be performed on XRecords are Add, Get, and Delete. There is no means to update (modify) an XRecord other than to delete and re-create it.

## AcadXRecord Object Methods

The AcadXRecord object inherits all the methods of the AcadObject object. It also supports the following methods.

| NAME | DESCRIPTION |
| --- | --- |
| GetXRecordData | Gets the extended record data associated with a dictionary. Parameters: XRecordDataType_As_Variant and XRecordDataValue_As Variant. |
| SetXRecordData | Sets the extended record data associated with a dictionary. Parameters: XRecordDataType_As_Variant and XRecordDataValue_As Variant. |

## AcadXRecord Object Properties

The AcadXRecord object inherits all the properties of the AcadObject object, as well as the common Application property. It also supports the following properties.

| NAME | RETURNS | DESCRIPTION |
| --- | --- | --- |
| Name | String | Gets or sets the name of the object within the dictionary. This name doesn't represent the class name of the object. |
| TranslateIDs | Boolean | Specifies whether or not translation of any contained object IDs occurs during deepClone or wblockClone operations. |

**NOTE**  *Because this object inherits from* AcadObject, *it supports the* Modified *event.*

## SecurityParams Object

The SecurityParams object is used to store settings for drawing security. The SecurityParams object is used to encrypt and digitally sign drawing files.

The object properties included are used to provide information about cryptography providers and other settings for drawing security. Additional information about cryptography providers is available on MSDN (msdn.microsoft.com).

| NAME | RETURNS | DESCRIPTION |
| --- | --- | --- |
| Action | Long | Gets or sets the desired security operation to be performed. Use one or more of the following constants for drawing encryption, drawing properties encryption, a digital signature, or a timestamp:<br><br>ACADSECURITYPARAMS_ENCRYPT_DATA = 0×00000001<br><br>ACADSECURITYPARAMS_ENCRYPT_PROPS = 0×00000002<br><br>ACADSECURITYPARAMS_SIGN_DATA = 0×00000010<br><br>ACADSECURITYPARAMS_ADD_TIMESTAMP = 0×00000020 |
| Algorithm | Long | Gets or sets the identifier of the encryption algorithm. This value can only be the following constant:<br><br>ACADSECURITYPARAMS_ALGID_RC4 = 0×00006801 |
| Comment | String | Gets or sets the comment to be included with a digital signature. |
| Issuer | String | Gets or sets the issuer of a digital certificate. |
| KeyLength | Long | Gets or sets the length of the encryption key, which is based upon the value in the ProviderName property. |
| Password | String | Gets or sets the encryption password. |
| ProviderName | String | Gets or sets the encryption provider name. More information about cryptography providers is available on MSDN. |

| NAME | RETURNS | DESCRIPTION |
|------|---------|-------------|
| ProviderType | Long | Gets or sets the encryption provider type. More information about cryptography providers is available on MSDN. |
| SerialNumber | String | Gets or sets the serial number of the digital certificate. |
| Subject | String | Gets or sets the subject name of the digital certificate. |
| TimeServer | String | Gets or sets the name of the time server to be used for a digital signature. If you don't set this property, the time from the local machine is used as the timestamp for the digital signature. |

## AcCmColor Object

The AcCmColor object represents colors within AutoCAD. You use the AcCmColor object to set colors and perform other color-related operations on objects.

### AcCmColor Object Methods

Unlike the other AutoCAD objects, the AcCmColor object doesn't inherit methods from any other AutoCAD objects. It supports the following methods.

| NAME | DESCRIPTION |
|------|-------------|
| SetColorBookColor | Sets the color name from an existing color book. Parameters: ColorName As String and ColorBook As String. |
| SetNames | Sets the color name and book name of the color. Parameters: ColorName As String and BookName As String. |
| SetRGB | Sets the RGB values of the True Color. Parameters: Red As Long, Green As Long, and Blue As Long. |

## *AcCmColor Object Properties*

Unlike the other AutoCAD objects, the AcCmColor object doesn't inherit properties from any other AutoCAD objects. It supports the following properties.

| NAME | RETURNS | DESCRIPTION |
| --- | --- | --- |
| Blue | Long | Gets the blue component, from 0 to 255, of AcCmColor. This property's value is read-only. |
| BookName | String | Gets the name of the color book that the color came from. This property's value is read-only. |
| ColorIndex | acColor enum | Gets or sets the default color designation in acByLayer. Use a color index number from 0 to 256, or one of the constants listed here:<br><br>acByBlock<br><br>acByLayer (not valid for the Layer object)<br><br>acRed<br><br>acYellow<br><br>acGreen<br><br>acCyan<br><br>acBlue<br><br>acMagenta<br><br>acWhite |
| ColorMethod | acColorMethod enum | Gets or sets the default color method in acColorMethodByLayer. To directly determine how a color is set, use the constants listed here:<br><br>acColorMethodByACI<br><br>acColorMethodByBlock<br><br>acColorMethodByLayer<br><br>acColorMethodByRGB<br><br>acColorMethodForeground |
| ColorName | String | Gets the name (if any) of the color. This property's value is read-only. |

| NAME | RETURNS | DESCRIPTION |
| --- | --- | --- |
| EntityColor | Long | Gets or sets the 32-bit AcCmEntityColor portion of the color. |
| Green | Long | Gets the green component, from 0 to 255, of AcCmColor. This property's value is read-only. |
| Red | Long | Gets the red component, from 0 to 255, of AcCmColor. This property's value is read-only. |

## *LayerStateManager Object*

The LayerStateManager object provides a set of functions for working with saved layer settings. The LayerStateManager object manipulates XRecord objects that define the properties of a layer. These XRecords are stored in the ACAD_LAYERSTATE dictionary, which is an extension dictionary in the drawing's Layers collection. (An *extension dictionary* is a mechanism for attaching data to objects. Every AutoCAD object can have an extension dictionary.)

After you retrieve the LayerStateManager object and associate a database with it, then you can access the object's methods. Use the SetDatabase method to associate a database with the LayerStateManager object.

### *LayerStateManager Object Methods*

Unlike the other AutoCAD objects, the LayerStateManager object doesn't inherit methods from any other AutoCAD objects. It supports the following methods.

| NAME | DESCRIPTION |
| --- | --- |
| Delete | Name representing the layer state to be deleted. Parameter: Name As String. |
| Export | Exports an AutoCAD drawing or a group of saved layer settings to a file. Parameters: Filename As String, Extension As String, and SelectionSet As SelectionSet. |
| Import | Imports a drawing or a group of saved layer settings from a file. Parameters: Filename As String, InsertionPoint As Variant, and ScaleFactor As Double. |

| NAME | DESCRIPTION |
|---|---|
| Rename | Renames a set of saved layer settings. Parameters: `OldName As String` and `NewName As String`. |
| Restore | Restores a group of layer property settings. Parmeter: `Name As String`. |
| Save | Saves a group of layer property settings. Parameters: `Name As String` and `Mask` (set `Mask` property as described in the next section). |
| SetDatabase | Gets AutoCAD database associated with the `LayerStateManager` object. |

## *LayerStateManager Object Properties*

Unlike the other AutoCAD objects, the `LayerStateManager` object doesn't inherit properties from any other AutoCAD objects. It supports the following properties.

| NAME | RETURNS | DESCRIPTION |
|---|---|---|
| Mask | Enum | Specifies the layer properties to be restored as a number representing the layer properties to be restored. The following table represents acceptable values for this property. |

| CONSTANT | LAYER PROPERTY | NUMERIC VALUE |
|---|---|---|
| AcLsAll | All layer properties | 65535 |
| AcLsColor | Color | 32 |
| AcLsFrozen | Frozen or thawed | 2 |
| AcLsLineType | Linetype | 64 |
| AcLsLineWeight | Lineweight | 128 |
| AcLsLocked | Locked or unlocked | 4 |
| AcLsNewViewport | New viewport layers frozen or thawed | 16 |
| AcLsNone | None | 0 |
| AcLsOn | On or off | 1 |
| AcLsPlot | Plotting on or off | 8 |
| AcLsPlotStyle | Plot style | 256 |

# APPENDIX B

# AutoCAD Constants Reference

THIS APPENDIX CONTAINS A LIST of all the enumerated types used in conjunction with the AutoCAD objects. The methods and properties (presented in Appendix A) that use them have been noted.

## Ac3DPolylineType

The following constants can be values for the Type property of the Acad3DPolyline object.

| CONSTANT | VALUE | DESCRIPTION |
| --- | --- | --- |
| acSimple3Dpoly | 0 | A simple polyline |
| acQuadSpline3Dpoly | 1 | A quadratic B-spline polyline |
| acCubicSpline3Dpoly | 2 | A cubic B-spline polyline |

## AcActiveSpace

The following constants can be values for the ActiveSpace property of the AcadDocument object.

| CONSTANT | VALUE | DESCRIPTION |
| --- | --- | --- |
| acModelSpace | 1 | The active space is model space. |
| acPaperSpace | 2 | The active space is paper space. |

## AcAlignment

The following constants can be values for the `Alignment` property of the
`AcadAttribute`, `AcadAttributeReference`, and `AcadText` objects.

| CONSTANT | VALUE | DESCRIPTION |
| --- | --- | --- |
| acAlignmentLeft | 0 | The attribute, attribute reference, or text is aligned with the insertion point. |
| acAlignmentCenter | 1 | The attribute, attribute reference, or text is aligned at the center. |
| AcAlignmentRight4 | 2 | The attribute, attribute reference, or text is aligned at the right. |
| acAlignmentAligned | 3 | The attribute, attribute reference, or text is aligned according to the points held in the `InsertionPoint` and `TextAlignmentPoint` properties. |
| acAlignmentMiddle | 4 | The attribute, attribute reference, or text is aligned at the middle, at a position slightly below middle-center. |
| acAlignmentFit | 5 | The attribute, attribute reference, or text is aligned to fit to the points held in the `InsertionPoint` and `TextAlignmentPoint` properties. |
| acAlignmentTopLeft | 6 | The attribute, attribute reference, or text is aligned at the top left. |
| acAlignmentTopCenter | 7 | The attribute, attribute reference, or text is aligned at the top center. |
| acAlignmentTopRight | 8 | The attribute, attribute reference, or text is aligned at the top right. |
| acAlignmentMiddleLeft | 9 | The attribute, attribute reference, or text is aligned at the middle left. |
| acAlignmentMiddleCenter | 10 | The attribute, attribute reference, or text is aligned at the middle center. |
| acAlignmentMiddleRight | 11 | The attribute, attribute reference, or text is aligned at the middle right. |
| acAlignmentBottomLeft | 12 | The attribute, attribute reference, or text is aligned at the bottom left. |

| CONSTANT | VALUE | DESCRIPTION |
| --- | --- | --- |
| acAlignmentBottomCenter | 13 | The attribute, attribute reference, or text is aligned at the bottom center. |
| acAlignmentBottomRight | 14 | The attribute, attribute reference, or text is aligned at the bottom right. |

# AcAlignmentPointAcquisition

The following constants can be values for the AlignmentPointAcquisition property of the AcadPreferencesDrafting object.

| CONSTANT | VALUE | DESCRIPTION |
| --- | --- | --- |
| acAlignPntAcquisitionAutomatic | 0 | Autoalignment points are acquired automatically. |
| acAlignPntAcquisitionShiftToAcquire | 1 | The user must use the Shift key to acquire autoalignment points. |

# AcAngleUnits

The following constants can be values for the AngleFormat property of the AcadDim3PointAngular object, and they can be supplied as the value for the second parameter of the AngleToReal and AngleToString methods of the AcadUtility object.

| CONSTANT | VALUE | DESCRIPTION |
| --- | --- | --- |
| acDegrees | 0 | Angle units are degrees. |
| acDegreeMinuteSeconds | 1 | Angle units are degrees, minutes, and seconds. |
| acGrads | 2 | Angle units are grads. |
| acRadians | 3 | Angle units are radians. |

## AcARXDemandLoad

The following constants can be values for the DemandLoadARXApp property of the
AcadPreferencesOpenSave object.

| CONSTANT | VALUE | DESCRIPTION |
|---|---|---|
| acDemandLoadDisable | 0 | Turns off demand loading. |
| acDemandLoadOnObjectDetect | 1 | Demand-loads the source application when you open a drawing that contains custom objects. This setting doesn't demand-load the application when you invoke one of the application's commands. |
| acDemandLoadCmdInvoke | 2 | Demand-loads the source application when you invoke one of the application's commands. This setting doesn't demand-load the application when you open a drawing that contains custom objects. |

## AcAttachmentPoint

The following constants can be values for the AttachmentPoint property of the
AcadMText object.

| CONSTANT | VALUE | DESCRIPTION |
|---|---|---|
| acAttachmentPointTopLeft | 1 | Left justified, spills down |
| acAttachmentPointTopCenter | 2 | Center justified, spills down |
| acAttachmentPointTopRight | 3 | Right justified, spills down |
| acAttachmentPointMiddleLeft | 4 | Left justified, spills up and down |
| acAttachmentPointMiddleCenter | 5 | Center justified, spills up and down |

| CONSTANT | VALUE | DESCRIPTION |
|---|---|---|
| acAttachmentPointMiddleRight | 6 | Right justified, spills up and down |
| acAttachmentPointBottomLeft | 7 | Left justified, spills up |
| acAttachmentPointBottomCenter | 8 | Center justified, spills up |
| acAttachmentPointBottomRight | 9 | Right justified, spills up |

## AcAttributeMode

The following constants can be values for the Mode property of the AcadAttribute object, and they can also be supplied as the value for the second parameter of the AddAttribute method of the AcadBlock, AcadModelSpace, and AcadPaperSpace objects.

| CONSTANT | VALUE | DESCRIPTION |
|---|---|---|
| acAttributeModeNormal | 0 | The default mode. In other words, it lacks any of the other modes listed here. |
| acAttributeModeInvisible | 1 | When the block is inserted, the attribute's values won't be visible. The system variable ATTDISP overrides this mode setting. |
| acAttributeModeConstant | 2 | Attribute values will have a fixed value for each block inserted. When set, prompting for the attribute is disabled. |
| acAttributeModeVerify | 4 | When you insert the block, AutoCAD will ask you to verify that the attribute value is correct. |
| acAttributeModePreset | 8 | The block is inserted using its default attribute values. You can't edit these values. |

## AcBooleanType

The following constants are values supplied as the value for the first parameter of the `Boolean` methods of the `Acad3DSolid` and `AcadRegion` objects.

| CONSTANT | VALUE | DESCRIPTION |
|---|---|---|
| acUnion | 0 | Performs a union operation |
| acIntersection | 1 | Performs an intersection operation |
| acSubtraction | 2 | Performs a subtraction operation |

## AcColor (and the ColorIndex Property of the AcCmColor Object)

The following constants can be values for these properties:

- The `AutoSnapMarkerColor` property of the `AcadPreferencesDrafting` object

- The `Color` property of the `AcadEntity` object (and all derived objects), and the `AcadGroup` and `AcadLayer` objects

- The `DimensionLineColor` property of the dimension objects that support it (all except `AcadDimOrdinate`), and the `AcadLeader` and `AcadTolerance` objects

- The `ExtensionLineColor` property of the dimension objects that support it (all except `AcadDimDiametric` and `AcadDimRadial`)

- The `GripColorSelected` and `GripColorUnselected` properties of the `AcadPreferencesSelection` object

- The `TextColor` property of the `AcadDimension` object (and all derived objects) and the `AcadTolerance` object

| CONSTANT | VALUE | DESCRIPTION |
|----------|-------|-------------|
| acByBlock | 0 | Objects are drawn in the default color until they're grouped into a block. When the block is inserted into a drawing, the objects inherit the value of the block's Color property. |
| acRed | 1 | Red. |
| acYellow | 2 | Yellow. |
| acGreen | 3 | Green. |
| acCyan | 4 | Cyan. |
| acBlue | 5 | Blue. |
| acMagenta | 6 | Magenta. |
| acWhite | 7 | White. |
| acByLayer | 256 | Object assumes color of layer on which it is drawn. |

## AcCmColor

The following constants can be supplied as values for the AcCmColor object as it relates to the TrueColor object. Only those constants marked with an asterisk (*), however, apply to the GradientColor1 and GradientColor2 properties for Hatch objects.

| CONSTANT | VALUE | DESCRIPTION |
|----------|-------|-------------|
| acColorMethodByACI* | 195 | Use traditional color index value. |
| acColorMethodByBlock* | 193 | |
| acColorMethodByLayer | 192 | |
| acColorMethodByRGB | 194 | Use RGB index values to define color. |
| acColorMethodForeground | 197 | |

## AcCoordinateSystem

You can supply the following constants as values for the second and third parameters of the `TranslateCoordinates` method of the `AcadUtility` object.

| CONSTANT | VALUE | DESCRIPTION |
| --- | --- | --- |
| acWorld | 0 | World Coordinate System (WCS) |
| acUCS | 1 | User Coordinate System (UCS) |
| acDisplayDCS | 2 | Display Coordinate System (DCS) |
| acPaperSpaceDCS | 3 | Paper Space Display Coordinate System (PSDCS) |
| acOCS | 4 | Object Coordinate System (OCS) |

## AcDimArrowheadType

The following constants can be values for these properties:

- The `Arrowhead1Type` and `Arrowhead2Type` properties of the dimension objects that support them (all except `AcadDimOrdinate` and `AcadDimRadial`)

- The `Arrowhead1Type` property of the `AcadTolerance` object

- The `ArrowheadType` property of the `AcadDimRadial` and `AcadLeader` objects

| CONSTANT | VALUE | DESCRIPTION |
| --- | --- | --- |
| acArrowDefault | 0 | The arrowhead is the default determined by the dimension style. |
| acArrowClosedBlank | 1 | The arrowhead is a closed empty triangle. |
| acArrowClosed | 2 | The arrowhead is a closed triangle with the dimension line inside. |
| acArrowDot | 3 | The arrowhead is a large filled circle. |
| acArrowArchTick | 4 | The arrowhead is a bold oblique line. |
| acArrowOblique | 5 | The arrowhead is an oblique line. |
| acArrowOpen | 6 | The arrowhead is a narrow open arrow. |

| CONSTANT | VALUE | DESCRIPTION |
| --- | --- | --- |
| acArrowOrigin | 7 | The arrowhead is a circle with the dimension line inside. |
| acArrowOrigin2 | 8 | The arrowhead comprises two circles with the dimension line inside. |
| acArrowOpen90 | 9 | The arrowhead is an open arrow with an internal angle of 90 degrees. |
| acArrowOpen30 | 10 | The arrowhead is an open arrow with an internal angle of 30 degrees. |
| acArrowDotSmall | 11 | The arrowhead is a small filled circle. |
| acArrowDotBlank | 12 | The arrowhead is a large empty circle. |
| acArrowSmall | 13 | The arrowhead is a small arrow. |
| acArrowBoxBlank | 14 | The arrowhead is an empty box. |
| acArrowBoxFilled | 15 | The arrowhead is a filled box. |
| acArrowDatumBlank | 16 | The arrowhead is a closed, empty, inward-pointing triangle. |
| acArrowDatumFilled | 17 | The arrowhead is a filled inward-pointing triangle. |
| acArrowIntegral | 18 | The arrowhead is an integral sign. |
| acArrowNone | 19 | There is no arrowhead. |
| acArrowUserDefined | 20 | The arrowhead is defined by the user. |

# AcDimCenterType

The following constants can be values for the CenterType property of the AcadDimDiametric and AcadDimRadial objects.

| CONSTANT | VALUE | DESCRIPTION |
| --- | --- | --- |
| acCenterMark | 0 | Marks the center with a small cross (+) |
| acCenterLine | 1 | Marks the center as the intersection of two perpendicular axes |
| acCenterNone | 2 | No center mark |

## AcDimFit

The following constants can be values for the `Fit` property of the dimension objects that support it (all except `AcadDimOrdinate`).

| CONSTANT | VALUE | DESCRIPTION |
|---|---|---|
| acTextAndArrows | 0 | Text and arrowheads are placed inside the extension lines. |
| acArrowsOnly | 1 | Arrowheads are placed inside the extension lines. The text is placed outside the arrowheads. |
| acTextOnly | 2 | Text is placed inside the extension lines. The arrowheads are placed outside the extension lines. |
| acBestFit | 3 | This option places the text and arrowheads in the best-fit location given the space available. |

## AcDimFractionType

The following constants can be values for the `FractionFormat` property of the `AcadDimension` object (and all derived objects) and the `AcadTolerance` object.

| CONSTANT | VALUE | DESCRIPTION |
|---|---|---|
| acHorizontal | 0 | Fraction displayed as "$\frac{1}{2}$" (with a horizontal divider) |
| acDiagonal | 1 | Fraction displayed as "$^{1}/_{2}$" (with a diagonal divider) |
| acNotStacked | 2 | Fraction displayed as "1/2" |

# AcDimHorizontalJustification

The following constants can be values for the HorizontalTextPosition property of the dimension objects that support it (all except AcadDimOrdinate).

| CONSTANT | VALUE | DESCRIPTION |
| --- | --- | --- |
| acHorzCentered | 0 | The text is centered along the dimension line between the extension lines. |
| acFirstExtensionLine | 1 | The text is next to the first extension line. |
| acSecondExtensionLine | 2 | The text is next to the second extension line. |
| acOverFirstExtension | 3 | The text is above and aligned with the first extension line. |
| acOverSecondExtension | 4 | The text is above and aligned with the second extension line. |

# AcDimLUnits

The following constants can be values for the UnitsFormat property of the dimension objects that support it (all except AcadDim3PointAngular and AcadDimAngular).

| CONSTANT | VALUE | DESCRIPTION |
| --- | --- | --- |
| acDimLScientific | 1 | Displays measurements in scientific notation |
| acDimLDecimal | 2 | Displays measurements in decimal notation |
| acDimLEngineering | 3 | Displays measurements in feet and decimal inches |
| acDimLArchitectural | 4 | Displays measurements in feet, inches, and fractional inches |
| acDimLFractional | 5 | Displays measurements in mixed-number (integer and fractional) notation |
| acDimLWindowsDesktop | 6 | Displays measurements in Windows Desktop format |

## AcDimPrecision

The following constants can be values for these properties:

- The AltTolerancePrecision and AltUnitsPrecision properties of the dimension objects that support them (all except AcadDim3PointAngular and AcadDimAngular)

- The PrimaryUnitsPrecision property of the dimension objects that support them (all except AcadDim3PointAngular and AcadDimAngular) and the AcadTolerance object

- The TextPrecision property of the AcadDim3PointAngular and AcadDimAngular objects

- The TolerancePrecision property of the AcadDimension object (and all derived objects)

| CONSTANT | VALUE | DESCRIPTION |
|---|---|---|
| acDimPrecisionZero | 0 | Accurate to no decimal places (0.) |
| acDimPrecisionOne | 1 | Accurate to one decimal place (0.0) |
| acDimPrecisionTwo | 2 | Accurate to two decimal places (0.00) |
| acDimPrecisionThree | 3 | Accurate to three decimal places (0.000) |
| acDimPrecisionFour | 4 | Accurate to four decimal places (0.0000) |
| acDimPrecisionFive | 5 | Accurate to five decimal places (0.00000) |
| acDimPrecisionSix | 6 | Accurate to six decimal places (0.000000) |
| acDimPrecisionSeven | 7 | Accurate to seven decimal places (0.0000000) |
| acDimPrecisionEight | 8 | Accurate to eight decimal places (0.00000000) |

# AcDimTextMovement

The following constants can be values for the TextMovement property of the AcadDimension object (and all derived objects).

| CONSTANT | VALUE | DESCRIPTION |
| --- | --- | --- |
| acDimLineWithText | 0 | The dimension line follows the text. |
| acMoveTextAddLeader | 1 | The text moves independently of the dimension line, with a leader drawn from the text to the dimension line. |
| acMoveTextNoLeader | 2 | The text moves independently of the dimension line, with no leader drawn from the text to the dimension line. |

# AcDimToleranceJustify

The following constants can be values for the ToleranceJustification property of the AcadDimension object (and all derived objects).

| CONSTANT | VALUE | DESCRIPTION |
| --- | --- | --- |
| acTolBottom | 0 | Displays the bottom tolerance value at the same level as the dimension text |
| acTolMiddle | 1 | Displays tolerance values half-size level with the dimension text |
| acTolTop | 2 | Displays the top tolerance value at the same level as the dimension text |

## AcDimToleranceMethod

The following constants can be values for the ToleranceDisplay property of the AcadDimension object (and all derived objects).

| CONSTANT | VALUE | DESCRIPTION |
|---|---|---|
| acTolNone | 0 | No tolerance values to be displayed with dimension text. |
| acTolSymmetrical | 1 | Use this constant to display tolerances when the positive and negative values are the same (e.g., 5.0 ± 0.2). |
| acTolDeviation | 2 | Use this constant to display tolerances when the positive and negative values are not the same. The positive value is displayed over the negative value. |
| acTolLimits | 3 | This constant incorporates tolerance values into the dimension value and displays the maximum dimension over the minimum. |
| acTolBasic | 4 | Basic draws a box around the dimension text, which is often used to indicate theoretically exact dimensions. |

## AcDimUnits

The following constants can be values for the AltUnitsFormat property of the dimension objects that support it (all except AcadDim3PointAngular and AcadDimAngular).

| CONSTANT | VALUE | DESCRIPTION |
|---|---|---|
| acDimScientific | 1 | Displays measurements in scientific notation |
| acDimDecimal | 2 | Displays measurements in decimal notation |

| CONSTANT | VALUE | DESCRIPTION |
| --- | --- | --- |
| acDimEngineering | 3 | Displays measurements in feet and decimal inches |
| acDimArchitecturalStacked | 4 | Displays measurements in feet, inches, and stacked (e.g., $\frac{1}{2}$) fractional inches |
| acDimFractionalStacked | 5 | Displays measurements in mixed-number notation, integers, and stacked (e.g., $\frac{1}{2}$) fractions |
| acDimArchitectural | 6 | Displays measurements in feet, inches, and fractional inches |
| acDimFractional | 7 | Displays measurements in mixed-number (integer and fractional) notation |
| acDimWindowsDesktop | 8 | Displays measurements in Windows Desktop format |

# AcDimVerticalJustification

The following constants can be values for the VerticalTextPosition property of the AcadDimension object (and all derived objects) and the AcadLeader object.

| CONSTANT | VALUE | DESCRIPTION |
| --- | --- | --- |
| acVertCentered | 0 | Centers the dimension text between the extension lines |
| acAbove | 1 | Places the dimension text above the dimension line except when the dimension line isn't horizontal and text inside the extension lines is forced horizontal |
| acOutside | 2 | Places the dimension text on the side of the dimension line farthest from the defining points |
| acJIS | 3 | Places the dimension text to conform to Japanese Industrial Standards (JIS) |

## AcDrawingAreaSCMCommand

The following constants can be values for the SCMCommandMode property of the AcadPreferencesUser object.

| CONSTANT | VALUE | DESCRIPTION |
|---|---|---|
| acEnter | 0 | Disables the Command shortcut menu. As a result, right-clicking in the drawing area when a command is in progress issues Enter. |
| acEnableSCMOptions | 1 | Enables the Command shortcut menu only when options are currently available from the command-line prompt. In a command-line prompt, options are enclosed in square brackets. If no options are available, right-clicking issues Enter. |
| acEnableSCM | 2 | Enables the Command shortcut menu. |

## AcDrawingAreaSCMDefault

The following constants can be values for the SCMDefaultMode property of the AcadPreferencesUser object.

| CONSTANT | VALUE | DESCRIPTION |
|---|---|---|
| acRepeatLastCommand | 0 | Disables the Default shortcut menu. As a result, right-clicking in the drawing area when no objects are selected and no commands are in progress issues Enter, which repeats the last issued command. |
| acSCM | 1 | Enables the Default shortcut menu. |

# AcDrawingAreaSCMEdit

The following constants can be values for the SCMEditMode property of the
AcadPreferencesUser object.

| CONSTANT | VALUE | DESCRIPTION |
|---|---|---|
| acEdRepeatLastCommand | 0 | Disables the Edit shortcut menu. As a result, right-clicking in the drawing area when one or more objects are selected and no commands are in progress issues Enter, which repeats the last issued command. |
| acEdSCM | 1 | Enables the Edit shortcut menu. |

# AcDrawingDirection

The following constants can be values for the DrawingDirection property of the
AcadMText object.

| CONSTANT | VALUE | DESCRIPTION |
|---|---|---|
| acLeftToRight | 1 | Text written from left to right |
| acRightToLeft | 2 | Reserved for future use |
| acTopToBottom | 3 | Text written from top to bottom |
| acBottomToTop | 4 | Reserved for future use |
| acByStyle | 5 | Reserved for future use |

## AcEntityName

The following constants can be values for the EntityName property of the AcadEntity object.

| CONSTANT | VALUE | DESCRIPTION |
| --- | --- | --- |
| ac3dFace | 1 | Acad3DFace object |
| ac3dPolyline | 2 | Acad3DPolyline object |
| ac3dSolid | 3 | Acad3DSolid object |
| acArc | 4 | AcadArc object |
| acAttribute | 5 | AcadAttribute object |
| acAttributeReference | 6 | AcadAttributeReference object |
| acBlockReference | 7 | AcadBlockReference object |
| acCircle | 8 | AcadCircle object |
| acDimAligned | 9 | AcadDimAligned object |
| acDimAngular | 10 | AcadDimAngular object |
| acDimDiametric | 12 | AcadDimDiametric object |
| acDimOrdinate | 13 | AcadDimOrdinate object |
| acDimRadial | 14 | AcadDimRadial object |
| acDimRotated | 15 | AcadDimRotated object |
| acEllipse | 16 | AcadEllipse object |
| acHatch | 17 | AcadHatch object |
| acLeader | 18 | AcadLeader object |
| acLine | 19 | AcadLine object |
| acMtext | 21 | AcadMText object |
| acPoint | 22 | AcadPoint object |
| acPolyline | 23 | AcadPolyline object |
| acPolylineLight | 24 | AcadLWPolyline object |
| acPolymesh | 25 | AcadPolygonMesh object |
| acRaster | 26 | AcadRasterImage object |

| CONSTANT | VALUE | DESCRIPTION |
| --- | --- | --- |
| acRay | 27 | AcadRay object |
| acRegion | 28 | AcadRegion object |
| acShape | 29 | AcadShape object |
| acSolid | 30 | AcadSolid object |
| acSpline | 31 | AcadSpline object |
| acText | 32 | AcadText object |
| acTolerance | 33 | AcadTolerance object |
| acTrace | 34 | AcadTrace object |
| acPViewport | 35 | AcadPViewport object |
| acXline | 36 | AcadXline object |
| acGroup | 37 | AcadGroup object |
| acMInsertBlock | 38 | AcadMInsertBlock object |
| acPolyfaceMesh | 39 | AcadPolyfaceMesh object |
| acMLine | 40 | AcadMLine object |
| acDim3PointAngular | 41 | AcadDim3PointAngular object |
| acExternalReference | 42 | AcadExternalReference object |

## AcExtendOption

The following constants can be supplied as the value for the third parameter of the IntersectWith method of the AcadEntity object, and those derived objects that support it (all except AcadPolygonMesh and AcadPViewport).

| CONSTANT | VALUE | DESCRIPTION |
| --- | --- | --- |
| acExtendNone | 0 | Doesn't extend either object |
| acExtendThisEntity | 1 | Extends the base object |
| acExtendOtherEntity | 2 | Extends the object passed as an argument |
| acExtendBoth | 3 | Extends both objects |

## AcHatchObjectType

These constants specify the type of Hatch.

| CONSTANT | VALUE | DESCRIPTION |
|---|---|---|
| acHatchObject | 0 | Classic |
| acGradientObject | 1 | Gradient |

## AcHatchStyle

The following constants can be values for the HatchStyle property of the AcadHatch object.

| CONSTANT | VALUE | DESCRIPTION |
|---|---|---|
| acHatchStyleNormal | 0 | Specifies standard style or normal. This option hatches inward from the outermost area boundary. If AutoCAD encounters an internal boundary, it turns off hatching until it encounters another boundary. |
| acHatchStyleOuter | 1 | Fills the outermost areas only. This style also hatches inward from the area boundary, but it turns off hatching if it encounters an internal boundary and doesn't turn it back on again. |
| acHatchStyleIgnore | 2 | Ignores internal structure. This option hatches through all internal objects. |

# AcHorizontalAlignment

The following constants can be values for the HorizontalAlignment property of the AcadAttribute, AcadAttributeReference, and AcadText objects.

| CONSTANT | VALUE | DESCRIPTION |
|---|---|---|
| acHorizontalAlignmentLeft | 0 | Aligns the attribute, attribute reference, or text at the left, the bottom edge of the text being on the baseline. |
| acHorizontalAlignmentCenter | 1 | Aligns the attribute, attribute reference, or text at the center, the bottom edge of the text being on the baseline. |
| acHorizontalAlignmentRight | 2 | Aligns the attribute, attribute reference, or text at the right, the bottom edge of the text being on the baseline. |
| acHorizontalAlignmentAligned | 3 | The attribute, attribute reference, or text is aligned according to the points held in the InsertionPoint and TextAlignmentPoint properties. |
| acHorizontalAlignmentMiddle | 4 | Aligns text at the middle. This isn't the same as acHorizontalAlignmentCenter, because the middle is defined as the midpoint between the top and bottom limits, the bottom referring to a position below the baseline. |
| acHorizontalAlignmentFit | 5 | The attribute, attribute reference, or text is aligned to fit to the points held in the InsertionPoint and TextAlignmentPoint properties. |

# AcInsertUnits

The following constants can be values for the ADCInsertUnitsDefaultSource and ADCInsertUnitsDefaultTarget properties of the AcadPreferencesUser object.

| CONSTANT | VALUE | DESCRIPTION |
|---|---|---|
| acInsertUnitsUnitless | 0 | No units |
| acInsertUnitsInches | 1 | Inches |
| acInsertUnitsFeet | 2 | Feet |
| acInsertUnitsMiles | 3 | Miles |
| acInsertUnitsMillimeters | 4 | Millimeters |
| acInsertUnitsCentimeters | 5 | Centimeters |
| acInsertUnitsMeters | 6 | Meters |
| acInsertUnitsKilometers | 7 | Kilometers |
| acInsertUnitsMicroinches | 8 | Microinches |
| acInsertUnitsMils | 9 | Mils |
| acInsertUnitsYards | 10 | Yards |
| acInsertUnitsAngstroms | 11 | Angstrom units |
| acInsertUnitsNanometers | 12 | Nanometers |
| acInsertUnitsMicrons | 13 | Microns (micrometers) |
| acInsertUnitsDecimeters | 14 | Decimeters |
| acInsertUnitsDecameters | 15 | Decameters |
| acInsertUnitsHectometers | 16 | Hectometers |
| acInsertUnitsGigameters | 17 | Gigameters |
| acInsertUnitsAstronomicalUnits | 18 | Astronomical units |
| acInsertUnitsLightYears | 19 | Light years |
| acInsertUnitsParsecs | 20 | Parsecs |

# AcISOPenWidth

The following constants can be values for the ISOPenWidth property of the AcadHatch object.

| CONSTANT | VALUE | DESCRIPTION |
|---|---|---|
| acPenWidthUnk | −1 | Unknown or nonstandard pen width |
| acPenWidth013 | 13 | 13/100th of a millimeter |
| acPenWidth018 | 18 | 18/100th of a millimeter |
| acPenWidth025 | 25 | 25/100th of a millimeter |
| acPenWidth035 | 35 | 35/100th of a millimeter |
| acPenWidth050 | 50 | 50/100th of a millimeter |
| acPenWidth070 | 70 | 70/100th of a millimeter |
| acPenWidth100 | 100 | 1 millimeter |
| acPenWidth140 | 140 | 1.4 millimeters |
| acPenWidth200 | 200 | 2 millimeters |

# AcKeyboardAccelerator

The following constants can be values for the KeyboardAccelerator property of the AcadPreferencesUser object.

| CONSTANT | VALUE | DESCRIPTION |
|---|---|---|
| acPreferenceClassic | 0 | Uses the AutoCAD classic keyboard |
| acPreferenceCustom | 1 | Uses the Windows standard keyboard |

## AcKeyboardPriority

The following constants can be values for the KeyboardPriority property of the AcadPreferencesUser object.

| CONSTANT | VALUE | DESCRIPTION |
|---|---|---|
| acKeyboardRunningObjSnap | 0 | Object snaps are strictly adhered to when typing in coordinates. |
| acKeyboardEntry | 1 | Keyboard entry values are strictly adhered to when typing in coordinates. |
| acKeyboardEntryExceptScripts | 2 | Keyboard entry values are strictly adhered to when typing in coordinates. However, when coordinates are entered through a script, running object snaps are adhered to. |

## AcLeaderType

The following constants can be values for the Type property of the AcadLeader object.

| CONSTANT | VALUE | DESCRIPTION |
|---|---|---|
| acLineNoArrow | 0 | A line with no arrow |
| acSplineNoArrow | 1 | A spline with no arrow |
| acLineWithArrow | 2 | A line with an arrow |
| acSplineWithArrow | 3 | A spline with an arrow |

# AcLineSpacingStyle

The following constants can be values for the LineSpacingStyle property of the AcadMText object.

| CONSTANT | VALUE | DESCRIPTION |
|---|---|---|
| acLineSpacingStyleAtLeast | 1 | Allows the spacing between different lines of text to adjust automatically, based on the height of the largest character in a line of text |
| acLineSpacingStyleExactly | 2 | Forces the line spacing to be the same size for all the lines in the text regardless of formatting overrides |

# AcLineWeight

The following constants can be values for these properties:

- The Lineweight property of the AcadEntity object (and all derived objects), the AcadDatabasePreferences, AcadGroup, and AcadLayer objects

- The DimensionLineweight property of the dimension objects that support it (all except AcadDimOrdinate) and the AcadLeader object

- The ExtensionLineweight property of the dimension objects that support it (all except AcadDimDiametric, AcadDimOrdinate, and AcadDimRadial)

| CONSTANT | VALUE | DESCRIPTION |
|---|---|---|
| acLnWtByLwDefault | −3 | Draws lines in the default lineweight. |
| acLnWtByBlock | −2 | Draws lines in the lineweight specified for the block (initial value). |
| acLnWtByLayer | −1 | Draws lines in the lineweight specified for the layer. |

*continues*

| CONSTANT | VALUE | DESCRIPTION |
|---|---|---|
| acLnWt000 | 0 | Plots with the thinnest lineweight available for the specified plotting device. (In model space, this is set with a width of one pixel.) |
| acLnWt005 | 5 | 5/100 millimeter. |
| acLnWt009 | 9 | 9/100 millimeter or 1/4 point. |
| acLnWt013 | 13 | 13/100 millimeter or 5/1000 inch. |
| acLnWt015 | 15 | 15/100 millimeter. |
| acLnWt018 | 18 | 18/100 millimeter, 1/2 point, or Pen Size 0000. |
| acLnWt020 | 20 | 2/10 millimeter or Pen Size 000. |
| acLnWt025 | 25 | $\frac{1}{4}$ millimeter, 1/100 inch, or 3/4 point. |
| acLnWt030 | 30 | 3/10 millimeter or Pen Size 00. |
| acLnWt035 | 35 | 35/100 millimeter, 1 point, or Pen Size 0. |
| acLnWt040 | 40 | 4/10 millimeter. |
| acLnWt050 | 50 | $\frac{1}{2}$ millimeter or Pen Size 1 |
| acLnWt053 | 53 | 53/100 millimeter or $1\frac{1}{2}$ points. |
| acLnWt060 | 60 | 6/10 millimeter or Pen Size 2. |
| acLnWt070 | 70 | 7/10 millimeter, $2\frac{1}{4}$ point, or Pen Size $2\frac{1}{2}$. |
| acLnWt080 | 80 | 8/10 millimeter or Pen Size 3. |
| acLnWt090 | 90 | 9/10 millimeter. |
| acLnWt100 | 100 | 1 millimeter or Pen Size $3\frac{1}{2}$. |
| acLnWt106 | 106 | 3 point. |
| acLnWt120 | 120 | 1.2 millimeters or Pen Size 4. |
| acLnWt140 | 140 | 1.4 millimeters. |
| acLnWt158 | 158 | $4\frac{1}{4}$ point. |
| acLnWt200 | 200 | 2 millimeters. |
| acLnWt211 | 211 | 6 point. |

# AcLoopType

The following constants can be supplied as the value for the second parameter of the InsertLoopAt method of the AcadHatch object.

| CONSTANT | VALUE | DESCRIPTION |
| --- | --- | --- |
| acHatchLoopTypeDefault | 0 | The loop type hasn't been specified. |
| acHatchLoopTypeExternal | 1 | The loop consists of external entities. |
| acHatchLoopTypePolyline | 2 | The hatch loop consists of a polyline. |
| AcHatchLoopTypeDerived | 4 | The loop was derived by AutoCAD's boundary tracer from a picked point. |
| acHatchLoopTypeTextbox | 8 | The loop consists of a box around an existing text object. |

# AcMenuFileType

The following constants can be supplied as the value for the parameter of the Save method of the AcadMenuGroup object or the second parameter for the property of the SaveAs method of the AcadDocument and AcadMenuGroup objects.

| CONSTANT | VALUE | DESCRIPTION |
| --- | --- | --- |
| acMenuFileCompiled | 0 | A compiled menu file (MNC file type) |
| acMenuFileSource | 1 | A source menu file (MNS file type) |

# AcMenuGroupType

The following constants can be values for the Type property of the AcadMenuGroup object.

| CONSTANT | VALUE | DESCRIPTION |
| --- | --- | --- |
| acBaseMenuGroup | 0 | A base menu group |
| acPartialMenuGroup | 1 | A partial menu group |

## AcMenuItemType

The following constants can be values for the Type property of the
AcadPopupMenuItem object.

| CONSTANT | VALUE | DESCRIPTION |
| --- | --- | --- |
| acMenuItem | 0 | Specifies a pop-up menu item |
| acMenuSeparator | 1 | Specifies a separator in a pop-up menu |
| acMenuSubMenu | 2 | Specifies a pop-up submenu |

## AcOleQuality

The following constants can be values for the OleQuality property of the
AcadPreferencesOutput object.

| CONSTANT | VALUE | DESCRIPTION |
| --- | --- | --- |
| acOQLineArt | 0 | Specifies line art quality (e.g., for an embedded spreadsheet) |
| acOQText | 1 | Specifies text quality (e.g., for an embedded Word document) |
| acOQGraphics | 2 | Specifies graphics quality (e.g., for an embedded pie chart) |
| acOQPhoto | 3 | Specifies photograph quality |
| acOQHighPhoto | 4 | High-quality photograph |

## AcPatternType

The following constants can be values for the PatternType property of the
AcadHatch object, and they can also be supplied as the value for the second para-
meter of the AddHatch method of the AcadBlock, AcadModelSpace, and
AcadPaperSpace objects and the SetPattern method of the AcadHatch object.

| CONSTANT | VALUE | DESCRIPTION |
|---|---|---|
| acHatchPatternTypeUserDefined | 0 | Defines a pattern of lines using the current linetype |
| acHatchPatternTypePreDefined | 1 | Selects the pattern name from those defined in the acad.pat file |
| acHatchPatternTypeCustomDefined | 2 | Selects the pattern name from a .pat file other than the acad.pat file |

# AcPlotPaperUnits

The following constants can be values for the PaperUnits property of the AcadLayout and AcadPlotConfiguration objects.

| CONSTANT | VALUE | DESCRIPTION |
|---|---|---|
| acInches | 0 | Units specified in inches |
| acMillimeters | 1 | Units specified in millimeters |
| acPixels | 2 | Units specified in pixels |

# AcPlotPolicy

The following constants can be values for the PlotPolicy property of the AcadPreferencesOutput object.

| CONSTANT | VALUE | DESCRIPTION |
|---|---|---|
| acPolicyNamed | 0 | No association is made between color and plot style name. Plot style name for each object is set to the default defined in the DefaultPlotStyleForObjects property. |
| acPolicyLegacy | 1 | An object's plot style name is associated with its color per the naming convention ACIx, where x is the color number of the object according to the AutoCAD color index. |

## AcPlotRotation

The following constants can be values for the PlotRotation property of the AcadLayout and AcadPlotConfiguration objects.

| CONSTANT | VALUE | DESCRIPTION |
|---|---|---|
| ac0degrees | 0 | These values are read counterclockwise relative to the X-axis. |
| ac90degrees | 1 | |
| ac180degrees | 2 | |
| ac270degrees | 3 | |

## AcPlotScale

The following constants can be values for the StandardScale property of the AcadLayout and AcadPlotConfiguration objects.

| CONSTANT | VALUE | DESCRIPTION |
|---|---|---|
| acScaleToFit | 0 | Scale to fit |
| ac1_128in_1ft | 1 | 1/128" : 1' |
| ac1_64in_1ft | 2 | 1/64" : 1' |
| ac1_32in_1ft | 3 | 1/32" : 1' |
| ac1_16in_1ft | 4 | 1/16" : 1' |
| ac3_32in_1ft | 5 | 3/32" : 1' |
| ac1_8in_1ft | 6 | 1/8" : 1' |
| ac3_16in_1ft | 7 | 3/16" : 1' |
| ac1_4in_1ft | 8 | 1/4" : 1' |

| CONSTANT | VALUE | DESCRIPTION |
|---|---|---|
| ac3_8in_1ft | 9 | 3/8" : 1' |
| ac1_2in_1ft | 10 | 1/2" : 1' |
| ac3_4in_1ft | 11 | 3/4" : 1' |
| ac1in_1ft | 12 | 1" : 1' |
| ac3in_1ft | 13 | 3" : 1' |
| ac6in_1ft | 14 | 6" : 1' |
| ac1ft_1ft | 15 | 1' : 1' |
| ac1_1 | 16 | 1 : 1 |
| ac1_2 | 17 | 1 : 2 |
| ac1_4 | 18 | 1 : 4 |
| ac1_8 | 19 | 1 : 8 |
| ac1_10 | 20 | 1: 10 |
| ac1_16 | 21 | 1: 16 |
| ac1_20 | 22 | 1: 20 |
| ac1_30 | 23 | 1 : 30 |
| ac1_40 | 24 | 1 : 40 |
| ac1_50 | 25 | 1 : 50 |
| ac1_100 | 26 | 1: 100 |
| ac2_1 | 27 | 2 : 1 |
| ac4_1 | 28 | 4 : 1 |
| ac8_1 | 29 | 8 : 1 |
| ac10_1 | 30 | 10 : 1 |
| ac100_1 | 31 | 100 : 1 |

# AcPlotType

The following constants can be values for the PlotType property of the AcadLayout and AcadPlotConfiguration objects.

| CONSTANT | VALUE | DESCRIPTION |
|---|---|---|
| acDisplay | 0 | Prints everything that is in the current display. |
| acExtents | 1 | Prints everything that falls within the extents of the currently selected space. |
| acLimits | 2 | Prints everything that is in the limits of the current space. |
| acView | 3 | Prints the view named by the ViewToPlot property. |
| acWindow | 4 | Prints everything in the window specified by the SetWindowToPlot method. |
| acLayout | 5 | Prints everything that falls within the margins of the specified paper size with the origin being calculated from the 0,0 coordinate location in the Layout tab. This option isn't available when printing from model space. |

# AcPolylineType

The following constants can be values for the Type property of the AcadPolyline object.

| CONSTANT | VALUE | DESCRIPTION |
|---|---|---|
| acSimplePoly | 0 | Specifies a simple polyline |
| acFitCurvePoly | 1 | Specifies a fit curve polyline |
| acQuadSplinePoly | 2 | Specifies a quadratic B-spline polyline |
| acCubicSplinePoly | 3 | Specifies a cubic B-spline polyline |

# AcPolymeshType

The following constants can be values for the Type property of the AcadPolygonMesh object.

| CONSTANT | VALUE | DESCRIPTION |
| --- | --- | --- |
| acSimpleMesh | 0 | Specifies a simple mesh with no surface fitting or smoothing |
| acQuadSurfaceMesh | 5 | Specifies a quadratic B-spline surface fit |
| acCubicSurfaceMesh | 6 | Specifies a cubic B-spline surface fit |
| acBezierSurfaceMesh | 8 | Specifies a Bezier surface fit |

# AcPreviewMode

The following constants can be values for the DisplayPlotPreview property of the AcadPlot object.

| CONSTANT | VALUE | DESCRIPTION |
| --- | --- | --- |
| acPartialPreview | 0 | Shows an accurate representation of the effective plot area relative to the paper size. The final location of the affected area on the paper depends on the plotter. |
| acFullPreview | 1 | Displays the drawing on the screen as it will appear when plotted on paper. Because this requires a regeneration of the drawing, it's slower than a partial preview. It's faster than the normal plot regeneration because AutoCAD performs no vector sorting or optimization. |

## AcPrinterSpoolAlert

The following constants can be values for the PrinterSpoolAlert property of the AcadPreferencesOutput object.

| CONSTANT | VALUE | DESCRIPTION |
| --- | --- | --- |
| acPrinterAlwaysAlert | 0 | Always alert and log errors. |
| acPrinterAlertOnce | 1 | Alert only the first error and log all errors. |
| acPrinterNeverAlertLogOnce | 2 | Never alert, but log all errors. |
| acPrinterNeverAlert | 3 | Never alert and don't log any errors. |

## AcProxyImage

The following constants can be values for the ProxyImage property of the AcadPreferencesOpenSave object.

| CONSTANT | VALUE | DESCRIPTION |
| --- | --- | --- |
| acProxyNotShow | 0 | Don't show the proxy image. |
| acProxyShow | 1 | Show the proxy image. |
| acProxyBoundingBox | 2 | Show the proxy image in a bounding box. |

## AcRegenType

The following constants can be supplied as the value for the parameter of the Regen method of the AcadDocument object.

| CONSTANT | VALUE | DESCRIPTION |
| --- | --- | --- |
| acActiveViewport | 0 | Regenerates drawing in active viewport only |
| acAllViewports | 1 | Regenerates drawing in all viewports |

# AcSaveAsType

The following constants can be values for the SaveAsType property of the AcadPreferencesOpenSave object.

| CONSTANT | VALUE | DESCRIPTION |
|---|---|---|
| acUnknown | −1 | This constant is read-only. The drawing type is unknown or invalid. |
| acR12_dxf | 1 | AutoCAD Release12/LT2 DXF (*.dxf). |
| acR13_dwg | 4 | AutoCAD Release13/LT95 DWG (*.dwg). |
| acR13_dxf | 5 | AutoCAD Release13/LT95 DXF (*.dxf). |
| acR14_dwg | 8 | AutoCAD Release14/LT97 DWG (*.dwg). |
| acR14_dxf | 9 | AutoCAD Release14/LT97 DXF (*.dxf). |
| acNative | 12 | A synonym for the current drawing release format. If you want your application to save the drawing in the format of whatever version of AutoCAD the application is running on, then use the acNative format. |
| acR15_dwg | 12 | AutoCAD 2000 DWG (*.dwg). |
| acR15_dxf | 13 | AutoCAD 2000 DXF (*.dxf). |
| acR15_Template | 14 | AutoCAD 2000 Drawing Template File (*.dwt). |
| ac2004_dwg | 24 | AutoCAD 2004 DWG (*.dwg). |

Note: The acR13_dwg, acR13_dxf, acR14_dwg, and acR14_dxf options aren't available in AutoCAD 2004

## AcSelect

The following constants can be supplied as the value for the first parameter in either of the Select or SelectByPolygon methods of the AcadSelectionSet object.

| CONSTANT | VALUE | DESCRIPTION |
|---|---|---|
| acSelectionSetWindow | 0 | Selects all entities completely inside a rectangular area whose corners are defined by Point1 and Point2 (Select method only). |
| acSelectionSetCrossing | 1 | Selects objects within and crossing a rectangular area whose corners are defined by Point1 and Point2 (Select method only). |
| acSelectionSetFence | 2 | Selects all entities crossing a selection fence. The fence is defined by coordinates in PointList. Fence mode is similar to CrossingPolygon mode except that AutoCAD doesn't close the last vector of the fence, and a fence can cross itself. Fence isn't affected by the PICKADD system variable (SelectByPolygon method only). |
| acSelectionSetPrevious | 3 | Selects the most recent selection set. This mode is ignored if you switch between paper and model space and attempt to use the selection set (Select method only). |
| acSelectionSetLast | 4 | Selects the most recently created visible entity (Select method only). |
| acSelectionSetAll | 5 | Selects all entities (Select method only). |

| CONSTANT | VALUE | DESCRIPTION |
|---|---|---|
| acSelectionSetWindowPolygon | 6 | Selects objects within a polygon defined by PointList (SelectByPolygon method only). |
| acSelectionSetCrossingPolygon | 7 | Selects objects within and crossing an area defined by a polygon. Use PointList to define the coordinates of the polygon. AutoCAD will close the last vector of the polygon. A polygon definition can't cross itself (SelectByPolygon method only). |

# AcTextFontStyle

The following constants an their combination can be values for the TextFontStyle property of the AcadPreferencesDisplay object.

| CONSTANT | VALUE | DESCRIPTION |
|---|---|---|
| acFontRegular | 0 | Specifies a normal font style |
| acFontItalic | 1 | Specifies italic style |
| acFontBold | 2 | Specifies bold style |
| acFontBoldItalic | 3 | Specifies both bold and italic styles |

# AcTextGenerationFlag

The following constants can be values for the TextGenerationFlag property of the AcadAttribute, AcadAttributeReference, and AcadText objects.

| CONSTANT | VALUE | DESCRIPTION |
|---|---|---|
| acTextFlagBackward | 2 | Text to be displayed backward |
| acTextFlagUpsideDown | 4 | Text to be displayed upside-down |

## AcToolbarDockStatus

The following constants can be values for the DockStatus property of the AcadToolbar object, or they can be supplied as the value for the parameter of the Dock method of the AcadToolbar object.

| CONSTANT | VALUE | DESCRIPTION |
|---|---|---|
| acToolbarDockTop | 0 | Toolbar docked at the top of the window |
| acToolbarDockBottom | 1 | Toolbar docked at the bottom of the window |
| acToolbarDockLeft | 2 | Toolbar docked at the left of the window |
| acToolbarDockRight | 3 | Toolbar docked at the right of the window |
| acToolbarFloating | 4 | Toolbar not docked at all |

## AcToolbarItemType

The following constants can be values for the Type property of the AcadToolbarItem object.

| CONSTANT | VALUE | DESCRIPTION |
|---|---|---|
| acToolbarButton | 0 | Specifies a generic button |
| acToolbarSeparator | 1 | Specifies a toolbar separator |
| acToolbarControl | 2 | Specifies a control button |
| acToolbarFlyout | 3 | Specifies a flyout button |

# AcUnits

The following constants can be supplied as the value for the second parameter of the `DistanceToReal` and `RealToString` methods of the `AcadUtility` object.

| CONSTANT | VALUE | DESCRIPTION |
|---|---|---|
| acDefaultUnits | −1 | Displays measurements in default units |
| acScientific | 1 | Displays measurements in scientific notation |
| acDecimal | 2 | Displays measurements in decimal notation |
| acEngineering | 3 | Displays measurements in feet and decimal inches |
| acArchitectural | 4 | Displays measurements in feet, inches, and fractional inches |
| acFractional | 5 | Displays measurements in mixed-number (integer and fractional) notation |

# AcVerticalAlignment

The following constants can be values for the `VerticalAlignment` property of the `AcadAttribute`, `AcadAttributeReference`, and `AcadText` objects.

| CONSTANT | VALUE | DESCRIPTION |
|---|---|---|
| acVerticalAlignmentBaseline | 0 | Align on the baseline. Note that the baseline isn't the same as the bottom. The baseline is defined at a level partway between the bottom position and the middle position. |
| acVerticalAlignmentBottom | 1 | Align at the bottom. |
| AcVerticalAlignmentMiddle | 2 | Align at the middle. This is midway between the bottom and the top positions. |
| AcVerticalAlignmentTop | 3 | Align at the top. |

## AcViewportScale

The following constants can be values for the StandardScale property of the AcadPViewport object.

| CONSTANT | VALUE | DESCRIPTION |
| --- | --- | --- |
| acVpScaleToFit | 0 | Scale to fit |
| acVpCustomScale | 1 | Custom scale |
| acVp1_1 | 2 | 1 : 1 |
| acVp1_2 | 3 | 1 : 2 |
| acVp1_4 | 4 | 1 : 4 |
| acVp1_8 | 5 | 1 : 8 |
| acVp1_10 | 6 | 1 : 10 |
| acVp1_16 | 7 | 1 : 16 |
| acVp1_20 | 8 | 1 : 20 |
| acVp1_30 | 9 | 1 : 30 |
| acVp1_40 | 10 | 1 : 40 |
| acVp1_50 | 11 | 1 : 50 |
| acVp1_100 | 12 | 1 : 100 |
| acVp2_1 | 13 | 2 : 1 |
| acVp4_1 | 14 | 4 : 1 |
| acVp8_1 | 15 | 8 : 1 |
| acVp10_1 | 16 | 10 : 1 |
| acVp100_1 | 17 | 100 : 1 |
| acVp1_128in_1ft | 18 | 1/128" : 1' |
| acVp1_64in_1ft | 19 | 1/64" : 1' |
| acVp1_32in_1ft | 20 | 1/32" : 1' |
| acVp1_16in_1ft | 21 | 1/16" : 1' |
| acVp1_32in_1ft | 22 | 3/32" : 1' |
| acVp1_8in_1ft | 23 | 1/8" : 1' |

| CONSTANT | VALUE | DESCRIPTION |
|----------|-------|-------------|
| acVp1_16in_1ft | 24 | 3/16" : 1' |
| acVp1_4in_1ft | 25 | 1/4" : 1' |
| acVp1_8in_1ft | 26 | 3/8" : 1' |
| acVp1_2in_1ft | 27 | 1/2" : 1' |
| acVp1_4in_1ft | 28 | 3/4" : 1' |
| acVp1in_1ft | 29 | 1" : 1' |
| acVp3in_1ft | 30 | 3" : 1' |
| acVp6in_1ft | 31 | 6" : 1' |
| acVp1ft_1ft | 32 | 1' : 1' |

# AcViewportSplitType

The following constants can be supplied as the value for the parameter of the Split method of the AcadViewport object.

| CONSTANT | VALUE | DESCRIPTION |
|----------|-------|-------------|
| acViewport2Horizontal | 0 | Splits the viewport horizontally into two equal sections. |
| acViewport2Vertical | 1 | Splits the viewport vertically into two equal sections. |
| acViewport3Left | 2 | Splits the viewport into two vertical halves. The left half is split horizontally into two equal sections. |
| acViewport3Right | 3 | Splits the viewport into two vertical halves. The right half is split horizontally into two equal sections. |
| acViewport3Horizontal | 4 | Splits the viewport horizontally into three equal sections. |
| acViewport3Vertical | 5 | Splits the viewport vertically into three equal sections. |

*continues*

| CONSTANT | VALUE | DESCRIPTION |
|---|---|---|
| acViewport3Above | 6 | Splits the viewport into two horizontal halves. The top half will be a single viewport. The bottom half is split vertically into two equal sections. |
| acViewport3Below | 7 | Splits the viewport into two horizontal halves. The bottom half will be a single viewport. The top half is split vertically into two equal sections. |
| acViewport4 | 8 | Splits the viewport horizontally and vertically into four equal sections. |

## AcWindowState

The following constants can be values for the WindowState property of the AcadApplication and AcadDocument objects.

| CONSTANT | VALUE | DESCRIPTION |
|---|---|---|
| acNorm | 1 | Neither maximized nor minimized |
| acMin | 2 | Minimized window |
| acMax | 3 | Maximized window |

# AcXRefDemandLoad

The following constants can be values for the XrefDemandLoad property of the AcadPreferencesOpenSave object.

| CONSTANT | VALUE | DESCRIPTION |
| --- | --- | --- |
| acDemandLoadDisabled | 0 | Turns off demand loading. The entire drawing is loaded. |
| acDemandLoadEnabled | 1 | Turns on demand loading and improves AutoCAD performance. Other users can't edit the file while it's being referenced. |
| acDemandLoadEnabledWithCopy | 2 | Turns on demand loading but uses a copy of the referenced drawing. Other users can edit the original drawing. |

# AcZoomScaleType

The following constants can be supplied as the value for the second parameter of the ZoomScale method of the AcadApplication object.

| CONSTANT | VALUE | DESCRIPTION |
| --- | --- | --- |
| acZoomScaledAbsolute | 0 | Scale factor is applied relative to the drawing limits |
| acZoomScaledRelative | 1 | Scale factor is applied relative to the current view |
| acZoomScaledRelativePSpace | 2 | Scale factor is applied relative to paper space units |

# APPENDIX C

# System Variables

AUTOCAD PROVIDES SEVERAL SYSTEM VARIABLES that let the user control user interface elements such as object snap mode, grids, and limits. This Appendix explains all of AutoCAD's system variables. It also demonstrates how to use the GetVariable and SetVariable methods to set and check a system variable's value. Each successive release of AutoCAD had introduced new system variables, modified existing ones, and removed others. Therefore, before you use a system variable, research it to determine whether your code needs to check the AutoCAD version to use the right system variable.

You can also use certain properties of AutoCAD objects to access some of these variables. This Appendix lists those properties.

## *The GetVariable Method*

Use the Document object's GetVariable method to retrieve a system variable's value. This method has the following syntax:

```
CurrentValue = DocumentObject.GetVariable(VariableName)
```

This method returns the value of the system variable you specify in the VariableName parameter. This parameter is a String.

This example retrieves and displays the ANGDIR system variable's current value. This variable's value determines whether AutoCAD measures angles counterclockwise or clockwise with respect to the current OCS.

```
Public Sub GetANGDIR()
Dim varAngleDirection As Variant

    varAngleDirection = ThisDrawing.GetVariable("ANGDIR")
    If varAngleDirection = 0 Then
        MsgBox "Angles are measured counterclockwise"
    Else
        MsgBox "Angles are measured clockwise"
    End If
End Sub
```

## *The SetVariable Method*

Use the Document object's SetVariable method to set a system variable. It has the following syntax:

```
DocumentObject.SetVariable VariableName, VariableValue
```

Table C-1 explains this method's parameters.

*Table C-1. SetVariable Method Parameters*

| NAME | DATA TYPE | DESCRIPTION |
| --- | --- | --- |
| VariableName | String | The name of the system variable |
| VariableValue | Variant | The system variable's new value |

This example lets the user set the ANGDIR system variable's value:

```
Public Sub SetANGDIR()
Dim strResponse As String

On Error Resume Next
    strResponse = InputBox("Please specify the direction that angles should " & _
    "be measured (Clockwise or Counterclockwise )", , "Counterclockwise")
    If UCase(strResponse) = "COUNTERCLOCKWISE" Then
        ThisDrawing.SetVariable "ANGDIR", 0
    ElseIf UCase(strResponse) = "CLOCKWISE" Then
        ThisDrawing.SetVariable "ANGDIR", 1
    ElseIf strResponse = "" Then
        MsgBox "You cancelled, the system variable setting has not been changed"
    Else
    MsgBox "The value you typed has not been recognized - " & _
        "the system variable setting has not been changed"
    End If
End Sub
```

# A

| NAME | DESCRIPTION |
| --- | --- |
| ACADLSPASDOC | Controls whether the acad.lsp file is loaded into every opened drawing or just the first one in the session. This variable's variable is also stored in the LoadAcadLspInAllDocuments property of the AcadPreferencesSelection object. |
| ACADPREFIX | Stores the directory path specified by the ACAD environment variable, including path separators where necessary. |
| ACADVER | Stores the AutoCAD version number. AutoCAD 2000 = 15.0, AutoCAD 2000i = 15.05, AutoCAD 2002 = 15.06, and AutoCAD 2004 = 16.0. This variable's value is also stored in the Version property of the AcadApplication object. |
| ACISOUTVER | Controls the ACIS version of .sat files created using the ACISOUT command. |
| ADCSTATE | Determines whether DesignCenter is active or not. |
| AFLAGS | Sets attribute flags for ATTDEF bit-code. This variable's value is also stored in the Mode property of the AcadAttribute object. |
| ANGBASE | Sets the base angle 0 with respect to the current UCS. |
| ANGDIR | Sets the positive angle direction from angle 0 with respect to the current UCS. |
| APBOX | Turns the AutoSnap aperture box on or off. This variable's value is also stored in the AutoSnapAperture property of the AcadPreferencesDrafting object. |
| APERTURE | Sets object snap target height in pixels. This variable's value is also stored in the AutoSnapApertureSize property of the AcadPreferencesDrafting object. |
| AREA | Stores the last area computed by AREA, LIST, or DBLIST. |
| ATTDIA | Controls whether -INSERT uses a dialog box when entering attribute values. |
| ATTMODE | Controls the display of attributes. |

| NAME | DESCRIPTION |
|------|-------------|
| ATTREQ | Determines whether INSERT uses default attribute settings during the insertion of blocks. |
| AUDITCTL | Controls whether AUDIT creates an audit report (.adt) file. |
| AUNITS | Sets angle units. |
| AUPREC | Sets the number of decimal places for angular units. |
| AUTOSNAP | Controls the AutoSnap marker, tooltip, and magnet. This variable's value is also stored in the AutoSnapMagnet, AutoSnapMarker, AutoSnapToolTip, and AutoTrackTooltip properties of the AcadPreferencesDrafting object. |

## B

| NAME | DESCRIPTION |
|------|-------------|
| BACKZ | Stores the current viewport's back clipping plane offset from the target plane. |
| BINDTYPE | Controls how XRef names are handled when binding them or when editing them in place. |
| BLIPMODE | Controls whether or not marker blips are visible. |

## C

| NAME | DESCRIPTION |
|------|-------------|
| CDATE | Sets the calendar's date and time. |
| CECOLOR | Sets the color of new objects. |
| CELTSCALE | Sets the linetype scaling factor for the current object. |
| CELTYPE | Sets the linetype of new objects. |

| NAME | DESCRIPTION |
|------|-------------|
| CELWEIGHT | Sets the lineweight of new objects. |
| CHAMFERA | Sets the first chamfer distance. |
| CHAMFERB | Sets the second chamfer distance. |
| CHAMFERC | Sets the chamfer length. |
| CHAMFERD | Sets the chamfer angle. |
| CHAMMODE | Sets the input method by which chamfers are created. |
| CIRCLERAD | Sets the default radius for a circle. |
| CLAYER | Sets the current layer. |
| CMDACTIVE | Stores the bit code that indicates whether an ordinary command, a transparent command, a script, or a dialog box is active. |
| CMDECHO | Controls whether prompts and input are echoed during the AutoLISP Command function. |
| CMDNAMES | Displays the names of active and transparent commands. |
| CMLJUST | Sets the justification of a multiline. |
| CMLSCALE | Sets the width of a multiline. |
| CMLSTYLE | Sets the style of a multiline. |
| COMPASS | Controls whether the 3-D compass is switched on or off for the current viewport. |
| COORDS | Controls when coordinates are updated on the status line. |
| CPLOTSTYLE | Sets the current plot style for new objects. |
| CPROFILE | Stores the current profile's name. |
| CTAB | Returns the name of the current model tab or layout tab in the drawing. |
| CURSORSIZE | Determines the size of the crosshairs as a percentage of the screen size. This variable's value is also stored in the CursorSize property of the AcadPreferencesDisplay object. |
| CVPORT | Sets the current viewport's identification number. |

# D

| NAME | DESCRIPTION |
|------|-------------|
| DATE | Stores the current date and time. |
| DBCSTATE | Stores the state of the dbConnect Manager, active or not active. |
| DBMOD | Indicates the status of drawing modifications using bit code. |
| DCTCUST | Displays the current custom dictionary's path and file name. |
| DCTMAIN | Displays the current main dictionary's file name. |
| DEFLPLSTYLE | Specifies the default plot style for new layers. This variable's value is also stored in the `DefaultPlotStyleForLayer` property of the `AcadPreferencesOutput` object. |
| DEFPLSTYLE | Specifies the default plot style for new objects. This variable's value is also stored in the `DefaultPlotStyleForObjects` property of the `AcadPreferencesOutput` object. |
| DELOBJ | Controls whether any objects used to create other objects are retained or deleted from the drawing database. |
| DEMANDLOAD | Specifies the conditions that cause AutoCAD to demand load a third-party application, if a drawing contains objects created in that application. This variable's value is also stored in the `DemandLoadARXApp` property of the `AcadPreferencesOpenSave` object. |
| DIASTAT | Stores the exit method of the most recently used dialog box. |
| DIMADEC | Controls the number of places of precision displayed for angular dimensions. |
| DIMALT | Controls the display of alternate units in dimensions. |
| DIMALTD | Controls the number of decimal places in alternate units. |
| DIMALTF | Controls the multiplier for alternate units. |
| DIMALTRND | Determines the rounding of alternate units. |
| DIMALTTD | Sets the number of decimal places for tolerance values in a dimension's alternate units. |

| NAME | DESCRIPTION |
|------|-------------|
| DIMALTTZ | Toggles suppression of zeros in tolerance values. |
| DIMALTU | Sets the units format for alternate units of all dimension style family members except angular. |
| DIMALTZ | Controls the suppression of zeros for alternate unit dimension values. |
| DIMAPOST | Specifies a text prefix and/or suffix to the alternate dimension measurement for all types of dimensions except angular. |
| DIMASO | Controls the associativity of dimension objects. (replaced by DIMASSOC in AutoCAD 2002 and later versions). |
| DIMASZ | Controls the size of dimension line and leader line arrowheads. |
| DIMATFIT | Determines how dimension text and arrows are arranged when space is not sufficient to place both within the extension lines. |
| DIMAUNIT | Sets the units format for angular dimensions. |
| DIMAZIN | Suppresses zeros for angular dimensions. |
| DIMBLK | Sets the arrowhead block displayed at the ends of dimension lines or leader lines. |
| DIMBLK1 | Sets the arrowhead for the first end of the dimension line when DIMSAH is on. |
| DIMBLK2 | Sets the arrowhead for the second end of the dimension line when DIMSAH is on. |
| DIMCEN | Controls drawing of circle or arc center marks and centerlines by DIMCENTER, DIMDIAMETER, and DIMRADIUS. |
| DIMCLRD | Assigns colors to dimension lines, arrowheads, and dimension leader lines. |
| DIMCLRE | Assigns colors to dimension extension lines. |
| DIMCLRT | Assigns colors to dimension text. |
| DIMDEC | Sets the number of decimal places displayed for a dimension's primary units. |
| DIMDLE | Sets the distance the dimension line extends beyond the extension line when oblique strokes are drawn instead of arrowheads. |

| NAME | DESCRIPTION |
|------|-------------|
| DIMDLI | Controls the spacing of dimension lines in baseline dimensions. |
| DIMDSEP | Specifies a single character decimal separator to use when creating dimensions whose unit format is decimal. |
| DIMEXE | Specifies how far to extend the extension line beyond the dimension line. |
| DIMEXO | Specifies how far extension lines are offset from origin points. |
| DIMFIT | Obsolete. Replaced by DIMATFIT and DIMTMOVE. Retained for backward compatibility only. |
| DIMFRAC | Sets the fraction format when DIMLUNIT is set to 4 or 5. |
| DIMGAP | Sets the distance around dimension text when the dimension line breaks to accommodate dimension text. |
| DIMJUST | Controls the horizontal positioning of dimension text. |
| DIMLDRBLK | Specifies the arrow type for leaders. |
| DIMLFAC | Sets a scale factor for linear dimension measurements. |
| DIMLIM | Generates dimension limits as the default text. |
| DIMLUNIT | Sets units for all dimension types except angular. |
| DIMLWD | Assigns lineweight to dimension lines. |
| DIMLWE | Assigns lineweight to extension lines. |
| DIMPOST | Specifies a text prefix and/or suffix to the dimension measurement. |
| DIMRND | Rounds all dimensioning distances to the specified value. |
| DIMSAH | Controls the display of dimension line arrowhead blocks. |
| DIMSCALE | Sets the overall scale factor applied to dimensioning variables that specify sizes, distances, or offsets. |
| DIMSD1 | Controls suppression of the first dimension line. |
| DIMSD2 | Controls suppression of the second dimension line. |
| DIMSE1 | Suppresses display of the first extension line. |
| DIMSE2 | Suppresses display of the second extension line. |
| DIMSHO | Controls redefinition of dimension objects while dragging. |

| NAME | DESCRIPTION |
|------|-------------|
| DIMSOXD | Suppresses drawing of dimension lines outside the extension lines. |
| DIMSTYLE | Shows the current dimension style. |
| DIMTAD | Controls the vertical position of text in relation to the dimension line. |
| DIMTDEC | Sets the number of decimal places to display in tolerance values for a dimension's primary units. |
| DIMTFAC | Sets a scale factor used to calculate the height of text for dimension fractions and tolerances. |
| DIMTIH | Controls the position of dimension text inside the extension lines for all dimension types except ordinate. |
| DIMTIX | Draws text between extension lines. |
| DIMTM | When DIMTOL or DIMLIM is on, sets the minimum tolerance limit for dimension text. |
| DIMTMOVE | Sets dimension text movement rules. |
| DIMTOFL | Controls whether a dimension line is drawn between the extension lines even if text is placed outside. |
| DIMTOH | Controls the position of dimension text outside the extension lines. |
| DIMTOL | Appends tolerances to dimension text. |
| DIMTOLJ | Sets the vertical justification for tolerance values relative to the nominal dimension text. |
| DIMTP | When DIMTOL or DIMLIM is on, sets the maximum tolerance limit for dimension text. |
| DIMTSZ | Specifies the size of oblique strokes drawn instead of arrowheads for linear, radial, and diameter dimensioning. |
| DIMTVP | Controls the vertical position of dimension text above or below the dimension line. |
| DIMTXSTY | Specifies the text style of the dimension. |
| DIMTXT | Specifies the height of dimension text, unless the current text style has a fixed height. |
| DIMTZIN | Controls the suppression of zeros in tolerance values. |

| NAME | DESCRIPTION |
|------|-------------|
| DIMUNIT | Obsolete. Replaced by DIMLUNIT and DIMFRAC. Retained for backward compatibility only. |
| DIMUPT | Controls options for user-positioned text. |
| DIMZIN | Controls the suppression of zeroes in the primary unit value. |
| DISPSILH | Controls display of silhouette curves of solid objects in Wireframe mode. This variable's value is also stored in the DisplaySilhouette property of the AcadDatabasePreferences object. |
| DISTANCE | Stores the distance computed by DIST. |
| DONUTID | Sets the default for the inside diameter of a torus (donut). |
| DONUTOD | Sets the default for the outside diameter of a torus (donut). |
| DRAGMODE | Controls the display of objects being dragged. |
| DRAGP1 | Sets the sampling rate for regen-drag input. |
| DRAGP2 | Sets the sampling rate for fast-drag input. |
| DWGCHECK | Determines whether a drawing was last edited by a product other than AutoCAD. |
| DWGCODEPAGE | Stores the same value as SYSCODEPAGE (retained for compatibility reasons). |
| DWGNAME | Stores the drawing name as entered by the user. |
| DWGPREFIX | Stores the drive or directory prefix for the drawing. |
| DWGTITLED | Indicates whether the current drawing has been named. |

# E

| NAME | DESCRIPTION |
|------|-------------|
| EDGEMODE | Controls how TRIM and EXTEND determine cutting and boundary edges. |
| ELEVATION | Stores the current elevation relative to the current UCS for the current viewport. |

| NAME | DESCRIPTION |
| --- | --- |
| EXPERT | Controls whether certain prompts are issued. |
| EXPLMODE | Controls whether EXPLODE supports nonuniformly scaled (NUS) blocks. |
| EXTMAX | Stores the upper-right point of the drawing extents. |
| EXTMIN | Stores the lower-left point of the drawing extents. |
| EXTNAMES | Sets the parameters for named object names (such as linetypes and layers) stored in symbol tables. This variable's value is also stored in the AllowLongSymbolNames property of the AcadDataBasePreferences object. |

# F

| NAME | DESCRIPTION |
| --- | --- |
| FACETRATIO | Controls the aspect ratio of faceting for cylindrical and conic ACIS solids. |
| FACETRES | Adjusts the smoothness of shaded and rendered objects and objects with hidden lines removed. This variable's value is also stored in the RenderSmoothness property of the AcadDatabasePreferences object. |
| FILEDIA | Suppresses display of file dialog boxes. |
| FILLETRAD | Stores the current fillet radius. |
| FILLMODE | Specifies whether multilines, traces, solids, hatches (including solid-fill hatches), and wide polylines are filled in. This variable's value is also stored in the SolidFill property of the AcadDatabasePreferences object. |
| FONTALT | Stores the alternate font that will be used when the specified font file can't be located. |
| FONTMAP | Specifies the font mapping file that will be used. |
| FRONTZ | Stores the front clipping plane offset from the target plane for the current viewport. |
| FULLOPEN | Indicates whether the current drawing is partially open or fully open. |

# G

| NAME | DESCRIPTION |
| --- | --- |
| GFCLR1 | Specifies the color for a one-color gradient fill or the first color for a two-color gradient fill. |
| GFCLR2 | Specifies the second color for a two-color gradient fill. |
| GFCLRLUM | Makes the color a tint (mixed with white) or a shade (mixed with black) in a one-color gradient fill. |
| GFCLRSTATE | Specifies whether a gradient fill uses one color or two colors. |
| GFNAME | Specifies the pattern of a gradient fill. |
| GFSHIFT | Specifies whether the pattern in a gradient fill is centered or is shifted up and to the left. |
| GRIDMODE | Specifies whether the grid is turned on or off. This variable's value is also stored in the GridOn property of the AcadPViewport and AcadViewport objects. |
| GRIDUNIT | Specifies the grid spacing for the current viewport. |
| GRIPBLOCK | Controls the assignment of grips in blocks. This variable's value is also stored in the DisplayGripsWithinBlocks property of the AcadPreferencesSelection object. |
| GRIPCOLOR | Controls the color of non-selected grips, which are drawn as box outlines. This variable's value is also stored in the GripColorUnselected property of the AcadPreferencesSelection object. |
| GRIPHOT | Controls the color of selected grips, which are drawn as filled boxes. This variable's value is also stored in the GripColorSelected property of the AcadPreferencesSelection object. |
| GRIPHOVER | Controls the fill color of a grip when the cursor pauses over the grip. |
| GRIPS | Controls the use of selection set grips for the Stretch, Move, Rotate, Scale, and Mirror grip modes. This variable's value is also stored in the DisplayGrips property of the AcadPreferencesSelection object. |
| GRIPSIZE | Sets the size of the grip box in pixels. This variable's value is also stored in the GripSize property of the AcadPreferencesSelection object. |
| GRIPTIPS | Controls the display of grip tips when the cursor hovers over grips on custom objects that support grip tips. |

# H

| NAME | DESCRIPTION |
| --- | --- |
| HALOGAP | Specifies the distance to shorten a haloed line. |
| HANDLES | Reports whether applications can access object handles. |
| HIDEPRECISION | Controls the accuracy of hides and shades. |
| HIDETEXT | Specifies whether text objects created by the TEXT, DTEXT, or MTEXT command are processed during a HIDE command. |
| HIGHLIGHT | Controls object highlighting. This variable's value does not affect objects selected with grips. |
| HPANG | Specifies the angle of the hatch pattern. This variable's value is also stored in the PatternAngle property of the AcadHatch object. |
| HPASSOC | Controls whether hatch patterns and gradient fills are associative. |
| HPBOUND | Controls the object type created by BHATCH and BOUNDARY. |
| HPDOUBLE | Specifies hatch pattern doubling for user-defined patterns. This variable's value is also stored in the PatternDouble property of the AcadHatch object . |
| HPNAME | Sets the default name for the hatch pattern. This variable's value is also stored in the PatternName property of the AcadHatch object. |
| HPSCALE | Specifies the scale factor for the hatch pattern. This variable's value is also stored in the PatternScale property of the AcadHatch object. |
| HPSPACE | Specifies the hatch pattern's line spacing for user-defined simple patterns. This variable's value is also stored in the PatternSpace property of the AcadHatch object. |
| HYPERLINKBASE | Specifies the path used for all relative hyperlinks in the drawing. |

# I

| NAME | DESCRIPTION |
|------|-------------|
| IMAGEHLT | Specifies whether the entire raster image or only the image frame is highlighted. This variable's value is also stored in the ImageFrameHighlight property of the AcadPreferencesDisplay object. |
| INDEXCTL | Controls whether layer and spatial indexes are created and saved in drawing files. |
| INETLOCATION | Stores the Internet location used by BROWSER and the Browse the Web dialog box. This variable's value is also stored in the DefaultInternetURL property of the AcadPreferencesFiles object. |
| INSBASE | Stores the insertion base point set by BASE. |
| INSNAME | Sets the default block name for INSERT. |
| INSUNITS | Specifies a value for the drawing units, when a block is dragged from the AutoCAD DesignCenter. |
| INSUNITSDEFSOURCE | Sets the source content's units value. This variable's value is also stored in the ADCInsertUnitsDefaultSource property of the AcadPreferencesUser object. |
| INSUNITSDEFTARGET | Sets the target drawing's units value. This variable's value is also stored in the ADCInsertUnitsDefaultTarget property of the AcadPreferencesUser object. |
| INTERSECTIONCOLOR | Specifies the color of intersection polylines. |
| INTERSECTIONDISPLAY | Specifies the display of intersection polylines. |
| ISAVEBAK | Increases the speed of incremental saves for large drawings. This variable's value is also stored in the CreateBackup property of the AcadPreferencesSaveOpen object. |
| ISAVEPERCENT | Determines the amount of wasted space tolerated in a drawing file. This variable's value is also stored in the IncrementalSavePercent property of the AcadPreferencesOpenSave object. |
| ISOLINES | Specifies the number of isolines per surface on objects. This variable's value is also stored in the ContourLinesPerSurface property of the AcadDatabasePreferences object. |

# L

| NAME | DESCRIPTION |
| --- | --- |
| LASTANGLE | Stores the end angle of the most recently drawn arc. |
| LASTPOINT | Stores the last point drawn. |
| LASTPROMPT | Stores the last string echoed to the command line. |
| LAYOUTREGENCTL | Specifies how the display list is updated in the Model tab and layout tabs. |
| LENSLENGTH | Stores the length of the lens (in millimeters) used in perspective viewing for the current viewport. This variable's value is also stored in the LensLength property of the AcadPViewport object. |
| LIMCHECK | Controls the creation of objects outside the drawing limits. |
| LIMMAX | Stores the upper-right drawing limits for the current space. This variable's value is also stored in the Limits property of the AcadDocument object. |
| LIMMIN | Stores the lower-left drawing limits for the current space. This variable's value is also stored in the Limits property of the AcadDocument object. |
| LISPINIT | In SDI mode, this specifies whether AutoLISP-defined functions and variables are preserved when a new drawing is opened. |
| LOCALE | Displays the ISO language code of the current AutoCAD version. |
| LOCALROOTPREFIX | Stores the full path to the root folder where local customizable files were installed. |
| LOGFILEMODE | Specifies whether or not the contents of the text window are written to a log file. This variable's value is also stored in the LogFileOn property of the AcadPreferencesOpenSave object. |
| LOGFILENAME | Specifies the path and name of the log file. |
| LOGFILEPATH | Specifies the path for the log files for all drawings in a session. This variable's value is also stored in the LogFilePath property of the PreferencesFiles object. |
| LOGINNAME | Displays the user's login name when AutoCAD is loaded. |
| LTSCALE | Sets the scale factor for the global linetype. |

| NAME | DESCRIPTION |
|------|-------------|
| LUNITS | Sets linear units. |
| LUPREC | Sets the number of decimal places displayed for linear units. |
| LWDEFAULT | Sets the lineweight's default value. |
| LWDISPLAY | Controls whether the lineweight is displayed in the Model or Layout tab. |
| LWSCALE | Controls whether or not the lineweight is scaled with the rest of the geometry when a layout is printed. This variable's value is also stored in the ScaleLineweights property of the AcadLayout and AcadPlotConfiguration objects. |
| LWUNITS | Controls whether lineweight units are displayed in inches or millimeters. |

## M

| NAME | DESCRIPTION |
|------|-------------|
| MAXACTVP | Sets the maximum number of viewports that can be active at one time. This variable's value is also stored in the MaxActiveViewports property of the AcadDatabasePreferences object. |
| MAXSORT | Sets the maximum number of symbol names or block names that can be sorted. |
| MBUTTONPAN | Controls the behavior of the third button or wheel on the pointing device. |
| MEASUREINIT | Sets the initial drawing units as English or metric. |
| MEASUREMENT | Sets drawing units as English or metric for the current drawing only. |
| MENUCTL | Controls the page switching of the screen menu. |
| MENUECHO | Sets menu echo and prompt control bits. |
| MENUNAME | Stores the menu file name, including the path. |
| MIRRTEXT | Controls how MIRROR reflects text. |

| NAME | DESCRIPTION |
|------|-------------|
| MODEMACRO | Displays a text string on the status line. |
| MTEXTED | Sets the primary and secondary text editors to use for AcadMText objects. |
| MTEXTFIXED | Controls the appearance of the Multiline Text Editor. |
| MTJIGSTRING | Sets the content of the sample text displayed at the cursor location when the MTEXT command is started. |
| MYDOCUMENTSPREFIX | Stores the full path to the My Documents folder for the user currently logged on. |

# N

| NAME | DESCRIPTION |
|------|-------------|
| NOMUTT | Controls whether message display (muttering) is suppressed in AutoCAD. |

# O

| NAME | DESCRIPTION |
|------|-------------|
| OBSCUREDCOLOR | Specifies the color of obscured lines. |
| OBSCUREDLTYPE | Specifies the linetype of obscured lines. |
| OFFSETDIST | Sets the default offset distance. |
| OFFSETGAPTYPE | Controls how to fill in gaps resulting from offsetting individual polyline segments. |
| OLEHIDE | Controls the display of OLE objects in AutoCAD. |
| OLEQUALITY | Controls the default quality level for embedded OLE objects. This variable's value is also stored in the OLEQuality property of the AcadPreferencesOutput object. |
| OLESTARTUP | Controls whether to load an embedded OLE object's source application when plotting. This variable's value is also stored in the OLELaunch property of the AcadDatabasePreferences object. |

| NAME | DESCRIPTION |
|------|-------------|
| ORTHOMODE | Constrains cursor movement to perpendicular axes. |
| OSMODE | Sets running object snap modes using bit codes. Specifies whether or not the lineweight is scaled with the rest of the geometry when a layout is printed. |
| OSNAPCOORD | Controls whether coordinates entered on the command line override running object snaps. This variable's value is also stored in the KeyboardPriority property of the AcadPreferencesUser object. |

## P

| NAME | DESCRIPTION |
|------|-------------|
| _PKSER | Stores the AutoCAD license serial number (e.g., "400-12345678"). |
| PALETTEOPAQUE | Controls whether windows can be made transparent. |
| PAPERUPDATE | Controls the display of a warning dialog when you try to print a layout with a paper size other than that specified for the plotter configuration file. |
| PDMODE | Controls how to display point objects. See Chapter 7 for more details. |
| PDSIZE | Sets the display size for point objects. See Chapter 7 for more details. |
| PEDITACCEPT | Suppresses display of the Object Selected Is Not a Polyline prompt in PEDIT. |
| PELLIPSE | Controls the ellipse type created with ELLIPSE. |
| PERIMETER | Stores the last perimeter value computed by AREA, LIST, or DBLIST. |
| PFACEVMAX | Sets the maximum number of vertices per face. |
| PICKADD | Controls whether subsequent selections replace the current selection set or add to it. This variable's value is also stored in the PickAdd property of the AcadPreferencesSelection object. |

| NAME | DESCRIPTION |
|------|-------------|
| PICKAUTO | Controls automatic windowing at the Select Objects prompt. This variable's value is also stored in the PickAuto property of the AcadPreferencesSelection object. |
| PICKBOX | Sets object selection target height. This variable's value is also stored in the PickBoxSize property of the AcadPreferencesSelection object. |
| PICKDRAG | Controls the method of drawing a selection window. This variable's value is also stored in the PickDrag property of the AcadPreferencesSelection object. |
| PICKFIRST | Controls whether you select objects before or after you issue a command. This variable's value is also stored in the PickFirst property of the AcadPreferencesSelection object. |
| PICKSTYLE | Controls the use of group selection and associative hatch selection. |
| PLATFORM | Indicates which platform of AutoCAD is being used. |
| PLINEGEN | Sets how linetype patterns generate around the vertices of a 2-D polyline. |
| PLINETYPE | Specifies whether optimized 2-D polylines are used. |
| PLINEWID | Stores the default width of the polyline. |
| PLOTID | Obsolete in AutoCAD 2000 and later versions; retained for backward compatibility. |
| PLOTLEGACY | Controls whether legacy plot scripts can be run. This variable's value is also stored in the PlotLegacy property of the AcadPreferencesOutput object. |
| PLOTROTMODE | Controls the orientation of plots. |
| PLOTTER | Obsolete in AutoCAD 2000 and later versions; retained for backward compatibility. |
| PLQUIET | Controls the display of optional dialog boxes and nonfatal errors for batch plotting and scripts. |
| POLARADDANG | Contains user-defined polar angles. |
| POLARANG | Sets the polar angle increment. |
| POLARDIST | Sets the snap increment when the SNAPSTYL system variable is set to 1 (polar snap). |

| NAME | DESCRIPTION |
|------|-------------|
| POLARMODE | Controls the settings for polar and object snap tracking. |
| POLYSIDES | Sets the default number of sides for POLYGON. |
| POPUPS | Displays the status of the currently configured display driver. |
| PRODUCT | Returns the product name. |
| PROGRAM | Returns the program name. |
| PROJECTNAME | Assigns a project name to the current drawing. |
| PROJMODE | Sets the current projection mode for trimming or extending. |
| PROXYGRAPHICS | Specifies whether to save images of proxy objects. |
| PROXYNOTICE | Displays a dialog box when a drawing is opened that contains custom objects created by an application that is not present on the system. This variable's value is also stored in the ShowProxyDialogBox property of the AcadPreferencesOpenSave object. |
| PROXYSHOW | Controls the display of proxy objects in a drawing. |
| PROXYWEBSEARCH | Specifies how AutoCAD checks for Object Enablers. |
| PSLTSCALE | Controls linetype scaling for the paper space. |
| PSPOOLALERT | Specifies whether to alert the user when output needs to be spooled through a system printer due to a conflict with an I/O port. Not used in AutoCAD 2004. This variable's value is also stored in the PrinterSpoolAlertproperty of the AcadPreferencesOutput object. |
| PSPROLOG | Assigns a name for a prolog section to be read from the acad.psf file when you are using PSOUT. This variable's value is also stored in the PostScriptPrologFile property of the PreferencesFiles object. |
| PSQUALITY | Controls the rendering quality of PostScript images. |
| PSTYLEMOD | Indicates whether the current drawing is in a Color Dependent or Named Plot Style mode. |
| PSTYLEPOLICY | Controls whether an object's color property is associated with its plot style. This variable's value is also stored in the PlotPolicy property of the AcadPreferencesOutput object. |

| NAME | DESCRIPTION |
|------|-------------|
| PSVPSCALE | Sets the view scale factor for all newly created viewports. |
| PUCSBASE | Stores the name of the UCS that defines the origin and orientation of orthographic UCS settings in paper space. |

# Q

| NAME | DESCRIPTION |
|------|-------------|
| QTEXTMODE | Controls how text is displayed. This variable's value is also stored in the TextFrameDisplay property of the DatabasePreferences object. |

# R

| NAME | DESCRIPTION |
|------|-------------|
| RASTERPREVIEW | Controls whether to save .bmp preview images. This variable's value is also stored in the SavePreviewThumbnail property of the AcadPreferencesOpenSave object. |
| REFEDITNAME | Indicates whether a drawing is in a reference-editing state and stores the reference file's name. |
| REGENMODE | Controls automatic drawing regeneration. |
| RE-INIT | Reinitializes the digitizer, digitizer port, and acad.pgp file. |
| REMEMBERFOLDERS | Controls the default path for the Look In or Save In option in standard file selection dialog boxes. |
| REPORTERRORS | Controls whether an error report can be sent to Autodesk if AutoCAD closes unexpectedly. |
| ROAMABLEROOTPREFIX | Stores the full path to the root folder where roamable customizable files were installed. |
| RTDISPLAY | Controls the display of raster images during real time ZOOM or PAN. This variable's value is also stored in the ShowRasterImage property of the AcadPreferencesDisplay object. |

# S

| NAME | DESCRIPTION |
| --- | --- |
| SAVEFILE | Stores the current autosave file name. |
| SAVEFILEPATH | Specifies the directory path for all automatic save files for the session. This variable's value is also stored in the AutoSavePath property of the AcadPreferencesFiles object. |
| SAVENAME | Stores the file name and directory path of a drawing after it is saved. |
| SAVETIME | Sets the automatic save interval in minutes. This variable's value is also stored in the AutoSaveInterval property of the AcadPreferencesOpenSave object. |
| SCREENBOXES | Stores the number of boxes in the drawing window's screen menu area. |
| SCREENMODE | Stores a bit code indicating the display's graphics and text state. |
| SCREENSIZE | Stores current viewport size in pixels. |
| SDI | Controls whether AutoCAD runs in single document interface (SDI) mode or in multiple-document interface (MDI) mode. This variable's value is also stored in the SingleDocumentMode property of the AcadPreferencesSelection object. |
| SHADEDGE | Controls the shading of edges in rendering. |
| SHADEDIF | Sets the ratio of diffuse reflective light to ambient light. |
| SHORTCUTMENU | Controls whether Default, Edit, and Command mode shortcut menus are available in the drawing area. This variable's value is also stored in the SCMCommandMode, SCMDefaultMode, SCMEditMode, and ShortCutMenuDisplay properties of the AcadPreferencesUser object. |
| SHPNAME | Sets a default shape name. |
| SIGWARN | Controls whether a warning is presented when a file with an attached digital signature is opened. |
| SKETCHINC | Sets the record increment for SKETCH. |
| SKPOLY | Determines whether SKETCH generates lines or polylines. |

| NAME | DESCRIPTION |
|------|-------------|
| SNAPANG | Sets snap and grid rotation angle for the current viewport. This variable's value is also stored in the SnapRotationAngle property of the AcadPViewport and AcadViewport objects. |
| SNAPBASE | Sets the snap and grid origin point for the current viewport relative to the current UCS. This variable's value is also stored in the SnapBasePoint property of the AcadPViewport and VAcadiewport objects. |
| SNAPISOPAIR | Controls the isometric plane for the current viewport. |
| SNAPMODE | Turns snap mode on and off. This variable's value is also stored in the SnapOn property of the AcadPViewport and AcadViewport objects. |
| SNAPSTYL | Sets the current viewport's snap style. |
| SNAPTYPE | Sets the current viewport's snap style. |
| SNAPUNIT | Sets the current viewport's snap spacing. |
| SOLIDCHECK | Turns solid validation on and off for the current session. |
| SORTENTS | Controls the OPTIONS command object sort order operations. This variable's value is also stored in the ObjectSortByPlotting, ObjectSortByRedraws, ObjectSortByPSOutput, ObjectSortByRegens, ObjectSortBySelection, and ObjectSortBySnap properties of the AcadDatabasePreferences object. |
| SPLFRAME | Controls the display of splines and spline-fit polylines. |
| SPLINESEGS | Sets the number of line segments to be generated for each spline-fit polyline. This variable's value is also stored in the SegmentPerPolyline property of the AcadDatabasePreferences object. |
| SPLINETYPE | Sets the type of curve generated by the Spline option of the PEDIT command. |
| STANDARDSVIOLATION | Specifies whether a user is notified of standards violations that exist in the current drawing. |
| STARTUP | Controls whether the Create New Drawing dialog box is displayed when starting a new drawing with the NEW and QNEW commands. |

| NAME | DESCRIPTION |
|------|-------------|
| SURFTAB1 | Sets the number of tabulations to be generated for RULESURF and TABSURF. |
| SURFTAB2 | Sets the mesh density in the N direction for REVSURF and EDGESURF. |
| SURFTYPE | Controls the type of surface-fitting to be performed by the Smooth option of the PEDIT command. |
| SURFU | Sets the surface density for PEDIT command's Smooth option in the M direction. |
| SURFV | Sets the surface density for PEDIT command's Smooth option in the N direction. |
| SYSCODEPAGE | Indicates the system code page specified in acad.xmf. |

# T

| NAME | DESCRIPTION |
|------|-------------|
| TABMODE | Controls the use of the tablet. |
| TARGET | Stores the location of the target point for the current viewport. |
| TDCREATE | Stores the local time and date the drawing was created. |
| TDINDWG | Stores the total editing time. |
| TDUCREATE | Stores the universal time and date the drawing was created. |
| TDUPDATE | Stores the local time and date of the last update/save. |
| TDUSRTIMER | Stores the user-elapsed timer. |
| TDUUPDATE | Stores the universal time and date of the last update/save. |
| TEMPPREFIX | Contains the directory name for temporary files. |
| TEXTEVAL | Controls the method of evaluation for text strings. |
| TEXTFILL | Controls the filling of TrueType fonts while plotting, exporting with the PSOUT command and rendering. |

| NAME | DESCRIPTION |
|------|-------------|
| TEXTQLTY | Sets the resolution of text outlines for TrueType fonts while plotting, exporting with the PSOUT command, and rendering. |
| TEXTSIZE | Sets the default height for new text objects drawn with the current text style. |
| TEXTSTYLE | Sets the name of the current text style. |
| THICKNESS | Sets the current 3-D solid thickness. |
| TILEMODE | Makes the Model tab or the Last Layout tab current. This variable's value is also stored in the ActiveSpace property of the AcadDocument object. |
| TOOLTIPS | Controls the display of tooltips. |
| TRACEWID | Sets the default trace width. |
| TRACKPATH | Controls the display of polar and object snap tracking alignment paths. This variable's value is also stored in the FullScreenTrackingVector and PolarTrackingVector properties of the AcadPreferencesDrafting object. |
| TRAYICONS | Controls whether a tray is displayed on the status bar. |
| TRAYNOTIFY | Controls whether service notifications are displayed in the status bar tray. |
| TRAYTIMEOUT | Controls the length of time (in seconds) that service notifications are displayed. |
| TREEDEPTH | Specifies the number of times the tree-structured spatial index can divide into branches. |
| TREEMAX | Limits memory consumption during drawing regeneration by limiting the number of nodes in the spatial index (oct-tree). |
| TRIMMODE | Controls whether AutoCAD trims selected edges for chamfers and fillets. |
| TSPACEFAC | Controls the multiline text line spacing distance, measured as a factor of text height. |
| TSPACETYPE | Controls the type of line spacing used in multiline text. |
| TSTACKALIGN | Controls the vertical alignment of stacked text. |
| TSTACKSIZE | Controls the height of stacked text fraction, as a percentage relative to the height of the selected text. |

# U

| NAME | DESCRIPTION |
|------|-------------|
| UCSAXISANG | Stores the default angle when rotating the UCS around one of its axes using the X, Y, or Z options of the UCS command. |
| UCSBASE | Stores the name of the UCS that defines the origin and orientation of orthographic UCS settings. |
| UCSFOLLOW | Generates a plan view whenever you change from one UCS to another. |
| UCSICON | Displays the UCS icon for the current viewport. |
| UCSNAME | Stores the name of the current coordinate system for the current viewport in the current space. |
| UCSORG | Stores the origin point of the coordinate system for the current viewport in the current space. This variable's value is also stored in the UCSIconAtOrigin property of the PViewport and Viewport objects. |
| UCSORTHO | Determines whether the related orthographic UCS setting is restored automatically when an orthographic view is restored. |
| UCSVIEW | Determines whether the current UCS is saved with a named view. |
| UCSVP | Determines whether the UCS in active viewports remains fixed or changes to reflect the currently active viewport. |
| UCSXDIR | Stores the X direction of the current UCS for the current viewport in the current space. This variable's value is also stored in the XVector property of the AcadUCS object. |
| UCSYDIR | Stores the Y direction of the current UCS for the current viewport in the current space. This variable's value is also stored in the YVector property of the AcadUCS object. |
| UNDOCTL | Stores a bit-code indicating the state of the Auto and Control options of the UNDO command. |
| UNDOMARKS | Stores the number of marks that have been placed in the UNDO control stream by the Mark option. |

| NAME | DESCRIPTION |
|------|-------------|
| UNITMODE | Controls the display format for units. |
| USERI1-5 | Stores and retrieves integer values. There are five variables of this type: USERI1, USERI2, ..., USERI5. |
| USERR1-5 | Stores and retrieves real numbers. There are five variables of this type: USERR1, USERR2, ..., USERR5. |
| USERS1-5 | Stores and retrieves strings. There are five variables of this type: USERS1, USERS2, ..., USERS5. |

# V

| NAME | DESCRIPTION |
|------|-------------|
| _VERNUM | Stores the internal build number of AutoCAD (such as "V.0.86"). |
| VIEWCTR | Stores the center of view in the current viewport. |
| VIEWDIR | Stores the viewing direction in the current viewport. |
| VIEWMODE | Controls the current viewport's view mode using a bit code. |
| VIEWSIZE | Stores the view's height in the current viewport. |
| VIEWTWIST | Stores the view's twist angle for the current viewport. |
| VISRETAIN | Controls the visibility, color, linetype, lineweight, and plot styles (if PSTYLEPOLICY is set to 0) of Xref-dependent layers and specifies whether nested Xref path changes are saved. This variable's value is also stored in the XrefLayerVisibility property of the AcadDatabasePreferences object. |
| VSMAX | Stores the upper-right corner of the current viewport's virtual screen. |
| VSMIN | Stores the lower-left corner of the current viewport's virtual screen. |

# W

| NAME | DESCRIPTION |
|------|-------------|
| WHIPARC | Controls whether the display of circles and arcs is smooth. |
| WHIPTHREAD | Controls whether to use an additional processor (known as multithreaded processing) to improve the speed of operations such as ZOOM and PAN that redraw or regenerate the drawing. |
| WMFBKGND | Controls the background of the output Windows metafile resulting from the WMFOUT command, and also the metafile format of objects placed on the clipboard or dragged and dropped into other applications. |
| WMFFOREGND | Controls the assignment of the foreground color of AutoCAD objects in other applications. |
| WORLDUCS | Indicates whether the UCS is the same as the WCS. |
| WORLDVIEW | Determines whether input to the 3DORBIT, DVIEW, and VPOINT commands is relative to the WCS (default), the current UCS, or the UCS specified by the UCSBASE system variable. |
| WRITESTAT | Indicates whether a drawing file is read-only or not, for developers who need to determine write status through AutoLISP. |

# X

| NAME | DESCRIPTION |
|------|-------------|
| XCLIPFRAME | Controls the visibility of XRef clipping boundaries. |
| XEDIT | Specifies whether the current drawing can be edited in place when another drawing references it. This variable's value is also stored in the XRefEdit property of the AcadDatabasePreferences object. |
| XFADECTL | Controls the fading intensity for references being edited in place. This variable's value is also stored in the XRefFadeIntensity property of the AcadPreferencesDisplay object. |

| NAME | DESCRIPTION |
|------|-------------|
| XLOADCTL | Turns Xref demand loading on and off and controls whether it opens the original drawing or a copy of the drawing. This variable's value is also stored in the XRefDemandLoad property of the AcadPreferencesOpenSave object. |
| XLOADPATH | Creates a path for storing temporary copies of demand-loaded Xref files. |
| XREFCTL | Controls whether AutoCAD writes external reference log (.xlg) files. |
| XREFNOTIFY | Controls the notification for changed or missing Xrefs. |

## Z

| NAME | DESCRIPTION |
|------|-------------|
| ZOOMFACTOR | Controls the incremental change in zoom with each IntelliMouse wheel action, whether forward or backward. |

# AutoCAD 2000, 2002, and 2004 Object Model Cross Reference

THIS APPENDIX LETS YOU CROSS REFERENCE the AutoCAD object model among AutoCAD 2000 through AutoCAD 2004. This cross reference gives you a more visual representation of the changes in the various versions of the object model. For full details about any of the objects, methods, properties, or events, see Appendix A.

## Objects Comparison

| 2000 | 2000I | 2002 | 2004 |
| --- | --- | --- | --- |
| 3DFace | 3DFace | 3DFace | 3DFace |
| 3DPoly | 3DPolyline | 3DPolyline | 3DPolyline |
| 3DSolid | 3DSolid | 3DSolid | 3DSolid |
| AcadState | AcadState | AcadState | AcadState |
| | | | AcCmColor |
| Application | Application | Application | Application |
| Arc | Arc | Arc | Arc |
| Attribute | Attribute | Attribute | Attribute |
| AttributeRef | AttributeRef | AttributeReference | AttributeReference |
| Block | Block | Block | Block |
| BlockRef | BlockRef | BlockRef | BlockRef |
| Blocks | Blocks | Blocks | Blocks |
| Circle | Circle | Circle | Circle |
| Database | Database | Database | Database |

| 2000 | 2000I | 2002 | 2004 |
|------|-------|------|------|
| DatabasePreferences | DatabasePreferences | DatabasePreferences | DatabasePreferences |
| Dictionaries | Dictionaries | Dictionaries | Dictionaries |
| Dictionary | Dictionary | Dictionary | Dictionary |
| Dim3PointAngular | Dim3PointAngular | Dim3PointAngular | Dim3PointAngular |
| DimAligned | DimAligned | DimAligned | DimAligned |
| DimAngular | DimAngular | DimAngular | DimAngular |
| DimDiametric | DimDiametric | DimDiametric | DimDiametric |
| DimOrdinate | DimOrdinate | DimOrdinate | DimOrdinate |
| DimRadial | DimRadial | DimRadial | DimRadial |
| DimRotated | DimRotated | DimRotated | DimRotated |
| DimStyle | DimStyle | DimStyle | DimStyle |
| DimStyles | DimStyles | DimStyles | DimStyles |
| Document | Document | Document | Document |
| Documents | Documents | Documents | Documents |
| Ellipse | Ellipse | Ellipse | Ellipse |
| ExternalReference | ExternalReference | ExternalReference | ExternalReference |
| | | | FileDependency |
| | | | FileDependencies |
| Group | Group | Group | Group |
| Groups | Groups | Groups | Groups |
| Hatch | Hatch | Hatch | Hatch |
| Hyperlink | Hyperlink | Hyperlink | Hyperlink |
| Hyperlinks | Hyperlinks | Hyperlinks | Hyperlinks |
| IDPair | IDPair | IDPair | IDPair |
| Layer | Layer | Layer | Layer |
| Layers | Layers | Layers | Layers |
| | LayerStateManager | LayerStateManager | LayerStateManager |
| Layout | Layout | Layout | Layout |
| Layouts | Layouts | Layouts | Layouts |

| 2000 | 2000I | 2002 | 2004 |
|---|---|---|---|
| Leader | Leader | Leader | Leader |
| LightweightPolyline | LightweightPolyline | LightweightPolyline | LightweightPolyline |
| Line | Line | Line | Line |
| Linetype | Linetype | Linetype | Linetype |
| Linetypes | Linetypes | Linetypes | Linetypes |
| MenuBar | MenuBar | MenuBar | MenuBar |
| MenuGroup | MenuGroup | MenuGroup | MenuGroup |
| MenuGroups | MenuGroups | MenuGroups | MenuGroups |
| MInsertBlock | MInsertBlock | MInsertBlock | MInsertBlock |
| MLine | MLine | MLine | MLine |
| ModelSpace | ModelSpace | ModelSpace | ModelSpace |
| MText | MText | MText | MText |
| PaperSpace | PaperSpace | PaperSpace | PaperSpace |
| Plot | Plot | Plot | Plot |
| PlotConfiguration | PlotConfiguration | PlotConfiguration | PlotConfiguration |
| PlotConfigurations | PlotConfigurations | PlotConfigurations | PlotConfigurations |
| Point | Point | Point | Point |
| PolyfaceMesh | PolyfaceMesh | PolyfaceMesh | PolyfaceMesh |
| PolygonMesh | PolygonMesh | PolygonMesh | PolygonMesh |
| Polyline | Polyline | Polyline | Polyline |
| PopupMenu | PopupMenu | PopupMenu | PopupMenu |
| PopupMenuItem | PopupMenuItem | PopupMenuItem | PopupMenuItem |
| PopupMenus | PopupMenus | PopupMenus | PopupMenus |
| Preferences | Preferences | Preferences | Preferences |
| PreferencesDisplay | PreferencesDisplay | PreferencesDisplay | PreferencesDisplay |
| PreferencesDrafting | PreferencesDrafting | PreferencesDrafting | PreferencesDrafting |
| PreferencesFiles | PreferencesFiles | PreferencesFiles | PreferencesFiles |
| PreferencesOpenSave | PreferencesOpenSave | PreferencesOpenSave | PreferencesOpenSave |
| PreferencesOutput | PreferencesOutput | PreferencesOutput | PreferencesOutput |

| 2000 | 2000I | 2002 | 2004 |
|---|---|---|---|
| PreferencesProfiles | PreferencesProfiles | PreferencesProfiles | PreferencesProfiles |
| PreferencesSelection | PreferencesSelection | PreferencesSelection | PreferencesSelection |
| PreferencesSystem | PreferencesSystem | PreferencesSystem | PreferencesSystem |
| PreferencesUser | PreferencesUser | PreferencesUser | PreferencesUser |
| PViewport | PViewport | PViewport | PViewport |
| Raster | Raster | Raster | Raster |
| Ray | Ray | Ray | Ray |
| Region | Region | Region | Region |
| RegisteredApplication | RegisteredApplication | RegisteredApplication | RegisteredApplication |
| RegisteredApplications | RegisteredApplications | RegisteredApplications | RegisteredApplications |
| | | | SecurityParams |
| SelectionSet | SelectionSet | SelectionSet | SelectionSet |
| SelectionSets | SelectionSets | SelectionSets | SelectionSets |
| Shape | Shape | Shape | Shape |
| Solid | Solid | Solid | Solid |
| Spline | Spline | Spline | Spline |
| Text | Text | Text | Text |
| TextStyle | TextStyle | TextStyle | TextStyle |
| TextStyles | TextStyles | TextStyles | TextStyles |
| Tolerance | Tolerance | Tolerance | Tolerance |
| Toolbar | Toolbar | Toolbar | Toolbar |
| ToolbarItem | ToolbarItem | ToolbarItem | ToolbarItem |
| Toolbars | Toolbars | Toolbars | Toolbars |
| Trace | Trace | Trace | Trace |
| UCS | UCS | UCS | UCS |
| UCSs | UCSs | UCSs | UCSs |
| Utility | Utility | Utility | Utility |
| View | View | View | View |
| Views | Views | Views | Views |

| 2000 | 2000I | 2002 | 2004 |
|---|---|---|---|
| Viewport | Viewport | Viewport | Viewport |
| Viewports | Viewports | Viewports | Viewports |
| XLine | XLine | XLine | XLine |
|  |  | XmlDatabase |  |
| XRecord | XRecord | XRecord | XRecord |

# Methods Comparison

| 2000 | 2000I | 2002 | 2004 |
|---|---|---|---|
| Activate | Activate | Activate | Activate |
| Add | Add | Add | Add |
| Add3DFace | Add3DFace | Add3DFace | Add3DFace |
| Add3DMesh | Add3DMesh | Add3DMesh | Add3DMesh |
| Add3DPoly | Add3DPoly | Add3DPoly | Add3DPoly |
| AddArc | AddArc | AddArc | AddArc |
| AddAttribute | AddAttribute | AddAttribute | AddAttribute |
| AddBox | AddBox | AddBox | AddBox |
| AddCircle | AddCircle | AddCircle | AddCircle |
| AddCone | AddCone | AddCone | AddCone |
| AddCustomObject | AddCustomObject | AddCustomObject | AddCustomObject |
| AddCylinder | AddCylinder | AddCylinder | AddCylinder |
| AddDim3PointAngular | AddDim3PointAngular | AddDim3PointAngular | AddDim3PointAngular |
| AddDimAligned | AddDimAligned | AddDimAligned | AddDimAligned |
| AddDimAngular | AddDimAngular | AddDimAngular | AddDimAngular |
| AddDimDiametric | AddDimDiametric | AddDimDiametric | AddDimDiametric |
| AddDimOrdinate | AddDimOrdinate | AddDimOrdinate | AddDimOrdinate |
| AddDimRadial | AddDimRadial | AddDimRadial | AddDimRadial |
| AddDimRotated | AddDimRotated | AddDimRotated | AddDimRotated |

| 2000 | 2000I | 2002 | 2004 |
|------|-------|------|------|
| AddEllipse | AddEllipse | AddEllipse | AddEllipse |
| AddEllipticalCone | AddEllipticalCone | AddEllipticalCone | AddEllipticalCone |
| AddEllipticalCylinder | AddEllipticalCylinder | AddEllipticalCylinder | AddEllipticalCylinder |
| AddExtrudedSolid | AddExtrudedSolid | AddExtrudedSolid | AddExtrudedSolid |
| AddExtrudedSolidAlongPath | AddExtrudedSolidAlongPath | AddExtrudedSolidAlongPath | AddExtrudedSolidAlongPath |
| AddFitPoint | AddFitPoint | AddFitPoint | AddFitPoint |
| AddHatch | AddHatch | AddHatch | AddHatch |
| AddItems | AddItems | AddItems | AddItems |
| AddLeader | AddLeader | AddLeader | AddLeader |
| AddLightweightPolyline | AddLightweightPolyline | AddLightweightPolyline | AddLightweightPolyline |
| AddLine | AddLine | AddLine | AddLine |
| AddMenuItem | AddMenuItem | AddMenuItem | AddMenuItem |
| AddMInsertBlock | AddMInsertBlock | AddMInsertBlock | AddMInsertBlock |
| AddMLine | AddMLine | AddMLine | AddMLine |
| AddMtext | AddMtext | AddMtext | AddMtext |
| AddObject | AddObject | AddObject | AddObject |
| AddPoint | AddPoint | AddPoint | AddPoint |
| AddPolyfaceMesh | AddPolyfaceMesh | AddPolyfaceMesh | AddPolyfaceMesh |
| AddPolyline | AddPolyline | AddPolyline | AddPolyline |
| AddPViewport | AddPViewport | AddPViewport | AddPViewport |
| AddRaster | AddRaster | AddRaster | AddRaster |
| AddRay | AddRay | AddRay | AddRay |
| AddRegion | AddRegion | AddRegion | AddRegion |
| AddRevolvedSolid | AddRevolvedSolid | AddRevolvedSolid | AddRevolvedSolid |
| AddSeparator | AddSeparator | AddSeparator | AddSeparator |
| AddShape | AddShape | AddShape | AddShape |
| AddSolid | AddSolid | AddSolid | AddSolid |
| AddSphere | AddSphere | AddSphere | AddSphere |

| 2000 | 2000I | 2002 | 2004 |
|---|---|---|---|
| AddSpline | AddSpline | AddSpline | AddSpline |
| AddSubMenu | AddSubMenu | AddSubMenu | AddSubMenu |
| AddText | AddText | AddText | AddText |
| AddTolerance | AddTolerance | AddTolerance | AddTolerance |
| AddToolbarButton | AddToolbarButton | AddToolbarButton | AddToolbarButton |
| AddTorus | AddTorus | AddTorus | AddTorus |
| AddTrace | AddTrace | AddTrace | AddTrace |
| AddVertex | AddVertex | AddVertex | AddVertex |
| AddWedge | AddWedge | AddWedge | AddWedge |
| AddXLine | AddXLine | AddXLine | AddXLine |
| AddXRecord | AddXRecord | AddXRecord | AddXRecord |
| AngleFromXAxis | AngleFromXAxis | AngleFromXAxis | AngleFromXAxis |
| AngleToReal | AngleToReal | AngleToReal | AngleToReal |
| AngleToString | AngleToString | AngleToString | AngleToString |
| AppendInnerLoop | AppendInnerLoop | AppendInnerLoop | AppendInnerLoop |
| AppendItems | AppendItems | AppendItems | AppendItems |
| AppendOuterLoop | AppendOuterLoop | AppendOuterLoop | AppendOuterLoop |
| AppendVertex | AppendVertex | AppendVertex | AppendVertex |
| ArrayPolar | ArrayPolar | ArrayPolar | ArrayPolar |
| ArrayRectangular | ArrayRectangular | ArrayRectangular | ArrayRectangular |
| AttachExternalReference | AttachExternalReference | AttachExternalReference | AttachExternalReference |
| AttachToolbarToFlyout | AttachToolbarToFlyout | AttachToolbarToFlyout | AttachToolbarToFlyout |
| AuditInfo | AuditInfo | AuditInfo | AuditInfo |
| Bind | Bind | Bind | Bind |
| Boolean | Boolean | Boolean | Boolean |
| CheckInterference | CheckInterference | CheckInterference | CheckInterference |
| Clear | Clear | Clear | Clear |
| ClipBoundary | ClipBoundary | ClipBoundary | ClipBoundary |
| Close | Close | Close | Close |

| 2000 | 2000I | 2002 | 2004 |
|------|-------|------|------|
| Copy | Copy | Copy | Copy |
| CopyFrom | CopyFrom | CopyFrom | CopyFrom |
| CopyObjects | CopyObjects | CopyObjects | CopyObjects |
| CopyProfile | CopyProfile | CopyProfile | CopyProfile |
| | | | CreateEntry |
| CreateTypedArray | CreateTypedArray | CreateTypedArray | CreateTypedArray |
| Delete | Delete | Delete | Delete |
| DeleteConfiguration | DeleteConfiguration | DeleteConfiguration | DeleteConfiguration |
| DeleteFitPoint | DeleteFitPoint | DeleteFitPoint | DeleteFitPoint |
| DeleteProfile | DeleteProfile | DeleteProfile | DeleteProfile |
| Detach | Detach | Detach | Detach |
| Display | Display | Display | Display |
| DisplayPlotPreview | DisplayPlotPreview | DisplayPlotPreview | DisplayPlotPreview |
| DistanceToReal | DistanceToReal | DistanceToReal | DistanceToReal |
| Dock | Dock | Dock | Dock |
| ElevateOrder | ElevateOrder | ElevateOrder | ElevateOrder |
| EndUndoMark | EndUndoMark | EndUndoMark | EndUndoMark |
| Erase | Erase | Erase | Erase |
| Eval | Eval | Eval | Eval |
| Evaluate | Evaluate | Evaluate | Evaluate |
| Explode | Explode | Explode | Explode |
| Export | Export | Export | Export |
| ExportProfile | ExportProfile | ExportProfile | ExportProfile |
| Float | Float | Float | Float |
| GetAcadState | GetAcadState | GetAcadState | GetAcadState |
| GetAllProfileNames | GetAllProfileNames | GetAllProfileNames | GetAllProfileNames |
| GetAngle | GetAngle | GetAngle | GetAngle |
| GetAttributes | GetAttributes | GetAttributes | GetAttributes |
| GetBitmaps | GetBitmaps | GetBitmaps | GetBitmaps |

| 2000 | 2000I | 2002 | 2004 |
|---|---|---|---|
| GetBoundingBox | GetBoundingBox | GetBoundingBox | GetBoundingBox |
| GetBulge | GetBulge | GetBulge | GetBulge |
| GetCanonicalMediaNames | GetCanonicalMediaNames | GetCanonicalMediaNames | GetCanonicalMediaNames |
| GetConstantAttributes | GetConstantAttributes | GetConstantAttributes | GetConstantAttributes |
| GetControlPoint | GetControlPoint | GetControlPoint | GetControlPoint |
| GetCorner | GetCorner | GetCorner | GetCorner |
| GetCustomScale | GetCustomScale | GetCustomScale | GetCustomScale |
| GetDistance | GetDistance | GetDistance | GetDistance |
| GetEntity | GetEntity | GetEntity | GetEntity |
| GetExtensionDictionary | GetExtensionDictionary | GetExtensionDictionary | GetExtensionDictionary |
| GetFitPoint | GetFitPoint | GetFitPoint | GetFitPoint |
| GetFont | GetFont | GetFont | GetFont |
| GetGridSpacing | GetGridSpacing | GetGridSpacing | GetGridSpacing |
| GetInput | GetInput | GetInput | GetInput |
| GetInteger | GetInteger | GetInteger | GetInteger |
| GetInterfaceObject | GetInterfaceObject | GetInterfaceObject | GetInterfaceObject |
| GetInvisibleEdge | GetInvisibleEdge | GetInvisibleEdge | GetInvisibleEdge |
| GetKeyword | GetKeyword | GetKeyword | GetKeyword |
| GetLocaleMediaName | GetLocaleMediaName | GetLocaleMediaName | GetLocaleMediaName |
| GetLoopAt | GetLoopAt | GetLoopAt | GetLoopAt |
| GetName | GetName | GetName | GetName |
| GetObject | GetObject | GetObject | GetObject |
| GetOrientation | GetOrientation | GetOrientation | GetOrientation |
| GetPaperMargins | GetPaperMargins | GetPaperMargins | GetPaperMargins |
| GetPaperSize | GetPaperSize | GetPaperSize | GetPaperSize |
| GetPlotDeviceNames | GetPlotDeviceNames | GetPlotDeviceNames | GetPlotDeviceNames |
| GetPlotStyleTableNames | GetPlotStyleTableNames | GetPlotStyleTableNames | GetPlotStyleTableNames |
| GetPoint | GetPoint | GetPoint | GetPoint |
| GetProjectFilePath | GetProjectFilePath | GetProjectFilePath | GetProjectFilePath |

| 2000 | 2000I | 2002 | 2004 |
|------|-------|------|------|
| GetReal | GetReal | GetReal | GetReal |
| GetRemoteFile | GetRemoteFile | GetRemoteFile | GetRemoteFile |
| GetSnapSpacing | GetSnapSpacing | GetSnapSpacing | GetSnapSpacing |
| GetString | GetString | GetString | GetString |
| GetSubEntity | GetSubEntity | GetSubEntity | GetSubEntity |
| GetUCSMatrix | GetUCSMatrix | GetUCSMatrix | GetUCSMatrix |
| GetVariable | GetVariable | GetVariable | GetVariable |
| GetWeight | GetWeight | GetWeight | GetWeight |
| GetWidth | GetWidth | GetWidth | GetWidth |
| GetWindowToPlot | GetWindowToPlot | GetWindowToPlot | GetWindowToPlot |
| GetXData | GetXData | GetXData | GetXData |
| GetXRecordData | GetXRecordData | GetXRecordData | GetXRecordData |
| HandleToObject | HandleToObject | HandleToObject | HandleToObject |
| Highlight | Highlight | Highlight | Highlight |
| Import | Import | Import | Import |
| ImportProfile | ImportProfile | ImportProfile | ImportProfile |
|  |  |  | IndexOf |
| InitializeUserInput | InitializeUserInput | InitializeUserInput | InitializeUserInput |
| InsertBlock | InsertBlock | InsertBlock | InsertBlock |
| InsertInMenuBar | InsertInMenuBar | InsertInMenuBar | InsertInMenuBar |
| InsertLoopAt | InsertLoopAt | InsertLoopAt | InsertLoopAt |
| InsertMenuInMenuBar | InsertMenuInMenuBar | InsertMenuInMenuBar | InsertMenuInMenuBar |
| IntersectWith | IntersectWith | IntersectWith | IntersectWith |
| IsRemoteFile | IsRemoteFile | IsRemoteFile | IsRemoteFile |
| IsURL | IsURL | IsURL | IsURL |
| Item | Item | Item | Item |
| LaunchBrowserDialog | LaunchBrowserDialog | LaunchBrowserDialog | LaunchBrowserDialog |
| ListARX | ListARX | ListARX | ListARX |
| Load | Load | Load | Load |

| 2000 | 2000I | 2002 | 2004 |
|---|---|---|---|
| LoadARX | LoadARX | LoadARX | LoadARX |
| LoadDVB | LoadDVB | LoadDVB | LoadDVB |
| LoadShapeFile | LoadShapeFile | LoadShapeFile | LoadShapeFile |
| Mirror | Mirror | Mirror | Mirror |
| Mirror3D | Mirror3D | Mirror3D | Mirror3D |
| Move | Move | Move | Move |
| New | New | New | New |
| ObjectIDToObject | ObjectIDToObject | ObjectIDToObject | ObjectIDToObject |
| Offset | Offset | Offset | Offset |
| Open | Open | Open | Open |
| PlotToDevice | PlotToDevice | PlotToDevice | PlotToDevice |
| PlotToFile | PlotToFile | PlotToFile | PlotToFile |
| PolarPoint | PolarPoint | PolarPoint | PolarPoint |
| Prompt | Prompt | Prompt | Prompt |
| PurgeAll | PurgeAll | PurgeAll | PurgeAll |
| PurgetFitData | PurgetFitData | PurgetFitData | PurgetFitData |
| PutRemoteFile | PutRemoteFile | PutRemoteFile | PutRemoteFile |
| Quit | Quit | Quit | Quit |
| RealToString | RealToString | RealToString | RealToString |
| RefreshPlotDeviceInfo | RefreshPlotDeviceInfo | RefreshPlotDeviceInfo | RefreshPlotDeviceInfo |
| Regen | Regen | Regen | Regen |
| Reload | Reload | Reload | Reload |
| Remove | Remove | Remove | Remove |
| | | | RemoveEntry |
| RemoveItems | RemoveItems | RemoveItems | RemoveItems |
| RemoveFromMenuBar | RemoveFromMenuBar | RemoveFromMenuBar | RemoveFromMenuBar |
| RemoveMenuFromMenuBar | RemoveMenuFromMenuBar | RemoveMenuFromMenuBar | RemoveMenuFromMenuBar |
| Rename | Rename | Rename | Rename |
| RenameProfile | RenameProfile | RenameProfile | RenameProfile |

| 2000 | 2000I | 2002 | 2004 |
|------|-------|------|------|
| Replace | Replace | Replace | Replace |
| ResetProfile | ResetProfile | ResetProfile | ResetProfile |
| | Restore | Restore | Restore |
| Reverse | Reverse | Reverse | Reverse |
| Rotate | Rotate | Rotate | Rotate |
| Rotate3D | Rotate3D | Rotate3D | Rotate3D |
| RunMacro | RunMacro | RunMacro | RunMacro |
| Save | Save | Save | Save |
| SaveAs | SaveAs | SaveAs | SaveAs |
| ScaleEntity | ScaleEntity | ScaleEntity | ScaleEntity |
| SectionSolid | SectionSolid | SectionSolid | SectionSolid |
| Select | Select | Select | Select |
| SelectAtPoint | SelectAtPoint | SelectAtPoint | SelectAtPoint |
| SelectByPolygon | SelectByPolygon | SelectByPolygon | SelectByPolygon |
| SelectOnScreen | SelectOnScreen | SelectOnScreen | SelectOnScreen |
| SendCommand | SendCommand | SendCommand | SendCommand |
| SetBitmaps | SetBitmaps | SetBitmaps | SetBitmaps |
| SetBulge | SetBulge | SetBulge | SetBulge |
| | | | SetColorBookColor |
| SetControlPoint | SetControlPoint | SetControlPoint | SetControlPoint |
| SetCustomScale | SetCustomScale | SetCustomScale | SetCustomScale |
| | SetDatabase | SetDatabase | SetDatabase |
| SetFitPoint | SetFitPoint | SetFitPoint | SetFitPoint |
| SetFont | SetFont | SetFont | SetFont |
| SetGridSpacing | SetGridSpacing | SetGridSpacing | SetGridSpacing |
| SetInvisibleEdge | SetInvisibleEdge | SetInvisibleEdge | SetInvisibleEdge |
| SetLayoutsToPlot | SetLayoutsToPlot | SetLayoutsToPlot | SetLayoutsToPlot |
| | | | SetNames |

| 2000 | 2000I | 2002 | 2004 |
|---|---|---|---|
| SetPattern | SetPattern | SetPattern | SetPattern |
| SetProjectFilePath | SetProjectFilePath | SetProjectFilePath | SetProjectFilePath |
| | | | SetRGB |
| SetSnapSpacing | SetSnapSpacing | SetSnapSpacing | SetSnapSpacing |
| SetVariable | SetVariable | SetVariable | SetVariable |
| SetView | SetView | SetView | SetView |
| SetWeight | SetWeight | SetWeight | SetWeight |
| SetWidth | SetWidth | SetWidth | SetWidth |
| SetWindowToPlot | SetWindowToPlot | SetWindowToPlot | SetWindowToPlot |
| SetXData | SetXData | SetXData | SetXData |
| SetXRecordData | SetXRecordData | SetXRecordData | SetXRecordData |
| SliceSolid | SliceSolid | SliceSolid | SliceSolid |
| Split | Split | Split | Split |
| StartBatchMode | StartBatchMode | StartBatchMode | StartBatchMode |
| StartUndoMark | StartUndoMark | StartUndoMark | StartUndoMark |
| TransformBy | TransformBy | TransformBy | TransformBy |
| TranslateCoordinates | TranslateCoordinates | TranslateCoordinates | TranslateCoordinates |
| Unload | Unload | Unload | Unload |
| UnloadARX | UnloadARX | UnloadARX | UnloadARX |
| UnloadDVB | UnloadDVB | UnloadDVB | UnloadDVB |
| Update | Update | Update | Update |
| | | | UpdateEntry |
| WBlock | WBlock | WBlock | WBlock |
| | | Xmlin | |
| | | Xmlout | |
| ZoomAll | ZoomAll | ZoomAll | ZoomAll |
| ZoomCenter | ZoomCenter | ZoomCenter | ZoomCenter |
| ZoomExtents | ZoomExtents | ZoomExtents | ZoomExtents |

| 2000 | 2000I | 2002 | 2004 |
|------|-------|------|------|
| ZoomPickWindow | ZoomPickWindow | ZoomPickWindow | ZoomPickWindow |
| ZoomPrevious | ZoomPrevious | ZoomPrevious | ZoomPrevious |
| ZoomScaled | ZoomScaled | ZoomScaled | ZoomScaled |
| ZoomWindow | ZoomWindow | ZoomWindow | ZoomWindow |

# Properties Comparison

| 2000 | 2000I | 2002 | 2004 |
|------|-------|------|------|
| | | | Action |
| Active | Active | Active | Active |
| ActiveDimStyle | ActiveDimStyle | ActiveDimStyle | ActiveDimStyle |
| ActiveDocument | ActiveDocument | ActiveDocument | ActiveDocument |
| ActiveLayer | ActiveLayer | ActiveLayer | ActiveLayer |
| ActiveLayout | ActiveLayout | ActiveLayout | ActiveLayout |
| ActiveLinetype | ActiveLinetype | ActiveLinetype | ActiveLinetype |
| ActiveProfile | ActiveProfile | ActiveProfile | ActiveProfile |
| ActivePViewport | ActivePViewport | ActivePViewport | ActivePViewport |
| ActiveSelectionSet | ActiveSelectionSet | ActiveSelectionSet | ActiveSelectionSet |
| ActiveSpace | ActiveSpace | ActiveSpace | ActiveSpace |
| ActiveTextStyle | ActiveTextStyle | ActiveTextStyle | ActiveTextStyle |
| ActiveUCS | ActiveUCS | ActiveUCS | ActiveUCS |
| ActiveViewport | ActiveViewport | ActiveViewport | ActiveViewport |
| ADCInsertUnitsDefaultSource | ADCInsertUnitsDefaultSource | ADCInsertUnitsDefaultSource | ADCInsertUnitsDefaultSource |
| ADCInsertUnitsDefaultTarget | ADCInsertUnitsDefaultTarget | ADCInsertUnitsDefaultTarget | ADCInsertUnitsDefaultTarget |
| | | | AffectsGraphics |
| | | | Algorithm |
| Alignment | Alignment | Alignment | Alignment |
| AlignmentPointAcquisition | AlignmentPointAcquisition | AlignmentPointAcquisition | AlignmentPointAcquisition |

| 2000 | 2000I | 2002 | 2004 |
|---|---|---|---|
| AllowLongSymbolNames | AllowLongSymbolNames | AllowLongSymbolNames | AllowLongSymbolNames |
| AltFontFile | AltFontFile | AltFontFile | AltFontFile |
| AltRoundDistance | AltRoundDistance | AltRoundDistance | AltRoundDistance |
| AltSuppressLeadingZeros | AltSuppressLeadingZeros | AltSuppressLeadingZeros | AltSuppressLeadingZeros |
| AltSuppressTrailingZeros | AltSuppressTrailingZeros | AltSuppressTrailingZeros | AltSuppressTrailingZeros |
| AltSuppressZeroFeet | AltSuppressZeroFeet | AltSuppressZeroFeet | AltSuppressZeroFeet |
| AltSuppressZeroInches | AltSuppressZeroInches | AltSuppressZeroInches | AltSuppressZeroInches |
| AltTabletMenuFile | AltTabletMenuFile | AltTabletMenuFile | AltTabletMenuFile |
| AltTextPrefix | AltTextPrefix | AltTextPrefix | AltTextPrefix |
| AltTextSuffix | AltTextSuffix | AltTextSuffix | AltTextSuffix |
| AltTolerancePrecision | AltTolerancePrecision | AltTolerancePrecision | AltTolerancePrecision |
| AltToleranceSuppressLeadingZeros | AltToleranceSuppressLeadingZeros | AltToleranceSuppressLeadingZeros | AltToleranceSuppressLeadingZeros |
| AltToleranceSuppressTrailingZeros | AltToleranceSuppressTrailingZeros | AltToleranceSuppressTrailingZeros | AltToleranceSuppressTrailingZeros |
| AltToleranceSuppressZeroFeet | AltToleranceSuppressZeroFeet | AltToleranceSuppressZeroFeet | AltToleranceSuppressZeroFeet |
| AltToleranceSuppressZeroInches | AltToleranceSuppressZeroInches | AltToleranceSuppressZeroInches | AltToleranceSuppressZeroInches |
| AltUnits | AltUnits | AltUnits | AltUnits |
| AltUnitsFormat | AltUnitsFormat | AltUnitsFormat | AltUnitsFormat |
| AltUnitsPrecision | AltUnitsPrecision | AltUnitsPrecision | AltUnitsPrecision |
| AltUnitsScale | AltUnitsScale | AltUnitsScale | AltUnitsScale |
| Angle | Angle | Angle | Angle |
| AngleFormat | AngleFormat | AngleFormat | AngleFormat |
| AngleVertex | AngleVertex | AngleVertex | AngleVertex |
| Annotation | Annotation | Annotation | Annotation |
| Application | Application | Application | Application |
| ArcLength | ArcLength | ArcLength | ArcLength |
| ArcSmoothness | ArcSmoothness | ArcSmoothness | ArcSmoothness |
| Area | Area | Area | Area |
| Arrowhead1Block | Arrowhead1Block | Arrowhead1Block | Arrowhead1Block |
| Arrowhead1Type | Arrowhead1Type | Arrowhead1Type | Arrowhead1Type |

| 2000 | 2000I | 2002 | 2004 |
|---|---|---|---|
| Arrowhead2Block | Arrowhead2Block | Arrowhead2Block | Arrowhead2Block |
| Arrowhead2Type | Arrowhead2Type | Arrowhead2Type | Arrowhead2Type |
| ArrowheadBlock | ArrowheadBlock | ArrowheadBlock | ArrowheadBlock |
| ArrowheadSize | ArrowheadSize | ArrowheadSize | ArrowheadSize |
| ArrowheadType | ArrowheadType | ArrowheadType | ArrowheadType |
| AssociativeHatch | AssociativeHatch | AssociativeHatch | AssociativeHatch |
| AttachmentPoint | AttachmentPoint | AttachmentPoint | AttachmentPoint |
| AutoAudit | AutoAudit | AutoAudit | AutoAudit |
| AutoSavePath | AutoSavePath | AutoSavePath | AutoSavePath |
| AutoSaveInterval | AutoSaveInterval | AutoSaveInterval | AutoSaveInterval |
| AutoSnapAperture | AutoSnapAperture | AutoSnapAperture | AutoSnapAperture |
| AutoSnapApertureSize | AutoSnapApertureSize | AutoSnapApertureSize | AutoSnapApertureSize |
| AutoSnapMagnet | AutoSnapMagnet | AutoSnapMagnet | AutoSnapMagnet |
| AutoSnapMarker | AutoSnapMarker | AutoSnapMarker | AutoSnapMarker |
| AutoSnapMarkerColor | AutoSnapMarkerColor | AutoSnapMarkerColor | AutoSnapMarkerColor |
| AutoSnapMarkerSize | AutoSnapMarkerSize | AutoSnapMarkerSize | AutoSnapMarkerSize |
| AutoSnapToolTip | AutoSnapToolTip | AutoSnapToolTip | AutoSnapToolTip |
| AutoTrackingVecColor | AutoTrackingVecColor | AutoTrackingVecColor | AutoTrackingVecColor |
| AutoTrackToolTip | AutoTrackToolTip | AutoTrackToolTip | AutoTrackToolTip |
| Backward | Backward | Backward | Backward |
| BasePoint | BasePoint | BasePoint | BasePoint |
| BatchPlotProgress | BatchPlotProgress | BatchPlotProgress | BatchPlotProgress |
| BeepOnError | BeepOnError | BeepOnError | BeepOnError |
| BigFontFile | BigFontFile | BigFontFile | BigFontFile |
| Block | Block | Block | Block |
| Blocks | Blocks | Blocks | Blocks |
| | | | Blue |
| | | | BookName |
| Brightness | Brightness | Brightness | Brightness |

| 2000 | 2000I | 2002 | 2004 |
|---|---|---|---|
| CanonicalMediaName | CanonicalMediaName | CanonicalMediaName | CanonicalMediaName |
| Caption | Caption | Caption | Caption |
| Center | Center | Center | Center |
| CenterMarkSize | CenterMarkSize | CenterMarkSize | CenterMarkSize |
| CenterPlot | CenterPlot | CenterPlot | CenterPlot |
| CenterType | CenterType | CenterType | CenterType |
| Centroid | Centroid | Centroid | Centroid |
| Check | Check | Check | Check |
| Circumference | Circumference | Circumference | Circumference |
| Clipped | Clipped | Clipped | Clipped |
| ClippingEnabled | ClippingEnabled | ClippingEnabled | ClippingEnabled |
| Closed | Closed | Closed | Closed |
| Color | Color | Color | Color |
| | | | ColorBookPath |
| | | | ColorIndex |
| | | | ColorMethod |
| | | | ColorName |
| Columns | Columns | Columns | Columns |
| ColumnSpacing | ColumnSpacing | ColumnSpacing | ColumnSpacing |
| | | | Comment |
| ConfigFile | ConfigFile | ConfigFile | ConfigFile |
| ConfigName | ConfigName | ConfigName | ConfigName |
| Constant | Constant | Constant | Constant |
| ConstantWidth | ConstantWidth | ConstantWidth | ConstantWidth |
| ContourlinesPerSurface | ContourlinesPerSurface | ContourlinesPerSurface | ContourlinesPerSurface |
| Contrast | Contrast | Contrast | Contrast |
| ControlPoints | ControlPoints | ControlPoints | ControlPoints |
| Coordinate | Coordinate | Coordinate | Coordinate |
| Coordinates | Coordinates | Coordinates | Coordinates |

| 2000 | 2000I | 2002 | 2004 |
|------|-------|------|------|
| Count | Count | Count | Count |
| CreateBackup | CreateBackup | CreateBackup | CreateBackup |
| CursorSize | CursorSize | CursorSize | CursorSize |
| CustomDictionary | CustomDictionary | CustomDictionary | CustomDictionary |
| CustomScale | CustomScale | CustomScale | CustomScale |
| Database | Database | Database | Database |
| DecimalSeparator | DecimalSeparator | DecimalSeparator | DecimalSeparator |
| DefaultInternetURL | DefaultInternetURL | DefaultInternetURL | DefaultInternetURL |
| DefaultOutputDevice | DefaultOutputDevice | DefaultOutputDevice | DefaultOutputDevice |
| DefaultPlotStyleForLayer | DefaultPlotStyleForLayer | DefaultPlotStyleForLayer | DefaultPlotStyleForLayer |
| DefaultPlotStyleForObjects | DefaultPlotStyleForObjects | DefaultPlotStyleForObjects | DefaultPlotStyleForObjects |
| DefaultPlotStyleTable | DefaultPlotStyleTable | DefaultPlotStyleTable | DefaultPlotStyleTable |
| Degree | Degree | Degree | Degree |
| Delta | Delta | Delta | Delta |
| DemandLoadARXApp | DemandLoadARXApp | DemandLoadARXApp | DemandLoadARXApp |
| Description | Description | Description | Description |
| Diameter | Diameter | Diameter | Diameter |
| Dictionaries | Dictionaries | Dictionaries | Dictionaries |
| DimensionLineColor | DimensionLineColor | DimensionLineColor | DimensionLineColor |
| DimensionLineExtend | DimensionLineExtend | DimensionLineExtend | DimensionLineExtend |
| DimensionLineWeight | DimensionLineWeight | DimensionLineWeight | DimensionLineWeight |
| DimLine1Suppress | DimLine1Suppress | DimLine1Suppress | DimLine1Suppress |
| DimLine2Suppress | DimLine2Suppress | DimLine2Suppress | DimLine2Suppress |
| DimLineInside | DimLineInside | DimLineInside | DimLineInside |
| DimLineSuppress | DimLineSuppress | DimLineSuppress | DimLineSuppress |
| DimStyles | DimStyles | DimStyles | DimStyles |
| Direction | Direction | Direction | Direction |
| DirectionVector | DirectionVector | DirectionVector | DirectionVector |
| Display | Display | Display | Display |

| 2000 | 2000I | 2002 | 2004 |
|---|---|---|---|
| DisplayGrips | DisplayGrips | DisplayGrips | DisplayGrips |
| DisplayGripsWIthinBlocks | DisplayGripsWIthinBlocks | DisplayGripsWIthinBlocks | DisplayGripsWIthinBlocks |
| DisplayLayoutTabs | DisplayLayoutTabs | DisplayLayoutTabs | DisplayLayoutTabs |
| DisplayLocked | DisplayLocked | DisplayLocked | DisplayLocked |
| DisplayOLEScale | DisplayOLEScale | DisplayOLEScale | DisplayOLEScale |
| DisplayScreenMenu | DisplayScreenMenu | DisplayScreenMenu | DisplayScreenMenu |
| DisplayScrollBars | DisplayScrollBars | DisplayScrollBars | DisplayScrollBars |
| DisplaySilhouette | DisplaySilhouette | DisplaySilhouette | DisplaySilhouette |
| DockedVisibleLines | DockedVisibleLines | DockedVisibleLines | DockedVisibleLines |
| DockStatus | DockStatus | DockStatus | DockStatus |
| Document | Document | Document | Document |
| Documents | Documents | Documents | Documents |
| Drafting | Drafting | Drafting | Drafting |
| DrawingDirection | DrawingDirection | DrawingDirection | DrawingDirection |
| DriversPath | DriversPath | DriversPath | DriversPath |
| Elevation | Elevation | Elevation | Elevation |
| ElevationModelSpace | ElevationModelSpace | ElevationModelSpace | ElevationModelSpace |
| ElevationPaperSpace | ElevationPaperSpace | ElevationPaperSpace | ElevationPaperSpace |
| Enable | Enable | Enable | Enable |
| EnableStartupDialog | EnableStartupDialog | EnableStartupDialog | EnableStartupDialog |
| EndAngle | EndAngle | EndAngle | EndAngle |
| EndParameter | EndParameter | EndParameter | EndParameter |
| EndPoint | EndPoint | EndPoint | EndPoint |
| EndSubMenuLevel | EndSubMenuLevel | EndSubMenuLevel | EndSubMenuLevel |
| EndTangent | EndTangent | EndTangent | EndTangent |
|  |  |  | EntityColor |
| ExtensionLineColor | ExtensionLineColor | ExtensionLineColor | ExtensionLineColor |
| ExtensionLineExtend | ExtensionLineExtend | ExtensionLineExtend | ExtensionLineExtend |
| ExtensionLineOffset | ExtensionLineOffset | ExtensionLineOffset | ExtensionLineOffset |

| 2000 | 2000I | 2002 | 2004 |
|------|-------|------|------|
| ExtensionLineWeight | ExtensionLineWeight | ExtensionLineWeight | ExtensionLineWeight |
| ExtLine1EndPoint | ExtLine1EndPoint | ExtLine1EndPoint | ExtLine1EndPoint |
| ExtLine1Point | ExtLine1Point | ExtLine1Point | ExtLine1Point |
| ExtLine1StartPoint | ExtLine1StartPoint | ExtLine1StartPoint | ExtLine1StartPoint |
| ExtLine1Suppress | ExtLine1Suppress | ExtLine1Suppress | ExtLine1Suppress |
| ExtLine2EndPoint | ExtLine2EndPoint | ExtLine2EndPoint | ExtLine2EndPoint |
| ExtLine2Point | ExtLine2Point | ExtLine2Point | ExtLine2Point |
| ExtLine2StartPoint | ExtLine2StartPoint | ExtLine2StartPoint | ExtLine2StartPoint |
| ExtLine2Suppress | ExtLine2Suppress | ExtLine2Suppress | ExtLine2Suppress |
| Fade | Fade | Fade | Fade |
| | | | Feature |
| FieldLength | FieldLength | FieldLength | FieldLength |
| | | | FileName |
| Files | Files | Files | Files |
| | | | FileSize |
| | | | FingerprintGUID |
| Fit | Fit | Fit | Fit |
| FitPoints | FitPoints | FitPoints | FitPoints |
| FitTolerance | FitTolerance | FitTolerance | FitTolerance |
| FloatingRows | FloatingRows | FloatingRows | FloatingRows |
| Flyout | Flyout | Flyout | Flyout |
| FontFile | FontFile | FontFile | FontFile |
| FontFileMap | FontFileMap | FontFileMap | FontFileMap |
| | | | FoundPath |
| ForceLineInside | ForceLineInside | ForceLineInside | ForceLineInside |
| FractionFormat | FractionFormat | FractionFormat | FractionFormat |
| Freeze | Freeze | Freeze | Freeze |
| FullCrcValidation | FullCrcValidation | FullCrcValidation | FullCrcValidation |
| | | | FullFileName |

| 2000 | 2000I | 2002 | 2004 |
|---|---|---|---|
| FullName | FullName | FullName | FullName |
| FullScreenTrackingVector | FullScreenTrackingVector | FullScreenTrackingVector | FullScreenTrackingVector |
| | | | GradientAngle |
| | | | GradientCentered |
| | | | GradientColor1 |
| | | | GradientColor2 |
| | | | GradientName |
| GraphicsWinLayoutBackgrndColor | GraphicsWinLayoutBackgrndColor | GraphicsWinLayoutBackgrndColor | GraphicsWinLayoutBackgrndColor |
| GraphicsWinModelBackgrndColor | GraphicsWinModelBackgrndColor | GraphicsWinModelBackgrndColor | GraphicsWinModelBackgrndColor |
| | | | Green |
| GridOn | GridOn | GridOn | GridOn |
| GripColorSelected | GripColorSelected | GripColorSelected | GripColorSelected |
| GripColorUnselected | GripColorUnselected | GripColorUnselected | GripColorUnselected |
| GripSize | GripSize | GripSize | GripSize |
| Groups | Groups | Groups | Groups |
| Handle | Handle | Handle | Handle |
| HasAttributes | HasAttributes | HasAttributes | HasAttributes |
| HasExtensionDictionary | HasExtensionDictionary | HasExtensionDictionary | HasExtensionDictionary |
| | | | HatchObjectType |
| HatchStyle | HatchStyle | HatchStyle | HatchStyle |
| Height | Height | Height | Height |
| HelpFilePath | HelpFilePath | HelpFilePath | HelpFilePath |
| HelpString | HelpString | HelpString | HelpString |
| HistoryLines | HistoryLines | HistoryLines | HistoryLines |
| HorizontalAlignment | HorizontalAlignment | HorizontalAlignment | HorizontalAlignment |
| HorizontalTextPosition | HorizontalTextPosition | HorizontalTextPosition | HorizontalTextPosition |
| HWND | HWND | HWND | HWND |
| HyperlinkDisplayCursor | HyperlinkDisplayCursor | HyperlinkDisplayCursor | HyperlinkDisplayCursor |
| HyperlinkDisplayTooltip | HyperlinkDisplayTooltip | HyperlinkDisplayTooltip | HyperlinkDisplayTooltip |

| 2000 | 2000I | 2002 | 2004 |
| --- | --- | --- | --- |
| Hyperlinks | Hyperlinks | Hyperlinks | Hyperlinks |
| ImageFile | ImageFile | ImageFile | ImageFile |
| ImageFrameHighlight | ImageFrameHighlight | ImageFrameHighlight | ImageFrameHighlight |
| ImageHeight | ImageHeight | ImageHeight | ImageHeight |
| ImageVisibility | ImageVisibility | ImageVisibility | ImageVisibility |
| ImageWidth | ImageWidth | ImageWidth | ImageWidth |
| IncrementalSavePercent | IncrementalSavePercent | IncrementalSavePercent | IncrementalSavePercent |
| Index | Index | Index | Index |
| InsertionPoint | InsertionPoint | InsertionPoint | InsertionPoint |
| Invisible | Invisible | Invisible | Invisible |
| IsCloned | IsCloned | IsCloned | IsCloned |
| IsLayout | IsLayout | IsLayout | IsLayout |
| | | | IsModified |
| ISOPenWidth | ISOPenWidth | ISOPenWidth | ISOPenWidth |
| IsOwnerXlated | IsOwnerXlated | IsOwnerXlated | IsOwnerXlated |
| IsPeriodic | IsPeriodic | IsPeriodic | IsPeriodic |
| IsPlanar | IsPlanar | IsPlanar | IsPlanar |
| IsPrimary | IsPrimary | IsPrimary | IsPrimary |
| IsQuiescent | IsQuiescent | IsQuiescent | IsQuiescent |
| IsRational | IsRational | IsRational | IsRational |
| | | | Issuer |
| IsXRef | IsXRef | IsXRef | IsXRef |
| Key | Key | Key | Key |
| KeyboardAccelerator | KeyboardAccelerator | KeyboardAccelerator | KeyboardAccelerator |
| KeyboardPriority | KeyboardPriority | KeyboardPriority | KeyboardPriority |
| | | | KeyLength |
| Knots | Knots | Knots | Knots |
| Label | Label | Label | Label |
| LargeButtons | LargeButtons | LargeButtons | LargeButtons |

| 2000 | 2000I | 2002 | 2004 |
|---|---|---|---|
| LastHeight | LastHeight | LastHeight | LastHeight |
| Layer | Layer | Layer | Layer |
| LayerOn | LayerOn | LayerOn | LayerOn |
| Layers | Layers | Layers | Layers |
| Layout | Layout | Layout | Layout |
| LayoutCreateViewport | LayoutCreateViewport | LayoutCreateViewport | LayoutCreateViewport |
| LayoutCrosshairColor | LayoutCrosshairColor | LayoutCrosshairColor | LayoutCrosshairColor |
| LayoutDisplayMargins | LayoutDisplayMargins | LayoutDisplayMargins | LayoutDisplayMargins |
| LayoutDisplayPaper | LayoutDisplayPaper | LayoutDisplayPaper | LayoutDisplayPaper |
| LayoutDisplayPaperShadow | LayoutDisplayPaperShadow | LayoutDisplayPaperShadow | LayoutDisplayPaperShadow |
| Layouts | Layouts | Layouts | Layouts |
| LayoutShowPlotSetup | LayoutShowPlotSetup | LayoutShowPlotSetup | LayoutShowPlotSetup |
| LeaderLength | LeaderLength | LeaderLength | LeaderLength |
| Left | Left | Left | Left |
| Length | Length | Length | Length |
| LensLength | LensLength | LensLength | LensLength |
| LicenseServer | LicenseServer | LicenseServer | |
| Limits | Limits | Limits | Limits |
| LinearScaleFactor | LinearScaleFactor | LinearScaleFactor | LinearScaleFactor |
| LineSpacingFactor | LineSpacingFactor | LineSpacingFactor | LineSpacingFactor |
| LineSpacingStyle | LineSpacingStyle | LineSpacingStyle | LineSpacingStyle |
| Linetype | Linetype | Linetype | Linetype |
| LinetypeGeneration | LinetypeGeneration | LinetypeGeneration | LinetypeGeneration |
| Linetypes | Linetypes | Linetypes | Linetypes |
| LinetypeScale | LinetypeScale | LinetypeScale | LinetypeScale |
| Lineweight | Lineweight | Lineweight | Lineweight |
| LineweightDisplay | LineweightDisplay | LineweightDisplay | LineweightDisplay |
| LoadAcadLspInAllDocuments | LoadAcadLspInAllDocuments | LoadAcadLspInAllDocuments | LoadAcadLspInAllDocuments |
| LocaleID | LocaleID | LocaleID | LocaleID |

| 2000 | 2000I | 2002 | 2004 |
|------|-------|------|------|
| Lock | Lock | Lock | Lock |
| LogFilePath | LogFilePath | LogFilePath | LogFilePath |
| LogFileOn | LogFileOn | LogFileOn | LogFileOn |
| LowerLeftCorner | LowerLeftCorner | LowerLeftCorner | LowerLeftCorner |
| Macro | Macro | Macro | Macro |
| MainDictionary | MainDictionary | MainDictionary | MainDictionary |
| MajorAxis | MajorAxis | MajorAxis | MajorAxis |
| MajorRadius | MajorRadius | MajorRadius | MajorRadius |
|  | Mask | Mask | Mask |
| MaxActiveViewports | MaxActiveViewports | MaxActiveViewports | MaxActiveViewports |
| MaxAutoCADWindow | MaxAutoCADWindow | MaxAutoCADWindow | MaxAutoCADWindow |
| MClose | MClose | MClose | MClose |
| MDensity | MDensity | MDensity | MDensity |
| Measurement | Measurement | Measurement | Measurement |
| MenuBar | MenuBar | MenuBar | MenuBar |
| MenuFile | MenuFile | MenuFile | MenuFile |
| MenuFileName | MenuFileName | MenuFileName | MenuFileName |
| MenuGroups | MenuGroups | MenuGroups | MenuGroups |
| Menus | Menus | Menus | Menus |
| MinorAxis | MinorAxis | MinorAxis | MinorAxis |
| MinorRadius | MinorRadius | MinorRadius | MinorRadius |
| Mode | Mode | Mode | Mode |
| ModelCrosshairColor | ModelCrosshairColor | ModelCrosshairColor | ModelCrosshairColor |
| ModelSpace | ModelSpace | ModelSpace | ModelSpace |
| ModelType | ModelType | ModelType | ModelType |
| MomentOfInertia | MomentOfInertia | MomentOfInertia | MomentOfInertia |
| MRUNumber | MRUNumber | MRUNumber | MRUNumber |
| MSpace | MSpace | MSpace | MSpace |
| MVertexCount | MVertexCount | MVertexCount | MVertexCount |

| 2000 | 2000I | 2002 | 2004 |
|---|---|---|---|
| Name | Name | Name | Name |
| NameNoMnemonic | NameNoMnemonic | NameNoMnemonic | NameNoMnemonic |
| NClose | NClose | NClose | NClose |
| NDensity | NDensity | NDensity | NDensity |
| Normal | Normal | Normal | Normal |
| NumberOfControlPoints | NumberOfControlPoints | NumberOfControlPoints | NumberOfControlPoints |
| NumberOfCopies | NumberOfCopies | NumberOfCopies | NumberOfCopies |
| NumberOfFaces | NumberOfFaces | NumberOfFaces | NumberOfFaces |
| NumberOfFitPoints | NumberOfFitPoints | NumberOfFitPoints | NumberOfFitPoints |
| NumberOfLoops | NumberOfLoops | NumberOfLoops | NumberOfLoops |
| NumberOfVertices | NumberOfVertices | NumberOfVertices | NumberOfVertices |
| NVertexCount | NVertexCount | NVertexCount | NVertexCount |
| ObjectARXPath | ObjectARXPath | ObjectARXPath | |
| ObjectID | ObjectID | ObjectID | ObjectID |
| ObjectName | ObjectName | ObjectName | ObjectName |
| ObjectSnapMode | ObjectSnapMode | ObjectSnapMode | ObjectSnapMode |
| ObjectSortByPlotting | ObjectSortByPlotting | ObjectSortByPlotting | ObjectSortByPlotting |
| ObjectSortByPSOutput | ObjectSortByPSOutput | ObjectSortByPSOutput | ObjectSortByPSOutput |
| ObjectSortByRedraws | ObjectSortByRedraws | ObjectSortByRedraws | ObjectSortByRedraws |
| ObjectSortByRegens | ObjectSortByRegens | ObjectSortByRegens | ObjectSortByRegens |
| ObjectSortBySelection | ObjectSortBySelection | ObjectSortBySelection | ObjectSortBySelection |
| ObjectSortBySnap | ObjectSortBySnap | ObjectSortBySnap | ObjectSortBySnap |
| ObliqueAngle | ObliqueAngle | ObliqueAngle | ObliqueAngle |
| OLELaunch | OLELaunch | OLELaunch | OLELaunch |
| OLEQuality | OLEQuality | OLEQuality | OLEQuality |
| OnMenuBar | OnMenuBar | OnMenuBar | OnMenuBar |
| OpenSave | OpenSave | OpenSave | OpenSave |
| Origin | Origin | Origin | Origin |
| OrthoOn | OrthoOn | OrthoOn | OrthoOn |

| 2000 | 2000I | 2002 | 2004 |
|------|-------|------|------|
| Output | Output | Output | Output |
| OwnerID | OwnerID | OwnerID | OwnerID |
| PaperSpace | PaperSpace | PaperSpace | PaperSpace |
| PaperUnits | PaperUnits | PaperUnits | PaperUnits |
| Parent | Parent | Parent | Parent |
|  |  |  | Password |
| Path | Path | Path | Path |
| PatternAngle | PatternAngle | PatternAngle | PatternAngle |
| PatternDouble | PatternDouble | PatternDouble | PatternDouble |
| PatternName | PatternName | PatternName | PatternName |
| PatternScale | PatternScale | PatternScale | PatternScale |
| PatternSpace | PatternSpace | PatternSpace | PatternSpace |
| PatternType | PatternType | PatternType | PatternType |
| Perimeter | Perimeter | Perimeter | Perimeter |
| PickAdd | PickAdd | PickAdd | PickAdd |
| PickAuto | PickAuto | PickAuto | PickAuto |
| PickBoxSize | PickBoxSize | PickBoxSize | PickBoxSize |
| PickDrag | PickDrag | PickDrag | PickDrag |
| PickFirst | PickFirst | PickFirst | PickFirst |
| PickfirstSelectionSet | PickfirstSelectionSet | PickfirstSelectionSet | PickfirstSelectionSet |
| PickGroup | PickGroup | PickGroup | PickGroup |
| Plot | Plot | Plot | Plot |
| PlotConfigurations | PlotConfigurations | PlotConfigurations | PlotConfigurations |
| PlotHidden | PlotHidden | PlotHidden | PlotHidden |
| PlotLegacy | PlotLegacy | PlotLegacy | PlotLegacy |
| PlotOrigin | PlotOrigin | PlotOrigin | PlotOrigin |
| PlotPolicy | PlotPolicy | PlotPolicy | PlotPolicy |
| PlotRotation | PlotRotation | PlotRotation | PlotRotation |
| PlotStyleName | PlotStyleName | PlotStyleName | PlotStyleName |

| 2000 | 2000I | 2002 | 2004 |
|---|---|---|---|
| Plottable | Plottable | Plottable | Plottable |
| PlotType | PlotType | PlotType | PlotType |
| PlotViewportBorders | PlotViewportBorders | PlotViewportBorders | PlotViewportBorders |
| PlotViewportsFirst | PlotViewportsFirst | PlotViewportsFirst | PlotViewportsFirst |
| PlotWithLineweights | PlotWithLineweights | PlotWithLineweights | PlotWithLineweights |
| PlotWithPlotStyles | PlotWithPlotStyles | PlotWithPlotStyles | PlotWithPlotStyles |
| PolarTrackingVector | PolarTrackingVector | PolarTrackingVector | PolarTrackingVector |
| PostScriptPrologFile | PostScriptPrologFile | PostScriptPrologFile | PostScriptPrologFile |
| Preferences | Preferences | Preferences | Preferences |
| Preset | Preset | Preset | Preset |
| PrimaryUnitsPrecision | PrimaryUnitsPrecision | PrimaryUnitsPrecision | PrimaryUnitsPrecision |
| PrincipalDirections | PrincipalDirections | PrincipalDirections | PrincipalDirections |
| PrincipalMoments | PrincipalMoments | PrincipalMoments | PrincipalMoments |
| PrinterConfigPath | PrinterConfigPath | PrinterConfigPath | PrinterConfigPath |
| PrinterDescPath | PrinterDescPath | PrinterDescPath | PrinterDescPath |
| PrinterPaperSizeAlert | PrinterPaperSizeAlert | PrinterPaperSizeAlert | PrinterPaperSizeAlert |
| PrinterSpoolAlert | PrinterSpoolAlert | PrinterSpoolAlert | PrinterSpoolAlert |
| PrinterStyleSheetPath | PrinterStyleSheetPath | PrinterStyleSheetPath | PrinterStyleSheetPath |
| PrintFile | PrintFile | PrintFile | PrintFile |
| PrintSpoolerPath | PrintSpoolerPath | PrintSpoolerPath | PrintSpoolerPath |
| PrintSpoolExecutable | PrintSpoolExecutable | PrintSpoolExecutable | PrintSpoolExecutable |
| ProductOfInertia | ProductOfInertia | ProductOfInertia | ProductOfInertia |
| Profiles | Profiles | Profiles | Profiles |
| PromptString | PromptString | PromptString | PromptString |
| | | | ProviderName |
| | | | ProviderType |
| ProxyImage | ProxyImage | ProxyImage | ProxyImage |
| QuietErrorMode | QuietErrorMode | QuietErrorMode | QuietErrorMode |
| RadiiOfGyration | RadiiOfGyration | RadiiOfGyration | RadiiOfGyration |

| 2000 | 2000I | 2002 | 2004 |
|------|-------|------|------|
| Radius | Radius | Radius | Radius |
| RadiusRatio | RadiusRatio | RadiusRatio | RadiusRatio |
| ReadOnly | ReadOnly | ReadOnly | ReadOnly |
| | | | Red |
| | | | ReferenceCount |
| RegisteredApplications | RegisteredApplications | RegisteredApplications | RegisteredApplications |
| RemoveHiddenLines | RemoveHiddenLines | RemoveHiddenLines | RemoveHiddenLines |
| RenderSmoothness | RenderSmoothness | RenderSmoothness | RenderSmoothness |
| Rotation | Rotation | Rotation | Rotation |
| RoundDistance | RoundDistance | RoundDistance | RoundDistance |
| Rows | Rows | Rows | Rows |
| RowSpacing | RowSpacing | RowSpacing | RowSpacing |
| SaveAsType | SaveAsType | SaveAsType | SaveAsType |
| Saved | Saved | Saved | Saved |
| SavePreviewThumbnail | SavePreviewThumbnail | SavePreviewThumbnail | SavePreviewThumbnail |
| ScaleFactor | ScaleFactor | ScaleFactor | ScaleFactor |
| ScaleLineweights | ScaleLineweights | ScaleLineweights | ScaleLineweights |
| SCMCommandMode | SCMCommandMode | SCMCommandMode | SCMCommandMode |
| SCMDefaultMode | SCMDefaultMode | SCMDefaultMode | SCMDefaultMode |
| SCMEditMode | SCMEditMode | SCMEditMode | SCMEditMode |
| SecondPoint | SecondPoint | SecondPoint | SecondPoint |
| SegmentPerPolyline | SegmentPerPolyline | SegmentPerPolyline | SegmentPerPolyline |
| Selection | Selection | Selection | Selection |
| SelectionSets | SelectionSets | SelectionSets | SelectionSets |
| | | | SerialNumber |
| | | | ShadePlot |
| ShortcutMenu | ShortcutMenu | ShortcutMenu | ShortcutMenu |
| ShortCutMenuDisplay | ShortCutMenuDisplay | ShortCutMenuDisplay | ShortCutMenuDisplay |
| ShowPlotStyles | ShowPlotStyles | ShowPlotStyles | ShowPlotStyles |

| 2000 | 2000I | 2002 | 2004 |
|---|---|---|---|
| ShowProxyDialogBox | ShowProxyDialogBox | ShowProxyDialogBox | ShowProxyDialogBox |
| ShowRasterImage | ShowRasterImage | ShowRasterImage | ShowRasterImage |
| ShowRotation | ShowRotation | ShowRotation | ShowRotation |
| ShowWarningMessages | ShowWarningMessages | ShowWarningMessages | ShowWarningMessages |
| SingleDocumentMode | SingleDocumentMode | SingleDocumentMode | SingleDocumentMode |
| SnapBasePoint | SnapBasePoint | SnapBasePoint | SnapBasePoint |
| SnapOn | SnapOn | SnapOn | SnapOn |
| SnapRotationAngle | SnapRotationAngle | SnapRotationAngle | SnapRotationAngle |
| SolidFill | SolidFill | SolidFill | SolidFill |
| StandardScale | StandardScale | StandardScale | StandardScale |
| StartAngle | StartAngle | StartAngle | StartAngle |
| StartParameter | StartParameter | StartParameter | StartParameter |
| StartPoint | StartPoint | StartPoint | StartPoint |
| StartTangent | StartTangent | StartTangent | StartTangent |
| StatusID | StatusID | StatusID | StatusID |
| StoreSQLIndex | StoreSQLIndex | StoreSQLIndex | StoreSQLIndex |
| StyleName | StyleName | StyleName | StyleName |
| StyleSheet | StyleSheet | StyleSheet | StyleSheet |
|  |  |  | Subject |
| SubMenu | SubMenu | SubMenu | SubMenu |
| SupportPath | SupportPath | SupportPath | SupportPath |
| SuppressLeadingZeros | SuppressLeadingZeros | SuppressLeadingZeros | SuppressLeadingZeros |
| SuppressTrailingZeros | SuppressTrailingZeros | SuppressTrailingZeros | SuppressTrailingZeros |
| SuppressZeroFeet | SuppressZeroFeet | SuppressZeroFeet | SuppressZeroFeet |
| SuppressZeroInches | SuppressZeroInches | SuppressZeroInches | SuppressZeroInches |
| System | System | System | System |
| TablesReadOnly | TablesReadOnly | TablesReadOnly | TablesReadOnly |
| TabOrder | TabOrder | TabOrder | TabOrder |
| TagString | TagString | TagString | TagString |

| 2000 | 2000I | 2002 | 2004 |
|------|-------|------|------|
| Target | Target | Target | Target |
| TempFileExtension | TempFileExtension | TempFileExtension | TempFileExtension |
| TempFilePath | TempFilePath | TempFilePath | TempFilePath |
| TemplateDwgPath | TemplateDwgPath | TemplateDwgPath | TemplateDwgPath |
| TempXRefPath | TempXRefPath | TempXRefPath | TempXRefPath |
| TextAlignmentPoint | TextAlignmentPoint | TextAlignmentPoint | TextAlignmentPoint |
| TextColor | TextColor | TextColor | TextColor |
| TextEditor | TextEditor | TextEditor | TextEditor |
| TextFont | TextFont | TextFont | TextFont |
| TextFontSize | TextFontSize | TextFontSize | TextFontSize |
| TextFontStyle | TextFontStyle | TextFontStyle | TextFontStyle |
| TextFrameDisplay | TextFrameDisplay | TextFrameDisplay | TextFrameDisplay |
| TextGap | TextGap | TextGap | TextGap |
| TextGenerationFlag | TextGenerationFlag | TextGenerationFlag | TextGenerationFlag |
| TextHeight | TextHeight | TextHeight | TextHeight |
| TextInside | TextInside | TextInside | TextInside |
| TextInsideAlign | TextInsideAlign | TextInsideAlign | TextInsideAlign |
| TextMovement | TextMovement | TextMovement | TextMovement |
| TextOutsideAlign | TextOutsideAlign | TextOutsideAlign | TextOutsideAlign |
| TextOverride | TextOverride | TextOverride | TextOverride |
| TextPosition | TextPosition | TextPosition | TextPosition |
| TextPrecision | TextPrecision | TextPrecision | TextPrecision |
| TextPrefix | TextPrefix | TextPrefix | TextPrefix |
| TextRotation | TextRotation | TextRotation | TextRotation |
| TextString | TextString | TextString | TextString |
| TextStyle | TextStyle | TextStyle | TextStyle |
| TextStyles | TextStyles | TextStyles | TextStyles |
| TextSuffix | TextSuffix | TextSuffix | TextSuffix |
| TextureMapPath | TextureMapPath | TextureMapPath | TextureMapPath |

| 2000 | 2000I | 2002 | 2004 |
|------|-------|------|------|
| TextWinBackgrndColor | TextWinBackgrndColor | TextWinBackgrndColor | TextWinBackgrndColor |
| TextWinTextColor | TextWinTextColor | TextWinTextColor | TextWinTextColor |
| Thickness | Thickness | Thickness | Thickness |
| | | | TimeServer |
| | | | TimeStamp |
| ToleranceDisplay | ToleranceDisplay | ToleranceDisplay | ToleranceDisplay |
| ToleranceHeightScale | ToleranceHeightScale | ToleranceHeightScale | ToleranceHeightScale |
| ToleranceJustification | ToleranceJustification | ToleranceJustification | ToleranceJustification |
| ToleranceLowerLimit | ToleranceLowerLimit | ToleranceLowerLimit | ToleranceLowerLimit |
| TolerancePrecision | TolerancePrecision | TolerancePrecision | TolerancePrecision |
| ToleranceSuppressLeadingZeros | ToleranceSuppressLeadingZeros | ToleranceSuppressLeadingZeros | ToleranceSuppressLeadingZeros |
| ToleranceSuppressTrailingZeros | ToleranceSuppressTrailingZeros | ToleranceSuppressTrailingZeros | ToleranceSuppressTrailingZeros |
| ToleranceSuppressZeroFeet | ToleranceSuppressZeroFeet | ToleranceSuppressZeroFeet | ToleranceSuppressZeroFeet |
| ToleranceSuppressZeroInches | ToleranceSuppressZeroInches | ToleranceSuppressZeroInches | ToleranceSuppressZeroInches |
| ToleranceUpperLimit | ToleranceUpperLimit | ToleranceUpperLimit | ToleranceUpperLimit |
| Toolbars | Toolbars | Toolbars | Toolbars |
| | | | ToolPalettePath |
| Top | Top | Top | Top |
| TotalAngle | TotalAngle | TotalAngle | TotalAngle |
| TranslateIDs | TranslateIDs | TranslateIDs | TranslateIDs |
| Transparency | Transparency | Transparency | Transparency |
| | | | TrueColor |
| TrueColorImages | TrueColorImages | TrueColorImages | TrueColorImages |
| TwistAngle | TwistAngle | TwistAngle | TwistAngle |
| Type | Type | Type | Type |
| UCSIconAtOrigin | UCSIconAtOrigin | UCSIconAtOrigin | UCSIconAtOrigin |
| UCSIconOn | UCSIconOn | UCSIconOn | UCSIconOn |
| UCSPerViewport | UCSPerViewport | UCSPerViewport | UCSPerViewport |
| UnitsFormat | UnitsFormat | UnitsFormat | UnitsFormat |

| 2000 | 2000I | 2002 | 2004 |
|---|---|---|---|
| UpperRightCorner | UpperRightCorner | UpperRightCorner | UpperRightCorner |
| UpsideDown | UpsideDown | UpsideDown | UpsideDown |
| URL | URL | URL | URL |
| URLDescription | URLDescription | URLDescription | URLDescription |
| URLNamedLocation | URLNamedLocation | URLNamedLocation | URLNamedLocation |
| UseLastPlotSettings | UseLastPlotSettings | UseLastPlotSettings | UseLastPlotSettings |
| User | User | User | User |
| UserCoordinateSystems | UserCoordinateSystems | UserCoordinateSystems | UserCoordinateSystems |
| UseStandardScale | UseStandardScale | UseStandardScale | UseStandardScale |
| Utility | Utility | Utility | Utility |
| Value | Value | Value | Value |
| VBE | VBE | VBE | VBE |
| Verify | Verify | Verify | Verify |
| Version | Version | Version | Version |
| | | | VersionGUID |
| VerticalAlignment | VerticalAlignment | VerticalAlignment | VerticalAlignment |
| VerticalTextPosition | VerticalTextPosition | VerticalTextPosition | VerticalTextPosition |
| ViewportDefault | ViewportDefault | ViewportDefault | ViewportDefault |
| ViewportOn | ViewportOn | ViewportOn | ViewportOn |
| Viewports | Viewports | Viewports | Viewports |
| Views | Views | Views | Views |
| ViewToPlot | ViewToPlot | ViewToPlot | ViewToPlot |
| Visible | Visible | Visible | Visible |
| VisibilityEdge1 | VisibilityEdge1 | VisibilityEdge1 | VisibilityEdge1 |
| VisibilityEdge2 | VisibilityEdge2 | VisibilityEdge2 | VisibilityEdge2 |
| VisibilityEdge3 | VisibilityEdge3 | VisibilityEdge3 | VisibilityEdge3 |
| VisibilityEdge4 | VisibilityEdge4 | VisibilityEdge4 | VisibilityEdge4 |
| Volume | Volume | Volume | Volume |
| Weights | Weights | Weights | Weights |

| 2000 | 2000I | 2002 | 2004 |
|---|---|---|---|
| Width | Width | Width | Width |
| WindowLeft | WindowLeft | WindowLeft | WindowLeft |
| WindowState | WindowState | WindowState | WindowState |
| WindowTitle | WindowTitle | WindowTitle | WindowTitle |
| WindowTop | WindowTop | WindowTop | WindowTop |
| WorkspacePath | WorkspacePath | WorkspacePath | WorkspacePath |
| XRefDatabase | XRefDatabase | XRefDatabase | XRefDatabase |
| XrefDemandLoad | XrefDemandLoad | XrefDemandLoad | XrefDemandLoad |
| XRefEdit | XRefEdit | XRefEdit | XRefEdit |
| XRefFadeIntensity | XRefFadeIntensity | XRefFadeIntensity | XRefFadeIntensity |
| XRefLayerVisibility | XRefLayerVisibility | XRefLayerVisibility | XRefLayerVisibility |
| XScaleFactor | XScaleFactor | XScaleFactor | XScaleFactor |
| XVector | XVector | XVector | XVector |
| YScaleFactor | YScaleFactor | YScaleFactor | YScaleFactor |
| YVector | YVector | YVector | YVector |
| ZScaleFactor | ZScaleFactor | ZScaleFactor | ZScaleFactor |

# Events Comparison

| 2000 | 2000I | 2002 | 2004 |
|---|---|---|---|
| Activate | Activate | Activate | Activate |
| AppActivate | AppActivate | AppActivate | AppActivate |
| AppDeactivate | AppDeactivate | AppDeactivate | AppDeactivate |
| ARXLoaded | ARXLoaded | ARXLoaded | ARXLoaded |
| ARXUnloaded | ARXUnloaded | ARXUnloaded | ARXUnloaded |
| BeginClose | BeginClose | BeginClose | BeginClose |
| BeginCommand | BeginCommand | BeginCommand | BeginCommand |
| BeginDoubleClick | BeginDoubleClick | BeginDoubleClick | BeginDoubleClick |

| 2000 | 2000I | 2002 | 2004 |
|------|-------|------|------|
| BeginFileDrop | BeginFileDrop | BeginFileDrop | BeginFileDrop |
| BeginLISP | BeginLISP | BeginLISP | BeginLISP |
| BeginModal | BeginModal | BeginModal | BeginModal |
| BeginOpen | BeginOpen | BeginOpen | BeginOpen |
| BeginPlot | BeginPlot | BeginPlot | BeginPlot |
| BeginQuit | BeginQuit | BeginQuit | BeginQuit |
| BeginRightClick | BeginRightClick | BeginRightClick | BeginRightClick |
| BeginSave | BeginSave | BeginSave | BeginSave |
| BeginShortcutMenuCommand | BeginShortcutMenuCommand | BeginShortcutMenuCommand | BeginShortcutMenuCommand |
| BeginShortcutMenuDefault | BeginShortcutMenuDefault | BeginShortcutMenuDefault | BeginShortcutMenuDefault |
| BeginShortcutMenuEdit | BeginShortcutMenuEdit | BeginShortcutMenuEdit | BeginShortcutMenuEdit |
| BeginShortcutMenuGrip | BeginShortcutMenuGrip | BeginShortcutMenuGrip | BeginShortcutMenuGrip |
| BeginShortcutMenuOsnap | BeginShortcutMenuOsnap | BeginShortcutMenuOsnap | BeginShortcutMenuOsnap |
| Deactivate | Deactivate | Deactivate | Deactivate |
| EndCommand | EndCommand | EndCommand | EndCommand |
| EndLISP | EndLISP | EndLISP | EndLISP |
| EndModal | EndModal | EndModal | EndModal |
| EndOpen | EndOpen | EndOpen | EndOpen |
| EndPlot | EndPlot | EndPlot | EndPlot |
| EndSave | EndSave | EndSave | EndSave |
| EndShortcutMenu | EndShortcutMenu | EndShortcutMenu | EndShortcutMenu |
| LayoutSwitched | LayoutSwitched | LayoutSwitched | LayoutSwitched |
| LISPCancelled | LISPCancelled | LISPCancelled | LISPCancelled |
| Modified | Modified | Modified | Modified |
| NewDrawing | NewDrawing | NewDrawing | NewDrawing |
| ObjectAdded | ObjectAdded | ObjectAdded | ObjectAdded |
| ObjectErased | ObjectErased | ObjectErased | ObjectErased |

| 2000 | 2000I | 2002 | 2004 |
|---|---|---|---|
| ObjectModified | ObjectModified | ObjectModified | ObjectModified |
| SelectionChanged | SelectionChanged | SelectionChanged | SelectionChanged |
| SysVarChanged | SysVarChanged | SysVarChanged | SysVarChanged |
| WindowChanged | WindowChanged | WindowChanged | WindowChanged |
| WindowMovedOrResized | WindowMovedOrResized | WindowMovedOrResized | WindowMovedOrResized |

# Index

See Appendix A, "AutoCAD Object Summary," for a comprehensive list of objects, collections, properties, methods, and events.